Shadman's Diaries

VOLUME 2

Fakhr al-Din Shadman in the early 1930s

Shadman's Diaries

VOLUME 2

In Pursuit of Western Civilization, 1933–1943

Fakhr al-Din Shadman

Preface & Persian Text Edited by

Kioumars Ghereghlou

MAGE PERSIAN EDITIONS

The publication of this six-volume series was supported by the generous subvention of Hassan and Mahvash Milani in memory of Zinat Shadman Milani.

Mage Persian Editions is an imprint of
Mage Publishers Inc
www.mage.com

Library of Congress Cataloging-in-Publication Data
Available at the Library of Congress

First hardcover edition
ISBN: 978-1-949445-89-3

Visit Mage online: www.mage.com
Email: as@mage.com

CONTENTS

Editor's Preface | ix

Persian Text | 1

Index | 387

EDITOR'S PREFACE

This is volume 2 of Seyyed Fakhr al-Din Shadman's diaries, and it contains a critical edition of two notebooks from the Shadman papers housed at the Stanford University Libraries. The primary goal of this preface is to provide readers with a comprehensive understanding of the historical context surrounding Shadman's diaries from 1933 to 1943.

The diaries in this volume cover almost a decade from December 15, 1933, when Shadman departed Tehran, to late March 1943, marking the beginning of the last year of his tenure as a technical assistant to ʿAli-Asghar Zarrin-Kafsh (d. 1969) and Fathollah Nuri Esfandyari (d. 1968), two prominent diplomats and government officials who led the Imperial Government of Iran's delegation with the Anglo-Persian Oil Company (APOC; renamed Anglo-Iranian Oil Company, or AIOC, in 1935) in London. The two notebooks, which serve as the base manuscripts for this edition, are identical in size and appearance, each measuring 4.5 x 6.75 inches. All footnotes to the Persian text have been added by the editor to provide readers with context about the text of the diaries' content, as well as the individuals, locations, and texts referenced within them.

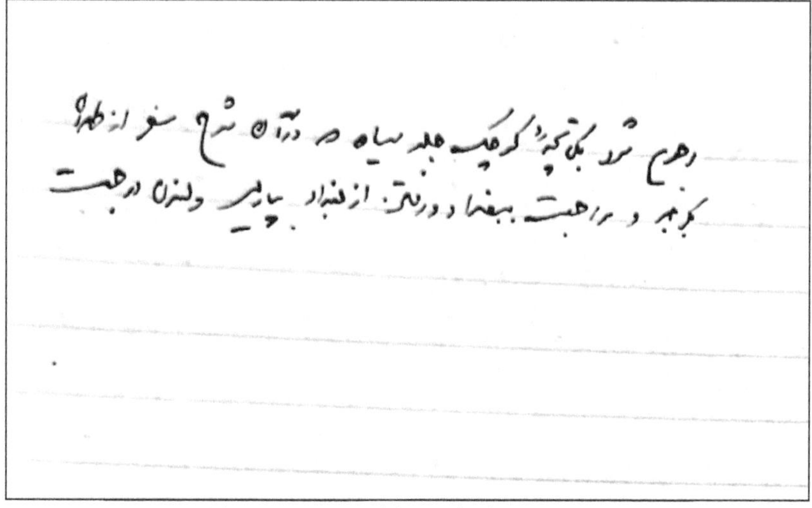

Fig. 1. The opening page of the notebook covering 1933-43.

It is reasonable to conclude that the diaries for the period under discussion were redacted by Shadman at a later date, most likely during the final years of Shadman's life when he held the position of professor of Islamic history and civilization at the Tehran University School of Theology. This hypothesis is supported by recurring calendar inconsistencies throughout the text (e.g., pp. 163 and 188), which suggest revisions and rewriting at a subsequent stage. Furthermore, the absence of any crossed-out word throughout the text, the misspelling of specific names from Shadman's student years at the London School of Economics (LSE), and the uniformity in the make and size of both notebooks collectively strengthen the likelihood that Shadman redacted the original text at a later period.

Around the time Shadman left for London in 1933, Reza Shah (r. 1925–41) was at the peak of his power and success, preparing to celebrate the eighth anniversary of his ascent to the throne as the founder of a new dynasty. Reza Shah's adversaries, notably the British and their allies within Iran, including the clergy, believed he would soon collapse under the weight of his own rule. As November 1933 drew to a close, a local source close to the British Legation in Tehran reported that pro-British circles in the capital were "alive" with rumors about the shah's declining health, with allegations circulating that he was terminally ill. The report claimed that "many people declare that he is suffering from cancer."[1] Throughout the summer and fall of 1933, a pervasive fear of an imminent tribal uprising spread through the capital, fueling an atmosphere of paranoia at the Pahlavi court. Just days before Shadman's departure, the shah ordered the political police to intensify their crackdown on influential tribal elements in the capital and key provincial centers across the south, including Isfahan, Chahar Mahal, Fars, and Khuzestan. Groups of Bakhtiari and Qashqai notables were subsequently arrested or held under house arrest.[2]

---

[1] *Printed Correspondence 1929–1938: Collection 28/File 39* (India Office Records and Private Papers, British Library, London), 178 (report no. 150). Available online: http://www.qdl.qa/en/archive/81055/vdc_100000000602.0x0003e4 (accessed November 9, 2024).

[2] *Printed Correspondence 1929–1938: Collection 28/File 39*, 184–87 (report no. 150). Reza Shah's suspicion of these local partners within the political system emerged at a time when tribal unrest was destabilizing neighboring Afghanistan, culminating in the assassination of Mohammad Nader Shah (r. 1922–33), a reformist ruler, on November 8, 1933, by a Hazara student. The forces involved in the regicide sought to restore the deposed king Amanollah (r. 1926–29). Louis Dupree, *Afghanistan* (Princeton: Princeton University Press, 1980), 458–76, at 474–75.

Shadman briefly outlines his travel itinerary at the beginning of his diaries. He left his family home in Pa-Menar, a historic neighborhood in downtown Tehran, on a Friday early morning. During the early part of the twentieth century, Pa-Menar, recognized as the site of the Russian Legation, also served as a key hub and marketplace for agricultural products from the Caspian provinces of the country. As Shadman grew up, this neighborhood was home to some of Iran's most prominent bureaucrats and religious figures, including Abo'l-Qasem Kashani (d. 1962), Mohammad Mosaddeq (d. 1967), Gholam-Hoseyn Sadiqi (d. 1991), Mohammad Tadayyon (d. 1951), Jalal Homa'i (d. 1980), and a minor cleric named Mohammad Saqafi Kalantari (d. 1985), who would later become Ayatollah Khomeini's (d. 1989) second father-in-law.[3]

How did Shadman—a former cleric, elementary school teacher, and novice judiciary clerk armed with a newly minted bachelor's degree in law from the School of Law and Political Science— come to be hired for a predominantly technical role in Reza Shah's delegation with the Anglo-Iranian Oil Company? Reza Shah's confidence in educated Iranians, particularly young and patriotic intellectuals like Shadman, was undoubtedly the main game changer. In addition, Shadman's diaries hint that, despite lacking technical expertise in fields like exploration, mechanical engineering, petroleum engineering, or earth science, Shadman had been hired because of a glowing recommendation from his well-connected friend, 'Abd al-Rahim Khalkhali (d. 1942). It is

---

[3] Zia al-Din Shadman to Farzaneh Milani, December 6, 1998, in private possession.

also likely that Shadman's boss in the judiciary, 'Ali-Akbar Davar (d. 1937), played a role in supporting his appointment to Iran's delegation with APOC. As with many others, patronage and favoritism played a pivotal role in his advancement. In addition to Khalkhali and Davar, Seyyed Hasan Taqizadeh (d. 1970) was instrumental in facilitating Shadman's recruitment as a delegate with APOC. Nearly a decade into his appointment, Shadman reflected on how, in the latter part of 1933, Khalkhali's encouragement and support played a decisive role in helping him overcome his doubts and fears, ultimately inspiring him to join the government delegation to London with APOC. Mourning Khalkhali's passing—news of which reached him in London through Taqizadeh in late August 1942—Shadman remembered his deceased mentor as one of his "dearest friends" who surpassed many in "foresight, goodwill, and patriotism" (p. 346). As Shadman emphasized, Khalkhali had connected him to a vibrant community of "learned and literary companions" in Tehran in the late 1920s and early 1930s (p. 347).

'Abd al-Rahim Khalkhali remains a relatively obscure figure in the intellectual history of early twentieth-century Iran. A prominent publisher, literary scholar, and journalist, Khalkhali pioneered modern scholarship on Hafez (d. c. 1390), the most celebrated lyric poet in the Persianate world, and his edition of the *Divan* of Hafez, based on the oldest known manuscript of the work, dated 1424, was a groundbreaking achievement. This publication established Khalkhali as the first scholar to authenticate Hafez's 496 *ghazals*—the number has stayed exactly the same since then. According to Mohammad Qazvini (d.

1949), an authority in Hafez studies, Khalkhali's pioneering edition allowed Iranians for the first time to "separate pure gold from worthless alloys, reintroducing readers to the captivating and luminous essence of the original poems Hafez had composed by dint of his resourceful and overflowing imagination."[4] In addition to his edition of the *Divan* of Hafez, Khalkhali produced the first critical edition of Nezam al-Molk Tusi's (d. 1092) *Siyasatnameh*, published by the Kaveh Bookstore in 1931.[5] Khalkhali, like Shadman, belonged to a *seyyed* family that traced its lineage back to the Prophet Mohammad. He began his career as a cleric-turned-educator, teaching at elementary and secondary schools in Rasht, the capital city of the Caspian province of Gilan. Born in 1871 in the rural suburbs of Khalkhal and raised in Ardabil, Khalkhali completed his education in a seminary in Rasht. Shortly before the Constitutional Revolution (1905–11), which gripped the country for nearly six years, Khalkhali moved to Tehran with one of his students, Ebrahim Purdavud (d. 1967), a young, talented poet who would later emerge as a leading scholar of Zoroastrian texts.[6]

---

[4]   Mohammad Qazvini, "Vafayat-e mo'aserin," *Yadgar* 3, no. 5 (December-January 1946–47/Day 1325 *sh.*): 38–49, at 44. See also Shams al-Din Mohammad Hafez, *Divan-e Khvajah Shams al-Din Mohammad Hafez Shirazi*, ed. Mohammad Qazvini and Qasem Ghani (Tehran: Chapkhaneh Majles, 1941/1320 *sh.*), kaf/ta-lam and 'ayn/jim-mim (editorial preface).

[5]   Abu 'Ali Hasan b. 'Ali Nezam al-Molk Tusi, *Siyasatnameh ya siyar al-moluk*, ed. 'Abd al-Rahim Khalkhali (Tehran: Ketabkhaneh Kaveh and Ketabkhaneh Ma'refat, 1931/1310 *sh.*). Khalkhali's other work is the Persian translation (from Arabic) of a monograph on the influence of idolatry and paganism on Christianity. See Mohammad-Taher Tanayyor, *Afsaneh'ha-ye bot'parasti dar a'yin-e kelisa* (Tehran: Dar al-Kotob al-Eslamiyeh, 1984/1363 *sh.*).

[6]   'Ali-Asghar Mostafavi, *Zaman va zendegi-e ostad Purdavud* (Tehran: Neda, 1993/1372 *sh.*), 17.

In Tehran, Khalkhali became actively involved in politics and journalism, collaborating with Seyyed Mohammad-Reza Shirazi (d. 1925) as co-editor of the *Mosavat* (Equality), the country's most radical newspaper during the chaotic reign of the Qajar Mohammad-ʿAli Shah (1907-9).[7] Khalkhali's reputation and influence as a publisher and literary scholar grew significantly following the release of his editions of the *Divan* of Hafez and Tusi's *Siyasatnameh* in 1927 and 1931. Khalkhali and Taqizadeh, both supporters of Shadman, were members of the left-leaning faction of the Constitutionalist coalition. Since 1904, their mentor, Seyyed Mohammad-Reza Shirazi, better known as Mosavat, served as a prominent member of the underground Revolutionary Committee.[8] Soon after Mohammad-ʿAli Shah's ascension to the throne, the Qajar ruler and his allies launched a merciless campaign to suppress constitutionalists and revolutionaries in Tehran and other parts of the country. In response, younger activists such as Khalkhali and Taqizadeh became radicalized and joined the Revolutionary Committee. Taqizadeh, seven years younger than Khalkhali, ranked among the most prominent representatives in Iran's newly established parliament, the *Majles*, leading the Social Democratic Party (*Ferqeh-e ejtemaʿiyun ʿammiyun*), founded by Heydar Khan Afshar Orumi (d. 1921), a Baku-educated communist electrical engineer better known as Heydar Khan ʿAmu-Oghli.[9]

---

[7] Mohammad Sadr Hashemi, *Tarikh-e jarayed va majallat-e Iran*, 4 vols. (Isfahan: Kamal, 1984/1363 *sh.*), 4: 208–9.

[8] Mahdi Malekzadeh, *Tarikh-e enqelab-e mashrutiyat-e Iran*, 7 vols. in three (Tehran: Entesharat-e ʿElmi, 1984/1363 *sh.*), 1: 236–45.

[9] On Heydar Khan's involvement in the establishment of the Social Democratic Party of Iran, see Alireza Sheikholeslami, "Ḥaydar Khan ʿAmu-Oḡli," *Encyclopaedia Iranica* 12 (2003): 69–70. Available online: https:/

The downfall of Mohammad-ʿAli Shah opened new opportunities for Khalkhali's professional advancement. From 1909 to 1915, he served as a high-ranking official in the Ministry of Finance, assisting legislators in establishing the Internal Audit Office (*Divan-e mohasebat*) to curb the corruption and excesses of the young and irresponsible Ahmad Shah and his close associates. Khalkhali remained close to Taqizadeh during their exile in Istanbul and Berlin from 1915 to 1917.[10] Upon returning from Turkey, Khalkhali reopened his bookstore on Naser-e Khosrow Street in downtown Tehran, naming it Kaveh in honor of the popular periodical published by Taqizadeh in Berlin between 1915 and 1921. During those years, the Kaveh Bookstore evolved into a vibrant hub, attracting young and emerging writers, poets, journalists, translators, and scholars such as Mojtaba Minovi (d. 1977), Ebrahim Purdavud, ʿAli-Asghar Zarrin-Kafsh, and Fakhr al-Din Shadman.[11] Shadman remains reticent about the specific circumstances under which

---

/iranicaonline.org/articles/haydar-khan-amu-ogli (accessed on December 2, 2024). Cf. Esmaʿil Raʾin, *Heydar Khan ʿAmu-Oghli* (Tehran: Moʾasseseh Tahqiq-e Raʾin, 1973/1352 *sh.*), 148–61.

[10] For more on the emigration of intellectuals and officials affiliated with the National Defense Committee, including Khalkhali and Taqizadeh, to Istanbul and Berlin, see ʿAbd al-Hoseyn Sheybani, *Khaterat-e mohajerat az dowlat-e movaqqat-e Kermanshah ta Komitah-e Melliyun-e Berlan*, ed. Iraj Afshar and Kaveh Bayat (Tehran: Shirazeh, 1999/1378 *sh.*).

[11] For more on Khalkhali's life and activities, see Hushang Ettehad and EIr, "Kalkali, Sayyed ʿAbd-al-Rahim," *Encyclopaedia Iranica* 15, fasc. 4 (2010): 405–8. Available online: https://iranicaonline.org/articles/kalkali–abd-al-rahim (accessed on May 2, 2024). In 1927, the Kaveh Bookstore was one of the 14 bookstores on Naser Khosrow Street. See Nader Motallebi Kashani, "Ketabforushan-e Tehran dar sal-e 1306," in *Ketabforushi*, ed. Iraj Afshar and ʿAbd al-Hoseyn Azarang, 2 vols. paginated as one (Tehran: Shehab-e Saqeb, 2004/1383 *sh.*), 603–7, at 606.

Khalkhali helped him commit to traveling to London. Nevertheless, considering Khalkhali's close friendship with Taqizadeh, Iran's chief negotiator in the 1933 Anglo-Iranian Oil Concession Agreement and the official who oversaw the formation of the Iranian delegation with APOC, it is safe to assume that Khalkhali likely played the decisive role in recommending Shadman's appointment as a delegate with the oil company in London.[12] Notably, Khalkhali had been a confidant of Taqizadeh since 1906, with Taqizadeh himself referring to him as "one of my best friends."[13]

The primary role of the Iranian delegation to APOC was to enhance Reza Shah's access to proceeds from the Company's sales of Iranian crude oil. The very formation of the delegation marked a historic win for the Iranian government. It granted its representatives, for the first time, regular and unlimited access to APOC's internal registers, holding the British accountable for managing and distributing royalties. The head of the delegation, along with his assistants, including Shadman, was permitted to gather detailed information on the Company's revenues, expenditures, projects, and investments. The Iranian chief delegate was also granted the privilege of attending all meetings of the Company's board of directors and principal shareholders. The head of the delegation had a say in all decisions concerning APOC's projects within Iran and was paid an annual salary of 2,000 pounds sterling. Regular access to the

---

[12] For more on the 1933 agreement, see H. Bamberg, *The History of the British Petroleum Company: The Anglo-Iranian Years, 1928–1954* (Cambridge: Cambridge University Press, 1994), 41–50.

[13] Hasan Taqizadeh, *Zendegi-e tufani: Khaterat-e Seyyed Hasan Taqizadeh*, ed. Iraj Afshar (Tehran: 'Elmi, 1993/1372 *sh.*), 203, also 74–5, 78, 83, 228.

Company's financial records and investment statements was essential. Under Article VI of the 1933 agreement, the Imperial Government of Iran held the right to verify all returns from the sale of Iranian crude. The same article also required APOC to adjust its annual payments to the Imperial Government of Iran according to fluctuations in the pound sterling's gold value on international markets.[14]

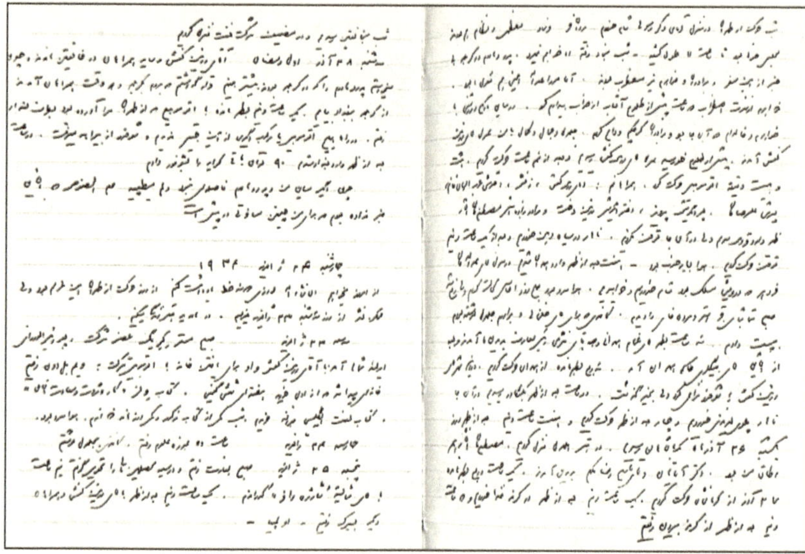

Fig. 2. The beginning of the 1933 diaries.

Aleksandr (Alek) Aqayan (d. 1963), a Swiss-educated lawyer of Armenian descent raised in Rasht and close to Khalkhali and other social democrat activists, visited Shadman upon his arrival in Kermanshah (p. 1). A seasoned constitutionalist and close associate

---

[14] Benjamin Shwadran, *The Middle East, Oil, and the Great Powers*, 3rd edition (New York: Wiley, 1974), 45. Cf. Bamberg, *The History of the British Petroleum Company*, 41–50. For more on the history of APOC and the 1933 concession, see Farhad Kazemi, "Anglo-Persian Oil Company," *Encyclopaedia Iranica* 2 (1985): 61–5. Available online: http://www.iranicaonline.org/articles/anglo-persian-oil-company (accessed on December 2, 2024).

of Yeprem Davidian Gantsaktsi (d. 1912), better known as Yeprem Khan, an Armenian military commander from Rasht who served as Tehran's police chief after Mohammad-'Ali Shah's downfall, Aqayan had played an active role in the arrest, trial, and execution of the infamous anti-constitutionalist Shaykh Fazlollah Nuri in the summer of 1909. Under Reza Shah, Aqayan became one of the architects behind Davar's criminal justice reforms. During this period, he was appointed professor of criminology at the newly established Tehran University. Towards the end of Reza Shah's reign, Aqayan founded the Iran Insurance Corporation, where he recruited Shadman shortly after his return from London in 1943.[15]

Zarrin-Kafsh's name appears frequently in Shadman's diaries between 1933 and 1943. During his initial months in London, Shadman received essential support from the Zarrin-Kafsh family, including food and lodging. Born in 1885 into a family of landed notables from Saneh (now Senehdej or Sanandej), the administrative center of Kurdistan Province, 'Ali-Asghar Zarrin-Kafsh was twenty-two years Shadman's senior. Like Shadman, he had earned his bachelor's degree from the School of Law and Political Science in Tehran. However, while Shadman aligned himself with pro-Soviet and pro-Islamist writers and activists such as Mohammad Farrokhi

---

[15] On Aqayan's life and career, see Habib Ladjevardi interview with Shahin Aghayan, October 25, 1985 (Paris, France), Iranian Oral History Collection, Harvard University, Transcript 1. Available online: https://nrs.lib.harvard.edu/urn-3:fhcl:608990 (accessed October 2, 2024). Cf. 'Abbas Moibarakiyan, *Chehreh'ha dar tarikhcheh-e nezam-e amuzesh-i 'ali-e hoquq va 'adliyeh-e novin* (Tehran: Peydayesh, 1998/1377 *sh.*), 110–11; Baqer 'Aqeli, *Sharh-e hal-e rejal-e siyasi va nezami-e mo'aser-e Iran,* 3 vols. (Tehran: Nashr-e Namak, 2020/1399 *sh.*), 1: 27; Abbas Milani, *Eminent Persians: The Men and Women Who Made Modern Iran, 1941–1979,* 2 vols. (New York: Syracuse University Press and Persian World Press, 2008), 1: 413–16.

Yazdi (d. 1939), Hasan 'Alavi (d. 1927), and 'Abd al-Hoseyn Hazhir (d. 1949), Zarrin-Kafsh began his journalistic career under the patronage of the former prime minister Seyyed Zia al-Din Tabataba'i (d. 1969), a right-wing pro-British nationalist. Following a similar career trajectory as Shadman's, Zarrin-Kafsh eventually joined the judiciary and served as a judiciary clerk in Tehran during the brief and transformative tenure of 'Ali-Akbar Davar, the founder of Iran's modern judiciary. Zarrin-Kafsh later transitioned from the judiciary to managerial roles in the Ministries of Interior and Finance. Despite their early disagreements and quarrels, particularly during their harrowing journey from Tehran to London (p. 28), Shadman and Zarrin-Kafsh remained close for many years.[16]

Shadman's appointment to the Iranian delegation with APOC was pursuant to Article VIII of the 1933 Anglo-Iranian Oil Concession Agreement.[17] The 1933 Anglo-Iranian Oil Concession Agreement came in the wake of Reza Shah's failed effort to end APOC's monopoly and secure greater Iranian control over its oil revenues. Unilaterally, he decided to annul the previous agreement in November 1932 to pressure British officials into renegotiation. Two of Shadman's mentors, Davar and Taqizadeh—then serving as Ministers of Finance and Foreign Affairs, respectively—alongside the Minister of Foreign Affairs, Mohammad-'Ali Forughi (d. 1942), Hoseyn 'Ala (d. 1964), Governor of the National Bank (Bank-e Melli), and Nasrollah Entezam from the Ministry of Foreign Affairs led the negotiations for a new concession agreement. Sir John Cadman (d. 1941) and his deputy, the

---

[16] On Zarrin-Kafsh, see Mobarakiyan, *Chehreh'ha*, 397–98; 'Aqeli, *Sharh-e hal-e rejal*, 2: 760.

[17] Shwadran, *The Middle East*, 45.

Scottish oilman William Fraser (d. 1970), represented APOC as the principal British negotiators. Dr. Edvard Beneš (d. 1948) of Czechoslovakia took over as *rapporteur* to reconcile the two delegations.[18] These talks, held at Iran's National Bank headquarters in downtown Tehran, extended through early spring 1933. The resulting agreement, signed on April 29, 1933, marked a short-term victory for Iran's financially strained government, raising its annual oil revenue share by roughly fifty percent—from approximately £650,000 in 1932 to £1,300,000 the following year. Within a few months, Taqizadeh and his allies appointed ʿAli-Asghar Zarrin-Kafsh as the chief delegate of the Imperial Government of Iran to APOC in London.[19]

Shadman's specific responsibilities as a technical assistant to the chief delegate remain unclear, leaving little detail about the extent or nature of his contributions in this role. While working for APOC in London, his role appeared administrative, largely involving paperwork. For instance, he was tasked with sorting job applications for a vacancy in the delegation's accounting department. Simultaneously, the Iranian Legation in London frequently enlisted his help. Tasks included translating a letter from the American art historian Arthur Upham Pope (d. 1969) to Reza Shah (January 24, 1935) and delivering historical maps from the

---

[18] Laurence P. Elwell-Sutton, *Persian Oil: A Study in Power Politics* (London: Lawrence and Wishart Ltd., 1955), 77–9.

[19] E. 2658/17/34 (May 22, 1933), Hoare to Simon, in *Anglo-Persian Oil Company's Concession Dispute with Persian Govt: Collection 28/File 55* (India Office Records and Private Papers, British Library, London). Available online: http://www.qdl.qa/en/archive/81055/vdc_100000000648.0x00000e (accessed January 25, 2022); Taqizadeh, *Zendegi-e tufani*, 262–67 and 277. See also Gregory Brew, "In Search of 'Equitability': Sir John Cadman, Reza Shah, and the Cancellation of the D'Arcy Concession, 1928–1933," *Iranian Studies* 50 (2017): 125–148.

London University School of Oriental Studies (SOS; later School of Oriental and African Studies or SOAS) to the Iranian Legation, as requested by Ambassador Hoseyn ʿAla. These maps were intended to strengthen the Iranian government's argument that the Iran-Iraq boundary in the Abadan region should be defined along the thalweg, or median line, of the Arvand River, also known as Shatt al-ʿArab. Supported by the United Kingdom, the Hashemite Kingdom of Iraq seized the opportunity to escalate the dispute to the League of Nations in 1934 (pp. 40–41).[20] ʿAla, shortly after assuming his ambassadorial role, encouraged Shadman to assist further with legation tasks and translations, fostering a close working relationship with the diplomatic corps (p. 54). This closeness, however, stirred jealousy among embassy staff, culminating in an anonymous accusation sent to Tehran in 1937, alleging political opposition to Reza Shah by both ʿAla and Shadman (p. 110).

Shadman's initial oil-related assignments in London were demanding and time-consuming. He had been tasked with studying, summarizing, and translating various reports and memoranda on the technical and financial aspects of oil and coal production in Iran. These reports had been authored by British officials, engineers, and scientists. More importantly, he had been commissioned to translate the Iran-related APOC financial records and ledgers prepared by Sir William McLintock (d. 1947), a senior accountant with the oil company (p. 9). Given Shadman's background as a former cleric and elementary school teacher, with

---

[20] See The United States of America Department of State, *International Boundary Study, No. 164: Iran-Iraq Boundary* (Washington DC: Office of the Geographer and Bureau of Intelligence and Research, 1978), 4.

studies in law (including the Shiʿa jurisprudence) and brief experience as a junior judiciary clerk, it remains unclear whether he possessed the technical expertise and scientific knowledge necessary to fully comprehend the content of more specialized reports, such as geological surveys, engineering communications, and technical guidelines. The lack of support and intense work pressure during the early months of his settlement in London appear to have triggered chronic stress, ultimately resulting in short bouts of nervous breakdown. The diaries from February, April, May, and June 1933 are filled with references to his distress and its accompanying physical symptoms (pp. 11, 13–15, 17). Shadman's accounts of coping with health issues are both terse and fragmented. His most repeated refrain is a stark and telling one: "I don't feel well."

Nevertheless, Shadman did not give up. He fought tirelessly to overcome the technical challenges of his role and close the gap in required expertise. He had at least one one-on-one meeting with Sir John Cadman to discuss technical details of coal oil and kerosene production in Iran. During his initial weeks in London, he immersed himself entirely in mastering the fundamentals of petroleum engineering, determined to build a robust understanding of APOC projects and investments (pp. 6–7). Additionally, he oversaw APOC's scholarship for Iranian students in various engineering programs across the UK (p. 2). His involvement in the APOC study abroad programs was primarily legal and administrative rather than technical in nature. On one occasion, Shadman traveled to Birmingham as an administrative advisor to visit Iranian students on APOC scholarships (p. 129). On another occasion, he assisted the Scotland Yard investigations into the drowning of a young Iranian student in Sunbury-on-Thames (p. 92).

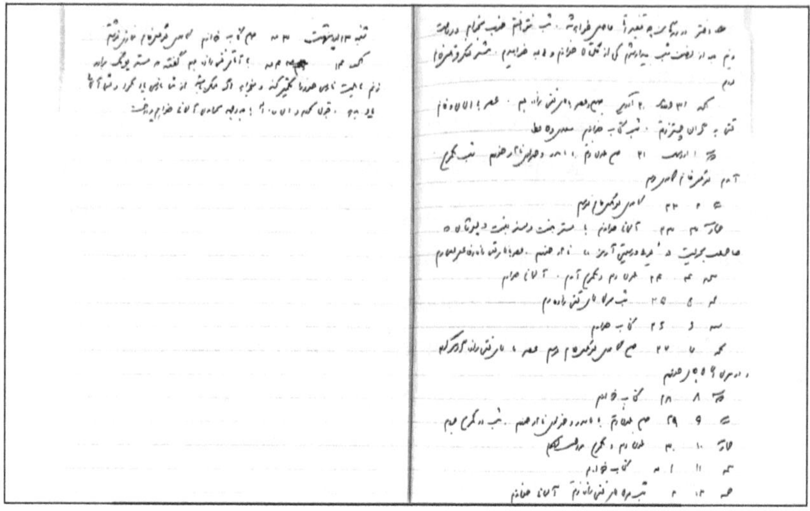

Fig. 3. The closing page of the notebook covering 1933–41.

January 24, 1943, a fine Wednesday, is the first day of Shadman's diaries abroad, marking the end of his seventh week in England.[21] During the first six weeks, he had stayed with the Zarrin-Kafshs at their spacious home on 147 Cromwell Road while frantically searching for rental accommodation in central London. Eight days later, Shadman found a single room at a boarding house in central London called Hotel Madrid, moving in the very same day. Eager to establish himself as a writer, he began corresponding with three prominent Iranian scholars and writers of his time—Hasan Taqizadeh, Mohammad Qazvini, and Qasem Ghani (d. 1952)—just three months after arriving in London. His relationship with Taqizadeh and Qazvini deepened over the next decade, developing

---

[21] *The Times* (January 24, 1934), 12.

into lasting friendships. These connections likely provided Shadman not only with invaluable mentorship and intellectual companionship but also with a supportive scholarly network that helped shape his emerging career as a writer and historian. Shadman expanded his network in the following weeks, initiating correspondence with two more influential writers and scholars, ʿAli Dashti (d. 1982) and Gholam-Reza Rashid Yasemi (d. 1951). These connections, noted in entries from April 10 and 11, 1934, further illustrate Shadman's dedication to engaging with the intellectual elite of his time.

While seeking a rental in London, Shadman placed an ad in the London *Times*, describing himself as a "young Persian writer." Interestingly, the ad omits his official role as a technician or administrative assistant with APOC, possibly reflecting his personal dissatisfaction with his position in the Iranian delegation.[22] Over the next nine years, as noted above, Shadman's diaries provide little to no detail about his employment and responsibilities as a technical assistant with the APOC. This omission can be taken to imply that, while his professional role may have provided financial stability, it held little personal or intellectual significance for him compared to his scholarly and literary pursuits. His meticulous documentation of correspondence with prominent writers and his dedication to fostering a network of intellectual connections within Iran and abroad appear to have eclipsed the routine aspects of his technical work with APOC.

Shadman's work at APOC did not diminish his quest to be recognized as a Persian writer among the Iranians of London. On August 16, 1934, he published a column in the London *Times* titled "Omar Khayyam: A Persian Writer's Opinion." In this brief

---

[22] *The Times* (January 15, 1934), 2.

note, written in response to a letter from Arthur Upham Pope published in the London *Times*, Shadman praised the English poet Edward FitzGerald (d. 1883) as "a genius who could understand the meaning, the real meaning of these pure Persian thoughts known under the poetic title of *Rubaiyat*." At the end of this column, he firmly refuted Pope's assertion that, without FitzGerald's translation, Iranians would have remained unaware of Khayyam's quatrains. Shadman's critical response underscored his conviction that Khayyam's verses held intrinsic significance within Persian culture, independent of Western translation and scholarship, while still acknowledging FitzGerald's remarkable ability to convey the essence of Persian thought to a broader audience. However, Shadman, ever a man of moderate views, deliberately steers clear of engaging with Khayyam's radically anti-religious worldview.[23]

In the early spring of 1934, Shadman visited the London University School of Oriental Studies.[24] Within a few days of this first visit, Sir Edward Denison Ross (d. 1940), the school's founder and first president, started a search for a Persian teacher at SOS. On 5 May 1934, the Iranian Legation in London suggested Shadman as the best candidate for the job, who accordingly accepted the

---

[23] *The Times* (August 16, 1934), 6.

[24] For years, Shadman avoided using the recently coined Persian term *daneshgah* for university or *université*. He adopted the term *daneshgah* shortly before his viva voce (p. 179). Years later, deeply enamored with the Arabic and Islamic dimensions of Iranian history, Shadman strongly and rather quixotically expressed his fiery opposition to the purge of Arabic words and constructs from the language advocated by intellectuals like Ahmad Kasravi (d. 1946), whom Shadman ridiculed and berated under the Hanavidi category—anti-Islamic intellectuals bent on purging Persian language of all Arabic words and constructs—as the "worst enemies" of Iranian culture and traditions. Seyyed Fakhr al-Din Shadman, *Taskhir-e tamaddon-e farangi* (Tehran: Chapkhaneh Majles, 1948/1327 *sh.*), 10 and 19–22.

offer. The same day, he met Foad Ruhani (d. 2004), then an APOC
employee who would become one of Shadman's closest friends for
the next decade and beyond. An accomplished translator and
scholar of Islam and the Bahá'í faith, Ruhani would later serve as
the first Secretary-General of OPEC from 1961 to 1964.[25]

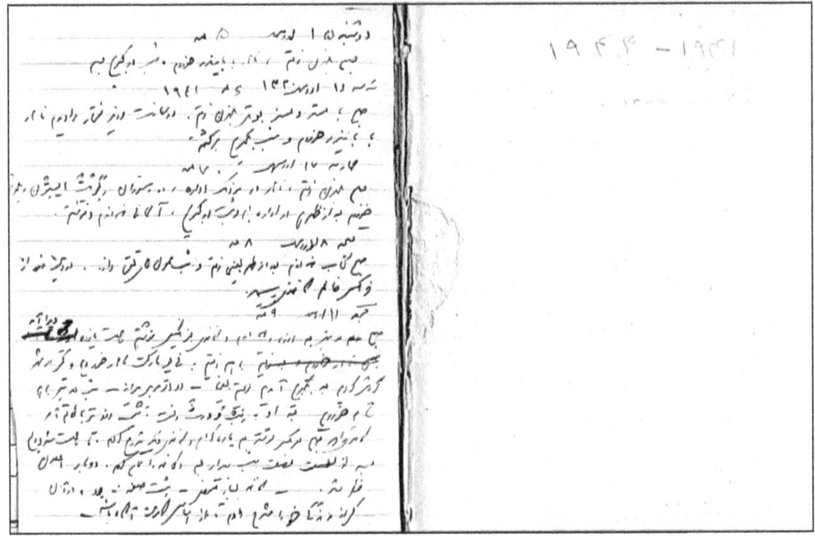

Fig. 4. The opening page of the notebook covering 1941–43.

From May 9, 1934, Shadman started teaching Persian for two to
three hours per week at SOS as Vladimir F. Minorsky's (d. 1966)
assistant. Their three students during the spring term were from
Bahrain, India, and Great Britain (pp. 9 and 13). A recent graduate
of the Persian program at SOS, who met Shadman early in June of
the same year during a school event, was a "young charming lady"
related by marriage to one of Sir Charles R. Darwin's (d. 1882)
sons (p. 16). Shadman continued teaching Persian for the next

---

[25] Milani, *Eminent Persians*, 1: 272–76.

nine years, even after the School of Oriental Studies relocated its operations from London to Cambridge during the Blitz, which lasted from September 1940 to May 1941.[26]

Besides working full-time and teaching part-time, by the end of May 1934, Shadman had taken it upon himself to transcribe and translate into Persian Taqizadeh's lectures in London. Inspired by Italian nationalist leader Giuseppe Mazzini's (d. 1872) movement *La Giovine Italia*, Taqizadeh's inaugural speech in London, delivered at the Royal Society of Arts on May 30, 1934, revolved around the concept of Young Iran (*Iran-e javan*) (p. 15). In 1935, Shadman devoted several weeks to reviewing Taqizadeh's various drafts and research notes, meticulously preparing a polished version of his monograph on calendar systems in pre-Islamic Iran, which was eventually published in Tehran in 1937 (pp. 75, 76, 83, and 87).[27] Recognizing Shadman's erudition and tireless efforts, Taqizadeh, in early June 1934, invited him to the Ferdowsi millennial celebration in Paris (p. 16). As part of this event, a series of public lectures were held at the Iranian Legation in London, where Taqizadeh and Shadman, joined by Arthur Upham Pope, the Director of the American Institute for Persian Art and Archaeology, invited local Iranian students and businessmen to support and participate in the upcoming Ferdowsi millennial

---

[26] See A. G. Watts, "City of Refuge: Evacuation of University of London Colleges to Cambridge during the Second World War," in *History of Universities XXXVI/1*, ed. Robin Darwell-Smith and Mordechai Feingold (Oxford: Oxford University Press, 2023), 180–214, at 199.

[27] Hasan Taqizadeh, *Gah'shomari dar Iran-e qadim* (Tehran: Ketabkhaneh Tehran, 1937/1316 *sh.*). In the acknowledgments section at the end of the foreword, Taqizadeh, thanks his friends Sir Denison Ross, the president of the School of Oriental Studies, and ʿAbbas Parviz, the publisher, but notably omits any mention of Shadman as his main collaborator.

celebration planned for later that year in Tehran and Mashhad (p. 21). This initiative aimed to foster a sense of national pride and cultural engagement among Iranians inside Iran and abroad, encouraging them to connect with their heritage and actively contribute to honoring the legacy of Ferdowsi.

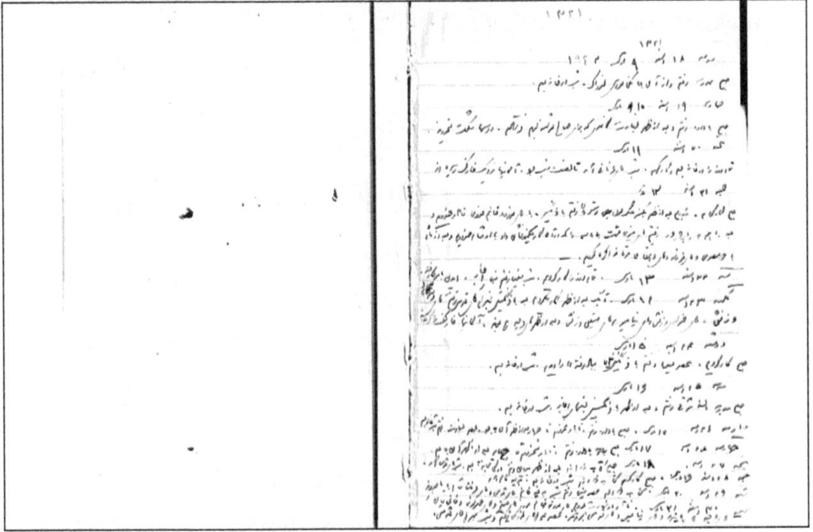

Fig. 5. The last page of the notebook covering 1941–43.

Shadman was later invited to recite parts of Ferdowsi's *Shahnamah* at a meeting held on October 4, 1934, for the House of Lords, organized by the Royal Asiatic Society. During the same session, David Samuel Margoliouth (d. 1937), the Laudian Professor of Arabic at the University of Oxford, and Reynold Alleyne Nicholson (d. 1945), professor of Persian and Arabic at the University of Cambridge, gave two lectures on the history of Persian and Arabic poetry (pp. 27–28). Two weeks later, Shadman attended a much bigger event held at the House of Lords, where he made a brief presentation in English on Ferdowsi and then recited part of the Rostam and Sohrab tragedy to the audience, which included luminaries such as the British diplomat Sir Horace Rumbold (d. 1941), Charles Cochrane-Baillie Lord Lamington (d. 1940), Aga Khan III (d. 1957), and the newly appointed Lord Privy Seal, Anthony Eden (d. 1977), who had studied Persian and Arabic at Oxford (p. 31).[28]

Impressed by Shadman's performance during that early House of Lords event, Hoseyn 'Ala—then serving as the governor of Iran's National Bank and soon-to-be-appointed ambassador to the United Kingdom—approached Shadman and requested him to write a response to an article published in the September 28 issue of the London *Times* by the renowned British travel writer and historian Robert Byron (d. 1941). Shadman accepted 'Ala's request, praising him in his diaries as "a polite and patriotic man" (p. 28). Byron's article, in which he gives an account of his recent travels in Fars, Qazvin, and Mashhad, opened with sharp criticisms of the Iranian officials. The acclaimed and perceptive historian and travel writer observed that "the study of monuments in [Iran] is not easy. To be English is a prime disadvantage." In particular, he expressed frustration and dismay that "photography in Persia is forbidden lest the malignant traveler should defame his hosts by advertising some picturesque but retrograde custom or type."[29] Within a week, the London *Times* published a brief note about Byron's article from Sir Coleridge Kennard (d. 1948), a diplomat who had served as the secretary of the British Legation in Tehran from 1909 to 1914.

---

[28] On Eden studying Persian and Arabic at Oxford, see Alan Campbell-Johnson, *Anthony Eden: A Biography* (New York: Washburn, 1939), 31.

[29] Robert Byron, "Middle Eastern Journey," *The Times* (28 September 1934), 15–16.

Coleridge affirmed Byron's negative account of how Iranian officials mistreated foreign travelers.[30]

Like all British diplomats and government agents stationed in Iran in the 1930s, Byron harbored a deep disdain for Reza Shah and vehemently opposed his centralizing and modernist reforms. His criticism was often accompanied by two-faced lamentation for the very forces—the corrupt pro-Qajar elites, tribal kingpins, and Shiite clerics—that had kept Iran weak, stagnant, and backward over the previous century. Despite his brilliance, Byron's perspective of Iran and its people was deeply influenced by an Orientalist bias. Writing from a perspective of civilizational superiority, he unhesitatingly portrayed Iranians as a monolithic and unchanging people. Byron's romanticized focus on Iran's landscapes and architectural monuments served as a mechanism for dehumanizing and othering its inhabitants. Distressed by Reza Shah's crackdown on unruly tribal khans in Fars and Isfahan, Byron expressed sympathy for the persecuted, many of them close allies of the British colonialists, and disparaged Reza Shah as a tyrant. The numerous challenges and mishaps he encountered during his travels in the country further deepened his contempt for Iranian officials. Iranian government officials were justified in their suspicions of Byron and his companion, Christopher Sykes (d. 1986), who had graduated from the School of Oriental Studies's Persian program less than a year before Shadman started teaching Persian there.[31] Shortly before entering

---

[30] Coleridge Kennard, "Travellers in Persia," *The Times* (5 October 1934), 10.

[31] Auberon Waugh, "Sykes, Christopher Hugh (1907–1986), Writer and Traveler," *Oxford Dictionary of National Biography* (September 23, 2004). Available online: https://doi-org.stanford.idm.oclc.org/10.1093/ref:odnb/39845 (accessed

Iran, Skyes, on the verge of being appointed as the London *Times* correspondent in Tehran, had been recruited as a spy by the British government. Unsurprisingly, this aroused Iranian authorities' suspicions about their every move within the country. Throughout their travels in Iran, Byron and Sykes, officially prohibited from using a camera, resorted to taking photographs clandestinely. To blend in more easily with the local population, they were compelled to wear the Pahlavi hat, which was mandated for all men in the country at the time, and Byron found it "detestable."[32]

After returning from Iran in the spring of 1935, Byron collaborated with Sykes and Harold Macmillan (d. 1986) to publish a novel titled *Innocence and Design* under the pseudonym Richard Waughburton. Set in the fictional pre-modern country of Media, where the local population "are instructed in a nationalism gross and fanatical, while kept in a state of savage ignorance concerning the outer world," the novel centers on the character of the country's tyrant, Potshaw (*padshāh*), and how the Russians sought to undermine British influence there. In *Innocence and Design*, Potshaw (also called Sanskrit Shah)— clearly a portrayal of Reza Shah—is depicted as a detested despot determined to oppress and degrade his people. Potshaw emerges

---

November 22, 2024). Sykes was even more outspoken in his criticism of Reza Shah's reforms. Reflecting on his travels in Iran during the 1930s, he made the unsubstantiated claim that "Reza Shah's policy at that time was not merely anti-clerical but anti-Islamic: indeed, he was toying with the idea of abolishing the Koran in Persia and of converting the religion of Zoroaster into a national church"! (Christopher Sykes, *Four Studies in Loyalty* [New York: William Sloane Associates, Inc., 1946], 43.)

[32] James Knox, *Robert Byron* (London: John Murray, 2003), 305–19.

as a madman who imposes "an undigested and hysterical code ... where-by ... all Medes, at all times and under all circumstances, are forced to appear in peacked [*sic*] skiing-caps."[33] Immediately after agreeing to write a response to Byron's article, Shadman faced harsh criticism and reproach from his boss, Zarrin-Kafsh, who thought he had committed to servicing 'Ala's request in an attempt to curry favor with him. Consequently, Shadman's intended response to Byron never materialized. In a moment of frustration and displeasure, Shadman vented in his diaries, claiming that many government employees of Zarrin-Kafsh's ilk "are either embezzlers and louts or [a bunch of] paranoid, naïve, and hapless [individuals]" (p. 28).

Similar to the situation in Iran, where Shadman had observed the formation, in 1928, of the country's first fascist party, the New Iran Party, under the leadership of 'Abd al-Hoseyn Teymurtash (d. 1933), fascism was gaining traction in British politics early in the 1930s. On January 21, 1934, the British Union of Fascists, led by Oswald Mosley (d. 1980), held one of its most infamous rallies at Birmingham's Bingley Hall, attracting ten thousand bigoted supporters, including two thousand black-shirts. Robert Bernays, a Conservative M.P., described those attending as "minor businessmen, returned exiles from Empire outposts, disgruntled Conservative women, a good proportion of rather hard-faced beribboned ex-servicemen" animated by Mosely's flamboyant speeches, criticized by Bernays for "a lack of personal touch, gaps in his knowledge and in the

---

[33] Richard Waughburton, *Innocence and Design* (London: Macmillan & Co., Ltd, 1935), 119–20,. See also Knox, *Robert Byron*, 333-34.

chain of his reasoning."[34] Mosley and his fascist followers frequently paraded through Hyde Park, exchanging Nazi-style salutes in public, with intense debates between fascists and their opponents, including the communists, becoming a common occurrence in city parks. Less than two months after he arrived in London, Shadman witnessed one of these anti-fascist gatherings in Hyde Park, capturing his sense of thrill and amazement in a single sentence: "I watched freedom with my own eyes!" (p. 5).

Alongside his duties as a delegate with APOC, Shadman also pursued his legal studies, focusing on international law. His April 1934 diaries reveal that he spent long hours daily preparing for the requirements for a *Doctorat de troisième cycle* in international law at the Sorbonne (pp. 5, 7, 9, and 10). Shortly before that, he had started gathering information on graduate programs in journalism in the UK and even visited the editorial offices of the *Evening Standard* on January 31, 1934. On October 17, 1934, he sought legal counsel on applying for a graduate degree at the Sorbonne and, within a day, submitted his application, spending 160 francs on admission fees (p. 29). One month later, Shadman received a letter confirming that he had been scheduled to take the entrance exams on November 26 in Paris. However, this first attempt was unsuccessful.

While in Paris, Shadman attended the Ferdowsi millennial celebration at the Sorbonne, a public event attended by over two

---

[34] Robert Bernays, "Fascism and the Answer," *Spectator* 152 (27 April 1934), 652–53, summarized in Philip Rees, *Fascism in Britain* (Sussex: Harvester Press, 1979), 52.

thousand guests, including the French President Albert François Lebrun (d. 1950), the Minister of Education André Mallarmé (d. 1956), the French scholar of Persian literature Henri Massé (d. 1969), and Shadman's friends and colleagues Mohammad Qazvini, Hossein ʿAla, and Vladimir Minorsky (p. 38). During his time in Paris, Shadman became friends with Yousef Khoshkish (d. 1980), a senior executive at Iran's National Bank, who had completed his banking and business management studies in Paris and London. Khoshkish met a tragic fate. Despite his achievements as the governor of Iran's National Bank in the 1960s and 1970s, he was arrested twenty months after the 1979 revolution and executed by the Islamic Republic's revolutionary guards.[35]

Undeterred by his failure in the Sorbonne's entrance exam, Shadman redoubled his efforts, pursuing his legal studies with renewed determination. Nearly every diary entry from the remainder of 1934 through the winter of 1935 highlights his preoccupation with studying legal texts in French. Shadman retook the entrance exam on May 22, 1935, and was subsequently admitted to the program (p. 52). Even before being admitted to the Sorbonne, Shadman knew that completing a degree in law in France "would not be useful." Despite experiencing buyer's remorse, he remained determined to fulfill the program requirements, regardless of the effort involved (p. 49). Shadman did not leave Paris until June 4, 1935, and by mid-November of

---

[35] "Khoshkish, the former President of the Central Bank, and two others are executed," *Ettelaʿat* (16 August 1980/25 Mordad 1359 *sh.*), 2. Absurdly, the revolutionary court had sentenced Khoshkish to death on charges of financial misconduct and alleged "genocide" (*halākat-e nasl*)!

the same year completed the required coursework for a *troisième cycle* degree. Initially, he intended to write a thesis on propaganda. Still, within a few days, he changed his mind and decided to concentrate his research on the organization of the British Foreign Office (pp. 67–69). While in Paris, Shadman delivered a presentation at the Collège de France, where he articulated his perspectives on which among the French, British, or German educational systems would best suit Iran (p. 70).

As Shadman took a more active role in the daily operations of the Iranian Legation in London, he became a regular participant in staff meetings. During one such meeting on July 4, 1935, those who attended, including ʿAla, deliberated on the possibility of establishing an Iran Society in London. Two weeks later, Basil Gray (d. 1989), the British art historian and head of the British Museum's Oriental Department, informed Shadman of his being appointed as honorary secretary of the Iran Society (pp. 56–57). ʿAla subsequently granted the Society permission to use the Iranian Legation at 10 Princes Gate, London, as its headquarters. One of the earliest meetings of the Society took place on November 19, 1935, at the Iranian Legation under the chairmanship of Hoseyn ʿAla. The others present in the same meeting, as the Society's records indicate, were ʿAli-Asghar Zarrin-Kafsh, Lord Lamington, Professor Reynold A. Nicholson, the English poet and dramatist Laurence Binyon (d. 1943), the British architect and diplomat Alfred C. Bossom (d. 1965), the Conservative M.P. Sir Edward H. Keeling (d. 1954), and Basil Gray.[36] On November 9, 1936, one year after that

---

[36] Iran Society, "The First 65 Years," https://iransociety.org/the-first-65-years/

inaugural meeting, Shadman participated for the first time in a meeting of the Iran Society held at the British Museum, during which Aga Khan III (d. 1957) delivered a lecture on the poetry of Hafez (p. 101).[37]

Soon after completing the coursework for a university doctorate at the Sorbonne,[38] Shadman decided, early in January 1936, to pursue a doctoral degree at a British institution of higher education (p. 73). Initially, he aspired to study for a graduate degree in journalism and even visited King's College London and University College London to explore their programs (pp. 74–75, 77). Ultimately, he decided to concentrate his doctoral studies on History. On January 23, Shadman toured the London School of Economics (LSE) to inquire about the school's History Department and doctoral admission requirements. About four months later, on May 12, 1936, he met with Professor Lionel C. Robbins (d. 1984), then head of the Department of Economics at LSE. Notably, Shadman misspelled Robbins's name as "Robinson" when rewriting his diaries years later. Six days later, he also met with Professor Sir Arnold Plant (d. 1978), an economics professor at LSE, to confirm if he was interested in supervising Shadman in writing a thesis on the history of the oil industry in Iran. Plant discouraged Shadman from pursuing this topic, citing the scarcity of archival materials. Less than a week later, on May 22, 1936, the LSE graduate admissions committee informed Shadman of his

---

(accessed November 12, 2024).

[37] For Aga Khan III's life and career, see an intimate tribute written by his son Sadruddin on the centenary of his birth: "The Aga Khan: From Curzon to Hitler, A Man Always at the Center of History," *The Times* (November 5, 1977), 14.

[38] We were unable to locate Shadman's thesis at the Sorbonne.

acceptance into the doctoral program in International History. At LSE, Professor Harold Laski (d. 1950), known for supporting international students, agreed to meet with Shadman to discuss potential topics for his doctoral research. Given Shadman's interest in the history of British diplomacy in Iran, Laski and his former student, Professor Robbins, decided to appoint Professor Sir Charles Kingsley Webster (d. 1961), a prominent British diplomat and historian, as Shadman's supervisor (pp. 84–85). Before the end of April 1936, Shadman had already started visiting the Public Record Office at Kew Gardens to complete research for his doctoral thesis (p. 113). Thirty-nine months later, on July 12, 1939, Shadman successfully defended his doctoral thesis (pp. 178–79). During the next three years, Fazlollah Nabil (also known as Nabil al-Dowleh), who served as Iran's acting Minister Plenipotentiary from 1938 to 1940 and later became chief of staff to Queen Farah, was one of Shadman's closest friends.[39]

Titled "The Relations of Britain and Persia, 1800–1815," Shadman's doctoral thesis was submitted to London University on June 9, 1939 (p. 175). His doctoral degree was officially awarded four months later, on October 28, 1939.[40] Shadman's focus on the relationship between Britain and Iran was likely influenced by his conversations with 'Abd-ol-Hoseyn Hamzavi (d. 1979), one of his close friends in London, who served as the press attaché at the Iranian Legation. Hamzavi, a graduate of the London University School of Economics, was working on an essay examining European powers' diplomacy in Iran, which he

---

[39] 'Aqeli, *Sharh-e hal-e rejal*, 3: 1606.
[40] *The Times* (October 28, 1939), 9.

later published as a monograph.[41] Be that as it may, Shadman's thesis is organized into three parts across seventeen chapters. It primarily examines a succession of diplomatic missions between the British Raj and early Qajar Iran, with several chapters dedicated to the broader international implications of British policy in Iran regarding Turkey, Russia, and France. The introduction, spanning forty pages, provides an overview of early nineteenth-century British diplomacy in Iran. Notably, Chapter II, the most extended section of the thesis at forty-eight pages, meticulously documents Sir John Malcolm's (d. 1833) first mission to Iran from 1799 to 1801, showcasing Shadman's commitment to a comprehensive account of this pivotal diplomatic effort.[42] Three years later, Shadman submitted a copy of his thesis to an editor at Longman & Green, hoping to have it published as a monograph; however, the project ultimately came to nothing (p. 271).

An avid traveler, Shadman visited Germany in August 1936, coinciding with the final week of the Games of the XI Olympiad. During his one-month stay, he toured Berlin, Stuttgart, and Potsdam. The Summer Olympic Games of 1936 brought together 49 nations and marked a historic milestone as the first Olympics to be broadcast on television, transforming the event into a global spectacle. Nearly all events were held at the newly constructed Olympiastadion in Berlin, which featured state-of-

---

[41] ʿAbd al-Hoseyn Hamzavi, *Persia and the Powers: An Account of Diplomatic Relations, 1941–1946* (London: Hutchinson & Co., 1946). For more on Hamzavi, see ʿAqeli, *Sharh-e hal-e rejal*, 1: 594.

[42] Seyyed Fakhr al-Din Shadman, "The Relations of Britain and Persia, 1800–1815" (Doctoral thesis, London University School of Economics, 1939), 75–123.

the-art facilities for the time. A few days after completing the draft of his article for the *Asiatic Review*, scheduled for publication the following year,[43] Shadman boarded a train from Liverpool Street Station to Harwich Town on the morning of Saturday, August 8, 1936. From Harwrich, he embarked on a ship to the Netherlands and arrived in Berlin that evening shortly before 8 p.m. While in Berlin, Shadman reunited with several close friends and acquaintances, including Javad, Taqizadeh's younger brother, and Dr. Hoseyn-Qoli Qezel-Ayagh (d. 1956), a former member of parliament and Iran's first forensic pathologist who had established the country's Office of Legal Medicine under ʿAli-Akbar Davar.[44]

On August 16, Shadman attended the closing ceremony of the 1936 Summer Olympics, a grand spectacle featuring soldiers and fireworks designed to showcase the Nazi regime's glorification of Hitler. During the remaining three weeks of his stay in Germany, Shadman made a brief journey to Potsdam, visiting Sanssouci Palace, and later toured Neues Schloss Palace near Stuttgart (pp. 92–5). While documenting the names of individuals he met in Berlin, Shadman deliberately avoided mentioning any potential encounters with leftist exiles, including Morteza ʿAlavi (d. 1941), a communist activist and the niece of his late friend Hasan ʿAlavi. Hasan ʿAlavi's sudden death in 1928 affected Shadman so profoundly that he wrote and published a fictionalized biographical account of his life.[45] Based in Berlin,

---

[43] Seyyed Fakhr al-Din Shadman, "Education in Iran," *Asiatic Review* 33, ser. 4 (1937): 165–73.

[44] ʿAqeli, *Sharh-e hal-e rejal*, 2: 1211.

[45] Seyyed Fakhr al-Din Shadman, *Ketab-e bi-nam* (Tehran: Matbaʿah-e Sirus,

Morteza ʿAlavi had established *Peykar*, a Persian-language periodical, in February 1931, advocating for a Marxist-Leninist revolution in Iran. ʿAlavi's political radicalism boarded on advocacy for violence. He openly called for the elimination of Reza Shah, whom he accused of serving as a puppet for British imperial interests. Shadman's friend and mentor, Hasan Taqizadeh, was a frequent target of ʿAlavi's scathing attacks, whom he denounced as one of the most corrupt officials of the "Pahlavi dictatorship." *Peykar* ceased publication after fifteen issues and was forcibly shut down by the German Reich judiciary under Curt Joël (d. 1945) in April 1932 following complaints from Iranian officials.[46]

The outbreak of World War II early in September 1939 plunged Iranians in London into the depths of panic and despair as they faced uncertainty about their safety, the fate of their homeland, and the broader implications of the conflict on their lives and futures. Blackouts had become routine as early as September 1939, disrupting daily life in London and instilling a sense of unease as the city prepared for the anticipated air raids during the early days of World War II. Food quality began to deteriorate, reflecting the impact of wartime rationing and supply chain disruptions, which limited access to fresh produce and other essentials, forcing people to adapt to increasingly scarce and substandard provisions. Overwhelmed by the uncertainties of war

---

1928/1307).

[46] Javad Karimi, "Peykar," *Daneshnameh-e Jahan-e Eslam*. Available online https:/ /rch.ac.ir/article/Details/13346 (accessed November 14, 2024). For more on Morteza ʿAlavi's life and fate, see Ahmad Ahqari, "Sharh-e hal va zendegi-e siyasi-ejtema'i-e Morteza ʿAlavi," *Radio Zamaneh* (January 24, 2012). Available online https://www.radiozamaneh.com/39635/ (accessed November 14, 2024).

and the emotional toll of living in a city gripped by fear and turmoil, Shadman struggled with despair and dejection almost every day in September, October, and November 1939. As the war intensified in Eastern Europe and England prepared to enter the conflict, Shadman received a telegraph from Tehran instructing him to travel to Trieste in northeastern Italy to manage the customs processing of a crude oil shipment from Iran. Horrified by this telegram and the prospect of traveling through war-torn Europe, he swiftly reached out to his friend Hazhir, a protégé of Taqizadeh and then serving as Vice-Minister of Finance, seeking his intervention to overrule this telegram—a request Hazhir successfully fulfilled (pp. 183-90).

During the early months of World War II, Shadman, no longer busy with thesis-related research and writing, had enough free time to engage in focused reading, immersing himself in books as a refuge from the anxiety and uncertainty of the unfolding global conflict. For several weeks, he read for hours every day, finding distraction and meaning in a diverse array of works such as Nezami's *Haft Peykar*, Tolstoy's *War and Peace*, and the poetry of Sa'di and Hafez. He had even acquired a copy of Hitler's *Mein Kampf*, which he read daily in September 1939, perhaps driven by a desire to understand the ideological underpinnings of the conflict engulfing the world (pp. 182 and 184).

As the complications arising from the outbreak of war intensified, the Iranian government informed Zarrin-Kafsh via telegram of his dismissal as the head of the delegation with the Anglo-Persian Oil Company. Shadman had been instructed to step in as the acting head of the delegation, taking over Zarrin-

Kafsh's responsibilities during this critical and turbulent period. On December 29, 1939, Zarrin-Kafsh granted Shadman access to the delegation's checkbooks and bank account, formally transferring his administrative authority as part of the transition in the leadership (p. 192, under December 14, 1939, and p. 194, under December 29 and 30). As the acting head of the delegation, Shadman traveled to Switzerland between January 26 and March 5, 1940. During his stay, he prepared the final draft of a detailed financial report on the sales of Iranian crude in consultation with Dr. Hegler, a Geneva-based international legal advisor. He was also hosted by Mohammad-ʿAli Jamalzadeh (d. 1997), further strengthening his connections within the expatriate community (pp. 196–200).

Shadman's frustration and anguish gradually subsided. By the end of the spring of 1940, he had already begun following the news of the conflict closely, immersing himself in the unfolding events of the war with renewed attentiveness. Like many Iranians at the time, he had concluded that Hitler would ultimately emerge as the victor in the war. The British and French, he observed, faced significant challenges in defeating the Nazi war machine, which he viewed as a highly efficient and unstoppable force (pp. 209–10). Anticipating the imminent victory of the Nazi regime and the potential opportunity to collaborate with German officials, he had even begun learning German, preparing himself for what he believed to be an inevitable shift in global power dynamics (pp. 211ff.). As the destruction in London became increasingly widespread, the Iranian Legation in London sustained damage from air raids, forcing Iranian diplomats and employees to evacuate to Cambridge, which, according to Shadman, was "a haven compared to London, from the point of view of air raids." He moved to Cambridge on 21 September 1940 (pp. 216 and 219).

Referring to Farangis Namazi (d. 1981), his future wife, Shadman confided in his diaries: "I have fallen in love with her manners and earnestness .... I cannot imagine what changes will appear in my life due to encountering this young lady" (p. 235). In Cambridge, Shadman, who was still diligently self-studying German, developed a romantic relationship with Farangis Namazi, a twenty-six-year-old Iranian student attending Oxford University. Their first meeting occurred on Sunday, March 23, 1941, during a lunch party hosted by Taqizadeh and his wife to celebrate the Iranian New Year, Nowruz. Shadman and Farangis Namazi had their first date approximately two weeks later, on April 7, at a local restaurant in Cambridge. Following their meal, they attended a screening of *Major Barbara*, a social satire produced and directed by Gabriel Pascal (d. 1954), at a nearby movie theater (pp. 232–33). On May 26, 1941, Shadman wrote to his father in Karbala to share his decision to marry Farangis Namazi (p. 241). Less than three years later, on December 27, 1942, Shadman and Namazi were married at the Iranian Legation. Ambassador Taqizadeh and his German-born wife, Atiyeh Jung, personally took responsibility for organizing their wedding celebration (pp. 372–73).

Farangis Namazi's name appears on nearly every page of Shadman's diaries from 1941—a testament to her profound influence. Her impact on broadening Shadman's intellectual horizons was remarkable. From the early weeks of her relationship with Shadman, Farangis, who would later become an authority in literary theory and translation studies, encouraged him to engage with scholarly trends related to classical Persian literature and language. Less than two months after falling in love with Farangis, Shadman began reading two texts: the collected essays of Mohammad Qazvini and an essay on the life and scholarship of Edward G. Browne (d. 1926), the renowned professor of Persian and Arabic at Cambridge University. Through Farangis, he found the opportunity to meet Sir Hamilton A. R. Gibb (d. 1971), Margoliouth's successor as the Laudian Professor of Arabic at Oxford University, during one of his trips to Oxford in June 1941. Farangis Namazi also played a key role in fostering Shadman's friendship with Harold Walter Bailey (d. 1996), a scholar of comparative linguistics and an expert on the Middle Iranian Saka language of Khotan. At the time, Bailey was working on his doctoral thesis, a critical edition of the Pahlavi *Greater Bundahishn*, completed in 1943. Shadman's reference to Bailey as a "professor" in 1941 suggests that he may have rewritten his diaries at a later date (p. 244–45).[47] On another occasion, Farangis Namazi introduced Shadman to the renowned English philologist Hector Munro Chadwick (d. 1947), who was then serving as the Elrington and Bosworth Professor of Anglo-Saxon at Cambridge University (p. 252).[48]

---

[47] See John Sheldon, "Bailey, Harold Walter," *Encyclopaedia Iranica*, July 20, 2002. Available online: https://iranicaonline.org/articles/bailey-harold-walter-1 (accessed November 24, 2024).

[48] William Telfer and John D. Haigh, "Chadwick, Hector Munro (1870–1947),

Similarly, it was through Farangis that Shadman formed a friendship with Walter Bruno Henning (d. 1967), a refugee from Nazi Germany and prominent scholar of Middle Persian languages and literature (pp. 356-57). Henning later supervised the doctoral thesis of Ehsan Yarshater (d. 2018), Shadman's colleague and close friend at Tehran University.[49] Influenced by Farangis's intellectual guidance, Shadman's readings from the fall of 1941 focused primarily on England and Germany's literary histories (pp. 281ff.). During this period, Shadman developed an interest in the works of Hans Werner Richter (d. 1993), a prominent German poet and writer who later established Gruppe 47, a literary platform dedicated to renewing German literature after World War II (p. 291). Moreover, the Japanese military successes in the East Asian theaters of war were so remarkable that, as the end of 1941 approached, he decided to delve into a monograph on the history of Japan (p. 288).

In the early summer of 1941, the first signs of the Allies' impending invasion of Iran began to emerge, causing Shadman considerable distress. In his diary entry for August 6, 1941, Shadman observed that there was "lots of debate" in the press and the British Parliament about Iran. He further noted that the British regarded Iran as "the center of German operations" (pp. 255–56). For the rest of August, Shadman's anxiety began to mount as the news of a potential military operation against Iran gained traction in

---

Literary Scholar," *Oxford Dictionary of National Biography*, September 23, 2004. Available online: https://doi-org.laneproxy.stanford.edu/10.1093/ref:odnb/32342 (accessed November 24, 2024).

[49] Mary Boyce, "Obituary: Walter Bruno Henning," *Bulletin of the School of Oriental and African Studies*, 30 (3): 781–85.

the mainstream British press. As the end of August approached, Shadman became overwhelmed by worry and stress over the dreadful news from Iran. He fell ill with what appeared to be influenza and remained bedridden for several days. As he had done two years earlier at the outbreak of World War II, he found refuge within the pages of books and immersed himself in reading for solace. Alongside the poems of Hafez and Saʿdi and Shakespeare's plays, which Farangis seems to have recommended, he began rereading Tolstoy's *War and Peace* (pp. 256–57). Shadman's response to the Allies' occupation of Iran was deeply emotional, reflecting his profound patriotism and pride as an Iranian. Overwhelmed by anxiety about the future of his homeland, he described Iran as a "wretched and defenseless" nation confronting an existential threat (p. 258). On August 25, 1941, upon hearing the news of the Soviet and British troops entering the soil of Iran, Shadman and Farangis felt so distraught and dejected that they spent hours walking through the streets of Cambridge "like maniacs":

> Until today, I didn't realize how deeply I love this wretched
> and hapless country. I wish I were in Iran to share in the grief
> of my fellow Iranians and, [if necessary], to die alongside
> them. I don't know what fate awaits our nation, but I am
> certain today that peace, friendship, and freedom are nothing
> more than empty words, and that power alone governs the
> world (p. 258).

That was Shadman's Machiavellian moment. More than four centuries ago, Niccolò Machiavelli (d. 1527), a humanist by training and a diplomat representing the court of Florence in France, experienced something strikingly similar. Dismissed and treated as "Mr. Nothing" in Paris, he came to the sobering realization that, without wealth and military power, "there might be no future for the Italian city-states."[50] In much the same way, Shadman, centuries later, confronted, like any other Iranian, a parallel truth in the summer of 1941. Shadman was not a chauvinist; to him, Iran represented "the virtues and vices of a great and time-honored ancient nation." To Shadman, nationalism was a concept far removed from jingoism and the pursuit of war. What he was attempting to articulate can broadly be understood as constructionist nationalism, a framework that emphasizes the role of modernity and the transformative power of contemporary institutions, including media and public education, in shaping national identity.[51] Nationalism was defined as the act of making life easier and better for one's fellow human beings. "Everyone who loves Iran and values global peace must strive to promote knowledge and science to the best of their ability. They should do all they can to create opportunities for progress, serving not only their own country but also contributing to the betterment of the world" (p. 346). In a long, passionate paragraph written nearly seven years later, in 1948, he articulated his pride in being Iranian as follows:

> We are who we are. Yesterday, we were Zoroastrians; today,
> we are Muslims. We have experienced both triumph and
> defeat. We have fought the Greeks, Romans, Arabs, Turks,
> Tatars, Russians, and British—and we have survived. One day,
> we liberated the Jews from slavery; another, we offered the
> throne of India to its defeated ruler. The imprisonment of

---

[50] Quentin Skinner, *Machiavelli: A Brief Insight* (New York: Sterling, 1981), 8–9.

[51] For a deeper exploration of constructionist nationalism, see Ernest Gellner's *Nations and Nationalism* (Oxford: Blackwell, 1983), chapter 7. See also Benedict Anderson's *Imagined Communities: Reflections on the Origin and Spread of Nationalism* (London: Verso, 2016), chapter 7, for a complementary perspective.

Roman Emperor Valerian is part of our past, just as Shah
Soltan-Hoseyn's helplessness, humiliation, and tragic fate
belong to it. Both Yazdgird III and Shah ʿAbbas the Great are
part of our legacy. Both Ferdowsi and Hushang Hanavidi are
Iranian, as are the Zoroastrian Arbab Rostam Kermani and
Shaykh ʿAbd-ol-Rasul Qaʾeni. We possess both virtues and
flaws. We are intelligent yet lazy, witty, sociable, libertine, and
merciful. We cherish sycophancy and pretense, favoring
generalities over specifics and words over their meanings. At
times, we are Helenists; at others, we revere the Arabs. One
day, we compose poetry praising the king, his vizier, or a
Turkish lover—male or female—and the next, we seek the
friendship of Europeans, naively asking for their guidance on
the path to progress.... We value honor so deeply that we are
willing to disgrace ourselves for the sake of fleeting splendor
in the eyes of others. We show kindness to strangers but are
easily deceived. We compose exceptional poetry but lack
respect for critical thinking. For twenty-five centuries, we
have grown accustomed to accepting the supremacy of
alcoholic, hedonistic, and corrupt elites and notables. Our
harmful words outnumber our harmful deeds. We have a
tendency to exaggerate and exhibit boldness. We are inheritors
of centuries of a nation's faith, traditions, language, ethics,
customs, sorrows, and joys.[52]

Shadman, appalled by the British and Soviet armies' brazen
violation of international laws, dismissed everything he read and
heard in the mainstream British news media about Iran as mere
"hogwash." Shadman believed that the pervasive lies and
demagoguery propagated by Western journalists and media,
combined with the public's unquestioning ignorance and gullibility,

---

[52] Shadman, *Taskhir-e tamaddon*, 97.

had reduced the moral and intellectual standing of the British to what he scornfully referred to as a nation of "African barbarians," a racist cliché reflective of the prejudiced language of his time (pp. 260 and 265). On one occasion, he and Farangis attended a public lecture at the Cambridge Guildhall delivered by a British priest named Gill, whom Shadman described as "narrow-minded, prejudiced, and ignorant." The audience was predominantly Jewish, and Mr. Gill's lecture focused on the conditions of Jews in Iran during Reza Shah's reign. The "biased" priest devoted much of his lecture to propagating a series of "baseless" claims about Reza Shah's alleged mistreatment of Jews in Iran. Shadman and Farangis were outraged by Mr. Gill's deliberate omission of how the ancient Iranian king, Cyrus the Great, had liberated the Babylonian Jews from Assyrian oppression. He was so incensed at this barrage of lies and unfounded accusations that he noted in his diary while reflecting on Reza Shah's decision to ban European missionary activities throughout Iran: "No one is more stupid and biased than these European priests, and it's the duty of every Iranians to prevent these egotistic, bigoted individuals from entering the country" (p. 266).

Shadman's stance on the issue of Westerners' presence in Iran grew increasingly rigid in the years that followed. Five years after returning to Iran, Shadman published his magnum opus, the treatise *Taskhir-e tamaddon-e farangi* (*Seizing Western Civilization*), in which he accused European and American "immigrants" in Iran of being a bunch of "fraudsters" (*shayyād*) bent on "sowing the seeds of mental corruption" within Iranian society. Railing against the hospitality Iranians used to extend to Westerners over the course of history and in a veiled criticism of the President Truman administration's Point Four Program, launched formally in January 1949, which facilitated the dispatch of hundreds of American technical assistants to Iran, he asked rhetorically: "Why should Avicenna's countrymen be so naive to assume that immigrants from Sweden, Denmark, Switzerland, and the United States have come to Iran to rebuild our country for our benefit, rather than their own?"[53]

By late August 1941, the intense focus on Iran in the British newspapers started to wane temporarily. In mid-September, however, the British media outlets resumed their criticism of Iran and Iranians, singling out Reza Shah as the root of all problems in the region (pp. 263–64). On a personal level, Reza Shah's forced abdication by the Soviet and British occupiers devastated Shadman:

> Although I never supported Reza Shah's dictatorship and some
> of his actions, his removal under these circumstances weighed
> heavily on me. Today, Iran's independence has been shattered,
> and only God knows when it can be restored. The only
> glimmer of hope lies in the possibility of Germany defeating
> Russia (p. 264).

In a moment of *Schadenfreude*, he expressed satisfaction at Russia's humiliating defeat by Nazi Germany, remarking that it was "so that they get their punishment after centuries of mistreating, massacring, and stealing land from their neighbors" (p. 272). The young Mohammad-Reza Shah's acceptance of the conditions of the occupation armies, including his pledge to strengthen the authority of local powerbrokers, deeply concerned Shadman. To him, this signified nothing less than the

---

[53] Shadman, *Taskhir-e tamaddon*, 96.

disintegration of Iran's territorial sovereignty (p. 265). A few months later, Shadman sorrowfully recorded the establishment of Soviet-backed separatist "governments" in Tabriz and Mahabad, viewing them as ominous precursors to the potential disintegration of Iran. Reflecting on the nation's fragile state, he lamented: "Our country is in a precarious situation, and no one knows what fate awaits it" (pp. 313 and 321).

In his assessment of Reza Shah's reign, included as a separate section at the end of the part containing his 1941–42 diaries, Shadman struggled to maintain an unwavering commitment to justice. Despite his effort to provide a balanced critique that reciognized both the achievements and the shortcomings of the monarch's rule, his analysis ultimately lacked impartiality. He acknowledged that "under Reza Shah, significant changes started to appear in the life and manners of Iranians, and buildings, roads, schools, and orphanages were constructed across the country." According to Shadman, Reza Shah, despite being illiterate, "was a smart and discerning man who enjoyed common sense." The shah, however, failed to pay attention to international affairs. Reza Shah, Shadman observed, "wielded absolute authority but refrained from abusing it." Reza Shah, Shadman added, "was a patriot, but his patriotism was not based on knowledge and practical wisdom." The founder of the Pahlavi dynasty "had an insatiable desire for acquiring land and wealth, which compelled him to surround himself with corrupt and unscrupulous individuals" (p. 310). Reza Shah's most devastating shortcoming, Shadman griped, was "destroying the character of the people of Iran." In his final assessment, Shadman concluded:

> [Reza Shah] destroyed self-confidence among the people,
> viewing himself as the sole pillar of the country.
> Consequently, when he was no longer in power, no institution
> or group of individuals was there to take charge of the nation's
> affairs. Despite all his accomplishments, I, as an Iranian,
> cannot forgive him for this failure. His greatest failure was his
> tolerance of sycophancy and his belief that Iran's very existence
> depended on his continued rule ... if he had not been driven
> by a thirst for acquiring land, he could have served the country
> more effectively. Had he been more knowledgeable about
> scientific advancements and global political affairs, he would
> not have marginalized talented and patriotic individuals....
> Reza Shah achieved a great deal over the past two decades.
> However, if Iran had enjoyed freedom, his accomplishments
> could have been carried out with greater impact (pp. 311-12).

Shadman's career stands in stark contradiction to his claim that Reza Shah's policies aimed to undermine the "character" and "self-confidence" of the Iranian people. His remarkable rise from a modest position as a junior judicial clerk to a role as part of the Iranian government's delegation with APOC would have been inconceivable without Reza Shah's final approval. Notably, Shadman's portrayal of Reza Shah as the destroyer of Iranians' character and self-respect sharply contrasts with the observations of Laurence P. Elwell-Sutton (d. 1984), a British employee of APOC, who served in Abadan from 1935 to 1938.[54] According to him,

---

[54] On his career, see "Obituary: Professor L.P. Elwell-Sutton (1912–84)," *British Society for Middle Eastern Studies Bulletin* 11 (1984): 212–13. Available online: https://doi.org/10.1080/13530198408705402 (accessed on December 4, 2024).

> Reza Shah's most striking success was the change he wrought
> in the outlook of Persians of all classes. Perhaps it is
> inaccurate to call it a change ... it would be more correct to see
> it as a revival of the fundamental elements in the Persian
> character .... He strove to revive in his people a sense of
> confidence and national self-respect. They must learn to look
> westerners in the face; they must have no grounds for feeling
> ashamed before the representatives of European civilisation ....
> Every device of education and propaganda, every art of press
> and radio, was used to instill into the people the virtues of
> pride, assurance and self-esteem. Europeans, accustomed to
> servility from orientals, could not stomach the new tone. But
> it was not intended to please them.[55]

Be that as it may, from a broader perspective, Shadman regarded the Pahlavi reign as one of the "most significant periods in Iranian history since the Mongol invasion" (p. 311).

Over the last three years of World War II, Shadman faced mounting financial difficulties as life in London and Cambridge grew increasingly challenging. Despite serving as the acting head of the Iranian delegation with AIOC, a role that undoubtedly required significant responsibility and effort, his salary was irregularly paid. On March 24, 1942, he telegraphed his younger brother, Jalal al-Din Shadman, in Tehran, requesting him to consult with their influential patron, Hazhir, about formally appointing him as the head of the delegation and resolving the issue of his long-overdue salary (p. 313).[56] Food

---

[55] Elwell-Sutton, *Persian Oil*, 62–3.

[56] On October 14, 1941, upon learning of the recently retired ambassador Mohammad-ʿAli Moqaddam's application to government officials in Tehran for his appointment as head of the Iranian delegation to the Anglo-Iranian Oil

shortages in London had reached such critical levels that basic items were almost impossible to come by. On April 8, 1942, Shadman experienced a rare moment of indulgence when he had his second egg after several months (p. 317). Jalal Shadman's efforts to lobby officials in Tehran for Shadman's appointment as the head of the delegation ultimately proved futile. On April 23, 1942, Taqizadeh received a telephone call from Tehran confirming the appointment of Fathollah Nuri Esfandyari as the head of the Imperial Government of Iran's delegation with AIOC (p. 322). A great-grandson of the disreputable Qajar-era grand vizier, Mirza Aqa Khan Nuri (d. 1865), Fathollah Nuri Esfandyari had completed his education in France and previously served as the Master of the Ceremonies at the Ministry of Foreign Affairs and the Inspector-General of the Ministry of Commerce.[57] Disgruntled and feeling marginalized, Shadman experienced a deep and bitter sense of disappointment. Upon hearing the news of Mr. Esfandyari's arrival in England, he griped that

> After eight years of hard work and study, I find myself in the
> same position I held eight years ago—as assistant to the head
> of the delegation. What's even stranger is that this role now
> comes with a salary cut, reducing my income by a third.
> Despite these setbacks, I refrain from complaining, as the
> country is in dire straits, and there seems to be no one in
> charge who is willing or able to address such grievances.
> Instead, I resolve to double my efforts and work even harder to

---

Company (AIOC), Shadman became so incensed that he described Moqaddam in his diary as "brazenly foolish," "ignorant," "shameless," and "greedy" (p. 274).

[57] ʻAqeli, *Sharh-e hal-e rejal*, 3: 1673–74.

achieve my goals. Perhaps, in the end, these changes will
bring about positive outcomes (p. 335).

The administrative instability and chaos in Iran during the last three years of World War II, coupled with the intensification of the Blitz in the months leading up to May 1941, drove Shadman to find solace in books. As previously noted, his relationship with Farangis Namazi, which eventually led to their marriage, significantly transformed Shadman's reading preferences, fostering a deeper appreciation for literature that aligned with her interests and values. Farangis's support encouraged and motivated Shadman to explore new genres and authors that he might not have considered otherwise. As the Blitz drew to a close, Shadman dedicated increasingly more time each day to reading, immersing himself in books as a means of distraction and intellectual engagement amidst the lingering aftermath of the air raids. Between August 1941 and January 1943, he read nearly 60 titles, either partially or in their entirety, spanning a range of languages, including English, Persian, German, French, Arabic, and Ottoman Turkish. History and literature were his favorite topics. "During these two years in Cambridge, I was engaged in reading literary and historical books," he admitted (p. 358).

A dabbler in fiction writing whose *Ketab-e bi-nam* (*A book without a name*), published in 1928, featured a frame tale revolving around the life of his deceased friend Hasan 'Alavi. Shadman was particularly drawn to novels and biographies, finding them the most engaging and captivating among his reading choices. Between September 1941 and March 1942, Shadman completed five major novels, reading them cover to cover. These included Gustave Flaubert's (d. 1880) *Madame Bovary*, Walter Scott's (d. 1832) *Ivanhoe: A Romance*, Stendhal's (d. 1842) *La Chartreuse de Parme*, Honoré de Balzac's (d. 1850) *Le Médecin de campagne*, and Alphonse Daudet's (d. 1897) *Lettres de mon moulin* (pp. 246, 297, 315, 318).

Shadman's focus on these titles was not accidental. All these novels are renowned for their stylistic excellence, distinguished by their unique narrative approaches and masterful storytelling. Whether through Flaubert's meticulous realism, Stendhal's profound psychological insight, or Daudet's richly evocative prose, each work showcases a distinctive voice that sets it apart from others. Internal evidence suggests that Shadman engaged with these literary texts as a means of studying the craft of storytelling and honing his skills to become a novelist. He references Edward M. Forster's (d. 1970) famous *Aspects of the Novel* on two occasions, a work he studied diligently to deepen his understanding of narrative structure and refine his approach to the art of novel writing (pp. 304 and 320).[58]

Biography was the other genre that captivated Shadman's interest. During the last two years of his time in London, he read biographies of Sir Thomas Herbert Shirley (d. 1682), Voltaire (d. 1778), Napoleon Bonaparte (d. 1821), Lord Tennyson (d. 1892) (two titles), and Anthony Trollope (d. 1882) (pp. 292, 295, 299, 309, 363). One title that stands out among

---

[58] Previously, he had read *A Survey of Modern Short Story* (p. 300). Three years earlier, he had crafted the plot of an Iran-related novel for an anonymous French writer based in London (p. 130). For Shadman's essay on the language of the novel (*Zaban-e dastan*), see Seyyed Fakhr al-Din Shadman, *Trazhedi-e farang* (Tehran: Chapkhaneh-e Arzhang, 1967/1346 *sh.*), 191–224.

Shadman's readings is Lin Yutang's (d. 1976) *The Importance of Living* (pp. 325, 326, 327, 328, 329). As a critic of Western civilization, Shadman, who published a collected volume titled *Trazhedi-e Farang* (*The tragedy of the West*) a few weeks before his death, discovered a kindred spirit in Yutang Lin's *The Importance of Living* (d. 1976).[59] Lin's critical perspective underscores the value of blending Eastern and Western philosophies to create a guide for achieving a balanced and fulfilling life. He draws extensively from Chinese philosophy, particularly Taoism and Confucianism while engaging Western thinkers like Bertrand Russell. A central theme in Lin's work is his critique of the Western obsession with work and productivity, which he contrasts with the Chinese emphasis on leisure, reflection, and the art of living well.[60]

In the final years of his time in London, Shadman's reading interests shifted notably, transitioning toward more scholarly and academic topics. His foundational readings in Iranian studies included Abu Reyhan Biruni's (d. after 1050) *Vestiges of the Past* (*Ketab-e asar al-baqiyah 'an al-qurun al-khaliyah*), Abo'l-Fazl Bayhaqi's (d. 1077) *Chronicle of the Reign of the Ghaznavid Sultan Mas'ud*, Nezami 'Aruzi's (d. 1161) *Chahar maqaleh*, 'Attar's biographical dictionary of Sufi notables, Joveyni's (d. 1283) chronicle, the *Jahangosha*, Mohammad b. 'Ali Ravandi's (d. 1245) historical writings on the formative phase of the Saljuqid rule in Iran, Rashid-al-Din Fazlollah's (d. 1318) *Compendium of Histories*, Hamdallah Mostowfi Qazvini's (d.

---

[59] The chapter on the tragedy of the West (*Trazhedi-e farang*, pp. 165–90) was first appeared in *Yaghma*, 14, no. 6 (August-September 1961/Shahrivar 1340 *sh.*).

[60] Yutang Lin, *The Importance of Living* (London: W. Heinemann, Ltd., 1939).

1340) *Tarikh-e gozideh*, Dowlatshah's (d. 1494) biographical dictionary of poets, and Haji Mirza Jani Kashani's (d. 1852) *Ketab-e Noqtat-al-Kaf*, a foundational narrative on the history of Babism edited by Edward G. Browne and Mohammad Qazvini (pp. 291, 320, 324, 325, 326, 327, 331). During the final months of his stay in Cambridge, Shadman developed a fleeting interest in Ottoman Turkish, particularly in how it had been influenced by Persian (p. 331). Nearly five years later, while voicing his opposition to the systematic purge of outdated Arabic words and constructs from Persian, Shadman highlighted Ottoman Turkish as an example to underscore classical Persian's enduring strength and influence.[61]

Additionally, Shadman read parts of or entire texts of Plato's *Republic* and Karl Marx's *Das Kapital* during the last year of his stay in London (pp. 330, 331, 332, 336). European history remained one of Shadman's enduring interests in the years that followed—evidenced by his translation from French into Persian of one of the scholarly textbooks written by the French historians Albert Malet (d. 1915) and Jules Isaac (d. 1963), *Histoire moderne* (2 vols.). His readings during 1942 included the recently deceased British historian Herbert A. L. Fischer's (d. 1940) *A History of Europe: Ancient and Medieval* (p. 345). Relatedly, his relentless attention to daily news about the Russian theater of war sparked his curiosity and led him to explore at least two scholarly monographs on Russian history—*La Russie Moscovite* by Sergeï F. Platonov (d. 1933), a prolific Russian historian and victim of Stalinist purges, and Alfred Nicolas Rambaud's (d. 1905) *Histoire*

---

[61] Shadman, *Taskhir-e tamaddon*, 87–88.

de la Russie depuis les origines jusqu'à nos jours (pp. 340, 350, 353). The systematic study of these pre-modern authors and historians helped Shadman, an expatriate who had spent nearly a decade living abroad, gain profound insights into the dynamics of continuity and change in Iran, as well as the evolution of the Persian language, its idioms, and literary forms. In the early fall of 1942, Shadman, acutely aware of the countless hours he spent reading each day, confided in his diary: "I must stop a student life devoted to reading and start writing" (p. 358).

PERSIAN TEXT

RIGHT TO LEFT FROM BACK OF THE BOOK

Shadman's Diaries

VOLUME 2

روزنوشت‌های شادمان

جلد ۲

آذر ۱۳۱۲ تا اسفند ۱۳۲۱ خورشیدی

سید فخرالدین شادمان

شب[1] حرکت از طهران در منزل آقای دکتر رسولی شام خوردم. یزدان‌فر، فرساد، معظمی، و نظام هم بودند. مجلس خوبی بود. تا ساعت ۱۱ طول کشید. شب بخانه رفتم امّا خوابم نمی‌برد. پدر و مادرم در کربلا بی‌خبر از این سفر و برادران و خواهرم نیز مضطرب بودند. آقا میرزا عبدالله امینی هم منزل ما بود. خواهرم از شدّت اضطراب دو ساعت پیش از طلوع آفتاب از خواب بیدارم کرد. در میان تاریکی و روشنی با خواهرم و خاله‌ام که آنجا بود و برادران کوچکم وداع کردم. جلال و جمال و کمال با من بمنزل آقای زرین‌کفش آمدند. پیش از طلوع خورشید بمنزل آقای زرین‌کفش رسیدیم و بعد از نیم ساعت حرکت کردم. هشت و بیست دقیقه اتومبیل حرکت کرد. همراهانم: آقای زرین‌کفش، زنش، دخترش عزیزالزمان خانم، پسرش علیرضاخان، پسر دیگرش پرویز، دختر دیگرش زرّین‌دخت، و برادرزاده‌اش مصطفی‌خان افشار. ظهر وارد قزوین شدیم ولی در آنجا توقف نکردیم. هفت بعد از ظهر وارد همدان شدیم. در منزل آقای عبدالله خان فروهر که درویش مسلک بود شام خوردیم و خوابیدیم. هوا سرد بود. صبح زود احساس کسالت کردم ولی رفع شد. صبح بتماشا قبر استر و مردخای را دیدیم. کاغذی که برای خلخالی و برادرم جلال نوشته بودم < را > بپست دادم. سه ساعت بظهر آقای غمام همدانی و آقای نثری رئیس معارف بدیدن ما آمدند و بعد از ایشان آقای بیگلری حاکم همدان آمد. سه ربع بظهر مانده از همدان حرکت کردیم. در این شهر آقای زرین‌کفش با شوفر نزاعی کرد ولی بخیر گذشت. دو ساعت بعد از ظهر بکنگاور رسیدیم. در آنجا ناهار پلوی لذیذی خوردیم و چهار بعد از ظهر حرکت کردیم و هفت ساعت و نیم بعد از ظهر روز یکشنبه ۲۶ آذر ماه بکرمانشاهان رسیدیم. در هتل هلال منزل کردیم. مصطفی خان افشار هم اطاق من بود. دکتر آقایان و آقای شیخ رضا ملکی بدیدن آمدند. یک ساعت و ربع بظهر مانده ۲۷ آذر از کرمانشاهان حرکت کردیم. یک

---

۱. صفحهٔ نخست این دفتر با این جمله آغاز می‌شود: رجوع شود بکتابچهٔ کوچک جلد سیاه که در آن شرح سفر از طهران بکربلا و مراجعت ببغداد و رفتن از بغداد بپاریس و لندن درجست.

ساعت و نیم بعد از ظهر در کرند غذا خوردیم و دو ساعت و نیم بعد از ظهر از کرند بیرون رفتیم. شب بخانقین رسیدیم و در مضیف شرکت نفت منزل کردیم.

سه‌شنبه ۲۸ آذر، اول رمضان - آقای زرین‌کفش و سایر همراهان در خانقین ماندند و چون می‌خواستم پدر و مادرم را که در کربلا بودند بیشتر ببینم، قرار گذاشتم که بروم بکربلا و هر وقت همراهان آمدند از کربلا ببغداد بیایم. یک ساعت و نیم بظهر مانده با اتومبیلی که از طهران مرا آورده بود بطرف بغداد رفتم. در راه هیچ اتومبیل یا مرکوب دیگری از آن قبیل ندیدم. شوفور از بیراهه می‌رفت. دو ساعت بعد از ظهر وارد بغداد شدم. ۹۰ تومان باقی کرایه را بشوفور دادم. چون دیگر میان من و پدر و مادرم فاصله‌ای نبود، دلم می‌طپید علی الخصوص که بایشان خبر نداده بودم که برای من چنین مسافرتی در پیش است.

چهارشنبه ۲۴ ژانویه ۱۹۳۴ - از امروز می‌خواهم انشاء الله روزی دو سه خط یادداشت کنم. از روز حرکت از طهران این عزم بود ولی ممکن نشد. از روز سه‌شنبه ۲۳ ژانویه می‌نویسم. در مادرید هتل زندگی می‌کنم.

سه‌شنبه ۲۳ ژانویه - صبح مستر کریگ عضو شرکت پسر رئیس الوزرای ایرلند شمالی آمد. با آقای زرین‌کفش و او برای یافتن خانه با اتومبیل شرکت به ویمبلدون رفتیم. خانه‌ای پیدا شد که از اول فوریه هفته‌ای شش گینی < اجاره می‌دهند >. کتاب ولز کار و ثروت و سعادت انسان[1] و کتاب لغت انگلیسی بفرانسه خریدم. شب کمی از کتاب مذکور و کمی روزنامه خواندم. هوا سرد بود.

چهارشنبه ۲۴ ژانویه - ساعت ده بموزه علوم رفتم. کاغذی بجلال نوشتم.

پنجشنبه ۲۵ ژانویه - صبح بسفارت رفتم و دوسیهٔ محصلین مالی را تحویل گرفتم. نیم ساعت با آقای شایسته شارژه دافر گذراندم. یک ساعت و نیم بعد از ظهر با آقای زرین‌کفش و همراهان دیگر بسیرک رفتیم - اولمپیا.

---

۱. مقصود این کتاب است: *The Work, Wealth and Happiness of Mankind* (by H. G. Wells).

جمعه ۶ بهمن، ۱۳۱۲، ۲۶ ژانویه - صبح با کمال کسالت و هول چاشت خوردم. آقای زرین‌کفش شش هفت کلمه بیشتر حرف نزد. بیشتر اوقات ناهار و شام این طور می‌گذرد. غذا را با خون دل می‌خورم. گاهی فکر می‌کنم چه زندگی خوشی! با این همسفر پیدا کردم. سکوت آقای زرین‌کفش گاهی راستی بکلی بچگانه است. بتماشای موزهٔ جنگ و نمایشگاه دائم محصولات امپراطوری انگلیس رفتم. شب هم با سکوت شام خورده شد.

شنبه ۷ بهمن ۲۷ ژانویه - کمی از کتب حقوقی خواندم. بعد بباغ وحش رفتم. عصر در هتل کتاب حقوقی خواندم. با آقای زرّین‌کفش بدیدن آقای محمّدآبادی بهتل مونتانا رفتیم. هفت بعد از ظهر بهتل مادرید مراجعت کردیم.

یکشنبه ۸ بهمن، ۲۸ ژانویه - صبح بتماشای وست مینستر ابی رفتم. در مادرید روزهای یکشنبه غذای بهتری می‌دهند. امشب یک جوجه برای پنج نفر آوردند و پهلوی پرتغال هم یک جعبه انگور بود.

دوشنبه ۹ بهمن، ۲۹ ژانویه - ساعت ده بتماشای مادام توسو رفتم. مجسمه مومی اشخاص بزرگ و معروف و اطاق وحشت را دیدم. آقای زرّین‌کفش گفته بود که اگر خانه‌ای بگیرند با ایشان زندگی کنم ولی امشب گفت که بهتر است یا در همین هتل و یا در خانه‌ای دیگر زندگی کنم. هنوز وضع زندگی من معین نیست تا خدا چه خواهد و بخت چه کند.

سه‌شنبه ۱۰ بهمن، ۳۰ ژانویه - ساعت ده بتماشای موزهٔ ویکتوریا رفتم امّا حالم خوب نبود. شش بعد از ظهر حساب از طهران تا این تاریخ را با آقای زرّین‌کفش روشن کردم. شب کمی از منتخب اشعار انگلیسی خواندم ببرادرم کاغذی نوشتم.

چهارشنبه ۱۱ بهمن، ۳۱ ژانویه - صبح بادارهٔ روزنامهٔ ایونینگ استاندارد رفتم و شمارهٔ ۷ و ۸ نوامبر ۱۹۳۴[1] را خریدم. در این شماره‌ها راجع بپادشاهان ایران مقالاتی بود. امروز کاغذی از خسرو خان اقبال رسید. این اولین کاغذیست که از طهران رسیده.

---

۱. در اصل: ۱۹۴۳

پنجشنبه ۱۲ بهمن، اول فوریه - ببهبودی و معظمی و یزدان‌فر و نقوی و دکتر رسولی کاغذ نوشتم. آقای زرّین‌کفش با خانوادهٔ خود دو ساعت بعد از ظهر از هتل مادرید به ویمبلدون بخانه‌ای که اجاره کرده است، رفت. تنها و افسرده بودم. عصر بی‌اختیار به رسل اسکویر رفتم. هوا سرد بود. در طالار عمومی شام خوردم. وقتی آقای زرین‌کفش در این هتل بود، بواسطهٔ اطفال کوچکش ما در اطاق مخصوص غذا می‌خوردیم. بعد از شام با دو زن انگلیسی و یک مرد انگلیسی همصحبت شدم. کمی از افسردگی بیرون آمدم. از اطاق نمرهٔ ۷ به اطاق نمرهٔ ۲۱ رفتم که یک طبقه بالاتر است.

جمعه ۱۳ بهمن، ۲ فوریه - با چند نفر آشنا شدم و زنی جوان را دیدم که زن طبیب است. از زنهای ایرانی پرسید. زنی دیگر موسم بمسیز هت که مدتها در امریکای جنوبی بوده است آشنا شد. زنی بسیار هوشمند و خوش محضر است و چهار زبان می‌داند. شب با مستر هریس نامی بتماشای یخ بازی رفتم.

شنبه ۱۴ بهمن، ۳ فوریه - صبح با مسیز هت به لستر اسکویر بدیدن تابلوهای نقاشی رفتم. در همان محله ناهار خوردم. بعد از شام با آقای محمدآبادی در پیکادلی گردش کردم.

یکشنبه ۱۵ بهمن، ۴ فوریه - حالم چندان خوب نبود. عصر به ماربل آرچ[1] رفتم. کسانی که نطق می‌کردند تماشایی بود. بجلال و بسعیدی کاغذی نوشتم.

دوشنبه ۱۶ بهمن، ۵ فوریه - حالم خوب نبود. بمحله هوبورن رفتم. اما زود مراجعت کردم. بعد از شام با مسیز هت راجع بموضوعات مختلف و ادبیات صحبت کردم.

سه‌شنبه ۱۷ بهمن، ۶ فوریه - حالم خوب نیست. عصر به ویمبلدون بمنزل آقای زرّین‌کفش رفتم.

---

۱. Marble Arch، بنایی است در زاویه شمال شرقی هاید پارک و باغ کنزینگتن در لندن.

چهارشنبه ۱۸ بهمن، ۷ فوریه - بعد از شام تا ساعت ده بعد از ظهر در مهمانخانه با آشنایان خود مذاکره می‌کردم. مسیز هت هم بود.

پنجشنبه ۱۹ بهمن ۱۳۱۲، ۸ فوریه - صبح بمیدلند بانک رفتم. ۷۵ لیره دادم و حساب جاری باز کردم. بعد از ظهر به بریتیش میوزیم رفتم.

جمعه ۲۰ بهمن، ۹ فوریه - تا دو بعد از ظهر در هتل حقوق اداری خواندم. هوا سرد بود.

شنبه ۲۱ بهمن، ۱۰ فوریه - صبح کتب حقوقی خواندم. بعد از ظهر بموزهٔ ویکتوریا و موزهٔ تاریخ طبیعی رفتم.

یکشنبه ۲۲ بهمن، ۱۱ فوریه - به هاید پارک رفتم و در پای نطق ناطقی ایستادم. آزادی را بچشم دیدم. عصر با مسیز هت به ریجنتز پارک رفتم. بمن انگلیسی درس می‌دهد و درسش بسیار مفید است.

دوشنبه ۲۳ بهمن، ۱۲ فوریه - صبح در سفارت با نواب و انتظام بودم. از آقای تقی‌زاده کاغذی رسید.

چهارشنبه ۲۵ بهمن، ۱۴ فوریه - حالم هیچ خوب نبود. از هتل بیرون نرفتم.

پنجشنبه ۲۶ بهمن، ۱۵ فوریه - تا دو بعد از ظهر کتاب حقوقی خواندم. شب در منزل آقای زرین‌کفش بودم.

جمعه ۲۷ بهمن، ۱۶ فوریه - صبح بدیدن محاکم عدلیه و شب با آقای محمدآبادی بتآتر رفتم.

شنبه ۲۸ بهمن، ۱۷ فوریه - عصر به بریتیش میوزیم و شب با نواب بسینما رفتم.

یکشنبه ۲۹ بهمن، ۱۸ فوریه - صبح در هاید پارک عصر در ریچموند گردش کردم.

دوشنبه ۳۰ بهمن، ۱۹ فوریه - صبح بسفارت رفتم. با نوری و نواب و یکتا بودم.

سه‌شنبه ۱ اسفند، ۲۰ فوریه - تا دو بعد از ظهر در هتل کتاب خواندم. عصر بموزهٔ ویکتوریا رفتم. ناهار در سفارت خوردم. زرین‌کفش، انتظام، نصر، محمدآبادی، گلمکانی، نواب، یکتا و سایر اعضای سفارت بودند. از جلال و از آقای خلخالی و آقای فلسفی کاغذ رسید. این اولین دفعه است که از جلال کاغذ رسیده است.

چهارشنبه ۴ اسفند، ۲۱ فوریه - روزنامه و کتاب خواندم.

پنجشنبه ۳ اسفند، ۲۲ فوریه - با مسیز هت بکلیسای وست مینستر رفتم.

جمعه ۴ اسفند، ۲۳ فوریه - با آقای محمدآبادی بودم.

شنبه ۵ اسفند، ۲۴ فوریه - برج لندن و جواهرات سلطنتی را دیدم.

یکشنبه ۶ اسفند، ۲۵ فوریه - مجموعه تابلوهای والاس را دیدم. امروز در هاید پارک بیکارها نمایشی می‌دادند.

دوشنبه ۷ اسفند، ۲۶ فوریه - صبح به ویمبلدون بدیدن آقای زرین‌کفش و تبریک خانمش رفتم که فارغ شده است. چهار و نیم بعد از ظهر سر جان کدمن رئیس شرکت را دیدم. مرد مؤدب مهربانیست. شب نزد آقای محمدآبادی رفتم.

سه‌شنبه ۸ اسفند، ۲۷ فوریه - صبح بسفارت رفتم. ناهار در پرینس آو ویلز هتل با آقای محمدآبادی خوردم. امینی پسر امین الدوله عصر با من بود.

چهارشنبه ۹ اسفند، ۲۸ فوریه - کتب راجع بنفت خواندم.

پنجشنبه ۱۰ اسفند، ۱ مارس - برای پدرم و جلال و یزدان و فلسفی کاغذ فرستادم. کتب راجع بنفت خواندم.

جمعه ۱۱ اسفند، ۲ مارس - بعد از ظهر بشرکت رفتم، با چند نفر آشنا شدم. شب بتئاتر الحمرا رفتم. بازی ژول سزار را دیدم.

شنبه ۱۲ اسفند، ۳ مارس - عصر بسفارت رفتم.

یکشنبه ۱۳ اسفند، ۴ مارس - در هاید پارک گردش کردم.

دوشنبه ۱۴ اسفند، ۵ مارس - تا دو بعد از ظهر کتاب حقوقی خواندم.

سه‌شنبه ۱۵ اسفند، ۶ مارس - صبح بسفارت رفتم. کمی با نصر و دیده‌بان و محمدآبادی مذاکره کردم. در هتل پرنس آو ویلز با محمدآبادی غذا خوردم. شب با مستر بنسن و یک کلنل انگلیسی و مسیز هت مذاکره کردم.

چهارشنبه ۱۶ اسفند، ۷ مارس - عصر بکتابفروشی لوزاک رفتم و شب بکافه روایال.

پنجشنبه ۱۷ اسفند، ۸ مارس - صبح بشرکت رفتم. با مستر کدمن برادر سر جان کدمن در باب استخراج نفت از زغال مذاکره کردم. عصر به بریتیش میوزیم رفتم.

جمعه ۱۸ اسفند، ۹ مارس - صبح بسفارت و شب بهتل محمدآبادی رفتم.

شنبه ۱۹ اسفند، ۱۰ مارس - تا دو ساعت بعد از ظهر کتاب خواندم. عصر با یکتا در باغ گردش کردم.

یکشنبه ۲۰ اسفند، ۱۱ مارس - عصر با یک انگلیسی بکلیسای سنت پول رفتم.

دوشنبه ۲۱ اسفند، ۱۲ مارس - هیچ از خانه بیرون نرفتم و دائم کتاب خواندم.

سه‌شنبه ۲۲ اسفند، ۱۳ مارس - صبح بشرکت رفتم. ناهار با مستر کدمن خوردم و تا چهار بعد از ظهر با او بودم. در باب استخراج نفت از زغال مذاکره کردم. از

جلال کاغذی رسید و در جوف آن کاغذی بود از پدرم از کربلا که بی‌نهایت متأثرم کرد. نتوانستم شام بخورم.

چهارشنبه ۲۳ اسفند، ۱۴ مارس - کتاب خواندم.

پنجشنبه ۲۴ اسفند، ۱۵ مارس - دو و نیم بعد از ظهر به پرنس او ویلز هتل رفتم و از آن جا با محمدآبادی بسفارت. جشن ولادت شاه بود. شب با محمدآبادی بودم. با هم شام خوردیم. بعد از شام یکتا آمد.

جمعه ۲۵ اسفند، ۱۶ مارس - چندین کاغذ نوشتم. عصر بمنزل آقای زرین‌کفش رفتم.

شنبه ۲۶ اسفند، ۱۷ مارس - برای تماشای مسابقۀ قایق‌رانی بین اکسفورد و کمبریج بکشتی نشستیم. مهمان شرکت بودم. آقای زرین‌کفش هم بود. عصر با شایسته و انتظام و زرین‌کفش بسفارت رفتم. شب با شایسته شام خوردم.

یکشنبه ۲۷ اسفند، ۱۸ مارس - صبح بهاید پارک و شب بمهمانخانۀ محمدآبادی رفتم.

دوشنبه ۲۸ اسفند، ۱۹ مارس - صبح بسفارت رفتم. از فرهت و از خسرو اقبال کاغذ رسیده بود.

سه‌شنبه ۲۹ اسفند، ۲۰ مارس - کتاب خواندم. بتقی‌زاده و محمدخان قزوینی و دکتر غنی کاغذی نوشتم.

چهارشنبه اول فروردین، ۲۱ مارس - صبح کتاب خواندم. عصر بسفارت رفتم. جمعی از ایرانیها بودند. شب در مهمانخانه راپورتهای سر ویلیام ماک‌لین‌توک را در باب مطالباتش از ایران مطالعه کردم.

پنجشنبه ۲ فروردین، ۲۲ مارس - صبح بسفارت رفتم. ناهار با دیده‌بان و محمدآبادی خوردم.

جمعه ۳ فروردین، ۲۳ مارس - صبح بمدرسهٔ السنهٔ شرقیه رفتم. شب کتب حقوقی خواندم.

شنبه ۴ فروردین، ۲۴ مارس - اوراق مربوط بمقالات ماک‌لین‌توک را ترجمه کردم. عصر انگلیسی خواندم. مسیز هت خیلی کمک می‌کند.

یکشنبه ۵ فروردین، ۲۵ مارس - ترجمه اوراق مربوط بماک‌لین‌توک مشغول بودم. عصر با دیده‌بان و امینی و محمّدآبادی به کی‌یو گاردنز رفتم.

دوشنبه ۶ فروردین، ۲۶ مارس - بترجمهٔ اوراق مربوط بماک لین توک مشغول بودم. خانم امین را که از بغداد تا اسلامبول همسفر ما بود، دیدم.

سه‌شنبه ۷ فروردین، ۲۷ مارس - از صبح تا شام بترجمه اوراق ماک لین توک مشغول بودم.

چهارشنبه ۸ فروردین، ۲۸ مارس - ترجمه کردم و کتاب می‌خواندم.

پنجشنبه ۹ فروردین، ۲۹ مارس - تمام روز گرم در کار ترجمه بودم. بعد از شام بهتل محمدآبادی رفتم. دیده‌بان و یکتا هم آمدند. محمدآبادی قرار است فردا بپاریس برود.

جمعه ۱۰ فروردین، ۳۰ مارس - صبح بکلیسای کاتولیکی رفتم و عصر به ریجنتز پارک.

شنبه ۱۱ فروردین، ۳۱ مارس - تا چندی بعد از ظهر در هتل مشغول تهیه ترجمه بودم. عصر بهاید پارک رفتم.

یکشنبه ۱۲ فروردین، ۱ آوریل - تا بعد از ظهر مشغول ترجمه بودم. بعد از ظهر بمنزل زرین‌کفش رفتم. بعد از شام در هتل، مجلس مهمانی کوچکی در هتل بود. دختر یکی از پیرزنهای مقیم هتل آمده بود.

دوشنبه ۱۳ فروردین، ۲ آوریل - تا دو بعد از ظهر کتاب حقوق می‌خواندم. عصر به کینگستون رفتم. شب امینی آمد بدیدنم.

سه‌شنبه ۱۴ فروردین، ۳ آوریل - حالم خوب نبود. در هتل ماندم و کتاب حقوق خواندم.

چهارشنبه ۱۵ فروردین، ۴ آوریل - خانم امین را در بولتون گاردنز دیدم. بعد از ظهر دیده‌بان نزد من آمد. شب کمی کتاب حقوقی خواندم. پسر مسیز هت بدیدن مادرش آمد.

پنجشنبه ۱۶ فروردین، ۵ آوریل - بپاکنویس ترجمۀ اوراق مربوط بماک لین توک مشغول بودم. در مونتانا هتل با اردلان و دیده‌بان صحبت کردم. از پدرم کاغذی رسید.

جمعه ۱۷ فروردین، ۶ آوریل - تا سه بعد از ظهر بپاکنویس ترجمه مشغول بودم. عصر در سفارت با انتظام و اردلان و یکتا صحبت کردم. کاغذی از زینت و ناصر و ضیاء رسید.

شنبه ۱۸ فروردین، ۷ آوریل - صبح از هتل بیرون نرفتم. کتاب خواندم.

یکشنبه ۱۹ فروردین، ۸ آوریل - تا دو بعد از ظهر کتاب حقوق خواندم. شب هم تا ساعت ۱۱ کتاب حقوق خواندم.

دوشنبه ۲۰ فروردین، ۹ آوریل - تا غروب در هتل بودم. شب هلن رفیق میسز هت آمد و کمی صحبت کردیم. مقداری کتاب انگلیسی خواندم.

سه‌شنبه ۲۱ فروردین، ۱۰ آوریل - صبح بسفارت رفتم. از دشتی و رشید یاسمی کاغذی رسیده بود. ناهار با یکتا به گلن رز گرین بمنزل زرین‌کفش رفتم. ناهار غذای ایرانی خوردیم.

چهارشنبه ۲۲ فروردین، ۱۱ آوریل - ناهار در منزل زرین‌کفش خوردم. محمدآبادی از پاریس مراجعت کرده شب کتاب انگلیسی خواندم.

پنجشنبه ۲۳ فروردین، ۱۲ آوریل - ناهار با محمدآبادی خوردم. از جلال و جمال و زینت السادات و دکتر محمود خان نجم آبادی و عباسقلی خان گلشائیان کاغذی رسیده بود با مقداری کتاب بی‌نام از ادارۀ هند. عصر با مسیز ویزلی هت بمنزل هلن رفتم. جشن ولادت هلن بود. شوهر مادر هلن قنسول اوروگوئه است. چندین مهمان بود. شب در محله چلسی غذا خوردم. حالم خوب نبود.

جمعه ۲۴ فروردین، ۱۳ آوریل - ناهار در منزل آقای زرین‌کفش خوردم. شب کتاب حقوق خواندم.

شنبه ۲۵ فروردین، ۱۴ آوریل - صبح نزد خانم امین رفتم و شب نزد محمدآبادی.

یکشنبه ۲۶ فروردین، ۱۵ آوریل - تا دو بعد از ظهر در مهمانخانه کتب حقوقی خواندم.

دوشنبه ۲۷ فروردین، ۱۶ آوریل - ناهار با محمدآبادی خوردم.

سه‌شنبه ۲۸ فروردین، ۱۷ آوریل - کتب حقوقی خواندم. بکتابفروشی فویلز رفتم.

چهارشنبه ۲۹ فروردین، ۱۸ آوریل - ناهار مهمان دیده‌بان بودم. عصر بمنزل زرین‌کفش رفتم.

پنجشنبه ۳۰ فروردین، ۱۹ آوریل - در هتل بودم و کتاب خواندم.

جمعه ۳۱ فروردین، ۲۰ آوریل - تا یک بعد از ظهر در هتل کتاب خواندم. ناهار در منزل زرین‌کفش فسنجان خوردم.

شنبه ۱ اردیبهشت، ۲۱ آوریل - از هژیر و امیر علائی و دکتر رسولی و دکتر متین دفتری کاغذی رسید.

یکشنبه ۲ اردیبهشت، ۲۲ آوریل - یکتا آتاشه سفارت بایران رفت. بمشایعت او بایستگاه ویکتوریا رفتم.

دوشنبه ۳ اردیبهشت، ۲۳ آوریل - از کمال و معاصر و اقبال و زینت السادات کاغذی رسید. بعد از ظهر بشرکت رفتم.

سه‌شنبه ۴ اردیبهشت، ۲۴ آوریل - به بریتیش میوزیم رفتم و بکتابفروشی لوزاک.

چهارشنبه ۵ اردیبهشت، ۲۵ آوریل - کتب حقوقی خواندم. بعد از ظهر بشرکت رفتم. بنزد اصغرزاده رفتم نبود. با برادرزاده‌اش صحبت کردم.

پنجشنبه ۶ اردیبهشت، ۲۶ آوریل - بعد از ظهر بتماشای نمایشگاه دیلی میل رفتم.

جمعه ۷ اردیبهشت، ۲۷ آوریل - باز نمایشگاه اولمپیا رفتم.

شنبه ۸ اردیبهشت، ۲۸ آوریل - از پدرم کاغذی داشت. شب کتب حقوقی خواندم.

یکشنبه ۹ اردیبهشت، ۲۹ آوریل - در هاید پارک احمدی منشی سفارت < را > با زن و دو بچه‌اش دیدم.

دوشنبه ۱۰ اردیبهشت، ۳۰ آوریل - کتاب و راپورت راجع باستخراج نفت از زغال خواندم. عصر با مسیز هت در قهوه‌خانهٔ کوچک نوک نزدیک کلیسا چای خوردم. شب ببلدیه محله کنزینگتون رفتم.

سه‌شنبه ۱۱ اردیبهشت، ۱ مه - بعد از ظهر بشرکت رفتم. آقای زرین‌کفش هم بود. شب بتأتر رفتم. بازی ربرت کلایو را دیدم.

چهارشنبه ۱۲ اردیبهشت، ۲ مه - حالم چندان خوب نبود. ناهار با زرین‌کفش در نزدیکی شرکت خوردیم.

پنجشنبه ۱۳ اردیبهشت، ۳ مه - ناهار با محمدآبادی خوردم.

جمعه ۱۴ اردیبهشت، ۴ مه - تا ظهر کتاب خواندم. بعد از ظهر بشرکت رفتم.

شنبه ۱۵ اردیبهشت، ۵ مه - صبح بسفارت رفتم. شایسته گفت سر دنیسن رس[1] مدیر مدرسه السنهٔ شرقیه برای فارسی درس دادن معلمی خواسته است و من شما را معرفی کرده‌ام. قبول کردم. عصر بعیادت محمدآبادی رفتم که ناخوش است. فؤاد روحانی و خانمش را دیدم. فؤاد روحانی از اعضای ایرانی شرکت است. شش ماهه بلندن آمده است. عصر با او و خانمش و دیده‌بان بباغ وحش رفتیم.

یکشنبه ۱۶ اردیبهشت، ۶ مه - صبح از مهمانخانه بیرون نرفتم. کتاب می‌خواندم.

دوشنبه ۱۷ اردیبهشت، ۷ مه - صبح بسفارت رفتم.

سه‌شنبه ۸ اردیبهشت، ۸ مه - بمدرسه السنهٔ شرقیه رفتم. قرار شد هفته‌ای سه ساعت درس بدهم.

چهارشنبه ۱۹ اردیبهشت، ۹ مه - ساعت ده و نیم بمدرسه السنهٔ شرقیه رفتم. سه شاگرد بود. یک بحرینی یک هندی و یک انگلیسی. مینورسکی معلم هم بود.

پنجشنبه ۲۰ اردیبهشت، ۱۰ مه - از پدرم و جلال و دکتر سیاسی و خواجه‌نوری کاغذی رسید. بعد از ظهر در مدرسه درس فارسی دادم. شب فیلم مرد نامرئی را دیدم.

---

۱. Sir Edward Denison Ross، مستشرق و زبانشناس (۱۸۷۱-۱۹۴۰). نخستین مدیر مدرسه السنهٔ شرقی.

جمعه ۲۱ اردیبهشت، ۱۱ مه – در باغ کنزینگتون کتاب حقوقی خواندم. حالم خوب نبود.

شنبه ۲۲ اردیبهشت، ۱۲ مه – حالم چندان خوب نیست. کتاب خواندم.

یکشنبه ۲۳ اردیبهشت، ۱۳ مه – کتاب خواندم.

دوشنبه ۲۴ اردیبهشت، ۱۴ مه – صبح بسفارت رفتم. از وکیلی کاغذی رسید. شب بتأتر رفتم. بازی جنایت و مجازات دوستویوسکی را که بازیگران فرانسوی نمایش می‌دادند، دیدم.

سه‌شنبه ۲۵ اردیبهشت، ۱۵ مه – عصر باداره رفتم. حالم چندان خوب نیست.

چهارشنبه ۲۶ اردیبهشت، ۱۶ مه – درس دادم و کتاب خواندم.

پنجشنبه ۲۷ اردیبهشت، ۱۷ مه – درس دادم، دو ساعت.

جمعه ۲۸ اردیبهشت، ۱۸ مه – بعد از ظهر با دیده‌بان و محمدآبادی و فؤاد روحانی و خانمش بیرون شهر رفتیم.

شنبه ۲۹ اردیبهشت، ۱۹ مه – تمام روز کتاب خواندم. مسیز ویزلی هت که بدیدن پدرش رفته بود مراجعت کرد.

یکشنبه ۳۰ اردیبهشت، ۲۰ مه – کتب حقوقی خواندم. فؤاد و خانمش را دیدم.

دوشنبه اول خرداد، ۲۱ مه – کتاب خواندم.

سه‌شنبه ۲ خرداد، ۲۲ مه – صبح باداره رفتم.

چهارشنبه ۳ خرداد، ۲۳ مه – صبح بمدرسهٔ علوم شرقیه رفتم و دو ساعت درس گفتم.

پنجشنبه ۴ خرداد، ۲۴ مه – صبح باداره و بعد از نهار بمدرسه رفتم. درس دادم.

جمعه ۵ خرداد، ۲۵ مه - با محمدآبادی مشق نظامی را در اولمپیا دیدم.

شنبه ۶ خرداد، ۲۶ مه - کتاب خواندم.

یکشنبه ۷ خرداد، ۲۷ مه - بمنزل زرین‌کفش رفتم. جوانی شیرازی < بنام > دکتر علوی در آنجا بود. احمد و زن و بچه‌هایش هم بودند.

دوشنبه ۸ خرداد، ۲۸ مه - بعد از ظهر بشرکت رفتم. شب کتاب خواندم.

سه‌شنبه ۹ خرداد، ۲۹ مه - ناهار با محمدآبادی خوردم. سخت چائیدم. حالم خوب نبود.

چهارشنبه ۱۰ خرداد، ۳۰ مه - از ساعت ۷ تا ساعت یک در مدرسه درس دادم. حالم صبح خوب نبود. با محمدآبادی و دیده‌بان بعمارت انجمن صنایع رفتیم. آقای تقی‌زاده در خصوص ایران جدید نطق کرد و باید آن را ترجمه کنم. مقداری از آن را ترجمه کردم. حالم هیچ خوب نیست. سر جان کدمن و سر دنیسن راس تشکر کردند ــ از نطق تقی‌زاده. شش بعد از ظهر بهتل ریتز رفتم. با آقای تقی‌زاده شام خوردم.

پنجشنبه ۱۱ خرداد، ۳۱ مه - از دو تا چهار بعد از ظهر در مدرسه درس دادم. شب با زرین‌کفش در ریتز شام خوردیم.

جمعه ۱۲ خرداد، اول ژوئن - ناهار با آقای تقی‌زاده و آقای محمدآبادی و آقای داریوش در سفارت خوردیم. حالم خوب نبود. شب بپاکنویس کردن نطق آقای تقی‌زاده مشغول بودم. شب بهتل ریتز رفتم ولی شام نخوردم چون که حالم خوب نبود.

شنبه ۱۳ خرداد، ۲ ژوئن - ساعت ده بهتل ریتز رفتم. با اتومبیل سفارت بهمراه آقای تقی‌زاده بگار راه آهن رفتم. شایسته و دیده‌بان و محمدآبادی و اردلان هم آمدند. قریب یک ساعت با آقای تقی‌زاده صحبت کردم. از من دعوت کرد که در موقع

جشن فردوسی بپاریس بروم. شب با دیده‌بان در کافه لانیز نزدیک ماربل آرچ بودم. از قضا انگلیسی که فارسی می‌دانست نزدیک ما نشسته بود.

یکشنبه ۱۴ خرداد، ۳ ژوئن - به هوبورن رفتم. قسمتهای قدیم این محله را تماشا کردم.

دوشنبه ۱۵ خرداد، ۴ ژوئن - با دیده‌بان در سنت جیمز پارک گردش کردیم. بواسطهٔ تولد شاه جشن بود.

سه‌شنبه ۱۶ خرداد، ۵ ژوئن - ناهار در سفارت با آقای شایسته خوردم.

چهارشنبه ۱۷ خرداد، ۶ ژوئن - عصر در مدرسه علوم شرقی جشن مختصری بود. سر دنیسن راس مرا بزنی جوان عروس یکی از پسرهای داروین که کمی فارسی خوانده بود، معرفی کرد.

پنجشنبه ۱۸ خرداد، ۷ ژوئن - صبح باداره رفتم.

جمعه ۱۹ خرداد، ۸ ژوئن - ناهار در منزل زرین‌کفش خوردم. محمدآبادی هم بود.

شنبه ۲۰ خرداد، ۹ ژوئن - با فؤاد و خانمش و محمدآبادی و دیده‌بان بگردش رفتم.

یکشنبه ۲۱ خرداد، ۱۰ ژوئن - با دیده‌بان و انگلیسی که از قضا پهلوی ما نشسته بود و فارسی می‌دانست ـ اسمش ویمن ـ بخانهٔ انگلیسی رفتم. پدر و مادرش را دیدیم.

دوشنبه ۲۲ خرداد، ۱۱ ژوئن - ناهار با محمدآبادی خوردم و عصر بمنزل کارلایل رفتم در محلهٔ چلسی. حمام دوران دیدم. جعبه‌ایست حلبی. شب بانجمن جغرافیایی رفتم. سر جان کدمن راجع بنفت ایران و عراق نطق کرد. در پایان نطق خود بآقای عسکری بانگلیسی و شایسته بفرانسه اظهار تشکر کرد.

سه‌شنبه ۲۳ خرداد، ۱۲ ژوئن - از صبح تا چهار رفته از ظهر درس انگلیسی خواندم. با شخص موسوم به مستر مود که مرد خوبیست آشنا شدم.

چهارشنبه ۲۴ خرداد، ۱۳ ژوئن - از ساعت ۱۱ تا یک ساعت بعد از ظهر درس دادم. حالم خوب نیست. در روزنامه تایمز نوشته شده است که بمناسبت ورود شاه بترکیه یک قطعه موسیقی بدستور و بفکر مصطفی کمال پاشا ساخته‌اند راجع بافسانه‌های قدیم ایران و ترکیه و چهارصد نوازنده آن را خواهند نواخت.

پنجشنبه ۲۵ خرداد، ۱۴ ژوئن - از پدرم و جلال کاغذ رسید.

جمعه ۲۶ خرداد، ۱۵ ژوئن - کتب حقوقی خواندم. با محمدآبادی ناهار خوردم. کاغذی بروزنامهٔ تایمز نوشتم.

شنبه ۲۷ خرداد، ۱۶ ژوئن ۳۴ - با اتوموبیل دیده‌بان باکسفورد رفتم. محمدآبادی کار داشت و نیامد. فؤاد روحانی و زنش در اکسفورد بودند. با ایشان اکسفورد و مدارسش را دیدم. شب در مهمانخانه‌ای خارج از اکسفورد خوابیدیم.

یکشنبه ۲۸ خرداد، ۱۷ ژوئن - صبح در اطاق مصفایی که پنجره‌هایش بباغ باز می‌شد، چاشت خوردیم. ساعت ۹ فؤاد و زنش آمدند. کمی در اطراف اکسفورد با اتوموبیل گردش کردیم. ناهار آش و خوراک جوجه لذیذ و خورش کرفس در منزل ناهار خوردیم. دختری انگلیسی دوست فؤاد و زنش نیز بود. شب کتب حقوقی که با خود آورده بودم، خواندم.

دوشنبه ۲۹ خرداد، ۱۸ ژوئن - با فؤاد و زنش بنواحی اکسفورد رفتم. در رستورانی مصفّا غذا خوردیم و بعد از آن باز چای و نان برداشتیم و بپارک اکسفورد رفتیم تا ساعت پنج بعد از ظهر همان جا بودیم. بعد خداحافظی کردیم و بلندن آمدیم.

سه‌شنبه ۳۰ خرداد، ۱۹ ژوئن - ناهار با محمدآبادی خوردم. بعد از ظهر باداره رفتم. انگلیسی خواندم.

چهارشنبه ۳۱ خرداد، ۲۰ ژوئن - حقوق و انگلیسی خواندم.

پنجشنبه ۱ تیر، ۲۱ ژوئن - از جلال کاغذی رسید. بعد از ظهر درس دادم.

جمعه ۲ تیر، ۲۲ ژوئن - کتب حقوقی خواندم.

شنبه ۳ تیر، ۲۳ ژوئن - تا چهار بعد از ظهر حقوق خواندم. عصر در پترسن پارک گردش کردم. شب هم حقوق خواندم.

یکشنبه ۴ تیر، ۲۴ ژوئن - حقوق خواندم. با محمدآبادی ناهار خوردم.

دوشنبه ۵ تیر، ۲۵ ژوئن - بکتابخانهٔ فویلز رفتم. چند کتاب خریدم. محلهٔ یهودیها را هم دیدم.

سه‌شنبه ۶ تیر، ۲۶ ژوئن - کتاب حقوقی خواندم.

چهارشنبه ۷ تیر، ۲۷ ژوئن - سر دنیسن رس را دیدم. کتب خود را باو دادم. کتب حقوقی خواندم.

پنجشنبه ۸ تیر، ۲۸ ژوئن - صبح بسفارت رفتم و بعد از ظهر بمدرسهٔ علوم شرقی. این آخرین درس بود و تعطیل شد. بعد از شام با محمدآبادی بپیکادلی رفتم.

جمعه ۹ تیر، ۲۹ ژوئن - با محمدآبادی در نایتز بریج چای خوردم. شام در هتل خوردم و تمام روز کتاب حقوقی خواندم.

شنبه ۱۰ تیر، ۳۰ ژوئن - به هندن برای تماشای نمایش و اعمال طیارات رفتم. ولیعهد انگلیس هم با طیاره آمد. از ظهر تا ساعت شش در آن جا بودم و شب با دیده‌بان و اردلان در ماربل آرچ غذا خوردیم.

یکشنبه ۱۱ تیر، اول ژوئیه - حقوق خواندم.

دوشنبه ۱۲ تیر، ۲ ژوئیه – با محمدآبادی بگار ویکتوریا رفتیم. محمدآبادی بپاریس رفت. عصر بمنزل زرین‌کفش رفتم. در جنگل مصنوعی نزدیک خانه‌اش گردش کردیم. شام در آنجا خوردم. ساعت ۱۱ بعد از ظهر بهتل آمدم.

سه‌شنبه ۱۳ تیر، ۳ ژوئیه – حقوق خواندم. دو سه روز است که در آلمان انقلابات سخت بر پا شده عده‌ای را کشته‌اند و جمعی را مجبور کرده‌اند بخودکشی.

چهارشنبه ۱۴ تیر، ۴ ژوئیه – دویست ریال چک برای طهران از بانک شاهی گرفتم. کتاب انگلیسی خواندم.

پنجشنبه ۱۵ تیر، ۵ ژوئیه – دویست ریال باکاغذی برای جلال فرستادم. بعد از ظهر باداره رفتم. مدتی با زرین‌کفش و مستر کریگ حرف زدم. شاه از ترکیه بایران مراجعت کرده.

جمعه ۱۶ تیر، ۶ ژوئیه – حقوق خواندم. ناهار در منزل زرین‌کفش خوردم. شب حقوق خواندم.

شنبه ۱۷ تیر، ۷ ژوئیه – حقوق و کتاب انگلیسی خواندم. عصر به پتنی بریج رفتم.

یکشنبه ۱۸ تیر، ۸ ژوئیه – تمام روز حقوق خواندم.

دوشنبه ۱۹ تیر، ۹ ژوئیه – با شایسته به اولد بوند استریت برای تماشای عکسهایی که با طیاره از نواحی مشرق برداشته‌اند < رفتم >. محمدآبادی از پاریس مراجعت کرده است. شب آلبرت هال رفتم. نمایش پارلمنت را دیدم. اوضاع پارلمنت را از اول تا امروز نشان می‌دادند.

سه‌شنبه ۲۰ تیر، ۱۰ ژوئیه – حقوق خواندم و انگلیسی.

چهارشنبه ۲۱ تیر، ۱۱ ژوئیه – بعد از ناهار بتماشای همتون کورت رفتم. مستر جان ویزلی هم بود.

پنجشنبه ۲۲ تیر، ۱۲ ژوئیه - از پدرم و پرویز کتابفروش کاغذی داشتم. تاریخ حقوق خواندم.

جمعه ۲۳ تیر، ۱۳ ژوئیه - تاریخ حقوق خواندم.

شنبه ۲۴ تیر، ۱۴ ژوئیه - بدیدن عمارت پارلمنت و وست مینستر ابی رفتم و کتب حقوقی خواندم.

یکشنبه ۲۵ تیر، ۱۵ ژوئیه - تمام روز و شب حقوق خواندم.

دوشنبه ۲۶ تیر، ۱۶ ژوئیه - کتاب خواندم.

سه‌شنبه ۲۷ تیر، ۱۷ ژوئیه - تاریخ حقوق خواندم.

چهارشنبه ۲۸ تیر، ۱۸ ژوئیه - تاریخ حقوق خواندم.

پنجشنبه ۲۹ تیر، ۱۹ ژوئیه - تاریخ حقوق و حقوق اساسی خواندم.

جمعه ۳۰ تیر، ۲۰ ژوئیه - از پدرم و جلال کاغذی رسید. با محمدآبادی ناهار خوردم و فیلم مادام دو باری را دیدم.

شنبه ۳۱ تیر، ۲۱ ژوئیه - عصر بخانه کلنل مک‌لین‌توک دعوت داشتم. از ایستگاه کینگز کراس[۱] رفتم. بسیاری از ایرانیها را در آنجا دیدم. مسابقهٔ فوتبال و تنیس هم بود. سر دنیسن رس، لاکهارت، و زرین‌کفش و جمعی دیگر از ایرانیها و انگلیسیها و چندین نفر از شاگردان قدیم بودند.

یکشنبه ۱ مرداد، ۲۲ ژوئیه - ببرادر و پدرم و جلال کاغذی نوشتم.

---

۱. کینز کرس

دوشنبه ۲ مرداد، ۲۳ ژوئیه - حقوق خواندم.

سه‌شنبه ۳ مرداد، ۲۴ ژوئیه - حقوق خواندم. حالم چندان خوب نبود.

چهارشنبه ۴ مرداد، ۲۵ ژوئیه - عبدالحسین سرداری همدرس مدرسهٔ حقوق طهران بهتل مادرید که من هم در آنم آمد. مدتی با او بودم.

پنجشنبه ۵ مرداد، ۲۶ ژوئیه - کتب حقوقی خواندم. شب با سرداری بهتل مونتانا رفتم که شاید سمیعی < را > که از طرف ادارهٔ نظمیه برای مطالعه آمده است، ببینیم. نبود. دولفوس رئیس الوزرای اطریش را نازیها کشتند.

جمعه ۶ مرداد، ۲۷ ژوئیه - صبح در باغ حقوق اساسی خواندم.

شنبه ۷ مرداد، ۲۸ ژوئیه - کتاب حقوق اساسی خواندم.

یکشنبه ۸ مرداد، ۲۹ ژوئیه - با محمدآبادی بمنزل زرین‌کفش رفتم. ناهار < را > در آنجا خوردیم. شب در هتل با مستر مود و مسیز بن‌سن و مسیز هت بودم و صحبت کردیم.

دوشنبه ۹ مرداد، ۳۰ ژوئیه - حقوق خواندم.

سه‌شنبه ۱۰ مرداد، ۳۱ ژوئیه - بعد از ظهر باداره رفتم. شب با سرداری گردش کردم.

چهارشنبه ۱۱ مرداد، ۱ اوت - با محمدآبادی و فؤاد و خانمش در رستوران هندی در شافتز بری او نیو غذا خوردیم. بعد از ظهر با محمدآبادی بسفارت ایران رفتم. زرین‌کفش و جمعی از تجار و محصلین بودند. پروفسور پوپ هم بود. در خصوص جشن فردوسی مذاکره می‌کردند. از سفارت با امینی بمنزل باقر خان سمیعی رفتم.

پنجشنبه ۱۲ مرداد، ۲ اوت - تلگرافی آمده که محمدآبادی و دیده‌بان اعضای هیأت خرید کشتی باید بایران مراجعت کنند. بعد از ظهر به برایتون هال هتل رفتم. لطفعلی صورتگر و امان‌پور و دکتر نعمت‌اللّهی را دیدم. در هتل با مسیز سند و مستر مور و مسیز بن سن و مسیز هت مدتی صحبت کردم. از پدرم و جلال کاغذی داشتم.

جمعه ۱۳ مرداد، ۳ اوت - شب با دیده‌بان و محمدآبادی و فؤاد و خانمش بریچموند رفتم.

شنبه ۱۴ مرداد، ۴ اوت - حقوق اساسی خواندم. بعد از ناهار فیلم ملکه کریستینا را دیدم. خوب بود.

یکشنبه ۱۵ مرداد، ۵ اوت - با محمدآبادی بمنزل زرین‌کفش رفتم. زرین‌کفش نبود. یک ساعت بعد از ظهر با قاسم‌زاده آمد. قاسم‌زاده مردیست بلند قد با لهجهٔ اصفهانی فارسی غلط حرف می‌زند. قریب بیست سال در لندن بوده تمام روز را او حرف زد و بکسی مهلت نداد. شام در هتل خوردم و بعد بهتل مونتانا رفتم. فؤاد و خانمش و برادر فؤاد و دختری فرانسوی دوست برادر فؤاد و سرداری و محمدآبادی و دیده‌بان هم بودند.

دوشنبه ۱۶ مرداد، ۶ اوت - بتماشای موزهٔ لندن رفتم.

سه‌شنبه ۱۷ مرداد، ۷ اوت - باداره رفتم. کتب حقوقی خواندم.

چهارشنبه ۱۸ مرداد، ۸ اوت - کتب حقوقی خواندم. عصر بکنار رود تمز رفتم. بعد از شام بهتل مونتانا رفتم. سرداری و فؤاد و زنش و برادر فؤاد و چند نفر دیگر بودند.

پنجشنبه ۱۹ مرداد، ۹ اوت - صبح کتاب خواندم. مسیز هت با پسرش بدیدن پدرش رفت. ناهار با محمدآبادی خوردم.

جمعه ۲۰ مرداد، ۱۰ اوت - حقوق اداری خواندم.

شنبه ۲۱ مرداد، ۱۱ اوت - حقوق خواندم.

یکشنبه ۲۲ مرداد، ۱۲ اوت - تا ساعت یازده کتاب خواندم.

دوشنبه ۲۳ مرداد، ۱۳ اوت - از پدرم و عبدالله میرزای دارا کاغذی از طهران رسید که ۶۸ تومان بحقوق من اضافه کرده‌اند.

سه‌شنبه ۲۴ مرداد، ۱۴ اوت - کتاب خواندم.

چهارشنبه ۲۵ مرداد، ۱۵ اوت - کتاب خواندم. شب فؤاد و خانمش و برادرش بهتل آمدند.

پنجشنبه ۲۶ مرداد، ۱۶ اوت - در تایمز کاغذی که در جواب پوپ نوشته بودم چاپ شده. از خلخالی کاغذی رسید. ناهار را با محمدآبادی خوردم. سمیعی هم بود. کاغذی بتقی‌زاده نوشتم.

جمعه ۲۷ مرداد، ۱۷ اوت - ناهار با محمدآبادی بودم. کتاب خواندم.

شنبه ۲۸ مرداد، ۱۸ اوت - تمام وقت کتاب خواندم.

یکشنبه ۲۹ مرداد، ۱۹ اوت - کتاب خواندم. شام در منزل زرین‌کفش بودم.

دوشنبه ۳۰ مرداد، ۲۰ اوت - کتاب خواندم. از پدرم کاغذی داشتم. با امینی و محمدآبادی گردش کردم. شب نزد فؤاد و خانمش و برادرش بودم.

سه‌شنبه ۳۱ < مرداد >، ۲۱ اوت - از جلال و دکتر باستان کاغذ رسید. ناهار با محمدآبادی خوردم. شب بهتل مونتانا رفتم نزد فؤاد و زنش.

چهارشنبه < ۱ شهریور >، ۲۲ اوت - کتاب خواندم.

پنجشنبه < ۲ شهریور >، ۲۳ اوت - از دشتی کاغذ رسید. عصر بمنزل پیرزنی انگلیسی رفتم نزدیک ریچموند. این پیرزن مدتی در هتل مادرید زندگی می‌کرد. اطاقش در خانه‌ای که دارد بسیار کوچک و سقفش کوتاه و بر رویهم خانهٔ محقریست امّا خیلی پاکیزه است. شب مونتانا نزد فؤاد رفتم.

جمعه ۲ شهریور، ۲۴ اوت - زرین‌کفش گفت که آقای تقی‌زاده را بطهران خواسته‌اند. بسیار متأسف شدم. شب بمنزل فؤاد رفتم.

شنبه ۳ شهریور، ۲۵ اوت - با محمدآبادی بودم.

یکشنبه ۴ شهریور، ۲۶ اوت - حقوق خواندم.

دوشنبه ۵ شهریور، ۲۷ اوت - از پدرم و جلال کاغذ رسید. با محمدآبادی بکتابفروشی لوزاک رفتیم. ناهار در حوالی بریتیش میوزیم خوردیم. شب با محمدآبادی بمنزل احمدی رفتم. اردلان عضو سفارت و دکتر علوی هم که هم منزل او هستند، بودند. تا ساعت ۱۱ در آنجا بودیم.

سه‌شنبه ۶ شهریور، ۲۸ اوت - کتب حقوقی خواندم.

چهارشنبه ۷ شهریور، ۲۹ اوت - صبح به پرینس آو ویلز هتل رفتم. محمدآبادی مشغول جمع کردن اثاث خود بود. ساعت ۹ و نیم اول بسفارت و بعد به ویکتوریا رفتم. احمدی و اردلان پیش از ما آمده بودند. زود خداحافظی کردند و رفتند ولی بعد فؤاد و زنش آمدند. ساعت ده و نیم ترن حرکت کرد. از رفتن محمدآبادی متأثر شدم چون که با او انس گرفته بودم. برگشتن پیاده با فؤاد و زنش به چلسی آمدم. شب بسینما رفتم.

پنجشنبه ۸ شهریور، ۳۰ اوت - به سمریتن هوس¹ بادارۀ مالیات بر عایدات رفتم. تمام روز در اداره کار کردم. شب حقوق خواندم.

جمعه ۹ شهریور، ۳۱ اوت - از خواهرم و ناصر و ضیاء کاغذ رسید. حقوق خواندم.

شنبه ۱۰ شهریور، اول سپتامبر - از محمدآبادی کارت‌پستال رسید. حقوق می‌خواندم.

یکشنبه ۱۱ شهریور، ۲ سپتامبر - حقوق خواندم. به بریتیش میوزیم رفتم.

دوشنبه ۱۲ شهریور، ۳ سپتامبر - ناهار در منزل زرین‌کفش بودم. مؤتمن، نورانی، مصباح و صالحی محصلین وزارت مالیه هم بودند.

سه‌شنبه ۱۳ شهریور، ۴ سپتامبر - آقای علاء سفیر ایران در لندن وارد شد. بدیدن او رفتم. شایسته و زرین‌کفش در سفارت بودند.

چهارشنبه ۱۴ شهریور، ۵ سپتامبر - در اداره کار کردم و حقوق خواندم.

پنجشنبه ۱۵ شهریور، ۶ سپتامبر - از جلال و فلسفی کاغذی رسید. شب در هتل مادرید با کلنل اسکاتلندی که متقاعد شده بود، صحبت کردم.

جمعه ۱۶ شهریور، ۷ سپتامبر - صبح ببا رفتم و حقوق خواندم. از صادق صوراسرافیل که از پاریس آمده کاغذی رسید که در اطراف لندن است.

شنبه ۱۷ شهریور، ۸ سپتامبر - بدیدن صور به ایلینگ² رفتم. شب حقوق خواندم.

یکشنبه ۱۸ شهریور، ۹ سپتامبر - در هاید پارک فاشیستها و کمونیستها نمایش می‌دادند. قریب هفت هزار آژان مأمور محافظت بودند. شب حقوق خواندم.

---

۱. Good Samaritan House.

۲. Ealing ناحیه‌ای در غرب لندن.

دوشنبه ۱۹ شهریور، ۱۰ سپتامبر - کتاب خواندم.

سه‌شنبه ۲۰ شهریور، ۱۱ سپتامبر - حقوق خواندم.

چهارشنبه ۲۱ شهریور، ۱۲ سپتامبر - حقوق می‌خواندم.

پنجشنبه ۲۲ شهریور، ۱۳ سپتامبر - از جلال و دشتی و هژیر کاغذ رسید.

جمعه ۲۳ شهریور، ۱۴ سپتامبر - در باغ درس خواندم.

شنبه ۲۴ شهریور، ۱۵ سپتامبر - کتاب خواندم.

یکشنبه ۲۵ شهریور، ۱۶ سپتامبر - در هتل با مستر مود و رفیق اسپانیاییش که
خوشمزه بود و با سایر دوستان هتل نشستیم و صحبت کردیم.

دوشنبه ۲۶ شهریور، ۱۷ سپتامبر - در هتل با کلنل اسکاتلندی و مستر مود و مسیز
بن سن و مسیز هت و مسیز هامت و پسرش که مراجعت کرده بودند مجلس گرمی
بود و رفیق اسپانیایی مستر مود حرکات خنده‌آور داشت.

سه‌شنبه ۲۷ شهریور، ۱۸ سپتامبر - شب با مستر مود و سایر دوستان هتل بسینما رفتم.

چهارشنبه ۲۸ شهریور، ۱۹ سپتامبر - حقوق خواندم.

پنجشنبه ۲۹ شهریور، ۲۰ سپتامبر - باز در هتل مجلس دوستانه گرم بود و اسپانیایی
وقت همه را خوش کرد.

جمعه ۳۰ شهریور، ۲۱ سپتامبر - اسپانیایی از هتل رفت. تمام روز حقوق خواندم.

شنبه ۳۱ شهریور، ۲۲ سپتامبر - در تایمز مقاله‌ای راجع بحافظ بقلم آقا خان خواندم.
درینک واتر و سر دنیسن راس برای جشن فردوسی بایران می‌روند.

یکشنبه ۱ مهر، ۲۳ سپتامبر - حقوق خواندم.

دوشنبه ۲ مهر، ۲۴ سپتامبر - حقوق خواندم.

سه‌شنبه ۳ مهر، ۲۵ سپتامبر - با امینی در باغ گردش کردم. حقوق خواندم.

چهارشنبه ۴ مهر، ۲۶ سپتامبر - حقوق خواندم. شب در هتل با کلنل در باب اسلام و اروپا حرف زدم.

پنجشنبه ۵ مهر، ۲۷ سپتامبر - از مدرسه السنۀ شرقیه کاغذی رسید باین مضمون که چون سر دنیسن رس و مینورسکی بایران می‌روند، بجای ایشان درس بدهم. بواسطه کمی وقت و لزوم خواندن کتب حقوقی از این دعوت خرسند نشدم و لیکن آن را قبول کردم. شب حقوق خواندم.

جمعه ۶ مهر، ۲۸ سپتامبر - کتاب خواندم.

شنبه ۷ مهر، ۲۹ سپتامبر - شب فؤاد و زنش بدیدنم آمدند.

یکشنبه ۸ مهر، ۳۰ سپتامبر - کاظمی وزیر خارجه دو روز پیش وارد لندن شد و امروز حرکت کرد و رفت.

دوشنبه ۹ مهر، ۱ اکتبر - منشی انجمن سلطنتی آسیا از من خواست که روز پنجشنبه چند بیت از شاهنامه در مجلس نطق بخوانم. پروفسور نیکلسن نطقی راجع بفردوسی می‌کند. قبول کردم.

سه‌شنبه ۱۰ مهر، ۲ اکتبر - حقوق خواندم.

چهارشنبه ۱۱ مهر، ۳ اکتبر - بمدرسه السنۀ شرقیه رفتم. مستر هوکر و زنش را دیدم. آمده‌اند درس فارسی بخوانند.

پنجشنبه ۱۲ مهر، ۴ اکتبر - آقای علاء خواهش کرد در مجلسی که بمناسبت جشن فردوسی در مجلس لردها بر پا می‌شود، اشعار فردوسی بخوانم. قبول کردم. چهار و ربع بعد از ظهر بمجمع رفتم. آقای علاء، سر پرسی سایکس و جمعی از علما و پروفسورها بودند. مسیز هت و مسیز استیون هم بودند و فؤاد با یک خانم انگلیسی هم آمده بود. پروفسور مارگولیوث استاد معروف عربی در اکسفورد قبلاً شرحی گفت و بعد پروفسور نیکلسن حرف زد. نطق سادهٔ جامعی کرد. در وسط نطقش برخاستم چد کلمه بانگلیسی گفتم و بعد ابیات را خواندم. آقای علاء و سر پرسی سایکس هم حرف زندند. مجلس ساعت شش تمام شد.

جمعه ۱۳ مهر، ۵ اکتبر - آقای علاء از من خواهش کرد که در جواب مقاله بایرن در روزنامه تایمز راجع بایران چیزی بنویسم.

شنبه ۱۴ مهر، ۶ اکتبر - حقوق خواندم. و مدتی بتهیه مقاله جوابیه مشغول بودم ولی در خصوص آنکه آیا این مقاله را چنانکه آقای علاء گفته امضا کنم بوسیله تلفون از آقای زرین‌کفش استعلام کردم ولی این شخص بدگمان که بسایه خود هم نظر بد دارد خیال کرد که من از داوطلب شده و از علاء خواسته‌ام که آن را امضا کنم و هیچ فکر نمی‌کرد که خلاف ادبست که من بعلاء دستور بدهم. اینست کار ایران! اکثر نوکران دولت یا دزدند و شریر یا بدگمان و ساده‌لوح و بیچاره. خواستم کاغذ تندی بزرین‌کفش بنویسم. دیدم وقت ضایع کردن است و دریغ است کلمه حکمت با آدم بدگمان گفتن.

یکشنبه ۱۵ مهر، ۷ اکتبر - حقوق خواندم.

دوشنبه ۱۶ مهر، ۸ اکتبر - در اداره با زرین‌کفش بتندی حرف زدم و گفتم که از او چها کشیده‌ام. سفر از طهران بلندن را بر من حرام کرد. خیلی خسته بودم.

سه‌شنبه ۱۷ مهر، ۹ اکتبر - صبح نزد علاء رفتم. راجع بمقاله صحبت کردم. مرد مؤدب وطن پرست خوبیست.

چهارشنبه ۱۸ مهر، ۱۰ اکتبر - بمدرسه رفتم. درس دادم. شب حقوق خواندم و بدیدن فؤاد رفتم.

پنجشنبه ۱۹ مهر، ۱۱ اکتبر - کتاب حقوقی خواندم.

جمعه ۲۰ مهر، ۱۳ اکتبر - فؤاد و خانمش را دیدم. حقوق خواندم.

شنبه ۲۱ مهر، ۱۳ اکتبر - کتاب خواندم.

یکشنبه ۲۲ مهر، ۱۴ اکتبر - با فؤاد و خانمش به بریتیش میوزیوم رفتم. کتب خطی شاهنامه و بعضی کتب دیگر را بمناسبت جشن فردوسی در معرض تماشا گذاشته بودند. ظفرنامه حمدالله مستوفی را هم دیدم.

دوشنبه ۲۳ مهر، ۱۵ اکتبر - کتاب خواندم.

سه‌شنبه ۲۴ مهر، ۱۶ اکتبر - از پدرم و جلال و جمال و زینت و سهیلی و پرویز کاغذ رسید. شب با صورتگر بودم.

چهارشنبه ۲۵ مهر، ۱۷ اکتبر - از وکیلی راجع بمدرسه حقوق پاریس کاغذی رسید.

پنجشنبه ۲۶ مهر، ۱۸ اکتبر - ۱۰۶ فرانک برای مدرسه حقوق فرستادم با دو کاغذ سفارشی یکی برای منشی مدرسه و دیگری برای تحویلدار. مدرسه السنهٔ شرقیه رفتم. ناهار نزدیک بریتیش میوزیوم خوردم. بعد از شام نزد فؤاد رفتم.

جمعه ۲۷ مهر، ۱۹ اکتبر - شب به پورتلند هتل بدیدن صورتگر رفتم. تا ساعت ۱۱ با او بودم.

شنبه ۲۸ مهر، ۲۰ اکتبر - فؤاد روحانی و خانمش بهتل من آمدند. چای خوردیم. می‌خواهند بایران مراجعت کنند. شب بهتل ایشان رفتم تا در رادیو نطق اشخاصی که راجع بایران بمناسبت جشن فردوسی حرف می‌زدند < را > بشنوم. ژنرال دنسترویل، سر آرنولد

ویلسن، مستر نیکلسن، سر دنیسن رس حرف زدند. فقط سر دنیسن رس مربوط حرف زد. موزیکی هم عجیب که نه موسیقی ایرانی بود و نه فرنگی شنیده می‌شد. از میس کندی منشی جمعیت آسیای وسطی مراسله‌ای رسید و مرا دعوت کرد که در روز ۳۱ اکتبر در مجلس ناهاری که در مجلس لردها خواهد بود قسمتی از شاهنامه را بخوانم.

یکشنبه ۲۹ مهر، ۲۱ اکتبر - حقوق خواندم. عصر در چلسی در کافه قنادی بسیار کوچک چای خوردم.

دوشنبه ۳۰ مهر، ۲۲ اکتبر - در مدرسه علوم شرقی درس دادم. با فؤاد و خانمش در باغ گردش کردم.

سه‌شنبه ۱ آبان، ۲۳ اکتبر - از خلخالی کاغذی رسید.

چهارشنبه ۲ آبان، ۲۴ اکتبر - با سر دنیسن رس قرار گذاشتم که قسمتی از اشعار راجع بجنگ رستم و سهراب را بخوانم. و او هم ترجمه اش را بخواند.

پنجشنبه ۳ آبان، ۲۵ اکتبر - با فؤاد و خانمش بتآتر رفتم.

جمعه ۴ آبان، ۲۶ اکتبر - با رفعتی در رستوران نزدیک مدرسه ناهار خوردم.

شنبه ۵ آبان، ۲۷ اکتبر - حقوق خواندم.

یکشنبه ۶ آبان، ۲۸ اکتبر - حقوق خواندم. شب تا ساعت ۱۱ با مستر مور و مستر هرس و میس جونسون و مستر برنز و دخترش و برادرزاده‌اش بازی کردم. شش بعد از نصف شب بیدار شدم برای کار و درس.

دوشنبه ۷ آبان، ۲۹ اکتبر - شب بپارک لین هتل رفتم. بمناسبت جشن فردوسی مجلسی بر پا بود. آقای علاء و سر پرسی سایکس و لرد لمینگتون و چند نفر دیگر از ایرانی و انگلیسی بودند. علاء و سر دنیسن رس نطق کردند. ابوالقاسم شیوا هم جوابی داد.

سه‌شنبه ۸ آبان، ۳۰ اکتبر - صبح کتاب خواندم. آقای علاء را دیدم. در باب ضیافت جمعه شب صحبت کردیم. در این شب باید بانگلیسی نطق کنم و قسمتی از شعرهای فردوسی را بخوانم. چهار بعد از ظهر بمدرسه السنه شرقیه رفتم. مجلسی بر پا بود. رئیس هیأت مدیره مدرسه و سر دنیسن رس و آقای علاء و پروفسور نیکلسن نطق کردند. رئیس مجلس نطق پروفسور مک گیل عضور آکادمی و یکی از نویسندگان انگلیسی بود که در خصوص کلیات ادبیات ایران نطق کرد.

چهارشنبه ۹ آبان، ۳۱ اکتبر - در این روز بمجلس لردها رفتم. جمع کثیری بناهار دعوت داشتند. در سر میز مستر انتونی ایدن که جوان و معروف بکفایت و لیاقت و همه کاره وزارت خارجه انگلیس است میان لیدی رمبولد و خانم علاء نشسته بود و پهلوی خانم علاء آقاخان. من هم پهلوی لیدی رمبولد نشسته بودم. سر ناهار اول لرد لمینگتون نطق کرد. چون رئیس جلسه بود آن را افتتاح کرد. اولاً بسلامت شاه انگلیس و بعد بسلامت شاه ایران و بعد بسلامت شعرا و مهمانها شراب خوردند. بعد انتونی ایدن که در اکسفورد فارسی خوانده است نطقی کرد. و بعد من شعرهای راجع بکشته شدن سهراب < را > خواندم و سر دنیسن رس از ترجمه اشعار ماثی‌یو ارنولد خواند. بعد سر هوراس رمبولد نطقی کرد و بعد از او آقاخان نطق مفصلی کرد. مجلس خوبی بود. سر غذا کارت صورت اغذیه یک مجلس از مجالس شاهنامه و آمدن تهمینه ببالین رستم که از حیث رنگ آمیزی بسیار تمام بود، چاپ کرده بودند. سه ساعت بعد از ظهر مجلس ختم شد. شب حقوق خواندم.

پنجشنبه ۱۰ آبان، ۱ نوامبر - از یزدان فر کاغذی رسید و از عباس آقا هم کاغذی رسید. در این ایام بمناسبت جشن هزارمین سال فردوسی مجالسی در لندن بر پاست.

جمعه ۱۱ آبان، ۲ نوامبر - کتاب خواندم. ساعت ده بسفارت رفتم. جمعی از رجال و اعیان بودن، اکثر دارای نشان و حمایل. تماشایی بود. سر دنیسن رس قبلاً مقدمه کسالت‌آوری گفت و بعد شعر درینک واتر در خصوص ایران و خیام را خواند و بعد

از آن شعر ملک الشعراء را. بعد من اولاً بانگلیسی نطق کردم و چند بیت از جنگ رستم و اشکبوس را خواندم. پوپ بعضی عکسهای معماری ایران را نشان داد. مجلس تا یک ساعت بعد از نصف شب بر پا بود.

شنبه ۱۲ آبان، ۳ نوامبر - کتاب خواندم.

یکشنبه ۱۳ آبان، ۴ نوامبر - ناهار در منزل زرین‌کفش خوردم. شب از هتل بیرون نرفتم. حقوق خواندم.

دوشنبه ۱۴ آبان، ۵ نوامبر - تاریخ حقوق خواندم.

سه‌شنبه ۱۵ آبان، ۶ نوامبر - صبح بسفارت و بعد از ظهر بشرکت رفتم. شب حقوق خواندم.

چهارشنبه ۱۶ آبان، ۷ نوامبر - ناهار با زرین‌کفش خوردم. کتاب خواندم.

پنجشنبه ۱۸ آبان، ۹ نوامبر - در استراند زیر باران ایستادم و لرد میر لندن با آژان و نظامی و قافله‌اش همه آمدند.

شنبه ۱۹ آبان، ۱۰ نوامبر - کتاب خواندم.

یکشنبه ۲۰ آبان، ۱۱ نوامبر - به وست مینیستر رفتم. بمناسبت و برای یادبود کشتگان جنگ مراسمی انجام یافت. همه سکوت مطلق بود بقدر دو دقیقه.

دوشنبه ۲۱ آبان، ۱۲ نوامبر - دو ساعت درس دادم. حقوق اداری خواندم.

سه‌شنبه ۲۲ آبان، ۱۳ نوامبر - نزدیک ظهر داماد مسیز استیون آمد. این مرد که کشیش و خیلی متعارف و مؤدب و پر حرف بود بسیار خوب فارسی حرف می‌زد. از ۱۹۰۳ تا ۱۹۲۰ در ایران بوده. در کرمان و یزد و اصفهان و کمی در طهران اقامت داشته.

چهارشنبه ۲۳ آبان، ۱۴ نوامبر - تا ساعت شش در اداره کار کردم. شب حقوق خواندم.

پنجشنبه ۲۴ آبان، ۱۵ نوامبر - تا نزدیک نصف شب کتاب خواندم.

جمعه ۲۵ آبان، ۱۶ نوامبر - صبح کاغذی از فاکولته حقوق پاریس رسید و تاریخ امتحان ــ ۲۶ نوامبر ــ را اعلام کرد. بعد از چای برای تهیه مقدمات سفر بیرون رفتم و تا چهار ساعت بعد از ظهر در تک و دو بودم. بقنسولخانه فرانسه در رس اسکویر و باداره گمرک برای گرفتن بلیط رفتم.

شنبه ۲۶ آبان، ۱۷ نوامبر - بعد از ناهار بمنزل زرین‌کفش رفتم. عباسقلی خان اردلان هم بود. صبح بمدرسه رفتم و درس دادم.

یکشنبه ۲۷ آبان، ۱۸ نوامبر - با ترن یازده بپاریس رفتم. دریا بین دوور و کاله آرام بود. دو ساعت و نیم بعد از ظهر بکاله رسیدم. در راه یک پروتستان با یک کاتولیک بحث داشتند، بحث مذهبی. شش و نیم بعد از ساعت وارد پاریس شدم. به Select Hotel رفتم. شب بمنزل اقبال در کوچه برآ رفتم. آقای مصدقی هم که اتّفاقاً در سلکت هتل شام می‌خورد، راهنمای من شد. شب با اقبال دو ساعت و نیم در شان ز لیزه و مون مارتر راه رفتیم. بسیار خسته شدم.

دوشنبه ۲۸ آبان، ۱۹ نوامبر - صبح کمی تاریخ حقوق خواندم و بعد بمدرسه حقوق رفتم. با آقای خسروپور بسفارت ایران رفتم. آقای عبدالله ریاضی و مرآت و وکیل را دیدم. شب مدتی با خسروپور در خیابان گردش کردم.

سه‌شنبه ۲۹ آبان، ۲۰ نوامبر - بعد از ظهر بمدرسه حقوق رفتم. پای امتحانات تماشا کردم. شب با شیدفر بودم و حقوق خواندم.

چهارشنبه ۳۰ آبان، ۲۱ نوامبر - صبح حقوق خواندم. بعد از ناهار با مصدقی بباغ لوک

سان بور[1] رفتم. بعد از یک ربع باز به هتل آمدم و تا یک بعد از نصف شب کتاب خواندم.

پنجشنبه اول آذر، ۲۲ نوامبر - بسیجی را دیدم. بعد از ظهر بمدرسه حقوق رفتم. تا نصف شب کتاب خواندم.

جمعه ۲ آذر، ۲۳ نوامبر - بسیار خسته بودم. کتاب خواندم.

شنبه ۳ آذر، ۲۴ نوامبر - تا پنج بعد از نصف شب کتاب خواندم. از خواندن بتنگ آمده‌ام. ششصد < صفحه > حقوق بین الملل را مطالعه کردم.

یکشنبه ۴ آذر، ۲۵ نوامبر - از آقای تقی زاده مراسله‌ای رسید. شب و روز کار کردم و کتاب خواندم.

دوشنبه ۵ آذر، ۲۶ نوامبر - شب هیچ نخوابیدم. روز امتحان دادم. قبول نشدم. در عرض دو سه ساعت باید قریب هشت هزار صفحه را جواب داد. شب آذر، باستان، شجاع نیا، و بسیجی آمدند. کمی صحبت کردیم.

سه‌شنبه ۶ آذر، ۲۷ نوامبر - صبح گردش کردم. شب با خسروپور و افضل‌پور بودم.

چهارشنبه ۷ آذر، ۲۸ نوامبر - با اقبال ببرج ایفل رفتم و شب بسینمای رکس.

پنجشنبه ۸ آذر، ۲۹ نوامبر - به سن مارتین یکی از مغازه‌های معروف پاریس رفتم و بعد از ظهر با خسروپور به آن والید < و > موزه جنگ < رفته > و قبر ناپلئون را دیدیم. در موزه جنگ یادگارهای سنت هلن، کلاه و مو و چکمه و لباس و میز کوچکی که در وقت نایب بودنش در نظام داشته و شمشیری که بر روی آن الفاظی بعربی است و پوست اسبی سفید عربی موسوم به وزیر و غیره < بود >. کلیسای آن والید عمارتیست بسیار عالی و قبر ناپلئون در محوطه

---

۱. مقصود Jardin du Luxembourg است.

گودی واقعست. راهنمایی که ما را در اطراف قبر که تصاویر اعمال ناپلئون است، برد و گرداند. هی می‌گفت ببینید اینجا جائیست که ناپلئون صلح را بملت می‌دهد یا این جا عدل می‌دهد ولی چون الکتریسیته نبود، چیزی نمی‌دیدیم. شب بتآتر سارا برنار رفتیم.

جمعه ۹ آذر، ۳۰ نوامبر - صبح بموزه لوک سان بور رفتم. در این موزه مجسمه‌ها و نقاشیهای مختلف علی الخصوص پرده‌های سبک جدید بسیار است. در بیرون موزه مجسمه‌ایست باسم سرما، مردی فقیر و زنی فقیر که لباس کافی ندارند و بهم چسبیده‌اند. سرما و بدبختی را خوب مجسم می‌کند. بعد از ظهر بمسجد و از آن جا بباغ نباتات رفتم. بعد از شام با غلامحسین امینی در کافه کوپر نشستیم.

شنبه ۱۰ آذر، ۱ دسامبر - بعد از ظهر با خسروپور و مصدقی بمغازه لافایت رفتم. بمناسبت نوئل آئین بسته بودند.

یکشنبه ۱۱ آذر، ۲ دسامبر - صبح با خسروپور بکلیسای سوربون رفتم. کاردینال وردیه اسقف اعظم پاریس بیاد کاردینال دو ریشلیو مراسم مذهبی انجام داد. نطقی کرد و در مقابل مجسمه ریشلیو رفت. وردی خواند و کارهای مهم ریشلیو را تذکر داد. جمعی از خانواده ریشلیو و اعضای آکادمی و پروفسورهای سوربون بودند. شب با وکیل در رستوران کولیزه شام خوردیم.

دوشنبه ۱۲ آذر، ۳ دسامبر - با نصراله عبادی و خسروپور گردش کردم.

سه‌شنبه ۱۳ آذر، ۴ دسامبر - < با > عبده و آزموده و میرهادیان و خسروپور بودم.

چهارشنبه ۱۴ آذر، ۵ دسامبر - با قرشی در لوک سان بور گردش کردم. با خسروپور به بوا دو بولون رفتم و شب به خوبی گذشت.

پنجشنبه ۱۵ آذر، ۶ دسامبر - صبح در خیابان گردش کردم و بعد از ظهر با خسروپور

بموزه لوور رفتم. بپدرم کاغذی نوشتم. شب با خسروپور و خوش کیش به کمدی فرانسز رفتم.

جمعه ۱۶ آذر، ۷ دسامبر - صبح گردش کردم و بعد از ظهر بمنزل امانی رفتم. با او بمنزل میرزا محمد خان < قزوینی > رفتم. شایگان و ملک اسماعیل و یک آلمانی هم آمدند. تا ساعت هشت آنجا بودیم.

شنبه ۱۷ آذر، ۸ دسامبر - با ملک اسماعیلی بکتابفروشی رفتم. چند کتاب خریدم. بعد از ظهر بسینما رفتم. فیلم سمفونی ناتمام را دیدم. شب با خسروپور بتآتر اودئون رفتم.

یکشنبه ۱۸ آذر، ۹ دسامبر - صبح به پانتئون رفتم که آن را سوفلو[1] معمار مشهور ساخته. در و دیوارش تصویر مذهبیست. در زیر زمین قبر بزرگان فرانسه است. قبر ولتر و روسو و ویکتور هوگو < و > سادی کارنو < و > سوفلو < و > برتلو و قبر زنش هم در آنجاست. راهنما یکایک را شرح می‌داد و تاریخچه هر یک را می‌گفت و گفت که این زن و شوهر خیلی بیکدیگر علاقه داشتند و از قضا هر دو در یک روز مردند و نظر بوصیت زنش که می‌خواست قبرش نیز با شوهرش باشد، او را در پانتئون دفن کردند. شب با خسروپور بسینما رفتم.

دوشنبه ۱۹ آذر، ۱۰ دسامبر - صبح بمدرسه حقوق رفتم. شیدفر را دیدم. با من در سلکت هتل ناهار خورد. عصر بسفارت رفتم. ابوالحسن خان و جواد خان فروغی را دیدم. از من خواستند که در جشن فردوسی چند بیت از شاهنامه بخوانم. شب با وکیل و کیهان شام خوردم.

سه‌شنبه ۲۰ آذر، ۱۱ دسامبر - صبح برای عوض کردن بلیط به پلاس مادلن رفتم و موزه اورانژری را دیدم. اکثر پرده‌ها از قرن هفدهم است. عصر ساعت شش میرزا محمد خان قزوینی بدیدنم آمد. شب با خسروپور بسینما رفتم.

---

۱. Jacques-Germain Soufflot معمار مشهور فرانسوی (۱۷۱۳-۱۷۸۰).

چهارشنبه ۲۱ آذر، ۱۲ دسامبر - بلیط مراجعت بلندن را عوض کردم. بکلیسای مادلن رفتم و بعد از ظهر با خسروپور بکتابخانه ملی بمناسبت جشن فردوسی نسخه‌های خطی و چاپی و نوشته‌های مربوط بایران را برای تماشا گذاشته بودند. وزیر معارف فرانسه هم برای افتتاح مراسم جشن آمد. شارژه دافر ایران نطق بالنسبه مفصلی بزبان فرانسه خواند. نطق وزیر معارف فرانسه مختصر بود. شب بسینمای پانتئون رفتم.

پنجشنبه ۲۲ آذر، ۱۳ دسامبر - صبح بسفارت رفتم. صدر را در آنجا دیدم. تا یک ساعت بعد از ظهر در سفارت با هم بودیم. در شان ز لیزه غذا خوردیم. بعد بهتل آمدم. چهار بعد از ظهر صدر بهتل من آمد. با هم بمنزل عبده رفتیم. آزموده هم آمد. شام با هم خوردیم.

جمعه ۲۳ آذر، ۱۴ دسامبر - ناهار در رستوران فلوریا با هشترودی خوردم. عصر بسفارت رفتم. با انتظام و جواد فروغی و ابوالحسن خان فروغی و وکیلی صحبت کردم. شب تاریخ و حقوق اداری خواندم.

شنبه ۲۴ آذر، ۱۵ دسامبر - صبح حقوق اداری خواندم. بسفارت رفتم. از منتخبات شاهنامه تألیف محمدعلی خان فروغی چند بیت برای خواندن در جشن فردوسی انتخاب کردم. حالم خوش نیست.

یکشنبه ۲۵ آذر، ۱۶ دسامبر - ببرج ایفل رفتم و بعد بموزه گیمه. پروفسور ماسه راجع به شاهنامه نطقی کرد. بد نبود. ابوالحسن خان هم نطقی کرد.

دوشنبه ۲۶ آذر، ۱۷ دسامبر - صبح با قرشی گردش کردم. ساعت پنج بعد از ظهر ببلدیه پاریس رفتم. سید کاظم خان صدر، ابوالحسن خان فروغی، جواد فروغی، علاء و اکثر شاگردها بودند. موزیک گارد ملی هم در سالون بود و نواهای شرقی می‌زد. علاء نطق خوب کرد. پیر < دو > نهسن هم نطق کرد و کتاب شاهنامه را که علاء بشهر پاریس تقدیم کرد، پذیرفت. پول فور Paul Fort شاعر فرانسوی هم نطق کرد و

شعرهایی که بمناسبت این جشن گفته بود، خواند. اشعار چاپ شده بود و بحضار دادند. حکیم الدوله هم از طرف بلدیه طهران نطق کرد. ابوالحسن خان فروغی هم نطق کرد. چندان خوب نبود. چنان می‌نمود که می‌خواست بدیگران ایراد بگیرد. قبل از فروغی، پر لی‌یو رئیس انجمن ایران نطق خوب مؤثر کرد. فروغی گفت که من هم شاعرم، من هم بلبلم. در سالون پذیرائی شیرینی و شربت و مشروب فراوان بود. مجلس خوبی بود. بعد از شام با خسروپور و خوش کیش به کازینو دو پاری با رفتم.

سه‌شنبه ۲۷[1] آذر، ۱۸ دسامبر - شیدفر در هتل با من ناهار خورد. بعد از ناهار پیاده به شان ز لیزه رفتم. هوا صاف بود و عمارت لوور و تویلری و خیابانها و باغها و مجسمه‌ها تماشای خاص داشت. پنج بعد از ظهر در کافه وبر نزدیک کلیسای مادلن چای خوردیم و بعد بهتل آمدم. بعد از شام لباس عوض کردم و به سوربون رفتم. ساعت ۹ رئیس جمهور وارد شد بمجلس جشن فردوسی ‹ که › در عمارت بزرگ آنفی تآتر سوربون بر پا بود. بیش از دو هزار نفر در آنفی تآتر بودند. گارد رپوبلیکن و موزیک آن برقرار بود و مستحفظ در گوشه و کنار بودند. در مقابل مجسمه فردوسی بود که بخرج شاگردان ایرانی ریخته شده است. بالای آن بیرقهای ایران و فرانسه بود. طرف چپ موزیک گارد جمهوری بود. در مقابل رئیس جمهور در صف اول کسانی که باید نطق کنند و چندین نفر از اشخاص محترم بودند. هانری ماسه، آبه برنار عضو آکادمی فرانسه، علاء، مالارمه وزیر معارف، پر لی‌یو رئیس انجمن ایران، سفیر افغانستان و چندین نفر دیگر. در صف بعد میرزا محمد خان قزوینی، پروفسور مینورسکی، و چندین معلم فاکولته نشسته بودند. در طرف راست رئیس جمهور خانم علاء بود. در صف بعد من نشسته بودم. جمیع شاگردهای مقیم پاریس و جمع بسیاری در آنفی تآتر بودند. وزیر معارف که در آخر خودش نطقی کرد، یکایک نطق کنندگان را معرفی کرد. اول پر لی‌یو نطق کرد. بسیار خوب و ساده و فصیح. بعد موزیک زدند. بعد از موزیک هانری ماسه نطق کرد. مریض بود و کمی کسالت آور.

بعد موزیک زدند. بعد از او آبه برنار بعد علاء و بعد وزیر معارف بعد موزیک زدند و رئیس جمهور و دیگران رفتند.

چهارشنبه ۲۸ آذر، ۱۹ دسامبر – صبح خطابه‌ای را که باید قبل از خواندن اشعار فردوسی قرائت کنم نوشتم و بردم که تایپ کنند. بعد از ظهر با مفتاح و ملک اسماعیل در کافه نشستم و بعد بسفارت رفتم. علاء را ملاقات کردم. شب با خسروپور و خوش کیش به نویی فو رفتم از قبیل فولی برژر چیزیست. بد نبود. روزنامه‌های فرانسه چنانکه باید راجع بجشن فردوسی چیزی ننوشتند.

پنجشنبه ۲۹ آذر، ۲۰ دسامبر – پنج بعد از ظهر صادق صدر آمد. در کافه مقابل هتل نشستیم و صبر کردیم. ساعت نه و نیم بسفارت رفتم. از ساعت ده مدعوین آمدند، قریب چهارصد نفر. موزیک ایرانی و فرنگی می‌زدند. بسیاری از معاریف بودند از قبیل مارشال فرانشه دس‌پره و ژنرال گورو. نطقی کردم و شعر خواندم. حالم دو روز است که بواسطه سرماخوردگی خوب نیست.

جمعه ۳۰ آذر، ۲۱ دسامبر – حالم خوب نیست. بعد از ظهر بسینما رفتم. شبهای مسکو را دیدم.

شنبه ۱ دی، ۲۲ دسامبر – چهار و نیم بظهر با خوش کیش به گار دو نور رفتم. آقای خوش کیش تا آن وقت با من بود. دریا آرام بود. دو ساعت در دوور معطل شدم. پنج بعد از ظهر بلندن رسیدم. در هتل تغییراتی پیدا شده. مسیز بن‌سن رفته مسیز هت مریض افتاده مستر مور و زنش باسپانیا رفته‌اند.

یکشنبه ۲ دی، ۲۳ دسامبر – بعد از ظهر بمنزل زرین‌کفش رفتم. شایسته هم آمد. با هم بهتل آمدیم. شب در سالون مدتی با میس بن‌سن و میس مورتون که دختری ایرلندی و خیلی خوش اخلاق است و مسیز هت صحبت کردم.

دوشنبه ۳ دی، ۲۴ دسامبر – از آقای تقی‌زاده و آقای خلخالی و آقای پرویز کاغذی داشتم. بقصر سنت جیمز رفتم برای تماشای هدایایی که بمناسبت عروسی پرنس جرج داده شده.

سه‌شنبه ۴ دی، ۲۵ دسامبر - صبح بمنزل زرین‌کفش رفتم. شب در هتل مادرید بساط عجیبی بر پا بود. خویشان میس ویلیامز صاحب مهمانخانه از ولز آمده بودند. بساط مهمانی مفصلی بر پا بود. بین میس مورتون و مسیز هت نشسته بودم. بد نگذشت. رقص و بازی در میان بود.

چهارشنبه ۵ دی، ۲۶ دسامبر - صبح بمنزل زرین‌کفش رفتم. تا پنج و نیم بعد از ظهر در آنجا بودم.

پنجشنبه ۶ دی، ۲۷ دسامبر - بعد از ظهر بشرکت رفتم. شب در هتل بودم.

جمعه ۷ دی، ۲۸ دسامبر - بیاض نامه‌های داوطلبان شغل محاسبی را مرتب می‌کردم. یکی نوشته بود به مادیات و گلکاری علاقه دارد و دیگری نوشته بود که مشغول بنایی‌ست. مدتی با مستر میلز که مشغول تحصیل و تهیه امتحانست حرف زدم.

شنبه ۸ دی، ۲۹ دسامبر - سرماخوردگی سخت داشتم. بسفارت رفتم. شایسته خواهش کرده کاغذی که پوپ بشاه نوشته < را > ترجمه کنم.

یکشنبه ۹ دی، ۳۰ دسامبر - اوراق مربوط بداوطلبان شغل محاسبی را مرتب کردم. بمنزل احمدی رفتم. نامدار و علوی و زرین‌کفش و خانواده‌اش هم آمدند. نامدار حضار را کمی خنداند.

دوشنبه ۱۰ دی، ۳۱ دسامبر - بعد از ظهر بشرکت رفتم و تا ساعت پنج و نیم بعد از ظهر کار کردم. شب در هتل بودم و با میس مورتون و مسیز هت و پسر پیرمردی هشتاد ساله که هر روز صبح زودتر از دیگران بعقب کار می‌رود، لوبو بازی کردیم.

سه‌شنبه ۱۱ دی، ۱ ژانویه - حقوق اداری خواندم.

چهارشنبه ۱۲ دی، ۲ ژانویه - حقوق اداری خواندم.

پنجشنبه ۱۳ دی، ۳ ژانویه - شایسته تلفون کرد. بسفارت رفتم. کاغذ علاء را داد که نوشته بود بمدرسه السنهٔ شرقیه بروم و مراسله پروفسور مینورسکی را که اکنون در پاریس است ببرم بمدرسه و نقشه‌های راجع بسرحد ایران و ترکیه را ببرم بسفارت که برای علاء بفرستند. چندی پیش دولت عراق از ایران بجامعه ملل شکایت کرده و باین سبب وزیر خارجه ایران و علاء بژنو رفته‌اند.

جمعه ۱۴ دی، ۴ ژانویه - کاغذی از دشتی رسید و در آن کسرایی و یاسمی و سعیدی و صورتگر و فریار و نفیسی چیزی نوشته بودند.

شنبه ۱۵ دی، ۵ ژانویه - حقوق اداری خواندم.

یکشنبه ۱۶ دی، ۶ ژانویه - شب نراقی بهتل آمد. با هم به ماربل آرچ رفتیم.

دوشنبه ۱۷ دی، ۷ ژانویه - شب با بعضی از اشخاص که در هتل بودند بازی کلکسیون کردم.

سه‌شنبه ۱۸ دی، ۸ ژانویه - کتب حقوق خواندم.

چهارشنبه ۱۹ دی، ۹ ژانویه - شب حقوق اداری خواندم.

پنجشنبه ۲۰ دی، ۱۰ ژانویه - شب در منزل لاک هارت شام خوردم.

جمعه ۲۱ دی، ۱۱ ژانویه - بسیار خسته‌ام. حالم خوب نیست.

شنبه ۲۲ دی، ۱۲ ژانویه - حالم چندان خوب نیست. عصر بموزه ویکتوریا رفتم.

یکشنبه ۲۳ دی، ۱۳ ژانویه - کمی انگلیسی خواندم.

دوشنبه ۲۴ دی، ۱۴ ژانویه - با عبدالحسین خان سرداری بمنزل رفتم. تا ساعت ۱۲ با او بودم.

سه‌شنبه ۲۵ دی، ۱۵ ژانویه - حقوق سیاسی خواندم.

چهارشنبه ۲۶ دی، ۱۶ ژانویه - در مدرسه السنهٔ شرقیه درس دادم.

پنجشنبه ۲۷ دی، ۱۷ ژانویه - حقوق اداری خواندم.

جمعه ۲۸ دی، ۱۸ ژانویه - در مدرسه درس دادم.

شنبه ۲۹ دی، ۱۹ ژانویه - حقوق اداری خواندم. مسیز هت نزد پدرش به ماین هد رفته.

یکشنبه ۳۰ دی، ۲۰ ژانویه - حقوق اداری خواندم.

دوشنبه ۱ بهمن، ۲۱ ژانویه - حقوق اداری خواندم. درس دادم.

سه‌شنبه ۲ بهمن، ۲۲ ژانویه - حقوق اداری خواندم.

چهارشنبه ۳ بهمن، ۲۳ ژانویه - حقوق اداری خواندم.

پنجشنبه ۴ بهمن، ۲۴ ژانویه - ترجمه کاغذ پوپ را بسفارت دادم.

جمعه ۵ بهمن، ۲۵ ژانویه - حقوق اداری خواندم.

شنبه ۶ بهمن، ۲۶ ژانویه - حقوق اداری خواندم.

یکشنبه ۷ بهمن، ۲۷ ژانویه - ناهار در منزل زرین‌کفش بود. شب با مستر هرز و میس مورتون و مسیز هت کلکسیون بازی کردیم.

دوشنبه ۸ بهمن، ۲۸ ژانویه - حقوق اداری خواندم. در روزنامه‌ها نوشتند که ایران خواهش کرده است آن را پرس و پرشیا نشناسند و ایران بخوانند.

سه‌شنبه ۹ بهمن، ۲۹ ژانویه - شب در اطاق مسیز هت دعوت داشتم. بعضی از سکنه هتل هم بودند.

چهارشنبه ۱۰ بهمن، ۳۰ ژانویه - حقوق اداری خواندم.

پنجشنبه ۱۱ بهمن، ۳۱ ژانویه - علاء را در سفارت دیدم. حقوق اداری خواندم.

جمعه ۱۲ بهمن، ۱ فوریه - حالم چندان خوب نیست. حسنعلی خان وزیری از امریکا وارد شد و بهتل مادرید آمد. تا ساعت ۱۱ با او بودم.

شنبه ۱۳ بهمن، ۲ فوریه - حقوق اداری خواند. وزیری شب باطاق من آمد.

یکشنبه ۱۴ بهمن، ۳ فوریه - حقوق اداری خواندم.

دوشنبه ۱۵ بهمن، ۴ فوریه - شب با وزیری بودم.

سه‌شنبه ۱۶ بهمن، ۵ فوریه - حقوق خواندم.

چهارشنبه ۱۷ بهمن، ۶ فوریه - حقوق اداری خواندم. مدتی هم با وزیری بودم.

پنجشنبه ۱۸ بهمن، ۷ فوریه - از پدرم کاغذی رسید. بهتل مونتانا بدیدن زنجانی و زنش رفتم.

جمعه ۱۹ بهمن، ۸ فوریه - شب با میس مورتون و مسیز هت و میس بن‌سن و مستر بولدر بازی کردم.

شنبه ۲۰ بهمن، ۹ فوریه - بمحله یهودیها رفتم برای تماشا.

یکشنبه ۲۱ بهمن، ۱۰ فوریه - حقوق خواندم.

دوشنبه ۲۲ بهمن، ۱۱ فوریه - در مدرسه درس دادم. کمی حقوق هم خواندم.

سه‌شنبه ۲۳ بهمن، ۱۲ فوریه - مذاکرات مجلس راجع بقانون هندوستان را خواندم.

چهارشنبه ۲۴ بهمن، ۱۳ فوریه - با وزیری و دیگران بازی کردم.

پنجشنبه ۲۵ بهمن، ۱۴ فوریه - حقوق خواندم.

جمعه ۲۶ بهمن، ۱۵ فوریه - تاریخ حقوق خواندم.

شنبه ۲۷ بهمن، ۱۶ فوریه - شب با وزیری و دیگران بازی کردیم.

یکشنبه ۲۸ بهمن، ۱۷ فوریه - با وزیری گردش کردم و شب حقوق خواندم.

دوشنبه ۲۹ بهمن، ۱۸ فوریه - ناهار با رفعتی خوردم. شب حقوق خواندم.

سه‌شنبه ۳۰ بهمن، ۱۹ فوریه - کتاب خواندم.

چهارشنبه اول اسفند، ۲۰ فوریه - در مدرسه درس دادم. با مسیز هت بمنزل دوستش هلن رفتیم و شوهر هلن هم بود.

پنجشنبه ۲ اسفند، ۲۱ فوریه - تاریخ حقوق خواندم.

جمعه ۳ اسفند، ۲۲ فوریه - با وزیری نمایشگاه امتعه انگلیسی رفتم.

شنبه ۴ اسفند، ۲۳ فوریه - تاریخ حقوق خواندم.

یکشنبه ۵ اسفند، ۲۴ فوریه - شب و روز کار کردم و تاریخ حقوق خواندم.

دوشنبه ۶ اسفند، ۲۵ فوریه - شب با وزیری در هتل بودم.

سه‌شنبه ۷ اسفند، ۲۶ فوریه - با وزیری بنمایشگاه رفتم و حقوق خواندم.

چهارشنبه ۸ اسفند، ۲۷ فوریه - درس دادم.

پنجشنبه ۹ اسفند، ۲۸ فوریه - جزوه تاریخ حقوق را تمام کردم.

جمعه ۱۰ اسفند، ۱ مارس - تا نصف شب حقوق خواندم.

شنبه ۱۱ اسفند، ۲ مارس - با وزیری فیلم عبدالحمید[1] را دیدم.

یکشنبه ۱۲ اسفند، ۳ مارس - با وزیری در منزل زرین‌کفش ناهار خوردم.

دوشنبه ۱۳ اسفند، ۴ مارس - عصر کمی حقوق خواندم. شام در ساووی هتل خوردم. معلمین مدرسه السنهٔ شرقیه و جمعی کثیر هندی و غیره بودند. علاء و سر دنیسن رس هم بودند.

سه‌شنبه ۱۴ اسفند، ۵ مارس - حقوق خواندم.

چهارشنبه ۱۵ اسفند، ۶ مارس - با وزیری در مدرسه صنایع گردش کردم.

پنجشنبه ۱۶ اسفند، ۷ مارس - حقوق خواندم.

جمعه ۱۷ اسفند، ۸ مارس - تا نصف شب کار کردم. خلاصه حقوق اداری را نوشتم.

شنبه ۱۸ اسفند، ۹ مارس - تا نصف شب حقوق می‌خواندم.

یکشنبه ۱۹ اسفند، ۱۰ مارس - تا نصف شب حقوق می‌خواندم.

---

۱. *Abdul the Damned* یا *Abdul Hamid*، محصول بریتانیا (۱۹۳۵) کارگردان کارل گرون.

دوشنبه ۲۰ اسفند، ۱۱ مارس - حقوق اداری را خلاصه کردم.

سه‌شنبه ۲۱ اسفند، ۱۲ مارس - حقوق خواندم و با وزیری بسفارت رفتم.

چهارشنبه ۲۲ اسفند، ۱۳ مارس - حقوق اداری خواندم.

پنجشنبه ۲۳ اسفند، ۱۴ مارس - تا نصف شب کار کردم. باداره هم رفتم.

جمعه ۲۴ اسفند، ۱۵ مارس - حقوق اداری خواندم.

شنبه ۲۵ اسفند، ۱۶ مارس - حقوق خواندم. عصر در چلسی گردش کردم. شب با وزیری بمنزل سرداری رفتم.

یکشنبه ۲۶ اسفند، ۱۷ مارس - تمام روز درس خواندم.

دوشنبه ۲۷ اسفند، ۱۸ مارس - صبح بمدرسه رفتم. درس دادم. عصر باداره رفتم. شب با وزیری بودم.

سه‌شنبه ۲۸ اسفند، ۱۹ مارس - حقوق خواندم.

چهارشنبه ۲۹ اسفند، ۲۰ مارس - حالم خوب نیست. درس می‌خوانم.

پنجشنبه ۳۰ اسفند، ۲۱ مارس - از مدینه از پدرم کاغذی داشتم. با وزیری کمی گردش کردم.

جمعه اول فروردین، ۲۲ مارس - با وزیری بعد از ظهر بسفارت رفتم. تا ساعت ۷ در آنجا بودم. شب حالم خوب نبود.

شنبه ۲ فروردین، ۲۳ مارس - عصر با وزیری بمنزل زرین‌کفش رفتم.

یکشنبه ۳ فروردین، ۲۴ مارس - عصر با وزیری و سرداری بودم.

دوشنبه ۴ فروردین، ۲۵ مارس - حقوق خواندم.

سه‌شنبه ۵ فروردین، ۲۶ مارس - حقوق خواندم.

چهارشنبه ۶ فروردین، ۲۷ مارس - در مدرسه درس دادم. شب حقوق خواندم. میس ویلیس و پدر و مادرش از الجزیره آمده‌اند. در هتل زندگی می‌کنند. میس ویلیس خیلی خوب فرانسه حرف می‌زند.

پنجشنبه ۷ فروردین، ۲۸ مارس - شب با وزیری و میس ویلیس و مسیز هت بودم. روز حقوق خواندم.

جمعه ۸ فروردین، ۲۹ مارس - تاریخ حقوق خواندم.

شنبه ۹ فروردین، ۳۰ مارس - حقوق خواندم.

یکشنبه ۱۰ فروردین، ۳۱ مارس - در باغ حقوق خواندم.

دوشنبه ۱۱ فروردین، ۱ آوریل - شب بعد از شام با مسیز هت و میس ویلیس و میس گریهام بمنزل میس مورتون رفتم. تا ساعت ۷ در آنجا بودم.

سه‌شنبه ۱۲ فروردین، ۲ آوریل - حقوق خواندم.

چهارشنبه ۱۳ فروردین، ۳ آوریل - عصر با وزیری به های گیت و از آنجا بباغ سر آلفرد دیویس بسیزده بدر رفتم. آقای علاء هم بود با اکثر ایرانیان. شب دختری نیمه انگلیسی نیمه شرقی که تحصیل می‌کند بهتل مادرید آمد.

پنجشنبه ۱۴ فروردین، ۴ آوریل - تاریخ حقوق می‌خوانم. سرم درد می‌کند. پستهای نظامی انگلیس که در خلیج فارس بود ببحرین انتقال یافت.

جمعه ۱۵ فروردین، ۵ آوریل - حقوق خواندم.

شنبه ۱۶ فروردین، ۶ آوریل - صبح بسفارت رفتم. حقوق خواندم.

یکشنبه ۱۷ فروردین، ۷ آوریل - صبح با صباحی کمی در باغ گردش کردم و پاروزنی کردم. ساعت ۹ با مسیز هت و وزیری بمنزل هلن رفیق مسیز هت رفتیم. تابلوهای کار شوهر مادرش را نشان داد.

دوشنبه ۱۸ فروردین، ۸ آوریل - حقوق خواندم. شب با وزیری و میس مورتون و مسیز هت باطاق مسیز هت رفتم. مهمان بودیم.

سه‌شنبه ۱۹ فروردین، ۹ آوریل - سخت سرما خورده‌ام. حالم هیچ خوب نیست. هیچ از هتل بیرون نرفتم. حقوق خواندم.

چهارشنبه ۲۰ فروردین، ۱۰ آوریل - حقوق خواندم. شب ثقة الدوله دیبا و زنش با وزیری بهتل آمدند و بعد رفتند.

پنجشنبه ۲۱ فروردین، ۱۱ آوریل - در باغ و در هتل حقوق خواندم.

جمعه ۲۲ فروردین، ۱۲ آوریل - شب با وزیری به هتل متروپول رفتم. بمناسبت شهادت امام حسین جشنی بر پا بود. آقای علاء هم بود. سر عبدالقادر و چندین نفر دیگر نطق کردند.

شنبه ۲۳ فروردین، ۱۳ آوریل - حقوق خواندم.

یکشنبه ۲۴ فروردین، ۱۴ آوریل - حقوق خواندم و مدتی با وزیری در ماربل آرچ گردش کردم. درسی که می‌خوانم چندان مفید نیست ولی باید کار شروع شده را تمام کنم.

دوشنبه ۲۵ فروردین، ۱۵ آوریل - حقوق خواندم.

سه‌شنبه ۲۶ فروردین، ۱۶ آوریل - شب با وزیری و مسیز هت و پگی ویلیس بودم.

چهارشنبه ۲۷ فروردین، ۱۷ آوریل - در هتل و باغ درس می‌خواندم.

پنجشنبه ۲۸ فرودین، ۱۸ آوریل - صبح حقوق بین الملل خواندم و باقی روز را هم کار کردم.

جمعه ۲۹ فروردین، ۱۹ آوریل - حقوق خواندم و با وزیری و سرداری بودم.

شنبه ۳۰ فروردین، ۲۰ آوریل - تمام روز حقوق خواندم.

یکشنبه ۳۱ فروردین، ۲۱ آوریل - تمام روز کار کردم و حقوق خواندم.

دوشنبه ۱ اردیبهشت، ۲۲ آوریل - حقوق خواندم.

سه‌شنبه ۲ اردیبهشت، ۲۳ آوریل - حقوق خواندم. مدتی با سرداری بودم.

چهارشنبه ۳ اردیبهشت، ۲۴ آوریل - حقوق خواندم.

پنجشنبه ۴ اردیبهشت، ۲۵ آوریل - مسیز هت که بدیدن پدرش رفته بود برگشت. حقوق خواندم.

جمعه ۵ اردیبهشت، ۲۶ آوریل - با وزیری بگالری نقاشی رفتم.

شنبه ۶ اردیبهشت، ۲۷ آوریل - با وزیری بودم. حقوق خواندم.

یکشنبه ۷ اردیبهشت، ۲۸ آوریل - کار کردم و تمام روز حقوق خواندم.

دوشنبه ۸ اردیبهشت، ۲۹ آوریل - ثنایی برادر زن زرین‌کفش که برای خرید اسلحه دو سال است در اروپاست، در اداره بود و او را دیدم.

سه‌شنبه ۹ اردیبهشت، ۳۰ آوریل - حقوق خواندم. شب با زرین‌کفش بمنزل او رفتم. علوی و ثنایی و زن ثنایی هم بود. علوی با ایشان بتآتر رفت و من با زرین‌کفش ماندم. تا ساعت ده صحبت کسالت آور کردیم.

چهارشنبه ۱۰ اردیبهشت، ۱ مه - با وزیری بودم.

پنجشنبه ۱۱ اردیبهشت، ۲ مه - تمام روز کتاب خواندم. حوصله‌ام از خواندن این مطالب دیگر سر آمده است.

جمعه ۱۲ اردیبهشت، ۳ مه - بمناسبت جشن بیست و پنجمین سال سلطنت جرج پنجم همه جا را آئین بسته‌اند. حقوق خواندم.

شنبه ۱۳ اردیبهشت، ۴ مه - حقوق خواندم.

یکشنبه ۱۴ اردیبهشت، ۵ مه - با وزیری و چند نفر دیگر به ماربل آرچ رفتم.

دوشنبه ۱۵ اردیبهشت، ۶ مه - به پل مل که دعوت داشتم برای تماشای جشن رفتم. ثنایی برادر زن زرین‌کفش هم بود.

سه‌شنبه ۱۶ اردیبهشت، ۷ مه - با وزیری بودم. فیلم میزرابل را دیدم.

چهارشنبه ۱۷ اردیبهشت، ۸ مه - با وزیری در فارج ناهار خوردیم. شب نراقی هم آمد.

پنجشنبه ۱۸ اردیبهشت، ۹ مه - حقوق خواندم.

جمعه ۱۹ اردیبهشت، ۱۰ مه - حقوق خواندم.

شنبه ۲۰ اردیبهشت، ۱۱ مه - حقوق خواندم.

یکشنبه ۲۱ اردیبهشت، ۱۲ مه - با وزیری بمنزل زرین‌کفش رفتم.

دوشنبه ۲۲ اردیبهشت، ۱۳ مه - از پدرم از کربلا کاغذی رسید. وزیری فردا بپاریس می‌رود. از مدرسه حقوق کاغذی رسید که ۲۲ مه در آنجا حاضر باشم.

سه‌شنبه ۲۳ اردیبهشت، ۱۴ مه - درس خواندم. پنج بظهر وزیری خداحافظی کرد و رفت.

چهارشنبه ۲۴ اردیبهشت، ۱۵ مه - پنج بعد از ظهر بیدار شدم. حالم خوب نیست. کار کردم.

پنجشنبه ۲۵ اردیبهشت، ۱۶ مه - پاسپورت[1] را بامضا رساندم. پول و بلیط برای سفر والد تهیه کردم.

جمعه ۲۶ اردیبهشت، ۱۷ مه - تمام روز کار کردم. شب هم از هتل بیرون نرفتم و درس خواندم.

شنبه ۲۷ اردیبهشت، ۱۸ مه - حقوق خواندم.

یکشنبه ۲۸ اردیبهشت، ۱۹ مه - صبح زود از اطاقم بیرون آمدم. با ترن ساعت ۱۱ از ویکتوریا بپاریس رفتم. حالم چندان خوب نبود. ساعت شش و ربع بپاریس رسیدم و در سلکت هتل منزل کردم.

---

۱. پاسپور

دوشنبه ۲۹ اردیبهشت، ۲۰ مه - تا چهارشنبه بعد از ظهر در اطاقم نشسته بودم و دروس را مرور می‌کردم. قریب نیم ساعت بمدرسه حقوق رفتم. حالم خوب نیست. نتوانستم غذا بخورم. شاید از کشتی حالم بهم خورده.

سه‌شنبه ۳۰ اردیبهشت، ۲۱ مه - تا یک بعد از نصف شب کار کردم. علی الخصوص بعضی از قسمت‌هایی که عوض شده و بواسطه نبودن در پاریس از آن اطلاع نداشتم، < را > خواندم.

چهارشنبه ۳۱ اردیبهشت، ۲۲ مه - صبح کمی درس خواندم. بعد از ناهار بمدرسه حقوق رفتم. از قضا لافریر معلم حقوق اداری که بسختگیری معروفست یکی از امتحان کنندگان بود. باو امتحان دادم و سایر درسها را نیز امتحان دادم و قبول شدم.

پنجشنبه ۱ خرداد، ۲۳ مه - ناهار با سید کاظم خان صدر خوردم. بعد از ظهر نزد اقبال رفتم . شب نزد خسروپور.

جمعه ۲ خرداد، ۲۴ مه - صبح بمدرسه حقوق و بعد از ظهر هم بمدرسه حقوق رفتم و از آنجا بمنزل اقبال و با هم بمنزل میرزا محمد خان قزوینی. اقبال خراسانی و برادرش بودند. شام با اقبال خوردم. شب کمی از کتاب اصول عقاید ثروت < را > خواندم.

شنبه ۳ خرداد، ۲۵ مه - صبح در مدرسه با شیدفر بودم. ناهار با علی‌آبادی خوردم.

یکشنبه ۴ خرداد، ۲۶ مه - در خیابان با بعضی از ایرانیها گردش کردم.

دوشنبه ۵ خرداد، ۲۷ مه - در سفارت حسنعلی خان وزیری را دیدم. با من بهتل آمد. ناهار با هم خوردیم. بعد بهتل او که نزدیک سفارت بود، رفتیم.

سه‌شنبه ۶ خرداد، ۲۸ مه - صبح بمدرسه حقوق سر امتحان اقتصاد رفتم و شب بمنزل رادمنش. اقبال خراسانی و برادرش هم آنجا بودند. تا ده و نیم بعد از ظهر در آنجا بودم.

چهارشنبه ۷ خرداد، ۲۹ مه - صبح با خراسانی مدتی در مقابل پانتئون راه رفتم و بعد از ظهر بمدرسه حقوق رفتم.

پنجشنبه ۸ خرداد، ۳۰ مه - بعد از ظهر با عباس اقبال به سن کلو رفتم که بقایی پسر میرزا شهاب را ببینم. جوان دیگری هم موسوم بسپهبدی بود. شب با صدر بمنزل عبده رفتم. با هم شام خوردیم.

جمعه ۹ خرداد، ۳۱ مه - صبح و بعد از ظهر بمدرسه حقوق رفتم. شب با اقبال خراسانی و برادرش و رادمنش بودم.

شنبه ۱۰ خرداد، ۱ ژوئن - بعد از ظهر با قریب پسر شمس العلما و ملک اسماعیلی در کافه نشستیم.

یکشنبه ۱۱ خرداد، ۲ ژوئن - صبح بوزیری تلفون کردم که با هم به ورسای برویم. قرار شد یکدیگر را در آن والید ببینیم. از آنجا با اتوموبیل به ورسای رفتیم. یک بعد از ظهر به ورسای رسیدیم و تا چهار بعد از ظهر در آنجا تابلوهای عمارت را تماشا کردیم. یک تابلو راجع بپذیرایی سفیر ایران توسط ناپلئون بود. تابلوی جنگهای ناپلئون و سایر محاربات را دیدم. تابلوهای راجع بجنگ الجزایر و تونس و مراکش بود. مجسمه‌های بسیاری در پارک دیدیم و هم در عمارات. ساعت چهار و نیم فواره‌ها بکار افتاد. باغچه سبزی خیلی عالی دارد. ساعت هفت و نیم در مقابل عمارت لوور از اتوموبیل پیاده شدیم. بعد از شام تا ساعت ۱۱ با شجاع نیا در کافه نشسته بودیم.

دوشنبه ۱۲ خرداد، ۳ ژوئن - با وزیری بنمایشگاه صنایع ایتالیا و نمایشگاه صنایع فرانسوی رفتیم. با اماموردی محصل ریاضی و علی‌آبادی محصل حقوق بالحمرا رفتم. شام را وزیری با من خورد.

سه‌شنبه ۱۳ خرداد، ۴ ژوئن - صبح زود از خواب بیدار شدم. حالم چندان خوب نبود. به گار دو نور رفتم. دو سه دقیقه دیر رسیدم. ترن کاله رفته بود. با خط دیگر به بولونی

رفتم. حالم خوب نبود. بعد از ظهر به بولونی رسیدم. یک ساعت در آنجا معطل شدم تا کشتی حرکت کرد. دریا آرام بود. یک ساعت و نیم در کشتی بودم. از فوکس تون بلندن آمدم. ساعت شش از پدرم کاغذی رسیده بود.

چهارشنبه ۱۴ خرداد، ۵ ژوئن - تا دو ساعت بعد از ظهر اقتصاد خواندم.

پنجشنبه ۱۵ خرداد، ۶ ژوئن - صبح حقوق خواندم.

جمعه ۱۶ خرداد، ۷ ژوئن - اقتصاد خواندم. شب بیرون نرفتم و اقتصاد خواندم.

شنبه ۱۷ خرداد، ۸ ژوئن - بخانه لیتون نقاش رفتم که قسمتی از آن را بسبک خانه‌های عربی ساخته چیزی شبیه بحوضخانه و کاشی و آیات قرآن.

یکشنبه ۱۸ خرداد، ۹ ژوئن - اقتصاد خواندم. ناهار در منزل زرین‌کفش خوردم. علوی هم بود.

دوشنبه ۱۹ خرداد، ۱۰ ژوئن - اقتصاد خواندم.

سه‌شنبه ۲۰ خرداد، ۱۱ ژوئن - علاء خواهش کرد که در کارهای سفارت با او کمک کنم و بعضی چیزها ترجمه کنم.

چهارشنبه ۲۱ خرداد، ۱۲ ژوئن - بادارهٔ عایدات رفتم. راجع بپولی که مرحوم علی خان قرض گرفته بود تحقیق کردم.

پنجشنبه ۲۲ خرداد، ۱۳ ژوئن - با زرین‌کفش نهار خوردم. اقتصاد خواندم.

جمعه ۲۳ خرداد، ۱۴ ژوئن - درس خواندم.

شنبه ۲۴ خرداد، ۱۵ ژوئن - اقتصاد خواندم. بعد از ظهر با میس پگی ویلیس و مسیز هت بسینما رفتم. فیلم سربازان بنگاله را دیدم.

یکشنبه ۲۵ خرداد، ۱۶ ژوئن - اقتصاد خواندم.

دوشنبه ۲۶ خرداد، ۱۷ ژوئن - از پدرم از کربلا کاغذی رسید. صبح درس خواندم. بعد از ظهر بمجمع آسیایی رفتم. فرانسوی راجع بمینیاتورهای ایران نطق کرد و همچنین در باب فردوسی.

سه‌شنبه ۲۷ خرداد، ۱۸ ژوئن - درس خواندم.

چهارشنبه ۲۸ خرداد، ۱۹ ژوئن - اقتصاد خواندم.

پنجشنبه ۲۹ خرداد، ۲۰ ژوئن - درس خواندم.

جمعه ۳۰ خرداد، ۲۱ ژوئن - در روزنامه تایمز نوشته بود که بحکم شاه اعضای ادارات باید کلاه فرنگی سر بگذارند و معلمات و دختران مدرسه‌ها باید بی‌حجاب بیرون بیایند.

شنبه ۳۱ خرداد، ۲۲ ژوئن - با مردی کانادایی که آدم خوبیست در باب مطالب مختلف حرف می‌زدم. شب نیز کمی درس خواندم.

یکشنبه ۱ تیر، ۲۳ ژوئن - صبح درس خواندم.

دوشنبه ۲ تیر، ۲۴ ژوئن - درس خواندم. شب با سرداری بودم.

سه‌شنبه ۳ تیر، ۲۵ ژوئن - بدیدن نفیسی (مشرف الدوله) رفتم. نظام الدین امان و زنش هم آمدند. مدتی با ایشان صحبت می‌کردیم.

چهارشنبه ۴ تیر، ۲۶ ژوئن - در پارک کتاب خواندم.

پنجشنبه ۵ تیر، ۲۷ ژوئن - اقتصاد خواندم.

جمعه ۶ تیر، ۲۸ ژوئن - شب با چند انگلیسی بتآتر واریته هوبورن رفتم.

شنبه ۷ تیر، ۲۹ ژوئن - درس خواندم. شب در چلسی گردش کردم.

یکشنبه ۸ تیر، ۳۰ ژوئن - بمنزل زرین‌کفش رفتم. دکتر علوی هم بود. عصر دکتر نیلی هم آمد. با او برگشتم.

دوشنبه ۹ تیر، ۱ ژوئیه - درس خواندم.

سه‌شنبه ۱۰ تیر، ۴ ژوئیه - کتاب اقتصاد خواندم.

چهارشنبه ۱۱ تیر، ۵ ژوئیه - کتاب خواندم.

پنجشنبه ۱۲ تیر، ۴ ژوئیه - از صدر کاغذی رسید. معلوم شد وارد لندن شده و در چی‌زل هرست زندگی می‌کند. نزد او رفتم. با او ناهار خوردم. با هم بسفارت رفتیم. در سفارت جلسه‌ای بود راجع باینکه آیا خوبست انجمن ایرانی تأسیس بشود یا نه.

جمعه ۱۳ تیر، ۵ ژوئیه - به چی‌زل هرست رفتم. با صدر ناهار خوردم. عصر بمدرسه السنهٔ شرقیه رفتم. جشن توزیع دیپلم و جایزه بود. شب به ساووی هتل دعوت داشتم. شرکت قریب سیصد نفر را دعوت کرده بود. سر جان سایمون نطقی کرد و سر جان کدمن و کشیشی هم دعا خواند و بعد مسخره و حقه بازی پیش آمد.

شنبه ۱۴ تیر، ۶ ژوئیه - با صدر به تیپ تری که دو ساعت راه است، رفتم. صدر آدرس این خانه را داشت و می‌خواست آن را ببیند که در آن منزل کند. رفتیم. خانه بدی نبود ولی دختر صاحبخانه که در آستانه در نشسته بود دیوانه می‌نمود.

یکشنبه ۱۵ تیر، ۷ ژوئیه - اقتصاد خواندم.

دوشنبه ۱۶ تیر، ۸ ژوئیه - کتاب خواندم.

سه‌شنبه ۱۷ تیر، ۹ ژوئیه - کتاب خواندم.

چهارشنبه ۱۸ تیر، ۱۰ ژوئیه - مقالات راجع ببحرین را ترجمه کردم. اقتصاد خواندم.

پنجشنبه ۱۹ تیر، ۱۱ ژوئیه - اقتصاد خواندم.

جمعه ۲۰ تیر، ۱۲ ژوئیه - اقتصاد خواندم.

شنبه ۲۱ تیر، ۱۳ ژوئیه - اقتصاد خواندم. دریفوس جهود فرانسوی مرد.

یکشنبه ۲۲ تیر، ۱۴ ژوئیه - اقتصاد خواندم. مدتی با سرداری بودم.

دوشنبه ۲۳ تیر، ۱۵ ژوئیه - از جلال کاغذی رسید. اقتصاد خواندم.

سه‌شنبه ۲۴ تیر، ۱۶ ژوئیه - با صدر بموزه ویکتوریا و موزه علوم و موزه تاریخ طبیعی رفتیم . از تیپ تری آمده بود.

چهارشنبه ۲۵ تیر، ۱۷ ژوئیه - اقتصاد خواندم.

پنجشنبه ۲۶ تیر، ۱۸ ژوئیه - به بریتیش میوزیم رفتم که مستر بازیل گری[1] منشی انجمن ایران را ببینم. مرا هم بسمت منشی انجمن ایران انتخاب کرده‌اند. حقوق مالی خواندم.

جمعه ۲۷ تیر، ۱۹ ژوئیه - در باغ درس خواندم.

شنبه ۲۸ تیر، ۲۰ ژوئیه - تمام روز و شب کار کردم.

یکشنبه ۲۹ تیر، ۲۱ ژوئیه - ناهار در منزل زرین‌کفش خوردم. اردلان هم بود.

---

۱. Basil Gray، متخصص تاریخ هنر ایران و مدیر بخش نقاشی‌های شرقی در موزه بریتانیا (۱۹۰۴-۱۹۸۹).

دوشنبه ۳۰ تیر، ۲۲ ژوئیه - صبح بسفارت نزد علاء رفتم. راجع بانجمن ایران مذاکراتی کردم.

سه‌شنبه ۳۱ تیر، ۲۳ ژوئیه - حقوق مالی خواندم.

چهارشنبه ۱ مرداد، ۲۴ ژوئیه - حالم خوب نبود. از هتل بیرون نرفتم. حقوق مالی خواندم.

پنجشنبه ۲ مرداد، ۲۵ ژوئیه - درس خواندم.

جمعه ۳ مرداد، ۲۶ ژوئیه - با صدر بهتل مون تانا رفتم. در آنجا منزل کرده شب با صدر شام خوردم در ماربل آرچ.

شنبه ۴ مرداد، ۲۷ ژوئیه - ناهار مهمان زنجانی بودم. صدر هم بود. شب با پگی ویلیس و گریهام بمنزل مسیز هستر رفتم.

یکشنبه ۵ مرداد، ۲۸ ژوئیه - ناهار با صدر در منزل زرین‌کفش خوردیم. شام در ماربل آرچ خوردیم.

دوشنبه ۶ مرداد، ۲۹ ژوئیه - از پدرم کاغذی رسید. ناهار و شام با صدر خوردم.

سه‌شنبه ۷ مرداد، ۳۰ ژوئیه - صدر بفرانسه رفت. بمشایعتش بویکتوریا رفتم. با علاء و بازیل گری در باب انجمن ایران مذاکره کردم.

چهارشنبه ۸ مرداد، ۳۱ ژوئیه - اقتصاد خواندم.

پنجشنبه ۹ مرداد، ۱ اوت - درس خواندم.

جمعه ۱۰ مرداد، ۲ اوت - قوانین و حقوق مستعمراتی خواندم.

شنبه ۱۱ مرداد، ۳ اوت - ناهار در منزل زرین‌کفش خوردم. احمدی و مصطفی خان افشار هم بودند.

یکشنبه ۱۲ مرداد، ۴ اوت - درس خواندم.

دوشنبه ۱۳ مرداد، ۵ اوت - با احمدی و بسیجی و رفعتی بودم. از جلال کاغذی رسید.

سه‌شنبه ۱۴ مرداد، ۶ اوت - درس خواندم.

چهارشنبه ۱۵ مرداد، ۷ اوت - تاریخ عقاید اقتصادی خواندم.

پنجشنبه ۱۶ مرداد، ۸ اوت - عقاید اقتصادی خواندم.

جمعه ۱۷ مرداد، ۹ اوت - صبح تاریخ عقاید اقتصادی خواندم. بعد به پدینگتن رفتم. بلیط دوسره برای اکسفورد خریدم. باکسفورد رفتم. در مدرسۀ بلیول کالج منزل کردم. شب بتآتر رفتم.

شنبه ۱۸ مرداد، ۱۰ اوت - صبح زود بیدار شدم. کمی درس خواندم. ببلدیه اکسفورد رفتم. اسم خود را در دفتر نمایندگان کنفرانس تربیتی ثبت کردم. پروگرامی بمن دادند. ناهار در رستوران کوچکی مقابل بلیول کالج خوردم. شب در عمارت بلدیه پذیرایی بود. از ۸ تا ده و نیم طول کشید. ۵۰۰ نماینده از ممالک مختلفه آمده بودند. در مدرسه شام خوردم و با یک معلم که از اهل ویلز است و در نزدیکی کمبریج معلمی می‌کند، آشنا شدم. پیش از خواب درس حقوق خواندم.

یکشنبه ۱۹ مرداد، ۱۱ اوت - در مدرسه چاشت خوردم. چاشت و شام و ناهاری که بما می‌دهند مثل چاشت و شام و ناهاریست که بشاگردان می‌دهند. عصر با دو هندی و یک انگلیسی قایق رانی کردم. بتماشای مدارس هم رفتم. شب به نی یو تئاتر رفتم. کنسرت[1] مفصلی بود.

---

۱. کنسر

دوشنبه ۲۰ مرداد، ۱۲ اوت - صبح زود بیدار شدم. درس حقوق خواندم. بعد از مجالس و کمیته‌های مختلف کنفرانس گردش کردم. وضع تدریس را رادیو را دیدم. بعد از ظهر بتماشای آثاری که شاگردهای مدارس ساخته بودند، رفتم. لرد هالیفاکس رئیس اونیورسیته آن را افتتاح کرد. شب بعد از شام به کلدونین[1] تئآتر مجلس کنفرانس بود. لرد هالیفاکس و چند تن دیگر حرف زدند.

سه‌شنبه ۲۱ مرداد، ۱۳ اوت - صبح مذاکرات راجع بمعلم هنر در مدارس را شنیدم. عصر به نی یو کالج رفتم. می‌رقصیدند. رقصهای قرن شانزدهم و هفدهم تماشایی بود. شب باز به کلدونین رفتم. لرد تویدزمیر حاکم کانادا که نویسندهٔ مشهوری است، نطق کرد و چندین نفر دیگر هم نطق کردند.

چهارشنبه ۲۲ مرداد، ۱۴ اوت - صبح باکسفورد میوزیم رفتم. بنطق برتراند راسل راجع بحق آزادی معلم در آموختن عقیده بشاگرد گوش کردم. با دو نفر هندی به همتون کورت رفتم.

پنجشنبه ۲۳ مرداد، ۱۵ اوت - صبح بعمارت بلدیه اکسفورد رفتم. بعد از ظهر در نی یو کالج گاردن پارتی بود. مستر جونز معلم اهل ولز که رفیق شده بود، با من بود. شب ببلدیه اکسفورد رفتم. مجلس رقص بود. در آن جا ایرانی باسم بهمنیار که در پاریس تحصیلات راجع بحقوق را تمام کرده بود، دیدم.

جمعه ۲۴ مرداد، ۱۶ اوت - بعد از ظهر به هدینگتن هیل هتل رفتم. اشعار قدیم انگلیسی می‌خواندند. باغ بزرگ خوبی بود. مستر جونز هم با من بود. شب به کلدونین رفتم. چندین نفر نطق کردند منجمله یکی از بومیان امریکایی با پر و لباس مخصوص خود. ساعت یازده بمدرسه بلیل کالج آمدم.

شنبه ۲۵ مرداد، ۱۷ اوت - صبح با رفیق هندی سوبرایمام با اتومبیل مخصوص بولایت شکسپیر رفتم. نه و نیم اتومبیل حرکت کرد. یک ساعت و نیم در راه بودیم

---

۱. شلدونین (در همه موارد اصلاح شد).

تا بقلعه کنیل ورث رسیدیم که تاریخیست. بعد از تماشای آن بطرف واریک کاسل رفتم و از آنجا به استراتفورد اپن ایون. خانه‌ای که مسقط الرأس اوست، بسیار مختصر است. بعد از پنج دقیقه بخانهٔ زن شکسپیر رسیدیم و از آنجا به هولی ترینیتی چرچ[1] رفتم. در دفتر آنجا اسم شکسپیر ثبت است و در هتل کلیسا هم عروسی کرده. با کانت کار هندی چای خوردیم. پنج بعد از ظهر باکسفور مراجعت کردم.

یکشنبه ۲۶ مرداد، ۱۸ اوت - در اکسفورد در خانه‌ای زندگی می‌کنم بنمرهٔ ۱۸ در کوچهٔ سنت جان. زنجانی و خانمش از لندن آمدند. با هم مدرسه‌ها را دیدیم. بلندن مراجعت کردیم.

دوشنبه ۲۷ مرداد، ۱۹ اوت - حقوق خواندم. مستوفی از دوستان اقبال بمادرید هتل آمده با او بودم.

سه‌شنبه ۲۸ مرداد، ۲۰ اوت - شب با سرداری بودم.

چهارشنبه ۲۹ مرداد، ۲۱ اوت - حقوق مالی خواندم.

پنجشنبه ۳۰ مرداد، ۲۲ اوت - یازده شاگرد که برای تحصیلات بلندن آمده‌اند < را > دیدم.

جمعه ۳۱ مرداد، ۲۳ اوت - درس می‌خواندم.

شنبه ۱ شهریور، ۲۴ اوت - درس خواندم

یکشنبه ۲ شهریور، ۲۵ اوت - درس خواندم.

دوشنبه ۳ شهریور، ۲۶ اوت - از پدرم و جلال و خلخالی کاغذی رسید. خبر رسیده بود که شنیده است که بجای زرین‌کفش و من، بدر و دیگری خواهند آمد.

---

۱. در اصل: چورچ

سه‌شنبه ۴ شهریور، ۲۷ اوت - درس خواندم. زرین‌کفش باداره نیامد. تلفون کردم علت < را > پرسیدم. معلوم شد کلفت ایرلندی که داشته بمرض حمله مرده. بعد از ظهر بمنزل زرین‌کفش رفتم.

چهارشنبه ۵ شهریور، ۲۸ اوت - صبح تاریخ مستعمرات و شب اقتصاد خواندم.

پنجشنبه ۶ شهریور، ۲۹ اوت - درس خواندم.

جمعه ۷ شهریور، ۳۰ اوت - تاریخ عقاید اقتصادی خواندم.

شنبه ۸ شهریور، ۳۱ اوت - صبح از هتل بیرون نرفتم و درس خواندم.

یکشنبه ۹ شهریور، ۱ سپتامبر - درس خواندم.

دوشنبه ۱۰ شهریور، ۲ سپتامبر - درس خواندم. احمد مستوفی هم بود.

سه‌شنبه ۱۱ شهریور، ۳ سپتامبر - درس خواندم. عبده و حسیبی آمدند. عصر بمجلس نطقی که برای همراهی بحبشه منعقد شده بود، رفتم. سر دنیسن راس هم بود.

چهارشنبه ۱۲ شهریور، ۴ سپتامبر - با زرین‌کفش بمنزل او رفتم. عبده و حسیبی هم قبلاً آمده بودند. شب با سید حسن ریاضی را دیدم. با هم شام خوردیم.

پنجشنبه ۱۳ شهریور، ۵ سپتامبر - در روایال پالاس هتل ناهار خوردم. مهمان شایسته بودم. وزیر مختار لهستان شده. اردلان عضو سفارت و تاجری عمامه بسر < بنام > حاج علیرضا هم بود. بعد با زرین‌کفش بمنزل زنجانی رفتم. بمناسبت رئیس شدن مهمانی می‌داد. علاء و خانمش و احمدی و دختر اردلان و اردلان هم بودند. تا یک بعد از نصف شب در آنجا بودم.

جمعه ۱۴ شهریور، ۶ سپتامبر - درس خواندم. دو ساعت درس دادم. شب بمنزل میس مورتون دعوت داشتم. جمعی دیگر هم بودند.

شنبه ۱۵ شهریور، ۷ سپتامبر - با عبده و دکتر ریاضی بودم. در ماربل آرچ غذا خوردیم.

یکشنبه ۱۶ شهریور، ۸ سپتامبر - درس می‌خواندم.

دوشنبه ۱۷ شهریور، ۹ سپتامبر - درس می‌خواندم.

سه‌شنبه ۱۸ شهریور، ۱۰ سپتامبر - درس می‌خواندم.

چهارشنبه ۱۹ شهریور، ۱۱ سپتامبر - درس خواندم. حسیبی و جلالی را دیدم.

پنجشنبه ۲۰ شهریور، ۱۲ سپتامبر - ناهار با عبده خوردم. خسته بودم. کاری نتوانستم بکنم.

جمعه ۲۱ شهریور، ۱۳ سپتامبر - ناهار با رفعتی و میتلند خوردم.

شنبه ۲۲ شهریور، ۱۴ سپتامبر - درس خواندم.

یکشنبه ۲۳ شهریور، ۱۵ سپتامبر - فؤاد روحانی آمد. بازبین هم اینجا بود. برای امتحان از آبادان آمده است.

دوشنبه ۲۴ شهریور، ۱۶ سپتامبر - با فؤاد بسینما رفتم. فیلم دیوید کپرفیلد را دیدم.

سه‌شنبه ۲۵ شهریور، ۱۷ سپتامبر - درس خواندم.

چهارشنبه ۲۶ شهریور، ۱۸ سپتامبر - درس خواندم.

پنجشنبه ۲۷ شهریور، ۱۹ سپتامبر - کاغذی از پدرم رسید با عکس او. یک سال پیش عکسی گرفته بودم و تنبلی می‌کردم که بفرستم. امروز آن را بطهران فرستادم پیش از آمدن کاغذ پدرم. تصادف عجیبی است.

جمعه ۲۸ شهریور، ۲۰ سپتامبر - درس خواندم.

شنبه ۲۹ شهریور، ۲۱ سپتامبر - در منزل زرین‌کفش ناهار خوردم. علیزاده هم در آنجا بود.

یکشنبه ۳۰ شهریور، ۲۲ سپتامبر - درس خواندم.

دوشنبه ۳۱ شهریور، ۲۳ سپتامبر - بمنزل زرین‌کفش رفتم. دکتر آصف الحکما تاجبخش هم بود. احمد مستوفی بپاریس رفت.

سه‌شنبه ۱ مهر، ۲۴ سپتامبر - راپورت کنفرانس اکسفورد را تهیه کردم. درس خواندم.

چهارشنبه ۲ مهر، ۲۵ سپتامبر - منوچهر فرمانفرمائیان آمد. می‌خواهد برود به بیرمنگام درس بخواند.

پنجشنبه ۳ مهر، ۲۶ سپتامبر - شب بمنزل زرین‌کفش رفتم. آصف الحکما هم آنجا بود.

جمعه ۴ مهر، ۲۷ سپتامبر - درس خواندم.

شنبه ۵ مهر، ۲۸ سپتامبر - درس خواندم. با فؤاد گردش کردم.

یکشنبه ۶ مهر، ۲۹ سپتامبر - با منوچهر فرمانفرمائیان گردش کردم.

دوشنبه ۷ مهر، ۳۰ سپتامبر - با فؤاد و فرمانفرمائیان بودم. درس خواندم.

سه‌شنبه ۸ مهر، ۱ اکتبر - با فؤاد روحانی غذا خوردیم. درس خواندم.

چهارشنبه ۹ مهر، ۲ اکتبر - درس خواندم و درس دادم.

پنجشنبه ۱۰ مهر، ۳ اکتبر - با فؤاد روحانی غذا خوردم. درس خواندم.

جمعه ۱۱ مهر، ۴ اکتبر - فؤاد قصد دارد روز شنبه بایران مراجعت کند. با او بودم.

شنبه ۱۲ مهر، ۵ اکتبر - درس خواندم.

یکشنبه ۱۳ مهر، ۶ اکتبر - درس خواندم.

دوشنبه ۱۴ مهر، ۷ اکتبر - درس خواندم.

سه‌شنبه ۱۵ مهر، ۸ اکتبر - درس خواندم. با دوستی انگلیسی بسینما رفتم. فیلم آنا کارنینا را دیدم.

چهارشنبه ۱۶ مهر، ۹ اکتبر - ناهار با مینورسکی خوردم. درس خواندم.

پنجشنبه ۱۷ مهر، ۱۰ اکتبر - در سفارت با بزیل گری در باب انجمن ایران حرف زدیم.

جمعه ۱۸ مهر، ۱۱ اکتبر[1]

شنبه ۱۹ مهر، ۱۲ اکتبر - تمام روز درس خواندم.

یکشنبه ۲۰ مهر، ۱۳ اکتبر - ناهار در منزل زرین‌کفش خوردم. دکتر علوی و قاسم زاده هم بودند.

دوشنبه ۲۱ مهر، ۱۴ اکتبر - درس خواندم. سرماخوردگی شدید داشتم. حالم خوش نبود.

سه‌شنبه ۲۲ مهر، ۱۵ اکتبر - درس خواندم.

چهارشنبه ۲۳ مهر، ۱۶ اکتبر - درس خواندم.

پنجشنبه ۲۴ مهر، ۱۷ اکتبر - درس خواندم.

جمعه ۲۵ مهر، ۱۸ اکتبر - درس خواندم.

شنبه ۲۶ مهر، ۱۹ اکتبر - شب و روز درس خواندم.

---

۱. در اصل خالی است.

یکشنبه ۲۷ مهر، ۲۰ اکتبر - درس خواندم.

دوشنبه ۲۸ مهر، ۲۱ اکتبر - سودآور آمد. با او به رمبرنت هتل رفتم.

سه‌شنبه ۲۹ مهر، ۲۲ اکتبر - درس خواندم.

چهارشنبه ۳۰ مهر، ۲۳ اکتبر - درس خواندم.

پنجشنبه ۱ آبان، ۲۴ اکتبر - درس خواندم.

جمعه ۲ آبان، ۲۵ اکتبر - درس خواندم.

شنبه ۳ آبان، ۲۶ اکتبر - درس خواندم.

یکشنبه ۴ آبان، ۲۷ اکتبر - درس خواندم. با سودآور بسینمای کرزن رفتم.

دوشنبه ۵ آبان، ۲۸ اکتبر - شام در منزل آقای زرین‌کفش بودم. روز درس خواندم.

سه‌شنبه ۶ آبان، ۲۹ اکتبر - درس خواندم.

چهارشنبه ۷ آبان، ۳۰ اکتبر - شب در سفارت مهمان بودم.

پنجشنبه ۸ آبان، ۳۱ اکتبر - درس خواندم.

جمعه ۹ آبان، ۱ نوامبر - از هتل بیرون نرفتم. درس خواندم.

شنبه ۱۰ آبان، ۲ نوامبر - درس خواندم. با سودآور به پرنس آو ویلز تآتر رفتم.

یکشنبه ۱۱ آبان، ۳ نوامبر - درس خواندم.

دوشنبه ۱۲ آبان، ۴ نوامبر - درس خواندم.

سه‌شنبه ۱۳ آبان، ۵ نوامبر - درس خواندم.

چهارشنبه ۱۴ آبان، ۶ نوامبر - درس خواندم.

پنجشنبه ۱۵ آبان، ۷ نوامبر[1] - دعوت امتحان رسید از مدرسهٔ پاریس. تا نصف شب درس خواندم. مقدمات سفر را فراهم کردم.

جمعه ۱۶ آبان، ۸ نوامبر - بلیط خریدم. مسیز هست که بدیدن پدرش رفته بود، آمد.

شنبه ۱۷ آبان، ۹ نوامبر - درس خواندم.

یکشنبه ۱۸ آبان، ۱۰ نوامبر - صبح زود بیدار شدم. بایستگاه ویکتوریا رفتم. دریا مواج بود. شش و ربع بعد از ظهر وارد پاریس شدم.

دوشنبه ۱۹ آبان، ۱۱ نوامبر - تمام روز را درس خواندم.

سه‌شنبه ۲۰ آبان، ۱۲ نوامبر - تا بعد از نصف شب درس خواندم. با شجاع نیا مدتی بودم.

چهارشنبه ۲۱ آبان، ۱۳ نوامبر - غیر از یک ساعت که بمدرسه حقوق رفتم، باقی اوقات را متصل درس خواندم. خسته شده‌ام.

پنجشنبه ۲۲ آبان، ۱۴ نوامبر - شب نخوابیدم و درس خواندم. بعد از ظهر امتحان دادم. از قضا در درسی که بیشتر زحمت کشیده بودم و آن را بهتر می‌دانستم نمره عالی نگرفتم. قبول شدم و از شر امتحانات خلاص شدم. شب با مفتاح و دو سه ایرانی دیگر به کوپل رفتم.

جمعه ۲۳ آبان، ۱۵ نوامبر - صبح در سفارت یکتا را دیدم. بعد از ظهر در مدرسه حقوق محمود مشاور را دیدم. از مدرسه حقوق بمنزل میرزا محمد خان قزوینی رفتم و شب با شیدفر بسینمای گومون.

---

۱. اکتبر

شنبه ۲۴ آبان، ۱۶ نوامبر - ناهار با عبده و جزائری و مشاور خوردم. مقبلی را در شان ز لیزه دیدم. او هم با ما شام خورد.

یکشنبه ۲۵ آبان، ۱۷ نوامبر - با شیدفر بودم.

دوشنبه ۲۶ آبان، ۱۸ نوامبر - صبح در خیابان گردش کردم. بعد از ظهر بمنزل یکتا رفتم و از آنجا بمنزل صدر. خوش‌بین هم در آن جا بود. شام در رستوران خوردیم و بعد به لیدو رفتم. تا دو بعد از نصف شب در آنجا بودم.

سه‌شنبه ۲۷ آبان، ۱۹ نوامبر - عصر بمدرسه حقوق رفتم. جمعی از ایرانیها امتحان می‌دادند.

چهارشنبه ۲۸ آبان، ۲۰ نوامبر - صبح بمدرسه حقوق رفتم. ناهار با عباس امامی خوردم و اماموردی. بعد از ظهر نزد احمد مستوفی رفتم و پنج بعد از ظهر یکی از طالارهای سوربون برای سعدی نطق جمال‌زاده. شب با جمال‌زاده شام خوردم و بعد به فولی برژر رفتم. یک بعد از نصف شب بهتل برگشتم.

پنجشنبه ۲۹ آبان، ۲۱ نوامبر - صبح دیر بیدار شدم. ناهار در منزل سید علی اکبر اخوی خوردم. جزائری هم بود. بمدرسه رفتم. موضوع پروپاگاند را برای تز انتخاب کردم.

جمعه ۳۰ آبان، ۲۲ نوامبر - بمنزل آصف الحکما رفتم. شب خسروپور و خوش‌کیش آمدند با من غذا خوردند.

شنبه ۱ آذر، ۲۳ نوامبر - صبح به لوور رفتم. شب با رادمنش و شیدفر و امینی به کوپول[1] رفتم.

یکشنبه ۲ آذر، ۲۴ نوامبر - صبح با صدیقی در خیابان گردش کردیم. به شان ز لیزه رفتم. راجع به تز شک داشتم. می‌خواهم تشکیلات وزارت امور خارجه

---

۱. La Coupole، رستورانی مشهور در پاریس.

انگلیس را موضوع تز کنم. به دولاپ راول تلفون کردم. قرار شد دوشنبه ساعت ۹ او را در خانه‌اش ببینم.

دوشنبه ۳ آذر، ۲۵ نوامبر - صبح بمنزل دولاپ راول رفتم. موضوع تز را با او مذاکره کردم. پسندید و قبول کرد که رئیس تز شود. بعد از ظهر با سید کاظم خان صدر به سوربون رفتم سر درس فلسفه. بعد با بقایی در چندین کتابخانه گردش کردم و چند کتاب راجع بفلسفه خریدم. شب هم مدتی در کافهٔ دوپون بودم.

سه‌شنبه ۴ آذر، ۲۶ نوامبر - با غیور بودم. و بعد با شیدفر و رادمنش و صدیقی بسینما دان تون رفتم.

چهارشنبه ۵ آذر، ۲۷ نوامبر - بسفارت رفتم. یکتا را دیدم. شب بمنزل سید حسن ریاضی رفتم.

پنجشنبه ۶ آذر، ۲۸ نوامبر - صبح کار کردم. باید نطق کنم برای محصلین. بعد از ظهر بکتابخانه سن ژنوی یو رفتم. شب با رادمنش و شیدفر و مفتاح به کافهٔ دوپن رفتم و تا یک ساعت بعد از نصف شب در آنجا بودم.

جمعه ۷ آذر، ۲۹ نوامبر - نطق تهیه می‌کردم. عصر بمنزل میرزا محمد خان رفتم. شب با رادمنش و شیدفر و رفعتی بکافه رفتم.

شنبه ۸ آذر، ۳۰ نوامبر - شب با رادمنش و شیدفر و مفتاح بودم. نطق هم تهیه کردم.

یکشنبه ۹ آذر، ۱ دسامبر - ناهار در منزل یکتا خوردم. شب با رادمنش و صدیقی و مفتاح و مانی به کوپُل رفتم.

دوشنبه ۱۰ آذر، ۲ دسامبر - بعد از ناهار با رادمنش بمنزل صدیقی رفتم و بعد بمدرسه حقوق. شیدفر تز خود را در خصوص پول ایران دفاع کرد و بعد با او دیگران بکافه رفتم.

سه‌شنبه ۱۱ آذر، ۳ دسامبر - بعد از ظهر با صدیقی بمنزل اقبال رفتم و شب با صدیقی و شیدفر و امینی و مفتاح و رفعتی به کوپل.

چهارشنبه ۱۲ آذر، ۴ دسامبر - ساعت پنج در کولژ دو فرانس راجع باینکه از سه نوع تربیت انگلیسی و آلمانی و فرانسوی کدام یک برای ایران نافعتر است نطقی کردم. بیش از یک ساعت طول کشید. شب با رادمنش و شیدفر و شجاع نیا در کافه‌ای تا ساعت ۱۰ نشستیم.

پنجشنبه ۱۳ آذر، ۵ دسامبر - ناهار با اقبال و صدیقی خوردیم. بعد با اقبال بمنزل دکتر ابوالقاسم نجم آبادی رفتم. چندین کتاب خریدم. شب با شیدفر و رفعتی و رادمنش بکافه تری یومف رفتم.

جمعه ۱۴ آذر، ۶ دسامبر - صبح با رادمنش بمنزل صدیقی و بعد با او بمدرسه حقوق رفتم. آقای حسینی تز خود < با عنوان > حقوق زن بموجب قانون اسلام و مذهب شیعه را دفاع کرد. هفت و نیم بعد از ظهر بهتل آمدم. طاهر رئیس اداره سرپرستی بدیدنم آمد. با هم در رستوران ماجیان ارمنی بادنجان سرخ کرده و دلمه خوردیم و بعد به سینما رفتم.

شنبه ۱۵ آذر،[1] ۷ دسامبر - با رادمنش بمنزل صدیقی رفتم. شب خسروپور و خوش‌کیش آمدند. با هم به نویی فو رفتم.

یکشنبه ۱۶ آذر، ۸ دسامبر - بعد از ناهار بمنزل صدیقی رفتم. رادمنش و مفتاح هم بود. شب با شیدفر بتأتر شات‌له[2] رفتم.

دوشنبه ۱۷ آذر، ۹ دسامبر - صبح بسفارت رفتم. با وزیر مختار و طاهر و شاهکار و یکتا خداحافظی کردم. بعد از ناهار با رادمنش بمنزل رادمنش رفتم و از آنجا به مادلن برای

---

۱. ۱۶ آذر. تا ۱۹ آذر اشتباه تکرار شده که تصحیح شد.

۲. Théatre du Châtelet، نام سرای اپرای مشهوری است در پاریس واقع در قصری به همین نام.

مراجعت بلندن بلیط خریدم و بعد بمنزل عبده رفتم. حسینی هم آمد. حسینی که تحصیلات حقوقی را تمام کرده عازم طهرانست. شب کمی از کتب فلسفه خواندم و خوابیدم.

سه‌شنبه ۱۸ آذر، ۱۰ دسامبر - در کافه سورس با صدیقی و شیدفر و مفتاح و عمید و دکتر نفیسی بودند. شب با امینی و مفتاح و شیدفر و رفعتی بسینما دان تون رفتم.

چهارشنبه ۱۹ آذر، ۱۱ دسامبر - چندین کتاب خریدم. بعد از ناهار با رادمنش بمنزل صدیقی رفتم و از آنجا بمریضخانه‌ای که صدر در آن جا بود و شب با رادمنش و صدیقی بکافه‌ای در مون مارتر.

پنجشنبه ۲۰ آذر، ۱۲ دسامبر - صبح چندین کتاب خریدم. بعد از ظهر اول بمنزل صدیقی بعد بکافه سورس و از آن جا با عبده و عمید و ملک اسماعیلی بمنزل مفتاح رفتم. شب با مهیمن در کوپل شام خوردم و ساعت ۱۰ مراجعت کردم.

جمعه ۲۱ آذر، ۱۳ دسامبر - بدیدن کاظم خان صدر رفتم. با خوش‌بین ناهار خوردم. بعد از ظهر با صادق صدر بودم و بعد بمنزل میرزا محمد خان رفتم. اقبال و بقایی و معظمی در آنجا بودند. شب با صدیقی و شیدفر و مفتاح و رفعتی بودم.

شنبه ۲۲ آذر، ۱۴ دسامبر - از گار دو نور بلندن آمدم. عبده در گار بود. چهار و نیم بعد از ظهر بمنزل رسیدم.

یکشنبه ۲۳ آذر، ۱۵ دسامبر - ناهار را بمنزل زرین‌کفش رفتم. افشار و رفعتی هم بودند. شب انگلیسی خواندم.

دوشنبه ۲۴ آذر، ۱۶ دسامبر - کتاب خواندم.

سه‌شنبه ۲۵ آذر، ۱۷ دسامبر - کتاب خواندم.

چهارشنبه ۲۶ آذر، ۱۸ دسامبر - بدیدن علاء بسفارت رفتم. با سودآور و نامدار بودم.

پنجشنبه ۲۷ آذر، ۱۹ دسامبر - ساعت ده بسفارت رفتم. تا یک بعد از نصف شب در آنجا بودم.

جمعه ۲۸ آذر، ۲۰ دسامبر - شب کتاب و روزنامه خواندم.

شنبه ۲۹ آذر، ۲۱ دسامبر - بپدرم و جلال کاغذ نوشتم.

یکشنبه ۳۰ آذر، ۲۲ دسامبر - کتاب خواندم.

دوشنبه ۱ دی، ۲۳ دسامبر - کتاب خواندم.

سه‌شنبه ۲ دی، ۲۴ دسامبر - کتاب خواندم.

چهارشنبه ۳ دی، ۲۵ دسامبر - بمناسب جشن ولادت مسیح جشن بود و در هتل مجلس خوبی بر پا بود. ساعت ۱۱ خوابیدم.

پنجشنبه ۴ دی، ۲۶ دسامبر - با آقای زاهدی بموزه رفتم.

جمعه ۵ دی، ۲۷ دسامبر - بسفارت برای مرتب کردن اوراق سفارت رفتم. ناهار با علوی و نامدار خوردم.

شنبه ۶ دی، ۲۸ دسامبر - کتاب خواندم. در سفارت بمرتب کردن اوراق پرداختم. انگلیسی خواندم.

یکشنبه ۷ دی، ۲۹ دسامبر - منوچهر فرمانفرمائیان آمد. در نزدیک ماربل آرچ اتومبیلی بما خورد ولی الحمد لله آسیبی نرسید.

دوشنبه ۸ دی، ۳۰ دسامبر - کتاب خواندم.

سه‌شنبه ۹ دی، ۳۱ دسامبر - با نامدار در هارودز غذا خوردم.

چهارشنبه ۱۰ دی، ۱ ژانویه - شب سرداری آمد. کتاب خواندم.

پنجشنبه ۱۱ دی، ۲ ژانویه - از پدرم کاغذی رسید. زرین‌کفش گفت که از سر جان کدمن شنیده‌ام شغل سفارت امریکا را برای من معیّن کرده‌اند. کمی افسرده شدم زیرا اگر در کار من هر تغییر پیدا شود، تحصیلاتم که در انگلیس باید انجام بگیرد، ناقص می‌ماند.

جمعه ۱۲ دی، ۳ ژانویه - کتاب می‌خواندم.

شنبه ۱۳ دی، ۴ ژانویه - بکتابخانه اونیورسیته لندن رفتم برای تحقیق راجع بگرفتن کتاب. کتاب خواندم.

یکشنبه ۱۴ دی، ۵ ژانویه - بعد از ظهر بمنزل زرین‌کفش رفتم. علوی و اصغرزاده و زنش هم بودند.

دوشنبه ۱۵ دی، ۶ ژانویه - صبح بسفارت و بعد از ظهر باداره رفتم.

سه‌شنبه ۱۶ دی، ۷ ژانویه - کتاب خواندم.

چهارشنبه ۱۷ دی، ۸ ژانویه - کتاب خواندم.

پنجشنبه ۱۸ دی، ۹ ژانویه - کتاب خواندم.

جمعه ۱۹ دی، ۱۰ ژانویه - آقای تقی‌زاده از برلن بلندن آمده. بعد از شام بدیدن آقای تقی‌زاده به کومرس کورت[1] هتل رفتم و تا ده و نیم آنجا بودم.

شنبه ۲۰ دی، ۱۱ ژانویه - کتاب خواندم.

یکشنبه ۲۱ دی، ۱۲ ژانویه - کتاب خواندم.

---

۱. مقصود Commercial Court است (همان Commercial & Admiralty Court).

دوشنبه ۲۲ دی، ۱۳ ژانویه - با آقای تقی‌زاده بمنزل زرین‌کفش رفتم.

سه‌شنبه ۲۳ دی، ۱۴ ژانویه - کتاب خواندم.

چهارشنبه ۲۴ دی، ۱۵ ژانویه - کتاب خواندم.

پنجشنبه ۲۵ دی، ۱۶ ژانویه - کتاب خواندم. از جلال و پدرم کاغذ رسید.

جمعه ۲۶ دی، ۱۷ ژانویه - کتاب می‌خواندم. فوستر.

شنبه ۲۷ دی، ۱۸ ژانویه - بدیدن آقای تقی‌زاده رفتم. تا نصف شب با او بودم.

یکشنبه ۲۸ دی، ۱۹ ژانویه - کتاب خواندم.

دوشنبه ۲۹ دی، ۲۰ ژانویه - با نامدار ناهار خوردم.

سه‌شنبه ۳۰ دی، ۲۱ ژانویه - کتاب خواندم. شاه انگلیس مرد.

چهارشنبه ۱ بهمن، ۲۲ ژانویه - اعلام سلطنت ادوارد. کتاب خواندم.

پنجشنبه ۲ بهمن، ۲۳ ژانویه - بمدرسهٔ اقتصاد لندن رفتم < تا > در باب دخول آن استفسار کنم.

جمعه ۳ بهمن، ۲۴ ژانویه - کتاب خواندم.

شنبه ۴ بهمن، ۲۵ ژانویه - کتاب خواندم.

یکشنبه ۵ بهمن، ۲۶ ژانویه - منوچهر فرمانفرمائیان با من ناهار خورد.

دوشنبه ۶ بهمن، ۲۷ ژانویه - شب بدیدن آقای تقی‌زاده رفتم. تا یازده و نیم بعد از ظهر نزد ایشان بودم.

سه‌شنبه ۷ بهمن، ۲۸ ژانویه - بتماشای تشییع جنازهٔ جرج جرج بماربل آرچ رفتم. ازدحام کثیری بود. تا ساعت ۱۰ کتاب خواندم.

چهارشنبه ۸ بهمن، ۲۹ ژانویه - کتاب خواندم.

پنجشنبه ۹ بهمن، ۳۰ ژانویه - آقای مینوی بهتل آمد. با او و رفعتی ناهار خوردم. سه و ربع بعد از ظهر بمدرسهٔ اقتصاد رفتم. راجع بورود به آن مذاکره کردم.

جمعه ۱۰ بهمن، ۳۱ ژانویه - از کینگز[۱] کالج در خصوص مدرسه روزنامه‌نگاری استفسار کردم.

شنبه ۱۱ بهمن، ۱ فوریه - زرین‌کفش مأمور شده است برای امور نفت به ژنو برود. ناهار در منزل زرین‌کفش بودم. علوی هم آمد.

یکشنبه ۱۲ بهمن، ۲ فوریه - مینوی با من ناهار خورد. به ویکتوریا رفتیم بمشایعت زرین‌کفش. عصر بمنزل آقای تقی‌زاده رفتم.

دوشنبه ۱۳ بهمن، ۳ فوریه - ناهار با حمزاوی و زنجانی و نامدار خوردم. به نزد آقای تقی‌زاده رفتم.

سه‌شنبه ۱۴ بهمن، ۴ فوریه - کتاب گاهشماری را برای آقای تقی‌زاده پاکنویس می‌کردم.

چهارشنبه ۱۵ بهمن، ۵ فوریه - تا ساعت هشت نزد آقای تقی‌زاده بودم. بعد بمنزل زرین‌کفش رفتم. تا ساعت ۱۰ در آنجا بودم.

پنجشنبه ۱۶ بهمن، ۶ فوریه - تا ساعت شش کتاب آقای تقی‌زاده را پاکنویس می‌کردم.

---

۱. کینز کالج. مقصود King’s College London است از مدارس روزنامه‌نگاری در بریتانیا.

جمعه ۱۷ بهمن، ۷ فوریه - کتاب آقای تقی‌زاده را پاکنویس کردم. شب نزد ایشان بودم.

شنبه ۱۸ بهمن، ۸ فوریه - کتاب خواندم و کتاب گاهشماری آقای تقی‌زاده را پاکنویس کردم.

یکشنبه ۱۹ بهمن، ۹ فوریه - با مینوی ناهار خوردم. کتاب خواندم و کتاب پاکنویس کردم.

دوشنبه ۲۰ بهمن، ۱۰ فوریه - پاکنویس کردم. مسیز ریدلی که بدیدن مادرش رفته بود آمد.

سه‌شنبه ۲۱ بهمن، ۱۱ فوریه - بمنزل زرین‌کفش و بعد به منزل آقای تقی‌زاده رفتم.

چهارشنبه ۲۲ بهمن، ۱۲ فوریه - بمدرسه السنهٔ شرقیه رفتم. راجع بانجمن و راجع بدرسی که می‌خواهم در اونیورسیته لندن بخوانم با او صحبت کردم.

پنجشنبه ۲۳ بهمن، ۱۳ فوریه - کتاب خواندم.

جمعه ۲۴ بهمن، ۱۴ فوریه - شب بمنزل آقای تقی‌زاده رفتم. تا نصف شب صفحاتی را که نوشته بودم مقابله می‌کردم.

شنبه ۲۵ بهمن، ۱۵ فوریه - کتاب آقای تقی‌زاده را پاکنویس کردم. کتاب خواندم.

یکشنبه ۲۶ بهمن، ۱۶ فوریه - حالم خوش نیست. کتاب خواندم.

دوشنبه ۲۷ بهمن، ۱۷ فوریه - کتاب خواندم و کتاب آقای تقی‌زاده را پاکنویس کردم.

سه‌شنبه ۲۸ بهمن، ۱۸ فوریه - کتاب خواندم.

چهارشنبه ۲۹ بهمن، ۱۹ فوریه - زرین‌کفش از سوییس مراجعت کرده در اداره بود.

پنجشنبه ۳۰ بهمن، ۲۰ فوریه - بیونیورسیتی کالج رفتم. از مدیر آن در باب ورود بمدرسه استعلام کردم.

جمعه ۱ اسفند، ۲۱ فوریه - تا نصف شب در منزل آقای تقی‌زاده بودم. کتاب خواندم.

شنبه ۲ اسفند، ۲۲ فوریه - کتاب خواندم. صبح از هتل بیرون نرفتم.

یکشنبه ۳ اسفند، ۲۳ فوریه - کتاب خواندم. حالم خوش نیست. بیرون نرفتم.

دوشنبه ۴ اسفند، ۲۴ فوریه - کتاب خواندم و کتاب آقای تقی‌زاده را پاکنویس کردم.

سه‌شنبه ۵ اسفند، ۲۵ فوریه - کتاب خواندم.

چهارشنبه ۶ اسفند، ۲۶ فوریه - جلسه راجع بانجمن ایران در سفارت ایران فکر شد. زرین‌کفش، سر دنیسن رس، پروفسور نیکلسن، لی اشتن، لاکهارت و من همه بودیم. مذاکراتی شد.

پنجشنبه ۷ اسفند، ۲۷ فوریه - شب بمنزل تقی‌زاده رفتم. تا نیم بعد از نصف شب نزد ایشان بودم.

جمعه ۸ اسفند، ۲۸ فوریه - از ساعت ۱۱ تا ۶ در باشگاه استد انگلیس بودم. تماشا می‌کردم.

شنبه ۹ اسفند، ۲۹ فوریه - کتاب خواندم.

یکشنبه ۱۰ اسفند، ۱ مارس - با آقای تقی‌زاده و خانم تقی‌زاده بمنزل زرین‌کفش رفتم.

دوشنبه ۱۱ اسفند، ۲ مارس - از پدرم و جلال کاغذی رسید. بطهران و کربلا جواب فرستادم.

سه‌شنبه ۱۲ اسفند، ۳ مارس - کتاب می‌خواندم.

چهارشنبه ۱۳ اسفند، ۴ مارس - بمنزل آقای تقی‌زاده رفتم.

پنجشنبه ۱۴ اسفند، ۵ مارس - بنمایشگاه چین رفتم. اتفاقاً کتابچی خان را در آنجا دیدم. زرین‌کفش باید دوباره بژنو برود.

جمعه ۱۵ اسفند، ۶ مارس - برای مشایعت زرین‌کفش بایستگاه ویکتوریا رفتم. بعد از ظهر در اداره بودم.

شنبه ۱۶ اسفند، ۷ مارس - کتاب خواندم.

یکشنبه ۱۷ اسفند، ۸ مارس - کتاب خواندم و کتاب آقای تقی‌زاده را پاکنویس کردم.

دوشنبه ۱۸ اسفند، ۹ مارس - شب در منزل آقای تقی‌زاده بودم.

سه‌شنبه ۱۹ اسفند، ۱۰ مارس - عصر بمنزل آقای تقی‌زاده رفتم. نوشته‌ها را با هم مقابله کردیم.

چهارشنبه ۲۰ اسفند، ۱۱ مارس - عصر بمدرسه السنهٔ شرقیه بجشن مدرسه رفتم.

پنجشنبه ۲۱ اسفند، ۱۲ مارس - با کتابچی خان و برادرش در رستوران هندی غذا خوردیم. چندین کاغذ تبریک عید نوشتم.

جمعه ۲۲ اسفند، ۱۳ مارس - کتاب خواندم.

شنبه ۲۳ اسفند، ۱۴ مارس - مقاله راجع بزنها را نوشتم و کتاب خواندم.

یکشنبه ۲۴ اسفند، ۱۵ مارس - بسفارت رفتم. جشن تولد شاه بود. تا ساعت شش و نیم در آنجا بودم.

دوشنبه ۲۵ اسفند، ۱۶ مارس - بنطق پروفسور سوئدی راجع بزردشت گوش کردم. رفعتی هم بود.

سه‌شنبه ۲۶ اسفند، ۱۷ مارس - کتاب خواندم. مقداری از کتاب آقای تقی‌زاده را پاکنویس کردم.

چهارشنبه ۲۷ اسفند، ۱۸ مارس - کتاب خواندم.

پنجشنبه ۲۸ اسفند، ۱۹ مارس - بعد از ظهر بمنزل آقای تقی‌زاده و شب بشام به ساووی هتل بمجلس مدرسه السنهٔ شرقیه رفتم. آقای علاء و سر دنیسن رس و سر عبدالقادر نطق کردند.

جمعه ۲۹ اسفند، ۲۰ مارس - کتاب خواندم و پاکنویس کردم.

شنبه ۱ فروردین، ۲۱ مارس - ناهار در سفارت خوردم. شب پرفسور سوئدی نایبرگ مهمان من بود. رفعتی هم بود.

یکشنبه ۲ فروردین، ۲۲ مارس - عصر بمنزل زرین‌کفش رفتم. دکتر علوی، اردلان عضو سفارت، افخمی، نامدار، احمدی و شاهرخی هم بودند.

دوشنبه ۳ فروردین، ۲۳ مارس - کتاب خواندم.

سه‌شنبه ۴ فروردین، ۲۴ مارس - عصر به ریچموند رفتم. کتاب خواندم.

چهارشنبه ۵ فروردین، ۲۵ مارس - عصر بمنزل آقای تقی‌زاده رفتم. صبح بانگلیسی چیزی نوشتم.

پنجشنبه ۶ فروردین، ۲۶ مارس - مدیر مجله آسیا از من خواست که برای مجله‌اش مقاله‌ای بنویسم.

جمعه ۷ فروردین، ۲۷ مارس - صبح بمنزل آقای تقی‌زاده رفتم.

شنبه ۸ فروردین، ۲۸ مارس - کتاب خواندم.

یکشنبه ۹ فروردین، ۲۹ مارس - در شافتس‌بری اَونی‌یو[1] چلوکباب خوردم. عصر با آقای تقی‌زاده بمنزل داراب خان رفتم.

دوشنبه ۱۰ فروردین، ۳۰ مارس - کتاب خواندم.

سه‌شنبه ۱۱ فروردین، ۳۱ مارس - با مینوی بمنزل سرداری رفتم.

____

۱. Shaftsbury Avenue، راسته‌ای از کاخ باکینگهام تا موزهٔ بریتانیا.

چهارشنبه ۱۲ فروردین، ۱ آوریل - صبح به بریتیش میوزیوم و شب بمنزل آقای تقی‌زاده رفتم.

پنجشنبه ۱۳ فروردین، ۲ آوریل - بسیزده بدر به همتون کورت رفتم.

جمعه ۱۴ فروردین، ۳ آوریل - به بریتیش میوزیوم رفتم.

شنبه ۱۵ فروردین، ۴ آوریل - با مینوی بکتابخانهٔ وزارت هند رفتم و شب بمنزل زنجانی رفتم. علاء و خانمش و زرین‌کفش و خانمش و اردلان و دخترش و شاهرخی و نامدار و بدر و قزوینی و جمعی دیگر بودند. تا سه بعد از نصف شب در آن جا بودم.

یکشنبه ۱۶ فروردین، ۵ آوریل - کتاب آقای تقی‌زاده را پاکنویس کردم. شب در هتل با مستر موریس که ژورنالیست است و از روسیه برگشته مذاکره کردم.

دوشنبه ۱۷ فروردین، ۶ آوریل - کتاب خواندم.

سه‌شنبه ۱۸ فروردین، ۷ آوریل - کتاب خواندم و مدتی با آقای تقی‌زاده بودم.

چهارشنبه ۱۹ فروردین، ۸ آوریل - کتاب آقای تقی‌زاده را پاکنویس کردم.

پنجشنبه ۲۰ فروردین، ۹ آوریل - کتاب آقای تقی‌زاده را پاکنویس کردم. شب با اشخاصی که در هتل هستند صحبت کردم. میسیز هت یکی از ایشان بدیدن پدرش به ماین هد رفته.

جمعه ۲۱ فروردین، ۱۰ آوریل - کتاب خواندم.

شنبه ۲۲ فروردین، ۱۱ آوریل - کتاب خواندم. به گولدرز گرین بدیدن رفعتی رفتم.

یکشنبه ۲۳ فروردین، ۱۲ آوریل - کتاب خواندم.

دوشنبه ۲۴ فروردین، ۱۳ آوریل - صبح به برومتن اراتری[1] بدیدن تماشای عروسی لورتا رفیق پگی ویلیس رفتم. مراسم عروسی کاتولیکی را دیدم.

سه‌شنبه ۲۵ فروردین، ۱۴ آوریل - شب بمنزل آقای تقی‌زاده رفتم.

چهارشنبه ۲۶ فروردین، ۱۵ آوریل - با آقای مینوی به بریتیش میوزیوم رفتم.

پنجشنبه ۲۷ فروردین، ۱۶ آوریل - به بریتیش میوزیوم رفتم. کتاب خواندم.

جمعه ۲۸ فروردین، ۱۷ آوریل - صبح بسفارت رفتم و شب بمنزل میس مورتون. شش نفر دیگر هم بودند همه ایرلندی و بلهجهٔ خوشی انگلیسی حرف می‌زدند. تا یک بعد از نصف شب در آن جا بودم.

شنبه ۲۹ فروردین، ۱۸ آوریل - به بریتیش میوزیوم رفتم. شب کتاب خواندم.

یکشنبه ۳۰ فروردین، ۱۹ آوریل - عصر به همتون کورت رفته کتاب خواندم.

دوشنبه ۳۱ فروردین، ۲۰ آوریل - کتاب خواندم.

سه‌شنبه ۱ اردیبهشت، ۲۱ آوریل - بعد از ظهر بمنزل جدید آقای تقی‌زاده رفتم.

چهارشنبه ۲ اردیبهشت، ۲۲ آوریل - کتاب خواندم.

پنجشنبه ۳ اردیبهشت، ۲۳ آوریل - کتاب خواندم. شب با بعضی از اهل هتل صحبت کردم.

جمعه ۴ اردیبهشت، ۲۴ آوریل - به بریتیش میوزیوم رفتم. عصر با سرداری و مینوی بودم.

شنبه ۵ اردیبهشت، ۲۵ آوریل - ناهار با حمزاوی و نامدار و زنجانی خوردم.

---

۱. Brompton Oratory، کلیسایی در محلهٔ چلسی لندن.

یکشنبه ۶ اردیبهشت، ۲۶ آوریل - کتاب خواندم. عصر به همتون کورت رفتم.

دوشنبه ۷ اردیبهشت، ۲۷ آوریل - کتاب خواندم.

سه‌شنبه ۸ اردیبهشت، ۲۸ آوریل - بمنزل آقای تقی‌زاده رفتم. با هم کتاب گاهشماری را مقابله کردیم.

چهارشنبه ۹ اردیبهشت، ۲۹ آوریل - بادارۀ جدید و کتابخانه و عمارت جدید مدرسه السنۀ شرقیه رفتم.

پنجشنبه ۱۰ اردیبهشت، ۳۰ آوریل - صبح کمی ترجمه انگلیسی قرآن را با متن آن مقابله کردم.

جمعه ۱۱ اردیبهشت، ۱ مه - کتاب خواندم.

شنبه ۱۲ اردیبهشت، ۲ مه - صبح برای دیدن خانه‌ای برای عبده به ریچموند رفتم و با یکی از اهل هتل برای خودم نیز در آنجا جستجو کردم که شاید خانه‌ای بدست بیاورم.

یکشنبه ۱۳ اردیبهشت، ۳ مه - با سجادی در هاید پارک قایقرانی کردم.

دوشنبه ۱۴ اردیبهشت، ۴ مه - کتاب خواندم.

سه‌شنبه ۱۵ اردیبهشت، ۵ مه - برای جستجوی خانه به سنت جان وود[1] و ابی رود[2] رفتم. جای مناسبی پیدا نکردم.

چهارشنبه ۱۶ اردیبهشت، ۶ مه - کتاب خواندم.

پنجشنبه ۱۷ اردیبهشت، ۷ مه - کتاب خواندم.

---

۱. St. John's Wood، محله‌ای در شمال لندن.

۲. Abbey Road، خیابانی در شمال لندن

جمعه ۱۸ اردیبهشت، ۸ مه - کتاب خواندم و بسینما رفتم. فیلم کپیتن بکر را دیدم.

شنبه ۱۹ اردیبهشت، ۹ مه - صبح کمی آلمانی خواندم.

یکشنبه ۲۰ اردیبهشت، ۱۰ مه - با قزوینی در هتل او ناهار خوردم.

دوشنبه ۲۱ اردیبهشت، ۱۱ مه - فلسفه خواندم.

سه‌شنبه ۲۲ اردیبهشت، ۱۲ مه - بمدرسهٔ اقتصاد رفتم. قرار شد روز پنجشنبه بدیدن رئیس قسمت اقتصاد بروم.

چهارشنبه ۲۳ اردیبهشت، ۱۳ مه - ناهار با نامدار خوردم. در آلبرت هال بتماشای توزیع تصدیقنامه و جوایز شاگردان یونیورسیته لندن رفتم.

پنجشنبه ۲۴ اردیبهشت، ۱۴ مه - بدیدن مستر ربنس[1] بمدرسهٔ اقتصاد رفتم. قرار شد معرفی نامه‌ام را بانجمن مخصوص این قبیل موضوعات بفرستند.

جمعه ۲۵ اردیبهشت، ۱۵ مه - کتاب خواندم.

شنبه ۲۶ اردیبهشت، ۱۶ مه - صبح به بریتیش میوزیوم و برای ناهار بمنزل زرین‌کفش رفتم. رفعتی و افشار هم بودند.

یکشنبه ۲۷ اردیبهشت، ۱۷ مه - کتاب خواندم. عصر بهاید پارک رفتم.

دوشنبه ۲۸ اردیبهشت، ۱۸ مه - صبح بمدرسه اقتصاد رفتم و پروفسور پلانت[2] را در اطاق کوچکش دیدم. اطاقش پر از کتاب و در گوشه‌اش یک تخت خواب بود. گفتم

---

۱. ربنسون. مقصود باید Lionel C. Robbins باشد (۱۸۹۸-۱۹۸۴). شاگرد لاسکی و استاد تاریخ اقتصادی در مدرسهٔ اقتصاد لندن.

۲. Sir Arnold Plant. اقتصاددان (۱۸۹۸-۱۹۷۸). از ۱۹۳۰ تا ۱۹۶۵ در مدرسهٔ اقتصاد لندن تدریس می‌کرد.

می‌خواهم در باب نفت تز بنویسم. گفت چون اسرارش را نمی‌توان منتشر کرد بهتر است فکر دیگر کنی. شب با قزوینی در هتل او شام خوردم. علیرضای ترک[1] معلم زبان ترکی هم آمد.

سه‌شنبه ۲۹ اردیبهشت، ۱۹ مه - به امرشام[2] رفتم. هوا و منظرهٔ بسیار خوب بود.

چهارشنبه ۳۰ اردیبهشت، ۲۰ مه - مستر ایمری یکی از اهل هتل به وست مینستر رفتم و با کشتی به همتون کورت رفتم. سه ساعت و نیم در راه بودیم.

پنجشنبه ۳۱ اردیبهشت، ۲۱ مه - شب قرآن خواندم.

جمعه ۱ خرداد، ۲۲ مه - از مدرسهٔ اقتصاد مراسله‌ای رسید و قبول شدن تقاضایم را اعلام کرد. بمنزل آقای تقی‌زاده رفتم.

شنبه ۲ خرداد، ۲۳ مه - کتاب خواندم.

یکشنبه ۳ خرداد، ۲۴ مه - شب به ریچموند بمنزل آقای علی اکبر اخوی رفتم که از پاریس آمده بود.

دوشنبه ۴ خرداد، ۲۵ مه - بمدرسه اقتصاد رفتم. پروفسور لاسکی[3] را دیدم. در خصوص موضوع تز مذاکره کردم و قرار شد تا روز سه‌شنبه در باب انتخاب موضوع فکر کنم. شب تورات خواندم.

سه‌شنبه ۵ خرداد، ۲۶ مه - کتاب خواندم.

---

۱. Ali Riza Bey، در ۱۹۲۱ کتابچه‌ای در آموزش مقدمات ترکی با عنوان *Kira'at Yaprakları* منتشر کرد.

۲. Amersham، قریه‌ای در حدود ۳۰ مایلی شمال‌غربی لندن.

۳. Harold Laski، استاد تاریخ سیاست و نظریه‌پرداز مارکسیست (۱۸۹۳-۱۹۵۰). از ۱۹۴۵ تا ۱۹۴۶ دبیر اول حزب کارگر انگلستان بود. در فاصله ۱۹۲۶ تا ۱۹۵۰ در مدرسهٔ اقتصاد لندن تدریس می‌کرد.

چهارشنبه ۶ خرداد، ۲۷ مه - با یکی از اهل هتل به اپسوم[1] رفتم بتماشای اسب دوانی. شب بسفارت رفتم. تابلوهای درویش را نشان می‌دادند. سر جان کدمن و سر دنیسن رس هم بودند.

پنجشنبه ۷ خرداد، ۲۸ مه - کتاب خواندم.

جمعه ۸ خرداد، ۲۹ مه - تا ساعت هفت در منزل آقای تقی‌زاده بودم و بعد بمنزل آقای زرین‌کفش رفتم. دیر بود در همانجا ماندم. تا دو بعد از نصف شب کتاب خواندم.

شنبه ۹ خرداد، ۳۰ مه - ناهار در منزل زرین‌کفش خوردم. عصر آقای تقی‌زاده هم آمد. همه با هم گردش کردیم.

یکشنبه ۱۰ خرداد، ۳۱ مه - به گولدرز گرین[2] بمنزل رفعتی رفتم. تنیس بازی می‌کردند.

دوشنبه ۱۱ خرداد، ۱ ژوئن - خواستم به وینزُر بروم ولی خیلی ازدحام بود. بکلیسای سن بارثولمیو رفتم و بمریضخانه سنت بارثولومیو[3] هم رفتم.

سه‌شنبه ۱۲ خرداد، ۲ ژوئن - صبح بسفارت و بعد بمدرسه اقتصاد رفتم. پروفسور لاسکی را دیدم. در باب تز گفتم می‌خواهم روابط ایران و انگلیس را انتخاب کنم و با مستر ربینس[4] رئیس قسمتش < که > به کارم مربوط است. گفت این موضوع را بخش تاریخ باید انتخاب کند. موضوع تز کار پر پیچ و خمی شده.

چهارشنبه ۱۳ خرداد، ۳ ژوئن - شب با آقای علاء برای شرکت در جشن تولد پیغمبر رفتم. چندین نفر نطق کردند. من هم نطق کردم. اول بانگلیسی و بعد بفارسی و بعد بانگلیسی. این اولین دفعه بود که بی یادداشت بانگلیسی نطق کردم.

---

۱. Epsom، شهرکی در ۱۵ مایلی جنوب لندن. اسبدوانی در نزدیکی آن در Epson Downs انجام می‌شود.

۲. Golders Green، محله‌ای ییلاقی حدود ۷ مایلی شمال لندن.

۳. St. Bartholomew's Hospital، بیمارستانی در مرکز لندن.

۴. ربن‌سن.

پنجشنبه ۱۴ خرداد، ۴ ژوئن - شب کتاب خواندم.

جمعه ۱۵ خرداد، ۵ ژوئن - به کاله‌دونین مارکت‌ رفتم و شب کتاب خواندم.

شنبه ۱۶ خرداد، ۶ ژوئن - به ریچموند بدیدن آقای علی اکبر اخوی رفتم. پسر کتابچی و یک دختر فرانسوی و چندین نفر دیگر هم بودند. تا ساعت ۱۰ با ایشان بودم. شب تورات خواندم.

یکشنبه ۱۷ خرداد، ۷ ژوئن - ناهار در منزل آقای تقی‌زاده خوردم. مقداری از کتاب گاهشماری را تصحیح کردم. شب با آقای تقی‌زاده و خانمش و آقای زرین‌کفش و خانمش بسینما رفتم. نصف شب بخانه برگشتم.

دوشنبه ۱۸ خرداد، ۸ ژوئن - کتاب خواندم.

سه‌شنبه ۱۹ خرداد، ۹ ژوئن - ناهار با نامدار خوردم. بعد از ظهر به پرتلند پلیس‌ رفتم. عکس ابنیهٔ ایران را دیدم. شب بهتل وان در بیلت رفتم بدیدن آقای کلانتری. آقای نبیل هم آمد. نایب اول سفارت است.

چهارشنبه ۲۰ خرداد، ۱۰ ژوئن - بموزهٔ لندن بانجمن ایران رفتم. شورای انجمن اول انعقاد یافت. جز من، لرد لمینگتون،‌ لی اشتون، گلبنکیان،‌ بزیل گری، ویلکنسن و پروفسور نیکلسن و لاکهارت هم بودند.

پنجشنبه ۲۱ خرداد، ۱۱ ژوئن - با نامدار و کلانتری بمسابقه اسبدوانی رفتم.

---

۱. Caledonian Market، بازارچهٔ دست دوم فروشی از ۱۸۵۲ تا ۱۹۳۹. امروزه به پارک تبدیل شده است.

۲. Portland Place، تالاری در لندن.

۳. Charles Wallace Alexander Napier Cochrane-Baillie (ولادت ۱۸۶۰ ـ وفات ۱۹۴۰) مشهور به Baron Lamington، حاکم سابق مستعمرات در کوئینزلند و بمبئی. رئیس انجمن ایران از ۱۹۱۱ تا ۱۹۳۵.

۴. Calouste Sarkis Gulbenkian (ولادت ۱۸۶۹ ـ وفات ۱۹۵۵) از ارامنهٔ عثمانی، دلال نفت. پس از مرگش در لیسبُن بنیادی بنامش تأسیس شدکه مجموعه‌ای از آثار ایران و ممالک خاورمیانه در آن نگهداری می‌شود.

جمعه ۲۲ خرداد، ۱۲ ژوئن - کتاب خواندم.

شنبه ۲۳ خرداد، ۱۳ ژوئن - شب با نامدار و کلانتری بسگدوانی رفتم.

یکشنبه ۲۴ خرداد، ۱۴ ژوئن - کتاب خواندم.

دوشنبه ۲۵ خرداد، ۱۵ ژوئن - بکتابخانهٔ شرکت رفتم. مدتی با کتابدار و مستر لاکهارت بودم.

سهشنبه ۲۶ خرداد، ۱۶ ژوئن - بعد از ظهر بنمایشگاه تابلوهای درویش رفتم.

چهارشنبه ۲۷ خرداد، ۱۷ ژوئن - کتاب خواندم.

پنجشنبه ۲۸ خرداد، ۱۸ ژوئن - شب بسگدوانی رفتم.

جمعه ۲۹ خرداد، ۱۹ ژوئن - عصر بدیدن آقای تقیزاده رفتم.

شنبه ۳۰ خرداد، ۲۰ ژوئن - با زرینکفش و مستر مایلز به نیو آرک رفتم برای دیدن شاگردها.

یکشنبه ۳۱ خرداد، ۲۱ ژوئن - پگی ویلیس که قریب دو سال در این هتل بود، رفت. روز شنبه هم میس پیرسن و میس جونسون که از هند برای تحصیل آمده بود، هر دو رفتند. ناهار در ریچموند با اخوی خوردم.

دوشنبه ۱ تیر، ۲۲ ژوئن - کتاب خواندم.

سهشنبه ۲ تیر، ۲۳ ژوئن - پوپ در باب معماری ایران در انجمن معماران نطق خوبی کرد. شب در ماربل آرچ با عبده و مینوی و رفعتی غذا خوردم. دکتر نفیسی هم بود.

چهارشنبه ۳ تیر، ۲۴ ژوئن - شب با کلنل لمسترن و مستر ایمری صحبت کردم.

پنجشنبه ۴ تیر، ۲۵ ژوئن - بعد از ظهر در سفارت جلسه شورای انجمن ایران منعقد شد. در باب نطق و سایر کارهای انجمن مذاکره شد.

جمعه ۵ تیر، ۲۶ ژوئن - کتاب خواندم. ساعت پنج بسفارت رفتم. مهمانی بود.

شنبه ۶ تیر، ۲۷ ژوئن - کتاب خواندم. مسیز ریزلی هت که یک هفته پیش بدیدن پدرش رفته بود، آمد. شب در هتل با اهل هتل صحبت کردم.

یکشنبه ۷ تیر، ۲۸ ژوئن - کتاب خواندم. مدتی هم باکلانتری بودم.

دوشنبه ۸ تیر، ۲۹ ژوئن - شب کتاب و چند روزنامه عربی خواندم.

سه‌شنبه ۹ تیر، ۳۰ ژوئن - عصر بمنزل آقای تقی‌زاده رفتم و تا ساعت ۱۱ با ایشان بودم.

چهارشنبه ۱۰ تیر، ۱ ژوئیه - از پدرم کاغذی[۱] رسید. بپدرم کاغذی نوشتم. کتاب خواندم.

پنجشنبه ۱۱ تیر، ۲ ژوئیه - به بریتیش میوزیم رفتم. کتاب خواندم.

جمعه ۱۲ تیر، ۳ ژوئیه - کتاب خواندم.

شنبه ۱۳ تیر، ۴ ژوئیه - کتاب خواندم.

یکشنبه ۱۴ تیر، ۵ ژوئیه - کتاب خواندم.

دوشنبه ۱۵ تیر، ۶ ژوئیه - شب بمنزل لیدی هدلی رفتم. نطقی بود راجع باوضاع بالکان.

سه‌شنبه ۱۶ تیر، ۷ ژوئیه - ناهار در سفارت خوردم. ژنرال نخجوان، شیرازی تاجری

---

۱. بپدرم.

که ۴۰ سال است ایران را ندیده، وزیر جنگ افغانستان، و مستر آلفرد بُسَم[1] هم بودند. شب با قزوینی شام خوردم.

چهارشنبه ۱۷ تیر، ۸ ژوئیه – کتاب خواندم. چیزی هم نوشتم.

پنجشنبه ۱۸ تیر، ۹ ژوئیه – بمنزل کلانتری رفتم. زن پر حرفی که بیک هندی شوهر کرده نیز بود.

جمعه ۱۹ تیر، ۱۰ ژوئیه – کتاب خواندم.

شنبه ۲۰ تیر، ۱۱ ژوئیه – کتاب خواندم.

یکشنبه ۲۱ تیر، ۱۲ ژوئیه – با حمزاوی در هتل قزوینی غذا خوردیم. عصر به آرلینگتون کاستل که ۳۵ میل تا لندن فاصله دارد، رفتم. غیر از اعضای جمعیت ایران جوان یک عده فنلاندی و اهل استونی و لیتوانی[2] هم بودند. زنهای فنلاندی با لباسهای ملی خود آمده بودند.

دوشنبه ۲۲ تیر، ۱۳ ژوئیه – کتاب خواندم و انگلیسی نوشتم.

سه‌شنبه ۲۳ تیر، ۱۴ ژوئیه – عصر بمنزل آقای تقی‌زاده رفتم. آقای سرداری و آقای زرین‌کفش و خانم زرین‌کفش هم بودند.

چهارشنبه ۲۴ تیر، ۱۵ ژوئیه – کتاب خواندم.

پنجشنبه ۲۵ تیر، ۱۶ ژوئیه – شب بسفارت رفتم. یک فرانسوی در باب مینیاتورهای ایران نطق می‌کرد.

---

۱. Alfred Charles Bossom، عضو پارلمان از حزب محافظه‌کار و معمار بریتانیایی (۱۸۸۱–۱۹۶۵).

۲. و اتونی

جمعه ۲۶ تیر، ۱۷ ژوئیه - کتاب خواندم و نوشتم.

شنبه ۲۷ تیر، ۱۸ ژوئیه - کتاب خواندم و نوشتم.

یکشنبه ۲۸ تیر، ۱۹ ژوئیه - آقای سپاسی را در فلیت استریت دیدم. از آلمان آمده بود. بمنزل زرین‌کفش هم رفتم. آقای تقی‌زاده و خانمش و آقای شیرازی و خانمش و افشار و دکتر علوی هم بودند.

دوشنبه ۲۹ تیر، ۲۰ ژوئیه - کتاب خواندم.

سه‌شنبه ۳۰ تیر، ۲۱ ژوئیه - با کلانتری و زنجانی بودم.

چهارشنبه ۳۱ تیر، ۲۲ ژوئیه - خوش کیش، افضل‌پور، و خسروپور از پاریس آمدند. ایشان را دیدم.

پنجشنبه ۱ مرداد، ۲۳ ژوئیه - کتاب خواندم.

جمعه ۲ مرداد، ۲۴ ژوئیه - بمنزل آقای تقی‌زاده رفتم. کتاب خواندم.

شنبه ۳ مرداد، ۲۵ ژوئیه - با دکتر علوی بودم.

یکشنبه ۴ مرداد، ۲۶ ژوئیه - با افضل‌پور و خسروپور بودم. شب بمنزل کلانتری رفتم.

دوشنبه ۵ مرداد، ۲۷ ژوئیه - کتاب خواندم. شب بمنزل آقای تقی‌زاده رفتم.

سه‌شنبه ۶ مرداد، ۲۸ ژوئیه - ویزای آلمان گرفتم. دکتر اخوی را دیدم. شب با آقای تقی‌زاده و خانم تقی‌زاده در منزل آقای زرین‌کفش بودم.

چهارشنبه ۷ مرداد، ۲۹ ژوئیه - کتاب خواندم.

پنجشنبه ۸ مرداد، ۳۰ ژوئیه - شب بمنزل زرین‌کفش رفتم. آقای علوی و صفوی هم بودند.

جمعه ۹ مرداد، ۳۱ ژوئیه - به سَن‌بری رفتم با مستر مایلز. فصیحی یکی از شاگردان غرق شده بود. در تحقیقات حضور داشتم.

شنبه ۱۰ مرداد، ۱ اوت - با زرین‌کفش و خانم زرین‌کفش بمسجد شاه جهان ووکینگ رفتم.

یکشنبه ۱۱ مرداد، ۲ اوت - عصر بهتل آقای شیرازی رفتم. آقای تقی‌زاده، خانم تقی‌زاده، آقای زرین‌کفش و زن و دخترش هم بودند.

دوشنبه ۱۲ مرداد، ۳ اوت - برای مجله آسیایی مقاله نوشتم.

سه‌شنبه ۱۳ مرداد، ۴ اوت - کتاب خواندم.

چهارشنبه ۱۴ مرداد، ۵ اوت - شب با قزوینی بودم.

پنجشنبه ۱۵ مرداد، ۶ اوت - بلیط آلمان خریدم.

جمعه ۱۶ مرداد، ۷ اوت - دو هزار مارک به ۸۹ لیره خریدم. شب با نبیل و کلانتری بودم.

شنبه ۱۷ مرداد، ۸ اوت - از لیورپول استریت با ترن ساعت ده حرکت کردم. از راه هریچ به فلشینگ رسیدم. ساعت هفت و کسری ببرلین وارد شدم. آقای سپاسی آمد. راهنمایی و مهربانی کرد.

یکشنبه ۱۸ مرداد، ۹ اوت - با سپاسی چای خوردم. ناهار در منزل دفتری بودم. صدر، خوش‌بین، بهرامی، تقی‌زاده برادر آقای تقی‌زاده، سپاسی، < و > عبدالله دفتری هم بودند. شب با سپاسی شام خوردم. بعد از ظهر هم با او و تقی‌زاده بفروشگاه که ۱۵ میلیون لیره برای آن خرج کرده‌اند، رفتیم. دختر و پسر بآهنگ موسیقی ورزش می‌کردند و خیلی عالی بود.

دوشنبه ۱۹ مرداد، ۱۰ اوت - عباس امیراصلانی را دیدم. با سپاسی در مغازهٔ معروفی ناهار خوردیم ــ در کورفو رستُران ــ و با او بکافه فمینا رفتم.

سه‌شنبه ۲۰ مرداد، ۱۱ اوت - با خوش‌بین و صدر در رستوران ایرانی غذا خوردیم. بعد از ظهر با ایشان بعمارت دکتر قزل ایاغ رفتم. شب بهتل اسپلاناد رفتم. جمعیت آلمانی و شرقی از ورزشکاران شرقی پذیرایی می‌کرد. آقای احمد سعیدی را دیدم. شب با صدر و خوش‌بین بودم.

چهارشنبه ۲۱ مرداد، ۱۲ اوت - صبح با صدر و خوش‌بین بسفارت و از آنجا برستوران احمد خان رفتم و بعد با خوش‌بین بمنزل مدیرالدوله ‹ و از آنجا › با عبدالله معظمی و سیروس و خوش‌بین به پوتسدام رفتم ولی پیاده نشدیم و با همان کسی که رفتیم برگشتیم. شب بمنزل برادرزن آقای تقی‌زاده رفتم. بسته‌ای که داشتم دادم.

پنجشنبه ۲۲ مرداد، ۱۳ اوت - با صدر و خوش‌بین بودم. بهرامی را هم دیدم. شب بایشان بمنزل احمد سعیدی رفتم.

جمعه ۲۳ مرداد، ۱۴ اوت - با صدر و خوش‌بین بعمارت دکتر قزل ایاغ رفتم. ناهار با خوش‌بین در رستوران احمد خان خوردم. شب با صدر و خوش‌بین و بهرامی ببیرون برلن رفتم. تا نصف شب آنجا بودم.

شنبه ۲۴ مرداد، ۱۵ اوت - بمشایعت سپاسی که بایران می‌رفت بایستگاه رفتم.

یکشنبه ۲۵ مرداد، ۱۶ اوت - با سهرابی به نمایشگاه بازیهای اولمپیک رفتم. پرش اسب را تماشا کردیم. ناهار در رستوران احمد خان خوردیم. بعد از ظهر[1] با صدر باز بنمایشگاه ورزشکاران رفتم. ستونهای نور می‌تاباندند و انسان احساس می‌کرد که زیر

---

۱. صدر

سقف است. ایران در این جشن شرکت نکرده بود. شب از بس تنم خارید ـ بواسطهٔ ساس ـ هیچ نخوابیدم.

دوشنبه ۲۶ مرداد، ۱۷ اوت - بعمارت دکتر قزل ایاغ رفتم. ناهار در رستوران احمد خان خوردم.

سهشنبه ۲۷ مرداد، ۱۸ اوت - صبح با صدر و عبدالله دفتری و سهرابی بمریضخانه بعیادت دکتر قزل ایاغ و از آنجا بدکان احمد خان رفتم. صدر ببلژیک رفت.

چهارشنبه ۲۸ مرداد، ۱۹ اوت - به اون تر دن لین دن[1] رفتم. موزه و علی الخصوص قسمت شرقی و شبه به عمارات یونان راکه در موزه ساختهاند دیدم.

پنجشنبه ۲۹ مرداد، ۲۰ اوت - با جمالزاده ناهار خوردم و شب هم با هم بودیم. دکتر کاویانی را هم دیدیم در رستوران.

جمعه ۳۰ مرداد، ۲۱ اوت - ناهار در رستوران احمد خان و شب در خانهٔ احمد سعیدی بودم.

شنبه ۳۱ مرداد، ۲۲ اوت - گردش کردم.

یکشنبه ۱ شهریور، ۲۳ اوت - ناهار با سعیدی و جمالزاده و زنش و امیرحسین قشقایی در کمینسکی خوردم و عصر با جمالزاده و زنش و خواهد و خواهرزادهاش نرگس و شوهرخواهرش و سعیدی و خانوادهاش در اطراف برلن گردش کردیم. شب در منزل سعیدی بودم.

دوشنبه ۲ شهریور، ۲۴ اوت - بعمارت قزل ایاغ رفتم. گردش کردم.

سهشنبه ۳ شهریور، ۲۵ اوت - با مقومی بباغ وحش رفتم. شب با عبدالله دفتری بودم.

---

۱. Unter den Linden، بولوار مشهوری در برلن.

چهارشنبه ۴ شهریور، ۲۶ اوت - با خوش‌بین بعمارت قزل ایاغ رفتم و عصر با علی اکبر دفتری بکافه.

پنجشنبه ۵ شهریور، ۲۷ اوت - با خوش‌بین و ناصر علوی به اون تر دن لین دن رفتم.

جمعه ۶ شهریور، ۲۸ اوت - با خوش‌بین بعمارت قزل ایاغ رفتم.

شنبه ۷ شهریور، ۲۹ اوت - در رستوران احمد خان ناهار خوردیم. بعد با وارسته به اون تر دن لین دن رفتم. شب در منزل علی اکبر دفتری بودم. عبدالله بهرامی و خوش‌بین و چند نفر دیگر هم بودند.

یکشنبه ۸ شهریور، ۳۰ اوت - با خوش‌بین و دفتری به پوتسدام رفتم. سان سوسی[1] و نویه شلوس[2] را دیدم.

دوشنبه ۹ شهریور، ۳۱ اوت - با عبدالله بهرامی و محمد اکبر و باقر وارسته بودم.

سه‌شنبه ۱۰ شهریور، ۱ سپتامبر - گردش کردم.

چهارشنبه ۱۱ شهریور، ۲ سپتامبر - جعبهٔ عکاسی خریدم. قزل ایاغ بدیدنم آمد.

پنجشنبه ۱۲ شهریور، ۳ سپتامبر - ناهار با خوش‌بین خوردم. عصر با هم بمنزل سعیدی رفتیم.

جمعه ۱۳ شهریور، ۴ سپتامبر - با خوش‌بین و دفتری بودم.

شنبه ۱۴ شهریور، ۵ سپتامبر - خوش‌بین[3] بپاریس رفت. تا گار او را مشایعت کردم. با

---

۱. Sanssouci، نام کاخی است در پوتسدام نزدیک برلن.

۲. Neues Schloss، نام کاخی است در پوتسدام در ضلع غربی پارک سان سوسی.

۳. خوش

دفتری در رستوران Schillow[1] شام خوردم. زنهایی که خدمت می‌کردند مقنعه مانند چیزی بر سر داشتند.

یکشنبه ۱۵ شهریور، ۶ سپتامبر - ناهار با تقی‌زاده و شام با اکبر دفتری و عبدالله بهرامی خوردیم و تا ده و نیم با هم بودیم. ساعت ۱۱ بایستگاه راه آهن آمدم. دفتری و گرگانی و آقا سید جواد تقی‌زاده هم آمدند. ساعت ۱۱ و ۷ دقیقه بترن نشستم. شب در ترن تخت خواب‌دار خوابیدم ولی خوش نگذشت. جوانب ترن را ندیدم.

دوشنبه ۱۶ شهریور، ۷ سپتامبر - در ترن چاشت خوردم. دوازده و ربع به فلشینگ رسیدم. شش ساعت و نیم در کشتی بودم. هوا طوفانی و کشتی دائم در لرزه بود. اغلب بد حال بودند. نتوانستم ناهار بخورم. هشت و نیم وارد هریج شدم. ۱۱ و نیم وارد هتل مادرید شدم.

سه‌شنبه ۱۷ شهریور، ۸ سپتامبر - بمنزل زرین‌کفش رفتم اما نبود. باسکاتلند رفته بود.

چهارشنبه ۱۸ شهریور، ۹ سپتامبر - شب بمنزل آقای تقی‌زاده رفتم.

پنجشنبه ۱۹ شهریور، ۱۰ سپتامبر - شب با دکتر علوی شام خوردیم.

جمعه ۲۰ شهریور، ۱۱ سپتامبر - با علوی بمشایعت دختر زرین‌کفش رفتم که برای تحصیل ببلژیک می‌رود.

شنبه ۲۱ شهریور، ۱۲ سپتامبر - با قزوینی ناهار خوردم. هلن که دختری از جنوب امریکا و رفیق مسیز ریزلی هت است، بهتل آمد و تا یازده در هتل بود.

یکشنبه ۲۲ شهریور، ۱۳ سپتامبر - با فؤاد و خانمش بودم.

Shillow .۱

دوشنبه ۲۳ شهریور، ۱۴ سپتامبر - کتاب خواندم.

سه‌شنبه ۲۴ شهریور، ۱۵ سپتامبر - برای دیدن اطاق بچندین جا رفتم. در وایتلی غذا خوردم.

چهارشنبه ۲۵ شهریور، ۱۶ سپتامبر - با دکتر علوی و فؤاد و خانمش بودم.

پنجشنبه ۲۶ شهریور، ۱۷ سپتامبر - با دکتر علوی بمسابقهٔ سگ‌دوانی رفتم.

جمعه ۲۷ شهریور، ۱۸ سپتامبر - ناهار با علوی و شام با فؤاد و خانمش خوردم.

شنبه ۲۸ شهریور، ۱۹ سپتامبر - کتاب خواندم.

یکشنبه ۲۹ شهریور، ۲۰ سپتامبر - به وتلند رفتم.

دوشنبه ۳۰ شهریور، ۲۱ سپتامبر - کتاب خواندم.

سه‌شنبه ۳۱ شهریور، ۲۲ سپتامبر - با علوی بودم. بسگ‌دوانی رفتم.

چهارشنبه ۱ مهر، ۲۳ سپتامبر - شب در منزل نامدار بودم. دکتر علوی و محمود میرزا هم بودند.[1]

پنجشنبه ۲ مهر، ۲۴ سپتامبر - شام در منزل آقای زرین‌کفش بودم. مدیرالدوله و دکتر معظمی هم بودند.

جمعه ۳ مهر، ۲۵ سپتامبر - شب در منزل آقای تقی‌زاده بودم.

شنبه ۴ مهر، ۲۶ سپتامبر - علوی سه اطاقش را بمن داد و خود بجای دیگری رفت.

---

۱. بود

یکشنبه ۵ مهر، ۲۷ سپتامبر - مشغول اسباب‌کشی بودم و خسته شدم. شام در منزل آقای زرین‌کفش خوردم.

دوشنبه ۶ مهر، ۲۸ سپتامبر - صبح انگلیسی خواندم. فیلم عربی وداد را دیدم.

سه‌شنبه ۷ مهر، ۲۹ سپتامبر - با علوی و نبیل ناهار خوردم.

چهارشنبه ۸ مهر، ۳۰ سپتامبر - رادیو در اطاقم کار گذاشتم. انگلیسی خواندم.

پنجشنبه ۹ مهر، ۱ اکتبر - شب با علوی به وایت سیتی رفتم.

جمعه ۱۰ مهر، ۲ اکتبر - با فؤاد و خانمش به شپردز بوش[1] بتماشای استودیوی فیلم‌برداری رفتم. شام با ایشان در مونتانا خوردم.

شنبه ۱۱ مهر، ۳ اکتبر - انگلیسی خواندم.

یکشنبه ۱۲ مهر، ۴ اکتبر - انگلیسی خواندم و با معلم انگلیسی به اُلد گیت رفتم.

دوشنبه ۱۳ مهر، ۵ اکتبر - فؤاد و خانمش بدیدنم آمدند.

سه‌شنبه ۱۴ مهر، ۶ اکتبر - کتاب خواندم.

چهارشنبه ۱۵ مهر، ۷ اکتبر - کتاب خواندم و چیزی نوشتم.

پنجشنبه ۱۶ مهر، ۸ اکتبر - کتاب خواندم.

جمعه ۱۷ مهر، ۹ اکتبر - بمنزل آقای تقی‌زاده رفتم و بمنزل زرین‌کفش. علوی چشمم را معاینه کرد.

---

۱. Shepherd's Bush، محله‌ای در غرب لندن.

شنبه ۱۸ مهر، ۱۰ اکتبر - کتاب خواندم. با نبیل و علوی بود.

یکشنبه ۱۹ مهر، ۱۱ اکتبر - بمشایعت علوی بایستگاه سنت پن کرس[1] رفتم.

دوشنبه ۲۰ مهر، ۱۲ اکتبر - کتاب خواندم، انگلیسی خواندم.

سه‌شنبه ۲۱ مهر، ۱۳ اکتبر - انگلیسی خواندم.

چهارشنبه ۲۲ مهر، ۱۴ اکتبر - برای نطق راجع بادبیات فارسی یادداشت کردم.

پنجشنبه ۲۳ مهر، ۱۵ اکتبر - بموزهٔ لندن برای جشن هزار سالهٔ متنبّی رفتم.

جمعه ۲۴ مهر، ۱۶ اکتبر - کتاب خواندم.

شنبه ۲۵ مهر، ۱۷ اکتبر - کتاب خواندم. با نبیل ناهار خوردم.

یکشنبه ۲۶ مهر، ۱۸ اکتبر - کتاب خواندم.

دوشنبه ۲۷ مهر، ۱۹ اکتبر - عصر بمنزل پروفسور وبستر[2] رفتم برای حضور در سمینار.

سه‌شنبه ۲۸ مهر، ۲۰ اکتبر - کتاب خواندم.

چهارشنبه ۲۹ مهر، ۲۱ اکتبر - نطقی راجع بشعر فارسی را که باید بانگلیسی بکنم، تهیه می‌کردم.

پنجشنبه ۳۰ مهر، ۲۲ اکتبر - انگلیسی خواندم.

جمعه ۱ آبان، ۲۳ اکتبر - عصر بمدرسهٔ اقتصاد رفتم. مقاله را تهیه می‌کردم.

---

۱. St Pancras، ایستگاه قطار مشهوری در شرق لندن نزدیک کتابخانه بریتانیا.

۲. Sir Charles K. Webster، دیپلمات و مورخ بریتانیایی (۱۸۸۶-۱۹۶۱). استاد در هاروارد و مدرسه اقتصاد لندن و رئیس آکادمی بریتانیا از ۱۹۵۴ تا ۱۹۵۰.

شنبه ۲ آبان، ۲۴ اکتبر - کتاب خواندم.

یکشنبه ۳ آبان، ۲۵ اکتبر - ناهار در منزل زرین‌کفش خوردم.

دوشنبه ۴ آبان، ۲۶ اکتبر - شب بمنزل فؤاد رفتم.

سه‌شنبه ۵ آبان، ۲۷ اکتبر - کتاب خواندم و نطق تهیه کردم.

چهارشنبه ۶ آبان، ۲۸ اکتبر - انگلیسی خواندم.

پنجشنبه ۷ آبان، ۲۹ اکتبر - چهار ساعت و نیم بعد از ظهر بخانهٔ نمرهٔ ۷۳ در واترلو اسکویر رفتم. قریب چهل پیرزن و دو مرد در آنجا بودند. در باب شعر فارسی نطق کردم. بعد بخانه آمدم. انگلیسی خواندم.

جمعه ۸ آبان،[1] ۳۰ اکتبر - بمدرسهٔ اقتصاد سر درس پروفسور وبستر رفتم. ناهار با جوانی فرانسوی که در منزل وبستر او را دیده بودم، خوردم. شب در منزل آقای تقی‌زاده بودم.

شنبه ۹ آبان، ۳۱ اکتبر - شنیدم که علاء را احضار کرده‌اند. متأسف شدم چون که وزیر مختار خوبیست.

یکشنبه ۱۰ آبان، ۱ نوامبر - باکلانتری و نبیل بودم.

دوشنبه ۱۱ آبان، ۳ نوامبر - صبح به بریتیش میوزیوم و عصر بمنزل وبستر رفتم.

سه‌شنبه ۱۲ آبان، ۴ نوامبر - کتاب خواندم و انگلیسی.

چهارشنبه ۱۳ آبان، ۵ نوامبر - عصر در منزل لاکهارت بودم. قریب بیست نفر مهمان داشت.

---

۱. ۷ آبان

پنجشنبه ۱۴ آبان، ۵ نوامبر - صبح نزد ریکتر[1] مدیر مجله آسیایی رفتم. مقاله‌ای را که می‌خواست باو دادم. از آنجا بوزارت امور خارجهٔ انگلیس رفتم. مستر استیفن کرلی را دیدم. رئیس کتابخانه است. گفت کمک خواهد کرد در باب تزم راجع بوزارت خارجهٔ انگلیس.

جمعه ۱۵ آبان، ۶ نوامبر - کتاب خواندم.

شنبه ۱۶ آبان، ۷ نوامبر - با نبیل و علوی و نامدار بودم.

یکشنبه ۱۷ آبان، ۸ نوامبر - با علوی و نبیل بودم.

دوشنبه ۱۸ آبان، ۹ نوامبر - در موزهٔ لندن اولین جلسهٔ انجمن ایران افتتاح شد. آقاخان نطقی راجع بحافظ کرد. شام با قزوینی خوردم.

سه‌شنبه ۱۹ آبان، ۱۰ نوامبر - انگلیسی خواندم.

چهارشنبه ۲۰ آبان، ۱۱ نوامبر - کتاب خواندم.

پنجشنبه ۲۱ آبان، ۱۲ نوامبر - شام با فؤاد و خانمش به چشر چیز به فلیت استریت[2] رفتم.

جمعه ۲۲ آبان، ۱۳ نوامبر - بمدرسهٔ اقتصاد سر درس پروفسور وبستر رفتم.

شنبه ۲۳ آبان، ۱۴ نوامبر - کتاب خواندم.

یکشنبه ۲۴ آبان، ۱۵ نوامبر - در منزل زرین‌کفش ناهار خوردم. آقای تقی‌زاده و خانمش هم بودند.

---

۱. ریشتر
۲. Cheshire Cheese، رستورانی در خیابان Fleet در مرکز لندن.

دوشنبه ۲۵ آبان، ۱۶ نوامبر - کتاب خواندم.

سه‌شنبه ۲۶ آبان، ۱۷ نوامبر - کتاب خواندم.

چهارشنبه ۲۷ آبان، ۱۸ نوامبر - کتاب خواندم.

پنجشنبه ۲۸ آبان، ۱۹ نوامبر - عصر بمنزل پروفسور وبستر رفتم.

جمعه ۲۹ آبان، ۲۰ نوامبر - بمدرسهٔ اقتصاد سر درس پروفسور وبستر رفتم.

شنبه ۳۰ آبان، ۲۱ نوامبر - عصر در سفارت کلاس درس فارسی بود. از سه تا پنج و نیم درس می‌دادم.

یکشنبه ۱ آذر، ۲۲ نوامبر - ناهار با نبیل و علوی خوردم و شام با مینوی.

دوشنبه ۲ آذر، ۲۳ نوامبر - کتاب خواندم.

سه‌شنبه ۳ آذر، ۲۴ نوامبر - کتاب خواندم.

چهارشنبه ۴ آذر، ۲۵ نوامبر - انگلیسی خواندم.

پنجشنبه ۵ آذر، ۲۶ نوامبر - شب بخانهٔ فؤاد رفتم.

جمعه ۶ آذر، ۲۷ نوامبر - عصر به ریتز هتل رفتم. جمعیت ایران بمناسبت رفتن آقای علاء مهمانی داد.

شنبه ۷ آذر، ۲۸ نوامبر - عصر با نبیل بمنزل آقای تقی‌زاده رفتم.

یکشنبه ۸ آذر، ۲۹ نوامبر - علوی به شفیلد رفت.

دوشنبه ۹ آذر، ۳۰ نوامبر - کتاب خواندم.

سه‌شنبه ۱۰ آذر، ۱ دسامبر - کتاب خواندم. حالم خوب نبود.

چهارشنبه ۱۱ آذر، ۲ دسامبر - کتاب خواندم. با مینوی بودم.

پنجشنبه ۱۲ آذر، ۳ دسامبر - عصر بمنزل پروفسور وبستر رفتم.

جمعه ۱۳ آذر، ۴ دسامبر - بمشایعت آقای علاء به ویکتوریا رفتم. خیلی بودند. شب فؤاد و خانمش بدیدنم آمدند.

شنبه ۱۴ آذر، ۵ دسامبر - عصر در سفارت درس فارسی دادم.

یکشنبه ۱۵ آذر، ۶ دسامبر - با کلانتری بودم.

دوشنبه ۱۶ آذر، ۷ دسامبر - انگلیسی خواندم.

سه‌شنبه ۱۷ آذر، ۸ دسامبر - کتاب خواندم.

چهارشنبه ۱۸ آذر، ۹ دسامبر - کتاب خواندم. شب بمنزل مسیز امیلی مونه رفتم. لاکهارت در باب بحریهٔ نادر نطق کرد.

پنجشنبه ۱۹ آذر، ۱۰ دسامبر - بمنزل پروفسور وبستر رفتم.

جمعه ۲۰ آذر، ۱۱ دسامبر - عصر بمنزل آقای تقی‌زاده رفتم. شب با دکتر مشرف الدوله نفیسی برستوران تروکادرو رفتم. نطق پادشاه انگلیس ادوارد را شنیدم که استعفا داد.

شنبه ۲۱ آذر، ۱۲ دسامبر - عصر در سفارت درس دادم. شب بدیدن روحانی رفتم.

یکشنبه ۲۲ آذر، ۱۳ دسامبر - شب بمنزل کلانتری رفتم.

دوشنبه ۲۳ آذر، ۱۴ دسامبر - انگلیسی خواندم.

سه‌شنبه ۲۴ آذر، ۱۵ دسامبر - شب با روحانی و خانمش به یونیورسیتی کالج رفتم. تئاتر حسن را دیدیم. در اطاقی که می‌خواستند چند شرقی داشته باشند، نامرئی بود. بر روی آن نوشته بودند «لا و له ایضا» بگمان آنکه باید شعری یا زینتی باشد.

چهارشنبه ۲۵ آذر، ۱۶ دسامبر - کتاب خواندم.

پنجشنبه ۲۶ آذر، ۱۷ دسامبر - حالم خوب نبود. اکثر وقت را در خانه بودم. انگلیسی خواندم.

جمعه ۲۷ آذر، ۱۸ دسامبر - کتاب خواندم.

شنبه ۲۸ آذر، ۱۹ دسامبر - علوی از شفلید آمد با او بمغازهٔ بربری[1] رفتم. پالتویی خریدم. ناهار با هم در سفارت خوردیم.

یکشنبه ۲۹ آذر، ۲۰ دسامبر - با علوی بمنزل زرین‌کفش رفتم.

دوشنبه ۳۰ آذر، ۲۱ دسامبر - کتاب خواندم.

سه‌شنبه اول دی، ۲۲ دسامبر - کتاب خواندم.

چهارشنبه ۲ دی، ۲۳ دسامبر - کتاب خواندم.

پنجشنبه ۳ دی، ۲۴ دسامبر - درس خواندم.

جمعه ۴ دی، ۲۵ دسامبر - کتاب و درس خواندم.

شنبه ۵ دی، ۲۶ دسامبر - کتاب خواندم. رخشانی هم بود.

یکشنبه ۶ دی، ۲۷ دسامبر - کتاب خواندم.

------

۱. Burberry، نام مغازه‌ای در لندن.

دوشنبه ۷ دی، ۲۸ دسامبر - شب با نامدار و رخشانی بسیرک رفتم.

سه‌شنبه ۸ دی، ۲۹ دسامبر - به بریتیش میوزیوم رفتم.

چهارشنبه ۹ دی، ۳۰ دسامبر - درس خواندم.

پنجشنبه ۱۰ دی، ۳۱ دسامبر - جلسه انجمن ایران بود. شب با مینوی بودم.

جمعه ۱۱ دی، ۱ ژانویه - به بریتیش میوزیوم رفتم. شب انگلیسی خواندم.

شنبه ۱۲ دی، ۲ ژانویه - کتاب خواندم.

یکشنبه ۱۳ دی، ۳ ژانویه - با علوی بمنزل زرین‌کفش و بعد بعیادت آقای تقی‌زاده رفتم.

دوشنبه ۱۴ دی، ۴ ژانویه - معلم انگلیسی بتعطیلی رفت. کتاب خواندم.

سه‌شنبه ۱۵ دی، ۵ ژانویه - کتاب خواندم.

چهارشنبه ۱۶ دی، ۶ ژانویه - کتاب خواندم.

پنجشنبه ۱۷ دی، ۷ ژانویه - به بریتیش میوزیوم رفتم.

جمعه ۱۸ دی، ۸ ژانویه - شب در منزل زرین‌کفش بودم.

شنبه ۱۹ دی، ۹ ژانویه - به بریتیش میوزیوم رفتم.

یکشنبه ۲۰ دی، ۱۰ ژانویه - شب با فؤاد و خانمش بودم.

دوشنبه ۲۱ دی، ۱۱ ژانویه - کتاب خواندم.

سه‌شنبه ۲۲ دی، ۱۲ ژانویه - کتاب خواندم.

چهارشنبه ۲۳ دی، ۱۳ ژانویه - معلم انگلیسی آمد. انگلیسی خواندم.

پنجشنبه ۲۴ دی، ۱۴ ژانویه - شب با فؤاد و خانمش بسینما رفتم.

جمعه ۲۵ دی، ۱۵ ژانویه - صبح بمدرسۀ اقتصاد و از آنجا بمنزل آقای تقی‌زاده رفتم.

شنبه ۲۶ دی، ۱۶ ژانویه - ناهار با علوی در سفارت خوردم.

یکشنبه ۲۷ دی، ۱۷ ژانویه - حالم خوب نیست. کمر و پایم درد می‌کرد.

دوشنبه ۲۸ دی، ۱۸ ژانویه - کتاب خواندم.

سه‌شنبه ۲۹ دی، ۱۹ ژانویه - کتاب خواندم.

چهارشنبه ۳۰ دی، ۲۰ ژانویه - حالم هیچ خوب نیست. کمردرد سخت دارم.

پنجشنبه ۱ بهمن، ۲۱ ژانویه - ناهار در منزل زرین‌کفش و عصر در خانۀ پروفسور وبستر بودم.

جمعه ۲ بهمن، ۲۲ ژانویه - صبح بمدرسۀ اقتصاد و شب بمنزل فؤاد رفتم.

شنبه ۳ بهمن، ۲۳ ژانویه - کتاب خواندم.

یکشنبه ۴ بهمن، ۲۴ ژانویه - با علوی بمنزل زرین‌کفش رفتم. زنجانی و نبیل و نامدار هم بودند.

دوشنبه ۵ بهمن، ۲۵ ژانویه - شب فؤاد و خانمش بدیدنم آمدند.

سه‌شنبه ۶ بهمن، ۲۶ ژانویه - کتاب خواندم.

چهارشنبه ۷ بهمن، ۲۷ ژانویه - کتاب خواندم.

پنجشنبه ۸ بهمن، ۲۸ ژانویه - کتاب خواندم.

جمعه ۹ بهمن، ۲۹ ژانویه - صبح بمدرسه و عصر بمنزل آقای تقی‌زاده رفتم.

شنبه ۱۰ بهمن، ۳۰ ژانویه - عصر درس دادم. کتاب خواندم.

یکشنبه ۱۱ بهمن، ۳۱ ژانویه - کتاب خواندم. با هورشید مورتس و زنش و نامدار بودم.

دوشنبه ۱۲ بهمن، ۱ فوریه - کتاب خواندم.

سه‌شنبه ۱۳ بهمن، ۲ فوریه - با نبیل و قزوینی و نامدار و حمزاوی در روایال پالاس هتل ناهار خوردم. شب بمنزل سر دنیسن رس رفتم.

چهارشنبه ۱۴ بهمن، ۳ فوریه - کتاب و انگلیسی خواندم.

پنجشنبه ۱۵ بهمن، ۴ فوریه - نامدار بپاریس رفت.

جمعه ۱۶ بهمن، ۵ فوریه - از کتابخانهٔ مدرسهٔ السنهٔ شرقیه بمنزل آقای تقی‌زاده رفتم.

شنبه ۱۷ بهمن، ۶ فوریه - با علوی بسفارت رفتم.

یکشنبه ۱۸ بهمن، ۷ فوریه - با علوی و مینوی ناهار در منزل زرین‌کفش خوردیم.

دوشنبه ۱۹ بهمن، ۸ فوریه - کتاب خواندم.

سه‌شنبه ۲۰ بهمن، ۹ فوریه - کتاب خواندم.

چهارشنبه ۲۱ بهمن، ۱۰ فوریه - کتاب خواندم.

پنجشنبه ۲۲ بهمن، ۱۱ فوریه - صبح بسفارت رفتم. نبیل را رنگ پریده دیدم. گفت مگر خبر نداری که داور سکته کرده است. متأثر شدم. ناهار با زنجانی خوردم.

جمعه ۲۳ بهمن، ۱۲ فوریه - کتاب خواندم.

شنبه ۲۴ بهمن، ۱۳ فوریه - با علوی و زنجانی در رستوران روسی ناهار خوردم.

یکشنبه ۲۵ بهمن، ۱۴ فوریه - کتاب خواندم.

دوشنبه ۲۶ بهمن، ۱۵ فوریه - بشنیدن نطق لارنس بینیُن راجع بمینیاتورهای ایران به برلینگ تن هوس' رفتم.

سه‌شنبه ۲۷ بهمن، ۱۶ فوریه - در خانه بودم. برای تز انگلیسی یادداشت می‌کردم.

چهارشنبه ۲۸ بهمن، ۱۷ فوریه - کتاب خواندم.

پنجشنبه ۲۹ بهمن، ۱۸ فوریه - کار کردم برای تز. عصر بمنزل پروفسور وبستر رفتم.

جمعه ۳۰ بهمن، ۱۹ فوریه - صبح بمدرسهٔ اقتصاد و عصر بمنزل آقای تقی‌زاده رفتم.

شنبه ۱ اسفند، ۲۰ فوریه - حالم خوب نبود. با علوی و کلانتری ناهار خوردم.

یکشنبه ۲ اسفند، ۲۱ فوریه - انگلیسی خواندم.

دوشنبه ۳ اسفند، ۲۲ فوریه - کمرم سخت درد می‌کرد. نتوانستم کار کنم.

سه‌شنبه ۴ اسفند، ۲۳ فوریه - کتاب خواندم.

چهارشنبه ۵ اسفند، ۲۴ فوریه - تصدیق لیسانس که از طهران فرستاده بودند، رسید.

---

۱. Burlington House، بنایی در مرکز لندن محل آکادمی سلطنتی هنرها.

پنجشنبه ۶ اسفند، ۲۵ فوریه - روحانی و خانمش بدیدنم آمدند.

جمعه ۷ اسفند، ۲۶ فوریه - برای مشایعت زنجانی به ویکتوریا رفتم.

شنبه ۸ اسفند، ۲۷ فوریه - برای تز کار کردم.

یکشنبه ۹ اسفند، ۲۸ فوریه - بمنزل آقای زرین‌کفش رفتم. آقای تقی‌زاده هم بود.

دوشنبه ۱۰ اسفند، ۱ مارس - با معلم انگلیسی باونیورسیتهٔ لندن رفتم. تصدیق لیسانس را دادم. ناهار با لاکهارت خوردم.

سه‌شنبه ۱۱ اسفند، ۲ مارس - کار کردم. شب بمنزل فؤاد رفتم.

چهارشنبه ۱۲ اسفند، ۳ مارس - با قزوینی ناهار خوردم. شب با فؤاد و خانمش بمدرسه‌ای که خانمش در آن درس می‌خواند، رفتم. رقص می‌کردند و اغلب حضّار سوئدی و نروژی و فنلاندی بودند.

پنجشنبه ۱۳ اسفند، ۴ مارس - انگلیسی خواندم.

جمعه ۱۴ اسفند، ۵ مارس - صبح بمدرسهٔ اقتصاد رفتم. علوی بدیدنم آمد.

شنبه ۱۵ اسفند، ۶ مارس - بسفارت رفتم. با نبیل و علوی ناهار خوردم. شب فؤاد بدیدنم آمد.

یکشنبه ۱۶ اسفند، ۷ مارس - صبح با علوی بمنزل زرین‌کفش رفتم. تا ساعت ۶ در آن جا بودم. شب با علوی بسفارت برگشتم. با هم برستوران اشمیت رفتیم.

۱
...

شنبه ۳۰ اسفند، ۲۰ مارس - نطقی در باب اسلام کردم.

---

۱. سه نقطه در اصل. پس از ۱۶ اسفند تا روز آخر آن ماه، مدخلی نوشته نشده است.

یکشنبه ۱ فروردین، ۲۱ مارس - با علوی از آقای تقی‌زاده و زرین‌کفش دیدن کردم. عصر بسفارت رفتم. شب با مینوی و سرداری به فورست او نی‌یو رستوران در هولبورن رفتم. اغلب هندیها در آنجا بودند. جشن بمناسبت نوروز بود.

دوشنبه ۲ فروردین، ۲۲ مارس - شب مهمان مستر ویلکنسون بودم. سرداری هم بود.

سه‌شنبه ۳ فروردین، ۲۳ مارس - با علوی بوزارت خارجه رفتم که تصدیقهایش را بگیرد. ناهار با او و نشاط و کلانتری خوردم.

چهارشنبه ۴ فروردین، ۲۴ مارس - با مینوی بمنزل سرداری رفتم.

پنجشنبه ۵ فروردین، ۲۵ مارس - با علوی ناهار خوردم.

جمعه ۶ فروردین، ۲۶ مارس - صبح بیرون نرفتم. حالم خوب نبود. شب علوی آمد.

شنبه ۷ فروردین، ۲۷ مارس - صبح بسفارت رفتم. در باب کاغذی که کسی بدولت ایران نوشته و مرا و علاء را متهم باعمال خلاف دولت کرده حرف زدم. بدیدن پناهی عضو سفارت رفتم.

یکشنبه ۸ فروردین، ۲۸ مارس - با علوی بودم. با هم بمنزل زرین‌کفش رفتم. ناهار در آنجا بودم.

دوشنبه ۹ فروردین، ۲۹ مارس - ناهار با علوی و نبیل و نشاط و کلانتری خوردم.

سه‌شنبه ۱۰ فروردین، ۳۰ مارس - کتاب خواندم.

چهارشنبه ۱۱ فروردین، ۳۱ مارس - کتاب خواندم.

پنجشنبه ۱۲ فروردین، ۱ آوریل - کتاب خواندم.

جمعه ۱۳ فروردین، ۲ آوریل - بکلیسای سنت مارتین این ز فیلد رفتم. مجلس تذکر جان درینک واتر بود. بعیادت آقای تقی‌زاده رفتم. تب شدید داشت.

شنبه ۱۴ فروردین، ۳ آوریل - ناهار با قزوینی خوردم. آقای آرام هم بود. بعد از ظهر به وان در بیلت هتل رفتم. با آقای قدس بمنزل آقای زرین‌کفش رفتم.

یکشنبه ۱۵ فروردین، ۴ آوریل - انگلیسی خواندم.

دوشنبه ۱۶ فروردین، ۵ آوریل - حالم خوب نبود. کتاب خواندم.

سه‌شنبه ۱۷ فروردین، ۶ آوریل - صورت کتابهای سفارت را مرتب کردم. شب انگلیسی خواندم.

چهارشنبه ۱۸ فروردین، ۷ آوریل - شب برستوران ویرا سوامی[1] رفتم. مجلس بزرگی بود.

پنجشنبه ۱۹ فروردین، ۸ آوریل - حالم هیچ خوب نبود. نتوانستم کار کنم.

جمعه ۲۰ فروردین، ۹ آوریل - کتاب و انگلیسی خواندم.

شنبه ۲۱ فروردین، ۱۰ آوریل - شب در سفارت دعوت داشتم. زرین‌کفش و خانمش و حمزاوی و خواهرش و دکتر علوی و شعاع و زنش هم بودند.

یکشنبه ۲۲ فروردین، ۱۱ آوریل - با علوی بمنزل زرین‌کفش رفتم. شب بمنزل نبیل.

دوشنبه ۲۳ فروردین، ۱۲ آوریل - کتاب خواندم و انگلیسی و یادداشت کردم برای تز.

---

۱. Veeraswamy، قدیمی‌ترین رستوران هندی لندن. در ۱۹۲۶ افتتاح شد.

سه‌شنبه ۲۴ فروردین، ۱۳ آوریل - با علوی بمریضخانه بعیادت آقای نشاط رفتم.

چهارشنبه ۲۵ فروردین، ۱۴ آوریل - به بریتیش میوزیوم رفتم. ناهار با مینوی خوردم.

پنجشنبه ۲۶ فروردین، ۱۵ آوریل - با دکتر علوی برای تماشای دارالمجانین رفتم. با دکتر ریندر طبیب دارالمجانین که همدرس علوی بوده، چای خوردیم.

جمعه ۲۷ فروردین، ۱۶ آوریل - کتاب خواندم.

شنبه ۲۸ فروردین، ۱۷ آوریل - ناهار در منزل زرین‌کفش خوردم. با آقای تقی‌زاده بسفارت بدیدن نبیل رفتم. رشته‌دارزاده و زنش و پناهی و زنش و علوی هم بودند.

یکشنبه ۲۹ فروردین، ۱۸ آوریل - با علوی بخانهٔ زرین‌کفش رفتم. پناهی و زنش و حمزاوی و زنش هم آمدند.

دوشنبه ۳۰ فروردین، ۱۹ آوریل - فؤاد و خانمش که از پاریس مراجعت کرده‌اند، بدیدنم آمدند. انگلیسی خواندم. *De Profundis* وایلد را خواندم.

سه‌شنبه ۳۱ فروردین، ۲۰ آوریل - شب با دکتر علوی و طبیبی که در دارالمجانین کار می‌کند، شام خوردم.

چهارشنبه ۱ اردیبهشت، ۲۱ آوریل - کتاب خواندم.

پنجشنبه ۲ اردیبهشت، ۲۲ آوریل - کتاب خواندم.

جمعه ۳ اردیبهشت، ۲۳ آوریل - شب با فؤاد و زنش بکلوبی نزدیک اولد[1] کورت رفتم.

شنبه ۴ اردیبهشت، ۲۴ آوریل - با علوی در چرچ استریت ناهار خوردم. کتاب خواندم.

---

۱. اولز

یکشنبه ۵ اردیبهشت، ۲۵ آوریل - با نبیل و پناهی و خانمش و علوی به کی‌یو گاردنز رفتم. آقای تقی‌زاده و زرین‌کفش و خانم تقی‌زاده و خانم زرین‌کفش هم بودند.

دوشنبه ۶ اردیبهشت، ۲۶ آوریل - با علوی بودم. با هم بمشایعت قزوینی رفتیم که بایران می‌رود. معظمی وارد شد.

سه‌شنبه ۷ اردیبهشت، ۲۷ آوریل - کتاب خواندم.

چهارشنبه ۸ اردیبهشت، ۲۸ آوریل - به ادارهٔ Public Record Office رفتم.

پنجشنبه ۹ اردیبهشت، ۲۹ آوریل - با غلامعلی معظمی و علوی بخرید رفتم.

جمعه ۱۰ اردیبهشت، ۳۰ آوریل - صبح بمدرسهٔ اقتصاد رفتم. کار کردم و کتاب خواندم.

شنبه ۱۱ اردیبهشت، اول مه - کتاب خواندم.

یکشنبه ۱۲ اردیبهشت، ۲ مه - با علوی و قدس و چند نفر دیگر به ریچ موند رفتم.

دوشنبه ۱۳ اردیبهشت، ۳ مه - کتاب خواندم.

سه‌شنبه ۱۴ اردیبهشت، ۴ مه - با علوی بودم.

چهارشنبه ۱۵ اردیبهشت، ۵ مه - در مدرسه السنهٔ شرقیه در کتابخانه کار کردم. شام با میسز ریزلی هت و پسرش جان خوردم.

پنجشنبه ۱۶ اردیبهشت، ۶ مه - انگلیسی خواندم. عصر بمنزل پروفسور وبستر رفتم.

جمعه ۱۷ اردیبهشت، ۷ مه - کتاب و انگلیسی خواندم.

شنبه ۱۸ اردیبهشت، ۸ مه - با پناهی ناهار خوردم. بمنزل عبدالله خان بهرامی رفتم که برای نمایندگی از طرف ایران آمده است.

یکشنبه ۱۹ اردیبهشت، ۹ مه - شب بدیدن روحانی رفتم.

دوشنبه ۲۰ اردیبهشت، ۱۰ مه - کتاب خواندم.

سه‌شنبه ۲۱ اردیبهشت، ۱۱ مه - با عبدالله بهرامی که برای نمایندگی ایران در تاجگذاری آمده بود، در خیابانهای پر از جمعیت گردش کردم.

چهارشنبه ۲۲ اردیبهشت، ۱۲ مه - پنج بعد از نصف شب با تاکسی به نایتز بریج رفتم و از آن جا بمحلی که بلیطش را داشتم. جای خوبی بود نزدیک قصر. اعضای سفارت هم بودند.

پنجشنبه ۲۳ اردیبهشت، ۱۳ مه - با علوی بودم.

جمعه ۲۴ اردیبهشت، ۱۴ مه - صبح بمدرسه و عصر بمنزل آقای تقی‌زاده رفتم.

شنبه ۲۵ اردیبهشت، ۱۵ مه - شب با عبدالله بهرامی بودم.

یکشنبه ۲۶ اردیبهشت، ۱۶ مه - با علوی بودم. در منزل قدس ناهار خوردم. شب هم با علوی بودم.

دوشنبه ۲۷ اردیبهشت، ۱۷ مه - کتاب خواندم.

سه‌شنبه ۲۸ اردیبهشت، ۱۸ مه - فؤاد و خانمش و علوی بدیدنم آمدند. صبح بکتابخانهٔ وزارت هند رفتم.

چهارشنبه ۲۹ اردیبهشت، ۱۹ مه - صبح بسفارت رفتم برای تهیه مقدمات نطق محتشم السلطنه. عصر بمنزل پروفسور وبستر رفتم.

پنجشنبه ۳۰ اردیبهشت، ۲۰ مه - بدیدن محتشم السلطنه رفتم. علوی بواسطهٔ تزریق سرم ضد حصبه حالت خوشی ندارد.

جمعه ۳۱ اردیبهشت، ۲۱ مه - صبح بمدرسه رفتم و نیم ساعت بعد از ظهر پروفسور وبستر را دیدم و در باب موضوع تز حرف زدم. عصر به دورچستر هتل برای دیدن ولیعهد حجاز و برادرش رفتم. شب با نبیل به پارک لین هتل رفتم بدیدن حسینقلی قره‌گوزلو.

شنبه ۱ خرداد، ۲۲ مه - شب با جزائری بودم.

یکشنبه ۲ خرداد، ۲۳ مه - ترجمه نطق محتشم السلطنه را دیدم. محتشم السلطنه و سهیلی را دیدم. با علوی ناهار و شام خوردم.

دوشنبه ۳ خرداد، ۲۴ مه - در سفارت تا نزدیک ظهر در خصوص نطقی که محتشم السلطنه باید بکند کار کردم. عصر بدیدن سودآور و ناصر رفتم و شب منزل روحانی.

سه‌شنبه ۴ خرداد، ۲۵ مه - محتشم السلطنه در لنکستر هوس نطق کرد و یک صد نفر بودند. شب با فؤاد و خانمش در رستوران هندی غذا خوردیم.

چهارشنبه ۵ خرداد، ۲۶ مه - بیشتر اوقات با علوی بودم.

پنجشنبه ۶ خرداد، ۲۷ مه - با حمزاوی و پناهی بمنزل یکی از تجار استن فور بریج رفتم. بمناسبت آمدن حاج محتشم السلطنه مهمانی دادند. بسیار خوب بود.

جمعه ۷ خرداد، ۲۸ مه - صبح بمدرسهٔ اقتصاد رفتم و شب در سفارت بودم. محسن قره‌گوزلو و حسینقلی قره‌گوزلو و اعضای سفارت بودند. تا ساعت ۱۱ در سفارت بودیم. در باب جوجه و لباس و این قبیل چرند و پرندها حرف می‌زدند و یک کلمه درست کسی نگفت.

شنبه ۸ خرداد، ۲۹ مه - کلانتری بایران رفت. پناهی و علوی و نبیل با من شام خوردند.

یکشنبه ۹ خرداد، ۳۰ مه - انگلیسی خواندم. شب با علوی شام خوردم.

دوشنبه ۱۰ < خرداد >، ۳۱ مه - صبح به بریتیش میوزیوم رفتم. با دکتر وکیل شام خوردم.

سه‌شنبه ۱۱ خرداد، ۱ ژوئن - صبح به بریتیش میوزیوم و شب با دکتر وکیل و نبیل و حمزاوی و دکتر علوی بسگ دوانی رفتم.

چهارشنبه ۱۲ خرداد، ۲ ژوئن - صبح به بریتیش میوزیوم رفتم و عصر با مینوی بودم. شب با علوی بسفارت رفتم.

پنجشنبه ۱۳ خرداد، ۳ ژوئن - عصر بخانه پروفسور وبستر رفتم و شب بدیدن سرهنگ اشرفی که از طرف ادارهٔ پلیس برای شرکت در کنفرانس پلیس آمده.

جمعه ۱۴ خرداد، ۴ ژوئن - صبح بمدرسه سر درس وبستر رفتم. شب بمنزل زرین‌کفش. امیرالدین و زنش دختر مدیر حبل‌المتین آمدند. ویلکنسن[1] خزانه‌دار انجمن ایران وفات یافت.

شنبه ۱۵ خرداد، ۵ ژوئن - صبح به بریتیش میوزیوم رفتم. شب علوی و فؤاد و خانمش بدیدنم آمدند.

یکشنبه ۱۶ خرداد، ۶ ژوئن - با علوی در منزل زرین‌کفش ناهار خوردم.

دوشنبه ۱۷ خرداد، ۷ ژوئن - شب بدیدن سرهنگ اشرفی رفتم.

سه‌شنبه ۱۸ خرداد، ۸ ژوئن - به بریتیش میوزیوم رفتم و بعد به وین‌زور کورت بمنزل رشید وهاب‌زاده. با من علوی و نبیل هم آمدند.

پنجشنبه ۱۹ خرداد، ۹ ژوئن - با علوی بمنزل زرین‌کفش و آقای تقی‌زاده رفتم. علوی با هر دو خداحافظی کرد. بعد با هم بسفارت رفتیم.

---

۱. Charles K. Wilkinson، متخصص تاریخ هنر. اثر اصلی او *The Miniature in Persian Art* است.

جمعه ۲۱ خرداد، ۱۱ ژوئن - با علوی بلیورپول استریت رفتم و با او در ترن نشستم. تا هریچ او را مشایعت کردم. روز گرم غم انگیزی بود. سه و نیم بعد از ظهر بلندن رسیدم.

شنبه ۲۲ خرداد، ۱۲ ژوئن - صبح به بریتیش میوزیوم رفتم.

یکشنبه ۲۳ خرداد، ۱۳ ژوئن - انگلیسی خواندم.

دوشنبه ۲۴ خرداد، ۱۴ ژوئن - انگلیسی خواندم.

سه‌شنبه ۲۵ خرداد، ۱۵ ژوئن - بعد از ظهر به بریتیش میوزیم رفتم. شب انگلیسی خواندم.

چهارشنبه ۲۶ خرداد، ۱۶ ژوئن - کتاب خواندم.

پنجشنبه ۲۷ خرداد، ۱۷ ژوئن - عصر بمنزل وبستر رفتم. حالم چندان خوب نبود.

جمعه ۲۸ خرداد، ۱۸ ژوئن - حالم خوب نبود. کتاب خواندم.

شنبه ۲۹ خرداد، ۱۹ ژوئن - از خانه بیرون نرفتم. انگلیسی و کتاب خواندم.

یکشنبه ۳۰ خرداد، ۲۰ ژوئن - حالم بدتر بود. خواستم با نبیل حرف بزنم، غش کردم. مرا آوردند باطاق. هیچ از خانه بیرون نرفتم.

دوشنبه ۳۱ خرداد، ۲۱ ژوئن - حالم کمی بهتر بود. بمحلۀ چلسی رفتم و شب کمی کار کردم.

سه‌شنبه ۱ تیر، ۲۲ ژوئن - عصر با زرین‌کفش بمنزل سر دنیس رس رفتم. سهیلی هم آمد. در باب انتخاب جانشین ویلکنسن مذاکره بود.

چهارشنبه ۲ تیر، ۲۳ ژوئن - انگلیسی خواندم. حالم چندان خوب نبود.

پنجشنبه ۳ تیر، ۲۴ ژوئن - شب در هلند پارک گردش کردم. بعد بخانه آمدم. کار کردم.

جمعه ۴ تیر، ۲۵ ژوئن - بخانه آقای تقی‌زاده رفتم. حالم چندان خوب نیست.

شنبه ۵ تیر، ۲۶ ژوئن - به بریتیش میوزیم رفتم. شب فؤاد و خانمش بدیدنم آمدند.

یکشنبه ۶ تیر، ۲۷ ژوئن - ناهار در منزل زرین‌کفش خوردم. عصر مستر همفریز دفتردار سفارت انگلیس در طهران و زنش آمد بخانهٔ زرین‌کفش. شب با فؤاد روحانی بودم.

دوشنبه ۷ تیر، ۲۸ ژوئن - صبح ببریتیش میوزیم رفتم. شب انگلیسی خواندم.

سه‌شنبه ۸ تیر، ۲۹ ژوئن - با فؤاد و خانمش در رستوران هندی غذا خوردیم.

چهارشنبه ۹ تیر، ۳۰ ژوئن - با مستر مایلز به لاف برو[1] < رفتم > برای رسیدگی بشکایات ۹ ایرانی که در آن جا درس می‌خوانند. شب دکتر علی اکبر دفتری را دیدم.

پنجشنبه ۱۰ تیر، ۱ ژوئیه - صبح با دفتری و آقا سید جواد تقی‌زاده بودیم. شب انگلیسی خواندم. ناهار در منزل پناهی بودم. آقای زرین‌کفش و خانمش هم بودند.

جمعه ۱۱ تیر، ۲ ژوئیه - کتاب خواندم. شام با مینوی در منزل آقای تقی‌زاده خوردم.

شنبه ۱۲ تیر، ۳ ژوئیه - با زرین‌کفش و الکین‌تون و مایلز ببیرمنگام رفتم برای حضور در مجلس جشن اونی‌ورسیته. بعضی از ایرانیها که در آنجا درس می‌خواندند تصدیق گرفتند.

دوشنبه ۱۴ تیر، ۵ ژوئیه - با فؤاد و زنش و فرانسیس گولدینگ که ما را دعوت کرده بود، در اکسفورد گردش کردیم. شب بلندن آمدیم. با هم در رستوران هندی غذا خوردیم. بعد بمنزل روحانی رفتیم.

---

۱. لاف برُ. مقصود دانشگاه لاف برو (Loughborough University) در حد فاصل لستر و ناتینگهام.

سه‌شنبه ۱۵ تیر، ۶ ژوئیه - شب انگلیسی خواندم.

چهارشنبه ۱۶ تیر، ۷ ژوئیه - شب انگلیسی خواندم.

پنجشنبه ۱۷ تیر، ۸ ژوئیه - بکلوب شرکت نفت در خارج لندن < به > لوور[1] سیدنم رفتم. قریب سیصد نفر بودند. زرین‌کفش و خانمش هم بودند.

جمعه ۱۸ تیر، ۹ ژوئیه - شب به ساووی هتل بمهمانی شرکت رفتم. کدمن و الکین‌تون نطق کردند. تقلید و شعبده‌بازی هم داشتند.

شنبه ۱۹ تیر، ۱۰ ژوئیه - به بریتیش میوزیم رفتم. با مینوی در رستوران هندی غذا خوردم.

یکشنبه ۲۰ تیر، ۱۱ ژوئیه - کتاب خواندم.

دوشنبه ۲۱ تیر، ۱۲ ژوئیه - کتاب خواندم.

سه‌شنبه ۲۲ تیر، ۱۳ ژوئیه - کتاب خواندم.

چهارشنبه ۲۳ تیر، ۱۴ ژوئیه - به بریتیش میوزیم رفتم. شب کتاب خواندم.

پنجشنبه ۲۴ تیر، ۱۵ ژوئیه - شب مستر اشتن ورث صاحبخانه که گاهی در تآتر بازی می‌کند، آمد. با هم در باب تآتر و ادبیات صحبت کردیم.

جمعه ۲۵ تیر، ۱۶ ژوئیه - صبح مقاله راجع بسعدی را نوشتم.

شنبه ۲۶ تیر، ۱۷ ژوئیه - به بریتیش میوزیم رفتم.

یکشنبه ۲۷ تیر، ۱۸ ژوئیه - عصر با روحانی و خانمش گردش کردم و شب در رستوران هندی غذا خوردم.

---

۱. لوو. Lower Sydenham محله‌ای در جنوب شرقی لندن.

دوشنبه ۲۸ تیر، ۱۹ ژوئیه - مقاله راجع بسعدی را نوشتم. شب انگلیسی خواندم.

سه‌شنبه ۲۹ تیر، ۲۰ ژوئیه - به بریتیش میوزیم رفتم. غروب انگلیسی خواندم.

چهارشنبه ۳۰ تیر، ۲۱ ژوئیه - صبح به بریتیش میوزیم و بعد از ظهر بجلسهٔ انجمن ایران رفتم.

پنجشنبه ۳۱ تیر، ۲۲ ژوئیه - بعد از ظهر بقصر باکینگهام به گاردن پارتی رفتم. جمع کثیری بودند. تماشایی بود. رجال و راجه‌های هندی و پسر متمهدی[1] بودند. تا ساعت شش در آنجا بودیم. با فؤاد و زنش در رستوران هندی غذا خوردیم و بعد بمنزل فؤاد رفتم.

جمعه ۱ مرداد، ۲۳ ژوئیه - روز به بریتیش میوزیم و شب با فؤاد و زنش بودم.

شنبه ۲ مرداد، ۲۴ ژوئیه - بعد از ظهر انگلیسی خواندم.

یکشنبه ۳ مرداد، ۲۵ ژوئیه - کتاب خواندم.

دوشنبه ۴ مرداد، ۲۶ ژوئیه - شب به گِروٗنر هوس[2] دعوت داشتم. مجلسی بمناسبت متقاعد شدن سر دنیسن بود. مستر جان رابینسون، لرد زِتلند،[3] و لرد لوینگستن هم بودند.

سه‌شنبه ۵ مرداد، ۲۷ ژوئیه - صبح بسفارت رفتم. بعد از ظهر با فؤاد و خانمش بودم. شب بسینما رفتم.

چهارشنبه ۶ مرداد، ۲۸ ژوئیه - صبح بکتابخانهٔ مدرسه السنهٔ شرقیه رفتم. شب با فؤاد و خانمش بودم.

---

۱. عبدالرحمان المهدی (۱۸۸۵-۱۹۵۹)، پسر محمد احمد بن عبدالله سودانی که در ۱۸۸۱ خود را مهدی خواند و چهار سال بعد، پس از چند ماه حبس، درگذشت. عبدالرحمان بعداً تاجر ثروتمندی شد. در دهه ۱۹۳۰ میلادی به قصد تبلیغ علیه ادعاهای سرزمینی مصر در سودان، باگروهی از حامیان خود موسوم به «انصار» به لندن سفر کرد.

۲. Grosvener House، هتلی در لندن.

۳. Lawrence Dundas مشهور به Earl of Ronaldshay از اعضای حزب محافظه‌کار (۱۸۷۶-۱۹۶۱).

پنجشنبه ۷ مرداد، ۲۹ ژوئیه - شب انگلیسی خواندم.

جمعه ۸ مرداد، ۳۰ ژوئیه - عصر بمنزل آقای تقی‌زاده رفتم.

شنبه ۹ مرداد، ۳۱ ژوئیه - عصر بدیدن مصطفی فاتح رفتم. زرین‌کفش و زنش هم بودند.

یکشنبه ۱۰ مرداد، ۱ اوت - با فاتح و زنش بمنزل زرین‌کفش رفتیم. شام با فؤاد و خانمش بودم.

دوشنبه ۱۱ مرداد، ۲ اوت - با فؤاد و خانمش بکمبریج رفتیم. ناهار بسیار بدی خوردیم. بعد از ظهر قایق‌رانی کردیم. شب بلندن آمدیم. در رستوران هندی غذا خوردیم.

سه‌شنبه ۱۲ مرداد، ۳ اوت - شب با فؤاد بکلوبی نزدیک منزل فؤاد رفتم. لاکهارت و فاتح هم بودند.

چهارشنبه ۱۳ مرداد، ۴ اوت - انگلیسی خواندم.

پنجشنبه ۱۴ مرداد، ۵ اوت - بکتابخانه وزارت هندوستان رفتم. شب انگلیسی خواندم.

جمعه ۱۵ مرداد، ۶ اوت - بکتابخانه وزارت هند رفتم. شب با فؤاد و خانمش بودم. نعیمی هم بود.

شنبه ۱۶ مرداد، ۷ اوت - با فاتح و زنش بمادام توسو رفتم.

یکشنبه ۱۷ مرداد، ۸ اوت - کتاب خواندم.

دوشنبه ۱۸ مرداد، ۹ اوت - بکتابخانه وزارت هند رفتم. شب انگلیسی خواندم.

سه‌شنبه ۱۹ مرداد، ۱۰ اوت - بکتابخانه هند رفتم. شب با فؤاد و زنش و نعیمی بودم.

چهارشنبه ۲۰ مرداد، ۱۱ اوت - عصر بدیدن مینوی بمریضخانه سنت تامس رفتم.

پنجشنبه ۲۱ مرداد، ۱۲ اوت - با فؤاد و خانمش شام خوردیم.

جمعه ۲۲ مرداد، ۱۳ اوت - صبح بکتابخانه وزارت هند رفتم.

شنبه ۲۳ مرداد، ۱۴ اوت - صبح بکتابخانه هند و شب با پناهی و خانمش بمنزل وهاب‌زاده رفتم. با اتومبیل نصیربک‌اف برگشتیم.

یکشنبه ۲۴ مرداد، ۱۵ اوت - با روحانی و خانمش و نعیمی بودم.

دوشنبه ۲۵ مرداد، ۱۶ اوت - صبح بکتابخانه هند رفتم. شب هم کتاب خواندم.

سه‌شنبه ۲۶ مرداد، ۱۷ اوت - کتاب خواندم.

چهارشنبه ۲۷ مرداد، ۱۸ اوت - بکتابخانه وزارت هند رفتم.

پنجشنبه ۲۸ مرداد، ۱۹ اوت - کتاب راجع باسلام که باید در باب آن مقاله‌ای مختصر بنویسم، خواندم.

جمعه ۲۹ مرداد، ۲۰ اوت - کتاب خواندم و کار کردم.

شنبه ۳۰ مرداد، ۲۱ اوت - با سجادی و رفعتی ناهار خوردم. کار کردم.

یکشنبه ۳۱ مرداد، ۲۲ اوت - با مینوی ناهار خوردم.

دوشنبه ۱ شهریور، ۲۳ اوت - شب بمنزل فؤاد رفتم. نعیمی هم آن جا بود.

سه‌شنبه ۲ شهریور، ۲۴ اوت - صبح بکتابخانه وزارت هند رفتم و بعد از ظهر باداره رفتم. شب انگلیسی خواندم.

چهارشنبه ۳ شهریور، ۲۵ اوت - بکتابخانه هند رفتم.

پنجشنبه ۴ شهریور، **۲۶ اوت** - ناهار با نبیل و سهیلی در منزل پناهی خوردم. شب بمنزل روحانی رفتم.

جمعه ۵ شهریور، **۲۷ اوت** - ناهار با نبیل و پناهی و خانمش خوردم.

شنبه ۶ شهریور، **۲۸ اوت** - کتاب خواندم.

یکشنبه ۷ شهریور، **۲۹ اوت** - کتاب خواندم.

دوشنبه ۸ شهریور، **۳۰ اوت** - مقاله راجع بکتاب شرح حال محمد و تاریخ اسلام برای مجله نفت نوشتم.

سه‌شنبه ۹ شهریور، **۳۱ اوت** - صبح بکتابخانه وزارت هند رفتم و شب بسینما. شهر خیوه را نشان می‌داد و کتیبه‌های فارسی بر بعضی عمارات بود.

چهارشنبه ۱۰ شهریور، **۱ سپتامبر** - کتاب خواندم.

پنجشنبه ۱۱ شهریور، **۲ سپتامبر** - دکتر نفیسی از طهران آمد. کتاب خواندم.

جمعه ۱۲ شهریور، **۳ سپتامبر** - شب بمنزل روحانی رفتم. قدس و همایون و اتحادیه هم در آن جا بودند.

شنبه ۱۳ شهریور، **۴ سپتامبر** - بعیادت پناهی بسفارت رفتم و بعد به اولمپیا بدیدن نمایشگاه تلوزیون. اتحادیه و فؤاد و چند نفر دیگر هم بودند.

یکشنبه ۱۴ شهریور، **۵ سپتامبر** - بعیادت پناهی رفتم.

دوشنبه ۱۵ شهریور، **۶ سپتامبر** - کتاب خواندم.

سه‌شنبه ۱۶ شهریور، **۷ سپتامبر** - بدیوان اسناد انگلیس Public Record Office رفتم.

چهارشنبه ۱۷ شهریور، ۸ سپتامبر - بدیوان اسناد رفتم.

پنجشنبه ۱۸ شهریور، ۹ سپتامبر - بدیوان اسناد رفتم. سپس در رستوران هندی با فؤاد و خانمش و نبیل غذا خوردیم.

جمعه ۱۹ شهریور، ۱۰ سپتامبر - صبح بعیادت پناهی و بعد با فؤاد و زنش بمنزل زرین‌کفش رفتم.

شنبه ۲۰ شهریور، ۱۱ سپتامبر - بدیوان اسناد رفتم.

یکشنبه ۲۱ شهریور، ۱۲ سپتامبر - شب با فؤاد و زنش در رستوران ایطالیایی نزدیک اورلز کورت غذا خوردم و بعد بمنزل نعیمی رفتم.

دوشنبه ۲۲ شهریور، ۱۳ سپتامبر - صبح بدیوان اسناد رفتم و عصر بمنزل آقای تقی‌زاده.

سه‌شنبه ۲۳ شهریور، ۱۴ سپتامبر - صبح انگلیسی خواندم. بعد بهارودز رفتم. کتب کتابخانه نی‌یو ویز را حراج می‌کردند. بعضی را خریدم.

چهارشنبه ۲۴ شهریور، ۱۵ سپتامبر - بدیوان اسناد رفتم.

پنجشنبه ۲۵ شهریور، ۱۶ سپتامبر - بدیوان اسناد رفتم. شب انگلیسی خواندم.

جمعه ۲۶ شهریور، ۱۷ سپتامبر - صبح بدیوان اسناد رفتم.

شنبه ۲۷ شهریور، ۱۸ سپتامبر - بدیوان اسناد رفتم.

یکشنبه ۲۸ شهریور، ۱۹ سپتامبر - عصر با نبیل و سهیلی به بری ۲۱ میلی لندن رفتم. چای خوردیم.

دوشنبه ۲۹ شهریور، ۲۰ سپتامبر - نعیمی بپاریس رفت.

سه‌شنبه ۳۰ شهریور، ۲۱ سپتامبر - بکتابخانه وزارت هند رفتم و شب بدیدن آقای جواد مهین کرمانی. با او شام خوردم.

چهارشنبه ۳۱ شهریور، ۲۲ سپتامبر - صبح بکتابخانه وزارت هند و شب بمنزل سر دنیسن رس بجلسه انجمن ایران رفتم.

پنجشنبه ۱ مهر، ۲۳ سپتامبر - تا پنج بعد از ظهر در کتابخانه هند بودم.

جمعه ۲ مهر، ۲۴ سپتامبر - صبح بکتابخانه هند و شب بمنزل آقای تقی‌زاده رفتم.

شنبه ۳ مهر، ۲۵ سپتامبر - صبح بکتابخانه هند رفتم. شام با فؤاد و خانمش و اتحادیه خوردیم.

یکشنبه ۴ مهر، ۲۶ سپتامبر - با فؤاد روحانی ناهار خوردم. عصر با هم بمنزل لاکهارت رفتیم.

دوشنبه ۵ مهر، ۲۷ سپتامبر - صبح بکتابخانه هند رفتم و شب در رستوران ایطالیایی نزدیک اورلز کورت با فؤاد و خانمش شام خوردم.

سه‌شنبه ۶ مهر، ۲۸ سپتامبر - شب انگلیسی خواندم.

چهارشنبه ۷ مهر، ۲۹ سپتامبر - حالم خوش نیست. با آقای جواد مهین بودم.

پنجشنبه ۸ مهر، ۳۰ سپتامبر - آقای مهین را دیدم. شب با روحانی بودیم.

جمعه ۹ مهر، اول اکتبر - مقدمات سفر پاریس را فراهم کردم. شب با روحانی و خانمش بودم.

شنبه ۱۰ مهر، ۲ اکتبر - با فؤاد و خانمش به ویکتوریا رفتیم. عزت خانم و لعل خانم هم بودند و با ایشان همسفر شدیم. با فؤاد و خانمش به ویکتوریا رفتیم. اسباب را فؤاد باشتباه در ترن گذاشته بود که قبلاً حرکت کرد ولی در دوور آنها را برای ما نگاه داشتند تا رسیدیم. ساعت شش و ده دقیقه بپاریس رسیدیم. عزت خانم اسباب و اثاث را گم کرده بود. عاقبت حمال پیدا کرد.[1] با فؤاد و خانمش در جستجوی هتل بودیم ولی پیدا نشد. حتی در سلکت هتل جا نبود. عاقبت ما سه در هتلی جا پیدا کردیم.

یکشنبه ۱۱ مهر، ۳ اکتبر - صبح بنمایشگاه بین الملل رفتیم. غرفهٔ عراق و ونزوئلا و پرو و مصر و نروژ و اسپانیا را دیدیم. با فؤاد و خانمش در رستوران هنگری غذا خوردیم. ساعت هفت به شان ز لیزه و از آنجا به کوپول[2] رفتیم.

دوشنبه ۱۲ مهر، ۴ اکتبر - بسفارت رفتم. یکتا و دکتر اردلان و نظام را دیدم. در رستوران جواد خان قیمه و چلو کباب و دوغ و خربزه خوردم. بگار سن لازار رفتم. نعیمی به ورسای رفت. با فؤاد در شان ز لیزه گردش کردم. اول شب در شان ز لیزه آقای جزائری را دیدم. باز برستوران جواد خان رفتیم. لعل خانم و عزّت خانم را دیدم. فؤاد و خانمش هم بعد آمدند. با ایشان و جزائری بکافه دو پون رفتیم.

سه‌شنبه ۱۳ مهر، ۵ اکتبر - صبح با روحانی و خانمش بنمایشگاه رفتیم. ناهار در رستوران جواد خان خوردیم. شب با نعیمی بودم.

چهارشنبه ۱۴ مهر، ۶ اکتبر - صبح بنمایشگاه رفتم. نعیمی را هم دیدیم. غرفهٔ بلژیک و ایطالیا را تماشا کردم. شب بمنزل یکتا رفتم. طائر، اردلان و نظام هم بودند.

پنجشنبه ۱۵ مهر، ۷ اکتبر - به بولوار سن میشل رفتم برای خرید کتاب. در رستوران

---

1. شد.
2. La Coupole، رستورانی مشهور در پاریس.

جواد خان غذا خوردیم. شب با فؤاد و خانمش به کاباره رفتم. دخترهایی به صورتی که بدنشان پر از جای انژکسیون بود، می‌رقصیدند. کمی ماندیم و بیرون آمدیم.

جمعه ۱۶ مهر، ۸ اکتبر - با مستر ریزلی در شان ز لیزه گردش کردم. قسمت مستعمرات را دیدم. بدیدن میرزا محمد خان قزوینی رفتم.

شنبه ۱۷ مهر، ۹ اکتبر - در منزل طائر ناهار خوردم. معاونی، انتظام، نظام و یکتا و خانمش و اردلان بودند. کتابچی خان هم بود. شام در رستوران جواد خان خوردم.

یکشنبه ۱۶ مهر، ۱۰ اکتبر - با فؤاد و خانمش بنمایشگاه رفتم و عصر بمنزل یکتا. نعیمی هم آمد.

دوشنبه ۱۷ مهر، ۱۱ اکتبر - عصر رفتم بمنزل مهیمن. نعیمی هم بود. شب بمنزل آقایی رفتم. خوش‌بین و جزائری و یکتا هم بودند.

سه‌شنبه ۲۰ مهر، ۱۲ اکتبر - فؤاد و خانمش و نعیمی به بروکسل رفتند. ناهار در منزل مادر معاونی خوردم. اردلان، نظام، انتظام، طائر، و یکتا هم بودند. هتل ما در کوچهٔ کنوانسیون است.

چهارشنبه ۲۱ مهر، ۱۳ اکتبر - صبح بهتل تراس هتل در خیابان گراند آرمه رفتم. عصر با عباس اقبال بودم.

پنجشنبه ۲۲ مهر، ۱۴ اکتبر - خوش‌بین را دیدم. شب بمنزل کتابچی خان رفتم. انتظام هم بود. باکتابچی خان و انتظام و زن کتابچی و پسرش بتآتر ساعت ده رفتم. خوب بود.

جمعه ۲۳ مهر، ۱۵ اکتبر - در رستوران جواد خان ناهار خوردم.

شنبه ۲۴ مهر، ۱۶ اکتبر - در رستوران جواد خان ناهار خوردم. انتظام و رضوی را هم دیدم. عصر بنمایشگاه رفتم و در همان جا شام خوردم.

یکشنبه ۲۵ مهر، ۱۷ اکتبر - نزدیک ظهر از ایستگاه حرکت کردم. سه و نیم بعد از ظهر بکاله رسیدم و هفت و نیم بعد از ظهر بلندن.

دوشنبه ۲۶ مهر، ۱۸ اکتبر - با نبیل ناهار خوردم. شب انگلیسی خواندم.

سه‌شنبه ۲۷ مهر، ۱۹ اکتبر - سر دنیسن رس برای انجمن ایران نطق کرد: نثر فارسی. چندان خوب نبود. با مینوی شام خوردم.

چهارشنبه ۲۸ مهر، ۲۰ اکتبر - آقای خوش‌کیش را دیدم.

پنجشنبه ۲۹ مهر، ۲۱ اکتبر - خوش‌کیش را دیدم. عصر بمنزل پروفسور وبستر رفتم.

جمعه ۳۰ مهر، ۲۲ اکتبر - بمدرسهٔ اقتصاد بدیدن وبستر رفتم و شب بمنزل آقای تقی‌زاده.

شنبه ۱ آبان، ۲۳ اکتبر - با نبیل ناهار خوردم. فیلم عبدالحمید ملعون را دیدم.

یکشنبه ۲ آبان، ۲۴ اکتبر - با مینوی بودم.

دوشنبه ۳ آبان، ۲۵ اکتبر - کتاب خواندم.

سه‌شنبه ۴ آبان، ۲۶ اکتبر - انگلیسی خواندم.

چهارشنبه ۵ آبان، ۲۷ اکتبر - کتاب خواندم.

پنجشنبه ۶ آبان، ۲۸ اکتبر - کار کردم و انگلیسی خواندم.

جمعه ۷ آبان، ۲۹ اکتبر - بمشایعت زرین‌کفش و خانمش که بپاریس می‌رفتند به ویکتوریا رفتم. شب انگلیسی خواندم و مقدمات تز انگلیسی را نوشتم.

شنبه ۸ آبان، ۳۰ اکتبر - عصر بمنزل آقای تقی‌زاده رفتم. آقای علی‌آبادی و سهیلی هم بودند.

یکشنبه ۹ آبان، ۳۱ اکتبر - با نبیل بودم و مدتی با آرام.

دوشنبه ۱۰ آبان، ۱ نوامبر - حالم خوش نیست. کار کردم و کتاب خواندم.

سه‌شنبه ۱۱ آبان، ۲ نوامبر - کتاب خواندم.

چهارشنبه ۱۲ آبان، ۳ نوامبر - شب در خانه بودم و کار کردم.

پنجشنبه ۱۳ آبان، ۴ نوامبر - عصر بمنزل وبستر رفتم.

جمعه ۱۴ آبان، ۵ نوامبر - شب بمنزل آقای تقی‌زاده رفتم.

شنبه ۱۵ آبان، ۶ نوامبر - کتاب خواندم.

یکشنبه ۱۶ آبان، ۷ نوامبر - با نبیل در رستوران هندی غذا خوردیم.

دوشنبه ۱۷ آبان، ۸ نوامبر - شب انگلیسی خواندم.

سه‌شنبه ۱۸ آبان، ۹ نوامبر - بکتابخانه وزارت هند رفتم.

چهارشنبه ۱۹ آبان، ۱۰ نوامبر - با مایلز به بیرمنگام بدیدن محصلین رفتم. احمد ارشد را هم در مریضخانه دیدیم که حالش خوب نیست. شب طالقانی و مرندی دو نفر از محصلین با ما شام خوردند.

پنجشنبه ۲۰ آبان، ۱۱ نوامبر - با مایلز بلندن آمدیم. شب انگلیسی خواندم.

جمعه ۲۱ آبان، ۱۲ نوامبر - بکتابخانه وزارت هند رفتم.

شنبه ۲۲ آبان، ۱۳ نوامبر - شب انگلیسی خواندم.

یکشنبه ۲۳ آبان، ۱۴ نوامبر - با نبیل بودم.

دوشنبه ۲۴ آبان، ۱۵ نوامبر - با مینوی و جزائری بودم.

سه‌شنبه ۲۵ آبان، ۱۶ نوامبر - به بریتیش میوزیم رفتم.

چهارشنبه ۲۶ آبان، ۱۷ نوامبر - به بریتیش میوزیم رفتم.

پنجشنبه ۲۷ آبان، ۱۸ نوامبر - ناهار با جزائری خوردم. عصر بمنزل وبستر رفتم.

جمعه ۲۸ آبان، ۱۹ نوامبر - کتاب خواندم.

شنبه ۲۹ آبان، ۲۰ نوامبر - ناهار با نبیل و پناهی و خانمش خوردم. شب با مستر مک رو در اطاق میس کاتن بودم که نامزد < یک > فرانسوی اهل جزیره موریس است.

یکشنبه ۳۰ آبان، ۲۱ نوامبر - با مینوی بودم.

دوشنبه ۱ آذر، ۲۲ نوامبر - بکتابخانه وزارت هند رفتم.

سه‌شنبه ۲ آذر، ۲۳ نوامبر - با جزائری در منزل زرین‌کفش شام خوردم.

چهارشنبه ۳ آذر، ۲۴ نوامبر - انگلیسی خواندم.

پنجشنبه ۴ آذر، ۲۵ نوامبر - بکتابخانه وزارت هند رفتم.

جمعه ۵ آذر، ۲۶ نوامبر - کتاب خواندم.

شنبه ۶ آذر، ۲۷ نوامبر - برای یک فرانسوی که می‌خواهد در باب ایران رمانی بنویسد، چیزی نوشتم.

یکشنبه ۷ آذر، ۲۸ نوامبر - با نبیل در رستوران اسپانیایی غذا خوردم.

دوشنبه ۸ آذر، ۲۹ نوامبر - با هژیر و نبیل شام خوردم.

سه‌شنبه ۹ آذر، ۳۰ نوامبر - با جزائری ناهار خوردم.

چهارشنبه ۱۰ آذر، ۱ دسامبر - ناهار با هژیر بودم. شام هم با او خوردم. عصر بخانه وبستر رفتم.

پنجشنبه ۱۱ آذر، ۲ دسامبر - در عمارت شرکت شل فیلمی که شرکت نفت ایران و انگلیس درست کرده است < را > دیدم. با جزائری ناهار خوردم.

جمعه ۱۲ آذر، ۳ دسامبر - با هژیر در سفارت بودم. سهیلی، خانمش و خواهرزنش و نبیل هم بودند.

شنبه ۱۳ آذر، ۴ دسامبر - با هژیر ناهار خوردم و شب هم با او بمنزل تقی‌زاده رفتم و بعد هم بماربل آرچ رفتم. قریب یک ساعت بر سر مستشرقین بحث می‌کردیم.

یکشنبه ۱۴ آذر، ۵ دسامبر - با هژیر بودم.

دوشنبه ۱۵ آذر، ۶ دسامبر - بکتابخانه هند رفتم. شام با هژیر و مینوی خوردم.

سه‌شنبه ۱۶ آذر، ۷ دسامبر - کتاب خواندم.

چهارشنبه ۱۷ آذر، ۸ دسامبر - بدیوان اسناد رفتم. انگلیسی خواندم.

پنجشنبه ۱۸ آذر، ۹ دسامبر - بدیوان اسناد رفتم. عصر با هژیر بودم. با هم شام خوردیم.

جمعه ۱۹ آذر، ۱۰ دسامبر - بدیوان اسناد رفتم. شام در منزل زرین‌کفش خوردم. هژیر و سهیلی و زنش و خواهرزنش و نبیل هم بودند.

شنبه ۲۰ آذر، ۱۱ دسامبر - بدیوان اسناد رفتم و ناهار و شام با هژیر بودم.

یکشنبه ۲۱ آذر، ۱۲ دسامبر - در خانه کار می‌کردم. بعد از ظهر با هژیر و مینوی به ریچموند رفتیم.

دوشنبه ۲۲ آذر، ۱۳ دسامبر - بدیوان اسناد رفتم. شب کار کردم و انگلیسی خواندم و چیز نوشتم.

***[1]**

شنبه ۱۱ دی، ۱ ژانویه - عصر با هژیر بمنزل آقای تقی‌زاده رفتم.

یکشنبه ۱۲ دی، ۲ ژانویه - ناهار با هژیر و مینوی رفتم.

دوشنبه ۱۳ دی، ۳ ژانویه - در دیوان اسناد کار کردم.

سه‌شنبه ۱۴ دی، ۴ ژانویه - در دیوان اسناد کار کردم. شب با هژیر بودم.

چهارشنبه ۱۵ دی، ۵ ژانویه - در دیوان اسناد کار کردم و شب با هژیر بودم.

پنجشنبه ۱۶ دی، ۶ ژانویه - روز در دیوان اسناد و شب با هژیر بودم.

جمعه ۱۷ دی، ۷ ژانویه - روز در دیوان اسناد و شب با هژیر بودم.

شنبه ۱۸ دی، ۸ ژانویه - صبح در دیوان اسناد کار کردم. بعد از ظهر با مینوی و هژیر ببرج لندن رفتم.

یکشنبه ۱۹ دی، ۹ ژانویه - شب با پناهی و زنش و نبیل بمنزل نصیرزاده رفتم. وهاب‌زاده هم بود.

دوشنبه ۲۰ دی، ۱۰ ژانویه - بدیوان اسناد رفتم. آقای علی اکبر بینا را دیدم. با او ناهار خوردم. شب با هژیر بودم.

سه‌شنبه ۲۱ دی، ۱۱ ژانویه - برای دیدن فیلم فارسی بشرکت شل رفتم. شب با هژیر بودم.

---

۱. از ۲۲ آذر تا ۱۱ دی مدخلی نوشته نشده است.

چهارشنبه ۲۲ دی، ۱۲ ژانویه - برای هژیر خرید کردم. با او بودم.

پنجشنبه ۲۳ دی، ۱۳ ژانویه - برای پر کردن صفحه مربوط بفیلم به شفردذ بوش[1] رفتم. عصر بمنزل وبستر رفتم. شب با هژیر بودم.

جمعه ۲۴ دی، ۱۴ ژانویه - در دیوان اسناد کار کردم. با هژیر بودم.

شنبه ۲۵ دی، ۱۵ ژانویه - صبح بدیوان اسناد رفتم و ناهار بمنزل پناهی. هژیر و نبیل هم بودند. شب با نبیل و هژیر بمنزل سرداری رفتیم و تا چهار بعد از نصف شب در آنجا بودیم.

یکشنبه ۲۶ دی، ۱۶ ژانویه - با نبیل بودم.

دوشنبه ۲۷ دی، ۱۷ ژانویه - صبح بکتابخانه هند و عصر بمجلس نطق بزیل گری راجع بمینیاتورهای ایران رفتم. شام با هژیر و نبیل خوردم.

سه‌شنبه ۲۸ دی، ۱۸ ژانویه - به پورت لند هتل رفتم. تا ده و نیم با صورتگر بودم.

چهارشنبه ۲۹ دی، ۱۹ ژانویه - بدیوان اسناد رفتم. با مهدوی و بینا و شیبانی بودم.

پنجشنبه ۳۰ دی، ۲۰ ژانویه - بدیوان اسناد رفتم. شب کتاب خواندم.

جمعه ۱ بهمن، ۲۱ ژانویه - بدیوان اسناد رفتم. شب انگلیسی خواندم و چیز نوشتم.

شنبه ۲ بهمن، ۲۲ ژانویه - در دیوان اسناد کار کردم.

یکشنبه ۳ بهمن، ۲۳ ژانویه - کتاب خواندم.

دوشنبه ۴ بهمن، ۲۴ ژانویه - بدیوان اسناد رفتم. شب انگلیسی خواندم و تز نوشتم.

---

۱. Shepherd's Bush، محله‌ای در غرب لندن.

سه‌شنبه ۵ بهمن، ۲۵ ژانویه - بدیوان اسناد رفتم. شب انگلیسی خواندم.

چهارشنبه ۶ بهمن، ۲۶ ژانویه - صبح بدیوان اسناد رفتم. شب به ساووی هتل رفتم و فیلم فارسی راجع بایران را نشان می‌دادند. سهیلی و اعضای سفارت بودند.

پنجشنبه ۷ بهمن، ۲۷ ژانویه - عصر بمنزل وبستر رفتم.

جمعه ۸ بهمن، ۲۸ ژانویه - عصر بمنزل آقای تقی‌زاده رفتم. آقای هژیر و آقای سهیلی هم آمدند.

شنبه ۹ بهمن، ۲۹ ژانویه - بدیوان اسناد رفتم. شب با هژیر بودم.

یکشنبه ۱۰ بهمن، ۳۰ ژانویه - شب با هژیر بمنزل زرین‌کفش رفتم. سهیلی و زن و خواهرزنش و قدس و آرام هم بودند.

دوشنبه ۱۱ بهمن، ۳۱ ژانویه - صبح بدیوان اسناد رفتم.

سه‌شنبه ۱۲ بهمن، ۱ فوریه - بمشایعت هژیر که ببرلن رفت، بویکتوریا رفتم. شب انگلیسی خواندم.

چهارشنبه ۱۳ بهمن، ۲ فوریه - بدیوان اسناد رفتم. شب تز نوشتم و انگلیسی خواندم.

پنجشنبه ۱۴ بهمن، ۳ فوریه - بدیوان اسناد رفتم. شب تز نوشتم.

جمعه ۱۵ بهمن، ۴ فوریه - بدیوان اسناد رفتم. شب انگلیسی خواندم.

شنبه ۱۶ بهمن، ۵ فوریه - در دیوان اسناد کار کردم.

یکشنبه ۱۷ بهمن، ۶ فوریه - کتاب خواندم.

دوشنبه ۱۸ بهمن، ۷ فوریه - بدیوان اسناد رفتم. شب انگلیسی خواندم.

سه‌شنبه ۱۹ بهمن، ۸ فوریه - بدیوان اسناد رفتم و عصر بمنزل بزیل گری.

چهارشنبه ۲۰ بهمن، ۹ فوریه - بدیوان اسناد رفتم. شب انگلیسی خواندم و تز نوشتم.

پنجشنبه ۲۱ بهمن، ۱۰ فوریه - بدیوان اسناد رفتم. شب انگلیسی خواندم و تز نوشتم.

جمعه ۲۲ بهمن، ۱۱ فوریه - بدیوان اسناد رفتم. شب تز نوشتم.

شنبه ۲۳ بهمن، ۱۲ فوریه - تز نوشتم.

یکشنبه ۲۴ بهمن، ۱۳ فوریه - با نبیل بودم.

دوشنبه ۲۵ بهمن، ۱۴ فوریه - بدیوان اسناد رفتم. تز نوشتم.

سه‌شنبه ۲۶ بهمن، ۱۵ فوریه - شب در منزل زرین‌کفش بودم. سهیلی هم بود.

چهارشنبه ۲۷ بهمن، ۱۶ فوریه - بدیوان اسناد رفتم. تز نوشتم.

پنجشنبه ۲۸ بهمن، ۱۷ فوریه - بمنزل وبستر رفتم. با صوفت همدرس مصری خود شام خوردم. کاغذی بخلخالی نوشتم.

جمعه ۲۹ بهمن، ۱۸ فوریه - صبح بدیوان اسناد و شب بمنزل آقای تقی‌زاده رفتم.

شنبه ۳۰ بهمن، ۱۹ فوریه - بدیوان اسناد رفتم.

یکشنبه ۱ اسفند، ۲۰ فوریه - با نبیل بودم.

دوشنبه ۲ اسفند، ۲۱ فوریه - شب تز نوشتم.

سه‌شنبه ۳ اسفند، ۲۲ فوریه - بدیوان اسناد رفتم و شب نطق پروفسور نیکلسن را شنیدم.

چهارشنبه ۴ اسفند، ۲۳ فوریه - بدیوان اسناد رفتم. شب تز نوشتم.

پنجشنبه ۵ اسفند، ۲۴ فوریه - بدیوان اسناد رفتم. شب تز نوشتم.

جمعه ۶ اسفند، ۲۵ فوریه - بدیوان اسناد رفتم.

شنبه ۷ اسفند، ۲۶ فوریه - با نبیل بودم.

یکشنبه ۸ اسفند، ۲۷ فوریه - با نبیل بودم.

دوشنبه ۹ اسفند، ۲۸ فوریه - بدیوان اسناد رفتم. حالم چندان خوب نیست.

سه‌شنبه ۱۰ اسفند، ۱ مارس - بدیوان اسناد رفتم.

چهارشنبه ۱۱ اسفند، ۲ مارس - بدیوان اسناد رفتم.

پنجشنبه ۱۲ اسفند، ۳ مارس - عصر بمنزل وبستر رفتم.

جمعه ۱۳ اسفند، ۴ مارس - بدیوان اسناد رفتم و شب بمنزل آقای تقی‌زاده.

شنبه ۱۴ اسفند، ۵ مارس - بدیوان اسناد رفتم. شب در منزل آقای زرین‌کفش بودم. آقای صفوی هم بود.

یکشنبه ۱۵ اسفند، ۶ مارس - کتاب خواندم.

دوشنبه ۱۶ اسفند، ۷ مارس - بدیوان اسناد رفتم. کاغذی بپدرم نوشتم.

سه‌شنبه ۱۷ اسفند، ۸ مارس - بدیوان اسناد رفتم. شب دندانم سخت درد گرفت. نتوانستم بخوابم.

چهارشنبه ۱۸ اسفند، ۹ مارس - بدیوان اسناد رفتم اما بعد از ده دقیقه کار کردن دندان

درد بی‌تابم کرد. رفتم بمنزل زرین‌کفش. کارم داشت. شب هم در آن جا خوابیدم. خیلی بد گذشت.

پنجشنبه ۱۹ اسفند، ۱۰ مارس - با زرین‌کفش نزد دندانساز رفتم. دندانم را کشید. بعد کار کردم. حالم هیچ خوب نیست.

جمعه ۲۰ اسفند، ۱۱ مارس - حالم خوب نیست. شب انگلیسی خواندم.

شنبه ۲۱ اسفند، ۱۲ مارس - صبح زرین‌کفش بعیادتم آمد. بعد از ظهر حالم بهتر شد. انگلیسی خواندم.

یکشنبه ۲۲ اسفند، ۱۳ مارس - بمنزل زرین‌کفش رفتم. ناهار در آن جا خوردم.

دوشنبه ۲۳ اسفند، ۱۴ مارس - شب تز نوشتم.

سه‌شنبه ۲۴ اسفند، ۱۵ مارس - شب بسفارت رفتم. مهمانی بود.

چهارشنبه ۲۵ اسفند، ۱۶ مارس - مختصری از تز برای وبستر نوشتم. عصر بدیدن فیلم اسنو وایت[1] رفتم. انگلیسی خواندم.

پنجشنبه ۲۶ اسفند، ۱۷ مارس - عصر بمنزل وبستر رفتم.

جمعه ۲۷ اسفند، ۱۸ مارس - انگلیسی خواندم.

شنبه ۲۸ اسفند، ۱۹ مارس - نزد دندان‌ساز رفتم. دندانم را پاک کرد. آرامم کرد. عصر به کریستال پالاس رفتم. شب انگلیسی خواندم.

یکشنبه ۲۹ اسفند، ۲۰ مارس - صبح انگلیسی خواندم. ناهار با نبیل خوردم.

---

[1]. *Snow White and the Seven Dwarfs*، محصول ۱۹۳۷ آمریکا.

دوشنبه ۱ فروردین، ۲۱ مارس - صبح انگلیسی خواندم. ناهار در منزل زرین‌کفش خوردم. بعد با او و صفوی و رضا خان و خانم زرین‌کفش بسفارت رفتم. تا ساعت ۷ در آنجا بودم. شب با نبیل بودم.

سه‌شنبه ۲ فروردین، ۲۲ مارس - بدیوان اسناد رفتم. شب انگلیسی خواندم.

چهارشنبه ۳ فروردین، ۲۳ مارس - بدیوان اسناد رفتم. شب انگلیسی خواندم.

پنجشنبه ۴ فروردین، ۲۴ مارس - شب بمنزل نصیرزاده رفتم. خسروشاهی، پناهی، < و > قدس هم بودند.

جمعه ۵ فروردین، ۲۵ مارس - بدیوان اسناد رفتم. شب انگلیسی خواندم.

شنبه ۶ فروردین، ۲۶ مارس - بدیوان اسناد رفتم. شب انگلیسی خواندم.

یکشنبه ۷ فروردین، ۲۷ مارس - انگلیسی خواندم.

دوشنبه ۸ فروردین، ۲۸ مارس - بدیوان اسناد رفتم.

سه‌شنبه ۹ فروردین، ۲۹ مارس - کتاب خواندم.

چهارشنبه ۱۰ فروردین، ۳۰ مارس - در دیوان اسناد کار کردم. شب انگلیسی خواندم.

پنجشنبه ۱۱ فروردین، ۳۱ مارس - شب بمنزل پناهی رفتم و قدس و نبیل و وهاب‌زاده و آرام و حمزاوی هم بودند.

جمعه ۱۲ فروردین، ۱ آوریل - انگلیسی خواندم.

شنبه ۱۳ فروردین، ۲ آوریل - بدیوان اسناد رفتم.

یکشنبه ۱۴ فروردین، ۳ آوریل - هیچ حالم خوب نبود. تب داشتم و درد. تا صبح نخوابیدم.

دوشنبه ۱۵ فروردین، ۴ آوریل - بزرین‌کفش تلفون کردم که نمی‌توانم باداره بیایم. سرماخوردگی عجیب داشتم.

سه‌شنبه ۱۶ فروردین، ۵ آوریل - حالم بسیار بد بود. صبح از خانه بیرون نرفتم.

چهارشنبه ۱۷ فروردین، ۶ آوریل - طبیب آمد. زرین‌کفش هم بعیادتم آمد.

پنجشنبه ۱۸ فروردین، ۷ آوریل - سرفه سخت دارم.

جمعه ۱۹ فروردین، ۸ آوریل - حالم بد است.

شنبه ۲۰ فروردین، ۹ آوریل - سرفه‌ام کمی بهتر شده ولی حالم خوب نیست.

یکشنبه ۲۱ فروردین، ۱۰ آوریل - از رختخواب بیرون نمی‌توانم بیایم. حالم خوب نیست.

دوشنبه ۲۲ فروردین، ۱۱ آوریل - حالم کمی بهتر شده.

سه‌شنبه ۲۳ فروردین، ۱۲ آوریل - کمی حالم بهتر است. عصر حدود نیم ساعت بیرون رفتم.

چهارشنبه ۲۴ فروردین، ۱۳ آوریل - حالم بهتر است. کتاب خواندم.

پنجشنبه ۲۵ فروردین، ۱۴ آوریل - کتاب خواندم.

جمعه ۲۶ فروردین، ۱۵ آوریل - کتاب خواندم.

شنبه ۲۷ فروردین، ۱۶ آوریل - کتاب خواندم.

یکشنبه ۲۸ فروردین، ۱۷ آوریل - در منزل زرین‌کفش ناهار خوردم. خود زرین‌کفش بفرانسه رفته است. آقای محمود قزل ایاغ و خانمش را دیدم.

دوشنبه ۲۹ فروردین، ۱۸ آوریل - کتاب خواندم.

سه‌شنبه ۳۰ فروردین، ۱۹ آوریل - بکتابخانه هند رفتم. عصر میرزا علی آقای یزدی و پسرش را دیدم.

چهارشنبه ۳۱ فروردین، ۲۰ آوریل - بکتابخانه وزارت هند رفتم.

پنجشنبه ۱ اردیبهشت، ۲۱ آوریل - بدیدن میرزا علی آقا رفتم. شام با نبیل بودم.

جمعه ۲ اردیبهشت، ۲۲ آوریل - بکتابخانه وزارت هند رفتم.

شنبه ۳ اردیبهشت، ۲۳ آوریل - بکتابخانه وزارت هند رفتم. عصر دکتر احتشام بدیدنم آمد.

یکشنبه ۴ اردیبهشت، ۲۴ آوریل - با نبیل بودم.

دوشنبه ۵ اردیبهشت، ۲۵ آوریل - در سفارت با سهیلی و سهرابی بودم. شب اسامی کتب مربوط به تز را مرتب کردم.

سه‌شنبه ۶ اردیبهشت، ۲۶ آوریل - بکتابخانه وزارت هند رفتم. شب بمنزل پناهی رفتم. دکتر نخعی و سهرابی و قدس هم بودند.

چهارشنبه ۷ اردیبهشت، ۲۷ آوریل - یک فصل از تز را شب پاکنویس کردم.

پنجشنبه ۸ اردیبهشت، ۲۸ آوریل - صبح بکتابخانه هند و عصر بمنزل وبستر رفتم.

جمعه ۹ اردیبهشت، ۲۹ آوریل - بمدرسه اقتصاد رفتم. وبستر را دیدم. مدت تز را یک سال تمدید کردم. شب انگلیسی خواندم.

شنبه ۱۰ اردیبهشت، ۳۰ آوریل - بکتابخانه وزارت هند رفتم. شب انگلیسی خواندم و تز نوشتم.

یکشنبه ۱۱ اردیبهشت، ۱ مه - در منزل زرین‌کفش ناهار خوردم. شب انگلیسی خواندم و تز نوشتم.

دوشنبه ۱۲ اردیبهشت، ۲ مه - سهیلی بطهران احضار شده. ناهار با مهدوی بودم. شب انگلیسی خواندم.

سه‌شنبه ۱۳ اردیبهشت، ۳ مه - با مهدوی ناهار خوردم. شب انگلیسی خواندم.

چهارشنبه ۱۴ اردیبهشت، ۴ مه - بکتابخانه وزارت هند رفتم. انگلیسی خواندم.

پنجشنبه ۱۵ اردیبهشت، ۵ مه - شب بمنزل آقای تقی‌زاده رفتم.

جمعه ۱۶ اردیبهشت، ۶ مه - صبح بکتابخانه وزارت هند و عصر بمجلس نطق اسکات راجع بسفرش در نواحی بحر خزر با بحریه جغرافیایی رفتم.

شنبه ۱۷ اردیبهشت، ۷ مه - بکتابخانه هند رفتم. شب انگلیسی خواندم.

یکشنبه ۱۸ اردیبهشت، ۸ مه - کتاب خواندم.

دوشنبه ۱۹ اردیبهشت، ۹ مه - شب با قدس و نخعی و نبیل در منزل زرین‌کفش شام خوردم.

سه‌شنبه ۲۰ اردیبهشت، ۱۰ مه - صبح انگلیسی خواندم و بعد بوزارت هند رفتم. شب مهمان نبیل بودم در رستوران هندی. سهیلی، صورتگر، و اعضای سفارت بودند.

چهارشنبه ۲۱ اردیبهشت، ۱۱ مه - صبح انگلیسی خواندم. عصر بسفارت رفتم. اغلب ایرانیهای مقیم لندن برای خداحافظی آمده بودند. هژیر از پاریس رسید. شام با هم خوردیم.

پنجشنبه ۲۲ اردیبهشت، ۱۲ مه - با هژیر بودم. برای مشایعت سهیلی و قدس که بایران می‌رفتند بایستگاه ویکتوریا رفتم. بعد با هژیر بخیاطی رفتم. چندین لباس خریدم. عصر بهتل ریتز بمجلس مهمانی که بمناسبت ولادت پیغمبر بود، رفتم و شب به کوادرنت رستوران مهمانی بمناسبت جشن بود.

جمعه ۲۳ اردیبهشت، ۱۳ مه - با هژیر بودم. عصر بمنزل وبستر رفتم. شام با هژیر بودم.

شنبه ۲۴ اردیبهشت، ۱۴ مه - با هژیر بودم.

یکشنبه ۲۵ اردیبهشت، ۱۵ مه - با سهرابی و نبیل بحوالی قصر وین‌زُر رفتم. در همان جا ناهار خوردیم. شام با هژیر بمنزل زرین‌کفش رفتیم. دکتر حافظی هم بود.

دوشنبه ۲۶ اردیبهشت، ۱۶ مه - با هژیر بودم.

سه‌شنبه ۲۷ اردیبهشت، ۱۷ مه - با هژیر بودم.

چهارشنبه ۲۸ اردیبهشت، ۱۸ مه - با هژیر بودم. شب با هم بمنزل آقای تقی‌زاده رفتیم.

پنجشنبه ۲۹ اردیبهشت، ۱۹ مه - با هژیر بودم. با هم بلندن کازینو رفتیم.

جمعه ۳۰ اردیبهشت، ۲۰ مه - با هژیر بودم. شب انگلیسی خواندم.

شنبه ۳۱ اردیبهشت، ۲۱ مه - عصر با هژیر به همتون کورت و شب بمنزل زرین‌کفش رفتم.

یکشنبه ۱ خرداد، ۲۲ مه - صبح انگلیسی خواندم. با نبیل و هژیر به گریت فوستر هتل رفتیم. خوش گذشت. شب هم با هژیر و نبیل بودم.

دوشنبه ۲ خرداد، ۲۳ مه - با هژیر بودم. شب با هم اول بمنزل آقای تقی‌زاده و بعد بمنزل زرین‌کفش رفتم.

سه‌شنبه ۳ خرداد، ۲۴ مه - بمشایعت هژیر به ویکتوریا رفتم. نبیل هم بود. شب با نبیل و پناهی و زنش و وهاب‌زاده در رستوران ارمنی که غذای شرقی دارد، در شافتزبری او نی‌یو شام خوردم.

چهارشنبه ۴ خرداد، ۲۵ مه - بوزارت هند و مدرسه اقتصاد رفتم. شب انگلیسی خواندم.

پنجشنبه ۵ خرداد، ۲۶ مه - عصر بمنزل وبستر رفتم. شب انگلیسی خواندم.

جمعه ۶ خرداد، ۲۷ مه - صبح بکتابخانه وزارت هند رفتم. شب در مهمانی سفارت بودم. صورتگر، زرین‌کفش، و وهاب‌زاده هم بودند.

شنبه ۷ خرداد، ۲۸ مه - بکتابخانه هند رفتم. شب انگلیسی خواندم.

یکشنبه ۸ خرداد، ۲۹ مه - صبح انگلیسی خواندم. شب با نبیل شام خوردم.

دوشنبه ۹ خرداد، ۳۰ مه - صبح بکتابخانه وزارت هند و شب بمهمانی سفارت رفتم.

سه‌شنبه ۱۰ خرداد، ۳۱ مه - صبح انگلیسی خواندم. شب کتاب خواندم.

چهارشنبه ۱۱ خرداد، ۱ ژوئن - در کتابخانه هند بودم.

پنجشنبه ۱۲ خرداد، ۲ ژوئن - در کتابخانه هند بودم.

جمعه ۱۳ خرداد، ۳ ژوئن - در کتابخانه وزارت هند بودم.

شنبه ۱۴ خرداد، ۴ ژوئن - با نبیل به اولمپیا بدیدن مشقهای نظامی رفتیم.

یکشنبه ۱۵ خرداد، ۵ ژوئن - با نبیل به وین‌زُر رفتم.

دوشنبه ۱۶ خرداد، ۶ ژوئن - با نبیل بودم.

سه‌شنبه ۱۷ خرداد، ۷ ژوئن - بکتابخانه وزارت هند رفتم.

چهارشنبه ۱۸ خرداد، ۸ ژوئن - شب انگلیسی خواندم.

پنجشنبه ۱۹ خرداد، ۹ ژوئن - عصر و شب انگلیسی خواندم.

جمعه ۲۰ خرداد، ۱۰ ژوئن - به کتابخانه هند رفتم. شب بمنزل آقای تقی‌زاده رفتم.

شنبه ۲۱ خرداد، ۱۱ ژوئن - به چسینگ‌تُن زو[1] رفتم. شب انگلیسی خواندم.

یکشنبه ۲۲ خرداد، ۱۲ ژوئن - با نبیل و صورتگر بمنزل داراب خان رفتم.

دوشنبه ۲۳ خرداد، ۱۳ ژوئن - انگلیسی خواندم.

سه‌شنبه ۲۴ خرداد، ۱۴ ژوئن - با مهدوی و صورتگر و مینوی بودم.

چهارشنبه ۲۵ خرداد، ۱۵ ژوئن - بکتابخانه وزارت هند رفتم. شب با آقای مهدوی بودم.

پنجشنبه ۲۶ خرداد، ۱۶ ژوئن - عصر به پُتنی[2] بگردش رفتم. شب انگلیسی خواندم.

جمعه ۲۷ خرداد، ۱۷ ژوئن - شب انگلیسی خواندم.

شنبه ۲۸ خرداد، ۱۸ ژوئن - بکتابخانه هند رفتم. با مهدوی و صورتگر و مینوی ناهار خوردم. شب انگلیسی خواندم.

---

۱. Chessington Zoo در حومه جنوب غربی لندن.

۲. Putney، محله‌ای در جنوب لندن.

یکشنبه ۲۹ خرداد، ۱۹ ژوئن - ناهار در منزل زرین‌کفش و شام با نبیل خوردم.

دوشنبه ۳۰ خرداد، ۲۰ ژوئن - به محل حراج کریستی رفتم. عکس تابلویی که تصویر محمد رضا بیک[1] سفیر ایران و کار واتو[2] می‌باشد، بدست آوردم. شب انگلیسی خواندم.

سه‌شنبه ۳۱ خرداد، ۲۱ ژوئن - عصر در پُتنی گردش کردم. شب انگلیسی خواندم.

چهارشنبه ۱ تیر، ۲۲ ژوئن - بکتابخانه هند رفتم. شب انگلیسی خواندم.

پنجشنبه ۲ تیر، ۲۳ ژوئن - با مهدوی و مینوی در کتابخانه هند بودم. شب با نبیل بودم.

جمعه ۳ تیر، ۲۴ ژوئن - خانوادهٔ زرین‌کفش بفرانسه رفتند. شب انگلیسی خواندم.

شنبه ۴ تیر، ۲۵ ژوئن - بکتابخانه هند رفتم. با مهدوی و مینوی ناهار خوردم. شب انگلیسی خواندم.

یکشنبه ۵ تیر، ۲۶ ژوئن - صبح با نبیل و عصر با مهدوی بودم.

دوشنبه ۶ تیر، ۲۷ ژوئن - صبح بکتابخانه وزارت هند بودم و شب انگلیسی خواندم.

سه‌شنبه ۷ تیر، ۲۸ ژوئن - با مهدی و مینوی ناهار خوردم. شب انگلیسی خواندم.

چهارشنبه ۸ تیر، ۲۹ ژوئن - بکتابخانه وزارت هند رفتم. شب در چلسی گردش کردم و انگلیسی خواندم.

پنجشنبه ۹ تیر، ۳۰ ژوئن - عصر با مینوی و مهدوی بودم. کمرم سخت درد می‌کرد.

---

۱. سفیر شاه سلطان حسین صفوی در فرانسه که پس از مراجعت به ایران بدستور شاه بقتل رسید.

۲. Jean-Antoine Watteau، نقاش و طراح فرانسوی (۱۷۲۱-۱۶۸۴).

جمعه ۱۰ تیر، ۱ ژوئیه - شب بمنزل آقای تقی‌زاده رفتم.

شنبه ۱۱ تیر، ۲ ژوئیه - با مایلز ببیرمنگام رفتم برای حضور در جشن اونیورسیته. باقر مستوفی دیپلم گرفت. شب بلندن آمدم. انگلیسی خواندم.

یکشنبه ۱۲ تیر، ۳ ژوئیه - صبح با مهدوی بودم. مینوی و زنش هم بودند.

دوشنبه ۱۳ تیر، ۴ ژوئیه - شب انگلیسی خواندم و برای تهیه تز کار کردم.

سه‌شنبه ۱۴ تیر، ۵ ژوئیه - صبح در کتابخانه هند و عصر با مهدوی بودم.

چهارشنبه ۱۵ تیر، ۶ ژوئیه - در کتابخانه هند کار کردم. شب انگلیسی خواندم.

پنجشنبه ۱۶ تیر، ۷ ژوئیه - بکتابخانه هند رفتم. شب انگلیسی خواندم.

جمعه ۱۷ تیر، ۸ ژوئیه - شب انگلیسی خواندم.

شنبه ۱۸ تیر، ۹ ژوئیه - بکتابخانه هند رفتم. شب انگلیسی خواندم.

یکشنبه ۱۹ تیر، ۱۰ ژوئیه - شب با نبیل و پناهی و خانمش و وهاب‌زاده بمنزل نصیرزاده رفتم.

دوشنبه ۲۰ تیر، ۱۱ ژوئیه - شب انگلیسی خواندم.

سه‌شنبه ۲۱ تیر، ۱۲ ژوئیه - شب انگلیسی خواندم و صحب در کتابخانه هند بودم.

چهارشنبه ۲۲ تیر، ۱۳ ژوئیه - صبح بکتابخانه هند رفتم. شب انگلیسی خواندم.

پنجشنبه ۲۳ تیر، ۱۴ ژوئیه - صبح بکتابخانه هند رفتم. شب انگلیسی خواندم.

جمعه ۲۴ تیر، ۱۵ ژوئیه - عصر بمجلس نطق مستر شرودر راجع بمساجد ایران رفتم.

شنبه ۲۵ تیر، ۱۶ ژوئیه - صبح بکتابخانه هند رفتم و شب انگلیسی خواندم.

یکشنبه ۲۶ تیر، ۱۷ ژوئیه - صبح انگلیسی خواندم. شب بمنزل آقای تقی‌زاده رفتم و در منزل زرین‌کفش خوابیدم.

دوشنبه ۲۷ تیر، ۱۸ ژوئیه - صبح انگلیسی خواندم. زود بخانه آمدم. عصر با نبیل به گاردن پارتی رفتم. شب انگلیسی خواندم.

سه‌شنبه ۲۸ تیر، ۱۹ ژوئیه - کمرم سخت درد می‌کرد. خیلی نخوابیدم. انگلیسی خواندم.

چهارشنبه ۲۹ تیر، ۲۰ ژوئیه - نزد طبیب رفتم. انگلیسی خواندم. بسیار خسته بودم.

پنجشنبه ۳۰ تیر، ۲۱ ژوئیه - برای دکتر علوی چند کتاب خریدم. با طائر و نبیل و پناهی ناهار خوردم. شب بمنزل آقای تقی‌زاده رفتم.

جمعه ۳۰ مرداد، ۲۲ ژوئیه - با مستر مایلز به نی‌یو آرک بدیدن محصلین رفتم. شب انگلیسی خواندم.

شنبه ۱ مرداد، ۲۳ ژوئیه - با نبیل و طائر رفتم به ایست بورن.[1] شب در ایست بورن ماندم.

یکشنبه ۲ مرداد، ۲۴ ژوئیه - در ایست بورن گردش کردم و از آنجا به فوکس‌تون رفتم. طائر بپاریس رفت. بلندن آمدیم.

دوشنبه ۳ مرداد، ۲۵ ژوئیه - بکتابخانه هند رفتم.

سه‌شنبه ۴ مرداد، ۲۶ ژوئیه - بکتابخانه هند رفتم و اول شب بمشایعت زرین‌کفش در خیابان که بفرانسه می‌رود بایستگاه واترلو.

---

۱. Eastbourne، شهر ساحلی و تفریحی در جنوب شرقی انگلستان.

چهارشنبه ۵ مرداد، ۲۷ ژوئیه - بکتابخانه وزارت هند رفتم.

پنجشنبه ۶ مرداد، ۲۸ ژوئیه - انگلیسی خواندم.

جمعه ۷ مرداد، ۲۹ ژوئیه - شب بدیدن آقای تقی‌زاده رفتم.

شنبه ۸ مرداد، ۳۰ ژوئیه - با مینوی و مهدوی و مستوفی ناهار خوردم.

یکشنبه ۹ مرداد، ۳۱ ژوئیه - صبح انگلیسی خواندم.

دوشنبه ۱۰ مرداد، ۱ اوت - صبح انگلیسی خواندم. ناهار با حمزاوی و پوروالی خوردم. شب انگلیسی خواندم.

سه‌شنبه ۱۱ مرداد، ۲ اوت - صبح انگلیسی خواندم. شب هم انگلیسی خواندم.

چهارشنبه ۱۲ مرداد، ۳ اوت - با مهدوی و مینوی و صورتگر و مستوفی ناهار خوردم. شب به ریچموند رفتم. انگلیسی هم خواندم.

پنجشنبه ۱۳ مرداد، ۴ اوت - با مینوی و مهدوی و مستوفی ناهار خوردم. شب با نبیل و پناهی بمنزل نصیرزاده رفتم.

جمعه ۱۴ مرداد، ۵ اوت - کتاب خواندم.

شنبه ۱۵ مرداد، ۶ اوت - با دکتر صدیق برادر صدیق اعلم ناهار خوردم.

یکشنبه ۱۶ مرداد، ۷ اوت - با نبیل بودم.

دوشنبه ۱۷ مرداد، ۸ اوت - با صورتگر و مهدوی و مینوی و مستوفی ناهار خوردم.

سه‌شنبه ۱۸ مرداد، ۹ اوت - ناهار و شام با مهدوی و مینوی خوردم.

چهارشنبه ۱۹ مرداد، ۱۰ اوت - ناهار با مینوی و مهدوی خوردم. شب انگلیسی خواندم.

پنجشنبه ۲۰ مرداد، ۱۱ اوت - ناهار با مینوی و مهدوی و صورتگر خوردم. شب انگلیسی خواندم.

جمعه ۲۱ مرداد، ۱۲ اوت - بمشایعت مهدوی رفتم. بفرانسه رفت. شب بمنزل آقای تقی‌زاده رفتم.

شنبه ۲۲ مرداد، ۱۳ اوت - بکتابخانه هند رفتم. با مستوفی و صورتگر ناهار خوردم. شب انگلیسی خواندم.

یکشنبه ۲۳ مرداد، ۱۴ اوت - با نبیل در رستوران هندی ناهار خوردم.

دوشنبه ۲۴ مرداد، ۱۵ اوت - شب انگلیسی خواندم.

سه‌شنبه ۲۵ مرداد، ۱۶ اوت - صبح بکتابخانه هند رفتم. ناهار با مینوی و صورتگر و مستوفی خوردم.

چهارشنبه ۲۶ مرداد، ۱۷ اوت - صبح رفتم بکتابخانه هند. با آقای رعدی و آقای پسیان و مستوفی و مینوی و صورتگر ناهار خوردم. شب آقای سجادی بدیدنم آمد. انگلیسی هم خواندم.

پنجشنبه ۲۷ مرداد، ۱۸ اوت - صبح مسیز ریزلی و جان پسرش بدیدنم آمدند. ناهار با مستوفی و مینوی و صورتگر خوردم.

جمعه ۲۸ مرداد، ۱۹ اوت - بکتابخانه هند رفتم.

شنبه ۲۹ مرداد، ۲۰ اوت - با صورتگر و مستوفی و رعدی و مینوی ناهار خوردم.

یکشنبه ۳۰ مرداد، ۲۱ اوت - با نبیل و وهاب‌زاده و زنش به ایست بورن رفتم.

دوشنبه ۳۱ مرداد، ۲۲ اوت - بکتابخانه وزارت هند رفتم. با مینوی و صورتگر و یزدی و مستوفی ناهار خوردم. شب بمنزل جدید مینوی رفتم. رعدی و صورتگر هم بودند.

سه‌شنبه ۱ شهریور، ۲۳ اوت - با مینوی ناهار خوردم. در کتابخانه هند کار کردم.

چهارشنبه ۲ شهریور، ۲۴ اوت - با مینوی و رعدی و صورتگر و پسیان ناهار خوردم. شب انگلیسی خواندم.

پنجشنبه ۳ شهریور، ۲۵ اوت - با مینوی بودم.

جمعه ۴ شهریور، ۲۶ اوت - تمام روز در بریتیش میوزیوم کار کردم. شب بمنزل آقای تقی‌زاده رفتم.

شنبه ۵ شهریور، ۲۷ اوت - با نبیل و آرام به Herne Bay[1] رفتم بدیدن زن سهیلی. در هتل St. George منزل کردم.

یکشنبه ۶ شهریور، ۲۸ اوت - در ساحل دریا گردش کردیم. در موقع مراجعت کلیسای بزرگ کن‌تربری[2] را دیدیم.

دوشنبه ۷ شهریور، ۲۹ اوت - با مینوی ناهار و با رعدی شام خوردم و بعد از شام بمنزل مینوی رفتم.

سه‌شنبه ۸ شهریور، ۳۰ اوت - با رعدی و پسیان و صورتگر چای خوردم. حالم خوب نیست.

---

1. Hearnn Bay
2. Canterbury Cathedral در کنت، مهمترین بنای مسیحی در انگلستان.

چهارشنبه ۹ شهریور، ۳۱ اوت - در بریتیش میوزیوم کار کردم.

پنجشنبه ۱۰ شهریور، ۱ سپتامبر - آقای محمدعلی هدایتی را دیدم. شب با مینوی و زنش بمنزل رعدی رفتیم.

جمعه ۱۱ شهریور، ۲ سپتامبر - در بریتیش میوزیوم بودم. شب در منزل مینوی بودم. ناصر فرهاد معتمد هم آمد.

شنبه ۱۲ شهریور، ۳ سپتامبر - دکتر نفیسی را دیدم.

یکشنبه ۱۳ شهریور، ۴ سپتامبر - در رستوران هندی با نبیل ناهار خوردیم و با قریب شارژه دافر پاریس و زن و دخترش به همتون کورت رفتم. شب با رعدی بودم.

دوشنبه ۱۴ شهریور، ۵ سپتامبر - در بریتیش میوزیوم کار کردم.

سه‌شنبه ۱۵ شهریور، ۶ سپتامبر - در بریتیش میوزیوم کار کردم.

چهارشنبه ۱۶ شهریور، ۷ سپتامبر - در بریتیش میوزیوم کار کردم.

پنجشنبه ۱۷ شهریور، ۸ سپتامبر - در بریتیش میوزیوم کار کردم. با صورتگر و مینوی ناهار خوردم.

جمعه ۱۸ شهریور، ۹ سپتامبر - به کتابخانه بریتیش میوزیوم رفتم. کار کردم و شب برای تز یادداشت کردم.

شنبه ۱۹ شهریور، ۱۰ سپتامبر - در کتابخانه بریتیش میوزیوم کار کردم.

یکشنبه ۲۰ شهریور، ۱۱ سپتامبر - کتاب خواندم.

دوشنبه ۲۱ شهریور، ۱۲ سپتامبر - در کتابخانه بریتیش میوزیوم کار کردم.

سه‌شنبه ۲۲ شهریور، ۱۳ سپتامبر - زرین‌کفش و خانواده‌اش از فرانسه مراجعت کردند.

چهارشنبه ۲۳ شهریور، ۱۴ سپتامبر - در بریتیش میوزیوم کار کردم و شب در خانه کار کردم برای تز.

پنجشنبه ۲۴ شهریور، ۱۵ سپتامبر - در بریتیش میوزیوم کار کردم.

جمعه ۲۵ شهریور، ۱۶ سپتامبر - روز در بریتیش میوزیوم و شب در خانه برای تز کار کردم.

شنبه ۲۶ شهریور، ۱۷ سپتامبر - در بریتیش میوزیوم و در خانه برای تز کار کردم.

یکشنبه ۲۷ شهریور، ۱۸ سپتامبر - صبح در خانه برای تز کار می‌کردم و عصر بمنزل زرین‌کفش رفتم.

دوشنبه ۲۸ شهریور، ۱۹ سپتامبر - صبح در بریتیش میوزیوم کار کردم. امان را در اداره دیدم.

سه‌شنبه ۲۹ شهریور، ۲۰ سپتامبر - به بریتیش میوزیوم رفتم. شب انگلیسی خواندم.

چهارشنبه ۳۰ شهریور، ۲۱ سپتامبر - صبح به اکسفورد رفتم. در نمره ۶۱ لیدی مارگرت هال منزل کردم و بعد بکنفرانس نمایندگان چهاردهمین کنفرانس ثبت و ضبط دفاتر و اوراق. یکی از نمایندگان که پهلوی من نشسته بود میس استایند نام داشت و برادرش در خدمت شرکت نفت ایران در ایرانست.

پنجشنبه ۳۱ شهریور، ۲۱ سپتامبر - ساعت هشت و نیم چاشت خوردم. در مقابلم اکسفورد خوش و خرم نمایان بود. صبح در مجالس کنفرانس حاضر شدم و بعد از ظهر بتماشای کارخانه اتومبیل سازی موریس رفتم. شام به کرایست کالج رفتم.

مهمانی از طرف دولت انگلیس بود و لرد استن هوپ[1] وزیر معارف از طرف دولت پذیرایی کرد.

جمعه ۱ مهر، ۲۳ سپتامبر - در باغ گردش کردم و بتماشای مطبعه اکسفورد یونیورسیتی پرس رفتم و شب ببلدیه اکسفورد. مجلس خوبی بود.

شنبه ۲ مهر، ۲۴ سپتامبر - در کنار رود گردش کردم. بتماشای کتابخانه بودلین رفتم.

یکشنبه ۳ مهر، ۲۵ سپتامبر - بتماشای ولادتگاه شکسپیر رفتم.

دوشنبه ۴ مهر، ۲۶ سپتامبر - بلندن آمدم. اوضاع بین المللی خوب نیست.

سه‌شنبه ۵ مهر، ۲۷ سپتامبر - برای اندازه گرفتن صورت و نقاب ضد گاز به های استریت رفتم. حالت اضطرابی مردم را گرفته است.

چهارشنبه ۶ مهر، ۲۸ سپتامبر - وحشت همه را گرفته است. در رستوران کوچکی نزدیک ایستگاه سنت جیمز ناهار خوردم. همه جنگ را نزدیک می‌بینند. عصر در روزنامه‌ها نوشته که هیتلر تجهیز قشون برای گرفتن ناحیه آلمانی درون چکوسلواکی را ۲۴ ساعت عقب انداخته و قرار است چمبرلن و دالادیه و موسولینی در مونیخ هیتلر را ببینند. مردم کمی امیدوار شده‌اند. شب بدیدن آقای زرین‌کفش و آقای تقی‌زاده رفتم.

پنجشنبه ۷ مهر، ۲۹ سپتامبر - به بریتیش میوزیوم رفتم. یادداشتهای راجع بکتب خطی فرنگی را که برای تز لازم داشتم تمام کردم. ناهار با مینوی و صورتگر و نفیسی خوردم.

جمعه ۸ مهر، ۳۰ سپتامبر - کار کردم برای تز.

---

۱. James Richard Stanhope, 7th Earl Stanhope وزیر در کابینه چمبرلین (۱۸۸۰-۱۹۶۷).

شنبه ۹ مهر، ۱ اکتبر - شب رفتم بسینمای لندن فیلم راجع بایران و یک فیلم دیگر را دیدم.

یکشنبه ۱۰ مهر، ۲ اکتبر - ناهار در منزل زرین‌کفش بودم. آقای تقی‌زاده و خانمش هم بودند.

دوشنبه ۱۱ مهر، ۳ اکتبر - ناهار با مینوی و مستوفی خوردم.

سه‌شنبه ۱۲ مهر، ۴ اکتبر - تمام روز در بریتیش میوزیم کار می‌کردم.

چهارشنبه ۱۳ مهر، ۵ اکتبر - تمام روز در بریتیش میوزیم کار می‌کردم.

پنجشنبه ۱۴ مهر، ۶ اکتبر - تمام روز در بریتیش میوزیم و شب در خانه کار می‌کردم.

جمعه ۱۵ مهر، ۷ اکتبر - تمام روز در بریتیش میوزیم و شب در خانه کار می‌کردم.

شنبه ۱۶ مهر، ۸ اکتبر - با نبیل در رستوران هندی غذا خوردیم. کار کردم.

یکشنبه ۱۷ مهر، ۹ اکتبر - با نبیل بودم.

دوشنبه ۱۸ مهر، ۱۰ اکتبر - در بریتیش میوزیم بودم.

سه‌شنبه ۱۹ مهر، ۱۱ اکتبر - ناهار در منزل زرین‌کفش بودم.

چهارشنبه ۲۰ مهر، ۱۲ اکتبر - در بریتیش میوزیم کار کردم. شب بسینما رفتم. فیلم پیگ‌ملیون[۱] را دیدم.

پنجشنبه ۲۱ مهر، ۳ اکتبر - تمام روز در بریتیش میوزیم و شب در خانه کار کردم.

---

۱. Pygmalion، محصول ۱۹۳۸ بریتانیا بر اساس نمایشنامه‌ای از جرج برنارد شاو.

جمعه ۲۲ مهر، ۴ اکتبر - روز در بریتیش میوزیم و شب در خانه آقای تقی‌زاده بودم.

شنبه ۲۳ مهر، ۱۵ اکتبر - عصر بسفارت افغان رفتم.

یکشنبه ۲۴ مهر، ۱۶ اکتبر - با نبیل بودم.

دوشنبه ۲۵ مهر، ۱۷ اکتبر - تا چهار بعد از ظهر در بریتیش میوزیم کار کردم. بعد با رفیق چینی خود بمنزل وبستر رفتم. شب با صفوت شام خوردم و بعد با هم بکلوب مصریها رفتیم. شب انگلیسی خواندم.

سه‌شنبه ۲۶ مهر، ۱۸ اکتبر - کار کردم برای تز.

چهارشنبه ۲۷ مهر، ۱۹ اکتبر - در بریتیش میوزیم کار کردم. شب کار کردم و کتاب و انگلیسی خواندم.

پنجشنبه ۲۸ مهر، ۲۰ اکتبر - در بریتیش میوزیم کار کردم. شب انگلیسی خواندم.

جمعه ۲۹ مهر، ۲۱ اکتبر - در بریتیش میوزیم کار کرد. عصر با مینوی بمجلس نطق پروفسور تولبت رایس[1] رفتم. در باب هنر ایران در قفقاز نطق کرد.

شنبه ۳۰ مهر، ۲۲ اکتبر - ناهار با مستوفی و چای با فرهاد معتمد خوردم. شب انگلیسی خواندم.

یکشنبه اول آبان، ۲۳ اکتبر - صبح انگلیسی خواندم. با نبیل بودم.

دوشنبه ۲ آبان، ۲۴ آبان - به بریتیش میوزیم رفتم. شب انگلیسی خواندم.

---

۱. David Talbot Rice، باستانشناس و مورخ هنر انگلیسی (۱۹۰۳-۱۹۷۲). در اکتشافات باستانشناختی در آسیای صغیر، ایران (شامل عراق)، و قبرس مشارکت داشت. آثار متعددی در باب ایران و بیزانس منتشر کرد.

سه‌شنبه ۳ آبان، ۲۵ اکتبر - صبح انگلیسی خواندم. بعد به کولین‌دیل[1] رفتم که شعبه بریتیش میوزیم است و در آن روزنامه‌ها و مجلات هست. تا غروب در آنجا کار کردم. شب انگلیسی خواندم.

چهارشنبه ۴ آبان، ۲۶ اکتبر - صبح انگلیسی خواندم. روز در کولین‌دیل کار کردم. روزنامه‌های فرانسه خواندم. شب انگلیسی خواندم.

پنجشنبه ۵ آبان، ۲۷ اکتبر - ناهار با مینوی و صورتگر و مستوفی خوردم. عصر رفتم بمنزل پروفسور وبستر. از آنجا با صفوت رفتم بکلوب مصریها.

جمعه ۶ آبان، ۲۸ اکتبر - بمجلس نطق مستر کِلَپ[2] رفتم. لرد کدمن رئیس مجلس بود.

شنبه ۷ آبان، ۲۹ اکتبر - صبح انگلیسی خواندم و شب فهرست اوراق تز را مرتب می‌کردم.

یکشنبه ۸ آبان، ۳۰ اکتبر - صبح انگلیسی خواندم. ناهار با سردار اکرم خوردم. نبیل و حمزاوی هم بودند.

دوشنبه ۹ آبان، ۳۱ اکتبر - صبح انگلیسی خواندم و تز نوشتم. شب هم تز نوشتم.

سه‌شنبه ۱۰ آبان، ۱ نوامبر - تا سه بعد از ظهر انگلیسی خواندم و تز نوشتم. شب با سردار اکرم بود. هاشم خان آوازه خوان در هتل پیکادلی می‌خواند.

چهارشنبه ۱۱ آبان، ۲ نوامبر - از صبح تا ساعت ۱۱ مشغول تهیه تز بودم.

پنجشنبه ۱۲ آبان، ۳ نوامبر - تمام روز مشغول خواندن انگلیسی و نوشتن تز بودم.

---

۱. Colindale، محله‌ای در حومه شمال غربی لندن.

۲. Frederick Gardner Clapp، زمین‌شناس نفت امریکایی (۱۸۷۹-۱۹۴۴) مشاور زمین‌شناسی شرکت‌های نفتی.

جمعه ۱۳ آبان، ۴ نوامبر - صبح و شب انگلیسی خواندم و کار کردم. عصر با مینوی و صورتگر بودم.

شنبه ۱۴ آبان، ۵ نوامبر - تا ساعت ۱۱ شب برای تز کار کردم و انگلیسی خواندم.

یکشنبه ۱۵ آبان، ۶ نوامبر - برای تز کار کردم. انگلیسی هم خواندم.

دوشنبه ۱۶ آبان، ۷ نوامبر - برای تز کار کردم. انگلیسی خواندم. آقای صدیق و آقای سجادی را هم دیدم.

سه‌شنبه ۱۷ آبان، ۸ نوامبر - آقای طرفه را دیدم. شب کار کردم و تز نوشتم.

چهارشنبه ۱۸ آبان، ۹ نوامبر - انگلیسی خواندم و برای تز کار کردم.

پنجشنبه ۱۹ آبان، ۱۰ نوامبر - با آقای دکتر طرفه بودم. برای تز هم کار کردم.

جمعه ۲۰ آبان، ۱۱ نوامبر - صبح انگلیسی خواندم و برای تز کار کردم. شب بدیدن آقای تقی‌زاده رفتم.

شنبه ۲۱ آبان، ۱۲ نوامبر - شب انگلیسی خواندم. روز بدیدن نمایشگاه کتاب رفتم.

یکشنبه ۲۲ آبان، ۱۳ نوامبر - صبح انگلیسی خواندم. ناهار با نبیل خوردم و عصر با آقای طرفه و مصطفوی بودم.

دوشنبه ۲۳ آبان، ۱۴ نوامبر - بمدرسه اقتصاد رفتم. شب انگلیسی خواندم.

سه‌شنبه ۲۴ آبان، ۱۵ نوامبر - از صبح تا غروب در دیوان اسناد بودم. شب انگلیسی خواندم.

چهارشنبه ۲۵ آبان، ۱۶ نوامبر - در دیوان اسناد کار کردم. شب اوراق فهرست مطالب تز را مرتب کردم.

پنجشنبه ۲۶ آبان، ۱۷ نوامبر - در بریتیش میوزیم کار کردم. شب انگلیسی خواندم و تز نوشتم.

جمعه ۲۷ آبان، ۱۸ نوامبر - در بریتیش میوزیم بودم. شب تز نوشتم و انگلیسی خواندم.

شنبه ۲۸ آبان، ۱۹ نوامبر - در بریتیش میوزیم بودم. شب انگلیسی خواندم و تز نوشتم.

یکشنبه ۲۹ آبان، ۲۰ نوامبر - صبح انگلیسی خواندم. ناهار با نبیل در پیکادلی هتل خوردم. شب انگلیسی خواندم.

دوشنبه ۳۰ آبان، ۲۱ نوامبر - شب انگلیسی خواندم و تز نوشتم.

سه‌شنبه ۱ آذر، ۲۲ نوامبر - در بریتیش میوزیم بودم. شب بمنزل زرین‌کفش رفتم. اصغرزاده و برادرش هم بودند.

چهارشنبه ۲ آذر، ۲۳ نوامبر - تمام روز مشغول نوشتن تز و انگلیسی خواندن بودم. شب بمنزل پناهی رفتم. آرام و نبیل و وحید هم بودند.

پنجشنبه ۳ آذر، ۲۴ نوامبر - تمام روز برای تز کار کردم و انگلیسی خواندم.

جمعه ۴ آذر، ۲۵ نوامبر - برای تز کار کردم و انگلیسی خواندم.

شنبه ۵ آذر، ۲۶ نوامبر - تمام روز کار کردم و تز نوشتم. تا دو ساعت و نیم بعد از نصف شب بیدار بودم و کار کردم.

یکشنبه ۶ آذر، ۲۷ نوامبر - صبح و شب تز نوشتم و کتاب و انگلیسی خواندم.

دوشنبه ۷ آذر، ۲۸ نوامبر - تمام روز تز نوشتم و انگلیسی خواندم.

سه‌شنبه ۸ آذر، ۲۹ نوامبر - تا ساعت ۱۱ شب برای تز کار کردم و انگلیسی خواندم.

چهارشنبه ۹ آذر، ۳۰ نوامبر - حالم چندان خوب نیست. کمی از یادداشتهای تز را برای وبستر ماشین کردم.

پنجشنبه ۱۰ آذر، ۱ دسامبر - عصر بمنزل وبستر رفتم و شب با صفوت بکلوب مصریها.

جمعه ۱۱ آذر، ۲ دسامبر - روز در بریتیش میوزیم و شب در خانه برای تز کار کردم. انگلیسی خواندم.

شنبه ۱۲ آذر، ۳ دسامبر - در بریتیش میوزیم بودم. کمر درد سخت داشتم. نتوانستم کار کنم.

یکشنبه ۱۳ آذر، ۴ دسامبر - صبح انگلیسی خواندم. شب بسفارت بمهمانی آرام رفتم. پناهی و نبیل و وهاب‌زاده هم بودند.

دوشنبه ۱۴ آذر، ۵ دسامبر - روز و شب کار کردم و تز نوشتم و انگلیسی خواندم.

سه‌شنبه ۱۵ آذر، ۶ دسامبر - تا ۱۱ بعد از ظهر کار کردم و انگلیسی خواندم.

چهارشنبه ۱۶ آذر، ۷ دسامبر - حتی وقت روزنامه خواندن ندارم. تا یازده و نیم تز نوشتم و انگلیسی خواندم.

پنجشنبه ۱۷ آذر، ۸ دسامبر - تمام روز کار کردم. انگلیسی خواندم و تز نوشتم.

جمعه ۱۸ آذر، ۹ دسامبر - صبح تز نوشتم و انگلیسی خواندم. عصر بمنزل وبستر رفتم و شب بمنزل آقای تقی‌زاده.

شنبه ۱۹ آذر، ۱۰ دسامبر - تمام روز و شب انگلیسی خواندم و تز نوشتم.

یکشنبه ۲۰ آذر، ۱۱ دسامبر - انگلیسی خواندم و تز نوشتم.

دوشنبه ۲۱ آذر، ۱۲ دسامبر - انگلیسی خواندم و تز نوشتم.

سه‌شنبه ۲۲ آذر، ۱۳ دسامبر - تمام روز در خانه بودم و کار کردم. ناهار با نبیل در روایال پالاس هتل خوردم.

چهارشنبه ۲۳ آذر، ۱۴ دسامبر - بمنزل فریا استارک[1] رفتم در چلسی. مینورسکی و زنش و سر پرسی سایکس و جمعی دیگر بودند.

پنجشنبه ۲۴ آذر، ۱۵ دسامبر - شب و روز کار کردم و تز نوشتم و انگلیسی خواندم.

جمعه ۲۵ آذر، ۱۶ دسامبر - در منزل زرین‌کفش دکتر راجی را دیدم.

شنبه ۲۶ آذر، ۱۷ دسامبر - تز نوشتم و انگلیسی خواندم. شب بمنزل زرین‌کفش رفتم. نبیل و پناهی و خانمش و آرام هم بودند. صدیقی با خواهرزاده‌اش سعادت اقبالیان و خانمش هم بودند.

یکشنبه ۲۷ آذر، ۱۸ دسامبر - روز و شب تز نوشتم و انگلیسی خواندم. ناهار با نبیل خوردم.

دوشنبه ۲۸ آذر، ۱۹ دسامبر - هوا سرد شده. تمام روز کار کردم و تز نوشتم و انگلیسی خواندم.

سه‌شنبه ۲۹ آذر، ۲۰ دسامبر - روز و شب کار کردم.

چهارشنبه ۳۰ آذر، ۲۱ دسامبر - کار کردم.

پنجشنبه ۱ دی، ۲۲ دسامبر - انگلیسی خواندم و تز نوشتم.

---

۱. Freya M. Stark، سیاح انگلیسی (۱۸۹۳-۱۹۹۳). نویسنده سفرنامه‌هایی درباره خاورمیانه و افغانستان.

جمعه ۲ دی، ۲۳ دسامبر - انگلیسی خواندم و تز نوشتم.

شنبه ۳ دی، ۲۴ دسامبر - تز نوشتم و انگلیسی خواندم. هیچ از خانه بیرون نرفتم.

یکشنبه ۴ دی، ۲۵ دسامبر - تز می‌نویسم. ناهار در منزل آقای تقی‌زاده بودم و عصر در منزل زرین‌کفش. شب انگلیسی خواندم.

دوشنبه ۵ دی، ۲۶ دسامبر - تز نوشتم و انگلیسی خواندم.

سه‌شنبه ۶ دی، ۲۷ دسامبر - ناهار در منزل زرین‌کفش خوردم. صبح و شب کار کردم و تز نوشتم و انگلیسی خواندم.

چهارشنبه ۷ دی، ۲۸ دسامبر - تمام روز تز نوشتم و انگلیسی خواندم.

پنجشنبه ۸ دی، ۲۹ دسامبر - تز نوشتم و انگلیسی خواندم.

جمعه ۹ دی، ۳۰ دسامبر - تز نوشتم و انگلیسی خواندم.

شنبه ۱۰ دی، ۳۱ دسامبر - تز نوشتم و انگلیسی خواندم.

یکشنبه ۱۱ دی، ۱ ژانویه - تز نوشتم و انگلیسی خواندم.

دوشنبه ۱۲ دی، ۲ ژانویه - صبح و شب انگلیسی خواندم و تز نوشتم.

سه‌شنبه ۱۳ دی، ۳ ژانویه - تمام روز و تا نصف شب تز نوشتم و انگلیسی خواندم.

چهارشنبه ۱۴ دی، ۴ ژانویه - تز نوشتم و انگلیسی خواندم. حالم خوب نیست.

پنجشنبه ۱۵ دی، ۵ ژانویه - تمام روز را کار کردم. انگلیسی هم خواندم. این روز پانصد صفحه از تز تمام شد.

جمعه ۱۶ دی، ۶ ژانویه - حالم چندان خوب نیست. کار کردم و تز نوشتم. دکتر فلاح را دیدم.

شنبه ۱۷ دی، ۷ ژانویه - سخت سرما خورده‌ام. حالم خوب نیست.

یکشنبه ۱۸ دی، ۸ ژانویه - شب کمی کار کردم.

دوشنبه ۱۹ دی، ۹ ژانویه - هیچ از خانه بیرون نرفتم. کمی کار کردم.

سه‌شنبه ۲۰ دی، ۱۰ ژانویه - با نبیل ناهار خوردم. خسته‌ام. کاری نکردم.

چهارشنبه ۲۱ دی، ۱۱ ژانویه - حالم چندان خوب نیست.

پنجشنبه ۲۲ دی، ۱۲ ژانویه - ناهار در روایال پالاس خوردم. کار کردم.

جمعه ۲۳ دی، ۱۳ ژانویه - با نبیل بودم.

شنبه ۲۴ دی، ۱۴ ژانویه - در سفارت مهمان بودم. اعضای سفارت افغان آقای فرخی و خانمش و نصیرزاده و خانمش، زرین‌کفش، وهاب‌زاده، وحید، آرام، پناهی و خانمش و صورتگر بودند.

یکشنبه ۲۵ دی، ۱۵ ژانویه - با نبیل در روایال پالاس هتل < ناهار > خوردم.

دوشنبه ۲۶ دی، ۱۶ ژانویه - کار کردم.

سه‌شنبه ۲۷ دی، ۱۷ ژانویه - تمام روز و تا نصف شب کار کردم.

چهارشنبه ۲۸ دی، ۱۸ ژانویه - تا نصف شب کار کردم.

پنجشنبه < ۲۹ دی >، ۱۹ ژانویه - تا نصف شب کار کردم.

جمعه ۳۰ دی،[1] ۲۰ ژانویه - عصر بمنزل وبستر رفتم. تا نصف شب کار کردم.

شنبه ۱ بهمن، ۲۱ ژانویه - با نبیل در روایال پالاس هتل ناهار خوردم.

یکشنبه ۲ بهمن، ۲۲ ژانویه - تا نصف شب کار کردم.

دوشنبه ۳ بهمن، ۲۳ ژانویه - بمدرسه اقتصاد رفتم. وبستر را دیدم. شب انگلیسی خواندم.

سه‌شنبه ۴ بهمن، ۲۴ ژانویه - صبح انگلیسی خواندم و شب تز نوشتم و انگلیسی خواندم.

چهارشنبه ۵ بهمن، ۲۵ ژانویه - صبح انگلیسی خواندم. ناهار با نبیل خوردم. شب بمنزل مستر ویلکنسن[2] رفتم. مستر هورشید هورتز و زنش و چند نفر دیگر هم بودند.

پنجشنبه ۶ بهمن، ۲۶ ژانویه - انگلیسی خواندم و تز نوشتم.

جمعه ۷ بهمن، ۲۷ ژانویه - انگلیسی خواندم و تا ساعت ۱۱ بعد از ظهر برای تز کار کردم و احتمال جنگ می‌رود. اخبار امیدبخش نیست.

شنبه ۸ بهمن، ۲۸ ژانویه - انگلیسی خواندم و تز نوشتم.

یکشنبه ۹ بهمن، ۲۹ ژانویه - صبح انگلیسی خواندم. ناهار در منزل زرین‌کفش خوردم. بدیدن آقای تقی‌زاده هم رفتم.

---

۱. از این روز تا ۳ بهمن، تاریخ خورشیدی یک روز خطا است. تصحیح شد.
۲. James V. S. Wilkinson، محقق نسخه‌های خطی و مینیاتور ایرانی در موزه بریتانیا (۱۸۸۵-۱۹۵۷).

دوشنبه ۱۰ بهمن، ۳۰ ژانویه - برای شنیدن موسیقی یک اوروگُئه‌ای به اییولین هال[1] رفتم. بعد از آن با حمزاوی و نبیل بودم. برستوران لا مزون و بعد به فلوریدا رفتم.

سه‌شنبه ۱۱ بهمن، ۳۱ ژانویه - انگلیسی خواندم و تز نوشتم.

چهارشنبه ۱۲ بهمن، ۱ فوریه - عصر بمنزل لاکهارت رفتم. شب در خانه انگلیسی خواندم و تز نوشتم.

پنجشنبه ۱۳ بهمن، ۲ فوریه - عصر بمنزل وبستر رفتم. شب انگلیسی خواندم و تز نوشتم.

جمعه ۱۴ بهمن، ۳ فوریه - تا ۱۱ بعد از ظهر تز نوشتم و انگلیسی خواندم.

شنبه ۱۵ بهمن، ۴ فوریه - تا اول شب انگلیسی خواندم و تز نوشتم. شب بمنزل پناهی رفتم. مهمانی بود.

یکشنبه ۱۶ بهمن، ۵ فوریه - با نبیل و نشاط ناهار خوردم.

دوشنبه ۱۷ بهمن، ۶ فوریه - پروفسور وبستر را دیدم. در باب تز مذاکره کردیم.

سه‌شنبه ۱۸ بهمن، ۷ فوریه - کار کردم.

چهارشنبه ۱۹ بهمن، ۹ فوریه - هیچ از خانه بیرون نرفتم. حالم خوب نبود.

پنجشنبه ۲۰ بهمن، ۱۰ فوریه - به پتنی رفتم. پس از مراجعت انگلیسی خواندم.

جمعه ۲۱ بهمن، ۱۱ فوریه - کتاب خواندم و انگلیسی.

شنبه ۲۲ بهمن، ۱۲ فوریه - صبح انگلیسی خواندم.

---

۱. Aeolian Hall، تالار موسیقی و آواز در مرکز لندن (دیگر دایر نیست).

یکشنبه ۲۳ بهمن، ۱۲ فوریه - صبح انگلیسی خواندم.

دوشنبه ۲۴ بهمن، ۱۳ فوریه - تز نوشتم و انگلیسی خواندم.

سه‌شنبه ۲۵ بهمن، ۱۴ فوریه - صبح انگلیسی خواندم و شب کار کردم برای تز.

چهارشنبه ۲۶ بهمن، ۱۵ فوریه - برای پدرم بکربلا پول و کاغذ فرستادم. شب انگلیسی خواندم و تز نوشتم.

پنجشنبه ۲۷ بهمن، ۱۶ فوریه - انگلیسی خواندم و تز نوشتم. بدیدن وبستر رفتم. شرح سفارت جونز را شروع کردم.

جمعه ۲۸ بهمن، ۱۷ فوریه - صبح و شب انگلیسی خواندم و تز نوشتم.

شنبه ۲۹ بهمن، ۱۸ فوریه - با ثاتی شام خوردم. شب تز نوشتم و انگلیسی خواندم.

یکشنبه ۳۰ بهمن، ۱۹ فوریه - صبح انگلیسی خواندم. ناهار در منزل زرین‌کفش بودم. عصر با خانم زرین‌کفش و دختر زرین‌کفش بمسجد شاه جهان به ووکینگ رفتم. شب با وحید شام خوردم.

دوشنبه اول اسفند، ۲۰ فوریه - صبح انگلیسی خواندم. ناهار با نبیل بودم و شب کار کردم.

سه‌شنبه ۲ اسفند، ۲۱ فوریه - صبح انگلیسی خواندم و برای تز کار کردم.

چهارشنبه ۳ اسفند، ۲۲ فوریه - شب انگلیسی خواندم و تز نوشتم.

پنجشنبه ۴ اسفند، ۲۳ فوریه - صبح کار کردم. جوهر روی قالیچه و اوراق یادداشت تز ریخته شد. روز و شب انگلیسی خواندم و برای تز کار کردم.

جمعه ۵ اسفند، ۲۴ فوریه - انگلیسی خواندم و تز نوشتم.

شنبه ۶ اسفند، ۲۵ فوریه - تا چهار بعد از ظهر برای تز کار کردم. انگلیسی هم خواندم. شب هم کار کردم و انگلیسی خواندم.

یکشنبه ۷ اسفند، ۲۶ فوریه - صبح انگلیسی خواندم و تز نوشتم. ناهار در منزل پناهی خوردم.

دوشنبه ۸ اسفند، ۲۷ فوریه - صبح انگلیسی خواندم و تز نوشتم. ناهار در سفارت خوردم. مهمانی بود و اکثر مدعوین نمایندگان مسلمان کنفرانس مسلمان فلسطین. شب تز نوشتم و انگلیسی خواندم.

سه‌شنبه ۹ اسفند، ۲۸ فوریه - تا ۱۱ بعد از ظهر تز نوشتم و انگلیسی خواندم.

چهارشنبه ۱۰ اسفند، ۱ مارس - تا ساعت یازده تز نوشتم و انگلیسی خواندم.

پنجشنبه ۱۱ اسفند، ۲ مارس - عصر بمنزل وبستر رفتم. حالم خوب نیست.

جمعه ۱۲ اسفند، ۳ مارس - در مدرسه اقتصاد وبستر را دیدم. در باب تز مذاکره کردیم. تا ساعت یازده بعد از ظهر تز نوشتم و انگلیسی خواندم.

شنبه ۱۳ اسفند، ۴ مارس - با نبیل و حمزاوی و پوروالی ناهار خوردم. انگلیسی خواندم و تز نوشتم.

یکشنبه ۱۴ اسفند، ۵ مارس - صبح انگلیسی خواندم و تز نوشتم. ناهار با نبیل و حمزاوی و پوروالی خوردم.

دوشنبه ۱۵ اسفند، ۶ مارس - حالم چندان خوب نیست. کم کار کردم. شب انگلیسی خواندم و تز نوشتم.

سه‌شنبه ۱۶ اسفند، ۷ مارس - انگلیسی خواندم. حالم چندان خوب نیست.

چهارشنبه ۱۷ اسفند، ۸ مارس - روز و شب تز نوشتم و انگلیسی خواندم.

پنجشنبه ۱۸ اسفند، ۹ مارس - بسیار خسته بودم. تمام وقت کار کردم. انگلیسی خواندم و تز نوشتم.

جمعه ۱۹ اسفند، ۱۰ مارس - بیش از سایر روزها کار کردم. انگلیسی خواندم و تز نوشتم.

شنبه ۲۰ اسفند، ۱۱ مارس - تمام روز کار کردم. انگلیسی خواندم و تز نوشتم.

یکشنبه ۲۱ اسفند، ۱۲ مارس - صبح انگلیسی خواندم و تز نوشتم. ناهار با نبیل خوردم و شب در منزل نبیل بودم.

دوشنبه ۲۲ اسفند، ۱۳ مارس - صبح تز نوشتم و انگلیسی خواندم. شب تز نوشتم و انگلیسی خواندم.

سه‌شنبه ۲۳ اسفند، ۱۴ مارس - بپدرم کاغذ نوشتم ببغداد. از صبح تا ساعت ۹ کار کردم. بعد به پارک لین رفتم بمحل مهمانی وزیر امور خارجه عراق بمناسبت کنفرانس فلسطین.

چهارشنبه ۲۴ اسفند، ۱۵ مارس - تمام روز کار کردم. انگلیسی خواندم. ساعت ده بعد از ظهر بسفارت رفتم مجلس مهمانی بمناسبت تولد شاه بود. تا سه بعد از نصف شب در آن جا بودم.

پنجشنبه ۲۵ اسفند، ۱۶ مارس - چنانکه باید پیشرفت نکرده‌ام و از فرنگ فایده نبردم. نقص تربیت در ایران و سایر عوامل بی تأثیر نیست. عزم کردم که بیشتر کار کنم تا بتوانم روزی بایران خدمت کنم. صبح انگلیسی خواندم و تز نوشتم. عصر بمنزل

پروفسور وبستر رفتم. مردم اروپا بسیار متوحشند. آلمان روز چهارشنبه چکوسلواکی را تصرف کرد.

جمعه ۲۶ اسفند، ۱۷ مارس - روز و شب انگلیسی خواندم و تز نوشتم.

شنبه ۲۷ اسفند، ۱۸ مارس - روز و شب انگلیسی خواندم و تز نوشتم.

یکشنبه ۲۸ اسفند، ۱۹ مارس - صبح و عصر و شب انگلیسی خواندم و کار کردم. با نبیل در روایال پالاس هتل ناهار خوردم.

دوشنبه ۲۹ اسفند، ۲۰ مارس - پروفسور وبستر را در مدرسه دیدم. در خصوص موقع تقدیم تز بمدرسه صحبت کردم. شب کار کردم. انگلیسی خواندم و تز نوشتم.

سه‌شنبه ۳۰ اسفند، ۲۱ مارس - صبح انگلیسی خواندم و تز نوشتم. ناهار در منزل زرین‌کفش خوردم. بساط هفت سین چیده بودند. آقای تقی‌زاده را دیدم.

چهارشنبه ۱ فروردین، ۲۲ مارس - تا عصر انگلیسی خواندم و تز نوشتم. عصر بسفارت رفتم برای تبریک عید. اکثر ایرانیها بودند. شب با آرام و وحید برستوران هندی رفتم.

پنجشنبه ۲ فروردین، ۲۳ مارس - عصر نطق پوپ را در باب ابنیه ایران شنیدم و باقی اوقات را انگلیسی خواندم و تز نوشتم.

جمعه ۳ فروردین، ۲۴ مارس - ناهار با نبیل خوردم. باقی وقت را انگلیسی خواندم و بتز نوشتن گذراندم.

شنبه ۴ فروردین، ۲۵ مارس - تمام روز را کار کردم. انگلیسی خواندم و تز نوشتم.

یکشنبه ۵ فروردین، ۲۶ مارس - با نبیل بودم. بعد از ظهر انگلیسی خواندم و تز نوشتم. شب با نبیل بمنزل نصیرزاده رفتم. وهاب‌زاده، زرین‌کفش، خانمش، عزّت خانم خانم پناهی، و خسروشاهی هم بودند.

دوشنبه ۶ فروردین، ۲۷ مارس - ناهار با نبیل خوردم. باقی وقت را تز نوشتم و انگلیسی خواندم.

سه‌شنبه ۷ فروردین، ۲۸ مارس - تا نصف شب انگلیسی خواندم و تز نوشتم.

چهارشنبه ۸ فروردین، ۲۹ مارس - صد و هشتاد و پنج لیره برای پدرم بکربلا فرستادم. تمام وقت تز نوشتم و انگلیسی خواندم.

پنجشنبه ۹ فروردین، ۳۰ مارس - ناهار با نبیل و نشاط خوردم. باقی وقت تز نوشتم و انگلیسی خواندم.

جمعه ۱۰ فروردین، ۳۱ مارس - روز و شب انگلیسی خواندم و تز نوشتم.

شنبه ۱۱ فروردین، ۱ آوریل - تمام روز کار کردم. انگلیسی خواندم و تز نوشتم.

یکشنبه ۱۲ فروردین، ۲ آوریل - روز انگلیسی خواندم و تز نوشتم. شام در منزل زرین‌کفش خوردم.

دوشنبه ۱۳ فروردین، ۳ آوریل - تز نوشتم و انگلیسی خواندم.

سه‌شنبه ۱۴ فروردین، ۴ آوریل - تز نوشتم و کار کردم.

چهارشنبه ۱۵ فروردین، ۵ آوریل - تز نوشتم و انگلیسی خواندم.

پنجشنبه ۱۶ فروردین، ۶ آوریل - تز نوشتم و انگلیسی خواندم.

جمعه ۱۷ فروردین، ۷ آوریل - تز نوشتم و انگلیسی خواندم. از این کار تزنویسی خسته شده‌ام.

شنبه ۱۸ فروردین، ۸ آوریل - روز و شب تز نوشتم و انگلیسی خواندم.

یکشنبه ۱۹ فروردین، ۹ آوریل - ناهار با نبیل خوردم. هوا بسیار عالی بود ولی بواسطه آنکه باید تز را تمام کنم، در خانه ماندم و کار کردم. انگلیسی هم خواندم.

دوشنبه ۲۰ فروردین، ۱۰ آوریل - ناهار در منزل زرین‌کفش خوردم. صبح و شب تز نوشتم و انگلیسی خواندم.

سه‌شنبه ۲۱ فروردین، ۱۱ آوریل - تز نوشتم و انگلیسی خواندم.

چهارشنبه ۲۲ فروردین، ۱۲ آوریل - تز نوشتم و انگلیسی خواندم.

پنجشنبه ۲۳ فروردین، ۱۳ آوریل - تز نوشتم و انگلیسی خواندم.

جمعه ۲۴ فروردین، ۱۴ آوریل - تز نوشتم و انگلیسی خواندم.

شنبه ۲۵ فروردین، ۱۵ آوریل - تز نوشتم و انگلیسی خواندم.

یکشنبه ۲۶ فروردین، ۱۶ آوریل - تا نصف شب کار کردم.

دوشنبه ۲۷ فروردین، ۱۷ آوریل - تز نوشتم و انگلیسی خواندم.

سه‌شنبه ۲۸ فروردین، ۱۸ آوریل - تز نوشتم و انگلیسی خواندم.

چهارشنبه ۲۹ فروردین، ۱۹ آوریل - عصر بمجلس نطق رفتم. آربری راجع بفراتی[1] شاعر نطق کرد. صبح و شب تز نوشتم و انگلیسی خواندم.

پنجشنبه ۳۰ فروردین، ۲۰ آوریل - تز نوشتم و انگلیسی خواندم.

جمعه ۳۱ فروردین، ۲۱ آوریل - تمام روز در خانه بودم. تز نوشتم و انگلیسی خواندم.

شنبه اول اردیبهشت، ۲۲ آوریل - انگلیسی خواندم و تز نوشتم.

یکشنبه ۲ اردیبهشت، ۲۳ آوریل - ناهار در رستوران هندی با نبیل خوردم. تمام وقت را تز نوشتم و انگلیسی خواندم.

دوشنبه ۳ اردیبهشت، ۲۴ آوریل - صبح انگلیسی خواندم و تز نوشتم. بعد رفتم بمدرسه. پروفسور وبستر را دیدم. قرار شد در ماه ژوئن تز را بمدرسه برای امتحان بفرستم.

سه‌شنبه ۴ اردیبهشت، ۲۵ آوریل - انگلیسی خواندم. شب تا ساعت سه و نیم بعد از نصف شب در سفارت بودم.

---

۱. مقصود محمد الفراتي شاعر اهل شام است (۱۸۸۰-۱۹۷۸).

چهارشنبه ۵ اردیبهشت، ۲۶ آوریل - برای ماشین کردن تز کسی را خواسته بودم. آمد. کار کردم. خسته بودم. حالم خوب نبود.

پنجشنبه ۶ اردیبهشت، ۲۷ آوریل - صبح کمی کار کردم. عصر بمنزل وبستر رفتم و شب بخانه آقای تقی‌زاده.

جمعه ۷ اردیبهشت، ۲۸ آوریل - کار کردم و تز نوشتم.

شنبه ۸ اردیبهشت، ۲۹ آوریل - حالم خوب نبود. کاری نکردم.

یکشنبه ۹ اردیبهشت، ۳۰ آوریل - حالم چندان خوب نیست. مقدمات تقدیم تز را فراهم کردم.

دوشنبه ۱۰ اردیبهشت، ۱ مه - صبح نزد پروفسور وبستر رفتم.

سه‌شنبه ۱۱ اردیبهشت، ۲ مه - صبح با شخصی که برای ماشین کردن آمده بود کار کردم. ناهار با صورتگر خوردم.

چهارشنبه ۱۲ اردیبهشت، ۳ مه - با شخصی که برای ماشین کردن آمده بود کار کردم.

پنجشنبه ۱۳ اردیبهشت، ۴ مه - تمام روز کار کردم با مستر نی‌لور.

جمعه ۱۴ اردیبهشت، ۵ مه - تمام روز کار کردم.

شنبه ۱۵ اردیبهشت، ۶ مه - تمام روز با شخصی که ماشین می‌کرد کار کردم.

یکشنبه ۱۶ اردیبهشت، ۷ مه - تا نصف شب کار کردم.

دوشنبه ۱۷ اردیبهشت، ۸ مه - قسمت آخر تز را تمام کردم.

سه‌شنبه ۱۸ اردیبهشت، ۹ مه - روز و شب کار کردم با شخصی که ماشین می‌کرد.

چهارشنبه ۱۹ اردیبهشت، ۱۰ مه - شب انگلیسی خواندم و تا نصف شب کار کردم.

پنجشنبه ۲۰ اردیبهشت، ۱۱ مه - ناهار با نبیل خوردم. انگلیسی خواندم و تا نصف شب کار کردم.

جمعه ۲۱ اردیبهشت، ۱۲ مه - عصر بمنزل وبستر رفتم. شب با صفوت شام خوردم. تا نصف شب کار کردم.

شنبه ۲۲ اردیبهشت، ۱۳ مه - روز و شب کار کردم. در رستوران روسی ناهار خوردم. انگلیسی خواندم.

یکشنبه ۲۳ اردیبهشت، ۱۴ مه - انگلیسی خواندم. فصول تز را مراجعه کردم.

دوشنبه ۲۴ اردیبهشت، ۱۵ مه - در مدرسه وبستر را دیدم. شب انگلیسی خواندم.

سه‌شنبه ۲۵ اردیبهشت، ۱۶ مه - عصر بادارهٔ ماشین رفتم و در باب ماشین کردن تمام تز مذاکره کردم. شب انگلیسی خواندم.

چهارشنبه ۲۶ اردیبهشت، ۱۷ مه - تا نصف شب کار کردم. انگلیسی هم خواندم. خسته بودم.

پنجشنبه ۲۷ اردیبهشت، ۱۸ مه - تا ساعت ۱۱ کار کردم. انگلیسی هم خواندم.

جمعه ۲۸ اردیبهشت، ۱۹ مه - تمام روز کار کردم. انگلیسی هم خواندم.

شنبه ۲۹ اردیبهشت، ۲۰ مه - صبح انگلیسی خواندم. شب با نبیل و پناهی و خانمش و وهاب‌زاده و خانمش و نصیرزاده و آرام بمنزل آقای زرین‌کفش رفتم. تا دو و نیم بعد از ظهر در آن جا بودم.

یکشنبه ۳۰ اردیبهشت، ۲۱ مه - انگلیسی خواندم. تا نصف شب کار کردم.

دوشنبه ۳۱ اردیبهشت، ۲۲ مه - مقدمه‌ای از تز را دادم ماشین کنند. تا نصف شب کار کردم.

سه‌شنبه ۱ خرداد، ۲۳ مه - انگلیسی خواندم و بمراجعه تز مشغول بودم.

چهارشنبه ۲ خرداد، ۲۴ مه - انگلیسی خواندم. تا نصف شب بر سر تز کار کردم.

پنجشنبه ۳ خرداد، ۲۵ مه - تا نصف شب کار کردم. انگلیسی هم خواندم.

جمعه ۴ خرداد، ۲۶ مه - انگلیسی خواندم و کار کردم.

شنبه ۵ خرداد، ۲۷ مه - صبح و شب کار کردم و انگلیسی خواندم. عصر بسفارت اسپانیا رفتم.

یکشنبه ۶ خرداد، ۲۸ مه - با نبیل در روایال پالاس هتل ناهار خوردم. قسمتی از تز را دادم ماشین کنند. انگلیسی خواندم و تا نصف شب کار کردم.

دوشنبه ۷ خرداد، ۲۹ مه - با نبیل ناهار خوردم. انگلیسی خواندم. تا نصف شب کار کردم.

سه‌شنبه ۸ خرداد، ۳۰ مه - شب و صبح انگلیسی خواندم و کار کردم.

چهارشنبه ۹ خرداد، ۳۱ مه - کار کردم.

پنجشنبه ۱۰ خرداد، ۱ ژوئن - بسیار خسته بودم. کاری نکردم. انگلیسی خواندم.

جمعه ۱۱ خرداد، ۲ ژوئن - ناهار با نبیل خوردم. انگلیسی خواندم و تز نوشتم.

شنبه ۱۲ خرداد، ۳ ژوئن - انگلیسی خواندم. قسمت آخر تز را مراجعه کردم.

یکشنبه ۱۳ خرداد، ۴ ژوئن - صبح زود مشغول کار شدم. قسمت اسامی کتب را نوشتم و

بعد رفتم بادارهٔ مخصوص تز ماشین کردن ــ ماشین ــ و باقی اوراق را دادم تا ماشین کنند. در این روز پس از سه سال کار و چندین ماه نوشتن شب و روز که گاهی تا بعد از نصف شب کار می‌کردم، تز تمام شد. عصر با نبیل به ایست بورن رفتم. حالم خوب نیست.

دوشنبه ۱۴ خرداد، ۵ ژوئن - انگلیسی خواندم.

سه‌شنبه ۱۵ خرداد، ۶ ژوئن - تا نصف شب تز را با نسخه اصلی مقابله کردم. انگلیسی هم خواندم.

چهارشنبه ۱۶ خرداد، ۷ ژوئن - بمقابله تز مشغول بودم. شب انگلیسی خواندم.

پنجشنبه ۱۷ خرداد، ۸ ژوئن - شانزده لیره و شش شیلینگ حق ماشین کردن تز را دادم و آن را بردم دادم صحافی کنند.

جمعه ۱۸ خرداد، ۹ ژوئن - تز مجلد را باونیورسیته لندن دادم. ناهار با مینوی خوردم. عصر با زرین‌کفش بمنزل سر دنیسن رس رفتم بجلسه انجمن ایران.

شنبه ۱۹ خرداد، ۱۰ ژوئن - ناهار در منزل زرین‌کفش خوردم و عصر با آقای تقی‌زاده و خانمش بباغی نزدیک گولدرز گرین رفتم.

یکشنبه ۲۰ خرداد، ۱۱ ژوئن - ناهار با نبیل خوردم. بعد از ظهر با او و پناهی به ایست بورن رفتم.

دوشنبه ۲۱ خرداد، ۱۲ ژوئن - انگلیسی خواندم.

سه‌شنبه ۲۲ خرداد، ۱۳ ژوئن - ناهار با زرین‌کفش و خانم زرین‌کفش و دخترش و مستر رابرتس در رستوران کوه نور خوردم. شب انگلیسی خواندم، از کتب وودهوس.[1]

---

۱. Sir Pelham Grenville Wodehouse، نویسنده و طنزپرداز بریتانیایی (۱۸۸۱-۱۹۷۵).

چهارشنبه ۲۳ خرداد، ۱۴ ژوئن - بپیکادلی بتماشای تابلوهای نقاشی رفتم.

پنجشنبه ۲۴ خرداد، ۱۵ ژوئن - شب در منزل آقای تقی‌زاده بودم. تا نصف شب با ایشان بودم. چلوکباب خوردیم. خانم تقی‌زاده خوب آن را پخته بود.

جمعه ۲۵ خرداد، ۱۶ ژوئن - صبح انگلیسی خواندم. شب با نبیل به الدرشوت تاتر[1] رفتم.

شنبه ۲۶ خرداد، ۱۷ ژوئن - ناهار در لستر اسکویر خوردم. انگلیسی خواندم. بدیدن فیلم مستر چیپز[2] رفتم. شب با نبیل بمنزل زرین‌کفش رفتم. مستر رابرتس و خواهرش هم بودند.

یکشنبه ۲۷ خرداد، ۱۸ ژوئن - کار کردم و کتاب خواندم.

دوشنبه ۲۸ خرداد، ۱۹ ژوئن - صبح انگلیسی خواندم.

سه‌شنبه ۲۹ خرداد، ۲۰ ژوئن - صبح انگلیسی خواندم.

چهارشنبه ۳۰ خرداد، ۲۱ ژوئن - صبح و شب انگلیسی خواندم.

پنجشنبه ۳۱ خرداد، ۲۲ ژوئن - صبح و شب انگلیسی خواندم.

جمعه ۱ تیر، ۲۳ ژوئن - صبح و شب انگلیسی خواندم.

شنبه ۲ تیر، ۲۴ ژوئن - انگلیسی خواندم. فیلم پطر کبیر[3] را دیدم.

یکشنبه ۳ تیر، ۲۵ ژوئن - صبح انگلیسی خواندم.

---

۱. Aldershot, Theater Royal، در فاصله ۱۸۹۱ تا ۱۹۵۹ فعال بود. بعداً تخریب شد.

۲. مقصود فیلم Goodbye, Mr. Chips است، درام رمانتیک محصول امریکا (۱۹۳۹).

۳. Peter the Great، فیلم تاریخی محصول شوروی (۱۹۳۷).

دوشنبه ۴ تیر، ۲۶ ژوئن - صبح و شب انگلیسی خواندم.

سه‌شنبه ۵ تیر، ۲۷ ژوئن - صبح و شب انگلیسی خواندم، کتاب شرح حال کرزن.[1]

چهارشنبه ۶ تیر، ۲۸ ژوئن - انگلیسی خواندم. ناهار در سیدندهم خوردم. مسابقه تنیس بین شاگردان ایرانی بود. شب هم انگلیسی خواندم.

پنجشنبه ۷ تیر، ۲۹ ژوئن - ناهار با فرمانفرمائیان خوردم. دوست او میس ربرتس هم بود.

جمعه ۸ تیر، ۳۰ ژوئن - کتاب خواندم.

شنبه ۹ تیر، ۱ ژوئیه - با زرین‌کفش و خانمش و مستر مایلز به بیرمنگام بمجلس جشن محصلین رفتیم.

یکشنبه ۱۰ تیر، ۲ ژوئیه - با نبیل بودم.

دوشنبه ۱۱ تیر، ۳ ژوئیه - کتاب خواندم.

سه‌شنبه ۱۲ تیر، ۴ ژوئیه - با قشقایی شام خوردم.

چهارشنبه ۱۳ تیر، ۵ ژوئیه - کتاب خواندم.

پنجشنبه ۱۴ تیر، ۶ ژوئیه - شب به گرونر هوس رفتم بمجلس مهمانی سالیانه جمعیت آسیای مرکزی. مهمان مستر رابرتس بودم. مکدونالد[2] وزیر مستعمرات در باب فلسطین نطقی کرد. و مستر هارولد نیکلسن در باب ایران و خیام. مجلس بدی نبود.

---

۱. احتمالاً مقصود کتاب هرولد جرج نیکولسُن (Harold George Nicolson) است که در ۱۹۳۴ منتشر شد، با عنوان: *Curzon: The Last Phase, 1919-1925*.

۲. Malcolm J. MacDonald، سیاستمدار و دیپلمات انگلیسی (۱۹۰۱-۱۹۸۱).

جمعه ۱۵ تیر، ۷ ژوئیه - شرح حال فیتز جرالد[1] < را > خواندم.

شنبه ۱۶ تیر، ۸ ژوئیه - با نبیل بودم. به وین‌زور بتماشای نمایشگاه فلاحت رفتم.

یکشنبه ۱۷ تیر، ۹ ژوئیه - با وحید ناهار خوردم.

دوشنبه ۱۸ تیر، ۱۰ ژوئیه - کتاب خواندم. شب رفتم بتآتر امپایر در هولبورن.[2]

سه‌شنبه ۱۹ تیر، ۱۱ ژوئیه - بعد از ظهر رفتم بتاتر بدیدن بازی *Grouse in June*.[3] و شب رفتم به پالی‌دیوم.[4]

چهارشنبه ۲۰ تیر، ۱۲ ژوئیه - صبح زود برخاستم. لباس پوشیدم. خواستم بند ارسی[5] را ببندم و بمجلس امتحان مدرسه برای گذراندن تز بروم. ناگهان کمر درد سختی احساس کردم. تا چند دقیقه مثل مرده قدرت حرکت نداشتم. بزحمت از اطاق بیرون رفتم و خود را بدر رساندم. در تاکسی نشستم و بدواخانه رفتم و از شوفر خواستم دوا فروش را نزد من بیاورد. دوا فروش آمد. باو گفتم که امروز باید امتحان بدهم و ناگهان کمر درد سختی مرا گرفته، دوای مسکن بدهد. دو قرص داد. خوردم و یک شیشه قرص داد که اگر لازم شد بخورم. پیش از ساعت ۱۱ بمدرسه اقتصاد رفتم. اطاق امتحان اطاق پروفسور وبستر بود. درد کمر سبک شده بود اما بزحمت راه می‌رفتم. ساعت ۱۲ امتحان شروع شد و بیش از سه ربع طول کشید. ممتحنین عبارت بودند از پروفسور وبستر، مستر سمنر[6] از اکسفورد، و سر دنیسن رس. در باب نقشه و اسامی کتب و اسامی کار و غیره سؤالاتی کردند. بعد از اطاق بیرون رفتم. وبستر

---

۱. Edward FitzGerald، شاعر و نویسنده انگلیسی (۱۸۸۳-۱۸۰۹). کتاب مورد اشاره احتمالاً باید اثری باشد از Francis Hindes Groome با عنوان: *Edward FitzGerald* (انتشار ۱۹۰۲).

۲. Holborn Empire Theater که در ۱۹۴۱ هدف بمباران آلمانیها قرار گرفت و مخروبه شد.

۳. بر اساس نمایشنامه کمدی اثر Norman C. Hunter،

۴. The London Palladium.

۵. مقصود پنجره مشبک است.

۶. Benedict H. Sumner، (۱۹۵۱-۱۸۹۳) استاد تاریخ در کالج بلیل (Balliol College)، اکسفرد.

گفت در بیرون منتظر نتیجه باش. بعد از دو دقیقه آمد و گفت که تبریک می‌گویم و مرا باطاق برد و دو ممتحن دیگر هم تبریک گفتند و در این روز با وجود این درد سخت خوشحال بودم که از شر امتحان خلاص شدم. بعد از ظهر دو نسخه تز را که ممتحنین داده بودند بدانشگاه بردم و بعد رفتم بمنزل نبیل. شب انگلیسی خواندم و کمی حالم بهتر بود.

پنجشنبه ۲۱ تیر، ۱۳ ژوئیه - صبح انگلیسی خواندم. ناهار با مستر رابرتس حسابدار شرکت خوردم. شب انگلیسی خواندم. هنوز کمی درد سخت دارم.

جمعه ۲۲ تیر، ۱۴ ژوئیه - صبح انگلیسی خواندم. ناهار با مستر رابرتس خوردم. شب به گرونرهوس رفتم بمهمانی شرکت. هزار و هفتصد نفر مهمان بود.

شنبه ۲۳ تیر، ۱۵ ژوئیه - صبح انگلیسی خواندم. کمر دردم فرق نکرده. شب هم انگلیسی خواندم.

یکشنبه ۲۴ تیر، ۱۶ ژوئیه - صبح انگلیسی خواندم. عصر و شب با نبیل بودم.

دوشنبه ۲۵ تیر، ۱۷ ژوئیه - شب انگلیسی خواندم.

سه‌شنبه ۲۶ تیر، ۱۸ ژوئیه - کتاب خواندم.

چهارشنبه ۲۷ تیر، ۱۹ ژوئیه - شب انگلیسی خواندم.

پنجشنبه ۲۸ تیر، ۲۰ ژوئیه - حالم کمی بهتر بود. انگلیسی خواندم. عصر قرار بود به گاردن پارتی بروم اما باران سخت می‌آمد و نرفتم. شب هم انگلیسی خواندم.

جمعه ۲۹ تیر، ۲۱ ژوئیه - صبح انگلیسی خواندم.

شنبه ۳۰ تیر، ۲۲ ژوئیه - صبح انگلیسی خواندم.

یکشنبه ۳۱ تیر، ۲۳ ژوئیه - صبح انگلیسی خواندم. ناهار در منزل زرین‌کفش و شب در منزل آقای تقی‌زاده بودم.

دوشنبه اول مرداد، ۲۴ ژوئیه - صبح انگلیسی خواندم. در این ایام برای فرستادن راپورت مفصلی بطهران خیلی کار هست.

سه‌شنبه ۲ مرداد، ۲۵ ژوئیه - صبح و شب انگلیسی خواندم.

چهارشنبه ۳ مرداد، ۲۶ ژوئیه - صبح و شب انگلیسی خواندم.

پنجشنبه ۴ مرداد، ۲۷ ژوئیه - صبح و شب انگلیسی خواندم.

جمعه ۵ مرداد، ۲۸ ژوئیه - صبح و شب انگلیسی خواندم.

شنبه ۶ مرداد، ۲۹ ژوئیه - صبح و شب انگلیسی خواندم.

یکشنبه ۷ مرداد، ۳۰ ژوئیه - صبح انگلیسی خواندم. ناهار با نبیل خوردم.

دوشنبه ۸ مرداد، ۳۱ ژوئیه - صبح انگلیسی خواندم. شب با جان ریزلی شام خوردم.

سه‌شنبه ۹ مرداد، ۱ اوت - صبح و شب انگلیسی خواندم. شب جان ریزلی آمد بدیدنم.

چهارشنبه ۱۰ مرداد، ۲ اوت - صبح انگلیسی خواندم.

پنجشنبه ۱۱ مرداد، ۳ اوت - صبح انگلیسی خواندم.

جمعه ۱۲ مرداد، ۴ اوت - صبح انگلیسی خواندم. شب بمنزل آقای تقی‌زاده رفتم. برادرزن آقای تقی‌زاده هم بودند.

شنبه ۱۳ مرداد، ۵ اوت - صبح و شب انگلیسی خواندم.

یکشنبه ۱۴ مرداد، ۶ اوت - صبح انگلیسی خواندم. شب در منزل نصیرزاده بودم. زرین‌کفش بود. آقای[1] پناهی و زنش و وهاب‌زاده و خانمش هم بودند.

دوشنبه ۱۵ مرداد، ۷ اوت - صبح انگلیسی خواندم.

سه‌شنبه ۱۶ مرداد، ۸ اوت - صبح و شب انگلیسی خواندم.

چهارشنبه ۱۷ مرداد، ۹ اوت - صبح انگلیسی خواندم. بعد بباغ وحش رفتم. تا سه ساعت بعد از ظهر در آن جا بودم. در بیکر استریت چای خوردم. شب هم انگلیسی خواندم.

پنجشنبه ۱۸ مرداد، ۱۰ اوت - بمنزل مینوی رفتم. لباس و جعبه عکاسیم را دزدیده بودند. بصاحبخانه شکایت کردم.

جمعه ۱۹ مرداد، ۱۱ اوت - انگلیسی خواندم. بپلیس شکایت کردم. چهار مفتش آمدند و تحقیق کردند.

شنبه ۲۰ مرداد، ۱۲ اوت - صبح انگلیسی خواندم. بعد به ریچموند رفتم. شب هم انگلیسی خواندم.

یکشنبه ۲۱ مرداد، ۱۳ اوت - صبح انگلیسی خواندم. در پیکادلی غذا خوردم. به اپینگ فورست[2] رفتم.

دوشنبه ۲۲ مرداد، ۱۴ اوت - صبح و شب انگلیسی خواندم.

سه‌شنبه ۲۳ مرداد، ۱۵ اوت - صبح انگلیسی خواندم. بعد به چلسی رفتم و از کافه رود تمز بباغ وست مینستر. ناهار در استراند خوردم. شب انگلیسی خواندم. جان ریزلی که دوست و مأنوس من بود، برای پنج هفته بدیدن مادر خود رفت.

---

۱. خانم
۲. Epping Forest، در حومه شمال‌شرقی لندن.

چهارشنبه ۲۴ مرداد، ۱۶ اوت - در سفارت مینوی و صورتگر را دیدم. با مینوی ناهار خوردم.

پنجشنبه ۲۵ مرداد، ۱۷ اوت - عصر به بریتیش میوزیم رفتم و با مینوی چای خوردم. شب به تآتر آلدویچ[1] رفتم. رقص هندی را تماشا کردم.

جمعه ۲۶ مرداد، ۱۸ اوت - با نبیل بودم.

شنبه ۲۷ مرداد، ۱۹ اوت - هفت پیکر نظامی خواندم. شب بمنزل زرین‌کفش رفتم.

یکشنبه ۲۸ مرداد، ۲۰ اوت - با نبیل بودم.

دوشنبه ۲۹ مرداد، ۲۱ اوت - اوضاع اروپا سخت شده. با نبیل بودم.

سه‌شنبه ۳۰ مرداد، ۲۲ اوت - خبر عقد اتحاد روس و آلمان منتشر شد و همه را متعجب کرد.

چهارشنبه ۳۱ مرداد، ۲۳ اوت - بتآتر امپایر در هولبورن رفتم.

پنجشنبه ۱ شهریور، ۲۴ اوت - ناهار با زرین‌کفش و اینچ‌بالد و مستر رابرتس خوردم. شب رفتم بسفارت. سرهنگ شیبانی و بایندر و معلم نبیل هم بودند. خطر جنگ نزدیک شده. آلمان و لهستان و فرانسه و انگلیس بتجهیز لشگر مشغولند.

جمعه ۲ شهریور، ۲۵ اوت - اوضاع سخت بنظر می‌رسد.

شنبه ۳ شهریور، ۲۶ اوت - سفیر انگلیس در آلمان از قیصر پیغامی آورد. روزولت دو پیام برای هیتلر فرستاده است. شاید راهی پیدا شود.

.Aldwych Theater ۱

یکشنبه ۴ شهریور، ۲۷ اوت - خطر جنگ کم نشده. با نبیل بودم.

دوشنبه ۵ شهریور، ۲۸ اوت - بمنزل زرین‌کفش رفتم. سفیر انگلیس جواب پیام هیتلر را ببرلین برد. خطر جنگ کم نشده.

سه‌شنبه ۶ شهریور، ۲۹ اوت - شاید بوساطت موسولینی کاری از پیش برود. خطر کم نشده.

چهارشنبه ۷ شهریور، ۳۰ اوت - بسیار افسرده‌ام.

پنجشنبه ۸ شهریور، ۳۱ اوت - اوضاع بد است و بسیار افسرده‌ام.

جمعه ۹ شهریور، ۱ سپتامبر - لندن را شب تاریک می‌کنند. امروز آلمان بلهستان حمله کرد و جنگی که میلیونها را از میان خواهد برد شروع شد. شب در منزل زرین‌کفش بودم.

شنبه ۱۰ شهریور، ۲ سپتامبر - ناهار با نبیل خوردم. بسیار افسرده‌ام.

یکشنبه ۱۱ شهریور، ۳ سپتامبر - از ساعت ۱۱ صبح جنگ انگلیس بآلمان اعلان شد. کتابها و اثاث خانه را جمع کردم. قرار است به نیویورک بروم. شب در سفارت بودم با نبیل و شیبانی (سرهنگ). شب اعلان خطر حمله هوایی شد. از تختخواب بیرون آمدیم. در تاریکی نشستیم.

دوشنبه ۱۲ شهریور، ۴ سپتامبر - شب ژان لارشه، مستر کمتون، میسز کمتون و دو سه نفر دیگر را بشام برستوران ماجستیک دعوت کردم. ناهار با نبیل خوردم.

سه‌شنبه ۱۳ شهریور، ۵ سپتامبر - با اهل خانه و همسایه‌های اطاق خداحافظی کردم. نه و نیم صبح با اتومبیل سفارت به نیویورک رفتم. سر راه اول بمنزل آقای تقی‌زاده و بعد بمنزل آقای نصیرزاده رفتم. دو ساعت بعد از ظهر به گودینگ‌تون هال[1] رسیدم که زرین‌کفش و خانواده‌اش در آن جا هستند. هیچ همصحبت و مؤنسی ندارم.

---

۱. Godington Hall.

چهارشنبه ۱۴ شهریور، ۶ سپتامبر - بسیار افسرده‌ام. غذا خوب نیست. کتاب جنگ و صلح تولستوی را خواندم.

پنجشنبه ۱۵ شهریور، ۷ سپتامبر - صبح با بعضی از محصلین به نیویورک که نزدیک است، رفتم. کتاب جنگ و صلح خواندم.

جمعه ۱۶ شهریور، ۸ سپتامبر - لشگر آلمان با سرعت در لهستان پیشرفت می‌کند.

شنبه ۱۷ شهریور، ۹ سپتامبر - بسیار بد می‌گذرد. غذا بد است و همصحبت ندارم.

یکشنبه ۱۸ شهریور، ۱۰ سپتامبر - سعدی و حافظ خواندم.

دوشنبه ۱۹ شهریور، ۱۱ سپتامبر - پیش از ظهر با آقای معظمی یکی از محصلین به نیویورک رفتم و قصر نیویورک را دیدم. از آقای تقی‌زاده کاغذی رسید مشعر بر منتهای تأثر او بود.

سه‌شنبه ۲۰ شهریور، ۱۲ سپتامبر - بسیار بد می‌گذرد. راه رفتم و کتاب خواندم.

چهارشنبه ۲۱ شهریور، ۱۳ سپتامبر- از هژیر و معظمی کاغذ رسید.

پنجشنبه ۲۲ شهریور، ۱۴ سپتامبر - تب داشتم. غذا نخوردم.

جمعه ۲۳ شهریور، ۱۵ سپتامبر - روز و شب در تختخواب بودم.

شنبه ۲۴ شهریور، ۱۶ سپتامبر - از کتاب هیتلر ــ ماین کمف[1] ــ کمی خواندم.

یکشنبه ۲۵ شهریور، ۱۷ سپتامبر - از کتاب هیتلر خواندم.

دوشنبه ۲۶ شهریور، ۱۸ سپتامبر - کتاب خواندم. حالم خوش نیست.

---

[1]. Mein Kempf، نبرد من.

سه‌شنبه ۲۷ شهریور، ۱۹ سپتامبر - زرین‌کفش خیلی اوقات تلخ بود. کمی از کتاب هیتلر را خواندم.

چهارشنبه ۲۸ شهریور، ۲۰ سپتامبر - در رستوران ساووی در نی‌یوآرک چای خوردم. هیتلر را خواندم.

پنجشنبه ۲۹ شهریور، ۲۱ سپتامبر - بکتابخانه این شهر کوچک نی‌یوآرک رفتم. کتابهای بسیار خوب دارد.

جمعه ۳۰ شهریور، ۲۲ سپتامبر - کتاب خواندم.

شنبه ۳۱ < شهریور >، ۲۳ < سپتامبر > - بعد از ظهر و بعد از شام از کادینگ‌تن هال بشهر نی‌یوآرک رفتم.

یکشنبه ۱ مهر، ۲۴ < سپتامبر > - قسمت مهمی از لهستان را آلمانها گرفته‌اند. شب در اطراف کادینگ‌تن هال در مهتاب راه رفتم.

دوشنبه ۲ < مهر >، ۲۵ < سپتامبر > - کتاب خواندم.

سه‌شنبه ۳ < مهر >، ۲۶ < سپتامبر > - کتاب خواندم.

چهارشنبه ۴ < مهر >، ۲۷ < سپتامبر > - کتاب خواندم.

پنجشنبه ۵ < مهر >، ۲۸ < سپتامبر > - کتاب خواندم.

جمعه ۶ < مهر >، ۲۹ < سپتامبر > - با زرین‌کفش به نی‌یوآرک بهتل رَم رفتم. مستر رابرتس و نامزدش را دیدیم.

شنبه ۷ < مهر >، ۳۰ < سپتامبر > - کتاب خواندم.

یکشنبه ۸ < مهر >، ۱ اکتبر - بکلیسای کوچک قشنگ نزدیک کادینگ‌تن هال[1] رفتم. کتاب خواندم.

دوشنبه ۹ < مهر >، ۲ اکتبر - زرین‌کفش و خانم زرین‌کفش و رضا خان بلندن رفتند. تا نیم بعد از نصف شب باخبار گوش دادم.

سه‌شنبه ۱۰ < مهر >، ۳ اکتبر - کتاب خواندم و با بعضی از محصلین به نی‌یوآرک رفتم.

چهارشنبه ۱۱ < مهر >، ۴ < اکتبر > - کتاب خواندم.

پنجشنبه ۱۲ < مهر >، ۵ < اکتبر > - کتاب خواندم.

جمعه ۱۳ < مهر >، ۶ < اکتبر > - کتاب خواندم. قرار بود به مارلبرو[2] بروم تا شاید از این زندان کادینگ‌تن هال[3] خلاص شوم اما کاغذی رسید که برایم هیچ جا نیست و نباید بروم. خیلی افسرده شدم و نتوانستم بخوابم.

شنبه ۱۴ مهر، ۷ اکتبر - تب داشتم. حالم هیچ خوب نبود و نتوانستم کاری کنم.

یکشنبه ۱۵ مهر، ۸ اکتبر - در تخت‌خواب افتاده بودم. کمی از کتاب هیتلر را خواندم. حالم هیچ خوب نیست و بواسطه اوضاع و پیشامدها بسیار نگرانم.

دوشنبه ۱۶ مهر، ۹ اکتبر - حافظ و کمی از کتاب هیتلر خواندم. ولی حالم بد و روحم افسرده است.

سه‌شنبه ۱۷ مهر، ۱۰ < اکتبر > - حالت مزاجیم کمی بهتر بود. از تخت‌خواب بیرون

---

۱. کادینگ
۲. مقصود Marlborough است، شهرکی در جنوب انگلستان.
۳. کادینگ‌هال

آمدم ولی از عمارت خارج نشدم. عصر خبری شنیدم که افسردگی و ملالم را صد برابر کرد. شنیدم که در رادیو می‌گویند ایران و افغانستان از جمع شدن قوای روس در قفقاز نگرانند.

چهارشنبه ۱۸ < مهر >، ۱۱ < اکتبر > - حالم خوب نیست. نتوانستم غذا بخورم.

پنجشنبه ۱۹ < مهر >، ۱۲ < اکتبر > - از پناهی کاغذی رسید. خداحافظی کرده بود. بایران می‌رود. می‌خواستم به وستن سیوپر مر' بروم ولی از آن جا هم کاغذ رسید که ممکن نیست.

جمعه ۲۰ < مهر >، ۱۳ < اکتبر > - حالم خوب نیست.

شنبه ۲۱ < مهر >، ۱۴ < اکتبر > - حالم خوب نیست.

یکشنبه ۲۲ < مهر >، ۱۵ < اکتبر > - کتاب خواندم ولی حالم خوب نیست.

دوشنبه ۲۳ < مهر >، ۱۶ < اکتبر > - کتاب خواندم.

سه‌شنبه ۲۴ < مهر >، ۱۶ < اکتبر > - کتاب خواندم.

چهارشنبه ۲۵ < مهر >، ۱۶ < اکتبر > - کتاب خواندم. چند روز است سخت باران می‌آید و بر ملالم می‌افزاید.

پنجشنبه ۲۶ < مهر >، ۱۷ < اکتبر > - حالم کمی بهتر است.

جمعه ۲۷ < مهر >، ۱۸ < اکتبر > - کتاب خواندم.

شنبه ۲۸ < مهر >، ۱۹ < اکتبر > - زرین‌کفش تلفون کرد از لندن. در کمبریج خانه‌ای گرفته‌اند. باید آن جا بروم. هر چه باشد از کادینگ‌تن هال بهتر است.

---

۱. مقصود Weston-super-Mare است، شهری بندری در حدود ۲۰ مایلی جنوب‌غربی بریستول.

یکشنبه ۲۹ مهر، ۲۲ اکتبر - حالم خوب نیست.

دوشنبه ۳۰ < مهر >، ۲۳ < اکتبر > - حالم خوب نیست.

سه‌شنبه ۱ آبان،[1] ۲۴ < اکتبر > - بکتاب خواندن وقت گذراندم. حالت روحی و مزاجیم خوب نیست.

چهارشنبه ۲ آبان، ۲۵ < اکتبر > - کتاب خواندم.

پنجشنبه ۳ آبان، ۲۶ < اکتبر > - کتاب خواندم.

جمعه ۴ < آبان >، ۲۷ < اکتبر > - زرین‌کفش هشت و نیم بعد از ظهر به کادینگ‌تن هال آمد. خانمش و رضا خان هم بودند. گفت تلگرافی از وزارت مالیه رسیده و خواسته‌اند که شادمان برای تحویل کردن بعضی اجناس به تریست[2] برود. از این خبر هیچ خوش‌وقت نشدم. چه سال عجیبی! غیر از روز ۱۲ ژانویه که امتحان دادم و قبول شدم، باقی اخبار همه نگرانی آورده است.

شنبه ۵ < آبان >، ۲۸ < اکتبر > - کتاب خواندم.

یکشنبه ۶ < آبان >، ۲۹ < اکتبر > - از کادینگ‌تن < هال > با سه اتومبیل بکمبریج رفتم. در راه باران می‌آمد. منزل زرین‌کفش در کمبریج تازه ساز و ظریفست. حالا در آن جا زندگی می‌کنم ولی باید هر چه زودتر بجایی دیگر بروم که تنهایی را بیشتر دوست دارم.

دوشنبه ۷ < آبان >، ۳۰ < اکتبر > - ناهار با آقای تقی‌زاده و خانمش خوردیم. ایشان هم در کمبریج منزل دارند. بسیار مهربانی کردند. حالت روحیم بهتر شد. باز کسی هست که با او بتوانم حرف بزنم.

―――――――――――――――――――

۱. ۳۱ مهر. روزهای بعد در تقویم خورشیدی یک روز عقب‌تر هستند. تصحیح شد.
۲. Trieste، شهری بندری در ایتالیا.

سه‌شنبه ۸ < آبان >، ۳۱ اکتبر - صبح بلندن رفتم. با نبیل غذا خوردم. تلگرافی بهژیر کردم که اقدام کند حکم فرستادن به تریست < را > لغو کنند.

چهارشنبه ۹ < آبان >، ۱ نوامبر - با نبیل ناهار خوردم. بمنزل قدیم خود کرمول رود نمره ۵۱ رفتم. حالت تأثر شدیدی حاصل شد. شب با نبیل بودم.

پنجشنبه ۱۰ < آبان >، ۲ نوامبر - زرین‌کفش بلندن آمد. با صالحی و مؤتمن که باید بایران بروند، مذاکره کردم. ناهار با زرین‌کفش و بایندر خوردم. حالت روحیم بسیار بد است.

جمعه ۱۱ < آبان >، ۳ نوامبر - بکمبریج تلفون کردم که آیا در باب لغو حکم رفتنم به تریست چیزی رسیده. عزت خانم گفت تلگرافی هست. آن را خواند. معلوم شد که لغو شده. حالم کمی بهتر شد. هیچ حوصله رفتن به تریست ندارم. شب با نبیل بودم.

شنبه ۱۲ < آبان>، ۴ < نوامبر > - با نبیل و معلمش به گرینیچ رفتم. تماشا کردیم. بد نگذشت.

یکشنبه ۱۳ < آبان >، ۵ < نوامبر > - با نبیل بودم.

دوشنبه ۱۴ < آبان >، ۶ < نوامبر > - با نبیل بودم.

سه‌شنبه ۱۵ < آبان >، ۷ < نوامبر > - با نبیل و حمزاوی به بورن موث رفتم. راه بسیار تماشایی بود. برگهای زرد زیر درختها قشنگ بود.

چهارشنبه ۱۶ < آبان >، ۸ < نوامبر > - با نبیل و آرام غذا خوردم. با نبیل بودم.

پنجشنبه ۱۷ < آبان >، ۹ < نوامبر > - با نبیل بودم در سفارت.

جمعه ۱۸ < آبان >، ۱۰ < نوامبر > - حالم کمی بهتر بود. با نبیل در سفارت بودم.

شنبه ۱۹ < آبان >، ۱۱ < نوامبر > - حالم هیچ خوب نبود. قرار بود به بورنم[1] بروم برای تعطیل ولی معلوم شد که هیچ جا نیست. امیدم از رفتن بتعطیل قطع شد. بسیار افسرده و ملولم.

یکشنبه ۲۰ < آبان >، ۱۲ < نوامبر > - ناهار با نبیل خوردم و با او بودم.

دوشنبه ۲۱ < آبان >، ۱۳ < نوامبر > - با نبیل بودم.

سه‌شنبه ۲۲ < آبان >، ۱۴ < نوامبر > - حالم هیچ خوب نیست. سرهنگ شیبانی از پاریس آمد و با او و نبیل بودم.

چهارشنبه ۲۳ < آبان >، ۱۵ < نوامبر > - حالت مزاجی و روحیم خوب نیست. شب با سرهنگ شیبانی و نبیل بودم.

پنجشنبه ۲۴ آبان، ۱۶ نوامبر - حالم خوب نیست. با نبیل و شیبانی بودم.

جمعه ۲۵ < آبان >، ۱۷ نوامبر - با نبیل بودم. در ماربل آرچ با مینوی شام خوردم. شب با شیبانی و نبیل و وهاب‌زاده و خانمش بودم.

شنبه ۲۶ < آبان >، ۱۸ < نوامبر > - با نبیل بودم.

یکشنبه ۲۷ < آبان >، ۱۹ < نوامبر > - با نبیل و شیبانی و بایندر و یاور سهراب بودم.

دوشنبه ۲۸ < آبان >، ۲۰ < نوامبر > - با نبیل بودم.

سه‌شنبه ۲۹ < آبان >، ۲۱ < نوامبر > - کتاب خواندم و با نبیل بودم.

چهارشنبه ۳۰ < آبان >، ۲۲ < نوامبر > - کتاب خواندم.

____

۱. Burnham.

پنجشنبه ۱ < آذر >، ۲۳ < نوامبر > - بکمبریج رفتم. شب اول در منزل زرین‌کفش بودم و در خانه نمره ۱۹ Millington Road منزل کردم.

جمعه ۲ آذر، ۲۴ نوامبر - صفوت همدرس خود را در کمبریج دیدم. ناهار با او و شام با آقای تقی‌زاده خوردم. حالم کمی بهتر شده است.

شنبه ۳ < آذر >، ۲۵ < نوامبر > - در کمبریج گردش کردم. شام در منزل زرین‌کفش خوردم.

یکشنبه ۴ < آذر >، ۲۶ < نوامبر > - بمنزل آقای تقی‌زاده رفتم.

دوشنبه ۵ < آذر >، ۲۷ < نوامبر > - در تآتر کمبریج بازی قیصر تصنیف شکسپیر را دیدم.

سه‌شنبه ۶ < آذر >، ۲۸ < نوامبر > - با آقای تقی‌زاده ناهار خوردم. شب بازی هملت را دیدم.

چهارشنبه ۷ < آذر >، ۲۹ < نوامبر > - با صفوت بودم.

پنجشنبه ۸ < آذر >، ۳۰ < نوامبر > - کتاب خواندم.

جمعه ۹ < آذر >، ۱ دسامبر - نبیل بکمبریج آمد. با او در یونیورسیتی آرمز هتل ناهار خوردم و عصر بمنزل آقای تقی‌زاده و شب بمنزل آقای زرین‌کفش رفتم و در همان جا خوابیدم.

شنبه ۱۰ آذر، ۲ دسامبر - در منزل آقای زرین‌کفش چاشت خوردم. نبیل هم بود. با او در یونیورسیتی آرمز هتل ناهار خوردم. عصر بلندن رفت.

یکشنبه ۱۱ < آذر >، ۳ < دسامبر > - کتاب خواندم.

دوشنبه ۱۲ < آذر >، ۴ < دسامبر > - شام در منزل زرین‌کفش خوردم و بعد بمنزل آقای تقی‌زاده رفتم.

سه‌شنبه ۱۳ < آذر >، ۵ < دسامبر > - با آقای تقی‌زاده و خانمش در رستوران دوروثی ناهار خوردم.

چهارشنبه ۱۴ < آذر >، ۶ < دسامبر > - کتاب خواندم. شب منزل صفوت رفتم.

پنجشنبه ۱۵ < آذر >، ۷ < دسامبر > - کتاب خواندم.

جمعه ۱۶ < آذر >، ۸ < دسامبر > - با صاحبخانه که مسیز بنت نام دارد خداحافظی کردم. بلندن آمدم و در منزل قدیم خود اطاقی گرفتم. بسیار کوچکتر و هیچ خوب نیست.

شنبه ۱۷ < آذر >، ۹ < دسامبر > - با نبیل بودم.

یکشنبه ۱۸ < آذر >، ۱۰ < دسامبر > - کتاب خواندم.

دوشنبه ۱۹ < آذر >، ۱۱ < دسامبر > - از نمره ۵۱ به نمره ۳۳ رفتم که خانه دیگریست. اطاق جدیدم بزرگست.

سه‌شنبه ۲۰ < آذر >، ۱۲ < دسامبر > - با نبیل بودم. ناهار با وحید خوردم.

چهارشنبه ۲۱ < آذر >، ۱۳ < دسامبر > - کتاب خواندم.

پنجشنبه ۲۲ < آذر >، ۱۴ < دسامبر > - صبح از کمبریج آقای زرین‌کفش تلفون کرد. افسرده بود. گفت دو تلگراف رسیده یکی آنکه بطهران برود و دیگر آنکه کار را بمن تحویل بدهد. از این خبر بی‌نهایت متأثر شدم زیرا در میان این جنگ و غوغا و سرما بردن یک خانواده هفت نفره بایران کار مشکلیست. زرین‌کفش از کمبریج آمد و چند تلگراف بوسیله سفارت بطهران مخابره کرد که شاید گشایشی در کارش شود.

جمعه ۲۳ آذر، ۱۵ دسامبر - زرین‌کفش در سفارت منزل داشت. خیلی افسرده بود.

شنبه ۲۴ < آذر >، ۱۶ < دسامبر > - با زرین‌کفش برستوران روسی رفتم.

یکشنبه ۲۵ < آذر >، ۱۷ < دسامبر > - با زرین‌کفش در رستوران روسی در پیکادلی غذا خوردم.

دوشنبه ۲۶ < آذر >، ۱۸ < دسامبر > - در سفارت ناهار خوردم. زرین‌کفش، باینـدر، و بعضی از اعضای سفارت هم بودند.

سه‌شنبه ۲۷ < آذر >، ۱۹ < دسامبر > - کتاب خواندم و مدتی با زرین‌کفش بودم.

چهارشنبه ۲۸ < آذر >، ۲۰ < دسامبر > - زرین‌کفش بکمبریج مراجعت کرد.

پنجشنبه ۲۹ < آذر >، ۲۱ < دسامبر > - شب با مینوی بودم. آقای عماد معاون کتابخانه مجلس هم در آن جا بود.

جمعه ۳۰ < آذر >، ۲۲ < دسامبر > - با نبیل بودم.

شنبه ۱ دی، ۲۳ < دسامبر > - با نبیل بودم.

یکشنبه ۲ < دی >، ۲۴ < دسامبر > - با نبیل بودم.

دوشنبه ۳ < دی >، ۲۵ < دسامبر > - کتاب خواندم. ناهار و شام با نبیل بودم.

سه‌شنبه ۴ < دی >، ۲۶ < دسامبر > - کتاب خواندم.

چهارشنبه ۵ < دی >، ۲۷ < دسامبر > - با شیبانی و نبیل بودم.

پنجشنبه ۶ < دی >، ۲۸ < دسامبر > - زرین‌کفش از کمبریج بلندن آمد. شب با زرین‌کفش و نبیل و شیبانی شام خوردم.

جمعه ۷ < دی >، ۲۹ < دسامبر > - زرین‌کفش اعتبار را بمن تحویل داد.

شنبه ۸ < دی >، ۳۰ < دسامبر > - زرین‌کفش اداره را تحویل داد. متأثر شدم. زرین‌کفش عصر بکمبریج رفت.

یکشنبه ۹ < دی >، ۳۱ < دسامبر > - با نبیل و شیبانی بودم.

دوشنبه ۱۰ دی، ۱ ژانویه - با نبیل و بایندر و شیبانی بودم.

سه‌شنبه ۱۱ < دی >، ۲ < ژانویه > - با نبیل و بایندر و شیبانی بودم.

چهارشنبه ۱۲ < دی >، ۳ < ژانویه > - کتاب خواندم.

پنجشنبه ۱۳ < دی >، ۴ < ژانویه > - بکمبریج بمنزل زرین‌کفش رفتم. شب آقای تقی‌زاده و خانمش و برادرزنش هم بودند.

جمعه ۱۴ < دی >، ۵ < ژانویه > - در منزل زرین‌کفش چاشت خوردم. شش و نیم بعد از ظهر بمنزل آقای تقی‌زاده رفتم. در مراجعت تاکسی پیدا شد. در میان مه غلیظ بمنزل زرین‌کفش مراجعت کردم. بسیار خسته شدم و بسیار در راه بد گذشت.

شنبه ۱۵ < دی >، ۶ < ژانویه > - بلندن مراجعت کردم.

یکشنبه ۱۶ < دی >، ۷ < ژانویه > - با نبیل و شیبانی بودم.

دوشنبه ۱۷ < دی >، ۸ < ژانویه > - کتاب خواندم.

سه‌شنبه ۱۸ < دی >، ۹ < ژانویه > - کتاب خواندم.

چهارشنبه ۱۹ < دی >، ۱۰ < ژانویه > - کتاب خواندم.

پنجشنبه ۲۰ < دی >، ۱۱ < ژانویه > - کتاب خواندم.

جمعه ۲۱ < دی >، ۱۲ < ژانویه > - با نبیل و حمزاوی و شیبانی و یاور آجودانی بودم.

شنبه ۲۲ < دی >، ۱۳ < ژانویه > - با نبیل و آجودانی و شیبانی بودم.

یکشنبه ۲۳ < دی >، ۱۴ < ژانویه > - با نبیل و آجودانی و شیبانی در سفارت ناهار خوردم. کتاب خواندم.

دوشنبه ۲۴ < دی >، ۱۵ < ژانویه > - کتاب خواندم. بسیار افسرده‌ام.

سه‌شنبه ۲۵ < دی >، ۱۶ < ژانویه > - با مستر مایلز ناهار خوردم.

چهارشنبه ۲۶ < دی >، ۱۷ < ژانویه > - کتاب خواندم و با شیبانی و نبیل بودم.

پنجشنبه ۲۷ < دی >، ۱۸ < ژانویه > - از ایران کاغذی رسید که باید برای مشاوره حقوقی بزوریخ بروم.

جمعه ۲۸ دی، ۱۹ ژانویه - با نبیل و حمزاوی و سرهنگ شیبانی بودم.

شنبه ۲۹ < دی >، ۲۰ < ژانویه > - با آرام بودم و با نبیل.

یکشنبه ۳۰ < دی >، ۲۱ < ژانویه > - با نبیل و آجودانی و شیبانی بودم.

دوشنبه ۱ بهمن، ۲۲ < ژانویه > - بکمبریج رفتم. آقای زرین‌کفش و بعد آقای تقی‌زاده را دیدم.

سه‌شنبه ۲ < بهمن >، ۲۳ < ژانویه > - با زرین‌کفش و آقای تقی< زاده > خداحافظی کردم. بلندن آمدم.

چهارشنبه ۳ < بهمن >، ۲۴ < ژانویه > - با شیبانی و آجودانی و نبیل شام خوردم.

پنجشنبه ۴ < بهمن >، ۲۵ < ژانویه > - مقدمات سفر بسوییس را فراهم کردم.

جمعه ۵ < بهمن >، ۲۶ < ژانویه > - شیبانی و آجودانی تا پاریس همسفر بودند. با ایشان و بایندر و نبیل به ویکتوریا رفتیم. با طیاره بپاریس رفتم. بعد از یک ساعت و نیم به لوبورژه[1] رسیدیم. در هتل دشان ز لیزه منزل کردیم. با شیبانی بمنزل اردلان رفتم که عضو سفارت پاریس بود. شب شیبانی ازگار دو لست[2] می‌رود. با او ساعت ده و ربع خداحافظی کردم. شام در تری‌یومف خوردم.

شنبه ۶ < بهمن >، ۲۷ < ژانویه > - برای زوریخ بلیط گرفتم. در سفارت اردلان و سرداری و سپهبدی را دیدم. ناهار با سرداری در کولیزه خوردم و شام با آجودانی در کولیزه خوردم.

یکشنبه ۷ بهمن، ۲۸ < ژانویه > - خوش‌کیش را دیدم. با او شام خوردم.

دوشنبه ۸ بهمن، ۲۹ < ژانویه > - از گار دو لست بزوریخ رفتم. سفر طولانی و کمی خسته کننده بود. در بازل[3] دو ساعت معطل شدم. در زوریخ در یکی از مهمانخانه‌های درجه اول ـ بل وو او لاک[4] ـ منزل کردم.

سه‌شنبه ۹ < بهمن >، ۳۰ < ژانویه > - مراسله وزارت مالیه را ترجمه کردم. عصر دکتر هنگلر را دیدم. دوسیه را باو دادم با توضیحات. شب بسینما رفتم.

چهارشنبه ۱۰ < بهمن >، ۳۱ < ژانویه > - در رستوران گیاه‌خواران غذا خوردم. شب بسینما رفتم.

پنجشنبه ۱۱ < بهمن >، ۱ فوریه - گردش کردم و شب کتاب خواندم.

---

۱. Le Bourget.
۲. Gare de l'Est.
۳. بال.
۴. Hotel Bellevue au Lac.

جمعه ۱۲ بهمن، ۲ فوریه - گردش کردم و کتاب خواندم.

شنبه ۱۳ < بهمن >، ۳ < فوریه > - در شهر گردش < کردم > و کتاب خواندم.

یکشنبه ۱۴ < بهمن >، ۴ < فوریه > - در رستوران کاپی‌قولی ناهار خوردم. در شهر گردش کردم.

دوشنبه ۱۵ < بهمن >، ۵ < فوریه > - از ده و نیم تا یک بعد از ظهر با دکتر هیگلر بودم و توضیحات دادم. ناهار با او بمنزلش رفتم. خانه‌ای بسیار خوب داد پر از قالی عالی و چینی. دو دخترش که در اونی‌ورسیته زوریخ درس می‌خوانند، آمدند. دختر بزرگ خوب فرانسه حرف می‌زد. شام در رستوران کاپی‌قول خوردم.

سه‌شنبه ۱۶ < بهمن >، ۶ < فوریه > - بژنو رفتم. ناهار با جمال‌زاده و عصر با وکیل و رعدی بودم.

چهارشنبه ۱۷ < بهمن >، ۷ < فوریه > - آقای رعدی را در Plage des Eaux-Vives دیدم. با هم به اونی‌ورسیته رفتیم. مهران را دیدیم. ناهار در منزل جمال‌زاده خوردیم و بعد از ناهار بمنزل وکیل رفتم. رعدی هم آمد. شام با جمال‌زاده و رعدی خوردم.

پنجشنبه ۱۸ بهمن، ۸ فوریه - در منزل مهران ناهار خوردم. بعد بمنزل وکیل رفتم. شام هم در منزل مهران بودم. رعدی و وصال و اسفندیاری و میرفخرایی هم بودند.

جمعه ۱۹ < بهمن >، ۹ < فوریه > - ناهار در منزل جمال‌زاده خوردم. جمشید جهانگیر هم آمد.

شنبه ۲۰ < بهمن >، ۱۰ < فوریه > - مدتی با رعدی راه رفتم. ناهار در منزل مهران خوردیم. جمال‌زاده، وکیل و خانمهایشان بودند. قرمه‌سبزی خوردیم و بعد از ظهر حافظ خواندیم و فال گرفتیم. شب با وکیل به کونسرواتوار رفتم. شاگردها تآتر

می‌دادند. بدری وزیری دختر کلنل علینقی‌خان هم یکی از بازیگرها بود و بد نبود. با جمشید جهانگیر شام خوردم.

یکشنبه ۲۱ < بهمن >، ۱۱ < فوریه > - با جمال‌زاده بمنزل دکتر وکیل رفتم. رعدی هم بود. چلوکباب خوردیم. شب دکتر یزدی را دیدم.

دوشنبه ۲۲ < بهمن >، ۱۲ < فوریه > - در دارالانشاء جامعه ملل آقای حکیمی را دیدم. ناهار در منزل جمال‌زاده خوردم. عصر با رعدی و وکیل بودم.

سه‌شنبه ۲۳ بهمن، ۱۳ فوریه - ناهار در منزل جواد فروغی خوردم. خانمش هم بود. عصر با رعدی و وکیل و مهران در کافهٔ وینا چای خوردم. بعد رفتم بمنزل آقای حکیمی. جمال‌زاده و خانمش هم بودند. در آن جا شام خوردم.

چهارشنبه ۲۴ < بهمن >، ۱۴ < فوریه > - ناهار در منزل جمال‌زاده خوردم. عصر با وکیل و رعدی بودم. با رعدی قسمت قدیم ژنو را تماشا کردیم. شب با رعدی شام خوردم و بعد بمنزل وکیل رفتم.

پنجشنبه ۲۵ < بهمن >، ۱۵ < فوریه > - ناهار در منزل جمال‌زاده خوردم. رعدی و جهانگیر هم بودند. ساعت هفت بعد از ظهر بزوریخ مراجعت کردم. شب کتاب خواندم.

جمعه ۲۶ < بهمن >، ۱۶ < فوریه > - موزه زوریخ را تماشا کردم. بعد از ظهربدیدن هیگلر رفتم. کتاب خواندم.

شنبه ۲۷ < بهمن >، ۱۷ < فوریه > - بپدرم کاغذ نوشتم. در رستوران کاپی‌قولی غذا خوردم.

یکشنبه ۲۸ < بهمن >، ۱۸ < فوریه > - نوشته و عقیده دکتر هیگلر را مطالعه کردم.

دوشنبه ۲۹ < بهمن >، ۱۹ < فوریه > - کتاب خواندم. ملاقات با هیگلر بواسطه مریضی او بتعویق افتاد.

سه‌شنبه ۳۰ < بهمن >، ۲۰ < فوریه > - کتاب خواندم و گردش کردم.

چهارشنبه ۱ اسفند، ۲۱ فوریه - به برن رفتم. در سفارت با انتظام ناهار خوردم. تا نیم بعد از نصف شب در آن جا بودم. با انتظام صحبت می‌کردم. شب آجودانی هم آمد. در هتل بل‌وو پالاس[1] منزل کردم.

پنجشنبه ۲ < اسفند >، ۲۲ < فوریه > - از هتل بل‌وو پالاس به هتل Bayeaux رفتم. شام با انتظام و آجودانی خوردم. بعد بسفارت رفتم. تا نصف شب صحبت کردم.

جمعه ۳ < اسفند >، ۲۳ < فوریه > - بموزه برن رفتم. قسمت شرقی آن بی‌تماشا نبود، علی الخصوص قباله فروش اسب دیدم باین مضمون که قول ناظر فروخت به میوزیم و این اسب نواده اسب پیغمبر است.

شنبه ۴ اسفند، ۲۴ فوریه - با اتوموبیل سفارت با انتظام در اطراف برن گردش کردیم. شب آجودانی و احمدی هم آمدند. تا دو و نیم بعد از نصف شب حرف زدیم.

یکشنبه ۵ اسفند، ۲۵ فوریه - بزوریخ رفتم. راپورت هیگلر را مطالعه کردم.

دوشنبه ۶ < اسفند >، ۲۶ < فوریه > - نزد هیگلر رفتم. توضیحات خواستم و قرار شد عقایدش را دوباره بنویسد.

سه‌شنبه ۷ < اسفند >، ۲۷ < فوریه > - به برن رفتم. دو بعد از ظهر به برن رسیدم. بسفارت رفتم. عروسی دختر سرهنگ شفایی بود با اختر زندی. مجلس بدی نبود.

---

1. Hotel Bellevue Palace.

چهارشنبه ۸ < اسفند >، ۲۸ < فوریه > - بتهیه راپورتی مشغول شدم که باید بوزارت مالیه بنویسم. شام با انتظام خوردم.

پنجشنبه ۹ < اسفند >، ۲۹ < فوریه > - شام با انتظام خوردم و روز بیشتر بتهیه راپورت مشغول بودم.

جمعه ۱۰ < اسفند >، ۱ مارس - ناهار با انتظام در منزل سرهنگ شیبانی خوردم.

شنبه ۱۱ < اسفند >، ۲ < مارس > - در سفارت بودم. بنوشتن راپورت مشغول شدم. شب در سفارت جشن عروسی بود. قریب پنجاه نفر آمدند. تا شش و نیم بعد از نصف شب در سفارت بودم و مجلس تا دیر وقت طول کشید. بسیار خسته شدم.

یکشنبه ۱۲ < اسفند >، ۳ < مارس > - بزوریخ رفتم. کتاب خواندم و گردش کردم.

دوشنبه ۱۳ < اسفند >، ۴ < مارس > - عصر بباغ وحش رفتم و اول شب با کشتی سواحل دریاچه زوریخ را تماشا کردم.

سه‌شنبه ۱۴ < اسفند >، ۵ < مارس > - مهیای سفر شدم و بپاریس حرکت کردم. در بین راه در Delle سرهنگ شیبانی را دیدم. با هم بپاریس رفتیم. ده و چهل و پنج دقیقه بعد از ظهر بپاریس رسیدیم. در هتل دشان ز لیزه منزل کردم. شام مختصری در تری‌یومف خوردم و خوابیدم.

چهارشنبه ۱۵ اسفند، ۶ مارس - ناهار با اختر زندی و تاراس در کولیزه خوردم و شب با سرداری.

پنجشنبه ۱۶ < اسفند >، ۷ < مارس > - صبح به کارتیه لاتن رفتم و مدرسه حقوق را دیدم و بیاد ایام درس و امتحان افتادم. ناهار با شیبانی بمنزل اردلان رفتم. شب با خوش‌کیش و عمید بودم.

جمعه ۱۷ < اسفند >، ۸ < مارس > - از میدان لا فایت به لوبورژه رفتم. با طیاره بلندن حرکت کردم. نیم ساعت بعد از ظهر بلندن رسیدم. عصر نبیل و مقدم وزیر مختار جدید را دیدم.

شنبه ۱۸ < اسفند >، ۹ < مارس > - کتاب خواندم و کارهای اداری رسیدگی کردم.

یکشنبه ۱۹ < اسفند >، ۱۰ < مارس > - بکمبریج رفتم. آقای تقی‌زاده و زرین‌کفش را دیدم و شب بلندن مراجعت کردم.

دوشنبه ۲۰ < اسفند >، ۱۱ < مارس > - ناهار با نبیل و بایندر خوردم.

سه‌شنبه ۲۱ < اسفند >، ۱۲ < مارس > - لرد کدمن را در وزارت معادن دیدم. برای کار اداری مذاکره کردم.

چهارشنبه ۲۲ < اسفند >، ۱۳ < مارس > - کتاب خواندم و گردش کردم.

پنجشنبه ۲۳ < اسفند >، ۱۴ < مارس > - صبح بدیدن وزیر مختار جدید رفتم. آقای زرین‌کفش، خانمش و عزت خانم و رضا خان از کمبریج بلندن آمدند. پانصد و هشتاد و یک لیره خرج سفر زرین‌کفش را باو دادم. شب با ایشان در رستوران هندی غذا خوردم.

جمعه ۲۴ < اسفند >، ۱۵ < مارس > - در رستوران وودن‌هوس با آقای زرین‌کفش و خانمش و عزت خانم و رضا خان و دکتر حافظی ناهار خوردم. عصر بسفارت بمجلس مهمانی رفتم بمناسبت ولادت شاه.

شنبه ۲۵ < اسفند >، ۱۶ < مارس > - در رستوران کوه نور با زرین‌کفش و خانمش و عزت خانم و دکتر حافظی ناهار خوردیم. زرین‌کفش و خانمش شب بکمبریج مراجعت کردند.

یکشنبه ۲۶ < اسفند >، ۱۷ < مارس > - با نبیل بودم.

دوشنبه ۲۷ < اسفند >، ۱۸ < مارس > - کتاب خواندم.

سه‌شنبه ۱۸ اسفند، ۱۹ مارس - شب به اوپرا رفتم. کتاب هم خواندم.

چهارشنبه ۲۹ < اسفند >، ۲۰ < مارس > - صبح در اداره با زرین‌کفش بودم. عصر با دکتر حافظی بمریضخانه چشم رفتم. چشمم جوشی داشت. عمل مختصری کرد. شام با نبیل و حمزاوی در کنزینگ‌تون هتل خوردم.

پنجشنبه ۱ فروردین، ۲۱ مارس - ناهار در سفارت خوردم. شب بمنزل مینوی رفتم. عصر در سفارت مهمانی بود.

جمعه ۲ فروردین، ۲۲ مارس - کتاب خواندم.

شنبه ۳ < فروردین >، ۲۳ < مارس > - ناهار با نبیل در کمبریج در منزل زرین‌کفش خوردم. بدیدن آقای تقی‌زاده هم رفتم. بلندن مراجعت کردم. در راه اتومبیل خراب شد و در نی‌یو اکسفورد استریت از کار افتاد. به ر‌کل تلفون کردیم. آمد ما را برد.

یکشنبه ۴ < فروردین >، ۲۴ < مارس > - با نبیل ناهار خوردم و کتاب خواندم.

دوشنبه ۵ < فروردین >، ۲۵ < مارس > - با نبیل بودم.

سه‌شنبه ۶ < فروردین >، ۲۶ < مارس > - زرین‌کفش از کمبریج آمد. با هم ناهار خوردیم. شب با زرین‌کفش در رستوران هندی شفیع شام خوردیم. نبیل هم بود.

چهارشنبه ۷ < فروردین >، ۲۷ < مارس > - در مریضخانه برآمدگی روی پلک چشمم را عمل کردند. چیز مهمی نبود. شب با زرین‌کفش و دکتر حافظی در رستوران روسی شام خوردیم.

پنجشنبه ۸ < فروردین >، ۲۸ < مارس > - آقای زرین‌کفش را دیدم. مشغول تهیه مقدمات سفر است.

جمعه ۹ < فروردین >، ۲۹ < مارس > - ناهار با نبیل و بایندر در رویال پالاس هتل خوردم.

شنبه ۱۰ < فروردین >، ۳۰ مارس - با دکتر حافظی بباغ وحش رفتم. شب با نبیل بودم.

یکشنبه ۱۱ < فروردین >، ۳۱ < مارس > - کتاب خواندم.

دوشنبه ۱۲ < فروردین >، ۱ آوریل - زرین‌کفش و خانواده‌اش از کمبریج به گرونر هتل آمدند که بایران بروند.

سه‌شنبه ۱۳ < فروردین >، ۲ < آوریل > - بدیدن زرین‌کفش و خانواده‌اش رفتم.

چهارشنبه ۱۴ < فروردین >، ۳ < آوریل > - ناهار در روایال پالاس هتل خوردیم. نبیل مهماندار بود. زرین‌کفش و خانمش و خانواده‌اش بودند. زرین‌کفش ساعت ۹ بعد از ظهر بایران رفت.

پنجشنبه ۱۵ < فروردین >، ۴ < آوریل > - آقای تقی‌زاده از کمبریج بلندن آمد. با ایشان و نبیل ناهار خوردم. از پدرم کاغذی رسید.

جمعه ۱۶ < فروردین >، ۵ < آوریل > - با نبیل و بایندر و شیبانی ناهار خوردم. شام با آقای تقی‌زاده در رستوران ناتینز بریج خوردم.

شنبه ۱۷ < فروردین >، ۶ < آوریل > - با نبیل و شیبانی و بایندر ناهار خوردم.

یکشنبه ۱۸ < فروردین >، ۷ < آوریل > - در جرج استریت ناهار و در ریجنت پالاس هتل شام خوردم. کتاب خواندم.

دوشنبه ۱۹ < فروردین >، ۸ < آوریل > - شام در سفارت با نبیل و شیبانی خوردم.

سه‌شنبه ۲۰ < فروردین >، ۹ < آوریل > - با نبیل بودم.

چهارشنبه ۲۱ < فروردین >، ۱۰ < آوریل > - با دکتر حافظی در هولبورن ناهار خوردم.

پنجشنبه ۲۲ < فروردین >، ۱۱ < آوریل > - ناهار با شیبانی و نبیل و بایندر خوردم.

جمعه ۲۳ < فروردین >، ۱۲ < آوریل > - با فرمانفرماییان در رستوران اسپانیایی شام خوردم.

شنبه ۲۴ < فروردین >، ۱۳ < آوریل > - با نبیل و شیبانی و بایندر بودم.

یکشنبه ۲۵ < فروردین >، ۱۴ < آوریل > - با بایندر و نبیل و حمزاوی بمنزل شیبانی رفتم و همه با هم بسفارت.

دوشنبه ۲۶ < فروردین >، ۱۵ < آوریل > - ناهار با نبیل بودم.

سه‌شنبه ۲۷ < فروردین >، ۱۶ < آوریل > - با نبیل بودم و کتاب خواندم.

چهارشنبه ۲۸ < فروردین >، ۱۷ < آوریل > - با نبیل بودم.

پنجشنبه ۲۹ < فروردین >، ۱۸ < آوریل > - کتاب خواندم.

جمعه ۳۰ < فروردین >، ۱۹ < آوریل > - با نبیل بودم.

شنبه ۳۱ فروردین، ۲۰ آوریل - با نبیل بودم.

یکشنبه ۱ اردیبهشت، ۲۱ آوریل - با نبیل بودم.

دوشنبه ۲ < اردیبهشت >، ۲۲ < آوریل > - با نبیل و بایندر در تروکادرو ناهار خوردم.

سه‌شنبه ۳ < اردیبهشت >، ۲۳ < آوریل > - با آقای اصغرزاده ناهار خوردم. شب با با نبیل بودم.

چهارشنبه ۴ < اردیبهشت >، ۲۴ < آوریل > - در الدویچ[1] بازی کینگ لیر را دیدم.

---

۱. الدویک. مقصود باید Aldwych بوده باشد.

پنجشنبه ۵ < اردیبهشت >، ۲۵ < آوریل > - با نبیل بودم.

جمعه ۶ < اردیبهشت >، ۲۶ < آوریل > - با مایلز ناهار خوردم.

شنبه ۷ < اردیبهشت >، ۲۷ < آوریل > - با شیبانی شام خوردم.

یکشنبه ۸ < اردیبهشت >، ۲۸ < آوریل > - با شیبانی و بایندر ناهار خوردم. بعد از آن رفتیم به کینگستون بمنزل بایندر و گردش کردیم. شب با شیبانی بودم.

دوشنبه ۹ < اردیبهشت >، ۲۹ < آوریل > - کتاب خواندم.

سه‌شنبه ۱۰ < اردیبهشت >، ۳۰ < آوریل > - ناهار با نبیل و شام با نبیل و بایندر و شیبانی بودم.

چهارشنبه ۱۱ < اردیبهشت >، ۱ مه - با نبیل بودم و کتاب خواندم.

پنجشنبه ۱۲ < اردیبهشت >، ۲ < مه > - کتاب خواندم.

جمعه ۱۳ < اردیبهشت >، ۳ < مه > - کتاب خواندم.

شنبه ۱۴ < اردیبهشت >، ۴ < مه > - با نبیل و شیبانی بودم.

یکشنبه ۱۵ < اردیبهشت >، ۵ < مه > - با نبیل بودم.

دوشنبه ۱۶ < اردیبهشت >، ۶ < مه > - ناهار با مستر کلگ و شب با آرام < شام > خوردم.

سه‌شنبه ۱۷ < اردیبهشت >، ۷ < مه > - در رستوران اسپانیایی ناهار خوردیم و فیلم بباد رفته[1] را دیدم.

---

۱. *Gone with the Wind*، محصول آمریکا (۱۹۳۹).

چهارشنبه ۱۸ < اردیبهشت >، ۸ < مه > - با نبیل بودم.

پنجشنبه ۱۹ اردیبهشت، ۹ مه - با نبیل بودم. آجودانی از سوییس آمده بود. با او و شیبانی بودم.

جمعه ۲۰ اردیبهشت، ۱۰ مه - با نبیل و شیبانی و آجودانی بودم.

شنبه ۲۱ < اردیبهشت >، ۱۱ < مه > - با نبیل و شیبانی و بایندر بودم.

یکشنبه ۲۲ < اردیبهشت >، ۱۲ < مه > - با نبیل بودم.

دوشنبه ۲۳ < اردیبهشت >، ۱۳ < مه > - بکمبریج رفتم. اشتباهاً در راه در بیشاپز استورتفورد[1] پیاده شدم. با تاکسی بکمبریج رفتم. در منزل آقای تقی‌زاده ناهار خودم. نبیل هم بود.

سه‌شنبه ۲۴ < اردیبهشت >، ۱۴ < مه > - با نبیل و شیبانی و حمزاوی بودم.

چهارشنبه ۲۵ < اردیبهشت >، ۱۵ < مه > - با نبیل و بایندر و شیبانی بودم.

پنجشنبه ۲۶ < اردیبهشت >، ۱۶ < مه > - با نبیل بودم.

جمعه ۲۷ < اردیبهشت >، ۱۷ < مه > - با نبیل بودم.

شنبه ۲۸ < اردیبهشت >، ۱۸ < مه > - با نبیل بودم.

یکشنبه ۲۹ < اردیبهشت >، ۱۹ < مه > - کار فرانسه و انگلیس بسیار سخت است.

دوشنبه ۳۰ < اردیبهشت >، ۲۰ < مه > - ناهار با نبیل و حمزاوی خوردم.

سه‌شنبه ۳۱ < اردیبهشت >، ۲۱ < مه > - با آقای نصیرزاده ناهار خوردم.

---

۱. بیشوپ استورفور، که مقصود باید Bishops-Stortford Station باشد.

چهارشنبه ۱ خرداد، ۲۲ < مه > - با نبیل بودم.

پنجشنبه ۲ < خرداد >، ۲۳ < مه > - با نبیل بودم.

جمعه ۳ < خرداد >، ۲۴ < مه > - در سفارت بودم با نبیل.

شنبه ۴ < خرداد >، ۲۵ < مه > - با نبیل بودم.

یکشنبه ۵ < خرداد >، ۲۶ < مه > - با نبیل بودم.

دوشنبه ۶ خرداد، ۲۷ مه - ناهار با نبیل و حمزاوی و بایندر در روایال پالاس هتل خوردم.

سه‌شنبه ۷ < خرداد >، ۲۸ < مه > - پادشاه بلژیک بآلمان تسلیم شد. با نبیل بودم.

چهارشنبه ۸ < خرداد >، ۲۹ < مه > - کتاب خواندم. با نبیل بودم.

پنجشنبه ۹ < خرداد >، ۳۰ < مه > - کتاب خواندم شب و روز.

جمعه ۱۰ < خرداد >، ۳۱ < مه > - کتاب خواندم.

شنبه ۱۱ < خرداد >، ۱ ژوئن - انگلیس در دن‌کرک[1] در مقابل حملات آلمان استقامت بسیار می‌کند.

یکشنبه ۱۲ < خرداد >، ۲ < ژوئن > - با نبیل بودم. کتاب خواندم.

دوشنبه ۱۳ < خرداد >، ۳ < ژوئن > - همه منتظرند که ایتالیا نیز وارد جنگ شود.

سه‌شنبه ۱۴ < خرداد >، ۴ < ژوئن > - کتاب خواندم.

چهارشنبه ۱۵ < خرداد >، ۵ < ژوئن > - شب با آرام شام خوردم.

Dunkirk .۱

پنجشنبه ۱۶ < خرداد >، ۶ < ژوئن > - کتاب خواندم.

جمعه ۱۷ < خرداد >، ۷ < ژوئن > - کتاب خواندم.

شنبه ۱۸ < خرداد >، ۸ < ژوئن > - کتاب خواندم. با نبیل بودم.

یکشنبه ۱۹ < خرداد >، ۹ < ژوئن > - با آرام و وحید به بورنم شیر[1] رفتم. در راه زیر درختها خوابیدیم. خوش گذشت.

دوشنبه ۲۰ < خرداد >، ۱۰ < ژوئن > - کتاب خواندم.

سه‌شنبه ۲۱ < خرداد >، ۱۱ < ژوئن > - با نبیل بودم و کتاب خواندم.

چهارشنبه ۲۲ < خرداد >، ۱۲ < ژوئن > - به سن‌بری[2] بدیدن قسمت تجربی رفتم.

پنجشنبه ۲۳ < خرداد >، ۱۳ < ژوئن > - آلمانی خواندم.

جمعه ۲۴ < خرداد >، ۱۴ < ژوئن > - کتاب خواندم.

شنبه ۲۵ خرداد، ۱۵ ژوئن - با نبیل بودم. اوضاع فرانسه بسیار بد است. آلمان پیش می‌رود.

یکشنبه ۲۶ < خرداد >، ۱۶ < ژوئن > - با نبیل بودم.

دوشنبه ۲۷ < خرداد >، ۱۷ < ژوئن > - می‌گویند که مارشال پتن مشغول مذاکره است که با آلمان صلح کند.

سه‌شنبه ۲۸ < خرداد >، ۱۸ < ژوئن > - با نبیل بودم.

---

۱. بورنم چیر. مقصود Burnhamshire است.
۲. مقصود Sunbury-on-Thames است.

چهارشنبه ۲۹ ‹ خرداد ›، ۱۹ ‹ ژوئن › - انگلیسیها می‌خواهند تنها با آلمان بجنگند و کارشان سخت است.

پنجشنبه ۳۰ ‹ خرداد ›، ۲۰ ‹ ژوئن › - فرانسه از ایطالیا خواسته که صلح کند. با نبیل بودم.

جمعه ۳۱ ‹ خرداد ›، ۲۱ ‹ ژوئن › - با آرام شام خوردم.

شنبه ۱ تیر، ۲۲ ‹ ژوئن › - فرانسه تسلیم شد.

یکشنبه ۲ تیر، ۲۲ ‹ ژوئن › - با نبیل بودم.

دوشنبه ۳ تیر، ۲۳ ‹ ژوئن › - فرانسه با ایطالیا صلح کرد.

سه‌شنبه ۴ تیر، ۲۴ ‹ ژوئن › - در شرکت بمناسبت جلسه سالیانه شرکت استخراج اویل با لرد کدمن و سر ویلیام فریزر و سایر مدیران شرکت ناهار خوردم.

چهارشنبه ۵ تیر، ۲۶ ‹ ژوئن › - با فرمانفرماییان و معظمی بودم.

پنجشنبه ۶ ‹ تیر ›، ۲۷ ‹ ژوئن › - با نبیل و بایندر بودم.

جمعه ۷ ‹ تیر ›، ۲۸ ‹ ژوئن › - کتاب خواندم.

شنبه ۸ ‹ تیر ›، ۲۹ ‹ ژوئن › - کتاب خواندم.

یکشنبه ۹ ‹ تیر ›، ۳۰ ‹ ژوئن › - با نبیل بودم.

دوشنبه ۱۰ ‹ تیر ›، ۱ ژوییه - با آقای تقی‌زاده که در لندن بود چای خوردم.

سه‌شنبه ۱۱ ‹ تیر ›، ۲ ‹ ژوییه › - کتاب خواندم.

چهارشنبه ۱۲ < تیر >، ۳ < ژوبیه > - شب آلمانی خواندم.

پنجشنبه ۱۳ تیر، ۴ ژوبیه - با نبیل بودم.

جمعه ۱۴ < تیر >، ۵ < ژوبیه > - با نبیل بودم.

شنبه ۱۵ < تیر >، ۶ < ژوبیه > - با نبیل بودم.

یکشنبه ۱۶ < تیر >، ۷ < ژوبیه > - با نبیل بودم.

دوشنبه ۱۷ < تیر >، ۸ < ژوبیه > - با بایندر ناهار خوردم.

سه‌شنبه ۱۸ < تیر >، ۹ < ژوبیه > - آلمانی خواندم.

چهارشنبه ۱۹ < تیر >، ۱۰ < ژوبیه > - شب بتآتر رفتم. بازی چو چین چا[۱] را دیدم.

پنجشنبه ۲۰ < تیر >، ۱۱ < ژوبیه > - آلمانی خواندم.

جمعه ۲۱ < تیر >، ۱۲ < ژوبیه > - کتاب خواندم.

شنبه ۲۲ < تیر >، ۱۳ < ژوبیه > - با نبیل بودم.

یکشنبه ۲۳ < تیر >، ۱۴ < ژوبیه > - در رستوران یونانی با نبیل و حمزاوی ناهار خوردم.

دوشنبه ۲۴ < تیر >، ۱۵ < ژوبیه > - با نبیل بودم.

سه‌شنبه ۲۵ < تیر >، ۱۶ < ژوبیه > - با نبیل بودم.

چهارشنبه ۲۶ < تیر >، ۱۷ < ژوبیه > - با مستر مایلز ناهار خوردم.

----

۱. چین چو چا. مقصود باید *Chu Chin Chow* باشد، نمایشنامه کمدی موزیکال به کارگردانی آسکر آش
(Oscar Asche) که نخستین بار در ۳ اوت ۱۹۱۶ اجرای عمومی داشت.

پنجشنبه ۲۷ < تیر >، ۱۹ < ژوییه > - معظمی، مستوفی، خلیلی و بینا با من ناهار خوردند.

جمعه ۲۸ < تیر >، ۲۰ < ژوییه > - با نبیل بودم.

شنبه ۲۹ < تیر >، ۲۱ < ژوییه > - با نبیل بودم.

یکشنبه ۳۰ < تیر >، ۲۲ < ژوییه > - با نبیل بودم.

دوشنبه ۳۱ < تیر >، ۲۳ < ژوییه > - از برن خبر رسید که فرزین یکی از صاحبمنصبها سرهنگ شیبانی را کشته است. خیلی افسرده شدم چونکه مرد نجیب خوبی بود.

سه‌شنبه ۱ مرداد، ۲۳ ژوییه - کتاب خواندم.

چهارشنبه ۲ < مرداد >، ۲۴ < ژوییه > - با نبیل و حمزاوی و بایندر ناهار خوردم.

پنجشنبه ۳ < مرداد >، ۲۵ < ژوییه > - شب آلمانی خواندم.

جمعه ۴ < مرداد >، ۲۶ < ژوییه > - با نبیل و بایندر شام خوردم.

شنبه ۵ < مرداد >، ۲۷ < ژوییه > - شب با نبیل بودم.

یکشنبه ۶ < مرداد >، ۲۸ < ژوییه > - با نبیل بودم.

دوشنبه ۷ < مرداد >، ۲۹ < ژوییه > - با نبیل و بایندر بودم.

سه‌شنبه ۸ < مرداد >، ۳۰ < ژوییه > - ناهار با مینوی و شام با نبیل خوردم.

چهارشنبه ۹ < مرداد >، ۳۱ < ژوییه > - شب آلمانی خواندم.

پنجشنبه ۱۰ < مرداد >، ۱ اوت - با نبیل ناهار خوردم.

جمعه ۱۱ < مرداد >، ۲ اوت - کتاب خواندم.

شنبه ۱۲ < مرداد >، ۳ < اوت > - با نبیل بودم.

یکشنبه ۱۳ < مرداد >، ۴ < اوت > - آلمانی خواندم.

دوشنبه ۱۴ < مرداد >، ۵ < اوت > - آلمانی خواندم.

سه‌شنبه ۱۵ < مرداد >، ۶ < اوت > - مقدم وزیر مختار را دیدم. تا ساعت ۱۰ با نبیل بودم.

چهارشنبه ۱۶ < مرداد >، ۷ < اوت > - کتاب خواندم.

پنجشنبه ۱۷ < مرداد >، ۸ < اوت > - آلمانی خواندم.

جمعه ۱۸ < مرداد >، ۹ < اوت > - با نبیل بودم.

شنبه ۱۹ < مرداد >، ۱۰ < اوت > - کتاب خواندم.

یکشنبه ۲۰ < مرداد >، ۱۱ < اوت > - کتاب خواندم.

دوشنبه ۲۱ مرداد، ۱۲ اوت - با نبیل بودم.

سه‌شنبه ۲۲ < مرداد >، ۱۳ < اوت > - کتاب خواندم.

چهارشنبه ۲۳ < مرداد >، ۱۴ < اوت > - کتاب خواندم.

پنجشنبه ۲۴ < مرداد >، ۱۵ < اوت > - آلمانی خواندم. در وقتی که درس می‌خواندم اعلام خطر حمله هوایی شد. روز بروز شدت این حملات بیشتر می‌شود.

جمعه ۲۵ < مرداد >، ۱۶ < اوت > - کتاب خواندم.

شنبه ۲۶ < مرداد >، ۱۷ < اوت > - با آقای مینوی بودم.

یکشنبه ۲۷ < مرداد >، ۱۸ < اوت > - با نبیل بکمبریج بمنزل آقای تقی‌زاده رفتم.

دوشنبه ۲۸ < مرداد >، ۱۹ < اوت > - با نبیل بودم.

سه‌شنبه ۲۹ < مرداد >، ۲۰ < اوت > - در شرکت ناهار خوردم و در مجلس صاحبان سهام شرکت حضور یافتم.

چهارشنبه ۳۰ < مرداد >، ۲۱ < اوت > - کتاب خواندم.

پنجشنبه ۳۱ < مرداد >، ۲۲ < اوت > - آلمانی خواندم. اعلام خطر هوایی شد.

جمعه ۱ شهریور، ۲۳ < اوت > - کتاب خواندم.

شنبه ۲ < شهریور >، ۲۴ < اوت > - با نبیل بودم.

یکشنبه ۳ < شهریور >، ۲۵ < اوت > - با نبیل بودم.

دوشنبه ۴ < شهریور >، ۲۶ < اوت > - کتاب خواندم.

سه‌شنبه ۵ < شهریور >، ۲۷ < اوت > - تیاتر رفتم. بازی *Devil and Daniel*[1] رفتم. وسط بازی اعلام خطر هوایی شد. آکتور آمد و گفت هر که می‌خواهد برود. کسی نرفت.

چهارشنبه ۶ < شهریور >، ۲۸ < اوت > - کتاب خواندم.

پنجشنبه ۷ شهریور، ۲۹ اوت - شب آلمانی خواندم. در سه شب اخیر آلمانیها بلندن حمله کردند و بمب انداختند.

---

۱. ظاهراً مقصود باید *The Devil and Daniel Webster* باشد، تصنیف داگلاس مور (Douglas Moore). نخستین بار در بهار ۱۹۳۹ در نیویورک به اجرا درآمد.

جمعه ۸ < شهریور >، ۳۰ اوت - بپدرم کاغذی نوشتم. شب بصدای ضد توپ هواپیما بیدار شدم. حملات شدیدتر شده است.

شنبه ۹ < شهریور >، ۳۱ اوت - کتاب خواندم.

یکشنبه ۱۰ < شهریور >، ۱ سپتامبر - کتاب خواندم. با نبیل به گریت فوسترز رفتم.

دوشنبه ۱۱ < شهریور >، ۲ < سپتامبر > - کتاب خواندم.

سه‌شنبه ۱۲ < شهریور >، ۳ < سپتامبر > - کتاب ادبیات روس خواندم.

چهارشنبه ۱۳ < شهریور >، ۴ < سپتامبر > - آلمانی خواندم.

پنجشنبه ۱۴ < شهریور >، ۵ < سپتامبر > - کتاب خواندم.

جمعه ۱۵ < شهریور >، ۶ < سپتامبر > - کتاب خواندم.

شنبه ۱۶ < شهریور >، ۷ < سپتامبر > - بیش از چهار صد نفر در حمله هوایی کشته شد. کتاب خواندم.

یکشنبه ۱۷ < شهریور >، ۸ < سپتامبر > - کتاب خواندم.

دوشنبه ۱۸ < شهریور >، ۹ < سپتامبر > - در چند شب اخیر سخت بلندن حمله هوایی می‌کنند. کتاب خواندم.

سه‌شنبه ۱۹ < شهریور >، ۱۰ < سپتامبر > - شب بمب‌باران سخت شد. کتاب خواندم.

چهارشنبه ۲۰ < شهریور >، ۱۱ < سپتامبر > - کتاب و آلمانی خواندم. از شدت صدای توپ ضد طیاره خوابم نبرد.

پنجشنبه ۲۱ < شهریور >، ۱۲ < سپتامبر > - از اطاق خود در موقع حمله بزیر زمین خانه رفتم. شش هفت نفر دیگر هم آمده‌اند. جز سلب آسایش فایده‌ای ندارد چونکه اگر بمب بر این خانه افتاد، کار ما طی خواهد شد.

جمعه ۲۲ < شهریور >، ۱۳ < سپتامبر > - کتاب خواندم.

شنبه ۲۳ < شهریور >، ۱۴ < سپتامبر > - کتاب خواندم. با نبیل بودم.

یکشنبه ۲۴ < شهریور >، ۱۵ < سپتامبر > - با نبیل بودم. شب در سفارت خوابیدیم.

دوشنبه ۲۵ < شهریور >، ۱۶ < سپتامبر > - با نبیل بودم.

سه‌شنبه ۲۶ < شهریور >، ۱۷ < سپتامبر > - صدای توپ ضد هواپیما شدیدتر بود. با نبیل بودم.

چهارشنبه ۲۷ < شهریور >، ۱۸ < سپتامبر > - آلمانی خواندم. شب با نبیل بود.

پنجشنبه ۲۸ < شهریور >، ۱۹ < سپتامبر > - کتاب خواندم.

جمعه ۲۹ < شهریور >، ۲۰ < سپتامبر > - با نبیل و بایندر ناهار خوردم.

شنبه ۳۰ < شهریور >، ۲۱ < سپتامبر > - صبح با سه چهار چمدان بکمبریج رفتم. با آقای تقی‌زاده ناهار خوردم. شام هم با ایشان خوردم و در منزلشان خوابیدم. در کمبریج هم اعلام خطر شد و بپناهگاه رفتیم ولی بمب نیفتاد.

یکشنبه ۳۱ < شهریور >، ۲۲ < سپتامبر > - به Garden House Hotel رفتم. چمدانها را گذاشتم. تا ساعت ۷ با آقای تقی‌زاده بودم. کمبریج از نظر حمله هوایی نسبت بلندن بهشت است. فراغ خاطر هست و بمب نیست.

دوشنبه ۱ مهر، ۲۳ < سپتامبر > - چای در منزل آقای تقی‌زاده خوردم. کتاب خواندم.

سه‌شنبه ۲ < مهر >، ۲۴ < سپتامبر > - کتاب خواندم.

چهارشنبه ۳ < مهر >، ۲۵ < سپتامبر > - کتاب خواندم.

پنجشنبه ۴ < مهر >، ۲۶ < سپتامبر > - کتاب خواندم. عصر در منزل آقای تقی‌زاده بودم. در اطراف کمبریج بمب انداخته‌اند.

جمعه ۵ < مهر >، ۲۷ < سپتامبر > - در Royal Hotel اطاق گرفتم. شام در منزل آقای تقی‌زاده خوردم. خانم چلوکباب خوب پخته بود. روز ولادت آقای تقی‌زاده بود.

شنبه ۶ < مهر >، ۲۸ < سپتامبر > - کتاب خواندم و با بعضی از اهل هتل صحبت کردم.

یکشنبه ۷ مهر، ۲۹ سپتامبر - عصر با آقای تقی‌زاده به گران‌چستر رفتم.

دوشنبه ۸ < مهر >، ۳۰ < سپتامبر > - بلندن رفتم. در اداره کار کردم. در نورماندی با نبیل و بایندر ناهار خوردم. کتابهایم را بسفارت بردم. با ترن کند از لندن بکمبریج رفتم. ساعت یازده و نیم رسیدم.

سه‌شنبه ۹ < مهر >، ۱۱ اکتبر - کتاب خواندم. اعلام خطر هوایی شد.

چهارشنبه ۱۰ < مهر >، ۲ < اکتبر > - عصر با آقای تقی‌زاده بسینما رفتم. شب نبیل را دیدم. از کمبریج آمده بود. بهتل او رفتم. تا ساعت یازده با هم بودیم.

پنجشنبه ۱۱ < مهر >، ۳ < اکتبر > - با نبیل عصر بمنزل آقای تقی‌زاده رفتم و شب بمنزل مینورسکی.

جمعه ۱۲ < مهر >، ۴ < اکتبر > - با نبیل بلندن رفتم. اسباب و اثاث خانه را جمع کردم و قسمتی را در سفارت گذاشتم. شب با نبیل بکمبریج آمدم.

شنبه ۱۳ > مهر >، ۵ > اکتبر > - با نبیل عصر بمنزل آقای تقی‌زاده رفتم.

یکشنبه ۱۴ > مهر >، ۶ > اکتبر > - با آقای تقی‌زاده و خانمش و نبیل به Ely رفتم. کلیسا را دیدیم. شب آقای تقی‌زاده و خانمش بهتل نبیل آمدند. همه با هم شام خوردیم.

دوشنبه ۱۵ > مهر >، ۷ > اکتبر > - با نبیل بلندن آمدم. با بایندر و او در لندن ناهار خوردیم. شب با نبیل به Caterham[1] رفتم. صدای توپ و بمب شنیده می‌شد. شب در کترم بودم.

سه‌شنبه ۱۶ > مهر >، ۸ > اکتبر > - با آقای تقی‌زاده و بایندر و نبیل در کافه روایال ناهار خوردیم و تا ایستگاه لیورپول آقای تقی‌زاده را مشایعت کردم. بعد با ترن به Caterham رفتم.

چهارشنبه ۱۷ > مهر >، ۹ > اکتبر > - با ترن به کترم رفتم. در کوچه‌های آن گردش کردم. شب نبیل هم آمد.

پنجشنبه ۱۸ مهر، ۱۰ اکتبر - مهمان بایندر بودم. نبیل و چند نفر دیگر هم بودند. نبیل عنقریب بایران می‌رود. شب بکمبریج مراجعت کردم. بمنزل آقای تقی‌زاده رفتم.

جمعه ۱۹ > مهر >، ۱۱ > اکتبر > - با نبیل بکمبریج آمدم و مقداری از کتب خود را آوردم.

شنبه ۲۰ > مهر >، ۱۲ > اکتبر > - با نبیل ناهار خوردم و عصر با او و آقای تقی‌زاده به گران‌چستر رفتم.

یکشنبه ۲۱ > مهر >، ۱۳ > اکتبر > - با نبیل در منزل آقای تقی‌زاده ناهار خوردم.

---

۱. شهرکی در جنوب لندن، حدود ۱۸ مایلی.

دوشنبه ۲۲ ‹ مهر ›، ۱۴ ‹ اکتبر › - با نبیل بلندن رفتم. شب بکمبریج آمدم.

سه‌شنبه ۲۳ ‹ مهر ›، ۱۵ ‹ اکتبر › - با نبیل بلندن رفتم و با او مراجعت کردم.

چهارشنبه ۲۴ ‹ مهر ›، ۱۶ ‹ اکتبر › - با نبیل و حمزاوی و بایندر و مستر گر ناهار خوردم. بمناسبت رفتن نبیل از وزیر مختار هم خواسته بودم که بیاید ولی برای پیدا کردن خانه به اسکاتلند رفته بود و عذر خواست. با نبیل بکمبریج آمدم.

پنجشنبه ۲۵ ‹ مهر ›، ۱۷ ‹ اکتبر › - با نبیل بلندن رفتم. اتوموبیلش در هت فیلد شکست. با ترن بلندن رفتیم. شب بکمبریج آمدم و بمنزل آقای تقی‌زاده رفتم.

جمعه ۲۶ ‹ مهر ›، ۱۸ ‹ اکتبر › - شب با نبیل بودم. به کمبریج آمده بود.

شنبه ۲۷ ‹ مهر ›، ۱۹ ‹ اکتبر › - از عصر تا ساعت ۱۱ در منزل آقای تقی‌زاده بودم. نبیل هم بود.

یکشنبه ۲۸ ‹ مهر ›، ۲۰ ‹ اکتبر › - با نبیل بودم.

دوشنبه ۲۹ ‹ مهر ›، ۲۱ ‹ اکتبر › - با نبیل بلندن رفتم. دیدم عمارت سفارت آسیب مختصر یافته ولی بسیار غم انگیز بود. شب با نبیل بکمبریج آمدم. کتابهایم را در شرکت امانت گذاشتم.

سه‌شنبه ۳۰ ‹ مهر ›، ۲۲ ‹ اکتبر › - بلندن رفتم و با نبیل مراجعت کردم و شب با او بود.

چهارشنبه ۱ آبان، ۲۳ ‹ اکتبر › - با خانم تقی‌زاده بتآتر رفتم. *Ladies &* *Gentlemen*[۱] را دیدیم. عصر بمنزل آقای تقی‌زاده رفتم. شب با نبیل بودم.

---

۱. نمایشنامه‌ای تصنیف چارلز مک‌آرثر (Charles MacArthur) و بن هگت (Bent Hecht). نخستین اجرای آن در کالیفرنیا بود.

پنجشنبه ۲ < آبان >، ۲۴ < اکتبر > - باداره رفتم و با بایندر ناهار خوردم. با نبیل بکمبریج آمدم.

جمعه ۳ آبان، ۲۵ اکتبر - کتاب خواندم و با نبیل بودم.

شنبه ۴ < آبان >، ۲۶ < اکتبر > - عصر با نبیل بمنزل آقای تقی‌زاده رفتم. شب با نبیل بودم.

یکشنبه ۵ < آبان >، ۲۷ < اکتبر > - با نبیل و آقای تقی‌زاده و خانمش اول به نی یو مارکت و بعد به گران‌چستر رفتم. بعد از شام با نبیل بمنزل آقای تقی‌زاده رفتم.

دوشنبه ۶ < آبان >، ۲۸ < اکتبر > - شب با نبیل بودم.

سه‌شنبه ۷ < آبان >، ۲۹ < اکتبر > - کتاب خواندم. شب با نبیل بودم.

چهارشنبه ۸ < آبان >، ۳۰ < اکتبر > - با نبیل بلندن رفتم. با بایندر و او ناهار خوردم. شب بکمبریج آمدم.

پنجشنبه ۹ < آبان >، ۳۱ < اکتبر > - بلندن رفتم و با ترن بکمبریج آمدم. شب با نبیل بودم.

جمعه ۱۰ < آبان >، ۱ نوامبر - شب با نبیل بودم. روز کتاب خواندم.

شنبه ۱۱ < آبان >، ۲ < نوامبر > - روز با نبیل بودم. عصر بمنزل آقای تقی‌زاده رفتم. شب هم با نبیل بودم.

یکشنبه ۱۲ < آبان >، ۳ < نوامبر > - از ساعت پنج تا یازده با نبیل در منزل آقای تقی‌زاده بودم.

دوشنبه ۱۳ < آبان >، ۴ < نوامبر > - تا یازده و نیم بعد از ظهر با نبیل بودم.

سه‌شنبه ۱۴ < آبان >، ۵ < نوامبر > - صبح با نبیل بلندن رفتم و شب با او و معلم انگلیسیش بکمبریج آمدم.

چهارشنبه ۱۵ < آبان >، ۶ < نوامبر > - کتاب خواندم و مدتی با نبیل بودم.

پنجشنبه ۱۶ < آبان >، ۷ < نوامبر > - صبح با نبیل بلندن رفتم. عصر بسینما رفتم. شب بکمبریج آمدم.

جمعه ۱۷ < آبان >، ۸ < نوامبر > - با آقای تقی‌زاده بسینما رفتم.

شنبه ۱۸ < آبان >، ۹ < نوامبر > - با نبیل بودم.

یکشنبه ۱۹ < آبان >، ۱۰ < نوامبر > - عصر با نبیل بمنزل آقای تقی‌زاده رفتم. تا ساعت ۱۱ با ایشان بودم. نبیل خداحافظی کرد و این آخرین شب اوست به کمبریج.

دوشنبه ۲۰ < آبان >، ۱۱ < نوامبر > - با نبیل بلندن رفتم. شب در فلت حمزاوی خوابیدیم. نبیل هم بود.

سه‌شنبه ۲۱ < آبان >، ۱۲ < نوامبر > - با اتومبیل سفارت پنج بعد از ظهر بایستگاه یوس‌تن[1] رفتیم و نبیل با ترن هشت بلیورپول رفت. شب بکمبریج آمدم. منزل آقای تقی‌زاده رفتم.

چهارشنبه ۲۲ < آبان >، ۱۳ < نوامبر > - کتاب خواندم.

پنجشنبه ۲۳ < آبان >، ۱۴ < نوامبر > - کتاب خواندم.

جمعه ۲۴ < آبان >، ۱۵ < نوامبر > - کتاب خواندم.

شنبه ۲۵ < آبان >، ۱۶ < نوامبر > - عصر بمنزل آقای تقی‌زاده رفتم.

یکشنبه ۲۶ < آبان >، ۱۷ < نوامبر > - عصر با آقای تقی‌زاده به گران‌چستر رفتم.

دوشنبه ۲۷ < آبان >، ۱۸ < نوامبر > - بلندن رفتم و بکمبریج آمدم.

سه‌شنبه ۲۸ < آبان >، ۱۹ < نوامبر > - حالم بد است. تب دارم و دندان درد.

چهارشنبه ۲۹ < آبان >، ۲۰ < نوامبر > - شب بمنزل آقای تقی‌زاده رفتم.

پنجشنبه ۳۰ < آبان >، ۲۱ < نوامبر > - کتاب خواندم.

جمعه ۱ آذر، ۲۲ < نوامبر > - کتاب خواندم.

شنبه ۲ < آذر >، ۲۳ < نوامبر > - با خانم تقی‌زاده چای خوردم. شب کتاب خواندم.

یکشنبه ۳ < آذر >، ۲۴ < نوامبر > - بلندن رفتم و بکمبریج آمدم.

دوشنبه ۴ < آذر >، ۲۵ < نوامبر > - کتاب خواندم.

سه‌شنبه ۵ < آذر >، ۲۶ < نوامبر > - بلندن رفتم و بکمبریج مراجعت کردم.

چهارشنبه ۶ < آذر >، ۲۷ < نوامبر > - شب بمنزل آقای تقی‌زاده رفتم.

پنجشنبه ۷ < آذر >، ۲۸ < نوامبر > - کتاب خواندم.

جمعه ۸ < آذر >، ۲۹ < نوامبر > - کتاب خواندم.

شنبه ۹ < آذر >، ۳۰ < نوامبر > - بعد از ظهر با خانم تقی‌زاده به باله رفتم. شب در منزل آقای تقی‌زاده بودم.

یکشنبه ۱۰ آذر، ۱ دسامبر - در هتل بودم و کتاب خواندم.

دوشنبه ۱۱ < آذر >، ۲ < دسامبر > - کتاب خواندم.

سه‌شنبه ۱۲ < آذر >، ۳ < دسامبر > - کتاب خواندم.

چهارشنبه ۱۳ < آذر >، ۴ < دسامبر > - کتاب خواندم.

پنجشنبه ۱۴ < آذر >، ۵ < دسامبر > - بلندن رفتم. با مینوی ناهار خوردم. عصر بکمبریج آمدم.

جمعه ۱۵ < آذر >، ۶ < دسامبر > - کتاب خواندم.

شنبه ۱۶ < آذر >، ۷ < دسامبر > - کتاب خواندم.

یکشنبه ۱۷ < آذر >، ۸ < دسامبر > - شب در منزل آقای تقی‌زاده شام خوردم.

دوشنبه ۱۸ < آذر >، ۹ < دسامبر > - کتاب خواندم.

سه‌شنبه ۱۹ < آذر >، ۱۰ < دسامبر > - کتاب خواندم.

چهارشنبه ۲۰ < آذر >، ۱۱ < دسامبر > - کتاب خواندم.

پنجشنبه ۲۱ < آذر >، ۱۲ < دسامبر > - کتاب خواندم.

جمعه ۲۲ < آذر >، ۱۳ < دسامبر > - بلندن رفتم و با بایندر ناهار خوردم. عصر بکمبریج آمدم.

شنبه ۲۳ < آذر >، ۱۴ < دسامبر > - عصر با آقای تقی‌زاده و خانمش به تآتر رفتم.

یکشنبه ۲۴ < آذر >، ۱۵ < دسامبر > - با آقای تقی‌زاده و خانمش و مسیز بنت

برای تماشای جلسه معتقدین باحضار ارواح رفتم. از آن جا بمنزل آقای تقی‌زاده رفتم.

دوشنبه ۲۵ < آذر >، ۱۶ < دسامبر > - بلندن رفتم و با بایندر و حمزاوی ناهار خوردم. عصر بکمبریج رفتم.

سه‌شنبه ۲۶ < آذر >، ۱۷ < دسامبر > - کتاب خواندم.

چهارشنبه ۲۷ < آذر >، ۱۸ < دسامبر > - بلندن رفتم. با بایندر ناهار خوردم. مراجعت کردم.

پنجشنبه ۲۸ < آذر >، ۱۹ < دسامبر > - با آقای تقی‌زاده و مینورسکی بلندن رفتم. شب مراجعت کردم.

جمعه ۲۹ آذر، ۲۰ دسامبر - کتاب خواندم.

شنبه ۳۰ < آذر >، ۲۱ < دسامبر > - بمنزل آقای تقی‌زاده رفتم.

یکشنبه ۱ دی، ۲۲ < دسامبر > - با آقای تقی‌زاده بکلیسای کینگز کالج و به تری‌نی‌تی رفتم. شب کتاب خواندم.

دوشنبه ۲ < دی >، ۲۳ < دسامبر > - بلندن رفتم. با بایندر ناهار خوردم. بکمبریج آمدم.

سه‌شنبه ۳ < دی >، ۲۴ < دسامبر > - کتاب خواندم.

چهارشنبه ۴ < دی >، ۲۵ < دسامبر > - کتاب خواندم. ناهار در منزل آقای تقی‌زاده خوردم. برادرزنش هم بود. در هتل بساط کریسمس[1] مرتب است.

____

۱. کریس مسز

پنجشنبه ۵ < دی >، ۲۶ < دسامبر > - کتاب خواندم.

جمعه ۶ < دی >، ۲۷ < دسامبر > - بلندن رفتم. با باینـدر و حمزاوی ناهار خوردم. شب بکمبریج آمدم.

شنبه ۷ < دی >، ۲۸ < دسامبر > - کتاب خواندم.

یکشنبه ۸ < دی >، ۲۹ < دسامبر > - کتاب خواندم.

دوشنبه ۹ < دی >، ۳۰ < دسامبر > - بلندن رفتم. با باینـدر ناهار خوردم. شب بکمبریج آمدم.

سه‌شنبه ۱۰ < دی >، ۳۱ دسامبر - بلندن رفتم. با حمزاوی و باینـدر ناهار خوردم.

چهارشنبه ۱۱ دی، ۱ ژانویه - با آقای تقی‌زاده و خانمش و مسیز بنت بسینما رفتم.

پنجشنبه ۱۲ < دی >، ۲ < ژانویه > - بلندن رفتم. با باینـدر و حمزاوی ناهار خوردم. بکمبریج آمدم.

جمعه ۱۳ < دی >، ۳ < ژانویه > - اَش‌بی دولازوش[1] رفتم. در Kettering ناهار خوردم. چهار بعد از ظهر به اَش‌بی رسیدم. در روایال هتل منزل کردم که هم اسم هتل کمبریج است.

شنبه ۱۴ < دی >، ۴ < ژانویه > - به داربی رفتم و کارخانه چینی‌سازی را تماشا کردم.

یکشنبه ۱۵ < دی >، ۵ < ژانویه > - قلعه نزدیک اَش‌بی دولازوش را دیدم.

دوشنبه ۱۶ < دی >، ۶ < ژانویه > - کتاب خواندم و بتماشای اَش‌بی دولازوش مشغول بودم.

---

۱. Ashby-de-la-Zouch، شهرکی در شمال شرقی بیرمنگام و شمال غربی لستر.

سه‌شنبه ۱۷ < دی >، ۷ < ژانویه > - بکمبریج برگشتم.

چهارشنبه ۱۸ < دی >، ۸ < ژانویه > - کتاب خواندم. رادیو در اطاقم گذاشتم و مونس خوبیست.

پنجشنبه ۱۹ < دی >، ۹ < ژانویه > - کتاب خواندم. با آقای تقی‌زاده بودم.

جمعه ۲۰ < دی >، ۱۰ < ژانویه > - بلندن رفتم و بکمبریج مراجعت کردم.

شنبه ۲۱ < دی >، ۱۱ < ژانویه > - کتاب خواندم.

یکشنبه ۲۲ < دی >، ۱۲ < ژانویه > - شب در منزل آقای تقی‌زاده بودم.

دوشنبه ۲۳ < دی >، ۱۳ < ژانویه > - بلندن رفتم. با بایندر ناهار خوردم و بکمبریج آمدم.

سه‌شنبه ۲۴ < دی >، ۱۴ < ژانویه > - کتاب خواندم.

چهارشنبه ۲۵ < دی >، ۱۵ < ژانویه > - عصر بمنزل آقای تقی‌زاده رفتم.

پنجشنبه ۲۶ < دی >، ۱۶ < ژانویه > - بلندن رفتم و عصر بکمبریج آمدم.

جمعه ۲۷ < دی >، ۱۷ < ژانویه > - کتاب خواندم.

شنبه ۲۸ < دی >، ۱۸ < ژانویه > - کتاب خواندم.

یکشنبه ۲۹ < دی >، ۱۹ < ژانویه > - عصر بمنزل آقای تقی‌زاده رفتم.

دوشنبه ۳۰ دی، ۲۰ ژانویه - کتاب خواندم.

سه‌شنبه ۱ بهمن، ۲۱ ژانویه - بلندن رفتم و بکمبریج آمدم.

چهارشنبه ۲ < بهمن >، ۲۲ < ژانویه > - کتاب خواندم.

پنجشنبه ۳ < بهمن >، ۲۳ < ژانویه > - بلندن رفتم. با باینِدر و حمزاوی ناهار خوردم. بکمبریج آمدم.

جمعه ۴ < بهمن >، ۲۴ < ژانویه > - بلندن رفتم. با بزیل گری و لاکهارت ناهار خوردم.

شنبه ۵ < بهمن >، ۲۵ < ژانویه > - با آقای تقی‌زاده بود.

یکشنبه ۶ < بهمن >، ۲۶ < ژانویه > - با آقای تقی‌زاده و خانم تقی‌زاده عصر به گران‌چستر رفتم.

دوشنبه ۷ < بهمن >، ۲۷ < ژانویه > - کتاب خواندم.

سه‌شنبه ۸ < بهمن >، ۲۸ < ژانویه > - کتاب خواندم.

چهارشنبه ۹ < بهمن >، ۲۹ < ژانویه > - کتاب خواندم.

شنبه ۱۰ < بهمن >، ۳۰ < ژانویه > - عصر بمنزل آقای تقی‌زاده رفتم.

یکشنبه ۱۱ < بهمن >، ۳۱ < ژانویه > - بلندن رفتم. با آقای آرام ناهار خوردم. شب بکمبریج آمدم.

شنبه ۱۲ < بهمن >، ۱ فوریه - کتاب خواندم.

یکشنبه ۱۳ < بهمن >، ۲ < فوریه > - کتاب خواندم.

دوشنبه ۱۴ < بهمن >، ۳ < فوریه > - بلندن رفتم و بکمبریج آمدم.

سه‌شنبه ۱۵ < بهمن >، ۴ < فوریه > - کتاب خواندم.

چهارشنبه ۱۶ < بهمن >، ۵ < فوریه > - کتاب خواندم.

پنجشنبه ۱۷ < بهمن >، ۶ < فوریه > - کتاب خواندم. شب بانجمن محصلین رفتم. در باب تربیت نطق می‌کردند.

جمعه ۱۸ < بهمن >، ۷ < فوریه > - بلندن رفتم. با بایندر ناهار خوردم. بکمبریج آمدم.

شنبه ۱۹ < بهمن >، ۸ < فوریه > - صبح مستر شتل‌ورث صاحبخانه لندن که بازیگر هم هست بهتل آمد. با من ناهار خورد. دو بعد از ظهر با ترن بلندن رفتم. مجلس مهمانی بمناسبت عروسیش بود. وزیر مختار هم آمده بود. با ترن هشت و ۲۲ دقیقه بکمبریج مراجعت کردم. در ایستگاه و در سکوی اطراف خط آهن چنان مردم از خطر حمله هوایی بپناه آمده بودند < که > رقت آور بود. اما نظم و ترتیب عجیب برقرار بود.

یکشنبه ۲۰ بهمن، ۹ فوریه - عصر بمنزل آقای تقی‌زاده رفتم.

دوشنبه ۲۱ < بهمن >، ۱۰ < فوریه > - بلندن رفتم و بکمبریج آمدم.

سه‌شنبه ۲۲ < بهمن >، ۱۱ < فوریه > - بلندن رفتم. با نیامیر نهار خوردم و عصر مهمانی سفارت مصر رفتم. شب بکمبریج آمدم. کتاب خواندم.

چهارشنبه ۲۳ < بهمن >، ۱۲ < فوریه > - بعد از شام بدیدن آقای تقی‌زاده رفتم.

پنجشنبه ۲۴ < بهمن >، ۱۳ < فوریه > - عصر با آقای تقی‌زاده بدیدن فیلم *Juarez*[1] رفتم.

جمعه ۲۵ < بهمن >، ۱۴ < فوریه > - آلمانی خواندم.

شنبه ۲۶ < بهمن >، ۱۵ < فوریه > - با آقای تقی‌زاده و خانمش و مسیز بنت و مستر بنت بسینما رفتم. فیلم دیکتاتور را دیدیم.

---

۱. درام تاریخی محصول ۱۹۳۹ امریکا به کارگردانی ویلیام دایترل (William Dieterle).

یکشنبه ۲۷ < بهمن >، ۱۶ < فوریه > - عصر با آقای تقی‌زاده بودم.

دوشنبه ۲۸ < بهمن >، ۱۷ < فوریه > - ناهار در لندن با بایندر و صاحب‌خانه‌اش خوردم. شب بکمبریج آمدم.

سه‌شنبه ۲۹ < بهمن >، ۱۸ < فوریه > - آلمانی خواندم.

چهارشنبه ۳۰ < بهمن >، ۱۹ < فوریه > - ناهار با مستر مایلز خوردم.

پنجشنبه ۱ اسفند، ۲۰ فوریه - بلندن رفتم. با سر ویلیام فریزر ناهار خوردم. شب بکمبریج آمدم.

جمعه ۲ < اسفند >، ۲۱ < فوریه > - کتاب خواندم.

شنبه ۳ < اسفند >، ۲۲ فوریه - کتاب خواندم.

یکشنبه ۴ < اسفند >، ۲۳ < فوریه > - کتاب خواندم.

دوشنبه ۵ < اسفند >، ۲۴ < فوریه > - کتاب خواندم.

سه‌شنبه ۶ < اسفند >، ۲۵ < فوریه > - بلندن رفتم. با بایندر و حمزاوی ناهار خوردم. بکمبریج آمدم.

چهارشنبه ۷ < اسفند >، ۲۶ < فوریه > - آلمانی خواندم. شب بمنزل آقای تقی‌زاده رفتم.

پنجشنبه ۸ < اسفند >، ۲۷ < فوریه > - آلمانی خواندم.

جمعه ۹ < اسفند >، ۲۸ < فوریه > - آلمانی خواندم.

شنبه ۱۰ < اسفند >، اول مارس - روز و شب کتاب خواندم.

یکشنبه ۱۱ < اسفند >، ۲ < مارس > - عصر بمنزل آقای تقی‌زاده رفتم. آلمانی خواندم.

دوشنبه ۱۲ < اسفند >، ۳ < مارس > - بلندن رفتم و بکمبریج آمدم. شب آلمانی خواندم.

سه‌شنبه ۱۳ < اسفند >، ۴ < مارس > - بلندن رفتم. با بایندر و حمزاوی و زنش ناهار خوردم. بکمبریج آمدم.

چهارشنبه ۱۴ < اسفند >، ۵ < مارس > - صبح آلمانی خواندم. عصر بمنزل آقای تقی‌زاده رفتم. پروفسور بیلی[1] هم بود. او رفت. شام در منزل آقای تقی‌زاده خوردم.

پنجشنبه ۱۵ < اسفند >، ۶ < مارس > - آلمانی خواندم. از نبیل کاغذی رسید.

جمعه ۱۶ < اسفند >، ۷ < مارس > - آلمانی خواندم.

شنبه ۱۷ < اسفند >، ۸ < مارس > - آلمانی خواندم. عصر با آقای تقی‌زاده بودم. شب مهمان پروفسور بیلی بودم در کویینز کالج.

یکشنبه ۱۸ < اسفند >، ۹ < مارس > - بنمایش گیلد هال کمبریج رفتم. بی‌تماشا نبود. سربازان چک نمایش می‌دادند.

دوشنبه ۱۹ < اسفند >، ۱۰ < مارس > - بلندن رفتم. با مقدم وزیر مختار راجع بکاری که می‌خواهد از گردن خود بردارد[2] مذاکره کردم. ناهار با بایندر خوردم. شب بکمبریج آمدم.

سه‌شنبه ۲۰ اسفند، ۱۱ مارس - بلندن رفتم. شب بمنزل آقای تقی‌زاده رفتم. از دورویی سفارت و کوشش در رفع مسئولیت اوقاتم تلخ بود.

---

۱. Harold Walter Bailey (م. ۱۹۹۶م) پژوهشگر زبانهای ختنی، سنسکریت، و ایرانی در دانشگاه لندن.

۲. بردارم

چهارشنبه ۲۱ < اسفند >، ۱۲ < مارس > - بلندن رفتم. مقدم وزیر مختار را دیدم. شب بکمبریج آمدم.

پنجشنبه ۲۲ < اسفند >، ۱۳ < مارس > - کتاب خواندم.

جمعه ۲۳ < اسفند >، ۱۴ < مارس > - با خانم تقی‌زاده و مستر بوتلر بلندن رفتم و با ایشان بکمبریج آمدم.

شنبه ۲۴ < اسفند >، ۱۵ < مارس > - آلمانی خواندم.

یکشنبه ۲۵ < اسفند >، ۱۶ < مارس > - عصر با آقای تقی‌زاده و خانمش به گران‌چستر رفتم. شب آلمانی خواندم.

دوشنبه ۲۶ < اسفند >، ۱۷ < مارس > - بلندن رفتم و شب بکمبریج آمدم.

سه‌شنبه ۲۷ < اسفند >، ۱۸ < مارس > - بلندن رفتم. با بایندر و حمزاوی ناهار خوردم. شب بکمبریج آمدم.

چهارشنبه ۲۸ < اسفند >، ۱۹ < مارس > - عصر بمنزل پروفسور مینورسکی رفتم و شب آلمانی خواندم.

پنجشنبه ۲۹ < اسفند >، ۲۰ < مارس > - بلندن رفتم. با بایندر و حمزاوی ناهار خوردم. شب بکمبریج آمدم.

جمعه ۱ فروردین، ۲۱ مارس - بلندن رفتم. اول به هرودز و از آنجا بسفارت رفتم. حمزاوی، زنش، آرام، وحید، نیامیر، و گلمکانی بودند. شب بکمبریج آمدم.

شنبه ۲ < فروردین >، ۲۲ مارس - آلمانی خواندم. عصر بدیدن آقای توپالیان رفتم که در منزل پروفسور چدویک معلم زبان قدیم انگلیسی است. پروفسور و زنش هم بودند. در باب ادبیات و زبان ایران صحبت کردیم.

یکشنبه ۳ < فروردین >، ۲۳ مارس - آلمانی خواندم. ناهار در منزل آقای تقی‌زاده خوردم. بعد با آقای تقی‌زاده و خانمش رفتم بمنزل مینورسکی. دختری ایرانی از خانواده نمازی آن جا بود. تا ساعت شش و نیم آن جا بودم. بعد با آقای تقی‌زاده راه رفتم. شب آلمانی خواندم.

دوشنبه ۴ < فروردین >، ۲۴ مارس - بلندن رفتم. با بایندر ناهار خوردم. شب بکمبریج آمدم.

سه‌شنبه ۵ < فروردین >، ۲۵ مارس - کتاب خواندم.

چهارشنبه ۶ < فروردین >، ۲۶ مارس - تمام روز آلمانی خواندم.

پنجشنبه ۷ < فروردین >، ۲۷ مارس - بلندن رفتم.

جمعه ۸ < فروردین >، ۲۸ مارس - با آقای تقی‌زاده بودم.

شنبه ۹ < فروردین >، ۲۹ مارس - بلندن رفتم. بکمبریج آمدم.

یکشنبه ۱۰ < فروردین >، ۳۰ مارس - با آقای تقی‌زاده راه رفتم. بعد از شام بمنزل آقای تقی‌زاده رفتم.

دوشنبه ۱۱ < فروردین >، ۳۱ مارس - بلندن رفتم. با بایندر ناهار خوردم. شب بکمبریج آمدم.

سه‌شنبه ۱۲ < فروردین >، ۱ آوریل - آلمانی خواندم.

چهارشنبه ۱۳ < فروردین >، ۲ < آوریل > - بلندن رفتم. با بایندر ناهار خوردم. شب بکمبریج آمدم.

پنجشنبه ۱۴ < فروردین >، ۳ < آوریل > - آلمانی خواندم.

جمعه ۱۵ < فروردین >، ۴ < آوریل > - آلمانی خواندم.

شنبه ۱۶ < فروردین >، ۵ < آوریل > - آلمانی خواندم. با آقای تقی‌زاده و خانمش و فرنگیس خانم نمازی به یونی‌ورسیتی آرمز هتل[1] رفتم. ناهار خوردیم. عصر بمنزل آقای تقی‌زاده رفتم.

یکشنبه ۱۷ < فروردین >، ۶ < آوریل > - از یازده تا یک بعد از ظهر با آقای تقی‌زاده بودم. عصر بمنزل پروفسور مینورسکی رفتم. فرنگیس خانم نمازی و یک شاهزاده هندی هم بودند. شب آلمانی خواندم.

دوشنبه ۱۸ < فروردین >، ۷ < آوریل > - صبح کتاب خواندم بعد بکتابخانه هفرز رفتم. نیم ساعت بعد از ظهر فرنگیس خانم نمازی آمد. با او در رستوران دوروثی ناهار خوردم. بعد رفتیم بسینما. دختر مؤدب، نجیبی است و باهوش. شب حالم خوب نبود.

سه‌شنبه ۱۹ < فروردین >، ۸ < آوریل > - فیلم میجر باربارا[2] را دیدم. شب بکمبریج آمدم. حالم چندان خوب نبود.

---

1. University Arms Hotel.

2. *Major Barbara*، کمدی محصول ۱۹۴۱ انگلستان.

چهارشنبه ۲۰ < فروردین >، ۹ < آوریل > - کتاب خواندم. با فرنگیس خانم نمازی ناهار خوردم. و از آن جا با هم رفتیم بسینما.

پنجشنبه ۲۱ < فروردین >، ۱۰ < آوریل > - صبح بلندن رفتم و شب بکمبریج آمدم.

جمعه ۲۲ < فروردین >، ۱۱ < آوریل > - صبح کتاب خواندم. بعد از ظهر بسینما و شب بمنزل آقای تقی‌زاده رفتم.

شنبه ۲۳ < فروردین >، ۱۲ < آوریل > - صبح کتاب خواندم. ناهار با فرنگیس خانم خوردم. بعد از ظهر با هم بودیم.

یکشنبه ۲۴ < فروردین >، ۱۳ < آوریل > - صبح با آقای تقی‌زاده در خیابانهای کمبریج گردش کردم. بعد از ناهار با فرنگیس خانم به گران‌چستر رفتم و بعد در کمبریج با هم شام خوردیم.

دوشنبه ۲۵ < فروردین >، ۱۴ < آوریل > - صبح کتاب خواندم و عصر با فرنگیس خانم کمی راه رفتم. بعد با هم در رستوران ایطالیایی شام خوردیم و بعد بمنزل آقای تقی‌زاده رفتیم. تا ساعت ده و ربع آن جا بودیم. بفرنگیس خانم بی‌نهایت انس گرفته‌ام. از اخلاق و ادب و معرفت این دختر ایرانی بسیار لذت می‌برم.

سه‌شنبه ۲۶ < فروردین >، ۱۵ < آوریل > - صبح بلندن رفتم. با بایندر و حمزاوی ناهار خوردم. شب بکمبریج آمدم. بعد از شام با فرنگیس خانم قریب یک ساعت و نیم راه رفتم. هوا ملایم و خوب بود. بسیار با هم حرف زدیم و خندیدیم و باو گفتم که مایلم با او زندگی کنم. کاشکی همه دخترهای ایرانی ادب و معرفت و وطن‌پرستی او را داشتند. تا ده و ربع با او بودم. شب کتاب خواندم.

چهارشنبه ۲۷ فروردین ، ۱۶ آوریل - صبح کتاب خواندم. ناهار در هتل خوردم. عصر

با فرنگیس خانم نمازی به Arts Theater رفتم. فیلم پی‌نوکی‌یو[1] را دیدیم. در رستوران آرتز شام خوردیم و تا ساعت سه و نیم راه رفتیم. هر چه با این دختر هوشمند بیشتر معاشرت می‌کنم بیشتر با او انس می‌گیرم و فریفته اخلاقش می‌شوم. هوا خوب بود و در خیابان خاموش راه رفتیم.

پنجشنبه ۲۸ ‹ فروردین ›، ۱۷ ‹ آوریل › – صبح آلمانی خواندم. شب بمنزل آقای تقی‌زاده رفتم. فرنگیس خانم نمازی هم آمد. تا ساعت ده نشستیم و صحبت کردیم. فرنگیس خانم را بمنزلش رساندم و خود بهتل رفتم.

جمعه ۲۹ ‹ فروردین ›، ۱۸ ‹ آوریل › – صبح آلمانی خواندم. از ساعت شش و نیم با فرنگیس خانم نمازی بودم. در رستوران آرتز تیاتر شام خوردیم و از آن جا بکافه‌ای رفتیم. تا ساعت ده در آن جا نشستیم و صحبت کردیم و بعد او را بخانه‌اش رساندم. از رفتن فرنگیس خانم باکسفورد افسرده‌ام چون با او بسیار انس گرفته‌ام و از صحبتش لذت می‌برم چرا که نکته‌سنج و خوب و خوش اخلاقست و نجیب و با وقار. در این روز شنیدم که ویلیام دربان سفارت کشته شده است. بسیار غمگین شدم.

شنبه ۳۰ ‹ فروردین ›، ۱۹ ‹ آوریل › – صبح کتاب خواندم. بعد کمی راه رفتم. ناهار زودتر خوردم. رفتم بایستگاه بلیط خریدم و با فرنگیس خانم نمازی به بلچلی[2] رفتم. قریب دو ساعت با هم بودیم. در بلچلی هم تا حرکت ترن باکسفورد یک ساعت با هم بودیم. در کافه کوچکی چای خوردیم. بعد با او وداع کردم. بعد از رفتن او بسیار دلتنگ شدم. در اقامت حدود ده روزه‌اش در کمبریج با او بسیار انس گرفته‌اند و عاشق اخلاق و وقارش شده‌ام. نمی‌دانم از ملاقات با این دختر در زندگی من چه تغییراتی حاصل خواهد شد. شب نتوانستم خوب بخوابم. دو ساعت و نیم بعد از نصف شب بیدار شدم. کمی از گلستان خواندم ولی بعد خوابیدم. بیشتر بفکر فرنگیس خانم بودم.

---

۱. *Pinocchio*، انیمیشن محصول ۱۹۴۰ امریکا.

۲. Bletchley، شهرکی در حدود ۵۰ مایلی جنوب غربی کمبریج.

یکشنبه ۳۱ فروردین، ۲۰ آوریل - صبح و عصر با آقای تقی‌زاده بودم. عصر با ایشان و خانم تقی <زاده> به گران‌چستر رفتم. شب کتاب خواندم، سعدی و حافظ.

دوشنبه ۱ اردیبهشت، ۲۱ < آوریل > - صبح بلندن رفتم. با بایندر و حمزاوی ناهار خوردم. شب بکمبریج آمدم. بفرنگیس خانم کاغذی نوشتم.

سه‌شنبه ۲ < اردیبهشت >، ۲۲ < آوریل > - کاغذی بفرنگیس خانم نوشتم.

چهارشنبه ۳ < اردیبهشت >، ۲۳ < آوریل > - آلمانی خواندم. با مستر بنت و مسیز بنت و پسرشان که صاحبمنصب بحریست در یونی‌ورسیتی آرمز ناهار خوردم. عصر با آقای تقی‌زاده و خانمش بسینما رفتم.

پنجشنبه ۴ < اردیبهشت >، ۲۴ < آوریل > - بلندن رفتم و بکمبریج آمدم. آلمانی خواندم.

جمعه ۵ < اردیبهشت >، ۲۵ < آوریل > - شب بمنزل آقای تقی‌زاده رفتم.

شنبه ۶ < اردیبهشت >، ۲۶ < آوریل > - کتاب خواندم.

یکشنبه ۷ < اردیبهشت >، ۲۷ < آوریل > - صبح کاغذی بفرنگیس خانم نوشتم. عصر با آقای تقی‌زاده گردش کردم و در منزل ایشان چای خوردم.

دوشنبه ۸ < اردیبهشت >، ۲۸ < آوریل > - کتاب خواندم.

سه‌شنبه ۹ < اردیبهشت >، ۲۹ < آوریل > - صبح بلندن رفتم و با بایندر ناهار خوردم. شب در کمبریج بودم.

چهارشنبه ۱۰ < اردیبهشت >، ۳۰ < آوریل > - بلندن رفتم و بکمبریج مراجعت کردم.

پنجشنبه ۱۱ < اردیبهشت >، ۱ < مه > - کتاب خواندم.

جمعه ۱۲ < اردیبهشت >، ۲ < مه > - شب بمنزل آقای تقی‌زاده رفتم. آلمانی خواندم.

شنبه ۱۳ < اردیبهشت >، ۳ < مه > - صبح کتاب خواندم. کاغذی بفرنگیس خانم نمازی نوشتم.

یکشنبه ۱۴ < اردیبهشت >، ۲ < مه > - با آقای تقی‌زاده بودم. گفتند که مستر یونگ برادرزنم مایلست فارسی خود را تکمیل کند و می‌خواهد اگر ممکن باشد از شما فارسی یاد بگیرد و بشما آلمانی یاد بدهد. قبول کردم و انشاء الله با جد و جهد بخواندن آلمانی خواهم پرداخت.

دوشنبه ۱۵ اردیبهشت، ۵ مه - صبح بلندن رفتم. ناهار با بایندر خوردم. شب در کمبریج بودم.

سه‌شنبه ۱۶ اردیبهشت ۱۳۲۰، ۶ مه ۱۹۴۱ - صبح با مستر و میسز بوتلر بلندن رفتم. در سفارت وزیر مختار را دیدم. ناهار با بایندر خوردم و شب بکمبریج برگشتم.

چهارشنبه ۱۷ اردیبهشت، ۷ مه - صبح بلندن رفتم. ناهار در نزدیک اداره در رستوران گریت ایسترن ریلوی خوردم. بعد از ظهر هم در اداره بودم و شب در کمبریج. آلمانی خواندم و نوشتم.

پنجشنبه ۱۸ اردیبهشت، ۸ مه - صبح کتاب خواندم. بعد از ظهر بسینما رفتم و شب منزل آقای تقی‌زاده. در این روز از فرنگیس خانم کاغذی رسید.

جمعه ۱۹ اردیبهشت، ۹ مه - صبح در هتل بودم. از آنجا بیرون آمدم و کاغذی بفرنگیس نوشتم. ساعت یازده وی آمد. با هم رفتیم به نی‌یو مارکت ناهار خوردیم و

کمی در شهر گردش کردم. بعد بکمبریج آمدیم. رفتیم بسینما. دو اتومبیل می‌راند. شب در هتل با هم شام خوردیم. بعد او به نب وورث[1] رفت. شب زودتر باطاقم آمدم. کاغذی را که صبح بفرنگیس نوشته بودم، پاره کردم و کاغذی دیگر شروع کردم. تا ساعت سه و ربع بعد از نصف شب بیدار بودم و کاغذ را تمام کردم. دو بار اعلان خطر شد. کاغذ بسیار مفصل ــ هشت صفحه ــ بود و در آن کمی از زندگی خود را شرح دادم تا از اساس کار من آگاه باشد.

شنبه ۲۰ اردیبهشت ۱۳۲۰، ۱۰ مه ۱۹۴۱ - صبح کتاب خواندم. ناهار با مسز لورنس خوردم. بعد از ظهر با هم بتئاتر رفتیم. بازی *Eight of Hearts* را دیدیم. شب در هتل بودم و کتاب خواندم.

یکشنبه ۲۱ اردیبهشت، ۱۱ مه - صبح روزنامه و کتاب خواندم. پیش از ظهر با آقای تقی‌زاده و بعد از ظهر با ایشان و خانم تقی‌زاده راه رفتیم. Caxton Gibbet دار قدیمی را که هنوز بحالت اول نگاه داشته‌اند، دیدیم. شب در هتل بودم.

دوشنبه ۲۲ اردیبهشت، ۱۲ مه - صبح رفتم بلندن. نتوانستم بعمارت بریتانیک هوس وارد بشوم. اطرافش را طناب کشیده بودند زیرا بمبی که هنوز نترکیده بود، در اطرافش انداخته بودند. سرایدار گفت که تمام پنجره‌های اطاقم در حمله هوایی شب یکشنبه شکسته. پیاده تا نزدیک هوبورن[2] رفتم. لندن را صدمه زیاد زده‌اند و اگر چندین بار دیگر اینطور حمله کنند، بسیار خرابی خواهد شد. شب در اخبار گفتند که هس معاون هیتلر باسکاتلند آمده است.

سه‌شنبه ۲۳ اردیبهشت، ۱۳ مه - صبح کتاب خواندم. بعد کمی در کمبریج گردش کردم. بعد از ظهر با مسز دولم و مسز بوتلر بسینما رفتم. شب در هتل بودم. روزنامه خواندم.

---

۱. Knebworth شهرستانی از توابع هرتفوردشر در میانه راه کمبریج به لندن.

۲.Holborn، از محلات مرکزی لندن.

چهارشنبه ۲۴ اردیبهشت، ۱۴ مه - تمام روز را در کمبریج بودم. بعد از ظهر بتئاتر رفتم و بالهٔ سدلرز ولز[1] را دیدم. شب در هتل بودم.

پنجشنبه ۲۵ اردیبهشت، ۱۵ مه - صبح زود بیدار شدم. چاشت خوردم. با مسیز بوتلر و شوهرش خداحافظی کردم زیرا باسکاتلند می‌روند. بعد رفتم بلندن. در اطاق کوچکی کار کردم چون اطاق معمولیم پاکیزه نبود. شب بکمبریج آمدم. رفتم تئاتر باله را دیدم.

جمعه ۲۶ اردیبهشت، ۱۶ مه - صبح در لندن بودم و کار کردم. نزدیک ظهر با آقای تقی‌زاده بکتابخانهٔ شرقی رفتم. مدتی در آنجا بودم و یک کتاب آلمانی راجع بایران را آقای تقی‌زاده برای من گرفت. عصر بسینما رفتم و شب در هتل بودم. اسباب را جمع آوری کردم برای رفتن باکسفورد.

شنبه ۲۷ اردیبهشت، ۱۷ مه - صبح زود بیدار شدم. بعد از خوردن چاشت، با ترن نه و ربع باکسفورد رفتم. ساعت یک و نیم بعد از ظهر رسیدم. فرنگیس در ایستگاه بود. با هم باطاقی که برایم دیده بود، رفتم. اثاثم را گذاشتم. بعد با هم ناهار خوردیم و بعد از ناهار با هم در پارک راه رفتیم و بسیار صحبت کردیم. آن بآن محبّت و عشقم باو زیادتر می‌شود و چنان می‌نماید که این دختر را موافق میل من آفریده است. اخلاق و وقار و نجابتش مرا روز به روز فریفته‌تر می‌کند. فرنگیس بلیط تآتر خریده بود. شب بتئاتر رفتیم با هم و بازی *Ladies in retirement*[2] را که در کمبریج دیده بودم، دیدیم. بسیار خوشم آمد چون سن بزرگتر بود و بازیگران جوان خوب بازی کردند که از دوباره دیدن آن لذت بردم. شب در رستوران هندی غذا خوردیم.

یکشنبه ۲۸ اردیبهشت، ۱۸ مه - صبح زود بیدار شدم. کمی در اکسفورد راه رفتم.

---

۱. Sadler's Wells، باشگاه رقص مشهوری در مرکز شهر لندن.

۲. بر اساس نمایشنامه‌ای از رجینالد دِنَم (Reginald Denham) و ادوارد پِرسی (Edward Percy) که در ۱۹۴۰ با بازی فلورا رابسن (Flora Robson) در نیویورک به روی صحنه رفت.

ساعت یازده فرنگیس آمد. با هم راه رفتیم و در رستوران ناهار خوردیم. بعد از ظهر بعد از مدتی انتظار با اتوموبیل به بورز هیل Boars Hill ¹ رفتم. هوا بسیار خوب بود. کمی در خیابانها راه رفتیم و صحبت کردیم و در خانه‌ای که قهوه‌خانه کرده بودند، چای خوبی خوردیم. شب در رستوران هتل غذا خوردیم و بعد در پارک راه رفتیم. بعد از رفتن فرنگیس، کمی در خیابان راه رفتم و بعد بخانه رفتم و پس از خواندن روزنامه خوابیدم.

دوشنبه ۲۹ اردیبهشت، ۱۹ مه - صبح کمی کتاب خواندم. یک ساعت بعد از ظهر با فرنگیس در رستورانی انگلیسی غذا خوردم. بعد رفتیم بسینما. فیلم Commander X را دیدیم. بعد او رفت برای درس و من رفتن به بلیئل ² کالج. پروفسور گیب و مستر ادواردز و زنش را که مدتها در ایران بوده‌اند، دیدم. صبح هم دکتر آربری Arberry را دیده بودم. بعد رفتم بتئاتر. منتظر فرنگیس شدم. کمی دیر آمد. نمایش Land of Smile را دیدیم. ریچارد توبر می‌خواند و بسیار خوب بود. شب شام نخوردم و اوقاتم چندان خوب نبود.

سه‌شنبه ۳۰ اردیبهشت، ۲۰ مه - صبح بکتابخانهٔ بودلین رفتم. اوراقی را که در ۱۸۰۳ در انگلستان بمناسبت قصد ناپلئون در باب حمله بانگلیس چاپ کرده بودند، خواندم. بسیار دیدنی بود. با فرنگیس در رستوران هندی ناهار خوردیم و بعد رفتیم بایستگاه لندن. در ساعت دو و سی و هشت دقیقه حرکت کرد. فرنگیس متأثر بود. در راه بفکر او بودم. این مدّت اقامت در اکسفورد بسیار بر من خوش گذشت و بیشتر بوقار و خوبی فرنگیس پی بردم. ترن ساعت شش بعد از ظهر بکمبریج رسید. شب کاغذی بفرنگیس نوشتم ولی نتوانستم آن را تمام کنم. خوابم برد.

چهارشنبه ۳۱ اردیبهشت، ۲۱ مه - صبح بقیه کاغذی را که شب شروع کردم به فرنگیس نوشتم. ناهار در هتل خوردم و بعد از ظهر بسینما و شب بتئاتر رفتم.

---

۱. دهکده‌ای است در ۵ کیلومتری جنوب غربی آکسفرد.
۲. Balliol College، قدیمی‌ترین کالج در سیستم دانشگاه آکسفرد.

پنجشنبه ۱ خرداد، ۲۲ مه - صبح رفتم بلندن. تا نیمساعت بعد از ظهر در اداره کار کردم. بعد با بایندر و حمزاوی ناهار خوردم. شب در کمبریج بمنزل آقای تقی‌زاده رفتم. تا ساعت یازده و نیم آنجا بودم.

جمعه ۲ خرداد، ۲۳ مه - صبح کمی روزنامه و کتاب خواندم. بعد از ظهر بسینما رفتم. امشب در هتل هم کتاب خواندم.

شنبه ۳ خرداد، ۲۴ مه - صبح کتاب خواندم. بعد از ظهر بسینما رفتم و شب زود باطاق آمدم. کتاب آلمانی راجع بایران < را > خواندم.

یکشنبه ۴ خرداد، ۲۵ مه - صبح با مستر مارتین و میسیز مارتین به گران‌چستر[1] رفتم و بعد از ظهر با آقای تقی‌زاده و خانمش بهمان جا رفتیم. شب کاغذی بپدرم نوشتم و آشنایی خود را با فرنگیس در آن شرح دادم. کاغذی را که بفرنگیس نوشته بودم، برایش فرستادم.

دوشنبه ۵ خرداد، ۲۶ مه - صبح کاغذی بسیار مفصل < در > ۱۲ صفحه بفرنگیس نوشتم. بعد از ظهر غمگین بودم. بسینما رفتم. ساعت شش مینوی بهتل آمد. باران می‌بارید. با هم بچندین مهمانخانه رفتیم. در یکی جا پیدا شد. شب با هم شام خوردیم و بعد رفتیم بمنزل آقای تقی‌زاده. تا نیمساعت بعد از نصف شب آنجا بودیم. بعد بهتل آمدم. تا سه ساعت بعد از نصف شب بیدار بودم. کاغذی دیگر بفرنگیس نوشتم. صبح کاغذی برای پدرم فرستادم و در باب قصهٔ عروسی با فرنگیس در آن شرحی نوشتم.

سه‌شنبه ۶ خرداد ۱۳۲۰، ۲۷ مه ۱۹۴۱ - صبح بکتابخانه رفتم. کتابهایم را عوض کردم. ناهار با مستر یونگ در فستیوال گریل خوردم و بعد از ظهر با مینوی بدیدن فیلم برادران کرامازوف رفتیم. عصر در دوروتی[2] چای و شب در اسکوچ هوس شام خوردیم. ساعت هشت و نیم بمنزل آقای تقی‌زاده رفتیم و تا نصف شب آنجا بودیم.

---

۱. Grantchester، دهکده‌ای قدیمی در حاشیه رودخانه کَم در کمبریج.
۲. The Dorothy Cafe، کافه‌ای در کمبریج در خیابان سیدنی (فعال از ۱۹۳۰ تا ۱۹۹۰).

چهارشنبه ۷ خرداد، ۲۸ < مه > ۱۹۴۱ - صبح کمی روزنامه خواندم. بعد با ترن نه و ده دقیقه به نب ورث Knebworth بمنزل ویرا رفتم. ناهار و شام در آنجا بودم. بعد از ظهر با ویرا و خواهرش بسینما رفتم، در هشت میلی نب ورث. سینما خوب و فیلم خوبی بود. شب پدر ویرا را دیدم. صبح پیش از چاشت کاغذی از فرنگیس رسیده بود. خواندم. بسیار غمگین شدم. تمام روز را بفکر او بودم و ناچار تبسم می‌کردم که اندوهم را ندانند. در سینما گریه‌ام افتاد. آنی از حال او فارغ نبودم.

پنجشنبه ۸ خرداد، ۲۹ مه ۱۹۴۱ - صبح بلندن رفتم. کمی در اداره بودم. بعد نزدیک سفارت با حمزاوی ناهار خوردم. بعد بسفارت رفتم. حالم خوب نبود و پریشان حال هم نتوانستم کار کنم. شب بکمبریج آمدم. تا ساعت یازده کتاب خواندم و خوابیدم. تأثیر کاغذ فرنگیس هر آن در وجودم بیشتر می‌شد.

جمعه ۹ خرداد، ۳۰ مه ۱۹۴۱ - صبح کمی روزنامه خواندم و بعد از ظهر بسینما رفتم. شب پس از شام رفتم که کووینز کالج[1] چون پروفسور بِیْلی، آقای تقی‌زاده، پروفسور مینورسکی و یک صاحبمنصب انگلیسی که کمی فارسی می‌دانست، بودند. تا ساعت ده و نیم آنجا بودم. بعد بهتل آمدم. تا نیم ساعت بعد از نصف شف با دکتر مارشال و دکتر برنز و مستر پول که در هتل زندگی می‌کنند، صحبت می‌کردیم. تمام روز و شب را بخیال فرنگیس بودم و بر رویهم حالم چندان خوش نیست.

شنبه ۱۰ خرداد، ۳۱ مه ۱۹۴۱ - صبح کتاب خواندم. بعد هانس برادرزن آقای تقی‌زاده آمد. با او آلمانی می‌خواندم. بعد از ظهر با آقای تقی‌زاده راه رفتم و در منزل ایشان چای خوردم. کاغذی بفرنگیس نوشتم.

یکشنبه ۱۱ خرداد، اول ژوئن - صبح کتاب خواندم و روزنامه. بعد قریب یک ساعت راه رفتم. بعد از ظهر در هتل بودم و عصر با مستر زگو و زنش در رودخانه پاروزنی

.Queen's College ۱

کردیم. دستم تاول کرد. درست یک ساعت پارو زدیم. بعد از شام بمنزل آقای تقی‌زاده رفتم و تا ساعت یازده و نیم آنجا بودم. در این روز محدود شدن لباس زن و مرد اعلان شد.

دوشنبه ۱۲ خرداد، ۲ ژوئن - صبح کمی روزنامه خواندم و کاغذی مفصل بفرنگیس نوشتم. در این روز کاغذی از او داشتم و حالم را خوش کرد. بعد از ظهر بسینما رفتم و شب در اطاقم تلگراف راجع بکشتی ارمنستان را تهیه می‌کردم که فردا باید مخابره شود.

سه‌شنبه ۱۳ خرداد، ۳ ژوئن - صبح بلندن و بسفارت رفتم. با حمزاوی و بایندر خوردم و شب بکمبریج آمدم. بعد از ظهر در اداره کار کردم. شب بعد از شام بکنار رود رفتم. مردم در قایقها و لب رود نشسته بودند و شعر می‌خواندند. در این هفته برسم قدیم مردم جشن می‌گیرند و در این شب اشعار قدیم < را > می‌خوانند. شب کاغذی بفرنگیس نوشتم.

چهارشنبه ۱۴ خرداد، ۴ ژوئن - صبح آلمانی خواندم و بعد از ظهر به کوبینز کالج رفتم باطاق پروفسور بِیْلی.[1] پروفسور مینورسکی و آقای تقی‌زاده و جمعی دیگر هم بودند. شخصی موسوم به وایت‌هد در باب سکه‌های هند صحبت کرد. شب کتاب خواندم و دو ساعت بعد از نصف شب خوابیدم. در این روز کاغذی بفرنگیس نوشتم.

پنجشنبه ۱۵ خرداد ۱۳۲۰، ۵ ژوئن ۱۹۴۱ - صبح بلندن باداره رفتم. تلگرافی بتهران در باب مرگ لرد کدمن کردم و کاغذی بزنش نوشتم. بعد رفتم بسفارت. با بایندر و حمزاوی ناهار خوردم و بکمبریج آمدم. صبح در راه با پروفسور مینورسکی و بعد از ظهر در راه با توپالیان و پروفسور مینورسکی بودم. شب در هتل بودم. در این روز کاغذی از فرنگیس داشتم.

---

۱. Harold W. Bailey، متخصص زبان‌های ایرانی میانه از جمله زبان سکایی ختن (۱۸۹۹-۱۹۹۶).

جمعه ۱۶ خرداد، ۶ ژوئن - صبح رفتم بیرون. اصلاح کردم و بلیط برای اکسفورد گرفتم. بعد از ظهر در هتل بودم. کتاب خواندم و شب رفتم بمنزل آقای تقی‌زاده. تا بیست دقیقه بعد از نصف شب آنجا بودم.

شنبه ۱۷ خرداد، ۷ ژوئن - صبح زود بیدار شدم. چاشت خوردم. با ترن نه و نیم بسمت اکسفورد رفتم. در راه رمان مادام بواری خواندم. یک ساعت در بلچلی منتظر ترن شدم. یک ساعت و بیست دقیقه بعد از ظهر باکسفورد رسیدم. فرنگیس بایستگاه آمده بود. با هم بهتل مایتر (Mitre) رفتیم. مهمانخانهٔ پاکیزهٔ خوبی است. با فرنگیس ناهار خوردم در همان هتل. بعد بکنار رودخانه رفتم. اول هوا خوب بود. در پارک راه رفتیم و حرف زدیم. همه جا خرم و همهٔ درختان سرسبز بودند. بعد از یکساعت راه رفتن، هوا بارانی شد. بهتل آمدیم. شام خوردیم. بعد از آن با هم رفتیم بتئاتر. بازی پیگ میلیون[۱] را دیدیم. شب و روز بسیار خوشی گذشت. شب کمی از بیست مقاله قزوینی < را > خواندم.

یکشنبه ۱۸ خرداد، ۸ ژوئن - صبح کمی کتاب خواندم و روزنامه. نزدیک ظهر فرنگیس آمد. با هم ناهار خوردیم. هوا بارانی بود. بعد از ظهر بیرون نرفتیم و حرف زدیم. شب در رستوران هندی شام خوردیم و بعد رفتیم بسینما. تا ساعت ده آنجا بودیم. بعد او بکالج و من بهتل آمدم و کتاب بیست مقاله قزوینی و مقالهٔ راجع بشرح حال ادوارد براون را خواندم.

دوشنبه ۱۹ خرداد، ۹ ژوئن - صبح کتاب فارسی خواندم ـ بیست مقاله. بعد بیرون به بلیول کالج رفتم. پروفسور گیب و پروفسور وبستر را دیدم. ناهار فرنگیس آمد. با هم بودیم و سه ساعت بعد از ظهر رفت چون باید سر درس حاضر شود. من تنها بسینما رفتم. فیلم *Kipps*[۲] را که از رمان ولز اقتباس شده است، دیده‌ام. بد نبود. شب با فرنگیس بتئاتر رفتیم. بالهٔ انگلیسی و لهستانی را دیدم و بعد ساعت نه و نیم بهتل آمدیم. بعجله شام خوردیم چون فرنگیس بایست ساعت ده در کالجش باشد. متصل باران می‌آمد.

---

۱. مقصود تئاتر Pygmalion است بر اساس اثری به همین نام از جرج برنارد شاو.

۲. کمدی درام محصول ۱۹۴۱ بر اساس قصه‌ای از هربرت ج. ولز (م. ۱۹۴۶).

سه‌شنبه ۲۰ خرداد، ۱۰ ژوئن - خسته بودم چون شب درست نخوابیده بودم. فرنگیس سه ربع بعد از ظهر آمد. با هم بشتاب ناهار خوردیم و حساب مهمانخانه را دادم و یک اطاق برای سه روز از روز ۳۰ ژوئن تا ۲ ژوئیه در همین هتل قبلاً اجاره کردم که باز دوباره باکسفورد بیایم. بعد با فرنگیس بایستگاه آمدم. ترن ساعت دو و سی و هشت دقیقه بعد از ظهر حرکت کرد. در راه بیشتر بفکر فرنگیس بودم. شب یک ربع بعد از شش بکمبریج رسیدم و شام خوردم ولی نه باشتها و بعد کمی روزنامه خواندم و یادداشت‌های چهار روز را نوشتم و باید کاغذی بفرنگیس در همین شب بنویسم.

چهارشنبه ۲۱ خرداد، ۱۱ ژوئن - صبح زود بیدار شدم. لباس سیاه عزا پوشیدم و بلندن رفتم. در کلیسای وست مینستر بمناسبت فوت لرد کدمن مجلس تذکری بود. جماعت بسیار آمده بودند. مجلس از ظهر شروع شد و تا نیمساعت بعد از ظهر طول کشید. ارگ و خوانندگان و دعا و شکوه مجلس انسان را بخیال می‌انداخت که اغنیاء حتّی در مرگشان نیز باید چیزهای خود دنیا را داشته باشند. بعضی از وزراء، رئیس بانک انگلستان، < و > تمام مدیران شرکت حاضر بودند. از کلیسا بسفارت رفتم. با آقای نیامیر در رستوران هندی غذا خوردم و بعد باداره و از آنجا بکمبریج < و > شب بسینما رفتم و دیر خوابیدم.

پنجشنبه ۲۲ خرداد، ۱۲ ژوئن ۱۹۴۱ - صبح بلندن رفتم. تا نیمساعت بعد از ظهر در اداره کار کردم. ناهار در پیکادلی با بایندر خوردم و شب بکمبریج آمدم. بعد از شام با میسز گورنی بتئاتر رفتم. Close Quarter بازی عجیبی بود. دو بازیگر، یکی زن و دیگر مرد بیشتر نداشت. شب دیر خوابیدم.

جمعه ۲۳ خرداد ۱۳۲۰، ۱۳ ژوئن - صبح کاغذی بفرنگیس نوشتم. ناهار در هتل خوردم و شب بمنزل آقای تقی‌زاده رفتم. پروفسور بیْلی، پروفسور مینورسکی و یک صاحب‌منصب انگلیسی که فارسی می‌دانست هم بودند. آنها ساعت یازده رفتند ولی من تا نیمساعت بعد از نصف شب ماندم و صحبت کردیم.

شنبه ۲۴ خرداد، ۱۴ ژوئن - صبح کمی کتاب خواندم. ساعت یازده ویرا آمد. با هم ناهار خوردیم در هتل و بعد بسینما رفتیم. شب در هتل شام خوردم و بعد با اتوبوس به گران‌چستر رفتم. کمی اتومبیل‌رانی بمن یاد داد. در تمام مدتی که با او بودم بفکر فرنگیس بودم. شب دیر خوابیدم. کاغذی را که شروع کرده بودم ــ برای فرنگیس ــ ناتمام ماند.

یکشنبه ۲۵ خرداد، ۱۵ ژوئن - صبح رفتم بمنزل مستر یونگ. آلمانی خواندم و عصر رفتم بمنزل آقای تقی‌زاده. تا ساعت هشت آنجا بودم. شب دیر خوابیدم.

دوشنبه ۲۶ خرداد، ۱۳۲۰، ۱۶ ژوئن ۱۹۴۱ - صبح رفتم بلندن. ناهار در رستوران روسی با آقای مینوی خوردم. بعد از ظهر مدتی با او در گرین پارک بودم. عصر بایستگاه آمدم. هوا گرم و ترن پر بود. در راه بسیار بد گذشت. صبح در اداره کار کردم و پیش از ظهر هم حمزاوی و بایندر را دیدم.

سه‌شنبه ۲۷ خرداد، ۱۳۲۰، ۱۷ ژوئن ۱۹۴۱ - صبح درس آلمانی خواندم. بعد از ظهر بسینما رفتم و شب در خانه بودم. هوا گرم و حالم بد بود. ساعت یازده ویرا تلفن کرد که مادر و خواهرش خواهند آمد به نی‌یو مارکت. شب بد خوابیدم.

چهارشنبه ۲۸ خرداد، ۱۸ ژوئن - صبح کمی کتاب خواندم. بعد ویرا و نورا و مادرشان آمدند. رفتیم به نی‌یو مارکت. جماعت بسیاری آمده بودند. ناهار خوردیم و اسب‌دوانی را تماشا کردیم. حال بالنسبه خوبی داشتم. قریب سه لیره باختم. شب منزل آقای تقی‌زاده رفتم. تا ساعت ۱۲ آنجا بودم. شب حالم بهتر بود و بهتر خوابیدم. بیشتر اوقات حتی در میان اسب‌دوانی هم بیاد فرنگیس بودم.

پنجشنبه ۲۹ خرداد، ۱۹ ژوئن - صبح کاغذی بفرنگیس نوشتم. بعد رفتم بمنزل فون نیگ برای درس آلمانی. بعد از ظهر رفتم بسینما و شب کتاب خواندم.

جمعه ۳۰ خرداد، ۲۰ ژوئن - صبح کتاب خواندم (کتاب مادام بواری). عصر نیز کتاب خواندم. شب بیست مقاله آقای قزوینی را خواندم. ساعت ۱۲ و نیم بعد از ظهر خوابیدم.

شنبه ۳۱ خرداد، ۲۱ ژوئن - صبح درس آلمانی خواندم. بعد از ظهر با مستر زگو Szego بکنار رود رفتیم و روی زمین نمناک خوابیدیم. بعد در گران‌چستر چای خوردیم. بعد از شام رفتم بمنزل آقای تقی‌زاده. تا ساعت ۱۲ آنجا بودم. حالم چندان خوش نبود. وقتی بهتل آمدم، تب داشتم. کاغذی بفرنگیس نوشتم. شب نتوانستم درست بخوابم.

یکشنبه اول تیر ماه ۱۳۲۰، ۲۲ ژوئن ۱۹۴۱ - صبح زود بیدار شدم. بسیار خسته و بد حال بودم. چاشت جز قهوه چیزی نخوردم و ناهار یک گیلاس شیر خوردم. بعد از ناهار باطاقم آمده و خوابیدم. تب شدید داشتم. شب هم نتوانستم خوب بخوابم. در این روز آلمان بروس حمله کرد.

دوشنبه ۲ تیر، ۲۳ ژوئن - صبح رفتم بلندن. ناهار با حمزاوی و بایندر خوردم و شب بکمبریج آمدم. حالم کمی بهتر بود و چند ساعت خوابیدم.

سه‌شنبه ۳ تیر، ۲۴ ژوئن - صبح حالم کمی بهتر بود. بنزد طبیب رفتم ــ دکتر یونگ‌لن ــ که آقای تقی‌زاده اسمش را داده بودند. خوب معاینه‌ام کرد و گفت چیزی مهم نیست. دوا داد. بعد از ظهر در مهمانخانه هم کتاب خواندم. از لندن تلفون رسیده بود که روز جمعه برای ناهار بسفارت بروم. جواب دادم که خواهم آمد. شب بمنزل آقای تقی‌زاده رفتم. ساعت ۱۱ برگشتم.

چهارشنبه ۴ تیر، ۲۵ ژوئن - صبح کتاب خواندم. بعد از ظهر از کمبریج بلندن تلفون کردم که خبر انتخاب سر ویلیام فریزر بریاست شرکت بدولت مخابره شود. شب کمی حالم بهتر بود.

پنجشنبه ۵ تیر، ۲۶ ژوئن - صبح کتاب میسیز هوکر را تصحیح کردم و بعد از ظهر بسینما رفتم. شب در هتل بودم. کتاب خواندم.

جمعه ۶ تیر، ۲۷ ژوئن - صبح رفتم بلندن. کمی در اداره کار کردم. بعد رفتم بسفارت.

آقای مقدم وزیر مختار، گلمکانی، بایندر، حمزاوی، آرام، وحید، نیامیر، و زن حمزاوی بودند. ناهار خوردیم و بعد با ترن پنج و بیست دقیقه بکمبریج آمدم. آلمانیها در خاک روس پیشرفت کرده‌اند.

شنبه ۷ تیر، ۲۸ ژوئن - صبح زود بیدار شدم. کمی خسته بودم. چاشت خوردم و بعد با ترن ۹ و نیم بطرف اکسفورد حرکت کردم. در بلچلی یک ساعت منتظر شدم و عاقبت یک ساعت و بیست دقیقه بعد از ظهر وارد اکسفورد شدم. فرنگیس در ایستگاه بود. با هم در مهمانخانه‌ای نزدیک ایستگاه ناهار خوردیم. دوست فرنگیس که در والینگ‌فورد Wallingford یکی از نقاط اطراف اکسفورد زندگی می‌کند، از او دعوت کرده بود که بخانه‌شان برود و مرا هم ببرد. در این سفر اکسفورد بهمین قصد آمدم که بآنجا برویم. بعد از خوردن ناهار خواستیم با تاکسی برویم ولی بهر که گفتیم و بهر جا تلفون کردیم فایده نداد و اتوبوس ساعت سه و ربع هم از دستمان رفت. ناچار با اتوبوس پنج و ربع که پر بود و کمی ناراحت به والینگ‌فورد رفتیم. از شدت اضطراب برای نیافتن تاکسی و گرمای هوا بسیار خسته شدیم. عاقبت شش ساعت و نیم بعد از ظهر به والینگ‌فورد رسیدیم. مستر اسلید Slade صاحبخانه با اتوموبیلش منتظرمان بود. مردی شصت ساله ولی بسیار تندرست و ساده و خوب بنظر می‌آمد. ما را بخانه‌اش که خارج والینگ‌فورد است، برد. خانه‌اش بسیار خوب و پاکیزه و بزرگ بود و باغی عالی و گلهای قشنگ داشت. اطاقی که بمن دادند، چشم‌انداز خوبی داشت. میسز هال دوست فرنگیس و عمه میسز اسلیدر که در حقیقت فرنگیس و من بمناسبت او دعوت شده بودیم و میسز اسلید ما را بسیار درست پذیرفتند. بعد از شام با فرنگیس بصحرا رفتیم. هوا بسیار معتدل و صحرا تماشایی بود. بیش از یک ساعت راه رفتیم. بسیار خوش گذشت. ساعت یازده بخانه آمدیم. فرنگیس چند دقیقه باطاق من آمد. صحبت کردیم. بعد کمی از کتاب شرح حال فلوبر را خواندم و خوابیدم.

یکشنبه ۸ تیر، ۲۹ ژوئن ۱۹۴۱ - صبح زود بیدار شدم. ساعت ۹ چاشت خوردم. با فرنگیس بیرون رفتیم. کمی راه رفتیم و بعد رفتیم بالای تپه‌ای که در دو طرفش آبادی

بود. قریب نیم‌ساعت آنجا بودیم و بسیار خوش بود. بعد از ناهار باز راه رفتیم. شب زودتر خوابیدم.

دوشنبه ۹ تیر، ۳۰ ژوئن - صبح زود بیدار شدم. مثل روز پیش صبح فرنگیس آمد. با هم رفتیم چاشت خوردیم و چون قرار بود با اتومبیل ده و بیست دقیقه صبح باکسفورد برویم، اسبابم را جمع کردم . با میسز هال و میسز اسلید خداحافظی کردم. مستر اسلید ما را با اتومبیلش به والینگ فورد آورد و با اتوبوس باکسفورد آمدیم. فرنگیس بکالجش رفت و من رفتم به مایتر هتل Mitre. فرنگیس برای ناهار آمد. بعد از ناهار در هتل نشستیم و شب هم در هتل شام خوردیم و بعد رفتیم بسینما. فرنگیس ساعت یازده بکالجش رفت و من آمدم بهتل.

سه‌شنبه ۱۰ تیر، اول ژوئیه - صبح ساعت ده و نیم فرنگیس آمد. با هم بباغ رفتیم ــ کرایست کالج ــ تا یک ساعت بعد از ظهر آنجا بودیم. هوا خوب بود و بسیار خوش گذشت. ناهار در مایتر خوردیم و بعد از ظهر در فویرز چای. شب رفتم بتئاتر < و > The Dancing Gear را که رقص و آواز داشت، دیدیم. خوب بود. بسیار طول کشید. فرنگیس شام نخورده بکالجش رفت و من در هتل شام خوردم.

چهارشنبه ۱۱ تیر، ۲ ژوئیه ۱۹۴۱ - صبح ساعت ۱۱ فرنگیس آمد. ناهار در هتل خوردیم و بعد رفتیم به Woodstock قصر Blenheim مقرّ دوک مال بورو را دیدیم و در کافهٔ محقری چای خوردیم. بعد آمدیم به اکسفورد. رفتیم به Worcester Collge. کمی راه رفتیم. شب در هتل شام خوردیم . بعد رفتیم بتأثر Playhouse < و > بازی Lilies in the field را دیدیم. ساعت ده بعد از ظهر تمام شد. قریب یک ساعت راه رفتیم. بعد آمدم بهتل.

پنجشنبه ۱۲ تیر، ۳ ژوئیه - فرنگیس ساعت ۱۱ آمد. با هم به بپارک رفتیم. ناهار در هتل خوردیم و بعد از ظهر بسینما رفتیم. شب در هتل شام خوردیم و بعد رفتیم بپارک. ساعت ده درهای پارک را می‌بندند و چون ما بعد از ساعت ده خواستیم بیرون

برویم، در ماندیم. عاقبت جوانی قبول کرد که ما را با قایق خودش بطرف دیگر مسافتی ببرد. و به ناچار از دیوار باغ بالا رفتیم.

جمعه ۱۳ تیر، ۴ ژوئیه - صبح فرنگیس آمد. ناهار در هتل خوردیم. بعد از ظهر در هتل بودیم و شب بسینما رفتیم.

شنبه ۱۴ تیر، ۵ ژوئیه - صبح زود بیدار شدم. فرنگیس ساعت ۱۱ آمد. اسبابهای او را از کالجش بایستگاه بردیم. بعد بهتل آمدیم. ناهار خوردیم و بعد از تفریغ حساب هتل، با فرنگیس با ترن دو و سی و هشت دقیقه بعد از ظهر بکمبریج آمدیم. ساعت شش و نیم وارد شدیم. شام خوردیم و بعد بمنزل آقای تقی‌زاده رفتیم. تا ساعت ۱۱ آنجا بودیم. بفرنگیس اطاقی دادند در هتل من، ولی دور از من.

یکشنبه ۱۵ تیر، ۵ ژوئیه - صبح ساعت ده با فرنگیس چاشت خوردیم. بعد روزنامه خواندم. ناهار در هتل خوردیم و عصر بمنزل آقای تقی‌زاده رفتم. تا ساعت هفت آنجا بودیم. شام در هتل خوردیم و بعد بیرون رفتیم.

دوشنبه ۱۶ تیر، ۶ ژوئیه - صبح بلندن رفتم. چندین کاغذ اداری نوشتم. در گریت ایسترن هتل ناهار خوردم. در این روز کاغذهای راجع بجنون گرگوریان را دیدم. مستر کلگ تلفون و پیشنهاد کرد روز سه‌شنبه ۸ ژوئیه با کلنل نتر بدیدن گرگوریان در مریضخانه نزدیک Lemington بروم و چون موضوع مهمی بود، قبول کردم. شب بکمبریج آمدم. با فرنگیس شام خوردیم و بعد با هم در صحرا راه رفتیم. نزدیک نصف شب بهتل آمدیم.

سه‌شنبه ۱۷ تیر، ۷ ژوئیه - صبح بسیار زود بیدار شدم. چاشت خوردیم و با پیرهن و زیر شلواری و سایر لوازم که برای ماندن در لندن و یا در لمنگتون برداشته بودم با مستر زگو و رفیق چکسلواکی او بلندن رفتم. با ترن هشت و بیست دقیقه از کمبریج حرکت کردم و ساعت ده بلندن رسیدم. یکسر به Paddington رفتم و منتظر کلنل نتر شدم. با

ترن یازده و پنج دقیقه به Lemington رفتیم. در ترن ناهار خوردم. با او صحبت کردم. مرد مؤدب خوبیست. مریضخانه‌ای که گرگوریان در آن است دو میل از Lemington دور است. با تاکسی بآنجا رفتیم. گرگوریان را دیدم و چون اطبا جنون او را تصدیق نکرده‌اند نمی‌توان او را بحکم جنون در مریضخانه نگاه داشت. متقاعدش کردیم که بماند. از حالات و حرکات او آثار سفه هویدا بود. می‌گفت بدوا معتقد نیستم و مسیح مرا معالجه خواهد کرد. باری پیش از ساعت چهار کارمان تمام شد. بعد با تاکسی از Hatton که مریضخانه در آنست به لمینگتون و از لمینگتون بلندن آمدم. ساعت شش بلندن رسیدم و چون ترن کمبریج در هشت و بیست و دو دقیقه حرکت می‌کرد، وقت برای شام خوردن داشتم. در گریت ایسترن هتل شام خوردم و بترن نشستم. اتّفاقاً مستر زگو را هم دیدم. با هم بکمبریج آمدیم. شب فرنگیس را در اطاقش دیدم.

چهارشنبه ۱۸ تیر، ۹ ژوئیه - صبح با فرنگیس چاشت خوردم. بعد با هم کمی روزنامه و کتاب خواندیم. بعد از ظهر بسینما رفتیم و شب پس از شام خوردن در هتل به صحرا رفتیم. ساعت ۱۲ بهتل آمدیم. خسته بودم و خوابیدم.

پنجشنبه ۱۹ تیر، ۱۰ ژوئیه - صبح با فرنگیس کتاب و روزنامه و شعر فارسی و انگلیسی خواندیم. بعد از ظهر در هتل بودیم و کتاب خواندیم. و شب به گران‌چستر رفتیم. ساعت یازده برگشتیم. شب کمی با فرنگیس بودم و بعد خوابیدم.

جمعه ۲۰ تیر، ۱۱ ژوئیه - صبح از هتل بیرون نرفتم. تا یکساعت بعد از ظهر با فرنگیس از حافظ و سعدی شعر و نثر خواندیم. بعد از ناهار بسینما رفتیم تا ساعت پنج و نیم بیرون آمدیم. هوا بسیار بد و گرم بود. بعد از شام هم بیرون نرفتیم. تا ساعت ۱۱ شب تنها در باغ نشستم و بعد کمی با فرنگیس بودم.

شنبه ۲۱ تیر، ۱۲ ژوئیه - صبح با فرنگیس کتاب خواندیم. بعد از ظهر در هتل بودیم و شب هم زودتر خوابیدم.

یکشنبه ۲۲ تیر، ۱۳ ژوئیه - صبح رفتم بعیادت آقای تقی‌زاده که چند روز در بستر افتاده بوده است. حالشان بهتر بود و بسیار خوشوقت شدم. ناهار با فرنگیس در هتل خوردم و عصر ساعت پنج رفتیم بمنزل آقای تقی‌زاده. تا ساعت هفت آنجا بودیم. حالت آقای تقی‌زاده بهتر بود چنانکه از تخت بیرون آمده بودند. شب در هتل بودیم.

دوشنبه ۲۳ تیر ۱۳۲۰، ۱۴ ژوئیه ۱۹۴۱ - صبح بلندن رفتم. در اداره کار کردم. ناهار در پیکادلی با بایندر خوردم. عصر در اداره کار کردم و شب بکمبریج آمدم.

سه‌شنبه ۲۴ تیر، ۱۵ ژوئیه - صبح کاغذ نوشتم و عصر با فرنگیس بمنزل پروفسور مینورسکی رفتم. شب در هتل بودیم.

چهارشنبه ۲۵ تیر، ۱۶ ژوئیه - صبح در هتل کتاب خواندم. بعد از ظهر با فرنگیس بسینما رفتیم و شب در هتل بودیم.

پنجشنبه ۲۶ تیر، ۱۷ ژوئیه - صبح رفتم بلندن. کاغذی بوزارت دارائی نوشتم. ناهار در پیکادلی با حمزاوی خوردم. بعد از ظهر بسینمای اخبار رفتم و شب بکمبریج آمدم. در این ایام کتاب مادام بواری را به دقّت می‌خوانم.

جمعه ۲۷ تیر، ۱۸ ژوئیه - صبح کتاب خواندیم. بعد از ظهر با فرنگیس راه رفتیم. شب در هتل بودم.

شنبه ۲۸ تیر، ۱۹ ژوئیه - صبح کتاب خواندیم. ساعت یازده و نیم با فرنگیس بمنزل پروفسور چَدْویک رفتم. ناهار در هتل خوردیم و بعد از ظهر در هتل بودیم. دائم باران می‌آمد. شب بیرون نرفتیم.

یکشنبه ۲۹ تیر، ۲۰ ژوئیه - صبح با فرنگیس بکلیسا رفتم. ناهار در هتل خوردیم. عصر در هتل بودیم. شب بعد از شام بمنزل آقای تقی‌زاده رفتیم. تا ساعت یازده آنجا بودیم.

دوشنبه ۳۰ تیر، ۲۱ ژوئیه - صبح رفتم بلندن. آقای وزیری تبار یکی از محصلین آمد. با او ناهار خوردم. بعد از ظهر هم در اداره کار کردم. شب بکمبریج آمدم. با فرنگیس شام خوردم. کمی راه رفتیم و زودتر خوابیدم.

سه‌شنبه ۳۱ تیر، ۲۲ ژوئیه - صبح کمی روزنامه خواندم. بعد از ظهر با فرنگیس بسینما رفتم و شب از هتل بیرون نرفتم.

چهارشنبه اول مرداد، ۲۳ ژوئیه - صبح در کمبریج با فرنگیس کتاب خواندیم و عصری در هتل بودیم.

پنجشنبه ۲ مرداد، ۲۴ ژوئیه - صبح رفتم بلندن. با مستر مایلز ناهار خوردم. عصری در اداره کار کردم. شب بکمبریج آمدم.

جمعه ۳ مرداد، ۲۵ ژوئیه - صبح کمی فرنگیس را استمالت دادم چون بواسطهٔ شنیدن خبر خوب نشدن امتحان فرانسه‌اش اوقات تلخ بود. بعد از ظهر کمی راه رفتیم و شب در هتل بودیم.

شنبه ۴ مرداد، ۲۶ ژوئیه - صبح کمی با فرنگیس کتاب خواندم. شب با او بمنزل پروفسور چَدْویک رفتم. تا ساعت ۱۰ آنجا بودیم. بد نگذشت. کمی در باب مسائل مختلف از قبیل زبان روسی و زبان هندی مذاکره شد. پروفسور چَدْویک و زنش بسیار خوشرو و فهیم و مهمان‌دارند.

یکشنبه ۵ مرداد، ۲۷ ژوئیه - صبح کتاب خواندم. بعد با فرنگیس کمی راه رفتیم. در این روزها کتاب مادام بواری را می‌خوانم.

دوشنبه ۶ مرداد ۱۳۲۰، ۲۸ ژوئیه ۱۹۴۱ - صبح کتاب خواندم با فرنگیس. عصر آقای مینوی آمد. با هم کمی راه رفتیم. بعد با فرنگیس بهتل آمدم.

سه‌شنبه ۷ مرداد، ۲۹ ژوئیه - صبح در هتل با فرنگیس روزنامه و کتاب خواندم. بعد از

ظهر با مینوی[1] و فرنگیس راه رفتم و بعد در هتل روایال شام خوردیم و بعد بمنزل آقای تقی‌زاده رفتیم. تا ساعت ۱۱ آنجا بودیم.

چهارشنبه ۸ مرداد، ۳۰ ژوئیه - صبح با فرنگیس کتاب خواندم. شب با او بمنزل مستر زگو رفتم.

پنجشنبه ۹ مرداد، ۳۱ ژوئیه[2] - صبح بلندن رفتم. با بایندر ناهار خوردم. شب بکمبریج آمدم. شب با فرنگیس بودم.

جمعه ۱۰ مرداد، ۱ اوت - صبح کمی کتاب خواندم. بعد از ظهر با فرنگیس بسینما رفتم. شب در هتل بودم.

شنبه ۱۱ مرداد، ۲ اوت - روز کتاب مادام بواری خواندم. شب با فرنگیس بمنزل آقای تقی‌زاده رفتم. پروفسور چَدْویک و زنش و پروفسور دیگری موسوم به جوبسون هم آمدند.

یکشنبه ۱۲ مرداد، ۳ اوت - صبح با فرنگیس راه رفتم و عصر با آقای تقی‌زاده و خانمش و فرنگیس به گران‌چستر رفتم. شب در هتل شام خوردیم. یکی از ایرانیان مقیم هندوستان که قرابتی با فرنگیس داد، با پسرعموی او بدیدن فرنگیس آمده بودند. بعد از شام، با آنها در کمبریج راه رفتیم.

دوشنبه ۱۳ مرداد، ۴ اوت - صبح با فرنگیس و رضای شیرازی ــ از ایرانیان مقیم هندوستان ــ < و > پسرعموی او خلیلی راه رفتم و بعد همه در هتل ناهار خوردیم. ایشان ساعت سه بعد از ظهر رفته و من و فرنگیس کمی راه رفتیم. شب از هتل بیرون نرفتم. حالم چندان خوب نبود. فرنگیس کمی از کتاب در راه هند را خواند.

سه‌شنبه ۱۴ مرداد، ۵ اوت - کمی از کتاب مادام بواری را خواندم. بعد از ظهر با

---

۲. ۱ اوت. تاریخ دو روز بعدی نیز اشتباه درج شده بود. تصحیح شد.

فرنگیس بسینما رفتم. فیلم *Little Old New York* را که راجع بزندگی در نیویورک بود دیدم و همچنین فیلم راجع بکشتی‌سازی معروف کووین مری. شب در هتل بودم. فرنگیس برایم کتاب فارسی خواند.

چهارشنبه ۱۵ مرداد، ۶ اوت - صبح با فرنگیس چاشت خوردم و بعد چون برای ثبت اسم و راپورت دادن فرنگیس می‌خواست به اکسفورد برود، با او به اکسفورد رفتم. با ترن نه و نیم حرکت کردیم. یک ساعت و نیم بعد از ظهر رسیدیم. کارش را انجام داد و بعد با ترن پنج بعد از ظهر بکمبریج آمدیم. ساعت شش و نیم رسیدیم. در این ایام در روزنامه‌ها و در مجلس انگلستان در باب ایران بحث زیاد می‌شود. ایران را مرکز کار آلمانیها می‌دانند.

پنجشنبه ۱۶ مرداد، ۷ اوت - صبح با فرنگیس بودم. بعد از ظهر بمنزل مستر یونگ رفتم. درس آلمانی خواندم. شب در هتل بودم.

جمعه ۱۷ مرداد ۱۳۲۰، ۸ اوت ۱۹۴۱ - صبح بلندن رفتم. با مستر مایلز و مستر کروناله ناهار خوردم. شب بکمبریج آمدم. با فرنگیس شام خوردم. در این روز خواندن رمان مادام بواری تمام شد. رمان جنگ و صلح تولستوی را شروع کردم.

شنبه ۱۸ مرداد، ۹ اوت - صبح در هتل بودم. بحساب بانک رسیدگی کردم. بعد از ظهر بمنزل مستر یونگ رفتم. درس آلمانی خواندم. شب با فرنگیس بمنزل آقای تقی‌زاده رفتم. تا نصف شب آنجا بودیم. وقت برگشتن باران می‌بارید.

یکشنبه ۱۹ مرداد، ۱۰ اوت - صبح روزنامه و کتاب خواندم. بعد با فرنگیس راه رفتم. شب در هتل بودم.

دوشنبه ۲۰ مرداد، ۱۱ اوت - صبح حالم بد بود. چاشت کمی خوردم و بعد تب و لرز سختی آمد. روز و شب در هتل بودم. فرنگیس پرستاریم می‌کرد. بعد از ظهر حالم کمی بهتر شد لیکن تب داشتم. شب خوب نخوابیدم.

سه‌شنبه ۲۱ مرداد، ۱۲ اوت - صبح لباس پوشیدم و چاشت خوردم ولی بعد از چاشت احساس ضعف کردم. باز باطاقم آمدم و در تخت خواب رفتم و روز و شب از اطاق خارج نشدم. فرنگیس پرستاریم می‌کرد. در این روز شعر و نثر فارسی و انگلیسی خواندم. از شاهنامه، حافظ، سعدی، شکسپیر، و غیر آنها. شب حالم کمی بهتر بود و بهتر خوابیدم.

چهارشنبه ۲۲ مرداد، ۱۳ اوت - صبح کمی حالم بهتر بود. ببانک رفتم. با رئیس بانک مذاکره کردم که دویست لیره برای نبیل بفرستند. بعد از ظهر بیرون رفتم. شب هم در هتل بودم. با فرنگیس کتاب می‌خواندم و در این ایام هر روز نام ایران در روزنامه‌هاست.

پنجشنبه ۲۳ مرداد ۱۳۲۰، ۱۴ اوت ۱۹۴۱ - صبح کمی از کتاب مستر هوکر را که برای آموختن فارسی نوشته است، تصحیح کردم. بعد از ظهر با فرنگیس بکلیسایی رفتیم و در آنجا رُجرز کشیش که در اصفهان بوده و فرنگیس او را می‌شناخت، نطقی در باب ایران کرد ـ راجع ببستن مدرسه‌های مذهبی و سخت‌گیریهای نظمیه و غیره. او را برای چای روز شنبه دعوت کردم. در این روز چندین فصل از جنگ و صلح تولستوی < را > خواندم. سه ساعت بعد از ظهر این روز اَتَلی معاون رئیس الوزاری انگلستان شرحی خواند در باب ملاقات میان روزولت و چرچیل و هشت ماده‌ای که راجع به آینده عالم تدوین کرده‌اند.

جمعه ۲۴ مرداد، ۵ اوت - صبح بعد از چاشت لرز کردم و تبی سخت آمد. در تخت خواب افتادم و بعد از ظهر طبیب آمد. معاینه‌ام کرد. گفت چیزی مهم نیست. انلفوانزاست. بعداً تب نداشتم. پیش از ظهر حالم بسیار بد بود ولی عصر کمی بهتر شد. اغلب اوقات فرنگیس در اطاقم بود و گاهی کتاب می‌خواند.

شنبه ۲۵ مرداد، ۱۶ اوت - صبح حالم کمی بهتر بود ولی از اطاق بیرون نرفتم. کتاب خواندم. پیش از ظهر آقای تقی‌زاده بعیادت آمدند. کمی صحبت کردیم و کاغذی که

از آقای نبیل برای ایشان آمده بود < را > بایشان دادم. بعد از ظهر مستر رُجِرز آمد. قریب یک ساعت و نیم نشست و در باب موضوعات مختلف صحبت کردیم. تمام روز فرنگیس با من بود.

یکشنبه ۲۶ مرداد، ۱۷ اوت - صبح حالم بهتر بود ولی از اطاق بیرون نرفتم. کتاب خواندم و بیشتر کتاب جنگ و صلح خواندم. در این روز سه بار در اخبار رادیو خبر راجع بایران را گفتند که چون یادداشتهایی که انگلیس و روس در باب خطر حضور آلمانیها در آن مملکت داده‌اند مؤثر نشده، دوباره خاطر نشان کرده و گفته‌اند که باید اقدامی مؤثر و فوری در این باب بشود.

دوشنبه ۲۷ مرداد ۱۳۲۰، ۱۸ اوت ۱۹۴۱ - صبح کتاب خواندم. حالم بهتر بود ولی از اطاق هیچ بیرون نرفتم. در این روز در تایمز و در دیلی‌تلگراف سرمقاله‌ای راجع بایران بود که می‌رساند اگر ایران آلمانیها را از مملکت بیرون نکند، روسها و انگلیسیها کار را بر ایران سخت خواهند گرفت و شاید لشکر وارد کنند. در این روز از کتاب جنگ و صلح تولستوی بسیار خواندم.

سه‌شنبه ۲۸ مرداد، ۱۹ اوت - بعد از چند روز خواندن در تخت خواب، از اطاق بیرون رفتم. بعد از ظهر با فرنگیس بدیدن فیلم دزد بغداد رفتیم و شب با او فرانسه خواندم.

چهارشنبه ۲۹ مرداد، ۲۰ اوت - صبح کتاب خواندم. عصر با فرنگیس بکتابخانهٔ عمومی و از آنجا برستوران دوروتی رفتیم. یک جوان از اهل مالزی آمد و در سر میز ما نشست. مسلمان بود و اسمش عبدالله بن محمد. در ژنو هم چندین ایرانی را دیده بود. قرار گذاشتیم باز یکدیگر را ببینیم.

پنجشنبه ۳۰ مرداد، ۲۱ اوت - صبح کتاب خواندم و روزنامه. در روزنامه‌ها در باب ایران بسیار می‌نویسند. در دیلی‌تلگراف سرمقاله‌ای بود مبنی بر اینکه اگر ایران بیادداشت انگلیس و روس راجع باخراج آلمانیها جواب مساعد ندهد، باید اقدام

مؤثری کرد چرا که صبر انگلستان بسر رسیده است. معلوم نیست برای ایران چه خیال بافته‌اند. بعد از ظهر با فرنگیس فرانسه خواندیم و شب در هتل بودیم.

جمعه ۳۱ مرداد، ۲۲ اوت - صبح در روزنامه‌ها راجع بایران مقالات و اخبار بسیار بود و از آنها چنان بر می‌آید که انگلیسیها و روسها باز می‌خواهند در ایران بیچاره و بی‌پناه دخالت کنند. بسیار اوقات تلخ بودم. شب بمنزل آقای تقی‌زاده رفتم و از حالت تأثر او بیشتر غمگین شدم. گفت برای من سخت است که ببینم نتیجهٔ پنجاه سال زحمت و فکر اینطور در معرض خطر باشد.

شنبه ۱ شهریور، ۲۳ اوت - صبح با فرنگیس کتاب خواندم. پیش از ظهر با آقای تقی‌زاده و فرنگیس راه رفتیم. بعد از ظهر در هتل بودیم. کتاب خواندم. اخبار راجع بایران چندان امیدبخش نبود.

یکشنبه ۲ شهریور، ۲۴ اوت - صبح با فرنگیس کتاب خواندم. بعد از ظهر بمنزل پروفسور مینورسکی رفتم و شب در خانه بودم. در این دو روز اخیر در رادیو راجع بایران هیچ خبری نبود.

دوشنبه ۳ شهریور ۱۳۲۰، ۲۵ اوت ۱۹۴۱ - صبح این روز خواستم بلندن بروم ولی نمی‌دانم چه شد که نرفتم. صبح کمی روزنامه خواندم و کمی از کتاب فارسی مستر هوکر را خواندم و تصحیح کردم. در این روز روزنامه‌ها و علی الخصوص تایمز در باب ایران مقالات و اخباری داشت که از آنها بوی خوش نمی‌آید و علی الخصوص سرمقالهٔ تایمز که بسیار معنی‌دار بود. ساعت یک بعد از ظهر در رادیو فرنگیس و من شنیدیم که قشون انگلستان و روس وارد ایران شده‌اند. بعد از ناهار با هم دیوانه‌وار در کوچه گشتیم. برای شنیدن اخبار در ساعت شش بهتل آمدیم. معلوم شد که در خلیج فارس لشکر ایران مقاومتی کرده است. بسیار بدحال شدیم. باز در اخبار عین آنچه در ساعت شش گفتند تکرار کردند و مستر کیلینگ عضو مجلس و عضو جمعیّت ایران در باب ایران نطقی کرد که بسیار خوب بود. از صناعت و تاریخ و عظمت ایران

گفت. تا امروز هرگز نمی‌دانستم که اینقدر این مملکت بدبخت و خراب و بیچاره را دوست دارم. کاشکی در ایران بودم و با ایرانیها در این غم بیشتر شریک می‌شدم و با آنها کشته می‌شدم. نمی‌دانم عاقبت کار مملکت بکجا خواهد کشید ولی از امروز فهمیدم که صلح و دوستی و آزادی جز حرف مفت چیزی نیست و در دنیا غیر از قدرت هیچ چیز حکمفرما نیست.

سه‌شنبه ۴ شهریور، ۲۶ اوت - صبح با حال بسیار بد صبح زود لباس پوشیدم و بلندن رفتم. شب نتوانستم درست بخوابم. در لندن قریب نیمساعت اداره بودم و بعد رفتم بسفارت. وزیر مختار را دیدم، بسیار بیچاره و عاجز و بی‌خبر. قریب نیمساعت با او بودم و بعد با بایندر و وحید در پیکادلی ناهار خوردم. بعد از ظهر با بایندر بسفارت رفتم و شب بکمبریج آمدم. بعد از اخبار ساعت سه، قریب یک ساعت با دو سه نفر انگلیسی بحث کردم. حالم بجا نبود و درست نمی‌دانستم چه می‌گویم. ایران را از چندین طرف گرفته‌اند و دیگر کار ما با خداست.

چهارشنبه ۵ شهریور، ۲۷ اوت - صبح روزنامه‌ها را خواندم. همه پر از اخبار راجع بتصرّف ایران بود. بعد از ظهر با فرنگیس بسینما رفتم ولی آنی از خیال ایران فارغ نبودم. شب در روزنامه خواندم که بایندر فرماندهٔ بحریهٔ کوچک ایران در خلیج فارس کشته شده است. شب بسیار خسته بودم و ساعت ده و نیم خوابیدم.

پنجشنبه ۶ شهریور، ۲۸ اوت - صبح با فرنگیس رفتم به پی‌تِر بُرو[1] که آقای تقی‌زاده را ببینم. چون ایشان بعد از ظهر می‌آمدند با فرنگیس بدیدن کلیسا رفتیم. گمان نمی‌بردم کلیسایی باین عظمت در پی‌تِر بُرو باشد. با فرنگیس در رستورانی غذا خوردیم. ساعت سه بعد از ظهر آقای تقی‌زاده و خانمشان آمدند. با هم چای خوردیم و تا ساعت پنج و نیم با هم بودیم. در موقع برگشتن، راه ایستگاه را گم کردیم و وقتی رسیدیم، ترن رفته بود و گفتند که یک ترن دیگر بکمبریج خواهد رفت و آنگاه با

---

۱. Peterborough، شهرکی در شمال‌غربی کمبریج به فاصلهٔ حدود ۴۵ مایل.

هم در ساعت یازده با تاکسی بکمبریج آمیدم. در ساعت سه شنیدیم که در ایران کابینه تغییر کرده و حکم کرده است که در مقابل لشکر انگلیس و روس مقاومتی نکنند. در نه و بیست دقیقه راجع بایران نطقی در رادیو کردند. بعد از اخبار، کمی در اطاق بزرگ نشستیم و ساعت یازده و نیم باطاقم آمدم و بعد از ساعت دوازده و شنیدن اخبار نصف شب، خوابیدم.

جمعه ۷ شهریور، ۲۹ اوت - صبح روزنامه خواندم و بعد بکتابخانه رفتم و تمام روزنامه‌های انگلیسی را که پر از اخبار راجع بایران بود، خواندم. ایران را از چندین طرف احاطه کرده‌اند و دیگر امیدی نیست و باید منتظر بود و دید که چه پیش خواهد آمد. یک ساعت بعد از نصف شب خوابیدم. از سرمقاله و مفاد اخبار چنان بر می‌آید که می‌خواهند کار را بر ایران سخت بگیرند. روسها کارشان سخت بنظر می‌آید و روزنامه‌ها و اخبار مردم را برای خبر بد آماده می‌کنند.

شنبه ۸ شهریور، ۳۰ اوت - صبح روزنامه خواندم. در باب ایران کمتر می‌نویسند ولی آنچه می‌نویسند دلخراش است. با فرنگیس بکتابخانه رفتم و تمام روزنامه‌های روز را خواندم. بعد از ظهر بمنزل عبدالله بن محمد از اهالی مالایا رفتم. قریب دو ساعت با او بودیم. بحث کردیم. بموسیقی مالایا و چین نگاه کردیم. زبان مالایا بخط عربی است و بسیاری لغت عربی داد. شب در اخبار شنیدیم که ایران هر نوعی مقاومتی را ترک کرده است و روس و انگلیس پیشنهادهای خود را بدولت خواهند داد. روسها تبریز، اورمیه، < بندر > پهلوی، و مشهد را گرفته‌اند. تا امروز چنین بدبختی برای ایران روی نداده بود.

یکشنبه ۹ شهریور، ۳۱ اوت - صبح اغلب روزنامه‌های انگلیس را خواندم. راجع بایران ترّهاتی داشت ولی از آن مهمتر مقالات و اخباری بود و چنان می‌نمود که مردم را برای خبر بد روس مهیّا می‌کنند و از این گذشته، در باب مخالفت بعضی از طبقات در امریکا با همراهی بانگلستان و از همه مهمتر نوشتن در باب عدم کفایت مهمّاتی

که از امریکا فرستاده می‌شود. بر رویهم کار انگلیسیها بسیار یأس‌آور بنظر می‌رسد. آقای وحید که بدیدن آقای تقی‌زاده آمده و او را نیافته بود بهتل آمد. با هم ناهار خوردیم. بعد فرنگیس بمنزل پروفسور مینورسکی رفت و من و وحید تا چهار ساعت و نیم بعد از ظهر با هم بودیم. و بعد بمنزل مینورسکی رفتم. تا ساعت هفت آنجا بودم. بعد با فرنگیس بهتل برگشتیم. اخبار را شنیدم. چندان امیدبخش نبود و چنان می‌نماید که روسها شکست فاحشی دیده‌اند و ممکن است در دو سه هفته لنینگراد و اودسا و کیِف از دست روسها برود.

دوشنبه ۱۰ شهریور، ۱ سپتامبر ۱۹۴۱ - صبح روزنامه خواندم و بعد با فرنگیس بکتابخانه رفتم و سایر روزنامه‌ها را خواندم. در باب ایران هنوز اخبار بسیار نوشته می‌شود. عصر بمنزل آقای تقی‌زاده رفتیم و ساعت هشت بهتل آمدیم. تمام شمال ایران بدست روسها افتاده است و لشکر روس تا قزوین و چالوس و شاهرود پیش آمده‌اند.

سه‌شنبه ۱۱ شهریور، ۲ سپتامبر - صبح کتاب و روزنامه خواند. بعد از ظهر با فرنگیس بسینما رفتیم و شب در هتل بودیم. بین ایران و انگلیس و روس قراردادی در شرف امضا است.

چهارشنبه ۱۲ شهریور، ۳ سپتامبر - صبح رفتم بلندن. در اداره کمی کار کردم. بعد رفتم بسفارت با وزیر مختار مذاکره کردم. ناهار با بایندر خوردم و شب بکمبریج آمدم. هنوز امضای قرارداد بین ایران و انگلیس و روس منتشر نشده است. قشون روس پیشتر نرفته‌اند.

پنجشنبه ۱۳ شهریور، ۴ سپتامبر - صبح روزنامه خواندم و بعد با فرنگیس بکتابخانه رفتم. بعد از ظهر با هم بسینما رفتیم و شب زودتر باطاقم آمدم. بسیار خسته بود. راجع بایران کمتر خبر می‌نویسند. فرمانده لشکر روس و فرمانده لشکر انگلیس در قزوین یکدیگر را ملاقات کرده و مجلس شادی بر پا کرده‌اند. ظاهراً ایران با امضای قراردادی که بر او تحمیل شده، موافقت کرده است.

جمعه ۱۴ شهریور، ۵ سپتامبر - صبح روزنامه و کتاب خواندم و بعد با فرنگیس بکتابخانهٔ عمومی رفتم. همه روزنامه‌های روز را دیدم. بعد از ظهر بمنزل آقای تقی‌زاده رفتیم و شب در هتل بودیم. هنوز خبر امضای قطعی قرارداد ایران و انگلیس و روس منتشر نشده است.

شنبه ۱۵ شهریور ۱۳۲۰، ۶ سپتامبر ۱۹۴۱ - صبح روزنامه خواندم و بعد با فرنگیس بادارهٔ پلیس رفتم چون فرنگیس می‌خواست در باب رفتن به ناتینگام اجازه بگیرد. از ادارهٔ پلیس بایستگاه رفتیم و او با ترن یازده و بیست دقیقه بدیدن یکی از دوستانش که او را دعوت کرده بود، رفت. بعد از ظهر بسینما رفتم و شب کتاب و روزنامه خواندم. از رفتن او متأثر شدم و در تنهایی در من اثر کرد. در باب ایران کمتر چیز نوشته می‌شود. خبری را که با آب و تاب شرح می‌دهند، ملاقات فرمانده روس و فرمانده انگلیس است در قزوین. هر روز امید ورود امریکا بجنگ برای انگلیسیها کمتر می‌شود و معلوم نیست که انگلیس پس از شکست روس چگونه و در کجا مقابل قشون آلمانی خواهد ایستاد.

یکشنبه ۱۶ شهریور، ۷ سپتامبر - صبح روزنامه خواندم. در ساعت یازده تا یک ساعت بعد از ظهر با آقای تقی‌زاده راه رفتم. عصر بمنزل آقای تقی‌زاده رفتم و شب در هتل بودم. تا ساعت یازده در باب جنگ با چند نفر از اهل هتل بحث می‌کردم. نبودن فرنگیس بسیار بمن تأثیر کرده است. از ایران خبری نیست و حتی در روزنامه‌ها هم کمتر از آن می‌نویسند.

دوشنبه ۱۷ شهریور، ۸ سپتامبر - صبح روزنامه خواندم. از آنها استنباط کردم که شرایط سخت دیگری بایران تحمیل کرده‌اند و شاید اگر ایران جزیی تغییری بخواهد، تهران را نیز روسها بگیرند. سه بعد از ظهر بسینما رفتم و شب در انتظار فرنگیس بودم. ساعت شش و چهل و پنج دقیقه بعد از ظهر آمد. بسیار خوشوقت شدم زیرا جدایی از او بر من سخت بود. آلمانیها لنینگراد را محاصره کرده‌اند و شاید تا ده دوازده روز دیگر آن را بگیرند.

سه‌شنبه ۱۸ شهریور ۱۳۲۰، ۹ سپتامبر ۱۹۴۱ - صبح کتاب خواندم. با فرنگیس بکتابخانه عمومی رفتم. روزنامه‌ها را خواندم. عصر با هم نطقی راجع بآثار عتیقهٔ روسیه را شنیدیم. شب در هتل بودیم.

چهارشنبه ۱۹ شهریور، ۱۰ سپتامبر - صبح کتاب و روزنامه خواندم و عصر با فرنگیس بدیدن فیلم یک روز در روسیه رفتم و شب بمنزل آقای تقی‌زاده. روز سه‌شنبه چرچیل نطقی مفصّل در مجلس کرد و در باب ایران هم شرحی بمیان آورد. از گفته‌هایش بدست می‌آید که بسیار از دولت ایران شکایت دارد. عقیده دارد تا ممکن است کار را بر ایران سخت بگیرد. روزنامهٔ تایمز هم بسخت‌گیری در کار ایران معتقد است.

پنجشنبه ۲۰ شهریور، ۱۱ سپتامبر - صبح با فرنگیس رفتم بلندن و تنها بسفارت رفتم. ناهار با بایندر و حمزاوی خوردم و بعد از ظهر هم در سفارت بودم. شب بکمبریج آمدم. به ایران اولتیماتوم داده‌اند که چهل و هشت ساعته سفارت آلمان و ایطالیا و رومانی و هنگری را ببندد و آلمانی‌هایی را که گذرنامهٔ سیاسی ندارند، بگیرد و بروس و انگلیس بسپارد.

جمعه ۲۱ شهریور، ۱۲ سپتامبر - صبح با فرنگیس روزنامه خواندم و بعد رفتم بکتابخانه. در باب شاه یکی دو روزنامه بسیار بد نوشته بودند. بعد از ظهر با فرنگیس رفتم بسینما. فیلم روسی چوپایف را که چهار سال پیش دیده بودم، دیدیم. شب در هتل بودیم.

شنبه ۲۲ شهریور، ۳ سپتامبر - صبح کتاب و روزنامه خواندم. بعد با فرنگیس بکتابخانهٔ عمومی رفتم. بعد از ظهر با فرنگیس و میسز طلعتی و دخترش در دورتی چای خوردیم. این زن روس ولی شوهرش پارسی و مقیم چین است و آنها را در لندن می‌شناختم. در وست کرمول رود[۱] زندگی می‌کردند در خانهٔ دوازده. در این روزها بشاه در روزنامه‌ها بسیار بد می‌نویسند.

---

۱. W Cromwell Rd، نام خیابانی در غرب لندن نزدیک محلهٔ چلسی (Chelsea).

یکشنبه ۲۳ شهریور ۱۳۲۰، ۱۴ سپتامبر ۱۹۴۱ - صبح با فرنگیس بودم. کتاب و روزنامه خواندیم و راه رفتم. عصر با هم بمنزل آقای تقی‌زاده رفتیم و شب در هتل بودیم. در روزنامه‌های یکشنبه باز در باب ایران شرحی نوشته‌اند و علی الخصوص با شاه روی خوشی نشان نمی‌دهند. شاید او را از میان بردارند.

دوشنبه ۲۴ شهریور، ۱۵ سپتامبر - صبح کتاب و روزنامه خواندم و بعد با فرنگیس بکتابخانهٔ عمومی رفتیم و روزنامه‌های روز همه را خواندیم. راجع بشاه و تغییراتی که ممکن است در ایران پیش آید، چیزهایی نوشته شده بود. بعد از ظهر با فرنگیس بسینما رفتم و شب در هتل بودیم. کار روسها روزبروز سخت‌تر می‌شود.

سه‌شنبه ۲۵ شهریور، ۱۶ سپتامبر - صبح با فرنگیس کتاب و روزنامه خواندیم. بعد با هم بکتابخانهٔ عمومی رفتیم و روزنامه‌های روز را خواندیم. یکساعت بعد از ظهر در اخبار شنیدیم که شاه استعفا داده است و از تهران بیرون رفته و لشکر روس و انگلیس وارد تهران خواهند شد. هر چند با استبداد و بعضی از اخلاق شاه هرگز موافق نبودم، از میان رفتن او باین وضع بر من گران آمد. استقلال ایران امروز نابود شده و خدا می‌داند که می‌توانیم دوباره استقلال داشته باشیم. ولی تنها روزن امیدی که هست شکست روسهاست از آلمانیها. روسها وقتی وارد ایران می‌شوند که خاک روس بدست لشکر آلمانی است و بیشتر پیش می‌آید. بعد از ظهر با فرنگیس بسینما رفتم و شب در هتل بودم.

چهارشنبه ۲۶ شهریور، ۱۷ سپتامبر - صبح کتاب و روزنامه خواندیم. بعد با فرنگیس بکتابخانهٔ عمومی رفتم. روزنامه‌ها را خواندم. همه پر از خبر راجع بایران و استعفای شاه بود و فحش و ناسزا باو. از ساعت یازده و نیم تا یک بعد از ظهر با آقای تقی‌زاده راه رفتیم و بعد بهتل آمدیم. عصر رفتیم به دوروتی و با عبدالله بن محمد که از اهل سنگاپور است، چای خوردیم. بموجب اخباری که می‌رسد ولیعهد را بسلطنت انتخاب کرده‌اند و هر چند قرار بود که دیروز قشون روس و انگلیس وارد تهران شوند، دیروز

عصر در اخبار گفتند که فرماندهٔ لشکر روس و انگلیس بتهران رفته‌اند و با آنکه قشون روس و انگلیس نزدیک تهرانند، هنوز وارد نشده‌اند. گویا در ورود آنها بتهران تردیدی حاصل شده است.

پنجشنبه ۲۷ شهریور ۱۳۲۰، ۱۸ سپتامبر ۱۹۴۱ - صبح بلندن رفتم. کمی در اداره بودم و بعد رفتم بسفارت. با وزیر مختار و حمزاوی و بایندر کمی صحبت کردم. از ایران بی‌خبر بودند. ناهار با بایندر و وحید خوردم و عصر دوباره بسفارت رفتم. شب بکمبریج آمدم. در روزنامه‌ها نوشته بودند که روسها با پاراشوت سرباز بتهران انداخته و تمام سربازخانه‌ها و ایستگاه راه آهن و سایر جاهای مهم را گرفته‌اند و قشون انگلیس هنوز وارد تهران نشده. دو سه روزنامه نوشته بودند که صاحب‌منصب روسی بیرون تهران جلوی قشون انگلیس را گرفته و بآنها گفته است که تهران را روسها تصرّف کرده‌اند. با آنکه روسها روزبروز شکست می‌خورند و محتاج بکمک انگلیس هستند، اینطور با انگلیس رفتار می‌کنند وای بوقتی که روسها فاتح شوند. شاه ظاهراً بمصر و از آنجا بامریکای جنوبی می‌رود. پسرش را بتخت نشانده‌اند و می‌گویند قول داده است موافق قانون اساسی حکومت کند. از اصلاحاتی که در نظر داشت پس دادن اراضی و کم کردن مالیات و ازدیاد قدرت حکومت محلی است که جز قطعه قطعه کردن ایران مقتضایی ندارد.

جمعه ۱۸ شهریور ۱۳۲۰، ۱۹ سپتامبر ۱۹۴۱ - صبح روزنامهٔ تایمز خواندم. در باب اوضاع ایران شرح مفصلی در تایمز بود. ظاهراً انگلیسها از ترس انقلاب داخلی هر چند از استعفای شاه خشنودند، نمی‌خواهند که ولیعهد از میان برود. ولی معلوم نیست که روسها چه راهی در نظر دارند. گویا چنانکه در روزنامه‌ها می‌نویسند بر سر تصرّف تهران بین انگلیسها و روسها اختلافی بوده است. اگر چه حقیقت معلوم نیست، آنچه مسلّم است آنکه روسها بتهران رفته و آن را تصرّف کرده و انگلیسها را بیرون تهران گذاشته‌اند. با فرنگیس بکتابخانهٔ عمومی رفتم. روزنامه‌ها را خواندم. در باب ایران ترّهاتی نوشته‌اند که انسان حیران می‌ماند. جنگ و منفعت ملّتی بزرگ و ظاهرساز مثل انگلیسها را بکار و گفتار عوام فریبانه‌ای برانگیخته است که بوحشی افریقایی می‌برازد

نه بروزنامه‌نویسها و روزنامه‌خوانهای انگلستان. شب با فرنگیس ببلدیهٔ کمبریج رفتم و در طالاری نطقی راجع بایران شنیدم. ناطق کشیشی بود موسوم به گیل Gill که برای مسیحی کردن یهودیها بایران رفته بوده. عکسهایی از ایران با خود آورده بود و آنها را نشان می‌داد ولی اغلب یهودیهای ایران را نشان می‌داد. ناطق مردی کوته‌نظر و مغرض و نادان بنظر می‌آمد. پیش از هر چیز گفت که چون شاه استعفا داده است آزادم هر چه می‌خواهم بگویم و گر نه امکان نداشت از ترس آنکه مبادا باو خبر بدهند، آنچه را باید شرح دهم. آنچه گفت مرض آلود و بی‌پا بود. اشاره‌ای کرد بکارهایی که شاه کرده بود ولی از آنها بزودی گذشت و هر چیز بدی را بشاه و هر نوع بدبختی و مرضی را بایران نسبت داد. در نظر حضّار که اغلب پیرزن و جهود بودند، ایران بعد از نطق او باید مثل یکی از ممالک پست افریقایی جلوه کرده باشد. چندان کوته‌نظر و مغرض بود که هر چند نطق با یهودیها رابطه داشت و با آنکه شرحی در باب اسارت یهود در بابل گفت، یک کلمه در باب آزاد شدن یهود بدست ایرانیها بر زبان نیاورد. از این آخوندهای فرنگی احمق‌تر و مغرض‌تر کسی در اروپا نیست و تکلیف هر ایرانی آنست که پای این خودپسندهای مغرض را بکلی از ایران ببرد. باری در تمام نطق که یک ساعت و نیم بطول کشید، جز بد بایران و ایرانی و بشاه چیزی نگفت. بعد از نطق فرنگیس و من نزد او رفتیم و تا گفتیم که ایرانی هستیم و جهود نیستیم، یک باره درمانده شد. باو گفتم که خوب نیست یک مسیحی این طور شاه را که یک فرد از پانزده میلیون ایرانی است نمایندهٔ ملّت ایران جلوه دهد. و نیز گفتیم که از نظر شما که مسیحی هستید، تصرّف تهران و سایر نواحی ایران چیست و آیا خیال می‌کنید که آمدن روسها بایران برای شما بهتر است، روسهایی که بخدا معتقد نیستند. با بیانی احمقانه گفت که بر اثر دوستی با ما آنها هم براه راست هدایت می‌شوند. از دیدن ما و گفته‌های ما بسیار ناراحت بود و منتظر بود که هر چه زودتر از چنگ ما خلاص شود. خدا ایران و تمام عالم را از شر این کشیشهای نادان و غرض‌ورز و کوتاه‌نظر فرنگی خلاص کند.

شنبه ۲۹ شهریور، ۲۰ سپتامبر - صبح با فرنگیس کتاب و روزنامه خواندیم و بعد بکتابخانهٔ عمومی رفتیم. روزنامه‌ها را خواندیم. پر بود از اخبار تصرّف شهر کِیف یکی

از سه شهر مهم روسیه که منظور آلمانیها بود. بعد از ظهر با فرنگیس بمنزل مسیز طلعتی رفتم ــ مسیز طلعتی و دخترش میس ال‌برن که در لندن هم منزل من بودند. تا شش و نیم بعد از ظهر آنجا بودیم و بیشتر در باب ایران صحبت بود. مسیز طلعتی زنی است روسی و شوهرش یکی از پارسیان هندوستان است که در چین زندگی می‌کند. او و دخترش را در لندن در خانه‌ای که زندگی می‌کردم، دیدم. چندین بار در کمبریج ملاقاتشان کردم ولی دیدن ایشان ممکن نشد. زن نجیب خوبی است. شب با فرنگیس بمنزل آقای تقی‌زاده رفتیم. تا ساعت یازده و نیم آنجا بودیم.

یکشنبه ۳۰ شهریور ۱۳۲۰، ۲۱ سپتامبر ۱۹۴۱ - صبح روزنامه خواندیم. بعد از ظهر با فرنگیس به گران‌چستر رفتم. شب در هتل بودم. در این روزها اخبار استعفای شاه و بتخت‌نشینی پسرش در روزنامه‌هاست. ظاهراً انگلیسها می‌خواهند پسرش را بر تخت نگاه دارند.

دوشنبه ۳۱ شهریور، ۲۲ سپتامبر - صبح کتاب و روزنامه خواندم. بعد از ظهر با فرنگیس بسینما رفتم. فیلم خلیج هودسن را دیدم که چندان خوب نبود. شب بسیار خسته بودم و زود خوابیدم.

سه‌شنبه ۱ مهر ۱۳۲۰، ۲۳ سپتامبر - صبح کتاب و روزنامه خواندم. بعد از ظهر با فرنگیس بسینما رفتم. فیلم *Le Bonheur*[1] را دیدم. شب در هتل بودیم. در این روز خبر تشکیل کابینهٔ جدید ایران را دوباره در دیلی‌تلگراف نوشته بودند. دکتر اشرف نفیسی وزیر مالیه شده است و دکتر عیسی صدیق وزیر معارف. حکمت وزیر صناعت و جهانبانی وزیر داخله. سهیلی وزیر خارجه و نخجوان وزیر جنگ.

چهارشنبه ۲ مهر، ۲۴ سپتامبر - صبح بلندن رفتم. کمی در اداره بودم و بعد رفتم بسفارت. آقای وزیر مختار را دیدم. با بایندر ناهار خوردم و شب بکمبریج آمدم. محاصرهٔ لنینگراد شدیدتر شده و شاید تا ده پانزده روز دیگر این شهر هم بدست آلمانیها بیفتد.

---

۱. در اصل: Bonheur.

پنجشنبه ۳ مهر، ۲۵ سپتامبر - صبح کتاب و روزنامه خواندم. بعد با فرنگیس بکتابخانهٔ عمومی رفتم. در این ایام خبرهایی از ترکیه در روزنامههای انگلیس بسیارست. فُن پاپن سفیر آلمان بانقره برگشته است و ظاهراً آلمانیها میخواهند بوعده و شفاعت ترکها را از اتحاد با انگلستان خارج کنند و شاید باین مقصود برسند چون در روسیه پیشرفت بسیار کردهاند و با اوضاع کنونی ترکها در چنگال آلمان بیچارهاند و اگر بخواهند با آلمانیها بجنگندند نه انگلیسها و نه روسها هیچیک نمیتوانند بترکیه کمک بدهند. بعد از ظهر با فرنگیس بسینما رفتم و شب در هتل بودم. شب بسیار گرم و بد بود و چندان خوب نمیتوانم بخوابم.

جمعه ۴ مهر ۱۳۲۰، ۲۶ سپتامبر - صبح روزنامه خواندم و بعد با فرنگیس بکتابخانه رفتم. بعد از ظهر با هم راه بسیار رفتیم و شب در هتل بودیم. در روزنامهها بدگویی بشاه کمتر شده است. هنوز از ایران خارج نشده است. در تایمز نوشته بود که انجمن مخصوص تخمین دارایی شاه در خارج ایران اظهار داشته است که او در بانکهای خارج پولی ندارد. در سایر روزنامهها هنوز در باب تموّل او چیزها مینویسند. آلمانیها حمله به کریمه را شروع کردهاند و در لنینگراد نیز پیشرفت میکنند. میگویند تا کنون بیش از پانصد هزار اسیر در ناحیهٔ کیف بدست آوردهاند.

شنبه ۵ مهر، ۲۷ سپتامبر - صبح با فرنگیس روزنامه و کتاب خواندیم. بعد بکتابخانهٔ عمومی رفتیم. بعد از ظهر بیرون شهر رفتیم، بجایی که جادهای قدیمی دارد بنام Roman Road. در دوروتی چای خوردیم. شب بمنزل آقای تقیزاده رفتیم. ژنرال وِیوِل[۱] برای مذاکره با چرچیل و سایر اعضای دولت بلندن آمده بود بهندوستان مراجعت کرد و در بین راه در تهران میماند که با صاحبمنصب روس مذاکره کند. در روزنامهها راجع بایران کمتر مینویسند.

یکشنبه ۶ مهر ۱۳۲۰، ۲۸ سپتامبر - صبح بعد از چاشت با فرنگیس بودم و روزنامههای

---

۱. Field Marshal Archibald P. Wavell (ولادت ۱۸۸۳ ـ وفات ۱۹۵۰) از فرماندهان ارشد ارتش بریتانیا.

یکشنبه را می‌خواندم. گفتند از لندن تلفونی هست. حمزاوی تلفون کرد و گفت که تلگرافی از تهران رسیده است و از آقای تقی‌زاده خواهش کرده‌اند که وزیر مختار شود و گفت که با زنش خواهد آمد. پیش از ظهر با آقای تقی‌زاده راه رفتم. بسیار در فکر بود. راستی هم باید در فکر باشد چونکه قبول و رد این پیشنهاد هر دو مهم و مؤثّر است، در کار خود آقای تقی‌زاده و کار ایران. آگر مان آقای تقی‌زاده را بوسیلهٔ سفارت انگلیس در تهران از دولت انگلستان خواسته‌اند و دولت انگلستان موافقت نموده است. نیم ساعت بعد از ظهر حمزاوی و خانمش آمده بودند. وقتی بهتل رسیدم ایشان را دیدم که با فرنگیس خانم حرف می‌زنند. با اتومبیل حمزاوی به یونی‌ورسی‌تی آرمز هتل[۱] رفتیم و ناهار خوردیم. تا ساعت چهار بعد از ظهر آنجا بودیم. بعد بمنزل آقای تقی‌زاده رفتیم. فرنگیس و زن حمزاوی را در اتومبیل بیرون باغ گذاشتیم و بمنزل آقای تقی‌زاده رفتیم. قریب یکساعت آنجا بودیم و حمزاوی شرحی در باب کار و اهمیّت قبول این شغل و خوشوقتی اعضای سفارت گفت. آقای تقی‌زاده با کمال آرامی و دقت گوش می‌کرد و تشکر نمود ولی گفت هنوز تصمیم قطعی نگرفته است علی الخصوص که متن تلگراف را روز شنبه آقای نیامیر در تلفون خوانده بود و خواهش کرده که آن را بفرستند که بیشتر دقّت شود. در این ایام که این تلگراف از تهران رسیده بود آقای مقدم وزیر مختار از لندن به کسویک[۲] بدیدن زن و فرزندش رفته بود ولی بمناسبت این تلگراف قرار بود که روز دوشنبه در لندن باشد. وقتی حمزاوی مطلبش تمام شد و می‌خواست برود، زنگ زدند. آقای تقی‌زاده بیرون رفت ببیند کیست. آمد و گفت که "آقای وزیرمختارند." حمزاوی ازین آمدن ناگهانی و بی‌موقع وزیر مختار مات و مبهوت شد. ایستاده بودیم که وزیر مختار آمد و او نیز سرگردان ماند. باری سه چهار کلمه بیشتر رد و بدل نشد. رفتیم. حمزاوی با زنش بلندن رفت. در هتل با فرنگیس چای خوردیم و شب در هتل بودم. روزنامه‌های یکشنبه را خواندم. از تصادف این روز در حیرت بودم.

---

۱. The University Arms Hotel، نام مهمانخانه‌ای در مرکز شهر کمبریج (اکنون نیز دایر است).

۲. Keswick شهر کوچکی در شمال‌غربی انگلستان.

دوشنبه ۷ مهر ۱۳۲۰، ۲۹ سپتامبر ۱۹۴۱ - صبح کتاب و روزنامه خواندم. بعد با فرنگیس بکتابخانهٔ عمومی رفتم. بعد از ظهر رفتیم بسینما و شب در هتل بودیم. کمی از کتاب *Dr. Jekyll and Mr. Hyde* را خواندم. در روزنامه‌ها نوشته بودند که شاه از بندرعباس با کشتی چاپاری بطرف هندوستان حرکت کرده است و از آنجا به شیلی خواهد رفت. در باب ایران اخبار کمتر شده است. غیر از سفر وِی‌وِل بتهران و ملاقاتش با فرماندهٔ لشکر روس در ایران چیز مهمی نوشته نمی‌شود. کار روسها روزبروز بدتر می‌شود. آلمانیها بقفقاز نزدیک می‌شوند.

سه‌شنبه ۸ مهر، ۳۰ سپتامبر - صبح با فرنگیس بودم. کتاب و روزنامه خواندم. بعد از ظهر بسینما رفتم و شب در هتل بودم. در این روز چرچیل در مجلس نطق کرد و در باب جنگ و آیندهٔ آن و گفت در نظر است با ایران قرارداد اتحادی بسته شود.

چهارشنبه ۹ مهر، اول اکتبر - رفتم بلندن. با باینِدر و حمزاوی و وحید ناهار خوردم. بعد از ظهر هم در سفارت بودم. صبح وزیر مختار را دیدم. مضطرب و بیچاره بود. در روزنامه‌ها در باب اتحاد با ایران چندان بحث نشده بود. فقط در روزنامه‌ای نوشته بود که قرارداد اتحاد با ایران ممکن است نظیر قرارداد اتحاد با مصر باشد. شب با فرنگیس بمنزل آقای تقی‌زاده رفتم. تلگرافی که آقای مقدم داده بود < را > بایشان رساندم. تا ساعت یازده آنجا بودم.

پنجشنبه ۱۰ مهر ۱۳۲۰، ۲ اکتبر ۱۹۴۱ - صبح با فرنگیس بودم. روزنامه و کتاب خواندیم و بعد رفتیم بکتابخانهٔ عمومی. روزنامه‌ها و مجلات را خواندیم. بعد از ظهر رفتم بتئاتر. بازی راجع بناپلئون را دیدم. بد نبود. *Napoleon Could Not Do It*. شب در هتل بودیم. کتاب خواندم.

جمعه ۱۱ مهر، ۳ اکتبر - صبح کتاب و روزنامه خواندم. بعد با فرنگیس بکتابخانهٔ عمومی رفتم. عصر در هتل بودیم و بعد رفتیم به دوروتی چای خوردیم. شب در هتل بودیم. در این روز هیتلر نطقی کرد ـ برای مدد بفقرا ـ و گفت که روسیه شکست

خورده و کارش تمام شده علی الخصوص که در ۴۸ ساعت اخیر کارهایی در میدان جنگ شرق شروع شده است که نتایج مهم خواهد داشت. در باب ایران خبری در روزنامه‌های انگلیسی نیست.

شنبه ۱۲ مهر، ۴ اکتبر – صبح با فرنگیس کتاب و روزنامه خواندم. بعد با هم بکتابخانهٔ عمومی رفتیم. بعد از ظهر در هتل بودیم و شب نیز کتاب خواندیم. در این روزها راجع بایران تقریباً خبری نوشته نمی‌شود و اوضاع روسیه روزبروز بدتر و سخت < می‌شود >.

یکشنبه ۱۳ مهر، ۵ اکتبر – صبح با فرنگیس و آقای تقی‌زاده راه رفتیم و بعد از ظهر با فرنگیس رفتیم بمنزل پروفسور مینورسکی. شب در هتل بودیم.

دوشنبه ۱۴ مهر، ۶ اکتبر – صبح با فرنگیس بودم و بعد از ظهر رفتم بسینما فیلم Nice Girl را دیدم. چندان خوب نبود. شب در هتل بودیم. کمی از کتاب تاریخ ادبیات انگلیسی را خواندم.

سه‌شنبه ۱۵ مهر ۱۳۲۰، ۷ اکتبر ۱۹۴۱ – صبح با فرنگیس بلندن رفتم. ناهار با فرنگیس و میس ویرا روبرتس خوردم و بعد از ظهر با هم رفتیم بسینمای اخبار. شب بکمبریج آمدیم. با فرنگیس رفتیم منزل آقای تقی‌زاده. در لندن بوسیلهٔ تلفون شنیدم که از تهران خبر رسیده است و از آقای تقی‌زاده خواهش کرده‌اند که وزارت مختار لندن را قبول کنند. کاشکی از چندین سال پیش او و امثال او را بکار می‌گماشتند. آلمانیها بطرف مسکو پیش می‌روند و چنانکه از روزنامه‌ها بدست می‌آید روسها هر چند مقاومت می‌کنند نتوانسته‌اند پیشرفت آلمانیها را مانع شوند.

چهارشنبه ۱۶ مهر، ۸ اکتبر – صبح کمی روزنامه خواندم. بعد با فرنگیس بیرون رفتیم. تز مدرسهٔ اقتصاد لندن را برای مستر هایار Highar عضو چاپخانهٔ Longman & Green فرستادم زیرا نوشته بود که می‌خواهد آن را بخواند. حالم

چندان خوب نبود. ناهار کمی سوپ خوردم. بعد در تخت خواب خوابیدم. تب کردم. فرنگیس با من بود و پرستاری می‌کرد. بسیار پریشانم زیرا فرنگیس برای تهیهٔ امتحان باید باکسفورد برود. قرار بود روز پنجشنبه ۹ اکتبر برود ولی چون حالم خوش نیست، آن را عقب انداخته است. رفتن از کمبریج بعد از این انس و الفت چندین ماهه بر من دشوار خواهد بود، علی الخصوص در این ایام که بدبختیهای ایران قلبم را حسّاس‌تر کرده است. روسهای بیچاره عقب می‌نشینند. بعد از چندین قرن آزار دادن همسایه و بدی و بدرفتاری و کشتن و تصرّف کردن خاک بیگانه خدا یکباره جزای اعمال اینها را بایشان نشان داده است. لابد حالا می‌فهمند که تصرّف خاک دیگران تنها راه بزرگی نیست. شاید تا سه چهار هفته دیگر مسکو بدست آلمانیها بیفتد.

پنجشنبه ۱۷ مهر ۱۳۲۰، ۹ اکتبر ۱۹۴۱ - حالم از روز پیش بهتر بود ولی احتیاطاً از اطاق بیرون نرفتم. فرنگیس هم رفتن باکسفورد را برای خاطر من بتعویق انداخت. تمام روز با من بود و کتاب می‌خواندیم. کتابی که در دست دارم و نصف آن را در یک روز و نیم خوانده‌ام کتاب Sir A. Wilson است: *S. W. Persia: A Political Officer's Diary 1907-1914* و در آن اطلاعات و نکته‌هایی راجع بایران و ایرانیان و فرنگیها علی الخصوص انگلیسیهایی که در مدّت مذکور در ایران بوده‌اند بسیار است. کار روسها سخت‌تر و پیشرفت آلمانها بطرف مسکو بیشتر شده است و چنانکه از اخبار بر می‌آید باید هفته‌های آخر روسیه باشد.

جمعه ۱۸ مهر، ۱۰ اکتبر - صبح حالم بهتر بود. از اطاق بیرون رفتم. کمی روزنامه خواندم و بعد با فرنگیس بکتابخانهٔ عمومی رفتیم و بعد از ظهر بسینما. *Bitter Sweet* را دیدیم. شب بمنزل مستر زگو Szego رفتیم. تا ساعت ۱۱ آنجا بودیم. کار روسیه بدتر شده است و هر چند در روزنامه‌های انگلیسی چنان وانمود می‌کنند که هنوز امید هست، از اخباری که می‌رسد می‌توان استنباط کرد که هفته‌های آخر روسیه است. از ایران هیچ خبری نیست. فقط در روزنامهٔ دیلی‌تلگراف نوشته بود که انگلستان توانسته

است بروسیّه بفهماند که باید حکومت ایران را قوی کرد و از طرز نوشتن خبر معلوم می‌شد که می‌خواهند بگویند روسیه پس از اوضاع اخیر و حملهٔ سخت آلمان سست‌تر شده است و در کار ایران شاید روزبروز مداخلهٔ انگلیس بیشتر شود.

شنبه ۱۹ مهر ۱۳۲۰، ۱۱ اکتبر ۱۹۴۱ - صبح کتاب و روزنامه خواندم. با فرنگیس پیش از ظهر بکتابخانه و بعد از ظهر بسینما رفتم. شب رفتم بمنزل زگو Szego. روسها هر روز شکست می‌خورند و آلمانیها بطرف مسکو پیش می‌روند. در این روز تلگرافی از پدرم رسید که خبر سلامت خود را باو تلگراف کنم و تلگراف کردم.

یکشنبه ۲۰ مهر، ۱۲ اکتبر - صبح با فرنگیس راه رفتم. هوا خوب ولی کمی سرد بود. با هم به گران‌چستر رفتیم. بعد از ظهر رفتیم بمنزل آقای تقی‌زاده. تا ساعت هفت و نیم آنجا بودیم. امشب شب آخر ماندن فرنگیس است زیرا باید روز دوشنبه ۱۳ اکتبر به اکسفورد برود. رفتن او علی الخصوص در این ایام که دلم بواسطهٔ حوادث ایران گرفته است، بر من بسیار ناگوار است. آلمانها پیشرفت می‌کنند و کار روسها روزبروز سخت‌تر می‌شود.

دوشنبه ۲۱ مهر، ۱۳ اکتبر - صبح زود برخاستم. با فرنگیس چاشت خوردم. بعد باطاق او رفتم. فرنگیس مشغول جمع کردن لوازم سفر شد. با او بایستگاه رفتم. ترن که باید یازده و بیست و پنج دقیقه حرکت کند، یک ربع دیرتر حرکت کرد. با فرنگیس وداع کردم و بعد بکتابخانهٔ عمومی رفتم و بعد از ظهر بسینما. شب در هتل بودم. رفتن فرنگیس بر من بسیار سخت است. بقدری با او انس گرفته‌ام که نمی‌دانم بی او چطور می‌توانم زندگی کنم. در کتابخانه، در اطاق، در سر میز، وقت کتاب و روزنامه خواندن همیشه در نظرم است. باز جای شکر باقی است که بعد از چند هفته می‌توانم او را ببینم. روسها عقب‌نشینی می‌کنند و کار روزبروز سخت‌تر می‌شود.

سه‌شنبه ۲۲ مهر، ۱۳۲۰، ۱۴ اکتبر ۱۹۴۱ - صبح روزنامه و کتاب خواندم. بعد بکتابخانه رفتم. آقای تقی‌زاده را دیدم. گفتند که آقای مقدم وزیر مختار که بیکار شده است، در

صدد برآمده که بجای آقای زرین‌کفش نمایندهٔ دولت در شرکت شود. اول در این باب با آقای تقی‌زاده باید مذاکره و از ایشان خواهش کرده است که همراهی کنند ولی خود آقای مقدم بموجب کاغذی که باآقای تقی‌زاده نوشته بتهران تلگراف کرده استدعا کرده است او را باین کار بگمارند. مرد دلیریست بی‌عقل و بی‌دانش. خود را برای هر کار مناسب می‌داند و اگر روزی بیکار باشد و فرماندهی لشکر بحری و بزّی و هوایی را برای گرفتن پول طمع کند، بی هیچ شرم خود را لایق آن معرفی می‌کند و از دولت می‌خواهد او را باین کارها بگمارند. باید دید که دولت چه خواهد کرد. در این روز از فرنگیس کاغذی رسید و باو جواب دادم. اوقاتم چندان خوش نبود. از طمع و بی‌شرمی مردم چه چیزها باید دید و شنید. شب در هتل بودم و کتاب شرح حال سر پرسی کوکس[۱] را خواندم. آلمانیها بسرعت بطرف مسکو پیش می‌روند.

چهارشنبه ۲۳ مهر، ۱۵ اکتبر - صبح بلندن رفتم. کمی در اداره کار کردم. ناهار با بایندر خوردم. با او و آقای وحید بسفارت رفتم. تا ساعت سه و نیم آنجا بودم. شب بکمبریج آمدم. بسته‌ای از فرنگیس رسیده بود. قرآن و کاغذی در آن بود. شب کاغذی باو نوشتم و زودتر خوابیدم. بسیار خواب پریشان دیدم. آلمانیها بمسکو نزدیکتر می‌شوند و از اخبار چنان بدست می‌آید که کار روسها اصلاح‌پذیر نیست.

پنجشنبه ۲۴ مهر، ۱۶ اکتبر - صبح چندین کاغذ نوشتم. بعد از ظهر بتئاتر رفتم. بازی *The First Mrs. Fraser*[۲] را دیدم. شب بمنزل آقای تقی‌زاده رفتم. آقای مینوی هم آنجا بود. ساعت یازده و نیم بهتل آمدم. یک ساعت بعد از نصف شب خوابیدم. در این روز اخبار راجع بروسیه خطر مسکو را بیشتر می‌نمایاند. سفارتخانه‌های مقیم مسکو بطرف مشرق شاید بشهر غازان می‌روند.

جمعه ۲۵ مهر ۱۳۲۰، ۱۷ اکتبر ۱۹۴۱ - صبح یکی دو کاغذ نوشتم. بعد روزنامه

---

۱. Major-General Sir Percy Z. Cox (ولادت ۱۸۶۴ ـ وفات ۱۹۳۷) از امرای بریتانیا در هند و خاورمیانه.

۲. در اصل: First Mrs. Fraser. نمایشنامه‌ای اثر سینت جان ارواین St. John Greer Ervine (ولادت ۱۸۸۳ ـ وفات ۱۹۷۱).

خواندم. ظهر بیرون رفتم. با مینوی ناهار خوردم. بعد از ظهر راه رفتیم. ساعت چهار بعد از ظهر آقای تقی‌زاده را در راه دیدیم. با هم بکافه رفتیم. چای خوردیم. در باب عربی، فارسی، ترجمه و از این قبیل مطالب حرف زدیم. ساعت پنج و نیم بعد بهتل آمدیم. لباس عوض کردم و بمنزل آقای تقی‌زاده رفتم. شام خوردیم و بعد پروفسور چدویک پروفسور انگلیسی قدیم با زنش و مستر توپالیان و زنش آمدند. تا ساعت یازده آنجا بودم. بعد بهتل آمدم. هوا بارانی و شب بسیار تاریک بود. روسها بتخلیهٔ اودسا اعتراف کرده‌اند و هنوز آلمانیها بطرف مسکو پیشرفت می‌کنند.

شنبه ۲۶ مهر، ۱۸ اکتبر - صبح کتاب آلمانی خواندم. بعد از ظهر بسینما رفتم. شب در هتل بودم. آلمانیها مدعی‌اند که بیش از ششصد هزار اسیر و هزار و صد تانک و بیش از پنج هزار توپ و مقدار مهمی مهمّات گرفته‌اند. کار روسها بدتر می‌شود.

یکشنبه ۲۷ مهر، ۱۹ اکتبر - صبح کتاب جنگ و صلح و روزنامه خواندم. بعد با زنی آلمانی قریب یک ساعت راه رفتم و آلمانی حرف زدم. بسیار مفید بود. بعد از ظهر در هتل بودم. ساعت شش به کرایست کالج باطاق Loewe[1] رفتم. قریب پانزده نفر شاگرد زن و مرد بودند. با یکی دو نفر در باب سیاست صحبت کردیم. در هتل شام خوردم و بعد بمنزل آقای تقی‌زاده رفتم. تا ساعت یازده و ربع آنجا بودم. چشم راستم کمی درد می‌کند و حال روحیم چندان خوب نیست.

دوشنبه ۲۸ مهر، ۲۰ اکتبر - صبح بلندن رفتم. وزیر مختار را ندیدم چون بدیدن زنش رفته بود. ناهار با حمزاوی و بایندر و وحید خوردم. بعد از ظهر در سفارت بودم. شب بکمبریج آمدم. آلمانیها پیشرفت می‌کنند.

سه‌شنبه ۲۹ مهر ۱۳۲۰، ۲۱ اکتبر ۱۹۴۱ - صبح کتاب خواندم و کاغذ نوشتم. بعد از

---

۱. مقصود Herbert M. J. Loewe (ولادت ۱۸۸۲ ـ وفات ۱۹۴۰) است که استاد زبانهای سامی در کمبریج و آکسفرد بود. امروزه مرکز مطالعات عبری و یهودی در دانشگاه آکسفرد بنام اوست.

ظهر هم کتاب جنگ و صلح خواندم. عصر بمنزل مستر زگو رفتم. شب با او رفتیم بسینما. آلمانیها مدعی‌اند که استالینو[1] را که شهری مهم و صنعتی است، گرفته‌اند.

چهارشنبه ۳۰ مهر، ۲۲ اکتبر - صبح بلندن رفتم. در سفارت با بایندر ناهار خوردم. بعد از ظهر باز بسفارت رفتم. در این روزها مقدّم را دیدم. در باب تلگرافی که راجع ببعضی نمایندگی بتهران کرده بود، چیزی نگفت. شب در کمبریج بودم. در این روز کاغذی از فرنگیس رسید.

پنجشنبه اوّل آبان، ۲۳ اکتبر - صبح با آقای تقی‌زاده و خانم و مسیز چدویک بلندن رفتم. ناهار با مستر مایلز خوردم. تمام روز را در اداره بودم و اوراق اداری را مرتب می‌کردم. با ترن پنج و چهل و نه دقیقه با آقای تقی‌زاده و خانم و میسز چدویک بکمبریج آمدیم. شب در هتل بودم. دیر خوابیدم. آلمانیها بچهل میلی مسکو رسیده‌اند. در کریمه و در جنوب هم کار روسها خراب است. در این روز از آقای تقی‌زاده شنیدم که در کاغذی مینوی بایشان نوشته که آقای فتح‌الله اسفندیاری بنمایندگی دولت در شرکت انتخاب شده است.

جمعه ۲ آبان، ۲۴ اکتبر - صبح چند کاغذ نوشتم. از فرنگیس کاغذی رسید. از ساعت یازده تا نیمساعت بعد از ظهر با زنی آلمانی راه رفتم و آلمانی حرف زدم. بعد از ظهر بسینما رفتم. در اخبار قسمتی از حوادث اخیر ایران را نشان می‌دادند: رفتن شاه جدید را بمجلس، قزوین، و ملاقات انگلیسها و روسها. شب در هتل بودم. روزنامه خواندم. خوابم گرفت شب زودتر خوابیدم. کار روسها بسیار بد است و تی‌موشن‌کو[2] را از فرماندهی لشکر مرکز که مدافع مسکو است، برداشته‌اند. در جنوب در نواحی دریای آزوف آلمانیها پیش می‌روند.

شنبه ۳ آبان، ۲۵ اکتبر - صبح کاغذ نوشتم. بعد از ظهر کتاب خواندم. عصر آقای

---

۱. منظور Stalino است، نام قدیم دونتسک در فاصلۀ ۱۹۲۴ تا ۱۹۶۱، واقع در شرق اوکراین.

۲. منظور Semyon K. Timoshenko (ولادت ۱۸۹۵ ـ وفات ۱۹۷۰) است، مارشال ارتش شوروی.

تقی‌زاده را در کوچه دیدم. با هم بخانه‌شان رفتم. بعد از شام رفتم منزل مستر زگو. تا نصف شب آنجا بودم. آلمانیها خارکف را گرفته‌اند و در حوالی مسکو به پیش می‌روند.

یکشنبه ۴ آبان، ۲۶ اکتبر - صبح روزنامه و کتاب جنگ و صلح خواندم. بعد از ظهر هم کتاب خواندم. عصر رفتم بیرون چای خوردم. آلمانیها در جنوب و مرکز پیش می‌روند.

دوشنبه ۵ آبان، ۲۷ اکتبر - صبح کتاب خواندم و روزنامه. بعد رفتم بکتابخانهٔ عمومی و بعد از ظهر بسینما. فیلم خوبی نبود. شب در هتل بودم و بیشتر بیاد فرنگیس. آلمانیها در همه جا علی الخصوص در جهت جنوب روسیه پیش می‌روند. امروز در اخبار گفتند که ۲۰ سرباز ژاپونی بسرحدّ روسها تجاوز کرده‌اند. عده‌ای مقتول شده‌اند.

سه‌شنبه ۶ آبان، ۲۸ اکتبر - صبح روزنامه خواندم. اوضاع روسها بد و کارشان هر روز بدتر می‌شود. جنگ در سراسر میدان سخت و پیشرفت آلمانیها روزبروز بیشتر می‌شود. کاغذی بپدرم نوشتم و تلگرافی در باب کارم بجلال کردم. بعد از ظهر بتئاتر رفتم. بازی *Cherry Orchard*[1] را دیدم. بعد بهتل آمدم. کاغذی بفرنگیس نوشتم. شب کتاب جنگ و صلح خواندم.

چهارشنبه ۷ آبان، ۲۹ اکتبر - صبح بلندن اول باداره و بعد بسفارت بدیدن آقای تقی‌زاده رفتم. ناهار با بایندر خوردم و عصر در سفارت بودم. شب با ترن پنج و سه ربع بکمبریج آمدم. شب کمی کتاب خواندم و بعد با یک صاحبمنصب بحری انگلیسی و زنش حرف زدم. ساعت ده و نیم دختری مست در اطاق تحریر آمد و تا یک ساعت بعد از نصف شب چرند و پرند گفت. از فرنگیس کارت پستال داشتم. اطاقی گرفته است. تلگراف کردم که جمعه خواهم آمد. کار روسها بد است.

پنجشنبه ۸ آبان، ۱۳۲۰، ۳۰ اکتبر ۱۹۴۱ - صبح بلندن رفتم. از ادارهٔ بهارودز و از هارودز بسفارت. با اتومبیل حمزاوی به ساووی رفتم. اعضای سفارت و آقای تقی‌زاده و آقای

---

۱. نمایشنامهٔ مشهوری بقلم آنتون چخوف.

مقدّم همه مهمان آقای گلبنکیان بودیم. ناهار خوب و لذیذ بود و سر میز در باب جنگ و ایران و مطالب دیگر صحبت شد. عصر بمنزل ۳۶ پرنسز گیت[1] رفتم بدیدن خانم تقی‌زاده. چای خوردم. اظهار دلتنگی کردند و حق هم با ایشان است چرا که با اوضاع جنگ در این خانهٔ بزرگ تنهایی بسیار مؤثر است. شب با ترن پنج و پنجاه و سه دقیقه بکمبریج آمدم. آلمانیها در کریمه پیش می‌روند و در حوالی مسکو نیز کار روسها سخت‌تر می‌شود.

جمعه ۹ آبان، ۳۱ اکتبر - صبح در کمبریج چای خوردم و کمی روزنامه خواندم. بعد با اسباب و لوازم کمی بایستگاه رفتم. بلیط اکسفورد خریدم و با ترن نه و بیست و پنج دقیقه باکسفورد رفتم. یک ساعت و بیست دقیقه بعد از ظهر باکسفورد رسیدم. فرنگیس در ایستگاه بود. با هم بمهمانخانهٔ محقّری موسوم به St. Giles Private Hotel رفتیم. جایی تنگ و تاریک و گران بود ولی چاره‌ای نداشتیم. شب با فرنگیس در رستوران هندی غذا خوردم. آلمانیها در کریمه پیشرفت می‌کنند.

شنبه ۱۰ آبان، اول نوامبر - صبح فرنگیس آمد. با هم راه رفتیم. با هم ناهار خوردیم و ساعت شش و نیم رفتیم بتئآتر. بازی Deep in the River را دیدیم. بد نبود. بعد در رستوران هندی غذا خوردیم.

یکشنبه ۱۱ آبان، ۲ نوامبر - صبح فرنگیس نزد من آمد. کمی در اطاق نشستم. صحبت کردیم. پیرمردی که کراواتش از یقه‌اش جدا و دیوانه وضع و لباس پاره بود، شروع بحرف زدن کرد. معلوم شد با زبان اسپرانتو آشنایی دارد. گفت موزه‌ای مخصوص زبان دارد و مایل است نشان بدهد. وقت نداشتم که بروم. بعد از ظهر با فرنگیس بودم. عصر عباس رضا یکی از ایرانیان مقیم هندوستان که فرنگیس دعوتش کرده بود، آمد. جوان محجوب خجولی بود. در باب ایران و حقوق و عشق ایرانیان هندوستان بایران صحبت کردیم. ایران چه غافل است! در تمام زبان فارسی یک کتاب بزبان فارسی در باب هندوستان نیست و هیچ مؤسسه‌ای نیست که در آن بتوان بهندوستان راجع اطلاعی بدست آورد.

---

۱. مقصود کوچهٔ Princes Gate است در ضلع جنوبی هاید پارک در لندن.

دوشنبه ۱۲ آبان، ۳ نوامبر - اول قرار بود که روز دوشنبه بکمبریج مراجعت کنم ولی خواستم این روز را هم بمانم. در مهمانخانه جا نبود. در مهمانخانهٔ دیگری نزدیک اولی اطاقی برای یک شب گرفتم. بعد از ظهر با فرنگیس بسینما رفتم. فیلم لیدی همیلتن را دیدم. خوب بود. شب تا ساعت ۹ با من بود.

سه‌شنبه ۱۳ آبان، ۴ نوامبر - صبح ساعت یازده فرنگیس بکتابخانهٔ عمومی آمد. با هم بکتابفروشی رفتیم. ناهار در رستوران هندی خوردیم. بعد با ترن دو و سی و هشت دقیقهٔ بعد از ظهر بکمبریج آمدم. از دو بعد از ظهر بایستگاه رفتم. فرنگیس هم بود. در ترن نشستیم صحبت کردیم. ساعت شش و نیم بکمبریج رسیدم. بسیار خسته بودم. در راه از کتاب صلح و جنگ خواندم. آلمانیها بسرعت در کریمه پیش می‌روند.

چهارشنبه ۱۴ آبان، ۵ نوامبر - صبح بلندن اول باداره و بعد بیبیکادلی و بعد از ظهر بسفارت رفتم. در اداره صندوقهای کتاب را باز کردم و کتاب فرهنگ انگلیسی بفرانسه و فرانسه بانگلیسی و کتاب تاریخ انگلستان را برای فرنگیس فرستادم. بعد از ظهر در سفارت آقای تقی‌زاده را دیدم. شب بکمبریج آمدم. با دکتر مارشال شطرنج بازی کردم.

پنجشنبه ۱۵ آبان ۱۳۲۰، ۶ نوامبر ۱۹۴۱ - صبح کاغذی بفرنگیس نوشتم. بعد از ظهر بسینما رفتم. فیلم *The Reluctant Dragon*[1] را دیدم که کار والت دیزنی است. چندان خوب نبود و بپای سایر فیلمهایش مانند اسنو وایت و غیر آن نمی‌رسید. شب در هتل بودم. روزنامهٔ آلمانی و فرانسوی و کتاب جنگ و صلح خواندم.

جمعه ۱۶ آبان، ۷ نوامبر - صبح کمی فرانسه خواندم و نوشتم و کمی آلمانی. بعد از ظهر کتاب جنگ و صلح خواندم و عصر در کافهٔ دوروتی چای خوردم. شب در هتل بودم. استالین در نطق دیشب خود گفت که چهار میلیون و نیم آلمانی کشته[2] و مجروح شده‌اند. آلمانیها در کریمه پیش می‌روند. از فرنگیس کاغذی رسید.

---

۱. در اصل: Reluctant Dragon.

۲. + و مقتول

شنبه ۱۷ آبان، ۸ نوامبر - صبح کتاب خواندم. کاغذی بفرنگیس نوشتم. بعد از ظهر در هتل بودم و کتاب جنگ و صلح خواندم. سه ساعت و سه ربع بعد از ظهر مستر جونز Jones بدیدنم آمد. این شخص را که پنج سال پیش در اکسفورد دیده بود، سه چهار هفته پیش ناگهان در کوچهٔ کمبریج دیدم و از او خواستم که بدیدنم بیاید. پنج سال پیش که بنمایندگی دولت در کنفرانس تربیت رفته بودم، مستر جونز را هم که یکی از نمایندگان بود، دیدم و با هم آشنا شدیم. در این روز با جونز کمی در باب تاریخ و تربیت صحبت کردیم. بعد از شام بمنزل آقای تقی‌زاده رفتم. تا ساعت ۱۱ آنجا بودم. آلمانیها در کریمه پیشرفت می‌کنند.

یکشنبه ۱۸ آبان، ۹ نوامبر - صبح روزنامه خواندم. ساعت یازده با زنی آلمانی راه رفتم و آلمانی حرف زدم. بعد از ظهر کتاب خواندم. شب دیر خوابیدم.

دوشنبه ۱۹ آبان، ۱۰ نوامبر - صبح رفتم بلندن. در اداره کار کردم. بعد بپیکادلی رفتم. حالم چندان خوب نبود. بسینمای اخبار رفتم. ناهار نخوردم. بعد از ظهر بسفارت رفتم. تا چهار و نیم آنجا بودم. شب بکمبریج آمدم. در ترن روشنایی کافی نبود. نتوانستم کتاب بخوانم. ساعت هفت و نیم بکمبریج رسیدم. آلمانیها در کریمه و در حوالی لنینگراد پیشرفت کرده‌اند.

سه‌شنبه ۲۰ آبان، ۱۱ نوامبر - صبح کاغذی بفرنگیس نوشتم و آلمانی خواندم. بعد از ظهر بسینما رفتم و شب حالم خوب نبود و زودتر باطاقم آمدم. کتاب خواندم و خوابیدم. در سه چهار روز اخیر کشتی‌های انگلیسی چندین کشتی آلمانی را غرق کرده‌اند. آلمانیها در کریمه و در نواحی لنینگراد پیشرفت می‌کنند.

چهارشنبه ۲۱ آبان، ۱۲ نوامبر - صبح کتاب خواندم، کتاب جنگ و صلح. پیش از ظهر قریب یک ساعت راه رفتم. بعد از ظهر جنگ و صلح خواندم و شب کمی فرانسه نوشتم و مدتی شطرنج بازی کردم. در این روز از فرنگیس کاغذی رسید و باو کاغذی نوشتم. آلمانیها در کریمه و بعضی از نواحی شمالی میدان جنگ پیش می‌روند.

پنجشنبه ۲۲ آبان، ۱۳ نوامبر - صبح زود بیدار شدم. امشب خوب نخوابیدم و از ساعت شش صبح بیدار بودم. بلندن رفتم. در جلسهٔ سالیانهٔ شرکت استخراج اولی حضور یافتم. بعد با ال کین تون[1] حرف زدم. از آنجا بسفارت رفتم. اعضای سفارت همه بناهار دعوت داشتند. تا ساعت سه و نیم آنجا بودم. ناهار خوبی بود. در باب بیچارگی ایران و بی‌سوادی مأمورین دولت و اعضای وزارت امور خارجه صحبت بود. از آنجا بدفتر سفارت رفتم. تا ساعت چهار و نیم آنجا بودم. شب با ترن پنج و بیست و پنج دقیقه که کند و بی‌چراغ بود بکمبریج آمدم. صبح کتاب نتوانستم بخوانم. امروز در تایمز در آخر سرمقاله نوشته است که تخلیهٔ بی‌موقع تهران بعضی از هواخواهان رژیم قدیم را بنیرنگ بازی واداشته است. معلوم نیست باز برای ایران بدبخت چه پیش آمدی خواهد شد.

جمعه ۲۳ آبان ۱۳۲۰، ۱۴ نوامبر ۱۹۴۱ - صبح کاغذ نوشتم و بعد بیرون رفتم. روزنامه‌ها را در کتابخانهٔ عمومی خواندم. بیشتر اخبار راجع بود بالغاء قانونی بی‌طرفی امریکا و از این ببعد کشتیهای امریکایی خواهند توانست که بتمام نواحی دنیا بروند. روسها کاری از پیش نبرده‌اند. کشتی آرک روایال غرق شده است. بعد از ظهر در خود احساس کسالت می‌کردم. از هتل بیرون نرفتم و بیش از صد صفحه از کتاب جنگ و صلح را خواندم. شب کمی فرانسه خواندم.

شنبه ۲۴ آبان، ۱۵ نوامبر - صبح روزنامه و کتاب خواندم. بعد از ظهر بسینما رفتم و شب در هتل بودم. در کریمه آلمانیها پیشرفت می‌کنند. کمی فرانسه خواندم.

یکشنبه ۲۵ آبان، ۱۶ نوامبر - صبح کتاب و روزنامه خواندم. پیش از ظهر با زنی آلمانی راه رفتم و قریب یکساعت حرف زدیم. آلمانی حرف زدم. بعد از ظهر بمنزل پروفسور مینورسکی رفتم. مستر Bowes رئیس کتابخانهٔ بوز در کمبریج و زنش و مستر جان کمنز (Cummings) معاون هئیت مدیره مدرسهٔ السنهٔ شرقیه هم بودند. در باب کتاب و ادبیات حرف زدیم، و بعد با مینورسکی و زنش راجع بجنگ و غیر آن. شام در هتل

---

۱. E. H. Elkington، رئیس وقت شرکت نفت ایران و انگلیس.

خوردم و بعد از اتمام بمنزل آقای تقی‌زاده رفتم. تا ساعت ده آنجا بودم. اوضاع کریمه بدتر شده است و شاید آلمانیها در این هفته آن را بکلی از دست روسها بیرون بیاورند.

دوشنبه ۲۶ آبان، ۱۷ نوامبر - صبح زود بیدار شدم. کمی آلمانی خواندم. بعد چاشت خوردم و منتظر شدم. اتوبوس آقای تقی‌زاده آمد. با ایشان و خانم تقی‌زاده بلندن رفتم. نزدیک لندن حالم بسیار بد بود ولی چیزی نگفتم. در ماربل آرچ پیاده شدم و باداره رفتم. مستر کلگ عضو شرکت نفت آمد. در باب منافع شرکت و تذکراتی که بدولت در این باب شده، مذاکره نمود. ناهار با بایندر خوردم و بعد از ظهر بسینمای اخبار رفتم و با ترن چهار و سه ربع بکمبریج آمدم. در لندن هوا بارانی بود. در این روز کاغذی از بانک میدلند رسید راجع بحوالهٔ ۱۷۵ لیره. ظاهراً مواجب سه ماهه است و سی و شش لیره کمتر از پیش است. این وضع با وجود گرانی وسائل زندگی در انگلستان قریب دوازده لیر از مواجب هر ماههٔ من کم کرده‌اند. آلمانیها شهر کرچ را گرفته‌اند و از این ببعد کار حمله بقفقاز برای ایشان آسانتر شده است.

سه‌شنبه ۲۷ آبان، ۱۷ نوامبر - صبح کتاب خواندم و کاغذی بفرنگیس نوشتم. بعد از ظهر بتأثر رفتم و بازی خنده‌آوری را که مربوط به وقایع معروف تاریخ انگلستان است دیدم موسوم به *The 1066 and all that*. در این روز کتاب جنگ و صلح تولستوی را تمام کردم. شب کمی شطرنج بازی کردم و کمی از کتاب تاریخ ادبیات انگلیسی خواندم.

چهارشنبه ۲۸ آبان، ۱۸ نوامبر - صبح با ترن بلندن رفتم. کمی در اداره کار کردم. از آنجا بسفارت (منزل شخص وزیر مختار) رفتم. حمزاوی و خانم حمزاوی، مستر گلبنکیان، و مستر هاکوپیان هم بودند. ناهار ایرانی با کباب و ماست و پلو خوردیم. عصر بسفارت و شب به پرینس آو ویلز رفتم. چندان خوب بود در Cadogan Hotel منزل کردم. لندن بیشتر روزها عادی است و علی الخصوص مردم در پیکادلی بسیار دیده می‌شوند. انگلیس در لیبی به آلمانیها و ایطالیایی‌ها حمله کرده است.

پنجشنبه ۲۹ آبان، ۱۹ نوامبر - صبح کتاب تاریخ ادبیات انگلیسی خواندم. در اطاقم

که بسیار گرم بود، چاشت خوردم. بعد به بریتیش میوزیم رفتم. مستر بازیل گری را دیدم. در باب جمعیت ایران مذاکره کردم. قرار شد جناب آقای تقی‌زاده را ملاقات کند. اطاقهای بریتیش میوزیم خالی، قفسه‌ها اغلب بی‌کتاب و دالانها و طالارها تاریک و هر چیزی غم آور بود. ناهار با بایندر خوردم و چهار ساعت بعد از ظهر بسفارت رفتم. ایرانیهای مقیم لندن را بچای دعوت کرده بودند. بیشتر تجّار بودند و هفت هشت نفر محصل هم آمده بودند. شب کمی در سفارت با آقای آرام و آقای وحید و آقای نیامیر صحبت کردم. بعد با آقای وحید شام خوردم و بهتل رفتم. کتاب تاریخ ادبیات انگلستان < را > خواندم. انگلیسها در افریقا پیشرفت کرده و آلمانیها را عقب زده‌اند.

جمعه ۳۰ آبان ۱۳۲۰، ۲۱ نوامبر ۱۹۴۱ - صبح کتاب تاریخ ادبیات خواندم. بعد بسفارت رفتم. با بایندر و حمزاوی ناهار خوردم و با ترن چهار و سه ربع بعد از ظهر بکمبریج آمدم. از فرنگیس کاغذی رسیده بود.

شنبه اوّل آذر، ۲۲ نوامبر - صبح کتاب خواندم. بعد از ظهر بسنما رفتم و شب آلمانی خواندم. آلمانیها شهر راستوف را گرفته‌اند و انگلیسیها در لیبی پیشرفت می‌کردند.

یکشنبه ۲ آذر، ۲۳ نوامبر - صبح روزنامه‌ها را خواندم. پر بود از اخبار جنگ لیبی. شب کمی کتاب خواندم و بعد باطاقم آمدم. بروزنامه‌های تایمز[1] که از ابتدای حمله بایران نگاه داشته بودم، مراجعه کردم و قسمتهای راجع بایران را پاره کردم که نگاه دارم.

دوشنبه ۳ آذر، ۲۴ نوامبر - صبح روزنامه خواندم و کتاب و کاغذی بفرنگیس و دیگری بآقای نیامیر نوشتم. بعد از ظهر بسینما رفتم و شب زود باطاقم آمدم. بروزنامه‌هایی که نگاه داشته بود، مراجعه کردم و قسمت‌های راجع بایران را پاره

---

[1]. را +

کردم که نگاه دارم. آلمانیها در حوالی مسکو پیشرفت کرده‌اند و شهری در چهل میلی مسکو تصرّف کرده‌اند. لحن انگلیسیها در باب پیشرفت در افریقا فرق کرده و سخن از خوب جنگیدن دشمن و آوردن مهمّات و سرباز است با طیّاره. باری، نیمساعت بعد از نصف شب خوابیدم. خوابهای پریشان دیدم. در خواب دیدم که هوا صاف بود و غروب که یکی با کمال ادب داری را نشان داد و از من خواست که با او بروم و بدارم بیاویزد. بی‌ترس بطرف دار روان شدم. در وسط راه بیدار شدم.

سه‌شنبه ۴ آذر، ۲۵ نوامبر ۱۹۴۱ - صبح تاریخ ادبیات انگلیس خواندم و بعد از ظهر بتأتر رفتم. بازی هملت را دیدم. بازیگر معروف Donald Wolfit هملت بود و بسیار خوب بازی کرد. شب در هتل بودم و کتاب تاریخ ادبیات خواندم. روسها در اطراف مسکو چندین جا عقب‌نشینی اختیار کرده‌اند. در افریقا هنوز کار جنگ میان انگلیس و آلمان یکسره نشده است.

چهارشنبه ۵ آذر، ۲۶ نوامبر - صبح بلندن رفتم. تلگرافی بتهران فرستادم. ناهار با بایندر خوردم. عصر با او بسفارت رفتم و شب بکمبریج آمدم. در منزل تاریخ ادبیات انگلیس خواندم. از فرنگیس کاغذی رسیده بود که افسردگی او را می‌رساند. جوابی دادم. آلمانیها در حوالی مسکو جلو می‌روند و پیشرفت انگلیسیها در افریقا ظاهراً متوقّف شده و در این ایّام در روزنامه‌ها سخن از تلفات بسیار طرفین است.

پنجشنبه ۶ آذر، ۲۷ نوامبر - صبح کتاب خواندم، تاریخ ادبیات انگلیس. مشغول خواندم بودم که مستر شَتِر وُرث بازیگر آمد. در باب تأتر و بازی هملت و رول او حرف زدیم. بعد از ظهر بتأتر رفتم. بازی ریچارد سوم را دیدم. خیلی بد بود. آلمانیها در روسیه پیشرفت می‌کنند و خطر مسکو روز بروز بیشتر می‌شود. تلگرافی بتهران فرستادم.

جمعه ۷ آذر ۱۳۲۰، ۲۸ نوامبر - صبح کتاب خواندم. ناهار با مستر شَتِر وُرث خوردم و

بعد از ظهر بسینما رفتم. شب در هتل بودم و کتاب خواندم. آلمانیها پیشرفت می‌کنند و مسکو سخت در خطر است.

شنبه ۸ آذر، ۲۹ نوامبر - صبح کتاب تاریخ ادبیات انگلیس خواندم. ناهار با مستر لوو یکی از محصلین اونیورسیته خوردم. در باب شکسپیر و ترجمه و غیر آن صحبت کردیم. بعد از ظهر کمی راه رفتم و نیز بمسابقهٔ بین اکسفورد و کمبریج رفتم. شب در هتل بودم و کتاب تاریخ ادبیات انگلیس خواندم. روسها شهر روسطوف را از آلمانیها گرفته‌اند. در روزنامه تایمز باز شرحی راجع بایران بود و شکایت از آنکه سیاست انگلستان در ایران چنانکه باید تند نیست.

یکشنبه ۹ آذر، ۳۰ نوامبر - صبح کتاب تاریخ ادبیات انگلیس خواندم و همچنین بعد از ظهر. قریب یک ساعت و نیم پیش از ظهر آلمانی خواندم و راه رفتم و آلمانی حرف زدم. شب بمنزل آقای تقی‌زاده رفتم. تا ساعت ده آنجا بودم. هنوز واقعهٔ مهم قطعی در لیبی پیش نیامده است.

دوشنبه ۱۰ آذر، اول دسامبر - صبح کتاب خواندم، تاریخ ادبیات انگلیس. بعد از ظهر بسینما رفتم و شب کتاب تاریخ خواندم. کاغذی بفرنگیس نوشتم. روسها مدعی‌اند که در جنوب آلمانیها را عقب زده‌اند و در مسکو حملات آلمان را دفاع کرده‌اند.

سه‌شنبه ۱۱ آذر، ۲ دسامبر - صبح بلندن آمدم. در سی و دومین جلسهٔ سالیانهٔ شرکت حاضر شدم و بیش از یک ربع طول نکشید. بعد با رؤسای شرکت ناهار خوردم. بعد از ظهر بسفارت رفتم و شب بسینما. فیلم *Plantasia* را که ولت دیزنی درست کرده است دیدم. چیز تازه‌ایست و ترقّیات مهم در پیش دارد. در حقیقت تجسّم موسیقی است. قطعات معروف موسیقی را گرفته و آنچه را که اصوات موسیقی ممکن است بنظر انسان آورده و تجسم داده است. در رستوران هندی شام خوردم و بعد بهتل آمدم، De Vere Hotel. در لیبی کار انگلیسیها چندان خوب نیست و در راستوف روسها پیشرفت کرده‌اند.

چهارشنبه ۱۲ آذر، ۳ دسامبر - صبح بسفارت رفتم. ناهار با بایندر خوردم و عصر هم در سفارت بودم. شب در ریجنتز پالاس قریب یک ساعت نشستم. بعد بهتل آمدم. کتاب تاریخ ادبیات انگلیس خواندم. آلمانیها در حوالی مسکو پیش و در راستوف عقب می‌روند. در افریقا لشگر انگلیس پیشرفتی نکرده است.

پنجشنبه ۱۳ آذر، ۴ دسامبر - صبح در مهمانخانه کمی کتاب تاریخ ادبیات خواندم. بعد با پادینگ‌تون رفتم. منتظر آمدن فرنگیس شدم. یازده و ربع آمد. کمی راه رفتیم. در رستوران هندی ناهار خوردیم. بعد بسینما رفتیم، در لستر اسکویر، و بعد بایستگاه. با ترن شش و ربع به اکسفورد رفت. از آنجا بیپکادلی آمدم. با آقای آرام برستوران کرنر در لستر اسکویر رفتم. تا ساعت نه و نیم آنجا بودیم. بعد هم صحبت کردیم. بد نگذشت.

جمعه ۱۴ آذر، ۵ دسامبر - صبح کتاب تاریخ ادبیات انگلیسی خواندم. بعد بسفارت رفتم. با بایندر ناهار خوردم. بعد از ظهر بسفارت رفتم و شب در مهمانخانهٔ دو وِر (De Vere) شام خوردم و زودتر باطاقم رفتم. خسته بودم. کتاب تاریخ ادبیات انگلیس خواندم. در جنوب میدان جنگ روسها خوب پیشرفت کرده‌اند.

شنبه ۱۵ آذر ۱۳۲۰، ۶ دسامبر ۱۹۴۱ - صبح از مهمانخانهٔ De Vere بسفارت رفتم و نیم‌ساعت بعد از ظهر باقامتگاه وزیر. با آقای تقی‌زاده و خانم بکمبریج آمدیم. در کمبریج ناهار خوردم. بعد کاغذی بفرنگیس فرستادم. بعد از شام بمنزل آقای تقی‌زاده رفتم. تا ساعت ده و نیم آنجا بودم. گفتند بفرنگیس خانم تلگراف کنم که او هم روز سه‌شنبه بلندن برای ناهار بیاید. تلگراف کردم و کاغذ نوشتم. بعد کمی فرانسه و کمی آلمانی خواندم.

یکشنبه ۱۶ آذر، ۷ دسامبر - صبح روزنامه و کتاب خواندم، تاریخ ادبیات انگلیسی. تنها کمی رفتم. بعد از ظهر کتاب تاریخ ادبیات خواندم. شب با مستر کِین شطرنج بازی کردم. در اخبار ساعت سه شنیدم که ژاپون به هاوایی حمله هوایی کرده است. میان امریکا و ژاپون جنگ درگرفته است.

دوشنبه ۱۷ آذر، ۸ دسامبر - صبح کتاب و روزنامه خواندم. روزنامه‌ها پر بود از اخبار راجع بجنگ میان ژاپون و آلمان. و در این روز روزولت در کنگره نطقی کرد و خواست که اجازهٔ اعلان جنگ بدهند و گفت که حالت جنگ بین ژاپون و امریکا برقرار است. بعد از ظهر بسینما رفتم و شب هم در هتل بودم. از فرنگیس تلگرافی رسید که روز سه‌شنبه بلندن خواهد آمد.

سه‌شنبه ۱۸ آذر، ۹ دسامبر - صبح زود بیدار شدم. با ترن ۹ بلندن رفتم. پیش از ظهر در اداره کار کردم. بعد از ظهر بایستگاه لیورپول استریت رفتم جایی که قرار گذاشته بودم. فرنگیس از اکسفورد آمده و در آنجا منتظر بود. با هم بسفارت رفتم. اعضای سفارت هم آمدند. خانم حمزاوی هم بود. ناهار ایرانی خوردیم. تا ساعت سه بعد از ظهر آنجا بودیم. بعد با ترن چهار و سه ربع بکمبریج آمدیم. اوضاع جنگ روز بروز در هم تر می‌شود. ژاپونیها بواسطه حملهٔ ناگهانی که کرده‌اند پیشرفتهایی نموده‌اند ولی در این جنگ هم عاقبت کار آلمان و متحدینش سخت خواهد شد.

چهارشنبه ۱۹ آذر، ۱۰ دسامبر - صبح روزنامه و کتاب خواندم. بعد از ظهر با فرنگیس بسینما رفتم. شب در هتل بودم. کتاب می‌خواندم (تاریخ ادبیات انگلیسی). در این روز چرچیل در مجلس گفت که کشتی پرینس آو ویلز و ری پالس[1] را ژاپونیها غرق کرده‌اند. ژاپونیها در مالزی و فیلیپین و در سیام پیشرفت می‌کنند. از جلال تلگرافی رسید و قسمت آخر آن درست فهمیدنی نبود.

پنجشنبه ۲۰ آذر، ۱۱ دسامبر - صبح کتاب خواندم. بعد با فرنگیس راه رفتم. بعد از ناهار کاغذها و روزنامه‌ها را در اطاقم مرتب کردم. شب در هتل بود و کتاب خواندم. در این روز آلمان و ایتالیا بامریکا اعلان جنگ دادند.

جمعه ۲۱ آذر، ۱۲ دسامبر - صبح کتاب و روزنامه خواندم. بعد با فرنگیس بکتابخانه

---

۱. *Repulse* (در اصل: ری پلس).

عمومی رفتم. چندین کتاب راجع بژاپون گرفتم. سه بعد از ظهر با هم بسینما رفتیم و شب در هتل بودیم. ژاپونیها در فیلیپین و مالزی کمی پیشرفت کرده‌اند.

شنبه ۲۲ آذر، ۱۳ دسامبر - صبح کتاب خواندم و بعد از ظهر از کتاب تاریخ سیاسی ژاپون یادداشت برداشتم. شب با فرنگیس بمنزل آقای تقی‌زاده رفتم. ساعت ده و نیم بهتل آمدیم.

یکشنبه ۲۳ آذر، ۱۳۲۰، ۱۴ دسامبر ۱۹۴۱ - صبح کتاب تاریخ ژاپون خواندم و از آن یادداشت برداشتم. ناهار آقای نیامیر و رفیقش آقای عرفانی (محصّل بانک) آمدند. بعد با هم کمی در کوچه‌های کمبریج راه رفتیم. باران می‌آمد. بعضی کالجها را دیدم. فرنگیس هم بود. بعد بمنزل پروفسور مینورسکی رفتیم. نبود. با فرنگیس بهتل آمدم. تاریخ ژاپون خواندم. روسها پیشرفت و انگلیسها در افریقا آلمانیها را تعقیب می‌کنند. در مالایا انگلیس عقب‌نشینی می‌کند. در فیلیپین امریکاییها جلوی ژاپونیها را گرفته‌اند.

دوشنبه ۲۴ آذر، ۱۵ دسامبر - صبح با فرنگیس بکتابخانهٔ دانشگاه رفتم. کمی کتاب خواندم. ناهار در هتل خوردیم و عصر کتاب خواندیم. شب در هتل بودم و کتاب خواندم. ژاپونیها در مالزی و انگلیسها در افریقا و روسها در میدان جنوبی و در حوالی مسکو پیشرفت می‌کنند.

سه‌شنبه ۲۵ آذر، ۱۶ دسامبر - صبح با فرنگیس بکتابخانه رفتم. ناهار در هتل خوردیم. دوباره بکتابخانه رفتیم. کتابخانهٔ اونیورسیته بسیار عالیست و اگر تمام عمر در آن کار کنم سیر نمی‌شوم. شب در هتل بودیم و کتاب خواندیم.

چهارشنبه ۲۶ آذر، ۱۷ دسامبر - صبح کتاب و روزنامه خواندیم. آقای عرفانی محصّل بانک آمد. تا یک ساعت بعد از ظهر نشست و صحبت کردیم. بعد از ظهر با فرنگیس بکتابخانهٔ دانشگاه رفتیم و ساعت چهار و نیم با او و عرفانی و خردجو محصّل دیگر بانک چای خوردیم. شب در هتل بودم و از کتاب راجع بژاپون یادداشت

می‌کردم. ژاپونیها پیشرفت نمی‌کنند. ساراراک را گرفته‌اند و در مالزی پیش می‌روند.

پنجشنبه ۲۷ آذر، ۱۸ دسامبر - صبح کتاب و روزنامه خواندم. بعد از ظهر با فرنگیس بسینما رفتم و شب در هتل بودم. ژاپونیها در مالایا و هنگ کنگ پیشرفت می‌کنند.

جمعه ۲۸ آذر، ۱۹ دسامبر - صبح بلندن رفتم. در اداره کار کردم. ناهار با بایندر در پیکادلی خوردم و بعد از آن بسفارت رفتم. تا ساعت پنج و نیم آنجا بودیم. با ترن پنج و چهل و نه دقیقه بکمبریج آمدم. جمعیت بسیار و ترن پر و هوا بد بود. بسیار خسته شدم. فرنگیس در رختخواب افتاده گرفتار زکام بود. کار آلمانیها در افریقا رو بشکست است. در روسیه هم پیشرفت با روسهاست. ژاپونیها پیشرفت خود را در دنبال نمی‌کنند.

شنبه ۲۹ آذر، ۲۰ دسامبر - صبح کتاب خواندیم. فرنگیس شب کسل بود. در اطاق ماند. بعد از ظهر چند کارت بمناسبت عید پیش رو برای دوستان انگلیسی فرستادم. عصر بکتابفروشی رفتیم. آقای عرفانی را در آنجا دیدم. از ساعت شش تا هفت با هم کمی راه رفتیم. بعد بهتل خودم آمدم. مدتی در اطاق فرنگیس بودم. کتاب خواندیم. بعد در اطاق خود تنها کتاب خواندیم و خوابیدیم. ژاپونیها پیشرفت می‌کنند ولی آلمانیها در روسیه و افریقا عقب می‌روند.

یکشنبه ۳۰ آذر، ۲۱ دسامبر - صبح باطاق فرنگیس رفتم. حالش چندان خوب نبود. طبیب خواستم. آمد. گفت خطری در میان نیست. چند حب داد که بخورد. بعد از ظهر حالش بهتر شد. با هم کتاب خواندیم. شب جدا از هم کتاب خواندیم. حالش خوب بود. هیتلر فرماندهی کلّ قشون را عهده‌دار شده است. فون بروشیش را از کار انداخته. ژاپونیها پیشرفت می‌کنند.

دوشنبه < ۱ > دی، ۲۲ دسامبر - صبح کتاب خواندم و بعد از ظهر کتاب ادبیات انگلیسی. شب فرنگیس حالش بهتر بود و از رختخواب بیرون آمد. با هم شام خوردیم. شب کتاب خواندم.

سه‌شنبه ۲ دی ۱۳۲۰، ۲۳ دسامبر ۱۹۴۱ - صبح کتاب خواندم. بعد از ظهر با فرنگیس بسینما رفتم. شب در هتل بودم. کتاب تاریخ ادبیات انگلیسی خواندم. در این ایّام عشق و علاقه بسیار بخواندن ادبیات یونانی و رومی در خود می‌یابم و چند کتاب در این دو موضوع خریده‌ام و ورقی چند از آنها را خوانده‌ام. می‌خواهم یک دورهٔ کامل ترجمه کتب مهم یونانی و لاتینی را بدست بیاورم و اگر ممکن باشد، ترجمه کنم و بخوانم.

چهارشنبه ۳ دی، ۲۴ دسامبر - صبح کتاب خواندم و بعد از ظهر با فرنگیس بسینما رفتم. شب هم کتاب تاریخ ادبیات و کمی آلمانی خواندم. مشهور است که مارشال پتن استعفا داده است. در مالزی و فیلیپین و هنگ کنگ کار انگلیس و امریکا چندان خوب بنظر نمی‌آید. در افریقا لشگر آلمان شکست خورده عقب می‌رود.

پنجشنبه ۴ دی، ۲۵ دسامبر - صبح کتاب تاریخ ادبیات خواندم. ناهار در هتل با فرنگیس خوردم. صبح بکلیسا رفتیم و بعد از ظهر در هتل بودیم. کتاب خواندیم. شب بعد از شام که بمناسبت کریسمس با شبهای دیگر فرق داشت، در اطاقی نشستیم و قریب پانزده نفر آمدند و سه چهار بریج بازی کردیم. میس گوردون که مادرش رفیق میز ماست، بازهای بیان می‌کرد. بد نبود. تا نصف شب نشستیم و صحبت کردیم. چائیده بودم. هنگ کنگ تسلیم ژاپون شده است. در فیلیپین ژاپونیها پیشرفت می‌کنند و در افریقا آلمانیها عقب می‌روند. مطابق اخبار روسها، کار آلمانیها در روسیه هم خراب است.

جمعه ۵ دی، ۲۶ دسامبر - صبح کتاب تاریخ ادبیات خواندم. بعد از ظهر با فرنگیس بسینما رفتم و شب در هتل بودیم. کتاب خواندیم. ساعت شش و نیم بنطق چرچیل که در واشنگتن در حضور اعضای سنا و مجلس نمایندگان حرف می‌زد، گوش کردیم. نطق مهمی بنظرم رسید. از این ببعد انگلیس از فکر اتحاد با فرانسه بیرون خواهد آمد و سعی خواهد کرد که با امریکا متحد شود و با امریکا

خواهد توانست که چند سال دیگر بزرگی خود را نگاه دارد منتهی باید تغییراتی در کار امپراطوری خود بدهد.

شنبه ۶ دی، ۲۷ دسامبر - صبح کتاب خواندم و بعد از ظهر و شب در هتل بودم. سرمایی سخت خوردهام و حالم چندان خوب نبود.

یکشنبه ۷ دی، ۲۸ دسامبر - حالم خوب نبود. صبح با فرنگیس و مستر فلات کِنْ یکی از هم مهمانخانهایها و زن و دخترش به گرانچستر رفتیم. بعد از ظهر در هتل بودم و شب از ساعت ده در هتل راجع بمذهب و خدا و سیاست بحثی درگرفت و تا یک ساعت بعد از نصف شب طول کشید.

دوشنبه ۸ دی، ۲۹ دسامبر - صبح کتاب خواندیم. بعد چون حالم چندان خوب نبود، باطاقم آمدم. شب با فرنگیس بمنزل پروفسور مینورسکی رفتیم. دو نفر دیگر هم بودند یکی عراقی که اسم خانوادگیش دوری بود. تا ساعت یازده و نیم نشستیم و بعد بهتل آمدیم.

سهشنبه ۹ دی، ۳۰ دسامبر - صبح از اطاقم بیرون نرفتم. فرنگیس تمام روز و شب با من بود. کتاب خواندیم مخصوصاً مقداری تاریخ بیهقی و .... باری، راشْتِر¹ را که روز دوشنبه شروع کرده بودم تمام کردم (شعر راشتر). حالم کمی بهتر بود. ژاپونیها در فیلیپین و مالزی پیشرفت میکنند و آلمانیها در لیبی مقاومت مینمایند.

چهارشنبه ۱۰ دی ۱۳۲۰، ۳۱ دسامبر ۱۹۴۱ - صبح بلندن رفتم و در اداره کار کردم. مستر کِلَگ آمد و کاغذهای مربوط بوصول مالیات سهام نفت را آورد. بعد از ظهر ببانک میدلند رفتم که در این باب دستور اقدام بدهم. ناهار با باینـدر و آرام خوردم و بعد بسفارت رفتم. تا ساعت چهار آنجا بودم. شب بکمبریج آمدم. مسیز گردون و دخترش و جمعی دیگر بودند. بمناسبت شب سال نو حرف زدیم و بازی کردیم. فرنگیس هم بود. یک ساعت بعد از نصف شب خوابیدم.

---

۱. مقصود هانس ورنر ریکتر (Hans Werner Richter) است، از سرآمدن جنبش ادبی «گروه ۴۷».

پنجشنبه ۱۱ دی، اول ژانویه - صبح کتاب خواندم. بعد از ظهر با فرنگیس بکتابخانه رفتم و شب در هتل بودیم. کتاب خواندیم.

جمعه ۱۲ دی، ۲ ژانویه - صبح کتاب خواندم. با فرنگیس کمی راه رفتم و کتاب خواندیم. شب در هتل بودم.

شنبه ۱۳ دی، ۳ ژانویه - صبح کتاب خواندم. بعد بکتابفروشی رفتم. کمی بکتابهای جدید نگاه کردم. بمناسبت جنگ طبع کتاب محدود شده است. شب کتاب شرح حال ولتر را خواندم.

یکشنبه ۱۴ دی،[1] ۴ ژانویه - صبح شرح حال ولتر را خواندم. بعد از چای با فرنگیس راه رفتم و شب در هتل بودیم.

دوشنبه ۱۵ < دی >، ۵ ژانویه - صبح در مهمانخانه بودم. کتاب خواندم، شرح حال ولتر، و روزنامه. بعد از ظهر با فرنگیس بسینما رفتم. فیلم دروغ بزرگ را دیدم. بد نبود. شب در هتل بودم و کتاب خواندم. ژاپونیها در مالزی پیش می‌روند. در افریقا لشگر آلمان عقب‌نشینی می‌کند.

سه‌شنبه ۱۶ دی، ۶ ژانویه - صبح کتاب خواندم و بعد از ظهر با فرنگیس بکتابخانهٔ اونیورسیته رفتم. شب در هتل بودیم.

چهارشنبه ۱۷ دی، ۷ ژانویه ۱۹۴۲ - صبح با فرنگیس بلندن رفتم. در اداره کار کردم. ناهار با بایندر و آرام خوردم. بعد از ظهر بمنزل آقای تقی‌زاده رفتم. از مریضخانه بخانه آمده (روز شنبه). تا چهار ساعت بعد از ظهر با ایشان بودم. شرح کسالت و عمل را گفتند. کمی ضعیف شده بود. تب و سرماخوردگی سخت داشتند. چون دیر شده بود با تاکسی به لیورپول استریت آمدم. فرنگیس منتظرم بود. جا پیدا نشد. دو ثلث راه را در راهرو ترن ایستاده بودیم. شب در هتل بودم. کتاب خواندم، شرح حال ولتر.

---

۱. ۱۳ دی. از این روز تا اول بهمن تقویم شمسی یک روز اختلاف دارد که تصحیح شد.

پنجشنبه ۱۸ دی، ۸ ژانویه - صبح با فرنگیس بکتابخانه دانشگاه کمبریج رفتم. کمی در باب ادبیات فرانسه و انگلیسی خواندم. بعد از ظهر هم با فرنگیس بکتابخانه رفتم. در قسمتِ کتب فارسی و عربی بودیم. چندین کتاب تماشایی دیدم. علی الخصوص کتابی بالفبای لاتین در ترجمهٔ کتاب ربنسن کروزو داشت از اردو بفارسی. شب در هتل بودیم. روسها پیشرفت می‌کنند ولی کار انگلیسها در مالزی چندان خوب نیست.

جمعه ۱۹ دی، ۹ ژانویه - صبح با فرنگیس بلندن رفتم. در اداره کار کردم. ناهار با بایندر خوردم و عصر در اداره بودم. کار کردم. شب با فرنگیس بکمبریج آمدم. از ساعت ده تا نصف شب شطرنج بازی کردم. در لندن از حال آقای تقی‌زاده جویا شدم. هنوز بستری است.

شنبه ۲۰ دی، ۱۰ ژانویه - صبح با فرنگیس بکتابخانهٔ دانشگاه رفتم. کتابهای فارسی و عربی خواندیم. بعد بهتل آمدیم. پیش از ناهار تلگرافی از جلال رسید در جواب تلگرافی که مخابره کرده بودم. نوشته بود که شش ماه بعد از ورود آقای اسفندیاری می‌توانم در انگلستان بمانم و بعد ازین باید بایران رفت. کمی در فکر فرو رفتم و لیکن هنوز درست معلوم نیست که خدا چه خواسته است. بعد از ظهر با مسیز گردون و دخترش و فرنگیس بسینما رفتم و شب در هتل بودیم.

یکشنبه ۲۱ دی ۱۳۲۰، ۱۱ ژانویه ۱۹۴۲ - صبح کتاب و روزنامه خواندم. پیش از ناهار با فرنگیس به گران‌چستر رفتم. هوا کمی سرد ولی خوب بود. بعد از ظهر کتاب خواندم و پیش از شام باز با فرنگیس راه رفتم. شب زودتر باطاقم آمدم و از کتاب ولتر چندین ورق خواندم.

دوشنبه ۲۲ دی، ۱۲ ژانویه - صبح کتاب خواندم. بعد با فرنگیس بکتابفروشی رفتم. چندین کتاب خریدم. بعد از ظهر با فرنگیس بسینما رفتم و شب بسیار خسته بودم. زودتر خوابیدم. در مالزی قشون انگلیس عقب‌نشینی می‌کنند و در روسیه لشگر آلمان.

سه‌شنبه ۲۳ دی، ۱۳ ژانویه - صبح کتاب خواندم. برف می‌آمد و هوا سرد. بود.

قسمتی از کتاب شرح حال ولتر را خواندم. بعد از ظهر شخصی موسوم به بوش از دوستان مستر کین که در مهمانخانه زندگی می‌کند، آمد. قریب سه ربع با او حرف زدیم. پروفسور ادوارد برون را می‌شناخت و نزد او کمی فارسی خوانده بود. قریب دو سال در هندوستان گذرانده بود. از کنسرواتورهای انگلیس بنظر می‌آمد. عصر با فرنگیس بکافهٔ ماتی‌یو رفتم. عرفانی محصّل نفت هم آمد. چای خوردیم. ساعت شش بهتل آمدیم. انگلیسیها در مالزی عقب‌نشینی می‌کنند.

چهارشنبه ۲۴ دی، ۱۴ ژانویه - صبح کتاب خواندم. بعد از ظهر با فرنگیس و مسیز گُردون بسینما رفتم. شب زودتر باطاقم آمدم و کتاب خواندم. کار انگلیس در مالزی چندان خوب نیست. روسها بعکس پیشرفت می‌کنند.

پنجشنبه ۲۵ دی، ۱۵ ژانویه - صبح با فرنگیس بلندن رفتم. در اداره کار کردم. چندین کاغذ نوشتم و بعد با فرنگیس بمنزل آقای تقی‌زاده رفتم. حال آقای تقی‌زاده بهتر شده بود. نیم‌ساعت بعد از ظهر آنجا بودیم. با فرنگیس در هارودز ناهار خوردیم و بعد به کرمول رود رفتیم که برای آمدن بلندن چندین جا را ببینیم. هیچ یک از جاهایی که اعلان آنها را خوانده بودم اطاق نداشت غیر از یکی و آن هم اطاق جنوبی نبود. بعد به پرینس او ویلز هتل رفتیم. آنها هم اطاق نداشتند ولی وعده دادند که اطاقی پیدا کنند. با ترن چهار و چهل و پنج دقیقه بکمبریج آمدم. شب در هتل بودم. شرح حال ولتر را خواندم و مدتی با دکتر مارشال صحبت کردم. ژاپونیها بطرف سنگاپور پیشرفت می‌کنند.

جمعه ۲۶ دی، ۱۶ ژانویه - صبح کتاب خواندم، شرح حال ولتر. بعد از ظهر با فرنگیس و عبدالله بن محمد از اهالی مالزی چای خوردیم. شب در مهمانخانه بودم.

شنبه ۲۷ دی، ۱۷ ژانویه - صبح کتاب خواندم. ناهار فرنگیس با مسیز گردون برای شنیدن نطق رفته بود. تنها ناهار خوردم. بعد از ناهار کمی کتاب خواندم و بعد به

کتابفروشی هفرز[1] رفتم. فرنگیس آنجا بود. کمی در آنجا بودیم و بعد بقهوه خانه رفتیم. آقای عرفانی محصل بانک آمد. با او بودیم. شب در هتل بودیم و کتاب خواندیم. ژاپونیها در مالزی پیشرفت می‌کنند.

یکشنبه ۲۸ دی، ۱۸ ژانویه - صبح زود بیدار شدم. کمی کتاب خواندم. بعد با فرنگیس چاشت خوردم و منتظر آمدن اتومبیل شدیم. هوا سرد بود و از رفتن فرنگیس به اکسفورد غمناک بودم. با هم بایستگاه رفتیم. با ترن ده و پنجاه و پنج دقیقه باکسفورد رفت. بهتل آمدم و کمی روزنامه خواندم و شرح حال ولتر. بعد از ظهر با مسیز گردون به آرتز تیاتر رفتم و فیلمی راجع به اوکرین دیدم بزبان روسی. بد نبود. شب در هتل هم کتاب خواندم. از رفتن فرنگیس به اکسفورد بسیار غمناک بودم. امیدوارم امسال کارش تمام شود.

دوشنبه ۲۹ دی ۱۳۲۰، ۱۹ ژانویه - صبح روزنامه خواندم و شرح حال ولتر را تمام کردم. بعد بکتابخانه عمومی رفتم. دو کتاب راجع بشرح حال لرد تنی‌سون[2] شاعر انگلیسی انتخاب کردم و در آنها نظر بدوستی تنی‌سون و فیتز جرالد شرحی راجع به فیتز جرالد است. بعد از ظهر و شب را بخواندن و یادداشت برداشتن راجع به فیتز جرالد گذراندم. کمی شطرنج بازی کردم . از ساعت یازده تا یک ساعت بعد از نصف شب با دکتر مارشال در باب سیاست و علم و فلسفه و بدبختی و جنگ حرف زدیم.

سه‌شنبه ۳۰ دی، ۲۰ ژانویه - از صبح تا وقت خواب کتاب شرح حال تنی‌سون خواندم و برای شرح حال فیتز جرالد یادداشت برداشتم. کاغذی بفرنگیس نوشتم.

چهارشنبه ۱ بهمن، ۲۱ ژانویه - بلندن آمدم. در اداره کار کردم. ناهار تنها در سیمسون خوردم و بعد از ظهر در سفارت بودم. شب بعد از شام که در پرینس او ویلز هتل خوردم بمنزل آقای تقی‌زاده رفتم و تا ساعت یازده آنجا بودم. شب روزنامه

---

1. Heffers Bookshop.
۲. Alfred Tennyson، شاعر بریتانیایی (۱۸۰۹-۱۸۹۲).

اطلاعات شماره‌های راجع بمذاکرات مجلس پس از تصرّف ایران بدست لشگر روس و انگلیس و مکاتبات میان دولت ایران و دولتین انگلیس و روس را خواندم و نیز رساله‌ای در باب آرایش و پیرایش زبان خواندم که در آن علل لزوم فرهنگستان و تدقیق لغات و غیر آن ذکر شده. ژاپونیها در مالزی و روسها در میدان جنگ شرق پیشرفت می‌کنند.

پنجشنبه ۲ بهمن ۱۳۲۰، ۲۲ ژانویه ۱۹۴۲ - صبح بسفارت رفتم. ناهار با بایندر و آرام خوردم. بعد از ظهر هم در سفارت بودم. ساعت پنج و نیم اخبار فارسی انگلیس را شنیدم. شب در هتل شام خوردم و بعد بسینمای اخبار رفتم. شب در اطاق کتاب خواندم. ژاپونیها پیشرفت می‌کنند. در افریقا هم انگلیسیها کمی عقب نشسته‌اند.

جمعه ۳ بهمن، ۲۳ ژانویه - صبح بسفارت رفتم. آقای تقی‌زاده را دیدم. ناهار با حمزاوی و بایندر و آرام در اکو دو فرانس[1] خوردم. بسیار خوب بود و نظر باوضاع جنگ قابل ملاحظه است که چنین رستورانهایی می‌تواند وجود داشته باشد. شب بکمبریج آمدم. آلمانیها در افریقا باز پیشرفت کرده‌اند و ژاپونیها در مالایا بسمت سنگاپور پیش می‌روند.

شنبه ۴ بهمن، ۲۴ ژانویه - صبح در باب فیتز جرالد یادداشت کردم. بعد بکتابفروشی رفتم. چندین جلد کتاب خریدم. بعد از ظهر بتأثر رفتم. بازی گود نایت چیل‌درن[2] که در واقع استهزاء رادیوی انگلیس بود، دیدم. بد نبود. شب در مهمانخانه بودم. کتاب خواندم و بصفحه‌های موسیقی دکتر مارشال گوش دادم و کمی شعر انگلیسی خواندم. کاغذی از فرنگیس رسید که کاغذی باو نوشتم.

یکشنبه ۵ بهمن، ۲۵ ژانویه - صبح کتاب و روزنامه خواندم. پیش از ناهار با مسیز مایر راه رفتم و قریب یک ساعت و نیم آلمانی حرف زدم. بعد از ظهر در هتل بودم و

---

۱. مقصود L'Ecu de France است از رستوران‌های مشهور در لندن.

۲. *Goodnight Children*.

کتاب خواندم. شب خسته بودم و زود خوابیدم. در افریقا و آسیا کار انگلیسیها چندان خوب نیست. روسها پیشرفت می‌کنند.

دوشنبه ۶ بهمن، ۲۶ ژانویه - صبح کتاب خواندم و برای زندگی فیتز جرالد یادداشت برداشتم. بعد برای تحقیق راجع برادیویی که آقای آرام می‌خواست، بکارخانهٔ پای (Pye) رفتم. چیزی که خواستیم نمی‌توانند بسازند. بعد از ظهر در هتل بودم. یادداشتهای راجع به فیتز جرالد را تمام کردم. شب زودتر باطاقم آمدم و خوابیدم. از امریکا بشمال ایرلند چندین هزار سرباز فرستاده‌اند.

سه‌شنبه ۷ بهمن، ۱۳۲۰، ۲۷ ژانویه ۱۹۴۲ - صبح کتاب خواندم و روزنامه، و کاغذ نوشتم. بعد از ظهر بکتابخانه عمومی رفتم و کتابهایی که داشتم عوض کردم. شب رمان *Ivanhoe* والتر اسکات را خواندم. آلمانیها در افریقا و ژاپونیها در مالایا پیشرفت می‌کنند.

چهارشنبه ۸ بهمن، ۲۸ ژانویه - صبح بلندن رفتم و از اداره بسفارت رفته آقای تقی‌زاده را دیدم و با باینندر و حمزاوی و آرام ناهار خوردم. بعد از ظهر در اداره کار کردم و شب بکمبریج آمدم. روز دویم مذاکرات پارلمان انگلیس است و به چرچیل حمله کرده‌اند که چرا در آسیا ـ مالزی و برمه ـ چنانکه باید خطر را پیش بینی نکرده است. از فرنگیس کاغذی رسید.

پنجشنبه ۹ بهمن، ۲۹ ژانویه - صبح چندین کاغذ نوشتم که یکی بدکتر نفیسی وزیر دارایی و دیگری بفرنگیس. بعد کتاب آی ون هو خواندم. عصر تنها بیش از یک ساعت راه رفتم. شب در مهمانخانه بودم. کتاب آی ون هو خواندم. در این روز مجلس انگلستان بکابینه چرچیل رأی اعتماد داد. رومل سردار آلمانی در افریقا پیشرفت می‌کند.

جمعه ۱۰ بهمن، ۳۰ ژانویه - صبح کتاب آی ون هو خواندم. بعد بکتابفروشی رفتم. چند کتاب منجمله کتاب راجع به ابن رشد تألیف ارنست رنان را خریدم. بعد از ظهر در هتل بودم و کتاب خواندم. بنغازی بدست آلمانیها افتاده است.

شنبه ۱۱ بهمن، ۳۱ ژانویه - صبح کتاب خواندم و بعد از ظهر بسینما رفتم. شب کتاب خواندم، آی ون هو. ژاپونیها پیشرفت می‌کنند. کاغذی بفرنگیس نوشتم.

یکشنبه ۱۲ بهمن، اول فوریه - تمام روز در هتل بودم و کتاب آی ون هو خواندم. آلمانیها در افریقا پیشرفت می‌کنند و ژاپونیها در مالایا و در برمه.

دوشنبه ۱۳ بهمن، ۲ فوریه - صبح کاغذی بتهران نوشتم. بعد از ظهر بسینما رفتم و بقیه وقت را بخواندن کتاب آی ون هو گذراندم. محاصره سنگاپور شروع شده است.

سه‌شنبه ۱۴ بهمن، ۳ فوریه - از صبح تا شب در مهمانخانه بودم و کتاب خواندم. رمان آی ون هو را تمام و کتابی راجع بانتقاد ادبی را شروع کردم. از فرنگیس که در لندن است (سه چهار روز) کاغذی رسید. آلمانیها در افریقا پیش می‌روند. در سنگاپور حمله بزرگ به سنگاپور هنوز شروع نشده. روسها با مقاومت بیشتر روبرو شده‌اند و در کریمه تخلیه فئودوزیا[1] را اعتراف کرده‌اند.

چهارشنبه ۱۵ بهمن، ۴ فوریه - صبح رفتم کار کردم. در اداره کار بلندن. با بایندر ناهار خوردم و عصر در سفارت آقای تقی‌زاده را دیدم. شب بکمبریج آمدم. آلمانیها در افریقا پیش می‌روند.

پنجشنبه ۱۶ بهمن، ۵ فوریه - صبح کتاب خواندم. بعد از ظهر به باله رفتم. بد نبود. *Les Patineurs* و *The Façade* و *The Haunted Ballroom*[2] را دیدم. شب زودتر باطاقم آمدم. شرح حال نی‌یوتن را خواندم.

جمعه ۱۷ بهمن، ۱۳۲۰، ۶ فوریه ۱۹۴۲ - صبح کتاب خواندم، شرح حال نی‌یوتن. بعد از ظهر بسینما رفتم و شب بسیار خسته بودم و زود باطاقم آمدم. کمی از کتاب خواندم. از فرنگیس کاغذی رسید و باو جواب دادم. رُمِل پیشرفت می‌کند و در مالایا ژاپونیها سنگاپور را شلیک می‌کنند.

---

۱. Feodosiya، شهری ساحلی در شبه جزیره کریمه.
۲. در اصل: Patineurs، Façade، و Haunted Ballroom.

سهشنبه ۱۸ بهمن، ۷ فوریه - از صبح تا شب در هتل بودم و کتاب و روزنامه خواندم. شب دکتر مارشال صفحههای گرامافون خود را آورد و قریب دو ساعت بموسیقی عالی گوش دادم. شرح حال رمان نویس انگلیسی Trollope¹ را خواندم.

یکشنبه ۱۹ بهمن، ۸ فوریه - صبح روزنامه خواندم. بعد با مسیز مایرز آلمانی به گرانچستر رفتم. در راه آلمانی حرف زدیم. بعد از ظهر کتاب خواندم، شرح حال ترولوپ. و بعد با آقای عرفانی محصل بانک دوباره به گرانچستر رفتم. در آنجا چای خوردیم. شب در مهمانخانه بودم و کتاب خواندم. روزنامههای یکشنبه چندان امیدبخش نبود.

دوشنبه ۲۰ بهمن، ۹ فوریه - صبح کتاب و روزنامه خواندم. بعد از ظهر بسینما رفتم. کتاب شرح حال ترولوپ را خواندم. ژاپونیها در جزیرۀ سنگاپور قشون وارد کردهاند.

سهشنبه ۲۱ بهمن، ۱۰ فوریه - صبح کتاب خواندم. شرح حال ترولوپ را تمام کردم. بعد از شام بمنزل پروفسور مینورسکی رفتم. هوا بارانی بود و سرد. در اطاق او کمی در باب ادبیات صحبت کردم و بعد قریب دو ساعت مشغول خواندن عکس چندین نوشتۀ فارسی بودیم از هزار سال پیش.

چهارشنبه ۲۲ بهمن، ۱۱ فوریه - صبح بلندن رفتم. در اداره کار کردم و بعد رفتم به پرینس آو ویلز هتل. در اطاق ۲۹۸ جا گرفتم. ناهار در سفارت خوردم. آقای تقیزاده دوباره تب کرده بودند و نتوانستند با ما ناهار بخورند. اعضای سفارت بودند و خانم. بعد از ناهار نزد آقای تقیزاده رفتم. با حال تب همه را پذیرفتند. در باب ایران و کتاب حرف زدیم. بعد باطاق دیگری رفتند. بعد بحثهای دیگری بمیان آمد. در ضمن گفت و شنید بآقای وحید سخن سخت گفتم و لکن بعد پشیمان شدم و دلم بر حالش سوخت. عصر با او و آقای آرام بسفارت مصر رفتم. مهمانی مفصّل بود. جمعی کثیر آمده بودند. بعد از آنجا با آقای آرام و آقای وحید بسینما رفتم و از سینما برستوران تا

---

۱. Anthony Trollope، داستان نویس بریتانیایی (۱۸۸۲-۱۸۱۵).

ساعت ده نشستیم و حرف زدیم و پیاده از پیکادلی به کنزینگ‌تون آمدیم. ژاپونیها وارد سنگاپور شده‌اند و لکن هنوز آن را بکلّی نگرفته‌اند.

پنجشنبه ۲۳ بهمن، ۱۲ فوریه - صبح بسفارت رفتم. با بایندر ناهار خوردم، در پیکادلی. و بعد از ظهر هم در سفارت بودم. شب در هتل شام خوردم و بعد از ساعت ۹ باطاقم رفتم. کتاب خواندم. در این روز از فرنگیس کاغذی رسید.

جمعه ۲۴ بهمن، ۱۳ فوریه - صبح بسفارت رفتم. روزنامه‌های فارسی را که گرفته بودم دادم. بعد باداره رفتم. تلگرافی بتهران در باب کار خودم و نیز در خصوص پولی که دو سال است نفرستاده‌اند، کردم. ناهار با بایندر خوردم. بعد از ظهر در اداره بودم. با ترن چهار و سه ربع بکمبریج آمدم. کمی کتاب خواندم و زودتر خوابیدم. کشتیهای آلمانی از برست از راه دریای مانش به آلمان رفته‌اند و در جنگ مهمی ۴۲ طیاره انگلیسی را نابوده کرده‌اند و می‌گویند که یک دستروریر۱ را غرق و یکی را از کار انداخته‌اند.

شنبه ۲۵ بهمن ۱۳۲۰، ۱۴ فوریه ۱۹۴۲ - صبح کتاب خواندم در باب تربیت، آینده تربیت. و بعد کمی راه رفتم. بعد از ظهر نیز همین کتاب را خواندم و یادداشت برداشتم. عصر با آقای عرفانی یکی از محصلّین بانک راه رفتم و شب در مهمانخانه بودم. بعد از ظهر فرنگیس از اکسفورد تلفون کرد چون از من کاغذی باو نرسیده بود. احوال پرسی کرد. شب بلندن تلفون کردم. از آقا و خانم تقی‌زاده احوال‌پرسی کردم. هنوز تب آقای تقی‌زاده پایین نیامده است.

یکشنبه ۲۶ بهمن، ۱۵ فوریه - صبح روزنامه و کتاب خواندم. کتاب تربیت را تمام کردم و چندین صفحه از کتاب راجع به قصه (*A Survey of Modern Short Story*) را خواندم. شب دکتر مارشال صفحه‌های گرامافون را آورده و موسیقی خوب شنیدیم. چرچیل نطق کرد در ساعت ۶ و خبر از دست رفتن سنگاپور را داد.

---

۱. Destroyer، مقصود ناوشکن است.

دوشنبه **۲۷ بهمن، ۱۶ فوریه** - صبح کتاب خواندم و روزنامه‌ها را. در همه شرحی در باب تصرف سنگاپور بدست ژاپونیها بود. بعد از ظهر بسینما رفتم و شب در هتل بودم. کتاب راجع به قصه را خواندم. بلندن تلفون کردم. حال آقای تقی‌زاده را پرسیدم که مدتیست بیمار است. تب قطع شده و امید بهبودی بیشتر هست.

سه‌شنبه ۲۸ بهمن، ۱۷ فوریه - صبح بکتابخانه رفتم و بعد از ظهر در هتل بودم و کتاب خواندم، شرح حال دانته. شب زودتر باطاقم رفتم و مجموعه نامه‌های کاترین مَنْس‌فیلد[1] را خواندم.

چهارشنبه ۲۹ بهمن، ۱۸ فوریه - صبح بلندن رفتم. در اداره کار کردم. ناهار با بایندر خوردم و بعد از ظهر بمنزل آقای تقی‌زاده رفتم. حالشان بهتر شده است. در این روز از فرنگیس کاغذی داشتم.

پنجشنبه ۳۰ بهمن، ۱۹ فوریه - صبح کتاب خواندم و بعد از ظهر با مستر بازیل گری بودم. کمی راه رفتیم و بعد چای خوردیم. در باب ایران و بدبختیهایی که بمناسبت تصرّف ایران پیش آمده صحبت کردیم. شب کتاب راجع بزبان انگلیسی خواندم. اوضاع جنگ در هم تر شده. ژاپونیها در برمه پیش می‌روند و در فیلیپین دوباره حمله‌های سخت < را > شروع کرده‌اند.

جمعه < ۱ > اسفند، ۲۰ فوریه - صبح زودتر برخاستم. دستور دادم که تاکسی بیاید. بعد از چاشت هر قدر منتظر شدم تاکسی سر وقت نیامد. چیزی نمانده بود که وقت ترن اکسفورد از دست برود. وقتی منتظر بودم که شاید تاکسی بیاید اتّفاقاً اتومبیل دیگری از مقابل در مهمانخانه گذشت و با آن بایستگاه رفتم. ترن سر وقت حرکت نکرد و گر نه نمی‌توانستم با ترن نه و نیم بروم. باری با عجله خود را به آن رساندم و ساعت یازده و نیم باکسفورد رسیدم. فرنگیس منتظر بود. با او به

---

۱. مقصود Kathleen Mansfield Murry است (نام او به صورت کاترین هم نوشته می‌شد)، نویسنده و روزنامه‌نگار نیوزلندی (۱۹۲۳-۱۸۸۸) و از چهره‌های برجستهٔ جنبش مدرنیست.

Mitre Hotel رفتم. ناهار خوردیم و شب بتاتر رفتم. بازی *Blithe Spirit*[1] را که مسخره احضار ارواح بود، دیدیم. بعد از آن بمهمانخانه آمدیم. شام خوردیم. فرنگیس را بخانه‌اش رساندم.

شنبه ۲ اسفند، ۲۱ فوریه - صبح فرنگیس آمد. بکتابخانهٔ بودلین رفتیم. اوراق و کتابها و نوشته‌های راجع بجنگ و علم جنگ و دفاع و حمله را دیدیم. کاغذی بود بانگلیسی از چارلز دویم پادشاه انگلیس بسلطان عثمانی در باب بدرفتاری ملوانان ترک در نواحی الجزایر. ناهار در رستوران هندی خوردیم و بعد از ظهر بتاتر دیگر اکسفورد رفتیم و بازی *Time and the Conways*[2] را دیدیم که پریستلی[3] نوشته است. شب در مهمانخانه نشستیم و حرف زدیم.

یکشنبه ۳ اسفند ۱۳۲۰، ۲۲ فوریه ۱۹۴۲ - صبح روزنامه خواندم و بعد فرنگیس آمده با هم کمی از مقاله‌ای را که ترجمه کرده بود خواندم. بعد از ظهر بکافهٔ فولرز رفتیم. وقتی چای می‌خوردیم مردی آمده و دیدیم که بحرفهای ما گوش می‌دهد. شبیه هندیها بود. بعد از آنکه چای خوردن تمام شد، پیش آمد و گفت که از هندوستان و برادر راجه پیر پورات است. فارسی حرف می‌زند و روان حرف می‌زند. با او بانجمن اکسفورد رفتیم. صحبت کردیم (در باب هندوستان و مسلمانها و هندوها و ...). بعد اطاقهای مختلف را نشان داد. کتابخانهٔ بسیار خوب < و > عالی دارد و میز اطاقهای پذیرایی و نوشتن و غیره همه خوب است. شب در هتل شام خوردیم و تا ساعت ده و نیم با هم بودیم. در این ایام ژاپونیها در برمه و سوماترا پیش می‌روند. پیشرفت روسها متوقف بنظر می‌آید و هنوز رُمل حمله تازه‌ای نکرده است.

دوشنبه ۴ اسفند، ۲۳ فوریه - صبح فرنگیس آمد. با هم بکتابخانه رفتیم و بعد در هتل ناهار خوردیم. بعد با ترن دو و سی و هشت دقیقه بکمبریج آمدم. پنج ساعت و

---

۱. نمایشنامه کمدی اثر Noël Coward، نمایشنامه‌نویس و کارگردان انگلیسی (۱۸۹۹-۱۹۷۳).

۲. در اصل: Time and Conways.

۳. John Boynton Priestley، داستان نویس و نمایشنامه نویس انگلیسی (۱۸۹۴-۱۹۸۴).

پنجاه دقیقه بعد از ظهر بکمبریج رسیدیم. فرنگیس بایستگاه آمد و ترن چند دقیقه دیر حرکت کرد. در راه کمی از کتابی که فرنگیس داده بود خواندم، کلنل شابر (Colonel Chabert).[1] شب خسته بودم و زودتر خوابیدم. ژاپونیها پیشرفت می‌کنند.

سه‌شنبه ۵ اسفند، ۲۴ فوریه - صبح کاغذی بفرنگیس نوشتم. بعد بکتابفروشی هِفِرز رفتم. بعد از ظهر کتاب خواندم و شب زودتر باطاقم آمدم و کتاب خواندم.

چهارشنبه ۶ اسفند، ۲۵ فوریه - صبح بلندن رفتم. پیش از ظهر آقای تقی‌زاده را دیدم. حالشان کمی بهتر بود و تب قطع شده است. ناهار با بایندر خوردم. بعد از ظهر در اداره بودم. با ترن چهار و چهل و پنج دقیقه بکمبریج آمدم. کتاب کلنل شابر بالزاک < را > خواندم.

پنجشنبه ۷ اسفند، ۲۶ فوریه - صبح کتاب خواندم و بعد برای سخن در باب مالیاتی که آقای زرین‌کفش از بابت خانه‌اش پرداخته ببلدیه کمبریج رفتم و بعد از ظهر بتاتر رفتم. بازی قتل در کلیسا[2] را دیدم. بسیار خوب بود. شب در هتل بودم. کتاب خواندم (رمان کلنل شابر را تمام کردم). نیز کتابی در باب اخلاق و آداب مردم در قرون وسطی خواندم.

جمعه ۸ اسفند، ۲۷ فوریه - صبح برای تحقیق مالیات بلدی خانه آقای زرین‌کفش به آن طرف شهر کمبریج رفتم بادارۀ صاحب خانه و در این باب تحقیق کردم. چون از موقع مراجعت از اکسفورد از فرنگیس کاغذی نداشتم بسیار نگران شدم و تلگراف کردم. ولی ظهر کاغذش رسید و شب تلفون کرد. آرام شدم. بعد از ظهر بسینما رفتم و شب در هتل بودم. کتاب خواندم.

شنبه ۹ اسفند، ۲۸ فوریه - صبح کتاب خواندم و کاغذی بفرنگیس نوشتم. بعد از

---

۱. داستان کوتاهی است بقلم Honoré de Balzac.

۲. Murder in the Cathedral، نمایشنامه‌ای منظوم از T.S. Eliot که نخستین بار در ۱۹۳۵ اجرا شد.

ظهر بسینما رفتم. دوباره فیلم فان تازیا را دیدم. شب در هتل بودم. بعد از شام دکتر مارشال چندین صفحهٔ خوب منجمله یک صفحه که در آن رباعیات خیام خوانده شده از اطاقش آورد و تا ساعت یازده و نیم بموسیقی گوش کردیم. اوضاع جنگ در بیرمانی[1] بسیار بد است و رانگون در خطر.

یکشنبه ۱۰ اسفند، اول مارس ۱۹۴۲ - صبح کتاب و روزنامه خواندم، کتاب راجع برمان و رمان‌نویسها بقلم Collins[2]. از یازده و نیم تا یک بعد از ظهر با مسیز میرز که از آلمان باین مملکت بپناه آمده است، راه رفتم و آلمانی صحبت کردم. بعد از ظهر در هتل بودم و کتاب خواندم. شب نیز کتاب خواندم و دیر خوابیدم. ژاپونیها بجاوه لشگر پیاده کرده‌اند.

دوشنبه ۱۱ اسفند ۱۳۲۰، ۲ مارس ۱۹۴۲ - صبح کتاب راجع برمان خواندم و بعد از ظهر نیز کتاب خواندم. عصر با عبدالله بن محمد محصل حقوق در کمبریج که از اهل مالایاست، چای خوردم و شب زودتر باطاقم رفتم. در رادیو بازی آنطونی و کلئوپاترا را شنیدم. بسیار خوب بود. ژاپونیها در جاوه پیش می‌روند و شاید تا چهار پنج روز دیگر آن را بگیرند.

سه‌شنبه ۱۲ اسفند، ۳ مارس - صبح کتاب خواندم و کاغذی بفرنگیس نوشتم. بعد از ظهر نیز کتاب خواندم، کتاب راجع بزبان. سه ساعت بعد از ظهر به فیتز ویلیام میوزیوم در کمبریج رفتم. مادر پطر پادشاه یوگوسلاوی آمد. مراسم افتتاح نمایشگاه آثار هنر یوگوسلاوی در حضور او باز شد. نقاشیهای جدید چیز مهم تازه‌ای نبود. پارچه‌ها و لباسهایی که دیدم نیز زیبایی تماشایی نداشت. تصویر اولیاء و مسیح و مریم کار دهقانهای یوگوسلاو بسیار ساده بود و بچگانه. از شمایلهای حضرت عباس و علی اکبر هم بچگانه تر. ایران از حیث این قبیل صنایع از یوگوسلاو و ممالک مثل آن

---

۱. اسم قدیم مملکت میانمار (برمه).
۲. مقصود Wilkie Collins است، داستان نویس و از پیشگامان داستان‌نویسی پلیسی (۱۸۲۴-۱۸۸۹).

بسیار برتر است. بیچاره ایران از علم و هنر گریزان نیست ولی کسی آن را بقدر کفاف از این سرچشمه آب نداده است. شب بعد از شام بعمارت بلدیه کمبریج رفتم و پادشاه جوان و رئیس الوزراء و معاون رئیس الوزرای یوگوسلاوی و رئیس British Council و معاون اونیورسیته کمبریج و پروفسور سی‌تون واتسون و دو سه نفر دیگر نطق کردند. شب دیر خوابیدم و کتاب خواندم.

چهارشنبه ۱۳ اسفند، ۴ مارس - صبح بلندن رفتم. در اداره کار کردم. ناهار با بایندر خوردم. بعد از ظهر بسفارت رفتم. حال آقای تقی‌زاده بهتر شده است. شب بکمبریج آمدم. بعد از شام بخانه پروفسور مینورسکی رفتم. تا ساعت یازده با او بود. گفتند ممکن است در مدرسه السنه شرقیه محتاج بمعلم فارسی باشند و از من پرسیدند آیا می‌توانم چند ساعتی درس بدهم. گفت می‌توانم. عکس خط فارسی داشت. کمی آن را خواندیم. اغلب کلمات بکل محو و یا چنان بد نوشته که خواندنی نبود. ژاپونیها در جاوه پیشرفت کرده‌اند.

پنجشنبه ۱۴ اسفند، ۵ مارس - صبح کاغذی بفرنگیس نوشتم و بعد بکتابخانه رفتم. رمان *La Chartreuse de Parme*[1] را گرفتم و چندین صفحه آن را خواندم. بعد از ظهر بسینما رفتم و شب در هتل بودم. کتاب خواندم.

جمعه ۱۵ اسفند، ۶ مارس - صبح کتاب خواندم و کمی از نوشته‌هایی که فرنگیس فرستاد بود را ترجمه کردم. بعد از ظهر هم کتاب خواندم، شارتْروز دو پارم. ساعت پنج بعد از ظهر بیرون رفتم. در عمارت بلدیه کمبریج نطق می‌کردند راجع بادبیات یوگوسلاو. دکتر الیزابت هیل زنی که یکی دو بار در منزل مینورسکی دیده بودم نطق می‌کرد. بد نبود. در یوگوسلاوی ادبیات بسه زبان کروات، اسلونی، و صربی است. بیشتر در باب ادبیات قرون وسطی و ذوق مردم بادبیات صحبت کرد. از ادبیات جدید چیزی نگفت. شب کتاب خواندم. و موزیک گوش کردم. ژاپونیها باتاویه را هم < در > جاوه گرفته‌اند.

---

۱. در اصل: Chartreuse de Parme. رمانی است در دو جلد از استاندال نویسنده فرانسوی.

شنبه ۱۶ اسفند، ۷ مارس - صبح کاغذی بفرنگیس نوشتم. صبح و عصر کتاب خواندم و شب در هتل بودم. ژاپنیها در جاوه و برمه پیشرفت میکنند.

یکشنبه ۱۷ اسفند، ۸ مارس- صبح روزنامه و کتاب خواندم. پیش از ظهر با مسیز مایرز راه رفتم. آلمانی حرف زدم. شب در هتل بودم و دکتر مارشال صفحههای گرامافون آورد. تا ساعت بعد از یازده موسیقی شنیدم و بعد مسیز حترنر صاحب هتل آمد. تا نیمساعت بعد از نصف شب با او و دکتر مارشال و دکتر ریورز صحبت کردم.

دوشنبه ۱۸ اسفند ۱۳۲۰، ۹ مارس ۱۹۴۲ - صبح کتاب خواندم. بعد از ظهر بسینما رفتم. عصر کاغذی از فرنگیس رسید. جوابش را فوراً فرستادم که زودتر باو برسد. شب در اطاقم بودم و کتاب خواندم. رانگون و جاوه از دست رفته است و در روزنامه خواندم که کابینهای در تهران بریاست آقای سهیلی تشکیل شده است.

سهشنبه ۱۹ اسفند، ۱۰ مارس - صبح کتاب خواندم. بعد از ظهر بسینما رفتم. فیلم *49th Parallel*[1] را دیدم. چندان خوب نبود. شب کتاب خواندم و تا نصف شب با دکتر مارشال صحبت کردم.

چهارشنبه ۲۰ اسفند، ۱۱ مارس - صبح بلندن رفتم. در اداره کار کردم. بعد رفتم به پرینس آو ویلز هتل و از آنجا بسفارت. با آقای نیامیر ناهار خوردم. بعد از ظهر در سفارت بودم و شب بعد از شام بمنزل آقای تقیزاده رفتم.

پنجشنبه ۲۱ اسفند، ۱۲ مارس - صبح باداره رفتم. ناهار با مستر کلگ خوردم و بعد از ظهر در اداره بودم. شب بسینما رفتم. فیلم سوواروف سردار معروف روسی را دیدم. بعد در رستوران هندی غذا خوردم و بهتل آمدم. روزنامههای شرق نزدیک را خواندم.

جمعه ۲۲ اسفند، ۱۳ مارس - صبح بسفارت رفتم. آقای تقیزاده را دیدم. با بایندر ناهار

---

۱. در اصل: Parallel ۴۹، فیلمی به کارگردانی مایکل پاول (Michael Powell) محصول ۱۹۴۲.

خوردم و بعد از ظهر باداره رفتم. با ترن چهار و چهل و پنج دقیقه بکمبریج آمدم. شب کمی روزنامه خواندم و زودتر باطاقم آمدم. در این ایام بواسطه اخبار بدی که می‌رسد، انگلیسیها هر چند خوب احساس خود را پنهان می‌کنند، ولی آثار اندک یأسی در آنها دیده می‌شود.

شنبه ۲۳ اسفند، ۱۴ مارس - صبح کتاب خواندم. بعد از ظهر بسینما رفتم و شب کتاب خواندم، شارل‌روز دو پارم. در این شب در اخبار عدد کشتیهای انگلیسی و متحدین که در جنگ جاوه از میان رفته است، گفته شد. گذشته از شکست، کشتیهایی که از میان رفته لطمهٔ سختی است. از ایران خبری نرسیده است ولی از آنچه در روزنامهٔ تایمز خواندم اوضاع خوب نیست. نوشته بود که فرماندهٔ قشون ایران در جنگ با کردها کشته شده. کاندید جدید ریاست آقای سهیلی معلوم نیست چه خواهد کرد و تا کی برقرار خواهد بود. در انگلیس غذا و احتیاجات زندگی روز بروز کمتر می‌شود. روزنامه‌ها را از روز دوشنبه ۱۶ مارس کم خواهند کرد. چندین ماه است که تخم مرغ نخورده‌ام. نه از حیث کمیّت بلکه کیفیت غذا هم نقصان پذیرفته است. روسها هر چند می‌گویند پیشرفت می‌کنند، معلوم نیست که وضعشان چیست.

یکشنبه ۲۴ اسفند، ۱۵ مارس - صبح کتاب خواندم، شارل‌روز دو پارم. پیش از ظهر با مسیز میرز آلمانی راه رفتم و آلمانی حرف زدم. بعد از ظهر هتل بودم و کتاب خواندم. عصر بیرون رفتم. هوا خوب بود. یک دم غروب آفتاب را در نزدیک گران‌چستر تماشا کردم. شب در هتل بودم و کتاب خواندم. روسها در این روزها چندان در باب پیشرفت خود حرف نمی‌زنند. هیتلر در نطق خود که بیاد کشتگان این جنگ و جنگ گذشته بود، گفته است که در تابستان روس[1] ازیشان خواهد بود. در انگلستان کمی مردم از فتح نومید شده‌اند.

دوشنبه ۲۵ اسفند، ۱۶ مارس - صبح کتاب خواندم و بعد از ظهر نیز تا سه و نیم کتاب

---

۱. را +۰.

خواندم. بعد بایستگاه رفتم. فرنگیس از ناتینگام آمد. با هم بمهمانخانه آمدیم. چای در بیرون خوردیم و شب در مهمانخانه بودیم. کتاب خواندم. در این ایام جنگ و علی الخصوص در این روزها که خبرهای بد راجع بایران بسیار است، بودن با فرنگیس برای من نعمتیست. کاشکی امتحانش تمام شده بود و میتوانستیم همه با هم باشیم. حالم چندان خوب نیست.

سه‌شنبه ۲۶ اسفند ۱۳۲۰، ۱۷ مارس ۱۹۴۲ - صبح کتاب خواندم و بعد با فرنگیس بتلگرافخانه رفتم. چندین تلگراف تبریک بطهران فرستادم. بعد از ظهر بسینما رفتیم. فیلم رویتر را دیدیم. بد نبود. و شب کتاب خواندم. در این روز خبر رسید که ژنرال ماک آرتور فرمانده لشگر آمریکایی و فیلیپینی در جزایر فیلیپین باسترالیا رفته و فرمانده آنجا شده است و این در تاریخ امپراتوری انگلستان حادثهٔ عجیبی خواهد بود. ناچار بانگلیسیهای فهیم سخت و ناگوار خواهد بود. از روس و افریقا خبر کم می‌رسد و شاید بمناسبت آنکه هوا در روس از سرمایش کاسته شده ممکن است چند روز جنگ کمتر و بعد حملهٔ آلمان سخت‌تر شود. امسال سال بدیست برای انگلیس و در بعضی آثار نومیدی دیده می‌شود. زغال و لباس و غذا هم کمتر بمردم می‌دهند. از میان رفتن کشتیهای انگلیسی اثرش کم کم هویدا می‌شود.

چهارشنبه ۲۷ اسفند، ۱۸ مارس - صبح با فرنگیس بلندن رفتم. در اداره کار کردم. بعد رفتم بسفارت. آقای تقی‌زاده را دیدم. با بایندر ناهار خوردم. بعد رفتم به هارودز. فرنگیس آنجا بود. با هم بدکان پوست‌فروشی رفتم. پوستی خریده بود. بقیه پولش را داد و بعد با ترن چهار و سه ربع بکمبریج آمدیم. شب کتاب خواندم.

پنجشنبه ۲۸ اسفند، ۱۹ مارس - صبح کتاب خواندم و بعد با فرنگیس کمی ترجمه کردم. بعد از ظهر با هم بتاتر رفتیم. بازی تاجر ونیز را دیدیم. بسیار خوب بود. علی الخصوص بازیگری که جهود شده بود، بسیار خوب بازی می‌کرد. شب کتاب شارتْروز دو پارم را خواندم و شب زودتر باطاقم آمدم. فرنگیس هم آمد. صحبت

کردیم و بیشتر در باب ایران بود. خبر مهم تازه‌ای نیست. در آلمان هم نان و چربی و بعضی از حوایج دیگر زندگی را کمتر کرده‌اند.

جمعه ۲۹ اسفند ماه، ۲۱ مارس ۱۹۴۲ - صبح کتاب خواندم. بعد با فرنگیس به هفرز رفتم. سه کتاب، منجمله کتاب شرح حال سر هربرت شرلی را خریدم. بعد از ظهر در هتل بودیم و من کتاب خواندم. این جمعه روز آخر سال ۱۳۲۰ بود.

در این سال در تاریخ ایران تغییری مهم ظاهر شد. در روز ۲۵ اوت لشگر روس و انگلیس بی آنکه اتمام حجتی بکنند، ببهانهٔ آنکه آلمانیها در ایران بمخالفت آنها برخاسته‌اند، بخاک ایران وارد شدند و نظم و ترتیب و اساس کار ایران را بر هم زدند. در روز سیم فروردین ماه این سال در خانهٔ پروفسور مینورسکی در کمبریج فرنگیس نمازی را دیدم و بعد، پس از چندین بار ملاقات در کمبریج و اکسفورد باو دل بستم و او را موافق دلخواه خود دیدم و رشتهٔ محبّت ما مستحکم شد. سعادت منست که در این گوشهٔ عالم دور از وطن با چنین دختر هوشمند، مهربان، و نجیبی آشنا شده‌ام که بروح و ذوق و فکر من آشنا است. اگر این بلایی که بر ایران وارد آمده است، نبود، این سال را بهترین سال زندگانی خود می‌دانستم. با این همه آشنایی و دوستی و عقد محبّت با فرنگیس بزرگترین و مهمترین واقعه زندگی منست و امیدوارم که بهمراهی او بتوانم برای ایران کاری کنم چه یقین دارم که اگر مملکت ایران از خطر این جنگ جان بدر برد، بمدد فرنگیس کاری خواهم کرد و باری از دوش این مملکت بیچاره برخواهم داشت.

در این سال وقایع مهم در عالم پیش آمد. آلمان بخاک روسیه حمله برد. انگلیس با روس متّحد شد. آلمان و ایطالیا بامریکا اعلان جنگ دادند. ژاپون در دسامبر وارد جنگ شد و در سه ماه امپراطوری انگلیس و هند را در مشرق در هم شکست. کشتیهای امریکایی را که در پرل هاربور لنگر انداخته بود، از میان برد. سنگاپور را که قلعه‌ای تسخیر نشدنی شناخته می‌شد، گرفت. جاوه را تصرف کرد. در این سال رضا شاه پهلوی استعفا داد و از ایران بیرون رفت. مدتی در جزیرهٔ ایل دو فرانس محبوس بود. بعد اجازه گرفت که بکانادا برود. ولیعهدش شاه شد و آقای تقی‌زاده بوزارت مختاری

ایران در انگلیس منصوب گردید. در این سال کمی آلمانی خواندم و چندین کتاب شعر و ادب و تاریخ. سال ۱۳۲۰ سالی بود عجیب و در زندگی من نیز بسیار مؤثر.

بودن در انگلیس و دیدن اوضاع جنگ و زندگی در میان مردم و دقت در احوال اشخاص بهترین فرصت است برای آنکه در جزییات امور این قسمت از فرنگی بچشم عبرت دیده شود و برای ایران درسی باشد.

در این سال بفکر افتادم که کتابی بنویسم باسم فردا و در آن چیزهایی را که برای پیشرفت ایران لازم می‌دانم شرح بدهم و بد و خوب گذشته و نقصها و عیبها و راه ترقی را بنمایم. کتابهایی چند در این باب خواندم و یادداشت برداشتم و هر وقت فکری بخاطرم آمد آن را یادداشت کردم. و باید این کار را دنبال کنم و کتابهای لازم را بخوانم و بعد کتابم را بنویسم.

بیشتر کتابهایی که در این سال خواندم راجع بادبیات بود. چند رمان از فرانسه و انگلیسی و روسی خواندم و نیز در نوشته‌های شکسپیر دقت کردم.

با فرنگیس کمی حافظ و سعدی و فردوسی خواندم. کاشکی امتحاناتش تمام شده بود و می‌توانستیم بیشتر با هم باشیم و بهتر کار کنیم.

از اوضاع ایران بی‌خبرم و بخواندن روزنامه‌های فارسی و یا بعضی از مقالات روزنامه‌های انگلیسی نمی‌توان حقیقت مطلب را دانست. پس آنچه در این باب می‌نویسم خیالی است و گمانی. با این همه نمی‌توانم باور کنم که ایرانیها از رفتن شاه و آشوبی که به میان آمده و سر و کار داشتن با دو لشگر خارجی خشنودند. در عهد رضا شاه تغییرات مهم در زندگی و اخلاق ایرانیها ظاهر شد و در مملکت عمارات و راهها و مدرسه‌ها و یتیم‌خانه‌ها ساخته شد. تغییراتی که در اخلاق و مراسم پیش آمد بعضی خوب بود و بعضی زیان آورده. رضا شاه مردی بود تیزهوش و صاحب رأی و هر چند بیسواد بود، عقل سلیم داشت. منتهی از اوضاع دنیا غافل بود. قدرت بی‌حد داشت و نسبت باین قدرت ظلم نکرد. در ملک خریدن و پول بدست آوردن حریص بود و باین واسطه ناچار شد که مردم ناپاک و دنی دور خود جمع کند. وطن پرست بود امّا وطن پرستیش بر اساس علم و معرفت نبود. امروز که سر نیزهٔ روس و انگلیس او

را از ایران بیرون انداخته و محبوس و یا سرگردان است، کسانی که چند ماه پیش چکمه‌اش را می‌بوسیدند و یا بزور او وکیل شده بودند، باو دشنام می‌دهند و ملک خریدن و ظلم و آزادی‌کشی او را بهزار رنگ و بهزار زبان جلوه می‌دهند.

رضا شاه پهلوی عیب بسیار داشت. امّا بزرگترین عیبش که عفوپذیر نیست آن بود که شخصیت مردم شریف را از میان برد. اطمینان بنفس را کشت. خود را محور امور ایران می‌دانست و خود را محور امور ایران کرد و روزی که از میان رفت مجمعی یا افرادی نبودند که بتوانند زمام امور ایران را بدست بگیرند و من که ایرانی هستم تمام خوبیهای او را باین خطای بزرگ نمی‌بخشم. خطای بزرگ این مرد آن بود که گفتهٔ متملّق را پذیرفت و خیال کرد که ایران بوجود او بسته است و نتوانست بفهمد که اوضاع دنیا باو این اختیار را داد. روزی که روس خواست او را از میان بردارد، بیچارگی او و سطحی بودن تغییرات او نمودار شد.

دورهٔ سلطنت پهلوی از نظر تغییرات اجتماعی یکی از مهمترین دوره‌های بعد از حملهٔ مغول است. بدیهای آن از میان خواهد رفت و قسمتی از خوبیهای آن خواهد ماند. با قدرتی که داشت می‌توانست خدمتهای بزرگ بکند. بزرگترین عیبش حرص و طمع او نبود. خطای بزرگ او خودپسندی او بود. وقتی او بسلطنت نشست، در ایران دزد بسیار بود و چندین مرد شریف زندگی می‌کردند که مردم بآنها عقیده و اطمینان داشتند. وقتی رضاشاه ایران را در بلا گذاشت و رفت، شمارهٔ دزدها کمتر نشده بود ولی چندین نفر هم نبودند که مردم بآنها اطمینان داشته باشند. اگر خود را می‌کشت بهتر بود. اگر حرص ملک خریدن نداشت، بیشتر خدمت می‌کرد. اگر از اوضاع عالم و پیشرفت علم و وضع سیاسی دنیا غافل نبود، مملکت را از مردم بزرگ و وطن‌پرست خالی نمی‌کرد.

مردم ایران بعد از حملهٔ مغول بی‌صفت و بداخلاق شده‌اند. سلطنت شاه عباس مثل برقی است در شب تاریک. سلسلهٔ قاجار خائن بودند و بیشرفِ تن پرور، و غیر از عباس میرزا دیگران بیشتر وقت را بعیش و نوش می‌گذرانیدند ولی بواسطهٔ نفوذ روس و انگلیس کاری نمی‌توانستند بکنند.

پس از جنگ ۱۹۱۴-۱۹۱۸ ایران بیست سال وقت داشت. در این بیست سال رضا شاه کارهای بسیار کرد و لیکن اگر در ایران آزادی بود، کارهای او بیشتر و بهتر انجام می‌گرفت. شاید راه و خط آهن اینقدر نبود، و لکن چیزی که از همه اینها بهتر است یعنی اخلاق و اطمینان و پیشرفت واقعی بیشتر بود.

سادگی رضاشاه پهلوی این بود که می‌خواست در این قرن که پادشاه بازی از میان رفته برای خود و فرزندان خود سلسلهٔ نویی ایجاد کند.

با این همه رضا شاه نمونهٔ مردم ایران بود. ضعف اخلاق مردم او را گستاخ کرد. تملّق او را از راه راست منحرف کرد و جهل او و مملکت را باین روز انداخت.

ایران فردا شاید از امروز بهتر شود. باید امیدوار بود و کار کرد.

شنبه اول فروردین ماه ۱۳۲۱، ۲۱ مارس ۱۹۴۲ - صبح با فرنگیس بلندن رفتم. در وراسوامی ناهار خوردیم و بعد بسینما رفتیم. بعضی از شاگردان و تجار هم بودند. عصر با اتومبیل آقای آرام بایستگاه لیورپول استریت رفتم. نیم دقیقه دیر بود و ترن شش و نیم از دست رفت. با آقای آرام بخانه‌اش رفتیم. نیمساعت آنجا بودیم. با ترن هشت و سی و دو دقیقه بکمبریج آمدیم. ده و نیم بعد از ظهر رسیدیم. شام مختصری خوردیم. پارسال در این روز تنها بودم و امسال فرنگیس با منست. با او روحم تنهایی را نمی‌شناسد و حال احساس می‌کنم که بکمک او می‌توانم کارهای مفید برای ایران انجام بدهم. در این روز از برادرم تلگرافی آمد باین مضمون که سفر آقای اسفندیاری بانگلستان مسلّم نیست و رتبهٔ هفت تصویب شده و نیز از آقای خلخالی و آقای پرویز و آقای علاء تلگرافی رسیده بود.

یکشنبه ۲ فروردین، ۲۲ مارس - صبح با فرنگیس راه رفتم. کتاب خواندم. بعد از ظهر بمنزل مینورسکی رفتم. نبود. در کافه‌ای چای خود خوردیم. شب کتاب خواندیم. در سختی کار انگلیسیها نصرتی پیدا نشده است.

دوشنبه ۳ فروردین، ۲۳ مارس - صبح با فرنگیس بلندن رفتم. صبح در اداره کار کردم. تنها در پیکادلی ناهار خوردم. بعد از ظهر بکتابخانهٔ فویلز رفتم. و نیز در لندن ترجمه جمهوری افلاطون را که در کمبریج یافت نمی‌شد، خریدم. با ترن چهار و سه ربع بکمبریج آمدیم. در این روز در روزنامه‌ای که روسها در لندن منتشر می‌کنند شرحی بود در باب آنکه بدروغ آلمانیها می‌گویند که روس می‌خواهد تهران را بگیرد و آذربایجان را هم بآذربایجان روس ملحق کند. راست و دروغ این اخبار معلوم نیست. آنچه مسلم است آنکه مملکت ما بروز بدی افتاده است و کسی نمی‌داند عاقبت چه خواهد شد.

سه‌شنبه ۴ فروردین، ۲۴ مارس - صبح کتاب خواندم. عصر ببرادرم تلگرافی کردم که اقدام کند < تا > پس از ۸ سال، شغل نمایندگی و حقوق آن را بمن بدهند. شب در

هتل بودم و کتاب خواندم و با فرنگیس در باب ایران و بدبختیهای ایران حرف زدم. در این روزها نام ترکیه در روزنامه‌ها بسیار ذکر می‌شود. گمان نمی‌رود که ترکها از این جنگ برکنار بمانند.

چهارشنبه ۵ مارس، ۲۵ مارس - صبح با فرنگیس بلندن رفتم. بسینمای اخبار رفتیم و از آنجا بسفارت. اعضای سفارت و خانم حمزاوی بودند. ناهار پلوی خوب خوردیم و بعد از ناهار باز در باب بیچارگی ایران و بیسوادی خواص ایران صحبت بمیان آمد. با ترن چهار و چهل و پنج دقیقه بعد از ظهر بکمبریج آمدیم. شب دیر خوابیدیم. ژاپونیها در برمه پیشرفت می‌کنند و کار روسها چندان خوب بنظر نمی‌رسد.

پنجشنبه ۶ مارس، ۲۶ مارس - صبح با فرنگیس کتاب خواندم. بعد با هم راه رفتیم. کتاب در راه هند و کتاب بی‌نام و مجله مهر را که در آن حکایت «نعمت جهل» بود < را > برای مسیز چدویک بردیم. عصر بسینما رفتم و شب در هتل بودم. کتاب خواندیم. چرچیل در نطقش گفته است که وضع کشتی‌رانی در اقیانوس اطلس سخت‌تر شده است. روسها پیشرفتی نکرده‌اند و سه چهار روز است می‌گویند در میدان جنگ تغییری حاصل نشده و آلمانیها حمله می‌کنند. ژاپونیها در برمه پیش می‌روند.

جمعه ۷ فروردین ۱۳۲۱، ۲۷ مارس ۱۹۴۲ - صبح روزنامه و کتاب خواندم. بعد با فرنگیس بیرون رفتم. برای ناهار در رستوران دوروتی رفتم. هیچ خوب نبود چنانکه نتوانستم آن را بخورم. بعد از ظهر بسینما رفتم و شب در اطاقم بودم. کتاب خواندم. چندین روز است که اخبار میدان جنگ روس بسیار کم شده است و از قرائن چنان بنظر می‌آید که آلمانیها مقاومت بیشتر می‌کنند و کار روسها خوب نیست. راجع بترکیه هم هر روز خبری هست و شاید تا چهار پنج هفته دیگر در ترکیه هم کار تغییراتی کند. از ایران خبری نرسیده است و در روزنامه‌ها هیچ اسم آن هم نیست.

شنبه ۸ فروردین، ۲۸ مارس - هوا خوب و آفتابی بود. با فرنگیس به ایلی Ely[1] رفتم با اتوبوس. راه خرّم بود و تماشایی. کلیسای بزرگ ایلی را دیدیم و در مهمانخانه‌ای ناهار خوردیم. عصر بکمبریج آمدیم. بسیار خوش گذشت. دوباره دیدن کلیسای ایلی زیبایی آن را در نظرم بهتر مجسم کرد.

یکشنبه ۹ فروردین، ۲۹ مارس - صبح کتاب خواندم و روزنامه. بعد از ظهر با فرنگیس به گران‌چستر رفتم. در آن جا چای خوردم و شب در مهمانخانه بودم. کتاب شارتروز دو پارم را خواندم. در این روز سر استافورد کریپز[2] طرحی را که دولت انگلیس برای هندوستان در نظر دارد علنی کرده است و از آنچه روزنامه‌ها نوشته‌اند دادن دومی‌نیون[3] بهندوستان در حکم شناختن استقلال هندوستان است زیرا بموجب اساس دومی‌نیون، هندوستان می‌تواند از انگلیس جدا شود.

دوشنبه ۱۰ فروردین، ۳۰ مارس - صبح کتاب و روزنامه خواندم و علی الخصوص مقالات و اخبار راجع بهندوستان را. انگلیسیها می‌خواهند بعد از جنگ بهندوستان حکومت دومی‌نیون بدهند و در حقیقت استقلال آن را شناخته‌اند ولی در این جنگ خود را مکلّف می‌دانند که هندوستان را حفظ کنند. پیشنهادهای انگلیس معقول است و خوب و اگر هندیها آن را بپسندند یکی از بزرگترین مشکلات انگلیس و یکی از سخت‌ترین مسائل دنیا حل شده است. بعد از ظهر با فرنگیس بسینما رفتم و شب در مهمانخانه بودم. حالم چندان خوب نبود و زودتر خوابیدم. کمی از کتاب شارت‌روز دو پارم را خواندم. نزدیک بآخر است.

سه‌شنبه ۱۱ فروردین، ۳۱ مارس - صبح کتاب خواندم، *Le Médecin de campagne*[4] بالزاک. بعد از ظهر در هتل بودم و کتاب خواندم. شب حالم چندان خوب نبود. زودتر خوابیدم و کمی از کتاب طبیب ده را خواندم.

---

۱. شهرکی باکلیسای جامع از توابع کمبریج.

۲. Sir Richard Stafford Cripps، سیاستمدار عضو حزب کارگر و دیپلمات بریتانیایی (۱۸۸۹-۱۹۵۲).

۳. Dominion، منظور حق حاکمیت سرزمینی است که به قلمروهای مستعمراتی سابق بریتانیا داده می‌شد.

۴. *Médecin de campagne*.

چهارشنبه ۱۲ فروردین، اول آوریل - صبح کتاب طبیب ده را خواندم. بعد از ظهر نیز در مهمانخانه بودم. ساعت چهار بعد از ظهر با فرنگیس در بیرون چای خوردم و بعد قریب یک ساعت راه رفتم. شب در هتل بودم و کتاب خواندم. در هندوستان هنوز با طرح پیشنهادی انگلیسیها موافقت نشده است و از آنچه از اخبار بدست می‌آید، هندیها می‌خواهند که از امروز کار دفاع مملکت را بدست بگیرند. روسها چندان پیشرفت نکرده‌اند و در باب ترکیه هر روز خبری هست. گمان نمی‌رود که امسال ترکیه را آسوده بگذارند.

پنجشنبه ۱۳ فروردین، ۲ آوریل - صبح با فرنگیس بلندن رفتم با ترنی که به کینگز کراس[1] می‌رود. این اولین دفعه‌ای بود که ازین راه بلندن سفر می‌کردم. هوا بسیار خوب بود. در لندن در رستوران فرانسوی ناهار خوردیم. از قضا *Blossom Time*[2] که در آن ریچارد توبر[3] می‌خواند در این روز داده می‌شد. دو و نیم بعد از ظهر بآنجا رفتیم. خوب بود. با ترن پنج و پنجاه دقیقه بکمبریج آمدیم. روز سیزده عید را امسال باین وضع گذراندم. خوب بود و خوش ولی دلم در ایران بود.

جمعه ۱۴ فروردین ۱۳۲۱، ۳ آوریل ۱۹۴۲ - صبح با فرنگیس بود. یادداشتهایی راجع بکتاب «فردا» را کمی مرتب کردم. بعد از ظهر با فرنگیس بیرون رفتم. با آقای عرفانی محصل بانک در کافه‌ای محقر نشستیم ـ بمناسبت آنکه روز جمعه که مطابق عقاید مسیحیها عیسی را بدار کشیده‌اند اغلب جاها بسته بود. و بعد راه رفتیم و در باب ایران بحث کردیم. از عجائب است که جوانهای ایرانی غافل از تاریخ ایران و سایر ممالک هر روز برای کار نکردن بهانه‌ای می‌تراشند. در این روزها بیشتر معتقدند که باید با ورزش ایران را اصلاح کرد. عرفانی جوان بی‌شوری نیست ولی افسوس که باید با هزار

---

۱. کینگز کروس.

۲. فیلم موزیک درام محصول انگلستان (۱۹۳۴).

۳. Richard Tauber، خواننده اتریشی (۱۸۹۱-۱۹۴۸).

دلیل و برهان جزئی چیزی[1] را بجوانهای ایران فهماند. ژاپونیها پیشرفت می‌کنند و هنوز در باب هندوستان خبر مسلّمی نرسیده است. نظر بپیشرفت ژاپونیها شاید انگلیسیها تا جایی که ممکن است با هندیها موافقت کنند.

شنبه ۱۵ فروردین، ۴ آوریل - صبح کتاب خواندم و بعد از ظهر با فرنگیس بکافه ماثی‌یو رفتم. آقای عرفانی هم آمد. تا ساعت شش آنجا بودیم. شب در هتل بودم. کمی آلمانی خواندم و مقداری از کتاب طبیب ده.

یکشنبه ۱۶ فروردین، ۵ آوریل - صبح کتاب و روزنامه خواندم. بعد با فرنگیس راه رفتم. آقای تقی‌زاده را در راه دیدم. خواهش کردند بعد از ظهر برای چای بخانه‌شان برویم. چهار ساعت بعد از ظهر رفتیم. برادر خانم تقی‌زاده و زن و بچه‌اش و مستر بِنِت هم بودند. تا ساعت هفت آنجا بودیم. شب در هتل بودم و کتاب خواندم. ژاپونیها در حمله پیشرفت و به کولومبو پایتخت سیلان حمله کرده‌اند. نتیجه مذاکرات سر استافورد کریپز در هندوستان هنوز بکلی معلوم نیست که چیست.

دوشنبه ۱۷ فروردین، ۶ آوریل - صبح کتاب خواندم. عصر با فرنگیس بمنزل پروفسور مینورسکی رفتم. دو زن انگلیسی هم آنجا بودند. تا ساعت هفت آنجا بودیم. شب در هتل بودم و کتاب *Le Médecin de campagne*[2] را خواندیم.

سه‌شنبه ۱۸ فروردین، ۷ آوریل - صبح کتاب خواندم. بعد از ظهر با فرنگیس بودم. در ماثی‌یو چای خوردیم و شب در هتل بودیم.

چهارشنبه ۱۹ فروردین، ۸ آوریل - صبح زود چاشت خوردم. در سر میزمان که مسیز گُردون و دخترش بود، زنی دیگر رفیق دخترش هم بود و تخم مرغ می‌خوردند. یکی هم بمن داد و این دومین تخم مرغی بود که بعد از چندین ماه خوردم. رفتم بلندن. در

---

۱. چیز

۲. *Médecin de campagne*.

اداره کمی کار کردم. بعد رفتم بسفارت. آقای تقی‌زاده را دیدم. با باینذر در پیکادلی ناهار خوردم. با ترن چهار و چهل و پنج دقیقه بعد از ظهر بکمبریج آمدم. شب کتاب خواندم (طبیب ده). سر استافورد کریپس در هندوستان هنوز در باب مذاکراتش اظهاری نداشته و آن را عقب انداخته است. روزولت هم شخصی را موسوم به کلنل جونسون[1] از طرف خود فرستاده است که میانه را بگیرد. ژاپونیها پیشرفت می‌کنند و روسها در ابلاغنامه‌های خود چیزی در باب فتح نمی‌نویسند. گویا آلمانیها خیال حمله بمصر و گرفتن مالت < را > دارند.

پنجشنبه ۲۰ فروردین، ۹ آوریل - صبح کتاب خواندم، کمی ترکی و کمی آلمانی و مقداری از طبیب ده. بعد از ظهر با فرنگیس بیرون رفتیم. در کافه ماثیو چای خوردیم. شب در هتل بودم. ساعت دوازده و نیم خوابیدم. ژاپونیها چندین کشتی تجارتی و دو کشتی جنگی انگلیسیها را غرق کرده‌اند.

جمعه ۲۱ فروردین، ۱۰ آوریل - صبح با فرنگیس کتاب خواندم و بعد از ظهر هم کتاب خواندیم و شب در هتل بودیم. در این روز خبر رد پیشنهاد انگلیسیها بهندیها منتشر شد. سر استافورد کریپز گفت که بانگلستان مراجعت خواهد کرد. در این روز کتاب طبیب ده را تمام کردم.

شنبه ۲۲ فروردین، ۱۱ آوریل - صبح کتاب خواندم و بعد از ظهر با فرنگیس و مسیز گُردون و دخترش بسینما رفتم. فیلم راجع بفتح لیبی را دیدیم و نیز فیلم باسم سانتافه تریل[2] که شرح حال جان برون[3] که معتقد بآزاد کردن سیاهان بود < را > دیدیم.[4] شب در هتل بودیم و کتاب خواندیم.

---

۱. Louis A. Johnson، سیاستمدار و حقوقدان امریکایی بعداً وزیر دفاع امریکا (۱۹۶۶-۱۸۹۱).

۲. Santa Fe Trail، فیلم وسترن محصول امریکا (۱۹۴۰).

۳. John Brown، شخصیت اصلی فیلم که نقش آن را Raymond Massey بازی می‌کرد.

۴. از سانتافه تریل ... تا ... دیدیم، در اصل خط خورده.

یکشنبه ۲۳ فروردین، ۱۲ آوریل - صبح کتاب خواندیم و در کمبریج رود[1] و گرانچستر راه رفتیم. شب در هتل بودیم. ژاپونیها در برمه پیشرفت می‌کنند.

دوشنبه ۲۴ فروردین، ۱۳ آوریل - صبح کتاب خواندم و بعد از ظهر با فرنگیس بسینما رفتم. در این روز کتاب *Lettres de mon moulin* تصنیف آلفونس دوده[2] را شروع کردم. کتاب خوبی است.

سه‌شنبه ۲۵ فروردین، ۱۴ آوریل - صبح با فرنگیس بباغ نباتات کمبریج رفتیم. قریب ده دقیقه با باغبان صحبت کردیم. بعد در گوشه‌ای نشستیم و شعر خواندیم. هوا خوب و آفتابی و زمین از سبزه پوشیده و گلهای عالم در اطراف شکفته بود. در میان آتش جنگ این آرامش لذت دیگری دارد. بعد از ظهر هم بباغ نباتات رفتیم و دیوان حافظ و گلستان را با خود بردیم. چندین غزل و چندین حکایت خواندیم. بسیار خوش گذشت. شب در هتل بودیم. در فرانسه لاوال[3] باز سر کار آمده است.

چهارشنبه ۲۶ فروردین، ۱۵ آوریل - صبح بباغ نباتات رفتم. فرنگیس هم بود. کمی راه رفتم و کمی از شعر حافظ خواندیم. من از کتاب *Lettres de mon moulin* چند صفحه خواندم. بعد از ظهر هم بباغ رفتیم. شب در هتل بودیم و کتاب خواندیم. در روزنامه تایمز خواندم که حسام الدین غفاری و داروگر و چند نفر دیگر من جمله یک کلنل ایرانی را باتهام رابطه داشتن با ژاپونیها گرفته‌اند.

پنجشنبه ۲۷ فروردین، ۱۶ آوریل - صبح و عصر با فرنگیس بکتابخانه دانشگاه کمبریج رفتیم. کتابهای فارسی خواندیم.

جمعه ۲۸ فروردین، ۱۷ آوریل - صبح با فرنگیس بکتابخانه دانشگاه رفتیم و کتابهای

۱. Cambridge Road، جاده‌ای در حومه شهر کمبریج.

۲. Alphonse Daudet، داستان‌نویس فرانسوی (۱۸۴۰-۱۸۹۷).

۳. Pierre Jean Marie Laval، سیاستمدار فرانسوی (۱۸۸۳-۱۹۴۵) و نخست وزیر دوران ویشی از ۱۸ آوریل ۱۹۴۲ تا ۲۰ اوت ۱۹۴۴. بعد از سقوط ویشی دستگیر، محاکمه، و اعدام شد.

فارسی علی الخصوص مقدمه کتاب تاریخ جهانگشا را خواندیم. بعد از ظهر با فرنگیس بباغ نباتات رفتم. کمی روزنامه آلمانی خواندم. در این روز ساعت چهار و نیم بعد از ظهر بمنزل پروفسور روبرتسون Robertson[1] معلم یونانی در ترینیتی کالج رفتم. قبلاً باو که می‌دانستم کمی فارسی می‌داند کاغذی بفارسی نوشتم و وقت خواستم که او را ببینم تا در باب ترجمه‌های انگلیسی و فرانسه کتابهای یونانی و لاتینی تحقیق کنم. جواب داد که روز جمعه بروم. در این روز بمنزل او که < در > < شماره > Bateman Street ۵۶ و نزدیک هتل بود رفتم. چای خوردیم و کمی در باب مطالب مختلف صحبت کردیم. بعد مرا بکتابخانه‌اش برد و بعضی از کتابهای فرانسه و انگلیسی ــ ترجمه از یونانی ــ را نشان داد و نیز چند کتاب فارسی خودش را نشان داد. کتابخانه بزرگ خوبی دارد و وقتی باطاق پر کتاب این معلم باذوق و دانشمند نگاه کردم بدبختی و جهل در ایران بنظرم آمد. در باب ادبیات فارسی و مقابله اشعار فارسی و یونانی حرف زدیم. از مستر چدویک شنیده بود که فرنگیس در کمبریج است. از من خواست که روز یکشنبه ۱۹ برای چای هر دو بمنزلش برویم و من این دعوت را قبول کردم.

شنبه ۱۹ فروردین ۱۳۲۱، ۱۸ آوریل ۱۹۴۲ - صبح بکتابخانه دانشگاه رفتم، با فرنگیس. و بعد از ظهر کتاب خواندیم. شب در هتل بودیم و کتاب Aspects of the Novel[2] را خواندم.

یکشنبه ۳۰ فروردین، ۱۹ آوریل - صبح کتاب و روزنامه خواندم و بعد با فرنگیس به گران‌چستر رفتم. بعد از ظهر ساعت چهار و نیم با فرنگیس بمنزل پروفسور روبرتسون رفتیم. دو پسرش و برادرزاده‌اش بودند. تا ساعت شش آنجا بودیم. در باب زبان فارسی و یونانی قدیم و ادبیات جدید یونانی صحبت کردیم. یکی از پسرانش

---

۱. Donald Struan Robertson، محقق ادبیات کلاسیک و استاد زبان یونانی در کمبریج (۱۸۸۵-۱۹۶۱).

۲. کتابی است از نویسنده مشهور انگلیسی ادوارد مُرگان فورستر (Edward M. Forster) بر اساس خطابه‌های او در کالج ترینیتی کمبریج، انتشار در ۱۹۲۷.

مدتی در یونان مشغول بحفاری بوده است. شب در هتل بودیم و کتاب خواندیم. روسها بگفتهٔ آلمانیها شکست خورده‌اند.

دوشنبه ۳۱ فروردین، ۲۰ آوریل - صبح عبارت زیر نقشه‌ای که در زمان مظفرالدین شاه کشیده شده بود < را > ترجمه کردم. آن را پروفسور رابرتسون بمن داد و خواهش کرد که ترجمه کنم. بعد با فرنگیس بیرون رفتم. ببانک و کتابفروشی رفتیم. دو کتاب یکی راجع بادبیات یونان و دیگری راجع بادبیات لاتین خریدم. بعد از ظهر با هم بکتابخانه دانشگاه کمبریج رفتم. من کمی کتاب فارسی ــ جهانگشای جوینی ــ خواندم. شب در هتل بودیم. لاوال کابینه‌ای تشکیل داده است و انگلیسیها از او در هراسند.

سه‌شنبه < ۱ > اردیبهشت، ۲۱ آوریل - صبح با فرنگیس بکتابخانه دانشگاه رفتم. کمی از کتاب تاریخ جهانگشا < را > خواندم. بعد از ظهر با فرنگیس بسینما رفتم. فیلم *La femme du boulanger*[۱] را دیدیم ــ زن نانوا ــ و شب در هتل بودیم. کتاب خواندیم. در اخباری که از پاریس شنیدم گفتند که کردستان بتشویق روسها اعلان استقلال داده‌اند و خود را مطیع طهران نمی‌دانند.

چهارشنبه ۲ اردیبهشت، ۲۲ آوریل ۱۹۴۲ - صبح تا عصر با فرنگیس بکتابخانه دانشگاه رفتم و کتاب خواندم. شب در هتل بودیم.

پنجشنبه ۳ اردیبهشت، ۲۳ آوریل - صبح با فرنگیس بلندن رفتیم. صبح و بعد از ظهر در اداره بودم. ساعت یازده مستر مایلز و شاگردهای ایرانی که در بیرمنگام تحصیل می‌کنند، آمدند. تا یک بعد از ظهر بودند. با مستر مایلز ناهار خوردم و بعد از ظهر کمی کار کردم. عصر با ترن چهار و چهل و پنج دقیقه بعد از ظهر بکمبریج آمدم. فرنگیس و پروفسور مینورسکی هم بودند. در راه پروفسور مینورسکی در باب رمانی که بزبان روسی در باب تاجیکستان نوشته شده است، حرف زد. صبح بآقای تقی‌زاده تلفون

---

۱. *Femme du boulanger*. عنوان دیگرش *The Baker's Wife*، محصول ۱۹۳۸ فرانسه.

کردم گفتند که آقای اسفندیاری با طیاره بعزم لندن از ایران حرکت کرده‌اند. ممکن است در راه معطل باشد. بهر حال زندگی انگلیسی من رو بتمام شدن است و معلوم نیست چه پیش آید ولی هر چه پیش آید کار خواهم کرد و برای ایران کار خواهم کرد.

جمعه ۴ اردیبهشت، ۲۴ آوریل - صبح با فرنگیس روزنامه خواندیم. بعد از ظهر بسینما رفتم. فیلم راجع بورزش و نظام روس را دیدیم. خوب بود. از تمام ممالک مختلف جزء روس دسته‌ای بودند که ورزش می‌کردند و می‌رقصیدند. از تاجیکستان و ترکستان و قفقاز و آذربایجان روس و گرجستان و غیر آن. شب در هتل بودم. انگلیسیها در برمه عقب نشسته‌اند. کار روسها چندان خوب بنظر نمی‌آید و راجع بآن خبری نیست.

شنبه ۵ اردیبهشت، ۲۵ آوریل - صبح با فرنگیس چاشت خوردم. بعد کمی راه رفتم و ناهار خوردم. با تاکسی بایستگاه رفتم. فرنگیس بلیط تا اکسفورد خرید و با ترن دو ساعت و پنج دقیقه رفت. از رفتن او بسیار متأثر شدم. کمی در کتابفروشی بوز اند بوز[1] بودم و بعد بخانه آمدم. کتاب خواندم. شب هم بعد از شام باطاقم آمدم و کتاب خواندم. از تنهایی در عذاب بودم. از زندگی در انگلستان خسته شده‌ام. امیدوارم هر چه زودتر این جنگ تمام شود و باز دنیا آرام شود و بتوانم بایران خدمت کنم.

یکشنبه ۶ اردیبهشت ۱۳۲۱، ۲۶ آوریل ۱۹۴۲ - صبح روزنامه خواندم و پیش از ظهر با آقای تقی‌زاده کمی راه رفتم و صحبت کردم. ناهار در هتل خوردم و شب در اطاقم بودم. کار کردم علی الخصوص کارهای شخصی. در این روز نبود فرنگیس بسیار در من مؤثر بود. امیدوارم هر چه زودتر امتحاناتش تمام بشود تا با هم باشیم و کار کنیم. در این روز هیتلر در سه بعد از ظهر نطقی مفصل کرد. قریب یک ساعت طول کشید و در ضمن بیان اوضاع جنگ و سختیهای زمستان روس بر لزوم عقب آمدن و تهدید انگلیس تقاضایی کرد مبنی بر خواستن قدرت مطلق راجع بقضات. نطق او در مجلس آلمان بود.

---

1. Bowes & Bowes، قدیمی‌ترین کتابفروشی انگلستان (تأسیس ۱۵۸۱).

دوشنبه ۷ اردیبهشت، ۲۷ آوریل - صبح زود بیدار شدم. با ترن هشت و بیست دقیقه بلندن رفتم و با ترن پنج و پنجاه دقیقه برگشتم. ناهار با بایندر خوردم و تمام روز را در اداره کار کردم.

سه‌شنبه ۸ اردیبهشت، ۲۸ آوریل - صبح زود با ترن هشت و بیست دقیقه بلندن رفتم و با ترن پنج و پنجاه دقیقه بکمبریج آمدم. ناهار با حمزاوی و بایندر خوردم و تمام روز را در اداره کار کردم. در این ایام انگلیسیها در آلمان و آلمانیها در انگلیس بیشتر از پیشتر بمب می‌اندازند. ژاپونیها در برمه پیشرفت می‌کنند.

چهارشنبه ۹ اردیبهشت، ۲۹ آوریل - صبح کتاب خواندم و بعد از ظهر بسینما رفتم. شب ساعت هفت و نیم در ترینیتی کالج مهمان پروفسور رابرتسون بودم. منتظرم بود. با هم باطاق نشیمن که بزرگ بود رفتیم. در این اطاق کتاب و روزنامه می‌خوانند. وقتی وارد شدم چند معلم که اغلب ایشان بسیار پیر بودند بخواندن روزنامه مشغول بودند. نایب رئیس مدرسه آمد. کمی حرف زد. بعد ساعت هشت باطاق غذاخوری رفتیم. بسیار بزرگ بود و گذشته از غیر محصلین در بالا که جای معلمهاست، دو میز بزرگ بود. بر سر یکی نایب رئیس نشست و من در دست راستش جا داشتم و در میز دیگر Dean مدرسه. پیش از شام، نایب رئیس و «دین» با هم دعای لاتین خواندند. بعد شام خوردیم، آش، ماهی، و شیرینی. شراب هم در سر سفره بود. کمی در باب ایران و شاه با هم حرف زدیم. بعد از شام نیز دعای لاتین خواندند و کمی با پروفسور رابرتسون در باغ گردش کردیم. قدیم‌ترین قسمت مدرسه را بمن نشان داد. بعد باطاق او رفتم. تا ساعت ده در باب ادبیات یونانی و لاتینی صحبت کردیم و نیز راجع بایران و ادبیات آن. بعد بهتل آمدم و تا نصف شب بصفحه‌های گرامافون دکتر مارشال گوش کردیم.

پنجشنبه ۱۰ اردیبهشت ۱۳۲۱، ۳۰ آوریل ۱۹۴۲ - صبح با ترن هشت و بیست دقیقه بلندن رفتم. ناهار با حمزاوی و بایندر خوردم و تا پنج و نیم بعد از ظهر کار کردم. با ترن پنج و پنجاه دقیقه بکمبریج آمدم. بعد از شام کمی کتاب خواندم. از فرنگیس کاغذی

رسیده بود. باو جوابی نوشتم و تا یک ساعت بعد از نصف شب با دکتر مارشال و دکتر ریٔوِر و دو نفر دیگر صحبت می‌کردم. ژاپونیها شهر لاشی‌یو[1] واقع در برمه را گرفته‌اند.

جمعه ۱۱ اردیبهشت، اول مه ۱۹۴۲ - صبح و عصر بکتابخانه رفتم. راحة الصدور و سلطنت غازان خان (از جامع التواریخ) خواندم.

شنبه ۱۲ اردیبهشت، ۲ مه - صبح بکتابخانه رفتم و بعد از ظهر در هتل بودم. کتاب خواندم. شب بمنزل آقای تقی‌زاده رفتم. تا ساعت یازده با ایشان حرف زدیم.

یکشنبه ۱۳ اردیبهشت ۱۳۲۱، ۳ مه ۱۹۴۲ - صبح روزنامه خواندم و پیش از ظهر با آقای تقی‌زاده کمی راه رفتم و کمی در باغ نشستیم صحبت کردیم. بعد از ظهر در هتل بودم و کتاب خواندم. ژاپونیها در برمه پیش می‌روند و من‌داله[2] دومین شهر بزرگ برمه را گرفته‌اند.

دوشنبه ۱۴ اردیبهشت، ۴ مه - صبح در اتوموبیل و در صحبت آقای تقی‌زاده و خانم تقی‌زاده بلندن رفتم. صبح و عصر در اداره کار کردم و شب بکمبریج آمدم. در مهمانخانه بودم و کتاب خواندم.

سه‌شنبه ۱۵ اردیبهشت، ۵ مه - صبح و بعد از ظهر بکتابخانه دانشگاه رفتم و کتب فارسی خواندم. شرع سلطنت غازان خان را تمام کردم و از اصلاحات او متعجب شدم که فکرش بچه اموری معطوف بوده و نسبت بآن عصر چه اصلاحات مهم و دقیقی کرده است. انگلیسها در جزیرهٔ مدگسکر[3] پیش می‌روند و لیکن فرانسویها می‌جنگند.

چهارشنبه ۱۶ اردیبهشت، ۶ مه - صبح بلندن رفتم. ناهار با بایندر خوردم و صبح و بعد از ظهر در اداره بودم. با ترن پنج و پنجاه دقیقه بکمبریج آمدم. شب کمی ترجمه

---

۱. Lashio، بزرگترین شهر استان شان (Shan) در شمال میانمار (برمه).

۲. Mandalay، در حدود ۶۳۰ کیلومتری پایتخت یانگُن.

۳. مقصود Madagascar است.

کردم. ساعت نصف شب خوابیدم. در این روز از فرنگیس کاغذی رسید. نوشته بود که از مادرش کاغذی دریافت کرده و در این کاغذ مادرش رضایت خود را بوصلت میان ما اظهار داشته. خوشوقت شدم چرا که برضای پدر و مادر اهمیت می‌دهم و حتی در این ایام هم که همه دم از خودسری می‌زنند، اطاعت پدر و مادر خوبست و در آن لذتی هست.

پنجشنبه ۱۷ اردیبهشت، ۷ مه - صبح بکتابخانه رفتم. کمی از لباب الألباب[1] و تذکره دولتشاه سمرقندی و تذکرة الاولیا را خواندم. بعد از ظهر هم بکتابخانه رفتم. شب برای فرنگیس مقاله‌ای ترجمه کردم. دکتر مارشال صفحه‌های گرامافون خوب زد. تا نصف شب کار می‌کردم. انگلیسیها در مدگسکر پیش می‌روند. یک کشتی انگلیسی غرق شده است.

جمعه ۱۸ اردیبهشت، ۸ مه - صبح و بعد از ظهر بکتابخانه رفتم. کاغذی از فرنگیس داشتم. نوشته بود در مهمانخانه مای‌تر[2] نتوانسته است جا بگیرد. در این روز کتابهای فارسی و عربی مطالعه کردم: لباب الألباب، تذکرة الأولیاء، معالم القربة في علم الحسبة،[3] کتاب البدیع،[4] کتاب الفاخر.[5] شب چندین صفحه از کتاب ‹ با عنوان › *The Importance of Living* تألیف نویسنده چینی موسوم به لین یوتانگ[6] خواندم. خوب و شیرین بود. هنوز نتیجه قطعی جنگ دریایی آمریکا و ژاپون معلوم نیست. ژاپونیها آن را فتح خود جلوه می‌دهند و آمریکاییها نیز آن را پیشرفت خود می‌گویند.

---

۱. تذکره‌ای است در احوال شعرا از نورالدین محمد عوفی بخاری، تألیف حدود ۶۱۸ قمری /۱۲۲۱م.

۲. مقصود Mitre است.

۳. اثری از محمد بن محمد القرشی مشهور به ابن الأخوة (م. ۷۲۹ق /۱۳۲۹م).

۴. اثر عبدالله بن المعتز مشهور به المرتضی بالله خلیفه عباسی که از ادبا و شعرای عصر خود بود. دوران خلافتش یک روزه بود. در جریان شورش غلامان در ۲۹۶ق /۹۰۹م به قتل رسید. او را مؤسس علم بدیع می‌دانند.

۵. اثری در امثال عرب از أبوطالب المفضّل بن سلمة بن عاصم (م. ۲۹۱ق /۹۰۴م)، از ادبای کوفه در اوایل عهد بنی‌عباس.

۶. Lin Yutang، زبانشناس، داستان‌نویس، و مترجم (۱۸۹۵-۱۹۷۶)، مخترع ماشین تایپ چینی.

شنبه ۱۹ اردیبهشت، ۹ مه - صبح بکتابخانه رفتم. کمی کتاب خواندم: چندین ورق از حواشی چهار مقاله و تاریخ گزیده. بعد از ظهر کمی کتاب خواندم. بعد بکتابفروشی رفتم. شب در هتل بودم. فرنگیس تلفون کرد. گفت نتوانسته است اطاقی بگیرد در اکسفورد.

یکشنبه ۲۰ اردیبهشت، ۱۰ مه - صبح کتاب و روزنامه خواندم. یک و نیم بعد از ظهر بمنزل پروفسور چَدویک رفتم. زنی بسیار زشت در آنجا بود، میس کورتیس و پروفسور Jepson معلم آشنای زبان در[۱] دانشگاه لیورپول و کمبریج. ساعت شش و نیم بمهمانخانه آمدم. کتاب خواندم. چرچیل نطقی کرد که اگر آلمانیها در روسیه گاز بکار برند، انگلستان هم این کار ‹ را › می‌کند.

دوشنبه ۲۱ اردیبهشت، ۱۱ مه - صبح بکتابخانه رفتم. حواشی چهار مقاله و کمی از تاریخ گزیده ‹ را › خواندم. بعد از ظهر هم بکتابخانه رفتم. از فرنگیس کاغذی رسیده بود. عصر جواب دادم.

سه‌شنبه ۲۲ اردیبهشت ۱۳۲۹، ۱۲ مه ۱۹۴۲ - صبح بلندن رفتم. کمی در اداره کار کردم و بعد رفتم به هارودز. با بایندر و صاحبخانه‌اش مستر داود ناهار خوردم. بعد رفتم بسفارت. آقای تقی‌زاده را دیدم و تا ساعت چهار و نیم در آنجا بودم. شب بکمبریج آمدم. کمی روزنامه فارسی و مقداری از کتاب اهمیّت زندگانی را خواندم. آلمانیها بشبه جزیره کرچ[۲] حمله کرده‌اند. ظاهراً حمله از روز جمعه شروع شده است و لشگر آلمان پیشرفتی کرده‌اند. سه کشتی انگلیسی در بحر متوسط[۳] غرق شده است.

چهارشنبه ۲۳ اردیبهشت، ۱۳ مه - صبح ببانک رفتم و چندین کاغذ نوشتم و بعد از

---

۱. دارالفنون خط خورده
۲. The Kerch Peninsula، در منتهای شرقی شبه جزیره کریمه در اوکراین.
۳. مقصود مدیترانه است.

ظهر بکتابخانه. کمی از مقدمه نقطة الکاف[1] را خواندم. شب در هتل بودم و کتاب اهمیت زندگی را خواندم. آلمانیها در کرچ پیشرفت کرده‌اند و مدعی‌اند که چهل هزار اسیر و چندین توپ و تانک گرفته‌اند.

پنجشنبه ۲۴ اردیبهشت، ۱۴ مه - صبح رفتم بلندن. ناهار با بایندر خوردم. بعد از ظهر در سفارت بودم و شب بکمبریج آمدم. کتاب اهمیت زندگی را خواندم.

جمعه ۲۵ اردیبهشت، ۱۵ مه - صبح رفتم بکتابخانه. چندین کتاب فارسی و عربی را مطالعه کردم. بعد از ظهر در کتابخانه بودم. آلمانیها در کرچ پیشرفت می‌کنند و روسها مدعی‌اند که بطرف خارکف پیش می‌روند.

شنبه ۲۶ اردیبهشت، ۱۶ مه - صبح با ترن نه و نیم باکسفورد رفتم. یک ساعت و بیست دقیقه بعد از ظهر باکسفورد رسیدم. با فرنگیس در راندولف Randolph هتل ناهار خوردم. بسیار خوب و کافی بود. بعد کمی در خیابان راه رفتم. ساعت شش و نیم رفتم بتأتر. بازی مکبث را دیدم. بازیگر معروف جان گیل‌گود[2] بازی می‌کرد. تأثر پر بود و مردم غافل از جنگ خوش بودند.

یکشنبه ۲۷ اردیبهشت، ۱۷ مه - صبح فرنگیس آمد. با هم بکلیسا رفتیم. در هتل ناهار خوردیم. عصر با یکی از بزرگ‌زادگان هندی چای خوردیم و بعد با او رفتم بکلوب محصلین اکسفورد. تا شش و نیم بعد از ظهر نشستیم < و > صحبت کردیم. شام در هتل با فرنگیس خوردم. شام راندولف بسیار خوب بود و عجیب است که در ایام جنگ کسانی که پول دارند می‌توانند اینطور خوش بگذرانند و خوش بخورند.

دوشنبه ۲۸ اردیبهشت، ۱۸ مه - صبح با فرنگیس راه رفتم. بپارک رفتیم و کتاب

---

۱. تاریخ ظهور باب اثر حاجی میرزا جانی کاشانی (م. ۱۲۶۸ق/۱۸۵۲م). مقدمه مفصل آن را ادوارد براون نوشته است. میرزا جانی کاشانی پس از واقعه سوء قصد بجان ناصرالدین شاه محبوس شد. نهایتاً در بقعه عبدالعظیم با قمه بدست محمدمهدی ملک‌التجار تبریزی (پدربزرگ حاج حسین ملک) به قتل رسید.
۲. Sir Arthur John Gielgud، بازیگر و کارگردان تئاتر (۱۹۰۴-۲۰۰۰).

خواندیم. بعد از ظهر نیز در پارک راه رفتیم و در کافه‌ای بسیار خوب چای خوردیم. غذا و شیرینی در آکسفورد بیشتر است از کمبریج. آلمانها در کرچ پیشرفت کرده‌اند و روسها می‌گویند که بطرف خارکف پیش می‌روند.

سه‌شنبه ۲۹ اردیبهشت، ۱۹ مه - صبح فرنگیس آمد. با هم بکتابفروشی Blackwell رفتم. بعد از ظهر در کافه کاوی‌نا[۱] چای خوردیم و شب در هتل بودیم. در این چند روز اقامت در اکسفورد بیشتر اوقات را با فرنگیس بودم و در باب ایران و زندگی خودمان و ادبیات حرفها زدیم. بسیار خوش بودم چرا که روح باو مأنوس شده است.

چهارشنبه ۳۰ اردیبهشت، ۲۰ مه - صبح کمی کتاب خواندم، شرح حال برون که در مقدمه یک مجموعه اسناد فارسی نوشته شده (ترجمه). ساعت ده صبح فرنگیس آمد. با هم بپارک رفتیم. در مقابل استخر نشستیم و بگلها و درختها نگاه کردیم. هوا خوب بود و خوش گذشت. بعد بکتابفروشی بلکول رفتیم. کتابهایی چند دیدیم. ناهار در هتل خوردیم و یک و سه ربع بعد از ظهر با هم بایستگاه آمدیم. تا دو و سی و هشت دقیقه فرنگیس با من بود. صحبت کردیم در باب ایران و شعر و اکسفورد و ایام خوش چند روزه. در راه جوانی ایرلندی محصل اکسفورد که بکمبریج می‌آمد، هم اطاقم بود. بسیار مخالف جهودها و روسها بود. عقایدی عجیب داشت. ساعت شش بعد از ظهر بکمبریج رسیدم. شام مختصری خوردم و بعد از غذاهای لذیذ هتل اکسفورد، بدهنم مزه‌ای نداشت. شب کمی از کتاب اهمیت زندگی خواندم. روسها مدعی‌اند که بطرف خارکف پیش می‌روند ولی اثری از این پیشرفت معلوم نیست.

پنجشنبه ۳۱ اردیبهشت ۱۳۲۱، ۲۱ مه ۱۹۴۲ - صبح بکتابخانه و بعد از ظهر بسینما رفتم. فیلم دکتر جکیل اند مستر هاید[۲] را دیدم. شب در مهمانخانه بودند. کتاب اهمیت زندگی را خواندم و دکتر مارشال صفحه‌های گرامافون جدیدی را گذاشت. نصف شب خوابیدم.

---

۱. مقصود ظاهراً باید Cavanaugh باشد.
۲. *Dr. Jekyll and Mr. Hyde*، محصول ۱۹۳۱ آمریکا، بکارگردانی روبن معمولیان.

جمعه ۱ خرداد، ۲۲ مه - صبح بلندن رفتم. ناهار با بایندر خوردم و بعد از ظهر با او بسفارت رفتم. آقای تقی‌زاده را دیدم در سفارت. بعد با بایندر و حمزاوی بمنزل بایندر رفتم. خانم حمزاوی هم بود. ساعت هشت شام خوردیم. مستر دود صاحبخانه بایندر کتهٔ خوبی پخته بود. شام پاکیزهٔ لذیذی خوردیم. حمزاوی و زنش بعد از ساعت ده رفتند. تا نصف شب با بایندر حرف می‌زدم. بعد خوابیدم. واقعه مهمی اتفاق نیفتاده. روسها مدعی‌اند که بطرف خارکوف پیش می‌روند.

شنبه ۲ خرداد، ۲۳ مه - صبح زود بیدار شدم. با بایندر و صاحب خانه‌اش چاشت خوردیم. بعد با بایندر بادارهٔ‌اش رفتم. قریب یک ساعت و نیم آنجا بودیم و بعد با هم بسفارت آمدیم. ناهار در سفارت با آقای تقی‌زاده و خانم خوردم و با اتومبیل همه بکمبریج آمدیم. سه و نیم بعد از ظهر رسیدیم. چای در منزل آقای تقی‌زاده خوردم. تا ساعت هفت آنجا بودم. از فرنگیس کاغذی رسیده بود. آلمانیها مدعی‌اند که پیشرفت روسها را متوقف کرده‌اند.

یکشنبه ۳ خرداد ۲۴،۱۳۲۱ مه ۱۹۴۲ - صبح روزنامه خواندم. پیش از ظهر با آقای تقی‌زاده راه رفتم. بعد از ظهر کمی خوابیدم و کتاب خواندم. شب در مهمانخانه بودم. کتاب خواندم. کتاب اهمیت زندگی را تمام کردم.

دوشنبه ۴ خرداد، ۲۵ مه - صبح و بعد از ظهر بکتابخانه دانشگاه رفتم. بعضی از کتب ترکی را مطالعه کردم. شب کتاب جمهوری افلاطون را شروع کردم و حدود نصف آن را خواندم. روسها بکلی کرچ را تخلیه کرده‌اند و آلمانیها مدعی‌اند که لشگر روس را محاصره کرده‌اند (نزدیک خارکوف).

سه‌شنبه ۵ خرداد، ۲۶ مه - صبح و عصر بکتابخانه دانشگاه رفتم و شرح بعضی از کتب فارسی را در کاتالوگ کتابهای خطی بریتیش میوزیم خواندم. پر از اطلاعات مفید است و بسیار لذت بردم. کاغذی از فرنگیس آمده بود. باو جواب دادم. کار روسها در فرانت خارکوف خوب نیست.

چهارشنبه ۶ خرداد، ۲۷ مه - صبح و عصر بکتابخانه رفتم و شرح کتب فارسی < را > خواندم. شب در مهمانخانه بودم. در این روز خبر رسید که در لیبی نیز لشگر ایتالیا و آلمان در حرکت هستند و پیشرفت کرده‌اند.

پنجشنبه ۷ خرداد، ۲۸ مه - صبح و عصر بکتابخانه رفتم و شرح کتب فارسی < را > خواندم. شب بسینما رفتم. فیلم رئیس الوزراء را دیدم. بد نبود. در این روز اخبار روس در مقال اخبار لیبی چندان رونقی ندارد. معلوم نیست که در اطراف خارکوف چه وقایعی اتفاق افتاده است. آلمانیها می‌گویند که روسها را محاصره کرده‌اند.

جمعه ۸ خرداد، ۲۹ مه - صبح کاغذی از فرنگیس رسید. جوابی فرستادم. صبح و عصر بکتابخانه رفتم. کاتالوگ کتب خطی بریتیش میوزیم را مطالعه کردم. شب در هتل بودم. جنگ سختی در لیبی در میان است و در روسیه هم اوضاع چندان خوب بنظر نمی‌رسد. آنچه مشخص است اینکه تی‌موشنکو[1] بکلی متوقف شده است.

شنبه ۹ خرداد ۱۳۲۱، ۳۰ مه ۱۹۴۲ - ساعت نه صبح بکتابخانه رفتم. تا یک ساعت بعد از ظهر کتاب خواندم. بعد از ظهر کمی کتاب خواندم و شب در مهمانخانه بودم. باقی مقاله‌ای را که فرنگیس فرستاده بود، ترجمه کردم.

یکشنبه ۱۰ خرداد، ۳۱ مه - صبح روزنامه خواندم و بعد از ظهر و شب جمهوری افلاطون را. در این روز خبر حمله انگلیس بشهر کولون[2] منتشر شد. چنانکه انگلیسیها می‌گویند بیش از هزار طیاره بمب افکن بشهر کولون[3] رفته آن را سوزانده‌اند. چهل و چهار بمب افکن برنگشتند.

---

۱. Semyon Timoshenko، مارشال شوروی و از امرای ارتش سرخ در جنگ جهانی دوم (۱۹۷۰-۱۸۹۵).

۲. کولونی. مقصود Cologne است.

۳. کولونی.

دوشنبه ۱۱ خرداد، اول ژوئن ۱۹۴۲ - صبح و بعد از ظهر بکتابخانه رفتم و کتب فارسی و عربی و ترکی را مطالعه کردم.

سه‌شنبه ۱۲ خرداد، ۲ ژوئن - صبح رفتم بلندن. نیمساعت بعد از ظهر به پیکادلی رفتم. فرنگیس از اکسفورد آمده بود. با او در رستوران فرانسوی ناهار خوردم و بعد کمی در باغ سنت جیمز نشستیم. بعد از ظهر بسفارت رفتم. آقای تقی‌زاده را دیدم و کمی با بایندر و حمزاوی و آرام صحبت کردم. با ترن پنج و چهل و نه دقیقه بکمبریج آمدیم. شب از کتاب جمهوری افلاطون چندین فصل خواندم. انگلیسیها باز بآلمان طیاره‌های بسیار فرستاده‌اند، هزار و سی و شش، و سی و پنج طیاره برنگشته است. این بار شهر اِسِن[1] را بمب انداخته‌اند.

چهارشنبه ۱۳ خرداد، ۳ ژوئن - صبح و عصر بکتابخانه رفتم. بعضی کتب ترکی و عربی را مطالعه کردم. شب در مهمانخانه شام خوردم و بعد رفتم به کینگز[2] کالج. در زیر پل هر سال جمعی می‌آیند و اشعار قدیمه می‌خوانند. مردم هم برای تماشا جمع می‌شوند. قایقهای بسیار پر از زن و مرد، اغلب جوان، دیده می‌شد. سه و ربع بعد از ظهر شروع بشعر بخواندن کردند. تا ده و نیم طول کشید. هوا بسیار خوب بود.

پنجشنبه ۱۴ خرداد، ۴ ژوئن - صبح و بعد از ظهر بکتابخانه رفتم. کتب ترکی و فارسی مطالعه کردم، علی الخصوص تذکره دولتشاه را. در افریقا گاهی آلمانیها و گاهی انگلیسیها پیشترفتی می‌کنند. در روس هنوز بعد از جنگ خارکوف در جای دیگر جنگ مهمی نشده است. در این روز از فرنگیس کاغذی رسید و باو جواب دادم.

جمعه ۱۵ خرداد، ۵ ژوئن - صبح و عصر بکتابخانه رفتم. کتابهای ترکی و فارسی خواندم. هر روز بیشتر معتقد می‌شود که زبان ترکی بکل تحت تأثیر فارسی بوده است

---

۱. Essen، شهری است صنعتی و پرجمعیت در غرب آلمان.

۲. کینز.

ولی ناچار تغییر الفبا این تأثیر را کم خواهد کرد. شب در مهمانخانه کتاب خواندم، جمهوری افلاطون. خبر مهمی در این روز نبود.

شنبه ۱۶ خرداد، ۶ ژوئن - صبح بکتابخانه رفتم. کتب ترکی را مطالعه کردم. بعد از ظهر کتاب خواندم و شب در مهمانخانه بودم.

یکشنبه ۱۷ خرداد، ۷ ژوئن - صبح روزنامه خواندم و بعد از ظهر با آقای عرفانی یکی از محصلین بانک قریب دو ساعت راه رفتم. شب در مهمانخانه بودم. هنوز جنگ سختی در لیبی بر پاست و معلوم نیست فتح با کیست.

دوشنبه ۱۸ خرداد، ۱۰ ژوئن - صبح و بعد از ظهر در کتابخانه بودم و کتاب عربی خواندم. کمی از تحریر اصول اقلیدس خواندم < و > چند ورق از کتاب شرح اشعار مشهور عرب.

سه‌شنبه ۱۹ خرداد ۱۳۲۱، ۹ ژوئن ۱۹۴۲ - صبح و بعد از ظهر بکتابخانه رفتم. بعضی از رسائل ابن سینا را خواندم و نیز بعضی کتابهای دیگر را مطالعه کردم. شب در مهمانخانه بودم. کمی از کتاب سرمایه کارل مارکس را خواندم. هنوز جنگ لیبی تمام نشده است و آلمانیها در سباستوپول حمله می‌کنند اما نتیجه‌ای قاطع بدست نیامده است.

چهارشنبه ۲۰ خرداد، ۱۰ ژوئن - صبح رفتم بکتابخانه و بعد از ظهر هم در آن جا بودم و کتابهای فارسی علی الخصوص تاریخ را مطالعه کردم.

پنجشنبه ۲۱ خرداد، ۱۱ ژوئن - صبح و بعد از ظهر بکتابخانه رفتم و کتاب خواندم، مخصوصاً کتابهای راجع بتاریخ.

جمعه ۲۲ خرداد، ۱۲ ژوئن - صبح و بعد از ظهر بکتابخانه رفتم. کمی از کتاب نفائس الفنون[1] را خواندم. کتاب پر اطلاع مفیدیست. در این روز خبر عهدنامه اتحاد بین روس

---

۱. نفائس الفنون فی عرائس العیون اثر شمس الدین محمد بن محمود آملی (م. ۷۵۳ق/۱۳۵۳م) به فارسی.

و انگلیس منتشر شد. این عهدنامه را در ۲۵ مه در لندن امضا کرده‌اند و مولوتوف وزیر خارجه روس در لندن آن را امضا کرده است. آمدن او بانگلیس و رفتنش بامریکا و مراجعت او از امریکا بانگلیس و برگشتنش بروس همه مخفی مانده بود. انگلیسیها در افریقا شکست خورده‌اند و بئر حکیم[1] بدست آلمانیها افتاده است. در روس نیز آلمانیها بسباستوپول و در حوالی خارکوف حمله‌های شدید می‌کنند. بآقای تقی‌زاده تلفون کردم. قرار شد روز دوشنبه ایشان را در لبنان ببینم.

شنبه ۲۳ خرداد، ۱۳ ژوئن - آلمانیها در سباستوپول و خار کف حمله‌های شدید می‌کنند و در افریقا نیز بطرف طبروک پیش می‌روند.

یکشنبه ۲۴ خرداد، ۱۴ ژوئن - صبح کتاب و روزنامه خواندم. عصر به گران‌چستر رفتم. وقت برگشتن مستر بِنِتْ را دیدم. با او بخانه‌اش رفتم و پدرش را که بعد از ۸ ماه خدمت در کشتی بمرخصی آمده است، دیدم. شب کتاب خواندم. کار انگلیسیها در افریقا چندان خوب نیست.

دوشنبه ۲۵ خرداد، ۱۵ ژوئن - صبح بلندن رفتم. کمی در اداره کار کردم و بعد رفتم بسفارت. آقای صیقل عضو سفارت و سرهنگ عطاپور آتاشه نظامی از ایران همان روز وارد شده بودند. آقای صیقل پاکتی بمن داد و در آن از پدرم و از جلال و کمال کاغذی بود. بسیار خوشوقت شدم. ناهار با آقای تقی‌زاده خوردم. شب در کمبریج کتاب خواندم. هنوز جنگ در سباستوپول و خارکوف تمام نشده ولی چنانکه از اخبار معلوم می‌شود آلمانیها پیشرفت می‌کنند.

سه‌شنبه ۲۶ خرداد، ۱۶ ژوئن - صبح و عصر بکتابخانه رفتم. کتب فارسی و عربی را مطالعه کردم. عصر آقای عرفانی را در کتابخانه دیدم. چای با هم خوردیم. حالم چندان خوب نبود. زودتر باطاقم رفتم و خوابیدم. در این روز از جلال تلگرافی رسید

---

۱. Bir Hakeim، واحه‌ای در جنوب‌شرقی طبروق و صحنه یکی از نبردهای اصلی بین قوای متفقین و لشگر آلمان در لیبی. به یادبود این نبرد نام یک پل و یکی از ایستگاه‌های مترو پاریس را به بئر حکیم تغییر دادند.

مشعر بر آنکه رتبه هفتم تصویب شده و ابلاغ شده ولی حقوق آن را نمی‌دهند و تقاضا کرده بود خبر سلامت را تلگراف کنم.

چهارشنبه ۲۷ خرداد، ۱۷ ژوئن - صبح و عصر بکتابخانه رفتم. از مرآت البلدان[1] ورقی چند خواندم. وضع انگلیسیها در افریقا چندان خوب نیست و آلمانیها پیشرفت می‌کنند.

پنجشنبه ۲۸ خرداد، ۱۸ ژوئن - صبح بلندن رفتم. از کتابخانهٔ فویلز یک فرهنگ ترکی بفرانسه و یک کتاب دستور فارسی که بانگلیسی نوشته شده و فرهنگ فارسی و انگلیسی جانسون[2] را خریدم. بعد بیپکادلی رفتم. بیست دقیقه بعد از ظهر فرنگیس که تازه از اکسفورد وارد شده بود آمد. با هم در رستوران هندی ناهار خوردیم و بعد بسینمای اخبار و از آنجا بهاید پارک رفتیم. عصر در ماربل آرچ چای خوردیم. با ترن پنج و پنجاه و نه دقیقه بکمبریج آمدیم. در این روز خبر رسید که انگلیسیها اتاریم و سیدی رزق[3] را که هر دو در نزدیکی تبروک است، تخلیه کرده‌اند.

جمعه ۲۹ خرداد ۱۳۲۱، ۱۹ ژوئن ۱۹۴۲ - صبح و عصر بکتابخانه رفتم. کتب عربی خواندم. شب کمی ترجمه کردم.

شنبه ۳۰ خرداد، ۲۰ ژوئن - صبح بلندن رفتم. کمی در کتابفروشیها بودم و بعد رفتم بسفارت. زنی ایرانی موسوم به عفت خانم که بمردی دانمارکی شوهر کرده است، بود. و بعد اعضای سفارت هم آمدند. آرام، وحید، حمزاوی و زنش، نیامیر، بایندر، سرهنگ عطاپور، صیقل، زن و دخترش. ناهار چلوکباب خوردیم و بعد از ظهر بیشتر در باب بدبختی و بی‌سرپرستی ایرانیها صحبت بمیان آمد. تا ساعت چهار و نیم بعد از ظهر در سفارت بودم. بعد با اتومبیل در صحبت آقای تقی‌زاده و خانم بکمبریج آمدیم.

---

۱. اثر محمدحسن اعتماد السلطنه (م. ۱۳۱۳ق /۱۸۹۶م) در جغرافیای تاریخی بلاد ایران.

۲. Francis Johnson، زبانشناس بریتانیایی (حدود ۱۷۹۵-۱۸۷۶م).

۳. Sidi Rezegh.

یکشنبه ۳۱ خرداد، ۲۱ ژوئن - صبح کتاب خواندم و روزنامه. یک بعد از ظهر آقای نیامیر و آقای عرفانی بکمبریج آمدند. با هم ناهار خوردیم. کمی راه رفتیم. بعد با آقای نیامیر بمنزل آقای تقی‌زاده رفتیم. طبروک بدست آلمانیها افتاده است و کار انگلیسیها در افریقا بسیار سخت شده است.

دوشنبه ۱ تیر، ۲۲ ژوئن - صبح دو دست لباس نزد خیاطی بردم که آستین آنها را کوتاه کند. بعد از ظهر بکتابخانه رفتم و کتب عربی خواندم. شب در مهمانخانه بودم. کاغذی بدکتر آربری[1] نوشتم و کمی ترجمه کردم. آلمانیها در سباستوپول پیشرفت کرده‌اند.

سه‌شنبه ۲ تیر ۱۳۲۱، ۲۳ ژوئن ۱۹۴۲ - صبح و بعد از ظهر بکتابخانه رفتم. کاغذی از فرنگیس رسید. بعد از شام باو جواب نوشتم. هنوز پاکت را نبسته بودم که پیشخدمت مهمانخانه گفت از لندن تلفون کرده بودند که بآن جا تلفون کنی. بسفارت تلفون کردم. خانم تقی‌زاده گفتند که آقای اسفندیاری وارد انگلیس شده است. ‹ با › این وضع استقلالی که داشتم از میان می‌رود. بعد از هشت سال زحمت و تحصیل دوباره همان مقامی که هشت سال پیش داشتم یعنی معاونت نمایندگی هستم و عجیب‌تر از این کم کردن حقوق منست که بقدر یک ثلث کم شده است. با این همه جای شکایت نیست چراکه مملکت در بدترین حالات است و کسی نیست که شکایت را بفهمد یا حوصلهٔ تأمل در این قبیل مطالب داشته باشد. باید بیشتر از پیشتر در پیشرفت مقاصد خود بکوشم و کار کنم. شاید این تغییرات مفید باشد.

چهارشنبه ۳ تیر، ۲۴ ژوئن - صبح بلندن رفتم. در سفارت آقای تقی‌زاده را دیدم. معلوم شد که آقای اسفندیاری و خانمش که از لیورپول با ترنی که دو و بیست دقیقه بعد از ظهر می‌رسد، بلندن می‌آیند. ناهار با بایندر و آرام و سرهنگ عطاپور خوردم. بعد با آرام در اتوبوس سفارت بایستگاه هریس‌تون رفتم. ترن سر وقت رسید. با آقای اسفندیاری و خانمش به هاید پارک هتل رفتم. تا پنج بعد از ظهر با ایشان بودم. هر دو مهربانی بسیار

---

۱. Arthur John Arberry، عضو آکادمی بریتانیا و محقق ادبیات عربی و فارسی (۱۹۶۹-۱۹۰۵).

کردند. کاغذی از پدرم و برادرم و دکتر علوی داشتم. شب بکمبریج آمدم. کاغذی بفرنگیس نوشتم. بسیار خسته بودم. آلمانیها در افریقا پیشرفت می‌کنند و انگلیسیها بیم آن دارند که مصر از دست برود. در خاک روس هم آلمانیها پیشرفت کرده‌اند.

پنجشنبه ۴ تیر، ۲۵ ژوئن - صبح و عصر بکتابخانه رفتم. کمی از کتاب آثار الباقیة عن القرون الخالیة بیرونی را خواندم. شب در هتل بودم. چند فصل از کتاب فتح غرناطه واشینگتون ایروینگ[1] را خواندم.

جمعه ۵ تیر ۱۳۲۱، ۲۶ ژوئن ۱۹۴۲ - صبح و عصر بکتابخانه رفتم. شب در مهمانخانه بودم. از کتاب جمهوری افلاطون خواندم. آلمانیها در افریقا و در روس پیشرفت می‌کنند. از دست رفتن تبروک در انگلیس تأثیر بسیار کرده است.

شنبه ۶ تیر، ۲۷ ژوئن - صبح با ترن هشت و بیست دقیقه بلندن رفتم. در هاید پارک هتل آقای اسفندیاری را دیدم. ناهار با او و خانمش خوردم. بعد از ظهر با آقای اسفندیاری بمنزل سرهنگ عطاپور رفتم. آقای آرام هم بود. قریب یکساعت آنجا نشستیم. بعد با ترن پنج و چهل و نه دقیقه بکمبریج آمدم. چرچیل از امریکا بانگلیس برگشته است.

یکشنبه ۷ تیر، ۲۸ ژوئن ۱۹۴۲ - صبح روزنامه خواندم. عصر کمی از کاغذی راجع بنفت ترجمه کردم. عصر بمنزل پروفسور مینورسکی رفتم. تقدیمی را که آقای علاء از طهران فرستاده و آقای اسفندیاری بمن داده بود، باو سپردم. شب در هتل بودم و کمی ترجمه کردم. آلمانیها در افریقا و روس پیشرفت می‌کنند.

دوشنبه ۸ تیر، ۲۹ ژوئن - صبح و عصر بکتابخانه رفتم و شب در هتل بودم. رومل[2] بسرعت بطرف اسکندریه پیش می‌آید.

---

۱. Washington Irving، نویسنده، مورخ، و دیپلمات امریکایی (۱۸۵۹-۱۷۸۳). اثری که در اینجا ذکر شده Chronicle of the Conquest of Granada است (انتشار در ۱۸۲۲).

۲. Erwin Rommel، فیلد مارشال آلمانی (۱۹۴۴-۱۸۹۱).

سه‌شنبه ۹ تیر، ۳۰ ژوئن – صبح بلندن رفتم. کمی در اداره کار کردم. بعد از ظهر رفتم سفارت و شب بکمبریج آمدم. ترجمه کاغذی را که آقای اسفندیاری داده بود، تمام کردم.

چهارشنبه ۱۰ تیر، اول ژوئیه – صبح رفتم بلندن. آقای اسفندیاری هم آمد. تا یک ساعت بعد از ظهر در اداره بودیم. بعد در مهمانخانه پیکادلی با هم ناهار خوردیم و از آنجا رفتیم بسفارت. آقای تقی‌زاده را در سفارت دیدم. عصر با ترن پنج و چهل و نه دقیقه بکمبریج آمدم. هوا بسیار گرم و ترن پر از نظامی بود. هنوز در افریقا نتوانسته‌اند پیشرفت رومل را متوقف کنند.[1]

پنجشنبه ۱۱ تیر، ۲ ژوئیه – صبح بلندن رفتم. در اداره بودم. آقای اسفندیاری آمد. با او و بعد مستر اِل‌کین‌تون بودم. ناهار در رستوران هندی خوردم. بعد از ظهر بسفارت رفتم. شب بکمبریج آمدم. رُمل هنوز در افریقا پیشرفت می‌کند. سباستوپول بدست آلمانیها افتاده است.

جمعه ۱۲ تیر، ۳ ژوییه – صبح بلندن رفتم. فرنگیس از اکسفورد آمد. با هم ناهار خوردیم، در رستوران فرانسوی. بعد از ظهر بسینما رفتم. ساعت پنج بعد از ظهر از او جدا شدم. با ترن پنج و پنجاه دقیقه بکمبریج آمدم. روزی خوش گذشت و از کسالت روحی بیرون آمدم. آلمانیها بسرعت ایام پیش پیش نمی‌روند. سردار انگلیسی با تمام قوای خود در العلمین شصت میلی اسکندریه بمقاومت پرداخته است و معلوم نیست که نتیجه جنگ چه خواهد بود. در روزنامه خواندم که در تهران خواسته‌اند آقای سهیلی رئیس الوزرا را بکشند.

شنبه ۱۳ تیر، ۴ ژوئیه – صبح کتاب خواندم. شب بمنزل آقای تقی‌زاده رفتم. تا ساعت ۱۱ آن جا بودم.

یکشنبه ۱۴ تیر، ۵ ژوئیه – صبح روزنامه و کتاب خواندم. عصر کمی راه رفتم و شب در هتل بودم. مقاله ترجمه کردم. انگلیسیها در العلمین مقاومت می‌کنند و قشون رُمِل متوقف شده است.

---

۱. + چهارشنبه ۱۰ تیر، اول ژوئیه – صبح بادارِه رفتم. آقای اسفندیاری آمد با او (خط خورده: و بعد مستر ال‌کین‌تون) کمی حرف زدم. بعد با آقای اسفندیاری در پیکادلی هتل غذا خوردم. بعد از ظهر با هم بسفارت رفتیم. شب بکمبریج آمدم.

دوشنبه ۱۵ تیر ۱۳۲۱، ۶ ژوئیه ۱۹۴۲ - صبح و بعد از ظهر بکتابخانه رفتم. سالنامه‌ها و کتابهای راجع بکمبریج را مطالعه کردم. شب در هتل بودم و کاغذی بفرنگیس نوشتم.

سه‌شنبه ۱۶ تیر، ۷ ژوئیه - صبح و عصر بکتابخانه رفتم و کتابهای راجع بکمبریج < را > خواندم.

چهارشنبه ۱۷ سپتامبر، ۸ ژوئیه - صبح بلندن رفتم. در اداره کمی کار کردم. ناهار با بایندر و آرام و عطاپور خوردم. بعد از ظهر دوباره باداره رفتم. کمی کار کردم. شب بکمبریج آمدم. آلمانیها در روس پیش می‌روند. شب بسیار دیر خوابیدم.

پنجشنبه ۱۸ تیر، ۹ ژوئیه - صبح بلندن رفتم. ناهار در گریت ایسترن هتل[1] خوردم. بعد از ظهر در اداره بودم. مستر مایلز آمد. شب بکمبریج آمدم و مقاله‌ای را که فرنگیس فرستاده بود، ترجمه کردم. حالم خوب نبود. بسیار خسته بودم.

جمعه ۱۹ تیر، ۱۰ ژوئیه - صبح و عصر بکتابخانه رفتم. حالم چندان خوب نبود. آلمانیها در روس پیشرفت می‌کنند.

شنبه ۱۶ تیر، ۱۱ ژوئیه - صبح کتاب خواندم و بعد از ظهر در هتل بودم. متصل باران می‌آمد و بسیار غمگین بودم. شب بمنزل آقای تقی‌زاده رفتم. تا ساعت ۱۲ آنجا بودم.

یکشنبه ۱۷ تیر، ۱۲ ژوئیه - صبح روزنامه خواندم. نزدیک ظهر با آقای تقی‌زاده راه رفتم. بعد از ظهر در هتل بودم. کمی آلمانی خواندم.

دوشنبه ۱۸ تیر، ۱۳ ژوئیه - صبح کتاب خواندم. بعد از ظهر بسینما رفتم و شب کتاب خواندم. آلمانیها بسرعت پیشرفت می‌کنند.

سه‌شنبه ۱۹ تیر ۱۳۲۱، ۱۴ ژوئیه ۱۹۴۲ - صبح روزنامه خواندم و کمی آلمانی. بعد

---

۱. Great Eastern Hotel، هتلی پنج ستاره در مرکز لندن.

از ظهر راه رفتم. حالم چندان خوب نیست. شب در هتل بودم. بعد باطاقم آمدم. میس بریجلند معلم انگلیسی نبیل تلفون کرد و قرار گذاشت که چهارشنبه ساعت هفت و نیم بعد از ظهر بیاید مرا ببیند. آلمانیها در جنوب روس پیشرفت می‌کنند. در مصل هنوز رُمِل در العالمین است.

چهارشنبه ۲۰ تیر، ۱۵ ژوئیه - صبح بلندن رفتم. تا یک ساعت بعد از ظهر با آقای اسفندیاری بودم. بعد از ناهار بسفارت رفتم. تا ساعت پنج بعد از ظهر آنجا بودم. شب بکمبریج آمدم. با میس بریجلند شام خوردم و بعد از ساعت ۹ با او بخانه‌اش در کیمبریج رود رفتیم. شب کمی کتاب خواندم. آلمانیها پیشرفت می‌کنند و کار روسها بسیار خراب بنظر می‌رسد.

پنجشنبه ۲۱ تیر، ۱۶ ژوئیه - صبح کتاب خواندم. بعد از ظهر بسینما رفتم. شب کتاب و علی الخصوص آلمانی خواندم. روسها هنوز عقب‌نشینی می‌کنند.

جمعه ۲۲ تیر، ۱۷ ژوئیه - صبح کتاب و روزنامه خواندم و بعد از ظهر کمی آلمانی. شب در هتل بودم.

شنبه ۲۳ تیر، ۱۸ ژوئیه - صبح و بعد از ظهر کتاب و آلمانی خواندم. شب بدیدن آقای تقی‌زاده رفتم. تا نصف شب آنجا بودم. آلمانیها در جنوب روس پیشرفت می‌کنند. شهر وروشیلوف‌گراد[۱] را گرفته‌اند.

یکشنبه ۲۴ تیر، ۱۹ ژوئیه - صبح کتاب خواندم و آلمانی. بعد از ظهر بمنزل پروفسور مینورسکی رفتم و شب در هتل بودم.

دوشنبه ۲۵ تیر ۱۳۲۱، ۲۰ ژوئیه ۱۹۴۲ - صبح بلندن رفتم. فرنگیس هم از اکسفورد آمد. با هم در رستوران هندی غذا خوردیم و بعد بسینما رفتیم. عصر در پیکادلی

---

۱. Voroshilovgrad، نام قدیم لوهانسک (Luhansk). امروزه جزء اوکراین است.

هتل چای خوردیم. با ترن پنج و چهل و نه دقیقه بکمبریج آمدم. شب کمی از کتاب *La Russie moscovite*[1] را که پروفسور مینورسکی بامانت داده بود، خواندم.

سه‌شنبه ۲۶ تیر، ۲۱ ژوئیه - صبح کتاب خواندم. بعد از ظهر بکتابخانه رفتم. تاریخ الحکمای قفطی[2] را مطالعه کردم. شب در هتل بودم.

چهارشنبه ۲۷ تیر، ۲۲ ژوئیه - صبح بلندن رفتم. در اداره کار کردم. آقای اسفندیاری هم بود. با باپندر ناهار خوردم و با او بسفارت رفتم. آقای تقی‌زاده را دیدم. با ترن پنج و چهل و نه دقیقه بکمبریج آمدم. در راه کتاب راجع بروس را خواندم. آلمانیها در جنوب روس پیشرفت می‌کنند و نزدیک راستوف هستند. انگلیسیها در افریقا بلشگر آلمانی حمله کرده‌اند.

پنجشنبه ۲۸ تیر، ۲۳ ژوئیه - صبح کتاب خواندم ـ آلمانی. بعد از ظهر کمی خوابیدم. حالم خوب نبود. از هتل بیرون رفتم و چای خوردم. شب در هتل بودم و کمی از کتاب راجع بروس را خواندم. آلمانیها در جنوب روس پیش می‌روند.

جمعه ۳۰ تیر، ۲۵ ژوئیه - صبح بکتابخانه رفتم و بعد از ظهر در هتل بودم و کتاب خواندم. شب هم کار کردم و کمی آلمانی خواندم. آلمانیها پیشرفت سریع می‌کنند. کاغذی بفرنگیس نوشتم.

یکشنبه ۳۱ تیر، ۲۶ ژوئیه - صبح روزنامه و کتاب خواندم. عصر آلمانی خواندم. بعد به گران‌چستر رفتم. شب در هتل بودم. کتاب *La Russie moscovite* را خواندم. کار روسها در جنوب بسیار سخت است و آلمانیها بسرعت پیش می‌روند.

---

۱. اثر Sergeï Fedorovich Platonov، (۱۸۶۰-۱۹۳۳) که در ۱۹۳۲ در پاریس منتشر شد. نویسنده از مشاهیر مورخان اواخر دوران تزاری بود. در ۱۹۳۰ به اتهام همدستی با ضد انقلاب دستگیر و در تبعید درگذشت.

۲. ابوالحسن علی بن یوسف القفطی (م. ۶۴۶ق/۱۲۴۸م)، مورخ و کتابشناس مصری. عنوان اصلی اثر او إخبار العلماء بأخبار الحکماء است و به شرح حال ۴۱۴ تن از اطبا، فلاسفه، و منجمان اختصاص دارد.

دوشنبه < ۱ > مرداد، ۲۷ ژوئیه - صبح کتاب و آلمانی خواندم. بعد از ظهر بسینما رفتم و شب قریب یک ساعت راه رفتم و تا یک ساعت بعد از نصف شب کتاب خواندم. از فرنگیس کاغذی رسید و جوابی باو نوشتم. شب در کمبریج بمب انداختند و چندین دکان و خانه را خراب کرده‌اند. آلمانیها وارد قفقاز شده‌اند.

سه‌شنبه ۲ مرداد، ۸ ژوئیه - صبح کتاب خواندم. بعد از ظهر بکتابخانه رفتم. شب آلمانی خواند. دیشب در کمبریج بمب انداخته‌اند. سه نفر کشته و چندین نفر مجروح شدند.

چهارشنبه ۳ مرداد، ۲۹ ژوئیه - صبح بلندن رفتم. صبح و عصر در اداره کار کردم و شب بکمبریج آمدم. از فرنگیس کاغذی رسیده بود. روز شنبه خواهد آمد. شب کمی آلمانی خواندم. یک ساعت بعد از نصف شب اعلام خطر کردند و عربده توپهای طیاره زن بلند شد. بیش از یک ساعت طول کشید. آلمانیها در جنوب روس پیشرفت می‌کنند.

پنجشنبه ۴ مرداد، ۳۰ ژوئیه - صبح آلمانی خواند. بعد از ظهر بکتابخانه رفتم و شب در هتل بودم و آلمانی خواندم. آلمانیها پیشرفت می‌کنند. در کمبریج چندین شب صدای طیاره و توپ بلند است.

جمعه ۵ مرداد ۱۳۲۱، ۳۱ ژوئیه ۱۹۴۲ - صبح و عصر بکتابخانه رفتم. کمی از تاریخ ادبیات عرب تألیف مستشرق آلمانی Hammer-Purgstall[1] را خواندم. شب در مهمانخانه بودم. کمی آلمانی خواندم. روسها در قفقاز عقب‌نشینی می‌کنند. کابینه ایران استعفا داده است و معلوم نیست در ایران چه بدبختی روی کرده.

شنبه ۶ مرداد، اول اوت ۱۹۴۲ - صبح آلمانی خواندم. بعد از ظهر هم آلمانی با کمی

---

۱. Joseph von Hammer-Purgstall، مستشرق اطریشی (۱۷۷۴-۱۸۵۶). اثر مورد اشاره در ۷ جلد بصورت ناتمام منتشر شد. عنوان آن به آلمانی *Literaturgeschichte der Araber. Von ihrem Beginne bis zu Ende des zwölften Jahrhunderts der Hidschret* است (۱۸۵۰-۱۸۵۶).

انگلیسی خواندم. عصر بایستگاه رفتم. منتظر آمدن فرنگیس بودم. ترنش نیم ساعت دیر آمد. بعد از شام با او بمنزل عبدالله بن محمد رفتم. تا یازده و نیم بعد از ظهر آنجا بودیم. یک صاحبمنصب انگلیسی و دختری انگلیسی که هر دو را در هتل دیده بودم، آمدند.

یکشنبه ۷ مرداد، ۲ اوت - صبح روزنامه خواندم. مدتی با فرنگیس راه رفتم. عصر هم راه رفتیم و کتاب خواندم. کمی آلمانی خواندم. شب در هتل بودیم.

دوشنبه ۸ مرداد، ۳ اوت - صبح روزنامه و کتاب خواندم. کمی راه رفتیم. آلمانیها در جنوب روس پیشرفت می‌کنند. هنوز از تشکیل کابینه در ایران خبری نیست.

سه‌شنبه ۹ مرداد، ۴ اوت - صبح کتاب و آلمانی خواندم. بعد از ظهر با فرنگیس بسینما رفتم و شب در هتل بودیم و کتاب خواندیم.

چهارشنبه ۱۰ مرداد، ۵ اوت - صبح بلندن رفتم. کمی در اداره کار کردم. ناهار نزدیک سفارت خوردم و بعد از ظهر بسفارت رفتم. آقای تقی‌زاده بمرخصی به بورن موث[1] رفته است. با ترن چهل و نه دقیقه بعد از پنج بکمبریج آمدم. با فرنگیس شام خوردم. بعد با هم به گران‌چستر رفتیم. کار روسها روزبروز خرابتر می‌شود. آلمانیها در قفقاز پیش می‌روند و در جهت استالینگراد پیشرفت کرده‌اند.

پنجشنبه ۱۱ مرداد، ۶ اوت - صبح و عصر کتاب خواندم و با فرنگیس بودم. در هندوستان تصمیم گرفته‌اند که از انگلیسیها جدا شوند.

جمعه ۱۲ مرداد، ۷ اوت - صبح بلندن رفتم. ناهار با بایندر خوردم. بعد از ظهر بسفارت رفتم. آقایان سرهنگ عطاپور، آرام، حمزاوی، وحید، و صیقل هم بودند. قریب دو ساعت در باب ایران صحبت کردیم.

---

۱. Bournemouth، شهری ساحلی در جنوب انگلستان.

شنبه ۱۳ مرداد، ۸ اوت - صبح کتاب خواندم. عصر با فرنگیس بمنزل پروفسور رابرتسون رفتیم. چندین کتاب فارسی و یک خنجر و یک قبله‌نما بما نشان داد. کمی در باب جنگ و فارسی صحبت کردیم. خوش گذشت. شب در هتل هم روزنامه‌های فارسی خواندم. در این روز گاندی از طرف کمیته حزب کنگرس[1] مأمور شد که استقلال هندوستان را اعلام کند. لرد لین‌لیث‌گو[2] اعلام نامه‌ای منتشر کرده است و بموجب آن می‌گوید که تکلیفش دفاع < از > هندوستان است و جمیع وسائل را بکار خواهد برد.

یکشنبه ۱۴ مرداد، ۹ اوت - صبح و بعد از ظهر با فرنگیس بودم و کتاب خواندیم. عصر به گران‌چستر رفتیم و شب در هتل بودم. گاندی، آزاد،[3] و نهرو و سایر رؤسای آزادیخواهان هندوستان را توقیف کرده‌اند و شاید این توقیف در هندوستان عواقب وخیمی داشته باشد. آلمانیها پیشرفت می‌کنند و ببحر خزر نزدیکتر می‌شوند. معلوم نیست آیا کابینه‌ای در ایران درست شده است یا نه.

دوشنبه ۱۵ مرداد ۱۳۲۱، ۱۰ اوت ۱۹۴۲ - صبح کتاب خواندم و کمی آلمانی. بعد از ظهر با فرنگیس بسینما رفتم و شب در هتل بودیم. آلمان پیشرفت می‌کند و در هندوستان تا کنون قریب سی نفر کشته و چندین صد نفر مجروح شده‌اند.

سه‌شنبه ۱۶ مرداد، ۱۱ اوت - صبح کتاب خواندم و بعد از ظهر کمی آلمانی. عصر با فرنگیس در کافهٔ کوچک نلی‌در چای خوردیم و بعد راه رفتیم. شب در هتل بودیم. آلمانیها بسرعت در قفقاز پیشرفت می‌کنند. و اوضاع هندوستان بد است. چنانکه

---

۱. منظور The Indian National Congress است.

۲. 2nd Marquess of Linlithgow، لقب Victor Alexander John Hope سیاستمدار بریتانیایی (۱۸۸۷-۱۹۵۲) که از ۱۹۳۶ تا ۱۹۴۳ فرماندار هند بود و از سرکوب خشونت‌بار مخالفان ابایی نداشت. برخی او را باعث قحطی ۱۹۴۳ بنگال می‌دانند که به مرگ سه میلیون نفوس هندی منجر شد.

۳. ابوالکلام آزاد الحسینی (۱۸۸۸-۱۹۵۸) از فعالان استقلال و یکپارچگی هندوستان و از همکاران وفادار گاندی و نهرو. پس از استقلال نخستین وزیر معارف هندوستان شد.

رادیوی انگلیس می‌گوید ۳۱ نفر مقتول و بیش از دویست نفر مجروح شده‌اند. در این روز خبر تشکیل کابینه قوام السلطنه را در روزنامه تایمز خواندم. نوشته بود آقای تقی‌زاده وزیر مالیه شده است ولی تا ورود ایشان بایران خود قوام السلطنه کفیل مالیه خواهد بود. وزرای دیگری که نام برده بود: ساعد وزیر خارجه، قره‌گوزلو عدلیه، کاظمی داخله. نام وزرای دیگر را ننوشته بودند.

چهارشنبه ۱۷ < مرداد >، ۱۲ اوت - صبح بلندن رفتم. با بایندر ناهار خوردم و بعد از ظهر در سفارت بودم. با آقایان بایندر و عطاپور و آرام و حمزاوی و صیقل کمی حرف زدم. شب بکمبریج آمدم. با فرنگیس شام خوردم. می‌گویند که در هندوستان آشوب کمتر شده است و لیکن در این ایام بهیچ خبری اطمینان نیست.

پنجشنبه ۱۸ مرداد، ۱۳ اوت - صبح کتاب خواندم. بعد از ظهر کمی آلمانی خواندم و شب در هتل بودم. روزها با فرنگیس بخواندن و ترجمه مشغولم. آلمانیها بسرعت بطرف بحر خزر پیش می‌روند.

جمعه ۱۹ مرداد، ۱۴ اوت - صبح کتاب و آلمانی خواندم. بعد از ظهر با فرنگیس بمنزل مسیز مایرز آلمانی رفتم و با او و پسرش مدتی صحبت کردیم. شب در هتل بودم.

شنبه ۲۰ مرداد، ۱۵ اوت - صبح و عصر کتاب خواندم. چای با فرنگیس در کافه ماتی‌یو خوردم. یک هندی هم بود. با او مدتی صحبت کردیم. شب در هتل بودیم.

یکشنبه ۲۱ مرداد، ۱۶ اوت - صبح با فرنگیس روزنامه و کتاب خواندم. بعد از ظهر به گران‌چستر رفتیم و شب در هتل بودیم. آلمانیها در قفقاز و در نزدیک استالینگراد پیش می‌روند.

دوشنبه ۲۲ مرداد، ۱۷ اوت - صبح و عصر کتاب خواندم و با فرنگیس بودم. حالم چندان خوب نبود. گوشم کمی درد می‌کرد. شب کمی آلمانی خواندم. آلمانیها در قفقاز و حوالی استالینگراد پیشرفت می‌کنند.

سه‌شنبه ۲۳ مرداد، ۱۸ اوت - صبح کتاب خواندم. با فرنگیس بباغ نباتات رفتم و کمی از کتاب تاریخ فیشر[1] را خواندم. شب در هتل بودم.

چهارشنبه ۲۴ مرداد، ۱۹ اوت - صبح با فرنگیس بلندن رفتم. تا نیمساعت بعد از ظهر در اداره بودم. بعد در نزدیک سفارت با باپندر و عطاپور و آرام ناهار خوردم. بعد از ظهر بسفارت رفتم. آقای تقی‌زاده را دیدم. قریب نیمساعت حرف زدیم. عصر با ترن پنج و چهل و نه دقیقه با فرنگیس بکمبریج آمدم. حالم کمی بهتر است. در این روز انگلیسیها ساعت هشت گفتند که یک دسته لشگر و هواپیما برای حمله به دِپ[2] فرستاده‌اند. عصر و شب اخبار بازگشت آنها راگفتند. آلمانیها مدعی‌اند که این حمله اتفاقی نبود و مقدمه هجوم باروپا برای تصرف آن بود ولی موفق نشدند. و می‌گویند ۱۵۰۰ نفر اسیر و جمیعی مقتول شده‌اند. چرچیل در روسیه بوده و با استالین ملاقات کرده است.

پنجشنبه ۲۵ مرداد ۱۳۲۱، ۲۰ اوت ۱۹۴۲ - صبح با فرنگیس کتاب و روزنامه خواندم. بعد از ظهر بتأتر رفتیم. مسیز مایرز که بمن آلمانی درس می‌داد و پسرش نیز آمدند. بازی را که جان درینک‌واتر[3] نوشته بود باسم *The Blue Bird*[4] دیدیم. شب در هتل بودیم و کار کردیم.

جمعه ۲۶ مرداد، ۲۱ اوت - صبح کتاب خواندم و بعد از ظهر با فرنگیس بمنزل یک هندی رفتیم. تا شش بعد از ظهر آنجا بودیم. شب در هتل بودیم و کتاب خواندیم. آلمانیها در قفقاز بپیش می‌روند و نیز در حوالی استالینگراد پیشرفت کرده‌اند.

---

۱. احتمالاً منظور هربرت فیشر (Herbert A. L. Fisher) مورخ بریتانیایی است (۱۸۶۵-۱۹۴۰). از جمله آثارش مجموعه‌ای سه جلدی در تاریخ اروپا است با عنوان *A History of Europe* (انتشار ۱۹۳۵).

۲. مقصود Dieppe Raid است، حمله آبی خاکی قوای متفقین به بندر دِپ در شمال فرانسه که در آن زمان در اشغال آلمان بود.

۳. John Drinkwater، شاعر و نمایشنامه‌نویس بریتانیایی (۱۸۸۲-۱۹۳۷).

۴. Blue Bird، اثر موریس مترلینک (انتشار ۱۹۰۸). انتساب آن به درینک‌واتر صحیح نیست.

شنبه ۲۷ مرداد، ۲۲ اوت - صبح کتاب خواندم و بعد از ظهر با فرنگیس بودم و راه رفتیم.

یکشنبه ۲۸ مرداد، ۲۳ اوت - صبح کتاب و روزنامه خواندیم. عصر بمنزل آقای تقی‌زاده رفتیم و تا ساعت شش و نیم آنجا بودیم. در باب اوضاع هندوستان و ایران مذاکره کردیم.

دوشنبه ۲۹ مرداد، ۲۴ اوت - صبح کتاب خواندم و بعد از ظهر راه رفتم. شب در هتل بودم. مستر چرچیل بلندن مراجعت کرده است. آلمانیها در قفقاز پیشرفت بسیار کرده‌اند.

سه‌شنبه ۳۰ مرداد، ۲۵ اوت ۱۹۴۲ - صبح کتاب خواندم و بعد از ظهر کتاب و آلمانی خواندم. عصر با فرنگیس قریب یک ساعت و نیم راه رفتم. آلمانیها در قفقاز و در حوالی استالینگراد پیشرفت می‌کنند و می‌گویند که بیرق آلمان را بر قله البرز در کوه‌های قفقاز برافراشته‌اند. پارسال روز ۲۵ اوت لشگر روس و انگلیس بی آنکه قبلاً اولتیماتوم داده باشند، ببهانه آنکه آلمانیها در ایران کارشکنی می‌کنند وارد ایران شدند. نظم و ترتیب در این مملکت از میان رفت. و در مدت یک سال قحط و غلا و شورش ایلات و گرانی و بدبختی دامنگیر ایران بوده است. در این یک سال همیشه روحم افسرده بود و نتوانستم کاری مهم از پیش ببرم و از امروز که ۲۶ اوت ۱۹۴۲ است باید جبران گذشته کنم و بیشتر درس بخوانم و بیشتر کار کنم، بگویم و بنویسم. در دنیای آینده برای ممالک بدبخت و مردم بی‌دانش جز بندگی کاری نیست و باید هر که ایران را می‌خواهد و صلح کلی عالم را دوست می‌دارد بقدر وسع خویش در پیشرفت علم و معرفت و در تهیه وسائل پیشرفت مردم از هر حیث بکوشد و بمملکت خود و از این راه بعالم خدمت واقعی کند.

چهارشنبه ۳۰ مرداد، ۲۶ اوت - صبح بلندن رفتم. در اداره کار کردم. ناهار تنها در رستوران ایطالیایی نزدیک سفارت خوردم. بعد از آن بسفارت رفتم. آقای تقی‌زاده را دیدم و کمی در سفارت بودم. در این روز خبر مرگ آقای سید عبدالرحیم خلخالی را از آقای تقی‌زاده شنیدم و بی‌نهایت متأثر شدم. خلخالی یکی از عزیزترین دوستانم بود و در بزرگواری و خیرخواهی و وطن‌دوستی کمتر نظیر داشت. آمدنم بفرنگستان

بتشویق و بهمراهی او بود. با او ساعتهای بسیار خوش گذرانده‌ام که همه در صحبت کتاب و دوستان عالم و نویسنده بود. خبر مرگ او دلم را لرزاند.

پنجشنبه ۳۱ مرداد ۱۳۲۱، ۲۷ اوت ۱۹۴۲ - صبح با فرنگیس بکتابفروشی هِفِرز رفتم و شاهنامه چاپ ماکان T. Macan[1] و چند جلد ترجمه موهل Jules Mohl را معاینه کردم. هر دو را سفارت برای وزارت معارف خریده و آقای تقی‌زاده خواهش کرد آنها را ببینم که بی‌عیب باشد. بعد از ظهر با فرنگیس و مسیز گوردون به امانوئل کالج رفتم. برای جمع‌آوری پول برای فرانسویان یک نوع گاردن پارتی بود. تماشا داشت. بالنسبه جمعیت بسیاری آمده بودند. آلمانیها در قفقاز پیشرفت می‌کنند و روسها مدعی‌اند که در حوالی مسکو بآلمانیها حمله کرده‌اند.

جمعه اول شهریور، ۲۸ اوت - صبح با فرنگیس بکتابفروشی هِفِرز رفتم. بقیه مجلدات شاهنامه ترجمه موهل را دیدم و عصر بباغ نباتات رفتم و کمی از مجلات عربی خواندم و شب در هتل بودم. هوا بسیار گرم بود. آلمانیها در قفقاز پیشرفت می‌کنند. از روزی که آقای تقی‌زاده خبر وفات خلخالی را دادند، بیشتر بیاد او هستم و بسیار از این خبر متأثرم.

شنبه ۲ شهریور، ۲۰ اوت - صبح با فرنگیس درس خواندیم. در باغ نباتات بودیم. کتاب خواندیم. عصر با او و یک کشیش و زنش بکافه دوروتی رفتیم. برادر کشیش که مدتی در هتل زندگی می‌کرد بعد آمد. تا ساعت شش آنجا بودیم. بعد با فرنگیس کمی راه رفتم. شب بمنزل آقای تقی‌زاده رفتیم. تا ساعت یازده آنجا بودیم. در باب شیرینی‌خوران صحبت شد و قرار شد هر روزی را که فرنگیس و من معین کنیم از اعضای سفارت و سه چهار نفر دیگر دعوت شود و شیرینی خوردن را رسماً اعلام کنند. ساعت دوازده و نیم خوابیدیم.

---

۱. Turner Macan، سرباز، زبانشناس و مترجم ایرلندی (۱۷۹۲-۱۸۳۶). در هند خدمت می‌کرد. در ۱۸۲۳ مأمور تنظیم آزمون زبان فارسی برای افسران بریتانیایی شد. اولین مصحح متن شاهنامه فردوسی است. تصحیح او در چهار جلد در ۱۸۲۹ در کلکته منتشر شد. قدیمی‌ترین نسخه هزار و یکشب را در ۱۸۳۰ میلادی کشف کرد.

یکشنبه ۳ شهریور، ۲۱ اوت - صبح روزنامه و کتاب خواندم. بعد با فرنگیس و مسیز گوردون بکلیسا رفتم. کشیش آلمانی بزبان انگلیسی وعظ کرد و بسیار خوب بود. تا بعد از ظهر در هتل بودیم و کتاب خواندیم. روسها مدعی‌اند که پیشرفت آلمانیها را در حوالی استالینگراد متوقف کرده‌اند و در قسمت شمالی میدان جنگ حمله می‌کنند.

دوشنبه ۴ شهریور، ۲۲ اوت - صبح کتاب خواندم و بعد از ظهر با فرنگیس بسینما رفتم. شب در هتل بودم و کتاب خواندم. آلمانیها در میدان جنگ استالینگراد پیشرفت می‌کنند.

سه‌شنبه ۵ شهریور، ۲۳ اوت - صبح کمی کتاب خواندم. بعد با فرنگیس بکتابفروشی هفرز رفتم و چندین جلد کتاب خریدم: ترجمه حافظ بآلمانی، تاریخ گزیده، لباب الألباب، تذکرة الاولیاء عطار، معاییر أشعار العجم. و دستور دادم که یک دوره مثنوی و ترجمه آن بانگلیسی را برایم بفرستند. بعد از ظهر کتاب خواندیم و بعد رفتم بکافه. عبدالله بن محمد که از اهل مالایا است نیز آمد. تا پنج ساعت و نیم بعد از ظهر آنجا بودم. شب در هتل بودیم و کتاب خواندیم.

چهارشنبه ۶ شهریور، ۲ سپتامبر - صبح زود برخاسته تنها بلندن رفتم. فرنگیس دیروز باکسفورد رفت که کتاب و لباس و هر چه را که در اکسفورد دارد با خود بکمبریج بیاورد و از کمبریج بلندن برویم. تا نیمساعت بعد از ظهر در اداره بودم. بعد برستوران کنزینگتون نزدیک سفارت رفتم. با سرهنگ عطارپور، و آقای آرام ناهار خوردم. بعد از ظهر بسفارت رفتم. آقای تقی‌زاده را دیدم. مدتی صحبت کردیم. صورت اسامی کسانی را که باید برای شیرینی‌خوران دعوت کنند باز مطالعه کردند و قرار شد که همه را خود آقای تقی‌زاده دعوت کنند و روز جمعه یازدهم سپتامبر را برای این کار معین کردند. شب بکمبریج آمدیم. بعد از شام بدیدن مستر فِریثزِر رفتم. در کی پی قهوه خوردم. بعد بهتل آمدم و تا یک ساعت بعد از نصف شب بدیدن اوراق کتابهایی که پریروز خریدم گذشت. آلمانیها در خاک روس پیشرفت می‌کنند و هنوز نتیجه جنگ مصر معلوم نیست.

پنجشنبه ۷ شهریور، ۳ سپتامبر ۱۹۴۲ - صبح بلندن رفتم. در اداره کار کردم. ناهار بسفارت رفتم. با خانم و آقای تقی‌زاده ناهار خوردم. عصر بسفارت رفتم. شب بکمبریج آمدم. فرنگیس از اکسفورد مراجعت کرده و تمام کتب و لباس و لوازم کارش را آورده بود. شب کمی کتاب خواندم. آلمانیها در روس پیش می‌روند.

جمعه ۸ شهریور، ۴ سپتامبر - صبح کمی کتاب خواندم. بعد با فرنگیس بکتابفروشی هفر رفتم. پول کتابهایی را که اول سپتامبر خریده بودم دادم. بعد از ظهر با فرنگیس بکافه ماتی‌یوز رفتم. دوستی هندی که معلم زبان هندوستانی است در مدرسه السنه شرقیه، آمد و تا ساعت پنج بعد از ظهر حرف می‌زدیم. شب در هتل بودم و در پشت کتابهایی که در کمبریج خریده بودم، اسم خود را نوشتم. یک ساعت بعد از نصف شب خوابیدم. در این روز کاغذی سفارشی از پدرم رسید و بسیار خوشوقتم کرد.

شنبه ۵ شهریور، ۵ سپتامبر - صبح کتاب خواندم. بعد از ظهر با فرنگیس بتأتر رفتم. بازی Arms and the Man را که برنارد شاو نوشته، دیدم. عصر با فرنگیس و مسیز گوردون چای خوردم. شب در هتل بودم.

یکشنبه ۱۰ شهریور ۱۳۲۱، ۶ سپتامبر ۱۹۴۲ - صبح کمی روزنامه خواندم. بعد با فرنگیس اول بمنزل مسیز بِنِت رفتم و کلید خانه آقای تقی‌زاده را گرفتم. کمی در آن جا بودیم. فرنگیس پیرهنی برید. بعد از ظهر با او بمنزل پروفسور مینورسکی رفتیم. تا ساعت هفت بعد از ظهر آن جا بودیم. آلمانیها مدعی‌اند که نوو روسیسک را در ساحل بحر اسود گرفته‌اند.

دوشنبه ۱۱ شهریور، ۷ سپتامبر - صبح روزنامه خواندم. بعد با فرنگیس بمنزل آقای تقی‌زاده رفتم. در آن جا او بخیاطی مشغول شد و من بکتاب خواندن مشغول شدم. ناهار در هتل خوردیم. بعد از ظهر هم بمنزل آقای تقی‌زاده رفتم. شب در هتل بودیم. کتاب خواندم. آلمانیها در قفقاز باز پیشرفت می‌کنند. انگلیسیها مدعی‌اند که در مصر رومل را عقب نشانده و او را مجبور کرده‌اند که بجای اول خودش برود. از ایران

خبری نیست. از مادر فرنگیس کاغذی رسیده بود. در وسط صفحه دویم آن یک قسمت را چیده بودند.

سه‌شنبه ۱۲ شهریور، ۸ سپتامبر - صبح با فرنگیس بمنزل آقای تقی‌زاده رفتیم و تا ظهر آنجا بودیم. فرنگیس خیاطی می‌کرد و من کتاب خواندم. بعد از ظهر هم در آن جا بودیم و شب در هتل. مستر چرچیل در مجلس انگلیس نطقی در باب جنگ و سفرش بروس و اوضاع جنگ در عالم کرده است. چندین شب است که در کمبریج اعلام خطر می‌کنند و صدای توپ طیاره‌زن بلند است. روز یکشنبه و دوشنبه و سه‌شنبه که بمنزل آقای تقی‌زاده رفتم نه خود ایشان و نه خانمشان هیچ یک در خانه نبودند. اجازه داده‌اند که فرنگیس بمنزل ایشان برود و از چرخ خیاطی استفاده کند.

چهارشنبه ۱۳ شهریور، ۹ سپتامبر - صبح تنها بلندن رفتم. تا نیمساعت بعد از ظهر در اداره کار کردم. ناهار با بایندر خوردم و بعد بسفارت رفتم. شب بکمبریج آمدم. در این روز کمی از کتاب تاریخ روس تألیف Rambaud¹ را خواندم. آلمانیها در استالینگراد پیشرفت می‌کنند.

پنجشنبه ۱۴ شهریور ۱۳۲۱، ۱۰ سپتامبر ۱۹۴۲ - صبح کتاب خواندم و روزنامه. بعد بکتابفروشی رفتم. یک دوره کتاب تاریخ ادبیات ایران² را دستور دادم برای سرهنگ عطاپور بفرستند. بعد از ظهر کتاب خواندم و عصر با فرنگیس بیرون رفتم. شب در هتل بودم. آلمانیها در نزدیک استالینگراد پیشرفت می‌کنند. چرچیل در باب هندوستان نطق کرده و گفته است که در هندوستان اوضاع موجب نگرانی نیست.

جمعه ۱۵ شهریور ۱۳۲۱، ۱۱ سپتامبر ۱۹۴۲ - در این روز مجلس شیرینی‌خوران

---

۱. مقصود Alfred Nicolas Rambaud است، مورخ فرانسوی (۱۸۴۲-۱۹۰۵). اثر اصلی او در تاریخ روسیه که از آکادمی فرانسه جایزه برد Histoire de la Russie depuis les origines jusqu'à nos jours است (انتشار در ۱۸۷۷).

۲. اثر چهار جلدی ادوارد براون، از انتشارات دانشگاه کمبریج.

دو مصمّم بودیم، از این روز ظاهراً نیز این تصمیم اعلام شد. این تغییر بزرگ که در زندگی من پیش آمده است فکر و وضع کار مرا نیز تغییر خواهد داد. باید بمدد فرنگیس که همعقیده و همفکر منست و ایران را مثل من دوست می‌دارد، برای مملکت بدبخت خود بیشتر کار کنم و شک ندارم که موفق خواهیم شد.

شنبه ۱۶ شهریور ۱۳۲۱، ۱۲ سپتامبر ۱۹۴۲ - صبح کتاب خواندم و روزنامه. بعد از ظهر با فرنگیس بسینما رفتم و شب بمنزل آقای تقی‌زاده. تا نصف شب آن جا بودیم. مسیز بِنِت و شوهرش و دو پسرش هم آمدند. آلمانیها در نواحی استالینگراد سخت می‌جنگند. روسها مدعی‌اند که در اغلب نقاط آنها را متوقف کرده‌اند.

یکشنبه ۱۷ شهریور، ۱۳ سپتامبر - صبح روزنامه و کتاب خواندم. بعد از ظهر با فرنگیس به گران‌چستر رفتم و شب در اطاق عمومی هتل نشستیم و کتاب خواندیم. آلمانیها در نواحی استالینگراد پیشرفت می‌کنند.

دوشنبه ۱۸ شهریور، ۱۴ سپتامبر - صبح کتاب خواندم و در باب کمبریج. بعد از ظهر هم کتاب و روزنامه خواندم. عصر با فرنگیس بکافه ماتی‌یوز رفتم. عبدالله بن محمد آمد. تا ساعت پنج و نیم بعد از ظهر آن جا بودیم. شب در هتل بودیم و کتاب تاریخ روس را خواندم. آلمانیها در استالینگراد پیشرفت می‌کنند و نیز مدعی‌اند که یک کاروان بزرگ کشتی را مورد حمله قرار داده‌اند.

سه‌شنبه ۱۹ شهریور، ۱۵ سپتامبر - صبح کتاب خواندم. بعد از ظهر با فرنگیس بسینما رفتم. فیلم *How Green Was My Valley*[1] را که در باب زندگی کارگران معدن ویلز است، دیدم. شب کتاب تاریخ روس خواندم. کار جنگ در استالینگراد روز بروز سخت‌تر می‌شوند. آلمانیها پیشرفت بسیار کمی کرده‌اند.

چهارشنبه ۲۰ شهریور، ۱۶ سپتامبر - صبح با فرنگیس بلندن رفتم. تا ظهر در اداره کار

---

۱. محصول ۱۹۴۱ آمریکا به کارگردانی جان فورد (۱۸۹۴-۱۹۷۳).

کردم. بعد با او در هاروودز ناهار خوردم. بعد از ظهر به کِنتون کورت[1] رفتم که ببینم آیا یک فلت[2] سه اطاقه دارند یا نه. یک فلت پنج اطاقه داشتند که بزرگ بود و دیگر فلتی خالی نبود. به فینچلی[3] رفتم و چندین جا را دیدم. هیچ جا فلت سه اطاقه وجود نداشت. خسته بکمبریج آمدیم. آلمانیها در استالینگراد پیشرفت می‌کنند و بموجب اخبار رادیوی پاریس در خود شهر استالینگراد جنگ است.

پنجشنبه ۲۱ شهریور، ۱۷ سپتامبر - صبح کتاب و روزنامه خواندم. بعد از ظهر با فرنگیس بسینما رفتم. شب در هتل بودم. آلمانیها در استالینگراد پیشرفت می‌کنند.

جمعه ۲۲ شهریور، ۱۸ سپتامبر - صبح کمی کتاب خواندم و مقداری از یادداشتهای راجع بکمبریج را. بعد از ظهر با فرنگیس بمنزل مسیز مایرز رفتم. تا شش و نیم بعد از ظهر آنجا بودیم و شب در هتل. تاریخ روس خواندم. آلمانیها در شهر استالینگراد جنگ می‌کنند.

شنبه ۲۳ شهریور ۱۳۲۱، ۱۹ سپتامبر ۱۹۴۲ - صبح کتاب خواندم و بعد از ظهر نیز کمی روزنامه و کتاب خواندم. با فرنگیس بودم و راه رفتیم. شب در هتل بودم. آلمانیها در استالینگراد پیشرفت می‌کنند.

یکشنبه ۲۴ شهریور، ۲۰ سپتامبر - صبح روزنامه و کتاب خواندم. بعد از ظهر با فرنگیس بعد از چای به گران‌چستر رفتم و شب در هتل بودیم. کتاب خواندیم. گلستان سعدی و قسمتی از تراژدی قیصر نوشته شکسپیر. آلمانیها در استالینگرادند ولی هنوز تمام شهر را نگرفته‌اند.

دوشنبه ۲۵ شهریور، ۲۱ سپتامبر - صبح با فرنگیس برای جستجوی فلت بلندن رفتم،

---

۱. Kenton Court، نام مجموعه‌ای آرپاتمانی در نزدیکی هاید پارک لندن.

۲. در مواردی فلات و در جاهای دیگر فلت. در همه جا بصورت فلت ضبط شد.

۳. Finchley، محله‌ای در شمال غربی مرکز لندن.

در های استریت و در ماربل آرچ. و بعد از ظهر در گلدرز گرین گردش کردم. اغلب هیچ نداشتند و یا فقط فلت‌های ۵ اطاقه. بسیار خسته شدیم و با ترن پنج و چهل و نه دقیقه بکمبریج آمدیم. عجب است که در لندن اینطور پر شده. آنهایی که نیمه خالی بود امروز از ایام صلح هم پرتر است.

سه‌شنبه ۲۶ شهریور، ۲۲ سپتامبر - صبح کتاب خواندم و کمی از مقاله کمبریج را نوشتم. بسیار خسته بودم. بعد از ظهر در هتل بودم و کتاب خواندم. عصر کمی راه رفتم. فرنگیس هم با من بود. ساعت هفت رفتیم به تأتر. بازی کینگ لیر[1] را دیدم. خوب بود. ساعت ده و نیم بهتل آمدیم. آلمانیها هنوز در کوچه‌های استالینگراد جنگ می‌کنند.

چهارشنبه ۲۷ شهریور، ۲۳ سپتامبر - صبح بلندن رفتم. در اداره بودم و بعد با آقای اسفندیاری و خانم اسفندیاری و بایندر در پیکادلی هتل ناهار خوردیم. بعد از ظهر بسفارت رفتم و شب بکمبریج آمدم.

پنجشنبه ۲۸ شهریور، ۲۴ سپتامبر - صبح با فرنگیس بلندن رفتیم. در منزل آقای صیقل ناهار خوردیم و فلتی را که باید بگیریم دیدیم. شب بکمبریج آمدیم. در این روز از خانم نمازی مادر فرنگیس تلگرافی در جواب تلگرافم رسید. بسیار گرم و خوب بود.

جمعه < ۲۹ شهریور >، ۱۵ سپتامبر - صبح کتاب خواندیم و بعد از ظهر نیز در هتل بودیم و کتاب خواندیم.

شنبه < ۳۰ شهریور >، ۱۶ سپتامبر - از صبح تا چهار ساعت و نیم بعد از ظهر ببستن کتابها مشغول بودم. قریب نصف آنها را با اتوموبیل سفارت بلندن فرستادم که در فلت آقای صیقل باشد تا وقتی بلندن برویم. روسها در استالینگراد خوب مقاومت می‌کنند و هنوز شهر بتصرف آلمانها در نیامده است.

یکشنبه < ۳۱ شهریور >، ۱۷ سپتامبر - صبح روزنامه خواندم و بعد کمی با فرنگیس بتصحیح ترجمه پرداختم. بعد از ظهر کتاب تاریخ روس خواندم و عصر تنها به گران‌چستر رفتم. دو ساعت راه رفتم. هنوز آلمانیها استالینگراد را بکلی تصرف نکرده‌اند. مقاومت روسها شدید است.

دوشنبه < ۱ مهر >، ۲۸ سپتامبر - صبح کتاب خواندم. بعد از ظهر با فرنگیس بسینما رفتم. فیلم پیت[1] را دیدیم. زندگی پیت رئیس الوزرای انگلیس را نشان می‌داد. بد نبود. فیلمی بود برای پروپاگاند. آلمانیها هنوز در استالینگراد می‌جنگند. می‌گویند یک میلیون آلمانی در استالینگراد است.

سه‌شنبه ۷ مهر ۱۳۲۱، ۲۹ سپتامبر - صبح کتاب خواندم و بعد از ظهر همی کمی کار کردم.

چهارشنبه ۸ مهر، ۳۰ سپتامبر - صبح بلندن رفتم. کمی در اداره کار کردم. بعد برای مذاکره در باب فلت به نورث اودلی استریت[2] رفتم. عاقبت قرار شد فلت را بگیرم. بعد از ظهر بسفارت رفتم و شب بکمبریج آمدم. هنوز استالینگراد بدست آلمانیها نیفتاده است اما کار دفاع کنندگان سخت است.

پنجشنبه ۹ مهر ۱۳۲۱، اول اکتبر ۱۹۴۲ - صبح با فرنگیس بلندن رفتم. کمی در سفارت بودم. اجاره‌نامه را امضا کردم. ناهار با بایندر و پروفسور مینورسکی در گلدن‌تون گریل خوردم. فرنگیس هم بود. بعد از ظهر با فرنگیس به هارودز رفتم و در باب موبل و سایر لوازم تحقیقاتی کردم. همه چیز گران شده است و بعضی چیزها اصلاً بدست نمی‌آید. آلمانیها باز در استالینگراد پیشرفت کرده‌اند.

جمعه ۱۰ مهر، ۲ اکتبر - صبح کتاب خواندم و بعد با فرنگیس کمی راه رفتم. عصر در باغ نباتات بودیم و شب در هتل کتاب خواندم. هنوز استالینگراد کاملاً بدست آلمانیها نیفتاده است.

---

۱. مقصود فیلمی است با عنوان *The Young Mr. Pitt*، محصول ۱۹۴۲ انگلستان.

۲. N Audley St، خیابانی در ضلع شمال شرقی هاید پارک.

شنبه ۱۱ مهر، ۳ اکتبر - صبح کتاب خواندم و بعد از ظهر و شب نیز در هتل بودم و کتاب تاریخ روس خواندم. استالینگراد هنوز بدست آلمانیها نیفتاده است.

یکشنبه ۱۲مهر، ۴ اکتبر - صبح کاغذی در باب اثاث خانه بآقای تقی‌زاده نوشتم. پیش از ظهر با فرنگیس به گران‌چستر رفتم و بعد از ظهر در هتل بودم. شب کتاب تاریخ روس خواندم. آلمانیها هنوز استالینگراد را نگرفته‌اند. استالین در جواب مخبر روزنامه‌ای گفته است که ایجاد یک میدان جنگ در اروپا که آلمانیها را بآن بکشد منتهای اهمیت را دارد.

دوشنبه ۱۳ مهر، ۵ اکتبر - صبح کتاب خواندم. بعد از ظهر بسینما رفتیم و شب در هتل بودم. آلمانیها کمی در استالینگراد پیشرفت کرده‌اند.

سه‌شنبه ۱۴ مهر، ۶ اکتبر - صبح و عصر کتاب خواندم. شب در هتل بودیم. آلمانیها در قفقاز پیشرفت می‌کنند ولی هنوز استالینگراد را بکلی نگرفته‌اند.

چهارشنبه ۱۵ مهر، ۷ اکتبر - صبح بلندن رفتم. در اداره کار کردم. ناهار با بایندر خوردم و بعد از ظهر بسفارت رفتم و آقای تقی‌زاده را دیدم. شب بکمبریج آمدم.

پنجشنبه ۱۶ مهر، ۸ اکتبر - صبح زود بیدار شدم و بجمع آوری بعضی از اسباب خانه مشغول شدم. چمدان‌های فرنگیس را بسته و با دو تاکسی بایستگاه رفتیم. یازده و نیم بلندن رسیدیم و از لیورپول استریت به فلت رفتم و چیزهایی را که با خود برده بودم، در آن جا گذاشتیم. ناهار در هارودز خوردیم و بعد سعات چهار و نیم بجمعیت آسیا رفتم. نطق پروفسور مینورسکی را در باب مطالعات و معلومات راجع به آسیا در روس بلشویکی را شنیدیم. آقای اسفندیاری هم بود. شب با ترن شش و سی و سه دقیقه با دکتر هنینگ[1] بکمبریج آمدیم. بسیار خسته بودم. آلمانیها اسرای انگلیسی را که در

---

۱. Walter Bruno Henning، محقق آلمانی متخصص در زبان‌های ایرانی میانه (۱۹۶۷-۱۹۰۸). در فاصله ۱۹۳۹ تا ۱۹۶۱، استاد مدرسه السنه شرقیه دانشگاه لندن بود.

دیپ گرفته‌اند، در زنجیر گذاشته‌اند باین سبب که می‌گویند انگلیسیها دستور داده‌اند دست اسرای آلمانی را ببندند.[1] انگلیسیها هم در تقابل می‌خواهند بهمان عدد از اسرای آلمانی را در زنجیر بگذارند. استالینگراد هنوز بکلی بدست آلمانیها نیفتاده است.

جمعه ۱۷ مهر، ۹ اکتبر - صبح کتاب خواندم و بعد از ظهر با فرنگیس کتاب خواندم. عصر میس گوردون و مادرش آمدند. همه با هم در کافه ماتی‌یو چای خوردیم. شب در هتل بودیم و کتاب خواندم.

شنبه ۱۸ مهر ۱۳۲۱، ۱۰ اکتبر ۱۹۴۲ - صبح کتاب و روزنامه خواندم. عصر باقی کتابهایم را توسط اتوبوس سفارت بلندن فرستادم. شب با فرنگیس بمنزل آقای تقی‌زاده رفتم. تا ساعت یازده آن جا بودیم.

یکشنبه ۱۹ مهر، ۱۱ اکتبر - صبح کتاب خواندم. عصر با فرنگیس بمنزل دکتر هنینگ رفتم. تا ساعت شش و نیم آن جا بودیم. خانه کوچک پاکیزه‌ای است. شب در هتل بودیم و دکتر مارشال صفحه‌های گرامافون گذاشت. تا ساعت یازده و نیم گوش می‌دادیم. هنوز استالینگراد بدست آلمانیها نیفتاده است.

دوشنبه ۲۰ مهر، ۱۲ اکتبر - صبح با فرنگیس بلندن رفتم. دربان فلت تلفون کرده بود که کلید فلت را برایش بفرستم چون می‌خواهند بتعمیر آن بپردازند. با ترن سی و سی و نه دقیقه بلندن رفتم. کلید را بدربان دادیم و بعد در باب اثاث و لوازم خانه با آقای صیقل بوسیله تلفون مذاکره کردم. دیدم موافق انصاف حرف نمی‌زند و نتوانستم او را متقاعد کنم از اثاث و لوازم کهنه < که > باو امانت داده شده پس بگیرم. بعد با فرنگیس بتمام هتلهای کرمِل رود و کنسینگتون که می‌دانستم رفتیم و قریب بیست جا را دیدم. اطاقی پیدا نشد. عاقبت دو اطاق در هتل مونتانا بدست آمد و آن را برای روز چهارشنبه گرفتیم. ناهار در مغازه دری اند تومز[2] خوردیم و خسته و اوقات تلخ ـ

---

۱. بسته‌اند.

۲. Derry & Toms، فروشگاهی زنجیره‌ای در لندن. در فاصله ۱۸۶۰ تا ۱۹۷۳ فعال بود.

از بی انصافی مردم ـ با ترن چهار و سه ربع بکمبریج آمدیم. من تا ساعت ۱۱ و نیم در اطاق نشسته بودم و با دکتر مارشال حرف می‌زدم.

سه‌شنبه ۲۱ مهر، ۱۳ اکتبر - صبح کمی روزنامه خواندم. بعد بکتابفروشی هفرز رفتم. با مستر شارپ که در قسمت کتب خطی و کتب شرقی کار می‌کند، خداحافظی کردم. مقاله‌ای را که پروفسور برون در مجله جنگ و صلح در باب نفت ایران و دخالت دولت انگیس در آن نوشته، بمن داد. ناهار در هتل خوردم و شب با بعضی دوستان هم مهمانخانه خداحافظی کردم. بسیار خسته بودم. دیر خوابیدم و زود بیدار شدم. رفتن از کمبریج پس از دو سال اقامت غم آور است.

چهارشنبه ۲۲ مهر ۱۳۲۱، ۱۴ اکتبر ۱۹۴۲ - صبح زود بیدار شدم. چمدانها را بهمراهی فرنگیس بسته بسیار خسته بودم. ساعت هشت تاکسی حاضر بود. با فرانسیس پیشخدمت هتل که مردی خوش خدمت و خوبیست و با سایر مستخدمین خداحافظی کردم و با ترن هشت و بیست دقیقه با فرنگیس بلندن آمدم. او را با چمدانها بهتل مونتانا فرستادم و خود باداره رفتم. تا نیم ساعت بعد از ظهر در اداره بودم. بعد بهتل مونتانا آمدم. ناهار خوردم و از آن جا بهارودز و از هارودز بسفارت رفتم. قریب نیم ساعت با آقای تقی‌زاده بودم. راجع بنکته‌هایی که وزارت دارایی در باب نفت می‌خواهند با شرکت مذاکره کنند و جوابهایی که شرکت نفت در این مدت بدولت داده، نظرهای خود را گفتند. شب در هتل مونتانا با فرنگیس شام خوردم و با جوانی عراقی بنام خالدی عضو سفارت عراق صحبت کردم. بعد از شام با فرنگیس بسینمای اخبار رفتم و زودتر خوابیدم. بعد از دو سال اقامت در کمبریج، دوباره بلندن آمده‌ام. در این دو سال در کمبریج بیشتر بخواندن کتابهای ادبی و تاریخی مشغول بودم و کمی آلمانی یاد گرفتم. در این شهر کوچک که یکی از بزرگترین مراکز علم دنیاست، ایام و شبهای خوش داشتم. فرنگیس را در آن جا دیدم. باید زندگی تحصیلی را که فقط بخواندن صرف می‌شد، کنار بگذارم و بنوشتن شروع کنم.

پنجشنبه ۲۳ مهر ۱۳۲۱، ۱۵ اکتبر ۱۹۴۲ - صبح زود بیدار شدم. شب خوب نتوانستم بخوابم. چاشت خوردم. چندان خوب نبود. با فرنگیس بمغازه دری اند تومز رفتم. مسیز گوردون همسفره روایال هتل و دخترش آمدند. تا ظهر با هم بودیم. بعد به فلت رفتم. دیدم از تمام لوازم و اثاث خانه‌ای که آقای زرین‌کفش و هشت نفر دیگر زندگی می‌کردند و اکنون بامانت به آقای صیقل داده شده، یک تخت خواب شکسته یک نفره و یک تخت خواب دو نفره و یک میز کثیف کوچک که آقای زرین‌کفش برای دختر هشت ساله‌اش خریده بود، برای من فرستاده‌اند. بسیار از این بی‌انصافی و بی‌ادبی متأثر شدم. از عجایب امور عالم است که یکی بی آنکه حقی داشته باشد، اینطور بخواهد بعجز و الحاح و اظهار بندگی از طرفی و جسارت و بی‌شرمی از طرف دیگر حق دیگران را پایمال کند. بعد از ظهر با فرنگیس به سلفریج[1] و به جان لوییس[2] رفتم. شب بسیار خسته بهتل آمدیم. شام خوردیم و تا ساعت نه و نیم در اطاق پذیرایی مهمانخانه بودیم. شب کمی روزنامه خواندم. درست نتوانستم بخوابم. در این روز دیدم که در و دیوار فلت بقدری ناپاک است که زندگی در آن لذتی ندارد. نزد مؤجر آن رفتم و قرار شد پانزده لیره بدهم که آن را پاکیزه کنند. در این ایام جنگ، نبودن جا در لندن انسان را محتاج کرده و مجبور می‌سازد که بهر قباحتی و یا اجحافی تن بدهد.

جمعه ۲۴ مهر، ۱۶ اکتبر - صبح باداره رفتم و ناهار با فرنگیس در هتل مونتانا خوردم. عصر به فلت رفتم. آقای اسفندیاری آمد. چیزهایی را که صیقل فرستاده بود بایشان نشان دادم. شب در هتل بودم و کتاب خواندم.

شنبه ۲۵ مهر، ۱۷ اکتبر - صبح کمی کار کردم و بعد با فرنگیس بمغازه می‌پل[3] و هیل[4] در توتنهم کورت[5] رود رفتم. بعضی چیزها از قبیل تخت خواب و غیر آن را

---

۱. Selfridges، نام فروشگاهی زنجیره‌ای در لندن.

۲. John Lewis & Partners، نام فروشگاه لوازم خانگی در لندن.

۳. Maple & Co، مغازه مبلمان و دست دوم فروشی در انگلستان که از ۱۸۴۱ تا ۱۹۹۷ فعال بود.

۴. Heal's.

۵. توتن کورت. مقصود Tuttenham Court Rd است، نام خیابانی در لندن.

دیدیم. همه چیز بسیار گران شده است. بعد از ظهر کمی کار کردیم. بعد بباغ کنزینگتون رفتیم. آقا و خانم تقی‌زاده را دیدیم. شب در هتل بودیم.

یکشنبه ۲۶ مهر، ۱۸ اکتبر - صبح کمی روزنامه خواندم. بعد از ظهر با فرنگیس بماربل آرچ رفتیم در پای معرکه‌ها و نطق‌ها و شب در هتل بودیم.

دوشنبه ۲۷ مهر، ۱۹ اکتبر - صبح با فرنگیس بمغازه مارکرز رفتم. میز و صندلی و مبل را دیدیم. قریب چهار صد و پنجاه لیره قیمت لوازم زندگی می‌شود. بعد به فلت رفتیم. برای رنگ و روغن زدن آن آمده بودند. عصر بترجمه مشغول بودیم و شب در هتل ماندیم. آلمانیها در استالینگراد پیشرفت کرده‌اند. در روزنامه ایونینگ نی‌یوز خواندم که کابینه ایران استعفا داده است.

سه‌شنبه ۲۸ مهر، ۲۰ اکتبر - صبح کمی کار کردم. با فرنگیس به فلت رفتم. عصر مشغول کار بودند. بعد بمغازه وایتلی و می‌پل رفتم. کارد و چنگال از می‌پل خریدیم و این اولین چیزی بود که برای فلت خریداری کردم. به هارودز رفتیم و قهوه خوردیم و لیوان آب خوری هم خریدیم. آلمانیها در استالینگراد پیشرفت کرده‌اند.

چهارشنبه ۲۹ مهر، ۲۱ اکتبر - صبح باداره رفتم. تا نیمساعت بعد از ظهر آن جا بودم. ناهار در هتل مونتانا با فرنگیس خوردیم. بعد از ظهر بیرون رفتیم. یک دست ظرف غذاخوری و یک دست چای‌خوری و یک قفسه کتاب خریدیم. شب در هتل بودیم. ژنرال اشمَت رئیس الوزرای افریقای جنوبی در این روز در مقابل اعضای مجلس لردها و مجلس نمایندگان نطق کرد در رادیو. از ساعت ۹ تا ساعت ۱۰ نطقش طول کشید.

پنجشنبه ۳۰ مهر ۱۳۲۱، ۲۲ اکتبر ۱۹۴۲ - صبح کار کردم. کتاب خواندیم. به فلت رفتم. بعد از ظهر بسفارت رفتم. آقای تقی‌زاده را دیدم. شب با فرنگیس بسینمای اخبار رفتم. شب کمی کار کردم. هنوز آلمانیها استالینگراد را نگرفته‌اند.

جمعه اول آبان، ۲۳ اکتبر ۱۹۴۲ - صبح کار کردم. بعد با فرنگیس به هارودز رفتم و

عصر ساعت پنج بمنزل آقای نوری اسفندیاری. صیقل هم آمد. تا ساعت ۷ بعد از ظهر بمذاکرات گذشت. بسیار خسته کننده هم گذشت و روحم را افسرده کرد. شب نتوانستم بخوابم. از سه ساعت و نیم بعد از نصف شب بیدار بودم.

شنبه ۲ آبان، ۲۴ اکتبر - حالت روحیم چندان خوب نبود. از بی‌شرمی و بی‌انصافی مردم بجان آمده‌ام. صبح با فرنگیس بودم. بعد از ظهر کمی کار کردم. بعد بسینما رفتیم. شرح حال گورکی را دیدیم که چندان خوب نبود. شب در هتل بودم. انگلیسیها در مصر و در ناحیه العالمین بقشون آلمان حمله کرده‌اند.

یکشنبه ۳ آبان، ۲۵ اکتبر - صبح کتاب خواندم. عصر با فرنگیس به ماربل آرچ رفتم. هوا بارانی بود. چای خوردیم و برگشتیم.

دوشنبه ۴ آبان، ۲۶ اکتبر - صبح باداره رفتم. کمی کار کردم. آقای اسفندیاری هم بود. نزدیک ظهر باران بسیار سخت می‌آمد و حالم چندان خوب نبود. لرز کردم. ناهار در هتل خوردم و سه و نیم بعد از ظهر با فرنگیس بسفارت رفتم. بمناسبت تولد شاه جشن بود. تا ساعت هفت در سفارت بودم. جمعیّت کثیری از اعیان و وزرا و سفرا آمده بودند. با سر استیفن گرلی رئیس کتابخانه وزارت خارجه در باب شعر خیام صحبت بمیان آمد و نیز با او راجع بمقاله‌ای که باید در خصوص تشکیلات وزارت امور خارجه انگلیس بنویسم مذاکره کردم و وعده راهنمایی داد. در میان باران شدید با فرنگیس بهتل آمدم. مطابق اطلاعاتی که در روزنامه‌ها مندرج است، در مصر لشگر انگلیس پیشرفت کرده است.

سه‌شنبه ۵ آبان، ۲۷ اکتبر - صحب به فلت رفتم. بعضی از لباسها را بآن جا بردم. بعد از ظهر بترجمه مشغول بودم. عصر با فرنگیس در هاید پارک راه رفتم و شب در هتل کار می‌کردم.

چهارشنبه ۶ آبان، ۲۸ اکتبر - صبح باداره رفتم. تا نیمساعت بعد از ظهر آن جا بودم.

در هتل با فرنگیس ناهار خوردم. بعد از ظهر بسینما رفتیم ـ سینمای اخبار. و عصر تنها بسفارت رفتم. پولی رسیده بود. حقوق شش ماه < را > گرفتم و کمی با عطارپور و بایندر حرف زدم. ساعت شش و نیم با فرنگیس بمنزل عفت خانم رفتم. شوهرش هم بعد آمد. بدیعه خانم مهتدی و دوستش که یک ملاح انگلیسی بود، نیز آمدند. خورش قرمه سبزی خوردیم. تا ساعت ده نشستیم و بعد بخانه آمدیم. از مصر اخباری که روزنامه‌ها می‌نویسند مشعر بر پیشرفت لشگر انگلیس است و لیکن هنوز خبر قطعی پیشرفت نرسیده است.

پنجشنبه ۷ آبان،[1] ۲۹ اکتبر - از صبح تا ده بعد از ظهر بترجمه جوابهایی که شرکت بسئوالات دولت در باب حق ماهیانه و ترفیع ایرانیان داده مشغول بودم و از مهمانخانه هیچ بیرون نرفتم.

جمعه ۸ آبان، ۳۰ اکتبر - صبح باداره رفتم. یکساعت و نیم بعد از ظهر بهتل آمدم. با فرنگیس ناهار خوردم. عصر بسینما رفتیم و بعد ساعت شش بعد از ظهر با هم به اِجوِر[2] آخرین ایستگاه یکی از راه آهنهای زیرزمینی لندن رفتیم. مستر رال‌ول‌ستن در آن جا منتظر ما بود. با او بخانه‌اش رفتم. قریب یک ربع راه بود. تا ساعت ده آن جا بودیم. زن ملیح خوبی دارد. در باب ایران و روس صحبت کردیم. بد نگذشت. با ترن ده و نیم برگشتیم.

شنبه ۹ آبان، ۳۱ اکتبر ۱۹۴۲ - صبح کمی کار کردم. بعد از ظهر با فرنگیس برستوران نورماندی رفتیم. مهمان آقای اسفندیاری بودیم. خانم اسفندیاری و یک چک بنام مستر پک هم بود. خوب فارسی حرف می‌زد و از ادبیات ایران و علی الخصوص عرفان اطلاع داشت و وضع حرف زدنش طبیعی و خوب بود. سه سال و نیم در ایران بوده است. دیدن او و فکرم را قوت داد که اگر فرنگیها بخواهند می‌توانند فارسی را خوب یاد بگیرند. بعد از ناهار کمی نشستیم. بعد مستر پک رفت و ما و

خانم و آقای اسفندیاری کمی در پارک گردش کردیم و بمرغها نان دادیم. از آن جا بخانه آقای اسفندیاری رفتیم. چای خوردیم و تا ساعت هفت بعد از ظهر آن جا بودیم.

یکشنبه ۱۰ آبان، اول نوامبر ۱۹۴۲ - صبح کمی ترجمه کردم. بعد برای دیدن یکی دو فلت با فرنگیس بیرون رفتیم. جز فلتهای ۵ اطاقه چیزی نیست. شب در هتل بودیم و کار کردیم. هنوز نتیجه قطعی جنگ مصر معلوم نیست.

دوشنبه ۱۱ آبان، ۲ نوامبر - صبح بهارودز رفتیم و کمی خرید کردیم. بعد از ظهر باداره رفتم. تا ساعت پنج آن جا بودم.

سه‌شنبه ۱۲ آبان، ۳ نوامبر - از صبح تا غروب در اداره بودم و کار کردم. ساعت شش بمنزل آقای اسفندیاری رفتم. تا ساعت هفت و نیم بعد از ظهر آن جا بودم. شب در هتل بودم. کتاب خواندم.

چهارشنبه ۱۳ آبان، ۴ نوامبر - صبح باداره رفتم و ناهار در هتل خوردم. بعد از ظهر بسفارت رفتم. تا ساعت پنج بعد از ظهر آنجا بودم. شب با فرنگیس بسینمای اخبار رفتیم. ساعت ده برگشتیم. انگلیسیها در میدان جنگ مصر و آلمانیها در قفقاز پیش می‌روند.

پنجشنبه ۱۴ آبان، ۵ نوامبر - صبح بسفارت رفتم. آقای اسفندیاری را در آنجا دیدم. در باب اثاث نمایندگی که باید مقداری از آن ‹ را › پس گرفته مذاکره کردم. عصر اول به فلت و بعد با فرنگیس بیپکادلی رفتم و شب هم در هتل بودم. کتاب شرح حال ناپلئون را خواندم. انگلیسیها در مصر پیشرفت کرده‌اند.

جمعه ۱۵ آبان، ۶ نوامبر - صبح باداره رفتم. صورت اثاثی را که می‌خواستم برای صیقل فرستادم. ناهار با فرنگیس در هتل خوردم. بعد از ظهر برای دیدن چند فلت بماربل آرچ رفتم. هیچ جا نبود. یکسر باداره‌ای که فلت کن‌تون کورت را اجاره می‌دهد ‹ رفتم › و اجاره‌نامه جدید را امضا کردم. شب در هتل بودم و در باب جنگ

و اوضاع عالم با جمعی صحبت می‌کردیم. هر یکی از حضار از مملکتی بود و در میان ایشان هیچ انگلیسی نبود. هنوز انگلیسیها در مصر پیشرفت می‌کنند.

شنبه ۱۶ آبان، ۷ نوامبر – صبح کمی کتاب خواندم. بعد با فرنگیس به هارودز رفتم و از آن جا بهتل نورماندی. آقای اسفندیاری و خانم اسفندیاری و مسیو پک چکسلواکی هم آمدند. با هم ناهار خوردیم. تا ساعت چهار بعد از ظهر در آن جا بودم. بعد بهتل آمدیم و کتاب خواندم و تا ساعت یازده و نیم بیدار بودم. انگلیسیها در مصر پیشرفت می‌کنند و تا امروز ۲۰ هزار اسیر گرفته‌اند.

یکشنبه ۱۷ آبان، ۸ نوامبر ۱۹۴۲ – صبح روزنامه خواندم و عصر به کی‌یو[1] رفتم. هوا خوب بود و برگهای زرد هم بر روی زمین و بر شاخه‌ها بود. تماشا داشت. شب در هتل بودم. سربازان امریکایی بافریقای شمالی که تحت حمایت و اداره فرانسویهاست حمله کرده و لشگر پیاده کرده‌اند. ژنرال ژیرو[2] که از دست آلمانیها فرار کرده در الجزایر است و خود را فرمانده قشون فرانسه می‌خواند.

دوشنبه ۱۸ آبان، ۹ نوامبر ۱۹۴۲ – صبح باداره رفتم و بعد از ظهر بسفارت. شب در هتل بودیم و کتاب شرح حال ناپلئون را خواندم. امریکاییها در شمال افریقای فرانسه و انگلیسیها در مصر پیشرفت می‌کنند.

سه‌شنبه < ۱۹ آبان >، ۱۰ نوامبر – صبح در هتل بودم و کتاب خواندیم.[3] بعد از ظهر بسفارت رفتم و شب در هتل بودم.

چهارشنبه ۲۰ آبان، ۱۱ نوامبر – صبح با فرنگیس بمغازه هارودز رفتم. موبلی خریدیم و آنچه را اول خریداری نمودیم ــ از مارکرز ــ پس دادیم. بعد باداره رفتم و بعد از ظهر

---

۱. Kew، باغ گیاهشناسی سلطنتی در غرب لندن.
۲. Henri Honoré Giraud، فرمانده قوای فرانسه آزاد در جنگ جهانی دوم (۱۹۴۹-۱۸۷۹).
۳. خط خورده: صبح با فرنگیس دوباره به هارودز برای خرید رفتیم. یک دست موبل خریدیم و ناچار آنچه را اول خریده بودیم پس دادیم.

بسفارت. شب در هتل بودم. آلمانیها تمام فرانسه را تصرف کرده‌اند و قشون انگلیس در مصر پیشرفت می‌نماید.

پنجشنبه ۲۱ آبان، ۱۲ نوامبر - صبح کمی کار کردم و بعد از ظهر با فرنگیس بدیدن فیلم بَمبی[1] رفتم. شب در هتل بودیم. آلمانیها در تونس با هواپیما قشون وارد کرده‌اند.

جمعه ۲۲ آبان، ۱۳ نوامبر ۱۹۴۲ - از صبح تا یک ساعت بعد از ظهر در هتل بودم و ترجمه می‌کردم. بعد از ظهر با فرنگیس بمغازه هارودز و بعد تنها بسفارت رفتم. شب در هتل بودم و کتاب خواندم. هنوز در تونس جنگ میان آلمانیها و امریکاییها و انگلیسیها در نگرفته است. کشتیهای فرانسوی در بندر تولون است ولی دارلان[2] از ایشان خواسته که بکشتیهای انگلیس و امریکا ملحق شوند.

شنبه ۲۳ آبان، ۱۴ نوامبر - صبح کمی کار کردم. بعد بهارودز رفتم و از آنجا برستوران نورماندی. عفت خانم و شوهرش آمدند. ناهار خوردیم. بعد بکلوب دانمارک رفتیم. چای خوردیم و شب بهتل آمدیم. تا ساعت یازده با بارون روم[3] روسی و خالدی عضو سفارت عراق و دیگران صحبت کردیم. انگلیسیها در افریقا پیشرفت می‌کنند.

یکشنبه ۲۴ آبان، ۱۵ نوامبر - صبح روزنامه خواندم. عصر با فرنگیس بسفارت رفتم. تا ساعت هفت بعد از ظهر با آقای تقی‌زاده و خانم تقی‌زاده بودیم. شب در هتل بودم و کتاب خواندم.

دوشنبه ۲۵ آبان، ۱۶ نوامبر - صبح کتاب خواندم. بعد با فرنگیس بهارودز رفتم. ناهار با فرنگیس و بایندر و مسیز داود صاحبخانه بایندر در نورماندی[4] خوردیم. عصر

---

۱. Bambi، انیمیشن محصول امریکا (۱۹۴۲)

۲. Jean Louis Xavier François Darlan، آدمیرال فرانسوی (۱۹۴۲-۱۸۸۱).

۳. در ادامه همین نام بصورت رون ضبط شده است.

۴. + ناهار

بسفارت رفتم و شب در هتل بودم. آدمیرال دارلان رییس کل عساکر فرانسه در شمال افریقا شده است و هواخواهان دوگل در انگلیس با او مخالفند.

سه‌شنبه ۲۶ آبان، ۱۷ نوامبر - صبح کتاب خواندم. بعد بهارودز رفتیم (با فرنگیس) و شب در خانه بودم.

چهارشنبه ۲۷ آبان، ۱۸ نوامبر - صبح باداره رفتم و ناهار در کنسینگتون رستوران خوردم. عصر در سفارت بودم. آقای تقی‌زاده نبود. کسالت داشت. شب در هتل بودم. با آقای خالدی عضو سفارت عراق و بارون روم روسی در باب روس و ایران و ترک مذاکره کردم. این هفته تمام تونس بدست انگلیسیها و امریکاییها نیفتاده است. دارلان در این ایام رییس قسمت شمال افریقاست و ژنرال ژیرو بنام او فرمانده کل قوا شده است.

پنجشنبه ۲۸ آبان، ۱۹ نوامبر - صبح روزنامه خواندم. در های استریت آقای مقدم وزیر < مختار > سابق ایران را دیدم که آمده است بلندن برای رفتن به بریستول و عزیمت بایران. ناهار با آقای آرام خوردم و شب در هتل بودم و کتاب خواندم. هنوز اخبار راجع بتونس منتشر نشده است. ظاهراً آلمانیها دفاع می‌کنند.

جمعه ۲۹ آبان، ۲۰ نوامبر - صبح کتاب خواندم و عصر با فرنگیس بدیدن سر حسّان سهروردی[۱] رفتم. شب کتاب خواندم.

شنبه ۳۰ آبان، ۲۱ نوامبر - صبح کتاب خواندم و ناهار با آقای اسفندیاری و خانم اسفندیاری و فرنگیس مهمان مستر پخ چک بودیم در رستوران نرماندی. چای هم با او خوردیم. شب در هتل بودیم. در این روز رادیو را در فلت کار گذاشتند.

---

۱. حسّان سهروردی مشهور به قیصر هند وزیر خارجه دولت هند بریتانیا. در ۱۹۳۲ مدال افتخار سن جان را دریافت کرد. از اقداماتش تأسیس مسجد شرق لندن بود. خاندان سهروردی ایرانی الاصل و از اشراف مسلمان هندند. تبار خود را به گروهی از اعراب مهاجم به ایران که در سهرورد از توابع زنجان ساکن شدند، می‌رساندند. مؤسس طریقت سهروردیه در ایران ابوالنجیب سهروردی (م. ۵۶۳ق/۱۱۶۸م) از این خاندان بود.

یکشنبه اول آذر، ۲۲ نوامبر - صبح ساعت ده بمنزل صیقل رفتم. کمی از اثاث خانه‌ای را که باید تحویل داد، بردم. بعد با فرنگیس بهتل آمدم. اتومبیل آقای عطاپور منتظر بود. با او و آقای آرام بمنزل عفت خانم و شوهرش رفتم. همه با هم ببیرون شهر رفتیم و در رستوران My Chef ناهار خوردیم. عصر در هتل بودیم.

دوشنبه ۲۳ نوامبر، ۲ آذر - صبح کتاب خواندم. با فرنگیس بهارودز رفتیم. شب در هتل بودم. با بارون و خالدی حرف زدیم.

سه‌شنبه ۲۴ نوامبر، ۳ آذر - صبح با فرنگیس بهارودز رفتم و بعد از ظهر در خانه بودم. ترجمه می‌کردم. شب در هتل بودیم. با بارون و خالدی در باب امور سیاسی حرف می‌زدیم.

چهارشنبه ۲۵ نوامبر، ۴ آذر - صبح باداره رفتم و عصر به فلت. شب در هتل بودم.

پنجشنبه ۲۶ نوامبر، ۵ آذر - صبح به فلت رفتم و تمام روز را در آنجا بودم. چراغهای الکتریک را کار گذاشته‌اند. فرنگیس جزیی سرماخوردگی داشت، بیرون نیامد.

جمعه ۲۷ نوامبر، ۶ آذر - صبح با فرنگیس به فلت رفتم. با هم در هتل ناهار خوردیم و عصر بمنزل سر حسّان سهروردی رفتیم. آقای نیامیر، عطاپور، آقای اسفندیاری، آقای حمزاوی و زنش، آقای آرام و دو نفر هندی و مسیز لعل[۱] زن معاون نماینده عالی هندوستان بودند. تا ساعت شش و نیم آن جا بودیم. شب تا ساعت ۱۱ با بارون و آقای خالدی در هتل حرف می‌زدیم. در این روز خبر رسید که آلمانیها بندر تولون را تصرف کرده‌اند و بحریه فرانسوی که در آنجا بود بدست فرانسویان غرق شد.

شنبه ۷ آذر ۱۳۲۱، ۲۸ نوامبر ۱۹۴۱ - صبح بسفارت رفتم و بعد از ظهر با فرنگیس بسینما. فیلم *A Yank at Eaton*[۲] را دیدیم. شب در هتل بودم و با بارون روم و خالدی در باب ایران و سیاست صحبت می‌کردیم.

---

۱. لال
۲. کمدی درام سینمایی محصول آمریکا (۱۹۴۲).

یکشنبه ۸ آذر، ۲۹ نوامبر - صبح در مهمانخانه بودم و عصر با فرنگیس به ماربل آرچ رفتیم. پای معرکه‌ها ایستادیم. هنوز در باب جنگ تونس خبر قطعی نرسیده است.

دوشنبه ۹ آذر، ۳۰ نوامبر - صبح باداره رفتم و عصر بمنزل آقای اسفندیاری. مستر همفریس عضو وزارت خارجه انگلیس که مدتی در ایران دفتردار سفارت بوده است، نیز در آن جا بود. مستر پیخْ اهل چکسلواکی هم آمد. شب در هتل بودم و کتاب اقتصادی خواندم.

سه‌شنبه ۱۰ آذر، اول دسامبر - صبح به فلت رفتیم و بعد از ظهر بسفارت. شب در هتل بودم و کتاب خواندم و کمی با بارون روم و خالدی صحبت کردیم. در باب تونس هنوز خبر قطعی نرسیده است.

چهارشنبه ۱۱ آذر، ۲ دسامبر - صبح باداره رفتم و بعد از ظهر بمغازه‌ها برای خرید لوازم خانه. شب در هتل بودم. هنوز از تونس خبر پیشرفت قطعی نرسیده است.

پنجشنبه ۱۲ آذر، ۳ دسامبر - صبح با فرنگیس بحراج رفتم و بعد از ظهر هم در حراج بودم. قفسه کتاب و فنجان خریدیم. اولین دفعه‌ای بود که در انگلیس حراج را دیدم. بسیار تماشایی بود دیدن مردم و جهودهایی که با هم عبری حرف می‌زدند. شب در هتل بودم . با بارون رون و خالدی صحبت کردم.

جمعه ۴ دسامبر، ۱۳ آذر - صبح به بوند استریت رفتم. با فرنگیس و چندین مغازه را دیدم. بعد بهارودز رفتیم و چند چیز لازم خریدیم. عصر در فلت بودیم. کمی کار کردم. شب در مهمانخانه بودیم و مذاکره می‌کردیم. در تونس آلمانیها پیشرفت کرده‌اند.

شنبه ۱۴ آذر، ۵ دسامبر - صبح کار کردم و با فرنگیس به فلت رفتم. اطاق کتابخانه را درست کردیم. شب در هتل بودم.

یکشنبه ۱۵ آذر، ۶ دسامبر - صبح به فلت رفتم. کمی ترجمه کردم. بعد از ظهر هم در فلت بودیم. کمی کار کردیم. اطاق خواب را تا اندازه‌ای مرتب کردیم. شب در هتل بودم. با بارون رون و خالدی حرف زدیم. در تونس کار متحدین چندان خوب نیست.

دوشنبه ۱۶ آذر، ۷ دسامبر - صبح به هارودز و از آنجا بسفارت رفتم. آقای تقی‌زاده را دیدم. در باب دعوت عروسی مذاکره کردم. بعد از ظهر با فرنگیس به فلت رفتم. در آن جا چای خوردیم. کمی کار کردم. شب در هتل بودم. با بارون رون و خالدی صحبت کردم. آقای قدس را که از ایران آمده بود، دیدم.

سه‌شنبه ۱۷ آذر، ۸ دسامبر - صبح در هتل بودم. کار کردم. نزدیک ظهر بسفارت رفتم. ناهار مهمان عطاپور بودم در کلوب نظامی معروف In and Out در پیکادلی. ناهار خوردیم. تا ساعت سه بعد از ظهر آن جا بودیم. بعداً با او به Davies & Son[1] رفتم که لباسی دستور بدهیم. تا شب در هتل بودم. با خالی و بارون و مسیز روزن صحبت کردیم. در تونس برای متحدین پیشرفتی نیست.

چهارشنبه ۱۸ آذر، ۹ دسامبر - صبح باداره رفتم. بعد از ظهر در هتل بودم. بعد نزد خیاط رفتم و با فرنگیس بسینمای اخبار. شب در هتل بودیم و حرف می‌زدیم.

پنجشنبه ۱۹ آذر، ۱۰ دسامبر - صبح و عصر با فرنگیس در فلت بودیم. کار کردیم. شب در هتل بودیم و مذاکره می‌کردیم.

جمعه ۲۰ آذر، ۱۱ دسامبر - صبح و عصر در فلت با فرنگیس بنوشتن مشغول بودیم و شب در هتل با بارون و مسیز روزن و خالدی در باب مسائل سیاسی صحبت می‌کردیم. در روزنامه ایونینگ استاندارد خواندم که بواسطه شورش مردم در تهران لشگر انگلیس وارد تهران شده، از آن عبور کرده و در خارج تهران اردو زده‌اند.

شنبه ۲۱ آذر، ۱۲ دسامبر - صحب با فرنگیس به فلت رفتم. کمی چیز نوشتم. فرنگیس زودتر رفت. تنها ناهار خوردم. بعد از ظهر با او در باغ سنت جیمز راه رفتم و پس از دیدن فیلم اخبار بهتل آمدیم. شب در هتل با خالدی و مسیز روزن و بعد با بارون رون در باب زمان بحث کردیم. در روزنامه تایمز راجع بشورش مردم در تهران

Davies & the Sons .1

شرح مختصری بود. نوشته بودند که مخالفین قوام السلطنه موجب آن بودند و پس از ورود یک بتالیون[1] انگلیسی نظم و ترتیب برقرار شد.

یکشنبه ۲۲ آذر ۱۳۲۱، ۱۳ دسامبر ۱۹۴۱ - صبح با فرنگیس به فلت رفتم. کمی ترجمه کردیم. ناهار در هتل خوردیم و بعد از ظهر باز به فلت رفتیم و تا شش و ربع آنجا بودیم. شب در هتل با بارون رون و خالدی و مسیز روزن حرف می‌زدیم.

دوشنبه ۱۴ دسامبر، ۲۳ آذر - صبح بهارودز رفتم و بعد از ظهر به خیاطی دیویس و از آنجا بسینما رفتیم. شب در هتل بودیم. با خالدی و بارون و مسیز روزن در باب ترکیه بحث می‌کردیم.

سه‌شنبه ۱۵ دسامبر، ۲۴ آذر - صبح و بعد از ظهر در فلت بودیم و بکار نوشتن مشغول. شب در هتل با بارون و مستر خالدی و بارون رون صحبت کردیم.

چهارشنبه ۱۶ دسامبر، ۲۵ آذر - صبح بادارہ رفتم. ناهار در گریت ایسترن هتل خوردم و بعد از ظهر در اداره بودم. صندوقهای کتاب را دیدم و کاغذهای بی‌فایده را از آنها خارج و پاره کردم. شب در هتل بودم.

پنجشنبه ۱۷ دسامبر، ۲۶ آذر - صبح بخیاطی رفتم و بعد از ظهر بسفارت و عصر در فلت بودیم و شب در هتل. بموجب اخباری که انگلیسیها منتشر می‌کنند رومل هنوز عقب‌نشینی می‌کند. می‌گویند قوای او را دو قسمت کرده‌اند و محاصره نموده‌اند.

جمعه ۱۸ دسامبر، ۲۷ آذر - صبح به فلت رفتم و بعد از ظهر هم در آنجا کمی کار کردم. حالم چندان خوب نبود. شب خسته بودم. کمی با بارون و خالدی حرف زدم. از ایران در روزنامه‌ها خبری نیست. در این روز قرارداد خرید اثاث خانه را امضا کردم.

شنبه ۱۹ دسامبر ۱۹۴۲، ۲۸ آذر ۱۳۲۱ - صبح به فلت رفتم و از آنجا بسفارت. با آقای

---

۱. باتالون. مقصود battalion است، به معنای گردان (یگان نظامی ۵۰۰ تا ۸۰۰ نفره).

قدس و عطاپور به نورماندی رفتم. فرنگیس هم در آن جا منتظر نشسته بود. با هم ناهار خوردیم. شب بعد از شام بسفارت نزد آقای تقی‌زاده رفتیم و تا ساعت ۷ آنجا بودیم. در باب تهیه مقدمات عروسی صحبت کردیم. قرار شد روز یکشنبه ۲۷ دسامبر که مصادف با عید غدیر است، عقد خوانده شود ـ عقد شرعی ـ و روز سه‌شنبه ۵ ژانویه ۱۹۴۳ نیز در ریتز مهمانی شود.

یکشنبه ۲۰ دسامبر ۱۹۴۳، ۲۹ آذر - صبح کمی خسته بودم. بعد با فرنگیس به فلت رفتم. اطاق خواب را درست کردیم. بعد از ظهر هم در فلت بودیم و شب در هتل.

دوشنبه ۲۱ دسامبر، ۳۰ آذر ۱۳۲۱ - صبح باداره رفتم. کمی کار کردم. ناهار در هتل با فرنگیس خوردم. بعد از ظهر بسفارت نزد خانم تقی‌زاده رفتم و با ایشان اول بهارودز و بعد گولد اسمیث اند سیلور اسمیث،[1] و از گولد اسمیث یک انگشتر الماس و یک انگشتر عروسی خریدم و بعد هم قوری و جای شیر و قنددان و جای قهوه ورشو خریدم. از آنجا بسفارت رفتم. آقای تقی‌زاده را دیدم. قرار شد که روز یکشنبه بجای آنکه عروسی مذهبی در فلت انجام پذیرد، در سفارت عروسی شود. بامام مسجد وکینگ نیز کاغذی نوشته شد که در آن روز بیاید. خودم نیز تلفون کردم. شب در هتل بودم و تا ساعت ده و نیم با بارون رون و خالدی و مسیز روزن حرف می‌زدیم.

سه‌شنبه ۲۲ دسامبر، اول دی ۱۳۲۱ - صبح با فرنگیس از خانه بیرون رفتم. در هارودز خرید کردیم. ناهار در هارودز خوردیم. بعد بسفارت رفتم. در باب دعوت به دورچستر مذاکره شد. عاقبت قرار شد در دورچستر مهمانی شود. ریتز وسائل مهمانی عروسی را ندارد. از سفارت به ریتز رفتم و با رییس آن مذاکره کردم. گفتند حتی مهمانی معمولی هم سخت است و نمی‌توانند. شب در هتل بودم. با خالدی و بارون رون و مسیز روزن حرف می‌زدیم. مسیز روزن گفت که از رادیوی آلمان شنیده است که باز در تهران انقلاب و قتل اتفاق افتاده است.

Goldsmiths & Silversmiths .۱

چهارشنبه ۲۳ دسامبر، ۲ دی - صبح به فلت رفتم. فرنگیس هم بود. موبل و سایر اثاثی را که از هارودز خریده بودیم آوردند. عصر بسینمای اخبار رفتیم و شب بمنزل آقای آرام. قدس، عطاپور، نیامیر، وحید، حمزاوی و خانمش و دختری فرانسوی که نزد نامزد آقای آرامست، نیز بودند. تا ساعت ده و نیم آن جا بودیم.

پنجشنبه ۲۴ دسامبر، ۳ دی - صبح بهارودز رفتم. فرنگیس هم بود. ناهار با هم در رستوران اسلامبول خوردیم و بعد با هم بهارودز رفتیم. خوردنی خریدیم. در این روز شنیدیم که در رادیوی آلمان گفته‌اند که سه نفر از اعضای دولت ایران را توقیف کرده‌اند.

جمعه ۲۵ دسامبر روز عید میلاد مسیح، ۳ دی ۱۳۲۱ - صبح کمی کتاب اقتصادی خواندم. بعد بایندر آمد. در حدود ظهر با فرنگیس بمنزل او رفتیم. ناهار و چای در آن جا خوردیم. مسیز داود صاحبخانه‌اش بسیار مهربانی کرد. پنج بعد از ظهر بایندر ما را بهتل آورد. کمی نشستیم و با بارون و خالدی صحبت کردیم. در این روز خبر کشته شدن شهردار تهران تکذیب شد.

شنبه ۲۶ دسامبر ۱۹۴۲، ۵ دی ۱۳۲۱ - بسیار سرد بود. تا دو ساعت و نیم بعد از ظهر در هتل بودیم و کتاب خواندیم. بعد به فلت رفتیم. تا ساعت شش و نیم بعد از ظهر آن جا بودیم. شب مدتی با خالدی و مسیز روزن حرف زدیم. جوانی فرانسوی بیست ساله که هنوز اسمش را منتشر نکرده‌اند دارلان را کشته است و خود او را هم بحکم محکمه نظامی کشته‌اند.

یکشنبه ۲۷ دسامبر ۱۹۴۲، ۱۸ ذیحجه روز عید غدیر، ۶ دی - در این روز مراسم عقد مذهبی در عمارت سفارت بعمل آمد. صبح در هتل مونتانا چاشت خوردیم. بعد اثاث و لوازم را بستیم و ساعت یازده صبح به فلت آوردیم. لباس عوض کردیم و بسفارت رفتیم. آقای قدس هم بود. ناهار با آقا و خانم تقی‌زاده و آقای قدس خوردیم و بعد از ظهر آقای اسفندیاری و خانم اسفندیاری هم آمدند. چهار ساعت بعد از ظهر امام

مسجد وکینگ آمد. مردی چهل ساله بود. پرگو ولی هوشیار بنظر می‌آمد. کمی در حضور خانم تقی‌زاده و خانم اسفندیاری[1] بتربیت اروپایی بد گفت و از اسلام تمجید کرد. در باب ترجمه قرآن و چیزهایی که مستشرقین بنام اسلام نوشته‌اند نیز تقریباً نطقی کرد. بعد آقای تقی‌زاده گفت بهتر است باصل مطلب یعنی عقد توجه کرد و اگر این اشاره نبود شاید یک ساعت دیگر هم امام حرف می‌زد. باری چند آیه از اول سوره النساء خواند و بعد بزبان انگلیسی از فرنگیس و من سه بار قبول خواست و بچهار صد لیره عقد کرد. صیغه عقد اَنْکَحت و زوّجت و غیر آن را نخواند. در باب لزوم مهر و علت آن نیز. در این موقع قریب ده دقیقه حرف زد و بعد رفت. مجلس پنج و نیم بعد از ظهر تمام شد. بعد با فرنگیس به فلت آمدیم. شام مختصری خوردیم و اخبار را گوش کردیم. روزنامه‌های فارسی خواندم. شب سرد بود. باید بیشتر از پیشتر بکوشم و حالا که همدم و همزندگی دارم وقتم را بیشتر صرف نوشتن کنم و شاید از این راه بزبان فارسی و ایران بتوانم خدمتی کنم.

دوشنبه ۲۸ دسامبر، ۷ دی - صبح با فرنگیس بودم. تلگرافی بتهران کردم که پدرم و حاج سید هادی افجه‌ای نیز در تهران صیغه عقد اسلامی را بخوانند. ناهار در هارودز خوردیم. عصر بسفارت رفتم. مدتی با بایندر بودم و بعد نزد قدس رفتم. تا ساعت شش و نیم با او بودم. با او بهتل پرینس او ویلز رفتم و از آنجا بمنزلش در کنزینگتون پالاس من‌شن.[2] شب در خانه بودم. آقای عطاپور آمد. تا ساعت ده بود. کمی صحبت کردیم.

سه‌شنبه ۲۹ دسامبر، ۸ دی - صبح در خانه بودم. کمی کار کردم و صورت اسامی مدعوین را مرتب کردم برای روز سه‌شنبه ۵ ژانویه که باید بمناسبت عروسی بهتل دورچستر بیایند. عصر با فرنگیس بیرون رفتم. کمی خرید کردیم و مدتی در اداره توزیع کارت غذا بودیم. شب در خانه بودم و کتاب خواندم.

---

۱. + کمی

Kensington Palace Mansion .۲

چهارشنبه ۳۰ دسامبر، ۹ دی - صبح بادارهٔ رفتم و یک ساعت و نیم بعد از ظهر بخانه آمدیم. بعد از ناهار بسفارت رفتم و تا ساعت ۵ آن جا بودم. شب در فلت بودم و کتاب خواندم.

پنجشنبه ۳۱ دسامبر ۱۹۴۲، ۱۰ دی ۱۳۲۱ - صبح کمی کار کردم. عصر بسفارت رفتم. کارتهای دعوت برای مجلس عروسی را آوردند. تا ساعت پنج بعد از ظهر در سفارت بودم و بمدد آقای حمزاوی و منشی سفارت آنها را نوشته بپست دادم. شب با فرنگیس بعد از شام بسفارت رفتم و ساعت یازده با خانم و آقای تقی‌زاده بودیم و صحبت می‌کردیم. ساعت پنج و نیم بعد از ظهر بخانه آمدم . دیدم صندوقهای کتاب را که در اداره بود فرستاده‌اند. تا ساعت هفت بجمع آوری و چیدن آنها بفلت مشغول بودم. شنیدم که دشتی را حبس و کاظمی را تبعید کرده‌اند. در این روز ناهار مهمان عباس رضای شوشتری بودم. فرنگیس هم بود و سر حسّان سهروردی هم آمده بود. تا سه ساعت بعد از ظهر در آن جا بودیم. از وضع لباس و حرکات مردم هیچ معلوم نمی‌شود که جنگ در میان است.

جمعه اول ژانویه ۱۹۴۳، ۱۱ دی - صبح کمی کتابها را مرتب کردم. از ساعت شش تا ۹ صبح یادداشتهای متفرقه‌ای را که با کتابها آورده بودند، از هم جدا کردم. بعد از ظهر با فرنگیس بیرون رفتم. در هارودز و هاروی نیکلز[1] خرید کردیم. سه قطعه پارچه خریدم که بوسیله آقای آرام بایران بفرستم. عصر بسفارت رفتم و شب در خانه بودم. کمی از کتاب اقتصاد تروشی را خواندم. موافق اخبار روس، آلمانیها هنوز در روس < دشمن را > عقب می‌رانند.

شنبه ۲ ژانویه ۱۹۴۳، ۱۲ دی ۱۳۲۱ - صبح کاغذی بپدرم و کاغذی بآقای علاء و کاغذی بدکتر حسن علوی و کاغذی به هژیر نوشتم. بعد آنها را بسفارت بردم که بوسیلهٔ آقای آرام بایشان داده شود. ناهار در خانه خوردم و بعد از ظهر بمرتب کردن

---

۱. Harvey Nichols، فروشگاه مشهور لباس‌های تجملاتی

کتابها مشغول شدم. شوفور ـ راکِل ـ کتابهایی را که نزدش گذاشته بودم آورد. تا ساعت پنج و نیم کتابها را مرتب کردم. بعد با فرنگیس بسینمای اخبار رفتیم. شب در منزل آقای عطاپور چای خوردیم و بعد او بمنزل ما آمد. تا ساعت ده بود.

یکشنبه ۳ ژانویه ۱۹۴۳، ۱۳ دی - صبح از خانه بیرون نرفتم. تمام روز بمرتب کردن کتب مشغول بودم. شب کمی کتاب اقتصاد تروشی را خواندم و زودتر خوابیدم.

دوشنبه ۴ ژانویه، ۱۴ دی - صبح در خانه بودم و کمی ترجمه کردم. بعد از ظهر بسفارت رفتم. جواب رقعه‌های دعوت و چندین تحفه را که فرستاده بودند گرفتم و آمدم. شب در منزل سرهنگ عطاپور بودم. قدس هم بود. بعد بخانه ما آمدند، تا ساعت ده و نیم.

سه‌شنبه ۵ ژانویه، ۱۵ دی - صبح در خانه کمی کار کردم. بعد بسفارت رفتم. باقی جوابهای دعوت را گرفت. مدتی با آقای تقی‌زاده بودم. گفتند ممکن است خانم بواسطه کسالتی که دارند نتوانند بمجلس پذیرایی دورچستر بیایند. باری، ساعت سه بعد از ظهر با فرنگیس به دورچستر رفتم. یک نفر از همدرسان فرنگیس آمده بود. بعد بعضی از مهمانها آمدند و کم کم مجلس شروع شد و تا یک ربع > بعد از هفت > بعد از ظهر ادامه داشت. آقای تقی‌زاده، خانم تقی‌زاده، آقای نوری، خانم نوری، آقای آرام، آقای وحید، آقای قدس، آقای حمزاوی، خانم حمزاوی، آقای بایندر، آقای عطاپور، آقای مینوی، آقای اصغرزاده، خانم اصغرزاده، آقای داراب خان، پروفسور مینورسکی، آقای وسترگارد و عفت خانم، مستر ویلیام فری رز و خانم فری رز و دخترش، آقای ال‌کین‌تون و مسیز ال‌کین‌تون، مستر کلگ و مسیز کلگ، آقای پخ، مستر جمسن و مسیز جمسن، و از دوستان کمبریج دکتر مارشال، میس گوردون و مسیز گوردون و جمعی دیگر بودند. بد نگذشت و بد نبود. شب در خانه بودیم. کمی از اشعار سعدی و فرخی خواندیم.

چهارشنبه ۶ ژانویه ۱۹۴۳، ۱۶ دی - صبح باداره رفتم. ناهار در خانه خوردم و بعد از ظهر بسفارت رفتم. آقای آرام منشی سفارت بعد از پنج سال و نیم خدمت در لندن

بطهران احضار شده و در این روز رفت. با او در سفارت وداع کردم. ساعت پنج بعد از ظهر بخانه آمدم. شب آقای عطاپور آمد. تا ساعت ده و نیم بود. صحبت می‌کردیم.

پنجشنبه ۷ ژانویه، ۱۷ دی - صبح کتاب خواندم و کمی کار کردم. بعد از ظهر با فرنگیس اول بمغازه می‌پل و بعد بهارودز رفتیم. چندین چیز خریدیم. شب در خانه بودم. کمی روزنامه و کتاب خواندم. در تونس آلمانیها باز کمی پیشرفت کرده‌اند.

جمعه ۸ ژانویه، ۱۸ دی - صبح کمی کار کردم. بعد از ظهر با فرنگیس بسفارت رفتم. در اطاق آقای قدس ازدواج را ثبت کردیم. شب بمنزل آقای قدس رفتیم و تا ساعت ده و نیم آن جا بودیم. در مذاکراتی که شد آقای سرهنگ عطاپور بسیار متغیر شد و از مجلس رفت. حمزاوی و خانم حمزاوی هم بودند. دیروز محمدحسن میرزا ولیعهد سابق ایران ناگهان مرد.

شنبه ۹ ژانویه، ۱۹ دی - صبح کتاب خواندم و ترجمه کردم. بعد از چای با فرنگیس بسینما رفتم و شب در خانه بودم. کمی از مقدمه کتاب فرست[1] را خواندم.

یکشنبه ۲۰ دی، ۱۰ ژانویه ۱۹۴۳ - صبح کمی ترجمه کردم. پیش از ظهر با فرنگیس بیرون رفتم. قریب یک ساعت راه رفتم. ساعت چهار بعد از ظهر آقای تقی‌زاده و خانم آمدند. تا ساعت شش بعد از ظهر بودند. اطاقها را دیدند. کمی در باب ایران صحبت کردیم.

دوشنبه ۲۱ دی، ۱۱ ژانویه - صبح باداره رفتم. تا یک ساعت بعد از ظهر آن جا بودم. ناهار در خانه خوردم. بعد از ظهر کمی با فرنگیس راه رفتم. شب در خانه بودم. مقاله تایمز را در باب اصلاحات وزارت امور خارجه خارج نویس کردم. در این روز پولهای دولت را که نزد من بود بآقای نوری تحویل دادم.

---

۱. مقصود احتمالاً Robert Lee Frost است، شاعر امریکایی که آثارش نخست در بریتانیا منتشر شد. کتاب مذکور در اینجا احتمالاً مجموعه اشعار اوست که در ۱۹۳۹ منتشر شد.

سه‌شنبه ۲۲ دی، ۱۲ ژانویه - صبح کمی کار کردم. بعد با فرنگیس بهارودز رفتم. آقای اسفندیاری و خانم اسفندیاری را دیدم. با ایشان ناهار خوردیم. بعد بسینما رفتیم. شب بمنزل آقای حمزاوی رفتم. شام خوردیم. آقای وسترگارد و خانمش عفت خانم هم بودند. تا ساعت ده و نیم آن جا بودیم. چنانکه شنیده‌ام سهیلی را در تهران کشته‌اند.

چهارشنبه ۱۳ ژانویه، ۲۳ < دی > - صبح باداره رفتم. ناهار در خانه خوردم. عصر آقای اسفندیاری و خانم اسفندیاری آمدند و تا ساعت شش بودند. شب در خانه بودم و بترجمه و نوشتن مشغول بودم.

پنجشنبه ۱۴ ژانویه، ۲۴ دی - صبح بسفارت رفتم. آقای تقی‌زاده را دیدم. در باب انجمن ایران صحبت کردند. بازیل گری ایشان را دیده بود. گویا می‌خواهند درباره انجمن ایران جنبشی داشته باشند.

جمعه ۱۵ ژانویه، ۲۵ دی - صبح باداره رفتم. ناهار در هتل نزدیک ایستگاه لیورپول خوردم و بعد از ظهر هم تا ساعت پنج در اداره بودم. کار می‌کردم. شب در خانه بودم. کتاب اقتصاد خواندم.

شنبه ۱۶ ژانویه، ۱۹۴۳، ۲۶ دی ۱۳۲۱ - صبح بسفارت رفتم. آقای نوری هم آمد. کاغذهایی چند که بود بوسیله سفارت بتهران فرستادیم. ناهار در خانه خوردم و بعد از ظهر هم در خانه بودم. شب کمی کتاب و کمی روزنامه خواندم.

یکشنبه ۱۷ ژانویه، ۲۷ < دی > - صبح در خانه بودم. کمی کار کردم. بعد از ظهر با فرنگیس یک ساعت و نیم راه رفتم. شب در خانه بودیم. آقای عطاپور آمد. مدتی نشسته صحبت کردیم. بعد از چهارده ماه که لندن از خطر هوایی برکنار بود، در این شب طیارات آلمانی آمدند و دو بار یکی از ساعت هشت و نیم تا نه و دیگری از ساعت پنج بعد از نصف شب تا پنج و نیم صدای توپ و طیاره بر پا بود. روسها مطابق اخبار انگلیسی پیشرفت می‌کنند. در افریقا نیز انگلیسیها پیشرفت کرده‌اند.

دوشنبه ۱۸ ژانویه، ۲۸ دی - صبح از خانه بیرون نرفتم. کاغذها را مرتب می‌کردم. کمرم کمی درد می‌کند.

سه‌شنبه ۱۹ ژانویه، ۲۹ دی - صبح نزد خیاط رفتم و از کتابفروشی فویلز کتاب خریدم و مدتی در چرین کروس رود[1] در کتابفروشیها بودم. ناهار در خانه خوردم. پنج بعد از ظهر مستر بازیل گری آمد. تا ساعت هفت نشست صحبت کردیم. در باب انجمن ایران مذاکره شد.

چهارشنبه ۲۰ ژانویه، ۳۰ دی - صبح باداره رفتم و بعد از ظهر بسفارت. شام قدس با ما بود. کمی صحبت کردیم و زودتر خوابیدم.

پنجشنبه اول بهمن ۱۳۲۱، ۲۱ ژانویه ۱۹۴۳ - صبح کمی ترجمه کردم. بعد بسفارت رفتم. با قدس و بایندر مهمان عطاپور بودیم. در مهمانخانه ریتز ناهار خوردیم. بعد از ظهر در سفارت بودم و شب در خانه ترجمه کردم. انگلیسیها در افریقا پیشرفت می‌کنند.

جمعه ۲ بهمن، ۲۲ ژانویه - از صبح تا چهار ساعت بعد از ظهر در خانه بودم و چیز می‌نوشتم. بعد پیاده بیپکادلی رفتم و با فرنگیس یک ساعت در سینمای اخبار بودیم. شب در خانه کار کردم و کمی از گزارش میلیسپو را که در ۱۹۲۹ نوشته است خواندم.

شنبه ۳ بهمن، ۲۳ ژانویه - صبح کمی ترجمه کردم. بعد از ظهر کتاب خواندم. چهار بعد از ظهر آقای نیامیر، آقای عرفانی، آقای وحید آمدند. تا ساعت هفت بودند و در باب ایران و لزوم کار کردن مردم با هم صحبت کردند. شب در خانه بودم و کتاب خواندم. طرابلس را انگلیسیها گرفته‌اند.

---

۱. Charing Cross Road، نام راسته‌ای درمرکز لندن.

یکشنبه ۴ بهمن، ۲۴ ژانویه - تمام روز را در خانه بودم و ترجمه کردم و کتاب خواندم. شب هم در خانه بودم و کار می‌کردم.

دوشنبه ۵ بهمن، ۲۵ ژانویه - صبح کمی کار کردم. بعد از ظهر با فرنگیس بکتابخانه لوزاک رفتم. چندین کتاب خریدم و نیز از کتابخانه کدگان بوک[1] کتابی خریدم. بعد بسینما رفتیم و شب در خانه بودیم.

سه‌شنبه ۶ بهمن، ۲۶ ژانویه - صبح و عصر در خانه بودم و کار کردم.

چهارشنبه ۷ بهمن، ۲۷ ژانویه - صبح باداره رفتم و شب با فرنگیس بمونتانا هتل. مهمان آقای خالدی عضو سفارت عراق بودیم. و بعد از شام با بارون رون و مسیز روزن تا ساعت یازده صحبت کردیم. در این روز خبر ملاقات روزولت و چرچیل در کازابلانکا منتشر شد. ژنرال دو گول و ژنرال ژیرو هم ملاقات کرده‌اند.

پنجشنبه ۸ بهمن، ۱۳۲۱، ۲۸ ژانویه ۱۹۴۳ - صبح بسفارت رفتم و بعد از ظهر در خانه بودم. دکتر آربری آمد. تا ساعت پنج و نیم بود. بعد از هفت با فرنگیس بسینمای اخبار رفتم و شب در خانه بودم.

جمعه ۹ بهمن، ۲۹ ژانویه - صبح کمی کار کردم. بعد از ظهر بسفارت رفتم. آقای تقی‌زاده را دیدم. شب در خانه بودم. کتاب و کمی آلمانی خواندم. عفت خانم وسترگارد در خانه ما بود.

شنبه ۱۰ بهمن، ۳۰ ژانویه - صبح کار کردم. بعد با فرنگیس بهارودز رفتیم. ناهار در رستوران ترکی خوردیم. بعد بخانه آمدیم و ساعت چهار بعد از ظهر بمنزل آقای وحید رفتیم. تا ساعت هفت و نیم آن جا بودیم. در این روز که گورینگ بنیابت هیتلر نطقی می‌کرد، طیارات انگلیسی ببرلین رفتند و بمب انداختند.

---

۱. بول. مقصود احتمالاً باید Leo Cadogan Rare Books بوده باشد.

یکشنبه ۱۱ بهمن، ۳۱ ژانویه - صبح کمی ترجمه کردم. بعد از ظهر آقای نیامیر آمد و با فرنگیس بمنزل آقای عرفانی رفتیم. تا ساعت ۸ آنجا بودیم. شب که برگشتیم دیدم که دو آژان منتظر ما ایستادهاند. در اطاق کتابخانه چراغ را روشن گذاشته بودیم. در غیاب ما آژان در را باز کرده و چراغ را خاموش کرده بود. در منزل آقای عرفانی در باب ایران و تحقیقات راجع بایران مذاکره بود.

دوشنبه ۱۲ بهمن ۱۳۲۱، اول فوریه ۱۹۴۳ - صبح کمی ترجمه کردم. عصری در خانه بودم. شب با فرنگیس بیپیکادلی رفتم. اخبار را دیدیم. شام در خانه خوردیم و کمی کتاب خواندیم، از قصاید فرخی و کمی از بوستان.

سهشنبه ۱۳ بهمن، ۲ فوریه - صبح زود برخاستم. بمدرسه السنه شرقیه رفتم در عمارت دانشگاه لندن و دو ساعت درس فارسی دادم. هشت نفر انگلیسی که هفت ماه پیش بیاد گرفتن فارسی شروع کردهاند حاضر بودند. اغلب خوب یاد گرفته بودند و اغلب مطالب مرا میفهمیدند. شکی نداشتم که یاد گرفتن فارسی سخت نیست و لیکن این پیشامد بر اطمینانم افزود. عصر در خانه بودم. آلمانیها در استالینگراد شکست خوردهاند.

چهارشنبه ۱۴ بهمن، ۳ فوریه - صبح باداره رفتم. بعد از ظهر در خانه بودم. شب حالم چندان خوب نبود. کمی سرم درد میکرد. زودتر خوابیدم.

پنجشنبه ۱۵ بهمن، ۴ فوریه - صبح بوزارت secretary رفتم. در باب خاک سرخی که دولت ایران میخواهد بفروشد، تحقیق کردم. بعد از ظهر در خانه بودم و کار کردم.

جمعه ۱۶ بهمن، ۵ فوریه - صبح بمدرسه السنه شرقیه رفتم. دو ساعت درس دادم. ناهار در خانه خوردم و شب هم در خانه بودم.

شنبه ۱۷ بهمن، ۶ فوریه - صبح کمی کار کردم. عصر با فرنگیس بمنزل آقای نوری رفتم. تدین، مینوی، و دکتر یونگ هم بودند. شب در خانه بودم. کتاب خواندم.

یکشنبه ۱۸ بهمن ۱۳۲۱، ۷ فوریه ۱۹۴۳ - ناهار مسیز گوردون دوست روایال هتل کمبریج آمد. ساعت چهار آقای عرفانی آمد و با او و فرنگیس بمنزل آقای نیامیر رفتیم. آقای وحید هم بود. تا ساعت هشت و نیم آن جا بودیم. کمی از روابط ایران و انگلیس را که قرار بود بیان کردم.

دوشنبه ۱۹ بهمن، ۸ فوریه - صبح کار کردم. عصر تنها بیرون رفتم و در سینمای اخبار بودم.

سه‌شنبه ۲۰ بهمن، ۹ فوریه - صبح بمدرسه رفتم. دو ساعت درس دادم و بعد از ظهر در خانه بودم.

چهارشنبه ۲۱ بهمن، ۱۰ فوریه - صبح باداره رفتم. آقای نوری نیامد. یک بعد از ظهر آمدم. بعد از ظهر در خانه بودم. شب آقای قدس آمد.

پنجشنبه ۲۲ بهمن، ۱۱ فوریه - صبح کمی ترجمه کردم. ناهار با فرنگیس در بیرون خوردیم. بعد از ظهر بسفارت مصر رفتم. مهمانی خوبی بود. اعضای سفارت ایران هم همه بودند. تا شش ساعت و نیم بعد از ظهر آن جا بودم و شب در خانه کار کردم. روسها پیشرفت می‌کنند. آی‌زن‌هوئر[1] فرمانده قوای متحدین در افریقا شده و ژنرال الکساندر[2] معاون او.

جمعه ۲۳ بهمن، ۱۲ فوریه - صبح کار کردم و بعد از ظهر هم در خانه بودم و کار کردم. شب با فرنگیس بمنزل آقای قدس رفتیم. تا ساعت ده و نیم آن جا بودیم. شب در خانه کمی روزنامه خواندیم و خوابیدیم.

شنبه ۲۴ بهمن، ۱۳ فوریه - صبح کتاب خواندم و ترجمه کردم. عصر بمنزل آقای قدس رفتیم. فرنگیس هم آمد. آقای نوری، خانم نوری، آقای حمزاوی، خانم حمزاوی، وحید، آقای وسترگارد و خانم وسترگارد هم بودند.

---

۱. Dwight D. Eisenhower، بعداً رییس جمهور امریکا.
۲. Field Marshal the Earl Alexander of Tunis، ژنرال بریتانیایی (۱۸۹۱-۱۹۶۹).

یکشنبه ۲۵ بهمن، ۱۴ فوریه - صبح کتاب و روزنامه خواندیم. کمی ترجمه کردم. بعد از ظهر با فرنگیس به دولفین اسکویر[1] بمنزل پروفسور وبستر رفتم. زنش و او بسیار گرم پذیرایی کردند. تا ساعت شش آن جا بودم. بعد بسینما رفتیم. شب آقای عرفانی آمد. تا ساعت ده و نیم بود. بعد شام خوردیم. روسها روستوف را گرفته‌اند.

دوشنبه ۲۶ بهمن، ۱۵ فوریه - صبح کمی ترجمه کردم. ناهار بایندر آمد. تا ساعت سه بعد از ظهر با ما بود. با او بسفارت رفتم و شب با قدس برگشتم. تا ساعت ده و نیم با او بودیم. کابینه قوام السلطنه استعفا داد و از قراری که در سفارت شنیدم سهیلی رییس الوزراء شده است.

سه‌شنبه ۲۷ بهمن، ۱۶ فوریه - صبح بمدرسه السنه شرقیه رفتم و بعد از ظهر در خانه بودم.

چهارشنبه ۲۸ بهمن، ۱۷ فوریه - صبح باداره رفتم و بعد از ظهر بجلسه شورای جمعیت ایران. آقای تقی‌زاده هم بودند. مستر هیل و مستر بازیل گری هم حضور داشتند. شب در خانه بودم. ترجمه کردم.

پنجشنبه ۲۹ بهمن، ۱۸ فوریه - صبح کمی ترجمه کردم. بعد از ظهر با فرنگیس بسینما رفتم. فیلم الف لیلة[2] را دیدم. چندان خوب نبود. امریکاییها در تونس شکست خورده‌اند. حال گاندی که از نظر اعتراضی روزه گرفته است، خوب نیست.

جمعه ۳۰ بهمن، ۱۹ فوریه - صبح کمی ترجمه کردم. بعد از ظهر کتاب خواندم. شب خالدی و بارون رون آشنایان هتل مونتانا آمدند.

شنبه ۱ اسفند، ۲۰ فوریه - صبح کمی کار کردم. عصر با فرنگیس بمنزل آقای نوری رفتم. آقای وحید، عفت خانم، آقای وسترگارد، آقای حمزاوی و خانمش هم بودند.

---

۱. Dolphin Square، مجموعه واحدهای آپارتمانی در غرب لندن (افتتاح در ۱۹۳۵).

۲. مقصود فیلم Arabian Nights است، محصول امریکا (۱۹۴۲).

شب بمنزل آقای تقی‌زاده رفتم. سرهنگ عطاپور، آقای نوری و خانم نوری، آقای حمزاوی و خانم حمزاوی هم بودند. تا نیمساعت بعد از نصف شب آن جا بودیم.

یکشنبه ۲ اسفند ۱۳۲۱، ۲۱ فوریه ۱۹۴۳ - صبح از خانه بیرون نرفتم. کمی ترجمه کردم و کمی کتاب خواندم. سرماخوردگی داشتم. حال گاندی بدتر شده است.

دوشنبه ۳ اسفند، ۲۲ فوریه - از خانه بیرون نرفتم. کتاب خواندم و ترجمه کردم. عصر دو زن انگلیسی که دوست فرنگیس بودند آمدند. آلمانیها در تونس پیشرفت می‌کنند.

سه‌شنبه ۴ اسفند، ۲۳ فوریه - صبح بترجمه و خواندن مشغول بودم. شب بمنزل آقای قدس رفتم. فرنگیس هم بود. آقای حمزاوی و خانمش و آقای وسترگارد و خانمش و آقای وحید و آقای نیامیر بودند. ساعت یازده برگشتیم. سرم درد می‌کرد.

چهارشنبه ۵ اسفند، ۲۴ فوریه - صبح باداره رفتم و بعد از ظهر با فرنگیس به هارودز و بعد بسینمای اخبار. انگلیسها در تونس آلمانیها را عقب رانده‌اند.

پنجشنبه ۶ اسفند، ۲۵ فوریه - صبح بسفارت رفتم. آقای تقی‌زاده را دیدم. در باب انجمن ایران صحبت کردیم. بعد از ظهر در خانه بودم. اشعار مسعود سعد سلمان را خواندم. گاندی هنوز در حبس است و نمی‌خواهد او را بیرون بیاورند. روسها ظاهراً زیاد پیشرفتی نمی‌کنند.

جمعه ۷ اسفند، ۲۶ فوریه - تمام روز را در خانه بودم و کار کردم.

شنبه ۸ اسفند، ۲۷ فوریه - صبح به بریتیش میوزیم رفتم. بازیل گری را دیدم و مدتی در کتابفروشی لوزاک[1] بودم. کتابهای تازه بسیاری داشت. چندین کتاب جدا کردم. عصر در خانه بودم. کتاب خواندم. شب مستر وستگارد و عفت خانم و قدس و حمزاوی و خانم حمزاوی شام آمدند. تا ساعت یازده بودند.

------

۱. Luzac & Co.

یکشنبه ۹ اسفند، ۲۸ فوریه - صبح از خانه بیرون نرفتم. کمی ترجمه کردم و کمی کتاب خواندم.

دوشنبه ۱۰ اسفند، اول مارس ۱۹۴۳ - صبح بسفارت رفتم و بعد از ظهر بکتابفروشی لوزاک. از کتب الیسن چند کتاب خریدم.

سه‌شنبه ۱۱ اسفند، ۲ مارس ۱۹۴۳ - صبح بمدرسه السنه شرقیه رفتم و از آن جا بکتابخانه لوزاک. بعد از ظهر کار کردم و چهار و نیم جلسه انجمن ایران بر پا شد. آقای تقی‌زاده، نوری، آقای قدس، پروفسور بیلی، دکتر آربری، و بازیل گری و مستر بوسوم و مستر هیل بودند. تا نصف شب کار می‌کردم.

چهارشنبه ۱۲ اسفند، ۳ مارس ۱۹۴۳ - صبح باداره رفتم. بعد از ظهر در خانه بودم. کار کردم. شب کمی کار کردم. بعد حمله هوایی شد. بپناهگاه رفتم. یک ساعت بیشتر در آن جا بودم. چهار بعد از نصف شب هم حمله هوایی شد ولی از تخت بیرون نرفتیم. گاندی بعد از ۲۱ روز در این روز روزه خود را شکست.

پنجشنبه ۱۳ اسفند، ۴ مارس ۱۹۴۳ - تمام روز را در خانه بودم و کار کردم. در یکی از دالونهای راه آهن زیرزمینی ۱۷۸ نفر کشته شده‌اند. در موقع شلیک یک زن از صدا می‌ترسد و می‌افتد و دیگران هم روی آن می‌افتند و ۱۷۸ نفر خفه می‌شوند.

جمعه ۱۴ اسفند، ۵ مارس - صبح باداره رفتم و بعد از ظهر در خانه بودم. عصر با فرنگیس بسینما رفتم.

شنبه ۱۵ اسفند، ۶ مارس - از صبح تا شب کار کردم. آلمانیها در شمال تونس پیشرفت کرده‌اند.

یکشنبه ۱۶ اسفند، ۷ مارس - صبح کار کردم. بعد از ظهر آقای وحید و عرفانی و نیامیر آمدند. تا ساعت هشت بودند. بعد با فرنگیس بمنزل آقای تقی‌زاده رفتم. تا ساعت یازده آن جا بودیم. بعد از نصف شب طیاره‌ای بالای لندن بود ولی زود رفت.

دوشنبه ۱۷ اسفند، ۸ مارس - هیچ از خانه بیرون نرفتم. کار کردم.

سه‌شنبه ۱۸ اسفند ۱۳۲۱، ۹ مارس ۱۹۴۳ - صبح بمدرسه رفتم و از آن جا بکتابفروشی لوزاک. شب در خانه بودم.

چهارشنبه ۱۹ اسفند، ۱۰ مارس - صبح باداره رفتم و بعد از ظهر بسفارت. کاغذی که برای صالح نوشته بودم فرستادم. روسها شکست می‌خورند.

پنجشنبه ۲۰ اسفند، ۱۱ مارس - تمام روز را در خانه بودم و کار کردم. شب آقای عرفانی آمد. تا نصف شب بود. آلمانیها بنزدیک خارکف رسیده‌اند.

جمعه ۲۱ اسفند، ۱۲ مارس - صبح کار کردم. سه ربع بعد از ظهر بکنزینگتون رستوران رفتم. با فرنگیس با آقای نوری و خانم نوری ناهار خوردیم و بعد با هم به اِجوِر رفتیم. آقای مینوی قسمت بی‌بی‌سی را که در آن کار می‌کند نشان داد. با او شام خوردیم و بعد از شام با دو مصری و آقای فرزاد و آقای دهقان مدتی مذاکره کردیم.

شنبه ۲۲ اسفند، ۱۳ مارس - تمام روز را کار کردیم. شب رفتیم بسینمای اخبار. ایدن بامریکا رفته.

یکشنبه ۲۳ اسفند، ۱۴ مارس - تا یک بعد از ظهر کار می‌کردم. بعد با فرنگیس بمنزل آقای قدس رفتم. آقای وسترگارد و زنش، آقای حمزاوی و زنش، آقای نیامیر، آقای صیقل و زنش، و بعد از ظهر آقای وحید هم بودند. آلمانیها خارکف را گرفته‌اند.

دوشنبه ۲۴ اسفند، ۱۵ مارس - صبح کار کردیم. عصر بسینما رفتم. با فرنگیس بباد رفته را دیدم. شب در خانه بودم.

سه‌شنبه ۲۵ اسفند، ۱۶ مارس - صبح بمدرسه السنه شرقی رفتم و بعد از ظهر با فرنگیس بسینمای اخبار. شب در خانه بودم.

چهارشنبه ۲۶ اسفند، ۱۷ مارس - صبح باداره رفتم. ناهار نخوردم. تا چهار بعد از ظهر آن جا بودم. عصر بسفارت رفتم. شب خانه بودم.

پنجشنبه ۲۷ اسفند، ۱۸ مارس - صبح کتاب خواندم. بعد از ظهر بیرون رفتم. در کتابخانه بودم. شب آقای قدس آمد.

جمعه ۲۸ اسفند، ۱۹ مارس - صبح کار کردم. کتاب خواندم. شب در خانه بودم. بدیعه خانم آمد.

شنبه ۲۹ اسفند، ۲۰ مارس - کتاب خواندم. عصر بسینما رفتم. شب بدیعه خانم، آقای قدس، و آقای عرفانی شام با ما بودند.

یکشنبه ۳۰ اسفند، ۲۱ مارس - ناهار در سفارت بودیم. آقای نوری، خانم نوری، آقای صیقل و آقای حمزاوی و خانمهایشان، آقای وحید، آقای بایندر و آقای قدس بودند. عصر بمنزل آقای نوری رفتیم و شب بمنزل آقای قدس.

نمایه

آبادان ۶۳

آبه برنار (Bernard du Boisrouvray) ۳۸، ۳۹

آتاتورک، مصطفی کمال پاشا ۱۷

آذربایجان ۳۲۲

آرام، غلام عباس ۱۱۱، ۱۳۴، ۱۳۸، ۱۵۰، ۱۵۸، ۱۶۰، ۱۶۲، ۱۶۹، ۱۹۵، ۲۰۸، ۲۰۹، ۲۲۷، ۲۴۸، ۲۸۳، ۲۸۶، ۲۹۱، ۲۹۹، ۳۱۳، ۳۳۴، ۳۳۵، ۳۳۶، ۳۳۸، ۳۴۲، ۳۴۴، ۳۴۵، ۳۴۸، ۳۵۱، ۳۶۶، ۳۷۲، ۳۷۴، ۳۷۵

آربری، آرتور جان ۱۷۱، ۲۴۰، ۳۳۵، ۳۷۹، ۳۸۴

آزاد، ابوالکلام ۳۴۳

آزموده ۳۵، ۳۷

آزوف ۲۷۶

آقاخان سوم، سلطان محمد شاه ۲۶، ۳۱

آقایان، الکساندر ۱

آلبرت هال ۱۹

آلبرت هال ۸۴

آلمان/آلمانیها ۱۹، ۹۱، ۹۲، ۱۶۸، ۱۸۲، ۱۸۳، ۱۸۴، ۲۰۸، ۲۰۹، ۲۱۰، ۲۴۸، ۲۵۷، ۲۶۳، ۲۶۴، ۲۶۷، ۲۶۸، ۲۷۰، ۲۷۱، ۲۷۲، ۲۷۴، ۲۷۵، ۲۷۶، ۲۷۷، ۲۷۸، ۲۷۹، ۲۸۰، ۲۸۱، ۲۸۲، ۲۸۳، ۲۸۴، ۲۸۵، ۲۸۶، ۲۸۷، ۲۸۹، ۲۹۱، ۲۹۳، ۲۹۶، ۲۹۷، ۲۹۸، ۳۰۰، ۳۰۹، ۳۱۳، ۳۱۴، ۳۲۳، ۳۲۶، ۳۲۷، ۳۲۹، ۳۳۰، ۳۳۱، ۳۳۲، ۳۳۳، ۳۳۴، ۳۳۵، ۳۳۶، ۳۳۷، ۳۳۸، ۳۳۹، ۳۴۰، ۳۴۱، ۳۴۲، ۳۴۳، ۳۴۴، ۳۴۵، ۳۴۶، ۳۴۷، ۳۴۸، ۳۴۹، ۳۵۰، ۳۵۲، ۳۵۳، ۳۵۵، ۳۵۶، ۳۶۰، ۳۶۳، ۳۶۵، ۳۶۶، ۳۶۷، ۳۶۸، ۳۷۴، ۳۷۶، ۳۷۷، ۳۸۰، ۳۸۳، ۳۸۴، ۳۸۵

آنقره ۲۶۸

آیزنهاور، دوایت ۳۸۱

ابن رشد ۲۹۷

اَتلی، کلمنت ۲۵۶

احمدی (منشی سفارت) ۱۲، ۲۴، ۵۹، ۶۲، ۸۰

اخوی، سید علی اکبر ۶۸، ۸۵، ۸۷، ۸۸، ۹۱

اردلان، عباسقلی ۱۰، ۱۵، ۲۴، ۳۳، ۵۷، ۶۲، ۸۰، ۸۱، ۱۲۶، ۱۲۷، ۱۹۶، ۲۰۰

ارمنستان ۲۴۳

ارنولد، ماثیو (Matthew Arnold) ۳۱

اروپا ۲۷، ۱۸۲

اسپانیا ۳۹، ۱۲۶

استارک، فریا ۱۶۰

استالین ۲۷۹، ۳۴۵، ۳۵۶

استالینگراد ۳۴۲، ۳۴۴، ۳۴۶، ۳۴۸، ۳۵۰، ۳۵۲، ۳۵۳، ۳۵۵، ۳۵۶، ۳۵۷، ۳۶۰، ۳۸۰

استالینو (دونتسک) ۲۷۶

استر و مردخای (بقعه) ۱

استراتفورد اپن ایون (Stratford-upon-Avon) ۶۱

استرالیا ۳۰۸

۳۸۷

استن هوپ، جیمز ریچارد ۱۵۳

اسفندیاری، حسن (محتشم السلطنه) ۱۱۴، ۱۱۵

اسفندیاری، فتح الله نوری (کارمند شرکت نفت/نماینده دولت ایران) ۵، ۲۷۶، ۲۹۳، ۳۲۲، ۳۳۵، ۳۳۶، ۳۳۷، ۳۳۸، ۳۵۱، ۳۵۳، ۳۵۶، ۳۵۹، ۳۶۱، ۳۶۳، ۳۶۴، ۳۶۶، ۳۶۷، ۳۶۸، ۳۷۲، ۳۷۵، ۳۷۶، ۳۷۷، ۳۸۰، ۳۸۱، ۳۸۲، ۳۸۳، ۳۸۴، ۳۸۵، ۳۸۶

اسکاتلند ۹۶، ۲۱۹، ۲۳۸، ۲۳۹

اسکندریه ۳۳۶

اسلامبول ۹

اسن ۳۳۱

اشتن، لی (Leigh Ashton) ۷۷، ۸۷

اشرفی، حسینقلی ۱۱۶

اصفهان ۳۲، ۲۵۵

افخمی (از کارکنان سفارت) ۸۰

افریقا ۲۸۳، ۲۸۴، ۲۸۸، ۲۸۹، ۲۹۰، ۲۹۶، ۲۹۷، ۲۹۸، ۳۰۸، ۳۳۱، ۳۳۳، ۳۳۴، ۳۳۵، ۳۳۶، ۳۳۷، ۳۶۰، ۳۶۴، ۳۶۶، ۳۷۷، ۳۷۸، ۳۸۱

افشار، مصطفی ۱، ۵۸، ۷۱، ۸۴، ۹۱

افغانستان ۳۸، ۹۰، ۱۵۵، ۱۶۲

افلاطون ۳۱۳، ۳۲۹، ۳۳۰، ۳۳۱، ۳۳۲، ۳۳۶

اقبال آشتیانی، عباس ۵۳، ۶۱، ۷۰

اقبال خراسانی، خسرو ۴، ۸، ۱۲، ۵۲، ۵۳، ۷۰

اقبال خراسانی، منوچهر ۵۲

اقبالیان، سعادت ۱۶۰

اکبر، محمد ۹۵

اکسفورد (شهر) ۱۷، ۵۹، ۶۴، ۱۱۸، ۱۵۲، ۱۵۳، ۲۳۵، ۲۳۹، ۲۴۰، ۲۴۴، ۲۴۸، ۲۵۵، ۲۷۲، ۲۷۸، ۲۸۰، ۲۸۵، ۲۹۵، ۳۰۰، ۳۰۱، ۳۰۲، ۳۰۳، ۳۰۹، ۳۲۲، ۳۲۶، ۳۲۷، ۳۲۷، ۳۳۱، ۳۴۸، ۳۴۹

البرز ۳۴۶

الجزایر ۵۳، ۳۶۴

الجزیره ۴۷

الدوری، عبدالعزیز ۲۹۱

العالمین ۳۳۷، ۳۶۱

الکساندر، فیلد مارشال ۳۸۱

الکینگتون، م. هـ (M. H. Elkington) ۱۱۶، ۱۱۹، ۲۸۱، ۳۳۷، ۳۷۵

امامی، عباس ۶۸

امان، نظام الدین ۵۵

امانوئل کالج (کمبریج) ۳۴۷

امریکا ۴۳، ۷۳، ۲۸۱، ۲۹۰، ۲۹۷، ۳۰۹، ۳۲۵، ۳۳۳، ۳۳۶، ۳۶۴، ۳۶۶، ۳۸۲، ۳۸۵

امریکای جنوبی ۲۶۵

امریکای جنوبی ۴

امیراصلانی، عباس ۹۳

امیرعلائی، شمس‌الدین ۱۲

امین (خانم) ۹، ۱۰، ۱۱

امین‌الدوله، علی ۶

امینی، غلامحسین ۳۵

امینی، محسن ۶، ۹، ۱۰، ۲۱، ۲۳، ۲۷، ۶۸، ۷۰

آن والید (کلیسا) ۳۴، ۵۳

انتظام، عبدالله ۵، ۶، ۸، ۱۰، ۳۷، ۱۲۷، ۱۹۹، ۲۰۰

انجمن ایران/جمعیت ایران (Iran Society) ۵۶، ۵۷، ۵۸، ۶۵، ۷۶، ۷۷، ۸۷، ۸۸، ۸۹، ۹۰، ۱۰۱، ۱۰۲، ۱۰۵، ۱۱۶، ۱۲۰، ۱۲۵، ۱۲۸، ۱۷۵، ۳۷۸، ۳۸۲، ۳۸۴

انجمن سلطنتی آسیا (Royal Asiatic Society) ۲۷، ۵۵

انجمن صنایع (Arts Council) ۱۵

اودسا ۲۶۱، ۲۷۵

اورمیه ۲۶۰

اوروگوئه ۱۱

اولمپیا (Olympia) ۲، ۱۲، ۱۵، ۱۲۳، ۱۴۳

اولمپیک ۹۳

ایدن، آنتونی ۳۸۵

ایدن، انتونی ۳۱

ایران ۴، ۹، ۱۲، ۱۵، ۱۶، ۱۹، ۲۱، ۲۲، ۲۵، ۲۶، ۲۸، ۲۹، ۳۱، ۳۲، ۳۳، ۳۷، ۳۸، ۴۰، ۴۳، ۵۵، ۵۶، ۶۴، ۷۰، ۸۶، ۸۷، ۸۸، ۹۰، ۹۳، ۹۴، ۱۱۳، ۱۱۴، ۱۱۵، ۱۳۰، ۱۳۱، ۱۳۳، ۱۳۴، ۱۴۲، ۱۴۵، ۱۴۶، ۱۵۲، ۱۵۴، ۱۵۵، ۱۶۷، ۱۶۹، ۱۷۷، ۱۸۷، ۱۹۲، ۱۹۵، ۲۰۴، ۲۳۲، ۲۳۹، ۲۴۱، ۲۵۶، ۲۵۷، ۲۵۸، ۲۵۹، ۲۶۰، ۲۶۱، ۲۶۳، ۲۶۴، ۲۶۵، ۲۶۶، ۲۶۷، ۲۶۹، ۲۷۰، ۲۷۱، ۲۷۲، ۲۷۳، ۲۷۸، ۲۸۱، ۲۸۳، ۲۸۵، ۲۹۳، ۲۹۶، ۲۹۹، ۳۰۱، ۳۰۴، ۳۰۵، ۳۰۷، ۳۰۸، ۳۰۹، ۳۱۰، ۳۱۱، ۳۱۲، ۳۱۳، ۳۱۴، ۳۱۶، ۳۱۷، ۳۲۰، ۳۲۱، ۳۲۳، ۳۲۸، ۳۳۴، ۳۴۱، ۳۴۲، ۳۴۳، ۳۴۴، ۳۴۶، ۳۴۹، ۳۵۱، ۳۵۲، ۳۵۸، ۳۶۰، ۳۶۲، ۳۷۲، ۳۷۳، ۳۷۶، ۳۸۰، ۳۸۱

ایرلند ۲، ۲۹۷

ایطالیا/ایطالیایی‌ها ۵۳، ۱۲۶، ۲۰۸، ۲۱۰، ۲۶۳، ۲۸۲، ۲۸۷، ۳۰۹، ۳۳۰

ایفل (برج) ۳۶، ۳۷

ایل دو فرانس (جزیره) ۳۰۹

ایلینگ ۲۵

ایونینگ استاندارد (روزنامه) ۴

بثر حکیم ۳۳۳

باتاویه/اندونزی ۳۰۵

بازل ۱۹۶

بالزاک، اونوره دو ۳۰۲، ۳۱۵

بالکان ۸۹

بالیوزی، حسن موقر ۳۵۱

بانک شاهی ۱۹

بایندر، غلامعلی ۲۵۹

بایندر، نصرالله ۱۸۲، ۱۸۹، ۱۹۰، ۱۹۴، ۱۹۶، ۲۰۱، ۲۰۳، ۲۰۴، ۲۰۵، ۲۰۶، ۲۰۷، ۲۰۸

۲۱۲، ۲۳۲، ۲۳۳، ۲۳۴، ۲۳۶، ۲۳۷، ۲۴۱،
۲۴۳، ۲۴۵، ۲۴۶، ۲۴۷، ۲۴۸، ۲۵۲، ۲۵۴،
۲۵۹، ۲۶۱، ۲۶۳، ۲۶۵، ۲۶۷، ۲۷۰، ۲۷۴،
۲۷۵، ۲۷۶، ۲۷۷، ۲۸۲، ۲۸۳، ۲۸۴، ۲۸۶،
۲۸۹، ۲۹۱، ۲۹۲، ۲۹۳، ۲۹۶، ۲۹۷، ۲۹۸،
۳۰۰، ۳۰۱، ۳۰۳، ۳۰۵، ۳۰۶، ۳۰۸، ۳۱۸،
۳۲۳، ۳۲۴، ۳۲۷، ۳۲۹، ۳۳۵، ۳۳۸، ۳۴۲،
۳۴۴، ۳۵۰، ۳۵۱، ۳۵۵، ۳۵۶، ۳۶۲، ۳۶۵،
۳۷۲، ۳۷۵، ۳۷۸، ۳۸۶

بحر اسود (دریای سیاه) ۳۴۹

بحر خزر ۱۴۱، ۳۴۳، ۳۴۴

بحر متوسط (مدیترانه) ۳۲۶

بحرین ۴۸، ۵۷

بَدر، محمود ۶۱، ۸۱

براون، ادوارد ۲۹۴، ۳۲۸، ۳۵۸

براون، جان ۳۱۸

برایتون هتل ۲۲

برتلو، مارسلن (Marcellin Berthelot) ۳۶

برج لندن ۶

برست ۳۰۰

برلن/برلین ۷۳، ۹۲، ۹۴، ۱۸۳، ۳۷۹

برمه/بیرمانی ۲۹۷، ۲۹۸، ۳۰۱، ۳۰۲، ۳۰۴،
۳۰۶، ۳۱۴، ۳۱۹، ۳۲۴

برن ۱۹۹، ۲۱۲

بروکسل ۱۲۷

بریستول ۳۶۶

بُسَم، آلفرد ۹۰

بغداد ۲، ۹، ۱۶۷

بقایی کرمانی، مظفر ۵۳، ۶۸، ۷۱

بلژیک ۹۴، ۹۶، ۱۲۶، ۲۰۸

بلیل کالج (آکسفورد) ۲۴۰، ۲۴۴

بلیول کالج (آکسفورد) ۵۹، ۶۰

بندر پهلوی ۲۶۰

بندرعباس ۲۷۰

بنغازی ۲۹۷

بهرامی، عبدالله ۹۲، ۹۵، ۹۶، ۱۱۳، ۱۱۴

بودلین (کتابخانه) ۲۴۰، ۳۰۱

بورن‌موث ۳۴۲

بوستان ۳۸۰

بولونی (پاریس) ۵۳، ۵۴

بی‌بی‌سی ۳۸۵

بیرمنگام ۱۱۸، ۱۲۹، ۱۴۶، ۱۷۶، ۳۲۱

بیرونی، ابوریحان ۳۳۶

بیلی، هرولد والتر ۲۳۰، ۲۴۲، ۲۴۳، ۲۴۵،
۳۸۴

بینا، علی‌اکبر ۱۳۲، ۱۳۳، ۲۱۱

بینیُن، لارنس (Laurence Binyon) ۱۰۸

بیهقی، ابوالفضل محمد بن حسین ۲۹۱

پارسیان هند ۲۶۷

پاریس ۱۱، ۱۶، ۱۹، ۲۵، ۲۸، ۳۳، ۳۷، ۳۸،
۵۱، ۶۰، ۶۴، ۶۷، ۹۱، ۹۵، ۱۲۵، ۱۲۶، ۱۲۸،
۱۴۱، ۱۵۱، ۱۹۰، ۱۹۶، ۲۰۰

پانتئون (پاریس) ۳۶، ۵۳

پترسن پارک (Peterson Park) ۱۸

پتن، مارشال ۲۰۹، ۲۹۰

پدینگتن (ایستگاه) ۵۹

پرس /پرشیا ۴۳

پرل هاربور ۳۰۹

پرنس آو ویلز هتل ۶، ۸، ۲۴

پرو ۱۲۶

پرویز، عباس ۲۰، ۳۹، ۳۱۳

پریستلی، جان بوینتن ۳۰۱

پل مل (Pall Mall) ۵۰

پلاس مادلن (پاریس) ۳۶

پلانت، سر آرنولد ۸۴

پناهی، ابوالقاسم ۱۱۰، ۱۱۱، ۱۱۳، ۱۱۵، ۱۱۸،
۱۲۱، ۱۲۳، ۱۳۰، ۱۳۲، ۱۳۸، ۱۴۰، ۱۴۳،
۱۴۶، ۱۴۷، ۱۵۸، ۱۶۰، ۱۶۲، ۱۶۶، ۱۶۹،
۱۷۳، ۱۷۵، ۱۸۱، ۱۸۷

پوپ، آرتور اوپهام (Arthur Upham Pope)
۲۱، ۳۲، ۴۲، ۸۸، ۱۶۹

پوتسدام ۹۳، ۹۵

پیر دو نه‌سن (Pierre de Nesson) ۳۷

تآتر ادوئون (Odéon) ۳۶

تئاتر الحمرا ۷

تئاتر سارا برنار (Sarah Bernhardt) ۳۵

تاجبخش، آصف الحکما ۶۴، ۶۸

تاجیکستان ۳۲۱، ۳۲۲

تبریز ۲۶۰

تربتی، عمادالدین ۱۹۳

ترکیه ۱۷، ۱۹، ۴۱، ۲۶۸، ۳۱۴، ۳۱۶، ۳۷۰

تریست ۱۸۸

ترینیتی کالج (کمبریج) ۳۲۳

تقی‌زاده، سید جواد ۹۲، ۹۶، ۱۱۸

تقی‌زاده، سید حسن ۵، ۸، ۱۵، ۳۴، ۳۹، ۷۳،
۷۴، ۷۵، ۷۶، ۷۸، ۷۹، ۸۰، ۸۱، ۸۲، ۸۳،
۸۵، ۸۶، ۸۷، ۸۸، ۹۰، ۹۱، ۹۲، ۹۶، ۹۷،
۱۰۱، ۱۰۲، ۱۰۳، ۱۰۵، ۱۰۶، ۱۰۷، ۱۰۹، ۱۱۰،
۱۱۱، ۱۱۲، ۱۱۳، ۱۱۴، ۱۱۶، ۱۱۷، ۱۱۸، ۱۲۱،
۱۲۴، ۱۲۸، ۱۲۹، ۱۳۱، ۱۳۲، ۱۳۴، ۱۳۵،
۱۳۶، ۱۴۱، ۱۴۲، ۱۴۳، ۱۴۴، ۱۴۶، ۱۴۷،
۱۴۸، ۱۵۰، ۱۵۳، ۱۵۴، ۱۵۵، ۱۵۷، ۱۵۹،
۱۶۱، ۱۶۳، ۱۶۸، ۱۷۵، ۱۷۶، ۱۸۰، ۱۸۳،
۱۸۸، ۱۹۱، ۱۹۲، ۱۹۴، ۲۰۱، ۲۰۳، ۲۰۴،
۲۰۵، ۲۱۰، ۲۱۴، ۲۱۶، ۲۱۸، ۲۱۹، ۲۲۰، ۲۲۱،
۲۲۲، ۲۲۳، ۲۲۴، ۲۲۵، ۲۲۶، ۲۲۷، ۲۲۸،
۲۲۹، ۲۳۰، ۲۳۱، ۲۳۲، ۲۳۳، ۲۳۴، ۲۳۵،
۲۳۶، ۲۳۷، ۲۳۸، ۲۳۹، ۲۴۱، ۲۴۳، ۲۴۴،
۲۴۵، ۲۴۶، ۲۴۷، ۲۴۹، ۲۵۲، ۲۵۴، ۲۵۵،
۲۵۸، ۲۵۹، ۲۶۱، ۲۶۲، ۲۶۴، ۲۶۷، ۲۶۸،
۲۶۹، ۲۷۱، ۲۷۳، ۲۷۴، ۲۷۵، ۲۷۷، ۲۷۸،
۲۷۹، ۲۸۱، ۲۸۲، ۲۸۵، ۲۸۶، ۲۸۸، ۲۹۲،
۲۹۳، ۲۹۴، ۲۹۶، ۲۹۸، ۳۰۰، ۳۰۱، ۳۰۶،
۳۰۸، ۳۰۹، ۳۱۷، ۳۱۸، ۳۲۱، ۳۲۴، ۳۲۶،
۳۲۹، ۳۳۱، ۳۳۲، ۳۳۵، ۳۳۷، ۳۳۸،
۳۳۹، ۳۴۰، ۳۴۴، ۳۴۶، ۳۴۷، ۳۴۸، ۳۴۹،
۳۵۰، ۳۵۱، ۳۵۲، ۳۵۶، ۳۵۸، ۳۶۰، ۳۶۵،
۳۷۱، ۳۷۳، ۳۷۴، ۳۷۵، ۳۷۶، ۳۷۷،

۳۸۴، ۳۸۳

توبر، ریچارد ۳۱۶

توپالیان، ساهاک ۲۳۲، ۲۴۳، ۲۷۵، ۲۸۲، ۲۸۳، ۲۹۶

تولستوی ۱۸۴، ۲۵۵، ۲۵۷

تونس ۵۳، ۳۶۵، ۳۶۶، ۳۶۷، ۳۶۸، ۳۶۹، ۳۷۷، ۳۸۲،۳۸۳، ۳۸۴

تویلری (باغ) ۳۸

تیموشنکو، سیمون ۲۷۶

ثقة الدوله دیبا، ابوالحسن ۴۸

جامعه ملل ۴۱

جانسن، لویی ۳۱۸

جاوه ۳۰۴، ۳۰۵، ۳۰۶، ۳۰۷، ۳۰۹

جزائری، شمس‌الدین ۶۸، ۱۲۸، ۱۳۰

جزیره موریس ۱۳۰

جشن فردوسی ۱۶، ۲۱، ۲۶، ۲۸، ۲۹، ۳۰، ۳۱، ۳۷، ۳۸، ۳۹

جمال‌زاده، محمدعلی ۱۹۷، ۱۹۸

جمال‌زاده، محمدعلی ۶۸، ۹۳

جمعیت آسیای وسطی (Central Asian Society) ۳۰

جهانبانی، امان الله ۲۶۷

چالوس ۲۶۱

چدویک، هکتور مونرو ۲۳۲، ۲۵۲، ۲۵۳، ۲۵۴، ۲۷۵، ۲۷۶، ۳۲۰، ۳۲۶

چرچیل، وینستن ۲۵۶، ۲۶۳، ۲۶۸، ۲۷۰، ۲۸۷، ۲۹۰، ۲۹۷، ۳۰۰، ۳۱۴، ۳۲۶، ۳۳۶،

۳۷۹، ۳۵۰، ۳۴۶، ۳۴۵

چکسلواکی ۱۶۸

چلسی (Chelsea) ۱۶، ۲۴، ۳۰، ۴۶، ۵۶

چمبرلن ۱۵۳

چین ۲۶۰، ۲۶۳، ۲۶۷

حافظ ۲۶، ۲۵۶، ۳۱۰، ۳۱۹

حبل المتین (روزنامه) ۱۱۶

حجاب ۵۵

حزب کنگره (هندوستان) ۳۴۳

حسیبی، کاظم ۶۲، ۶۳

حکمت، علی اصغر ۲۶۷

حکیم الدوله (حسن ادهم) ۳۸

حکیمی، ابوالحسن ۱۹۸

حمزاوی، عبدالحسین ۷۵، ۸۲، ۹۰، ۱۰۷، ۱۱۱، ۱۱۲، ۱۱۵، ۱۱۶، ۱۳۸، ۱۴۸، ۱۵۶، ۱۶۴، ۱۶۶، ۱۸۹، ۱۹۵، ۲۰۲، ۲۰۵، ۲۰۷، ۲۰۸، ۲۱۱، ۲۱۹، ۲۲۱، ۲۲۴، ۲۲۵، ۲۲۷، ۲۲۹، ۲۳۰، ۲۳۱، ۲۳۲، ۲۳۴، ۲۳۶، ۲۴۱، ۲۴۲، ۲۴۳، ۲۴۶، ۲۴۷، ۲۴۸، ۲۵۲، ۲۶۳، ۲۶۵، ۲۶۹، ۲۷۰، ۲۷۵، ۲۷۷، ۲۸۲، ۲۸۳، ۲۸۷، ۲۹۶، ۲۹۷، ۳۱۴، ۳۲۳، ۳۲۹، ۳۳۱، ۳۳۴، ۳۴۲، ۳۴۴، ۳۵۱، ۳۶۷، ۳۷۲، ۳۷۳، ۳۷۴، ۳۷۵، ۳۷۶، ۳۷۷، ۳۸۱، ۳۸۲، ۳۸۳، ۳۸۵، ۳۸۶

خارکف ۲۷۷، ۳۲۷، ۳۲۹، ۳۳۰، ۳۳۱

۳۳۳، ۳۸۵

خانقین ۲

خسروپور ۳۳، ۳۵، ۳۷، ۳۸، ۳۹، ۵۲، ۶۸،

۹۱

خسروشاهی، علی ۱۶۹

خلخالی، عبدالرحیم ۱، ۶، ۳۹، ۶۱، ۳۱۳،

۳۴۶، ۳۴۷

خلیج فارس ۴۸، ۲۵۸، ۲۵۹

خواجه‌نوری، ابراهیم ۱۳

خوش‌بین، غلامحسین ۹۲، ۹۳، ۹۴، ۹۵، ۱۲۷

خوش‌کیش، یوسف ۳۶، ۳۸، ۳۹، ۶۸، ۷۰،

۹۱، ۱۲۸، ۱۹۶، ۲۰۰

خیام ۳۱، ۱۷۷، ۳۰۴، ۳۶۱

خیوه ۱۲۳

دارا، عبدالله میرزا ۲۳

داراب خان ۸۰

دارلان، ژان لویی گزاویه فرانسوا ۳۶۵، ۳۶۶،

۳۷۲

داروگر، غلامرضا ۳۱۹

داروین ۱۶

داریوش، پرویز ۱۵

دالادیه ۱۵۳

دانشگاه اکسفورد ۸، ۲۸، ۳۱، ۱۵۳، ۱۷۸

دانشگاه کمبریج ۸، ۳۰۵، ۳۲۶

دانمارک ۳۶۵

داور، علی‌اکبر ۱۰۸

دریفوس، آلفرد ۵۷

درینک‌واتر، جان (John Drinkwater) ۲۷،

۳۱، ۱۱۱، ۳۴۵

دشتی، علی ۱۱، ۲۴، ۲۶، ۴۱، ۳۷۴

دفتری، عبدالله ۹۲، ۹۴

دفتری، علی اکبر ۹۵، ۹۶، ۱۱۸

دنسترویل، لیونل (Lionel Dunsterville) ۲۹

دهقان، عباس ۳۸۵

دوده، آلفونس ۳۱۹

دوستویوسکی ۱۴

دوگل، شارل ۳۶۶، ۳۷۹

دوور (بندر) ۳۹، ۱۲۶

دیپ (بندر) ۳۴۵، ۳۵۷

دیده‌بان ۷، ۱۱، ۱۸، ۲۲

رابرتسون، دانلد ۳۲۰، ۳۲۱، ۳۲۳، ۳۴۳

راجی، عبدالحسین ۱۶۰

رادمنش، رضا ۵۳، ۶۸، ۶۹، ۷۰

رانگون ۳۰۶

رایس، دیوید تالبوت ۱۵۵

ربنس، لیونل ۸۴، ۸۶

رخشانی (از کارکنان سفارت) ۱۰۴، ۱۰۵

رسل اسکویر ۴

رشید یاسمی، غلامرضا ۱۱، ۴۱

رضا شاه ۸، ۱۷، ۱۹، ۳۱، ۵۵، ۷۸، ۱۶۷،

۲۶۳، ۲۶۴، ۲۶۵، ۲۶۶، ۲۶۷، ۲۶۸، ۳۰۹،

۳۱۰، ۳۱۱، ۳۱۲، ۳۲۳، ۳۶۱

رضا شوشتری، عباس ۲۷۸، ۳۷۴

رعدی آذرخشی، غلامعلی ۱۴۹، ۱۵۰، ۱۵۱،

۱۹۷، ۱۹۸

رفعتی (از کارکنان سفارت) ۳۰، ۴۴، ۵۹، ۶۳،

۷۰، ۸۴، ۸۶

رمبرنت هتل ۶۶

رمبو، آلفرد نیکلاس ۳۵۰

رنان، ارنست ۲۹۷

روحانی، فؤاد ۱۳، ۱۴، ۱۶، ۱۷، ۲۱، ۲۲، ۲۳،
۲۴، ۲۷، ۲۹، ۳۰، ۶۳، ۹۶، ۹۷، ۹۸، ۱۰۰،
۱۰۱، ۱۰۲، ۱۰۳، ۱۰۳، ۱۰۵، ۱۰۶، ۱۰۹، ۱۱۱،
۱۱۴، ۱۱۵، ۱۱۸، ۱۱۹، ۱۲۰، ۱۲۱، ۱۲۲، ۱۲۳،
۱۲۴، ۱۲۵، ۱۲۶، ۱۲۷

روزولت، فرانکلین دلانو ۲۵۶، ۳۱۸، ۳۷۹

روستوف (روسطوف/راستوف) ۲۸۵، ۲۸۶،
۳۴۰، ۳۸۲

روسو، ژان ژاک ۳۶

روسیه/روسها ۸۱، ۱۸۲، ۱۸۷، ۲۴۸، ۲۵۷،
۲۵۸، ۲۶۰، ۲۶۱، ۲۶۲، ۲۶۴، ۲۶۵، ۲۶۷،
۲۶۸، ۲۷۰، ۲۷۱، ۲۷۳، ۲۷۴، ۲۷۶، ۲۷۸،
۲۸۵، ۲۸۸، ۲۸۹، ۲۹۰، ۲۹۳، ۲۹۴، ۲۹۶،
۳۰۲، ۳۰۷، ۳۰۹، ۳۱۳، ۳۱۴، ۳۱۸، ۳۲۱،
۳۲۲، ۳۲۸، ۳۲۹، ۳۳۰، ۳۳۹، ۳۴۰، ۳۴۱،
۳۴۲، ۳۴۵، ۳۴۸، ۳۴۹، ۳۵۲، ۳۶۲، ۳۷۴،
۳۷۷، ۳۸۲، ۳۸۳، ۳۸۵

رومانی ۲۶۳

رومل، اروین ۲۹۷، ۲۹۸، ۳۰۲، ۳۳۶، ۳۳۷،
۳۴۹، ۳۷۰

ریاضی، سید حسن ۳۳، ۶۲، ۶۳، ۶۹

ریجنتز پارک ۵، ۹

ریچموند (محله) ۵

ریکتر، چارلز ۱۰۱

ریکتر، هانس ۲۹۱

زردشت ۷۹

زرین‌کفش، پرویز ۱

زرین‌کفش، زرّین‌دخت ۱

زرین‌کفش، عزیزالزمان ۱

زرین‌کفش، علی اصغر ۱، ۲، ۳، ۴، ۶، ۸، ۹،
۱۱، ۱۲، ۱۳، ۱۵، ۱۶، ۱۹، ۲۱، ۲۲، ۲۳، ۲۵،
۲۸، ۳۲، ۴۰، ۴۲، ۴۵، ۵۰، ۵۱، ۵۴، ۵۶، ۵۷،
۵۸، ۶۱، ۶۲، ۶۴، ۶۵، ۶۶، ۷۱، ۷۳، ۷۵،
۷۶، ۷۷، ۸۰، ۸۱، ۸۴، ۸۶، ۸۷، ۹۰، ۹۱،
۹۲، ۹۶، ۹۸، ۱۰۰، ۱۰۱، ۱۰۴، ۱۰۵، ۱۰۶،
۱۰۷، ۱۰۹، ۱۱۰، ۱۱۱، ۱۱۲، ۱۱۳، ۱۱۶، ۱۱۸،
۱۱۹، ۱۲۱، ۱۲۸، ۱۳۱، ۱۳۴، ۱۳۵، ۱۳۶،
۱۳۷، ۱۳۸، ۱۳۹، ۱۴۰، ۱۴۱، ۱۴۲، ۱۴۵،
۱۴۷، ۱۵۲، ۱۵۳، ۱۵۴، ۱۵۸، ۱۶۰، ۱۶۱،
۱۶۲، ۱۶۳، ۱۶۵، ۱۶۸، ۱۶۹، ۱۷۰، ۱۷۳،
۱۷۵، ۱۷۶، ۱۷۷، ۱۸۰، ۱۸۱، ۱۸۲، ۱۸۳،
۱۸۵، ۱۸۶، ۱۸۷، ۱۸۸، ۱۸۹، ۱۹۱، ۱۹۲،
۱۹۳، ۱۹۴، ۲۰۱، ۲۰۲، ۲۰۳، ۲۰۴، ۲۷۴،
۳۰۳، ۳۵۹

زرین‌کفش، علیرضا ۱

زندی، اختر ۱۹۹، ۲۰۰

زوریخ ۱۹۵، ۱۹۶، ۱۹۷، ۱۹۸، ۲۰۰، ۲۱۰، ۲۱۱،
۲۱۶، ۲۱۷، ۲۱۸، ۲۱۹، ۲۲۰، ۲۲۲، ۲۲۳،
۲۲۴، ۲۲۵، ۲۲۶، ۲۲۷، ۲۲۸، ۲۲۹، ۲۳۰،
۲۳۱، ۲۳۲، ۲۳۳، ۲۳۴، ۲۳۷، ۲۴۱، ۲۴۳،

۲۴۵، ۲۴۶، ۲۵۲، ۲۵۴، ۲۵۹، ۲۶۱، ۲۷۰،
۲۷۶، ۲۷۷، ۲۸۲، ۲۸۳، ۲۸۶، ۲۹۱، ۲۹۲،
۲۹۳، ۲۹۶، ۲۹۸، ۳۰۰، ۳۰۱، ۳۰۵، ۳۰۶،
۳۰۸

ژاپن/ژاپونی‌ها ۲۷۷، ۲۸۶، ۲۸۷، ۲۸۸، ۲۸۹،
۲۹۰، ۲۹۱، ۲۹۲، ۲۹۳، ۲۹۴، ۲۹۵، ۲۹۶،
۲۹۷، ۲۹۸، ۲۹۹، ۳۰۰، ۳۰۱، ۳۰۲، ۳۰۴،
۳۰۵، ۳۰۶، ۳۰۹، ۳۱۴، ۳۱۷، ۳۱۸، ۳۱۹،
۳۲۳، ۳۲۴، ۳۲۵

ژنو ۴۱، ۷۵، ۱۹۷، ۱۹۸، ۲۵۷

ژیرو، آنری اُنوره ۳۶۴، ۳۶۶، ۳۷۹

ساعد مراغه‌ای، محمد ۳۴۴

سان سوسی (کاخ) ۹۵

سایکس، سر پرسی ۲۸، ۳۰، ۱۶۰،

سایمون، سر جان (Sir John A. Simon) ۵۶

سباستوپول (سواستوپول) ۳۳۲، ۳۳۳، ۳۳۵،
۳۳۷

سپاسی ۹۱، ۹۲، ۹۳

سپهبدی، فرهاد ۵۳، ۱۹۶

سر دنیسن راس ۱۳، ۱۵، ۲۰، ۲۶، ۲۷، ۳۰،
۳۱، ۴۵، ۶۲، ۷۷، ۷۹، ۸۶، ۱۰۷، ۱۱۷،
۱۲۰، ۱۲۸، ۱۷۵، ۱۷۸

سر هوراس رمبولد (Sir Horace Rumbold)
۳۱

سردار اکرم قراگوزلو، منصورعلی ۱۵۶

سرداری، عبدالحسین ۲۱، ۴۲، ۴۷، ۴۹، ۵۷،
۶۱، ۷۲، ۸۰، ۸۲، ۹۰، ۱۱۰، ۱۳۳، ۱۹۶، ۲۰۰

سعدی ۶۸، ۱۱۹، ۱۲۰، ۲۵۶، ۳۱۰، ۳۵۲، ۳۷۵

سعیدی، احمد ۹۳، ۹۴

سمرقندی، دولتشاه ۳۲۵

سمریتن هوس ۳۵

سمنر، بندیکت ۱۷۸

سمیعی، باقر خان ۲۱، ۲۲

سن ژنوی‌یو (Sainte-Geneviève) ۶۹

سنت هلن (جزیره) ۳۴

سنگاپور ۲۹۴، ۲۹۶، ۲۹۸، ۲۹۹، ۳۰۰، ۳۰۱،
۳۰۹

سهروردی، حسان ۳۶۶، ۳۶۷، ۳۷۴

سهیلی، علی ۲۹، ۱۱۵، ۱۱۷، ۱۲۴، ۱۲۸، ۱۳۱،
۱۳۴، ۱۳۵، ۱۴۰، ۱۴۱، ۱۴۲، ۲۶۷، ۳۰۶،
۳۰۷، ۳۳۷، ۳۷۷، ۳۸۲

سودآور، صمد ۶۶، ۷۱، ۱۱۵

سوربون ۳۵، ۳۸، ۶۸، ۶۹

سوفلو، ژاک ژرمن ۳۶

سوماترا ۳۰۲

سوییس ۷۷، ۱۹۶

سیاسی، علی‌اکبر ۱۳

سیام ۲۸۷

سی‌تون واتسون، رابرت ویلیام (Robert William Seton-Watson) ۳۰۵

سیدی رزق ۳۳۴

سیزده بدر ۴۸

سیلان ۳۱۷

شادمان، جلال ۱، ۶، ۸، ۱۱، ۱۳، ۱۷، ۱۸، ۱۹،

۲۰، ۲۲، ۲۳، ۲۶، ۲۹، ۵۷، ۶۱، ۷۲، ۷۴،
۷۷، ۲۸۷، ۲۹۳، ۳۳۳

شادمان، جمال ۱، ۱۱، ۲۹

شادمان، زینت ۱۰، ۱۲، ۲۵، ۲۹

شادمان، ضیاء ۱۰، ۲۵

شادمان، کمال ۱، ۳۳۳

شادمان، ناصر ۱۰، ۲۵

شان ز لیزه ۳۳، ۳۷، ۳۸، ۶۸، ۱۲۶، ۱۲۷

شاهرخی (از کارکنان سفارت) ۸۰، ۸۱

شاهرود ۲۶۱

شاهنامه ۳۴۷

شایسته، محمد (از کارکنان سفارت/سفیر ایران در لهستان) ۸، ۱۳، ۱۵، ۱۶، ۴۰، ۴۱، ۶۲

شایگان، سید علی ۳۶

شرکت شل ۱۳۱، ۱۳۲

شرکت نفت ایران و انگلیس ۲، ۸۵، ۱۱۹، ۱۳۱، ۱۵۲، ۲۸۲، ۳۵۸

شرودر، اریک ۱۴۴۶

شکسپیر ۶۱، ۱۵۳، ۱۹۱، ۲۵۶، ۲۸۵، ۳۱۰، ۳۵۳

شیبانی، حبیب الله ۱۸۲، ۱۸۳، ۱۹۰، ۱۹۳، ۱۹۴، ۱۹۵، ۱۹۶، ۲۰۰، ۲۰۴، ۲۰۵، ۲۰۶، ۲۰۷، ۲۱۲

شیدفر، زین‌العابدین ۳۳، ۳۶، ۳۸، ۵۲، ۶۷، ۶۸، ۶۹، ۷۰، ۷۱

شیرازی، رضا ۲۵۴

شیعه ۷۰

شیلی ۲۷۰

شیوا، ابوالقاسم ۳۰

صالح، جهانشاه ۳۸۵

صدر، سید صادق، ۳۹، ۵۶، ۵۷، ۵۸

صدر، سید کاظم ۳۶، ۳۷، ۵۲، ۵۳، ۶۹، ۷۱، ۹۳، ۹۴

صدیق اعلم، عیسی ۱۴۸، ۲۶۷

صدیقی، غلامحسین ۶۸، ۶۹، ۷۰، ۷۱، ۱۶۰

صفوت، امیرحسین ۱۵۵، ۱۵۹، ۱۷۳، ۱۹۱، ۱۹۲

صوراسرافیل، صادق ۲۵

صورتگر، لطفعلی ۲۲، ۲۹، ۴۱، ۱۴۱، ۱۴۳، ۱۴۴، ۱۴۸، ۱۴۹، ۱۵۰، ۱۵۳، ۱۵۶، ۱۵۷، ۱۶۲، ۱۸۲

طبروک (طبرق) ۳۳۳، ۳۳۴، ۳۳۵، ۳۳۶

طرابلس (لیبی) ۳۷۸

طهران/تهران ۱، ۲، ۳، ۱۹، ۲۱، ۲۲، ۲۸، ۳۲، ۳۸، ۶۳، ۷۷، ۱۰۸، ۱۱۸، ۱۲۳، ۱۴۱، ۱۸۰، ۱۹۲، ۲۴۳، ۲۶۲، ۲۶۴، ۲۶۵، ۲۶۸، ۲۶۹، ۲۷۰، ۲۷۶، ۲۸۱، ۳۰۶، ۳۰۸، ۳۲۱، ۳۳۶، ۳۶۹، ۳۷۱، ۳۷۶، ۳۷۷

عبادی، نصراله ۳۵

عبدالرحمان المهدی ۱۲۰

عبدالقادر (Sir Sheikh Abdul Qadir) ۷۹

عبده، جلال ۳۵، ۳۷، ۵۳، ۶۲، ۶۳، ۶۸، ۷۱

عثمانی ۳۰۱

عراق ۱۶، ۴۱، ۱۲۶، ۱۶۷، ۳۷۹

عطار (شاعر) ۳۴۸

علاء، حسین ۲۵، ۲۸، ۳۰، ۳۱، ۳۷، ۳۸، ۳۹، ۴۰، ۴۳، ۴۸، ۵۴، ۵۷، ۵۸، ۶۲، ۷۱، ۷۹، ۸۱، ۸۶، ۱۰۲، ۱۰۳، ۱۱۰، ۳۱۳، ۳۳۶، ۳۷۴

علوی، حسن ۱۵، ۲۴، ۹۵، ۹۶، ۹۸، ۹۹، ۱۰۱، ۱۰۴، ۱۰۶، ۱۰۷، ۱۰۸، ۱۰۹، ۱۱۰، ۱۱۱، ۱۱۲، ۱۱۳، ۱۱۴، ۱۱۵، ۱۱۶، ۱۱۷، ۱۴۷، ۳۳۶، ۳۷۴

علی‌آبادی، عبدالحسین ۵۲، ۵۳، ۱۲۸

علیرضا بی ۸۵

عمید، موسی ۷۱، ۲۰۰

غازان ۲۷۴

غازان خان ۳۲۴

غفاری، حسام الدین ۳۱۹

غمام همدانی ۱

غنی، قاسم ۸

فئودوزیا ۲۹۸

فاتح، مصطفی ۱۲۱

فاشیستها ۲۵

فراست، رابرت لی ۳۷۶

فرانسه ۱۶، ۳۳، ۱۴۷، ۱۵۲، ۱۸۲، ۲۰۹، ۲۱۰، ۲۹۰، ۳۶۶

فرانشه دس‌پره، لویی فلیکس فرانسوا (Louis-Félix-François Franchet d'Espèrey) ۳۹

فرخی سیستانی ۳۷۵، ۳۸۰

فردوسی ۲۷، ۳۱، ۳۸، ۳۹، ۵۵، ۳۱۰

فرزاد، مسعود ۳۸۵

فرمانفرمائیان، منوچهر ۶۴، ۷۲، ۷۴، ۲۰۵، ۲۱۰

فرهاد معتمد، ناصر ۱۵۱

فرهت ۸

فروغی، ابوالحسن ۳۷، ۳۸

فروغی، جواد ۳۷، ۱۹۸

فروغی، محمدعلی ۳۷

فروهر، عبدالله ۱

فریار، عبدالله ۴۱

فریزر، ویلیام ۲۱۰، ۲۲۹، ۲۴۷

فلاح، رضا ۱۶۲

فلسطین ۱۶۶، ۱۶۷، ۱۷۷

فلسفی، نصرالله ۶، ۲۵

فن پاپن، فرانتس ۲۶۸

فور، پل ۳۷

فولی برژر (Folies Bergère) ۳۹، ۶۸

فون براوخیچ، والتر هاینریک آلفرد هرمان (Walther Heirich Alfred Hermann von Brauchitsch) ۲۸۹

فویلز (Foyles) ۱۱، ۱۸

فیتزجرالد، ادوارد ۱۷۸، ۲۹۵، ۲۹۶، ۲۹۷

فیلیپین ۲۸۷، ۲۹۰، ۲۹۱، ۳۰۸

قاجار، محمدحسن میرزا ۳۷۶

قدس نخعی، حسین ۱۱۳، ۱۲۳، ۱۳۴، ۱۳۸، ۱۴۰، ۱۴۱، ۳۶۹، ۳۷۲، ۳۷۵، ۳۷۸، ۳۸۱،

۳۸۴، ۳۸۶

قراگوزلو، علی‌رضا بهاء الملک ۳۴۴

قره‌گوزلو، حسینقلی ۱۱۵

قره‌گوزلو، محسن ۱۱۵

قریب گرگانی، شمس العلما محمدحسین ۵۳

قریب گرگانی، محمد ۵۳

قزل ایاغ، حسینقلی ۹۳، ۹۴، ۹۵

قزل ایاغ، محمود ۱۴۰

قزوین ۱، ۲۶۱، ۲۶۲، ۲۷۶

قزوینی، محمد ۸، ۳۶، ۳۸، ۵۲، ۶۷، ۶۹،
۷۱، ۸۱، ۸۴، ۸۵، ۹۰، ۹۲، ۹۶، ۱۰۷، ۱۱۱،
۱۱۳، ۱۲۷، ۲۴۴، ۲۴۶

قشقایی، امیرحسین ۹۴

قشقایی، ناصر ۱۷۷

قفطی، ابوالحسن علی ۳۴۰

قفقاز ۱۵۵، ۱۸۷، ۲۷۰، ۲۸۲، ۳۲۲، ۳۴۱،
۳۴۲، ۳۴۳، ۳۴۴، ۳۴۵، ۳۴۶، ۳۴۷، ۳۴۹،
۳۵۶، ۳۶۳

قوام السلطنه ۳۴۴، ۳۷۰، ۳۸۲

قیصر ۱۸۲

کاردینال دو ریشلیو ۳۵

کاردینال وردیه (Jean Verdier) ۳۵

کارلایل ۱۶

کاظمی، سید باقر مهذب الدوله ۲۷، ۳۴۴،
۳۷۴

کاکس، سر پرسی ۲۷۴

کاله (بندر) ۳۳

کانادا ۶۰، ۳۰۹

کتابچی خان، آنتوان ۷۸، ۱۲۷

کتابخانه ملی فرانسه ۳۷

کدمن، سر جان ۶، ۷، ۱۵، ۱۶، ۵۵، ۷۳، ۸۶،
۱۱۹، ۱۵۶، ۲۰۱، ۲۱۰، ۲۴۳، ۲۴۵

کرایست کالج (اکسفورد) ۲۴۹

کربلا ۱، ۲، ۸، ۵۱، ۵۵، ۷۷، ۱۶۵، ۱۶۹

کرج ۲۸۲، ۳۲۶، ۳۲۷، ۳۲۹

کردستان ۳۲۱

کرلی، استیفن ۱۰۱

کرمان ۳۲

کرمانشاهان ۱

کرمانی، میرزا شهاب ۵۳

کرند ۲

کریپس، استافورد ۳۱۵، ۳۱۸

کریگ، جیمز (رئیس الوزرای ایرلند) ۲

کریمه ۲۶۸، ۲۷۶، ۲۷۸، ۲۷۹، ۲۸۰، ۲۸۱،
۲۸۲، ۲۹۸

کلانتری (از کارکنان سفارت) ۸۷، ۸۸، ۸۹،
۹۰، ۹۲، ۱۰۰، ۱۰۳، ۱۰۸، ۱۱۰، ۱۱۵

کلاه فرنگی ۵۵

کلپ، فردریک گاردنر ۱۵۶

کلن (کولون) ۳۳۰

کلیسای سنت پول ۷

کمبریج ۵۹، ۱۲۱، ۱۸۷، ۱۸۸، ۱۸۹، ۱۹۱،
۱۹۳، ۱۹۵، ۲۰۱، ۲۰۳، ۲۰۴، ۲۰۶، ۲۱۴،
۲۱۶، ۲۱۷، ۲۱۹، ۲۲۱، ۲۲۲، ۲۲۳، ۲۲۴،

۲۲۵، ۲۲۶، ۲۲۸، ۲۲۹، ۲۳۰، ۲۳۱، ۲۳۲،
۲۳۳، ۲۳۴، ۲۳۵، ۲۳۶، ۲۳۷، ۲۳۸، ۲۳۹،
۲۴۰، ۲۴۲، ۲۴۳، ۲۴۵، ۲۴۸، ۲۵۰، ۲۵۱،
۲۵۲، ۲۵۴، ۲۵۹، ۲۶۰، ۲۶۱، ۲۶۶، ۲۶۷،
۲۷۱، ۲۷۲، ۲۷۴، ۲۷۶، ۲۷۸، ۲۷۹، ۲۸۰،
۲۸۱، ۲۸۳، ۲۸۵، ۲۸۷، ۲۸۹، ۲۹۱، ۲۹۳،
۲۹۴، ۲۹۷، ۳۰۰، ۳۰۲، ۳۰۴، ۳۰۷، ۳۱۳،
۳۱۴، ۳۱۵، ۳۱۶، ۳۱۹، ۳۲۰، ۳۲۱، ۳۲۳،
۳۲۴، ۳۲۸، ۳۳۳، ۳۳۴، ۳۳۵، ۳۳۶،
۳۳۷، ۳۳۸، ۳۳۹، ۳۴۱، ۳۴۵، ۳۴۸، ۳۴۹،
۳۵۰، ۳۵۱، ۳۵۲، ۳۵۳، ۳۵۵، ۳۵۶، ۳۵۷،
۳۵۸، ۳۸۱

کمدی فرانسز ۳۶

کمنز، جان ۲۸۱

کمونیستها ۲۵

کنزینگتون (Kensington) ۱۲، ۱۴

کنگاور ۱

کنیل ورث (Kenilworth) ۶۱

کولژ دو فرانس ۷۰

کویینز کالج (کمبریج) ۲۴۳

کیف ۲۶۱

کیف ۲۶۶، ۲۶۸

کینگز کالج (کمبریج) ۷۵، ۳۳۱

کینگز کراس ۲۰

کینگستون (Kingston upon Thames) ۱۰

کی‌یو گاردنز (Kew Gardens) ۹

گار دو نور (Gare du Nord) ۵۳، ۶۷

گاندی، مهاتما ۳۴۳، ۳۸۲، ۳۸۳، ۳۸۴

گرجستان ۳۲۱

گرلی، استیفن ۳۶۱

گری، بازیل (Basil Gray) ۵۷، ۵۸، ۶۵، ۸۷، ۱۳۳، ۱۳۵، ۲۲۷، ۲۸۳، ۳۷۷، ۳۷۸، ۳۸۲، ۳۸۳

گلبنکیان، کالوست (Calouste Gulbenkian) ۸۷

گلبنکیان، کالوست ۲۷۸، ۲۸۲

گلستان ۳۵۲

گلشائیان، عباسقلی ۱۱

گورکی، ماکسیم ۳۶۱

گورو، ژانرال هانری ژوزف اوژن (Henri Joseph Eugène Gouroud) ۳۹

گورینگ، هرمان ۳۷۹

گیب، همیلتن الکساندر راسکین ۲۴۰، ۲۴۴

گیل‌گود، جان ۳۲۷

لا کوپول (رستوران) ۶۸، ۶۹

لاسکی، هارولد ۸۵، ۸۶

لاف برو (Loughborough) ۱۱۸

لافریر (معلم حقوق سوربون) ۵۲

لاکهارت، لارنس ۲۰، ۴۱، ۷۷، ۸۷، ۸۸، ۱۰۰، ۱۰۳، ۱۰۹، ۱۶۴، ۲۲۷

لرد تویدزمیر (Lord Tweedsmuir) ۶۰

لرد هالیفاکس (Edward Wood, 1st Earl of Halifax) ۶۰

لستر اسکویر ۴

لمینگتون، لرد (Charles W. A. Napier

Cochrane-Baillie) ۳۰، ۳۱، ۸۷

لنینگراد ۲۶۱، ۲۶۲، ۲۶۷، ۲۸۰

لهستان ۶۲، ۱۸۲، ۱۸۳، ۱۸۴، ۱۸۵

لو بورژه ۱۹۶، ۲۰۱

لوئو، هربرت ۲۷۵

لوزاک (ناشر) ۷، ۲۴، ۳۷۹، ۳۸۳، ۳۸۴،

۳۸۵

لوکسان‌بور (باغ) ۳۳، ۳۶

لوکسان‌بور (موزه) ۳۵

لوور (موزه) ۳۸، ۵۳

لیبی ۲۸۲، ۲۸۳، ۳۱۸، ۳۳۰، ۳۳۲

لیتون (Frederic Leighton) ۵۴

لیدی رمبولد (Etheldred Constantia, Lady

Rumbold) ۳۱

لین‌لیث‌گو (مارکیز) ۳۴۳

لیورپول ۲۲۱، ۳۲۶، ۳۳۵

لی‌یو، پر ۳۸

ماداگاسکار ۳۲۴

مادام برتلو (Mme Sophie Caroline

Berthelot) ۳۶

مادام توسو (Madame Tussauds) ۳

مادرید هتل ۲، ۳، ۲۱، ۲۴، ۲۵، ۴۰، ۴۳، ۴۸

ماربل آرچ ۴، ۱۶، ۱۸، ۴۹، ۵۰، ۵۸، ۶۳، ۷۲،

۷۵

مارکس، کارل ۳۳۲

مارگولیوث ۲۸

ماسه، هانری ۳۷، ۳۸

ماک‌لین‌توک، سر ویلیام (Sir William

McLintock) ۹، ۱۰، ۲۰

مالارمه، استفان (Stéphane Mallarmé) ۳۸

مالایا ۲۸۸، ۲۸۹، ۲۹۶، ۲۹۷، ۲۹۸، ۳۰۴،

۳۴۸

مالزی ۲۸۷، ۲۸۸، ۲۹۰، ۲۹۱، ۲۹۲، ۲۹۳،

۲۹۴، ۲۹۵، ۲۹۷

مانش ۳۰۰

متروپول (هتل) ۴۸

متنبّی (شاعر) ۹۹

متین‌دفتری، احمد ۱۲

محمدآبادی (از کارکنان سفارت) ۳، ۴، ۶، ۷،

۸، ۹، ۱۱، ۱۳، ۱۴، ۱۵، ۱۶، ۱۷، ۱۸، ۱۹، ۲۰،

۲۱، ۲۲، ۲۳، ۲۴، ۲۵

محمدرضا شاه/ولیعهد ۲۶۵، ۲۷۶، ۳۰۹

مدرسه اقتصاد لندن ۷۴، ۷۵، ۸۴، ۸۵، ۸۶،

۹۹، ۱۰۰، ۱۰۱، ۱۰۲، ۱۰۶، ۱۰۸، ۱۰۹، ۱۱۳،

۱۱۵، ۱۲۸، ۱۴۱، ۱۴۳، ۱۵۷، ۱۶۳، ۱۶۶،

۱۷۸، ۲۷۱

مدرسه السنه شرقیه/مدرسه علوم شرقیه

(School of Oriental Studies) ۹، ۱۳، ۱۴،

۱۵، ۱۶، ۱۸، ۲۷، ۲۹، ۳۰، ۳۱، ۴۱، ۴۲، ۴۵،

۷۶، ۷۷، ۷۹، ۸۲، ۱۰۷، ۱۱۳، ۱۲۰، ۲۸۱،

۳۰۵، ۳۴۹، ۳۸۰، ۳۸۵

مدرسه حقوق (سوربون) ۵۱، ۵۲، ۵۳

مدیرالدوله، محمود ۹۷

مدینه ۴۶

مرآت، اسماعیل ۳۳

مراکش ۵۳

مستوفی، احمد ۶۱، ۶۲، ۶۴، ۶۸، ۱۴۸، ۱۴۹،
۱۵۴، ۱۵۶، ۲۱۲

مستوفی، حمدالله ۲۹

مسجد شاه جهان (ووکینگ) ۹۲، ۱۶۵، ۳۷۱،
۳۷۳

مسعود سعد سلمان ۳۵۱، ۳۸۳

مسکو ۲۷۱، ۲۷۲، ۲۷۳، ۲۷۴، ۲۷۵، ۲۷۶،
۲۷۷، ۲۷۸، ۲۸۴، ۲۸۵، ۲۸۶، ۲۸۸

مشاور، محمود ۶۷، ۶۸

مشهد ۲۶۰

مصباح ۲۵

مصدقی ۳۳، ۳۵

مصر ۱۲۶، ۲۶۵، ۲۷۰، ۲۹۹، ۳۴۸، ۳۴۹،
۳۶۱، ۳۶۳، ۳۶۴، ۳۶۵

مظفرالدین شاه ۳۲۱

معظمی، عبدالله ۱۸۴

معظمی، غلامعلی ۱، ۷۱، ۹۷، ۱۱۳، ۱۸۴،
۲۱۰، ۲۱۱

مفتاح، داود ۳۹، ۶۷، ۶۹، ۷۰، ۷۱

مقدم، محمدعلی ۲۰۱، ۲۱۳، ۲۳۰، ۲۴۸، ۲۶۹،
۲۷۰، ۲۷۳، ۲۷۴، ۲۷۶، ۳۶۶

مک‌آرتور، داگلاس ۳۰۸

مکدونالد، مالکم ۱۷۷

مک‌گیل ۳۱

ملک اسماعیلی ۳۶، ۵۳

ملک الشعرا بهار، محمدتقی ۳۲

ملکه کریستینا (فیلم) ۲۲

ملکی، شیخ رضا ۱

مهتدی، بدیعه ۳۵۱، ۳۶۲، ۳۸۶

مهدوی، یحیی ۱۴۱، ۱۴۴، ۱۴۵، ۱۴۶، ۱۴۸،
۱۴۹

مهین کرمانی، جواد ۱۲۵

مورتس، هورشید ۱۰۷

موزهٔ بریتانیا/بریتیش میوزیم ۵، ۷، ۲۴، ۲۵،
۲۹، ۵۷، ۸۱، ۸۲، ۸۴، ۸۹، ۱۰۰، ۱۰۵، ۱۱۶،
۱۱۷، ۱۱۸، ۱۱۹، ۱۲۰، ۱۳۰، ۱۵۰، ۱۵۱، ۱۵۲،
۱۵۳، ۱۵۴، ۱۵۵، ۱۵۶، ۱۵۸، ۱۵۹، ۱۸۲،
۲۸۳، ۳۲۹، ۳۸۳

موزهٔ تاریخ طبیعی ۴، ۵۷

موزهٔ جنگ (Imperial War Museum) ۳

موزهٔ علوم (Science Museum) ۲

موزهٔ لندن ۲۲

موزهٔ ویکتوریا و آلبرت (Victoria and
Albert Museum) ۳، ۴، ۶، ۴۱، ۵۷

موسولینی ۱۵۳، ۱۸۳

مولوتوف، ویاچسلاو میخائیلوویچ ۳۳۳

مون مارتر ۳۳

مونیخ ۱۵۳

میدلند بانک ۵

میرزا عبدالله امینی ۱

میرهادیان ۳۵

میزرابل (فیلم) ۵۰

میلسپو، آرتور ۳۷۸

مینورسکی، ولادیمیر ۱۳، ۲۷، ۴۱، ۶۵، ۱۶۰، ۲۲۴، ۲۳۱، ۲۳۲، ۲۳۳، ۲۳۴، ۲۴۲، ۲۴۳، ۲۴۵، ۲۵۲، ۲۷۱، ۲۸۱، ۲۸۸، ۲۹۱، ۲۹۹، ۳۰۵، ۳۰۹، ۳۱۳، ۳۱۷، ۳۲۱، ۳۳۶، ۳۳۹، ۳۴۰، ۳۴۹، ۳۵۱، ۳۵۵، ۳۵۶، ۳۷۵

مینوی، مجتبی ۷۵، ۷۶، ۸۰، ۸۱، ۸۲، ۱۰۲، ۱۰۵، ۱۰۷، ۱۱۰، ۱۱۶، ۱۱۸، ۱۱۹، ۱۲۱، ۱۲۲، ۱۳۰، ۱۳۱، ۱۳۲، ۱۴۴، ۱۴۵، ۱۴۶، ۱۴۸، ۱۴۹، ۱۵۰، ۱۵۱، ۱۵۳، ۱۵۴، ۱۵۵، ۱۵۶، ۱۵۷، ۱۷۵، ۱۸۱، ۱۸۲، ۱۹۰، ۲۱۲، ۲۱۴، ۲۲۳، ۲۴۱، ۲۴۶، ۲۵۳، ۲۷۴، ۲۷۵، ۲۷۶، ۳۵۱، ۳۷۵، ۳۸۰، ۳۸۵

ناپلئون ۳۴، ۳۵، ۵۳

نادرشاه ۱۰۳

نازیها ۲۱

نامدار (از کارکنان سفارت) ۴۰، ۷۱، ۷۲، ۷۴، ۷۵، ۸۰، ۸۱، ۸۲، ۸۷، ۸۸، ۹۷، ۱۰۱، ۱۰۶، ۱۰۷

نبیل، فضل الله ۸۷، ۹۲، ۹۸، ۹۹، ۱۰۰، ۱۰۱، ۱۰۲، ۱۰۶، ۱۰۷، ۱۰۸، ۱۰۹، ۱۱۰، ۱۱۱، ۱۱۲، ۱۱۳، ۱۱۵، ۱۱۶، ۱۱۷، ۱۲۳، ۱۲۴، ۱۲۸، ۱۲۹، ۱۳۰، ۱۳۱، ۱۳۲، ۱۳۳، ۱۳۵، ۱۳۶، ۱۳۷، ۱۳۸، ۱۴۰، ۱۴۱، ۱۴۲، ۱۴۳، ۱۴۴، ۱۴۵، ۱۴۶، ۱۴۷، ۱۴۹، ۱۵۰، ۱۵۱، ۱۵۴، ۱۵۵، ۱۵۷، ۱۵۸، ۱۶۰، ۱۶۲، ۱۶۳، ۱۶۴، ۱۶۵،

میزرابل ستون راست:

۱۶۶، ۱۶۷، ۱۶۸، ۱۶۹، ۱۷۰، ۱۷۱، ۱۷۳، ۱۷۴، ۱۷۵، ۱۷۶، ۱۷۷، ۱۷۸، ۱۷۹، ۱۸۲، ۱۸۳، ۱۸۹، ۱۹۰، ۱۹۱، ۱۹۲، ۱۹۳، ۱۹۴، ۱۹۵، ۱۹۶، ۲۰۱، ۲۰۲، ۲۰۳، ۲۰۴، ۲۰۵، ۲۰۶، ۲۰۷، ۲۰۸، ۲۰۹، ۲۱۰، ۲۱۱، ۲۱۲، ۲۱۳، ۲۱۴، ۲۱۵، ۲۱۶، ۲۱۷، ۲۱۸، ۲۱۹، ۲۲۰، ۲۲۱، ۲۳۰، ۲۵۶، ۲۵۷، ۳۳۹

نجم آبادی، ابوالقاسم ۷۰

نجم‌آبادی، محمود ۱۱

نخجوان، محمد ۸۹، ۲۶۷

نروژ ۱۲۶

نظامی ۱۸۲

نعمت اللّهی ۲۲

نفیسی، اشرف ۲۶۷

نفیسی، سعید ۴۱

نفیسی، مشرف‌الدوله حسن ۵۵، ۷۱، ۸۸، ۱۰۳، ۱۲۳، ۱۵۳، ۲۹۷

نمازی، فرنگیس ۲۳۲، ۲۳۳، ۲۳۴، ۲۳۵، ۲۳۶، ۲۳۷، ۲۳۸، ۲۳۹، ۲۴۰، ۲۴۱، ۲۴۲، ۲۴۳، ۲۴۴، ۲۴۵، ۲۴۶، ۲۴۷، ۲۴۸، ۲۴۹، ۲۵۰، ۲۵۱، ۲۵۲، ۲۵۳، ۲۵۴، ۲۵۵، ۲۵۶، ۲۵۷، ۲۵۸، ۲۵۹، ۲۶۰، ۲۶۱، ۲۶۲، ۲۶۳، ۲۶۴، ۲۶۶، ۲۶۷، ۲۶۸، ۲۷۰، ۲۷۱، ۲۷۲، ۲۷۳، ۲۷۴، ۲۷۶، ۲۷۷، ۲۷۸، ۲۷۹، ۲۸۰، ۲۸۲، ۲۸۴، ۲۸۶، ۲۸۷، ۲۸۹، ۲۹۰، ۲۹۱، ۲۹۲، ۲۹۸، ۳۰۱، ۳۰۲، ۳۰۳، ۳۰۵، ۳۰۶، ۳۰۸، ۳۰۹، ۳۱۳، ۳۱۴، ۳۱۵، ۳۱۶، ۳۱۸

۳۱۹، ۳۲۰، ۳۲۱، ۳۲۲، ۳۲۳، ۳۲۵، ۳۲۶،
۳۲۷، ۳۲۸، ۳۲۹، ۳۳۰، ۳۳۱، ۳۳۵،
۳۳۶، ۳۳۷، ۳۳۹، ۳۴۰، ۳۴۱، ۳۴۲، ۳۴۳،
۳۴۴، ۳۴۶، ۳۴۷، ۳۴۸، ۳۴۹، ۳۵۰، ۳۵۱،
۳۵۲، ۳۵۳، ۳۵۴، ۳۵۵، ۳۵۷، ۳۵۹، ۳۶۱،
۳۶۲، ۳۶۳، ۳۶۵، ۳۶۶، ۳۶۷، ۳۶۸،
۳۶۹، ۳۷۰، ۳۷۱، ۳۷۳، ۳۷۴، ۳۷۵،
۳۷۶، ۳۷۷، ۳۷۹، ۳۸۰، ۳۸۱، ۳۸۳،
۳۸۴، ۳۸۵

نهرو، جواهر لعل ۳۴۳

نوو روسیسک ۳۴۹

نویه شلوس (کاخ) ۹۵

نویی فو (Nuits Fauves) ۳۹، ۷۰

نیامیر، کاظم ۲۲۸، ۲۳۲، ۲۴۵، ۲۴۸، ۲۶۹،
۲۸۳، ۲۸۸، ۳۰۶، ۳۳۴، ۳۳۵، ۳۷۸،
۳۸۰، ۳۸۱، ۳۸۳، ۳۸۵

نیبرگ، هنریک ساموئل (Henrik Samuel
Nyberg)

نیکلسن، رینولد آلین (Reynold Alleyne
Nicholson) ۲۷، ۳۰، ۳۱، ۷۷، ۸۷، ۱۳۵،
۱۷۷

نیو کالج (اکسفورد) ۶۰

نیویورک ۲۵۵

هامر پورگشتال، یوزف فون ۳۴۱

هاوایی ۲۸۶

های گیت ۴۸

هاید پارک ۵، ۶، ۷، ۹، ۱۲، ۲۵، ۸۳، ۸۴،

۳۳۴، ۳۳۵، ۳۶۱

هتل ریتز ۱۵

هتل مونتانا ۳، ۱۰، ۲۱، ۲۲، ۲۳، ۲۴، ۴۳، ۵۸،

هدایتی، محمد علی ۱۵۱

هژیر، عبدالحسین ۱۲، ۲۶، ۱۳۰، ۱۳۱، ۱۳۱،
۱۳۳، ۱۴۱، ۱۴۲، ۱۴۳، ۱۸۴، ۱۸۹،

هس، رودلف ۲۳۸

هشترودی، محسن ۳۷

همتون کورت (Hampton Court) ۱۹، ۸۱،
۸۵

همتون کورت (اکسفورد) ۶۰

همدان ۱

هندن (Hendon) ۱۸

هندوستان ۴۳، ۸۸، ۲۶۷، ۲۶۸، ۲۷۰، ۲۷۸،
۲۹۴، ۳۰۱، ۳۰۹، ۳۱۵، ۳۱۷، ۳۱۸، ۳۴۲،
۳۴۳، ۳۴۴، ۳۴۶، ۳۵۰، ۳۶۷

هنگ کنگ ۲۸۹، ۲۹۰

هنگری (مجارستان) ۲۶۳

هنینگ، والتر برونو ۳۵۶

هوبورن/هولبورن (محله) ۴، ۱۶، ۵۶، ۱۱۰،
۱۷۸، ۱۸۲، ۲۰۵، ۲۳۸

هورتز، هورشید ۱۶۳

هوگو، ویکتور ۳۶

هیتلر ۱۵۳، ۱۸۲، ۱۸۳، ۱۸۴، ۱۸۵، ۱۸۶،
۲۳۸، ۲۷۰، ۲۸۹، ۳۰۷، ۳۲۲، ۳۷۹

هیل، الیزابت ۳۰۵

واتو، ژان آنتوان ۱۴۵

وارسته، باقر ۹۳، ۹۵

واریک کاسل (Warwick Castle) ۶۱

واشنگتن ۲۹۰

وایلد، اسکار (Oscar Wilde) ۱۱۲

وبستر، سر چارلز ۹۹، ۱۰۰، ۱۰۱، ۱۰۲، ۱۰۳، ۱۰۶، ۱۰۸، ۱۱۳، ۱۱۵، ۱۱۷، ۱۲۸، ۱۲۹، ۱۳۱، ۱۳۴، ۱۳۶، ۱۳۷، ۱۴۰، ۱۴۱، ۱۴۲، ۱۵۵، ۱۶۳، ۱۶۴، ۱۶۵، ۱۶۶، ۱۶۸، ۱۷۲، ۱۷۸، ۲۴۴

ورسای ۵۳، ۱۲۶

وروشیلوف‌گراد (لوهانسک) ۳۳۹

وزیری، حسنعلی ۴۳، ۴۴، ۴۵، ۴۶، ۴۷، ۴۸، ۴۹، ۵۰، ۵۱، ۵۲، ۵۳

وزیری، علیقلی ۱۹۸

وست‌مینستر اَبی (Westminster Abbey) ۳، ۶، ۳۲

ولتر ۳۶

ولز ۶۰

ولز، هربرت جرج ۲

ولفیت، دانلد ۲۸۴

ونزوئلا ۱۲۶

وهاب‌زاده، رشید ۱۱۶، ۱۲۲، ۱۳۸، ۱۴۳، ۱۴۶، ۱۵۰، ۱۶۲، ۱۶۹، ۱۸۱، ۱۹۰

ویکتوریا (Victoria Station) ۱۹، ۲۴، ۵۱، ۵۸، ۶۷، ۱۰۳، ۱۰۹، ۱۲۶، ۱۳۴، ۱۴۲

ویلسن، آرنولد ۲۹

ویلکنسن، ادوارد (Edward Wilkinson) ۸۷، ۱۱۱، ۱۱۶، ۱۶۳

ویمبلدون ۲، ۳، ۶

وی‌ول، آرچیبالد ۲۶۸، ۲۷۰

یزد ۳۲

یزدان‌فر ۱، ۶

یزدی، میرزا علی ۱۴۰

یکتا (کارمند سفارت) ۵، ۶، ۷، ۸، ۹، ۱۱، ۱۲، ۶۷، ۶۸، ۷۰، ۱۲۶، ۱۲۷

یهودیها ۱۸، ۴۳، ۲۶۶، ۳۲۸، ۳۶۸

یوگوسلاوی ۳۰۴، ۳۰۵

یونان ۹۴، ۳۲۱

یونگ، هانس ۲۳۷، ۲۴۲، ۲۴۶، ۲۵۵، ۳۸۰

یونیورسیته لندن/دانشگاه لندن ۷۳، ۷۶، ۸۴، ۱۰۹، ۱۷۵، ۳۸۰

یونیورسیتی کالج ۷۷، ۱۰۴